D1200523

ROME IN THE EAST

ROME IN THE EAST

The transformation of an empire

Warwick Ball

London and New York

First published 2000
by Routledge
11 New Fetter Lane, London EC4P 4EE

Simultaneously published in the USA and Canada
by Routledge
29 West 35th Street, New York, NY 10001

Routledge is an imprint of the Taylor & Francis Group

Typeset in Bembo by RefineCatch Limited, Bungay, Suffolk
Printed in Great Britain by Bell and Bain Ltd., Glasgow

British Library Cataloguing in Publication Data
A catalogue record for this book is available from the British Library

Library of Congress Cataloging in Publication Data
Ball, Warwick
Rome in the East / Warwick Ball.
p.   cm.
Includes bibliographical references and index.
1. Rome – Civilization – Middle Eastern influences.   2. Rome –
Civilization – Christian influences.   I. Title.
DG77.B317   1999
937 – dc21   99–21402
CIP

ISBN 0–415–11376–8

TO RALPH PINDER-WILSON

CONTENTS

CONTENTS

PLATES

LIST OF FIGURES AND FAMILY TREES

Figures

Family trees

PREFACE

This book began some six years ago. It was to be a straightforward work of synthesis, intended to summarise and discuss the relationship between the historical evidence and the material remains of the eastern bounds of the Roman Empire and beyond. The material remains alone of this area deserved a higher place in the orbit of Roman architecture, being some of the most extensive and spectacular in the Roman world.

As work progressed, however, it soon became apparent that there were things that needed to be said about the presence, role and character of Rome in the East. In particular, much of the material remains could only be satisfactorily explained from a Near Eastern archaeological viewpoint, rather than the more usual Classical and Western. This in turn seemed to demand an Eastern perspective for Rome in the East as a whole, and with it a resulting reappraisal and new emphasis. In reassessing the interaction of Rome and the East and its legacy, it further became apparent that much new comment could usefully be made on the legacy of Roman civilisation as a whole and the beginnings of Europe. In some ways this represents a challenge to previous views, in other ways it will present new evidence for old theories (and new theories of old evidence), but it is only another perspective.

The germ of this book probably began many years ago when I found myself being required to restore a monumental Roman arch at Jerash, the North Tetrapylon. After many years of the familiar shapes, forms and norms of Near Eastern archaeology and architecture, I suddenly found myself confronted by the far less familiar forms of that rather daunting beast, Classical architecture – and imperial Roman to boot. As well as the technical problems of producing a 'new' monument out of an apparently meaningless mass of rubble was the academic problem of working out what this Roman building looked like – and why. Here at least I was on familiar ground: a tetrapylon, or four-way arch, I knew from Iran, the *chahartaq* or Persian equivalent being one of the most fundamental 'building blocks' of Persian architecture. From there, I began to look at the other buildings at Jerash not as the Roman buildings they appeared to be, but as Near Eastern buildings, simply to find some common ground with my own architectural knowledge. This applied in particular to that most ubiquitous feature of Roman cities in the East, the colonnaded street, when those long daunting lines of very Roman colonnades simply melted away to appear as something I had been used to for years: eastern bazaar streets. The rest followed.

With such a long gestation and even longer background, the book naturally owes much to many more than I could possibly acknowledge. I would like to thank Wendy Ball, Leonard Harrow, Stan Kennon, E. Mary Smallwood, David Whitehouse and in particular Routledge's anonymous readers, who read versions of the manuscript, made much valuable comment and picked up on many a blunder and howler. I must also apologise to them for the advice ignored, the blunders that remained and the howlers that crept in afterwards. I would also like to thank Leslie Florence, for printing the photographs, Miranda Ball, for work on the line drawings, and Tom Chandler, for meticulous copyediting. I owe a particular debt of gratitude to Richard Stoneman, Coco Stevenson and Kate Chenevix Trench of Routledge for tolerating with such good grace a manuscript that was over double its intended length and years late in delivery. Indeed, Richard Stoneman's enthusiasm for and encouragement of the book has been a source of support since its inception. Finally, although not directly connected to this work, I owe especial thanks to Ralph Pinder-Wilson who provided very concrete and much needed encouragement years ago when first embarking upon an academic career, and ever since has been one of the wisest and most stimulating academic mentors I have been privileged to know.

At this point in most works of self-indulgence such as this one, most authors pay tribute to their long-suffering family for putting up with both book and author for so long. Mine put up with more and suffered more than most, and I owe much to Wendy, Oliver, Eleanor and Aidan over the years. True, without them the book might well have been finished years before. But far more truly, without them there would be little point in creative work in the first place. I hope this work is as much an expression of love for them as self-indulgence for myself.

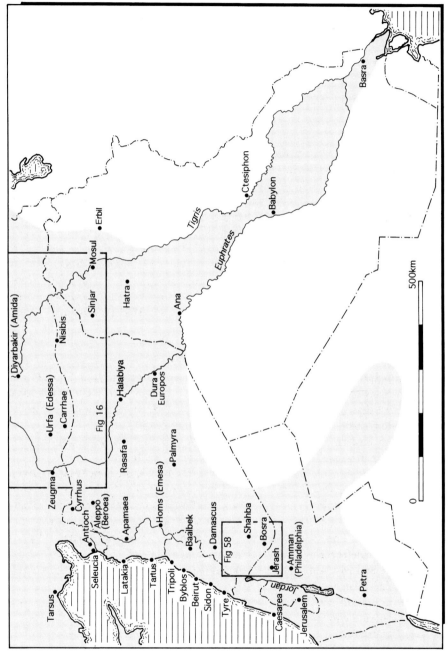

Figure 1 General map to illustrate Rome in the East. Shaded area shows approximate limits of the Empire at its greatest extent

1

INTRODUCTION

We look to Rome for our own European cultural roots. But Rome itself looked East (Figure 1). The Roman East had an immense impact upon Europe in a way that no other part of the empire had. Christianity is the most obvious, but there were many other ways, more subtle but equally important, that the East dominated Rome from the beginning of its imperial expansion. The East was Rome's greatest source of wealth. In the East was the only other great power – Iran – which ever matched Rome, both culturally and militarily. After contact with eastern royalty Rome itself became a monarchy. From mythological origins in Troy to Syrian emperors of Rome to oriental religious, intellectual and architectural influences, the East transformed Rome. Through this contact, Near Eastern civilisation transformed Europe. The story of Rome is a story of a fascination for the East, a fascination that amounted to an obsession. This is the story of that fascination.

Background

Alexander's conquests opened up the Mediterranean world, and ultimately Europe, to the ancient civilisations of the East. From this interchange Europe received a revolutionary new eastern idea that would change the course of its history: Christianity. Alexander's conquest is often called the end of the ancient Near East,[1] but surely it was a new beginning. Near Eastern civilisation lived on under the gloss of a Macedonian and subsequently Roman veneer – indeed it remained a very vital force.

Pompey the Great annexed the Seleucid Empire in 64 BC, and Rome soon became an empire with an emperor to rule it. But the sophisticated world of the Near East where these rather raw Roman soldiers and administrators first found themselves was immeasurably older than Rome – far older, even, than the world of Greek civilisation which the Romans felt heirs to. The Near East had been seeing great empires come and go for thousands of years before the Romans: Persian, Babylonian, Assyrian, not to mention Egyptian, Hittite and Mitanni empires before them and the first outward expansions of the Sumerian, Akkadian and Eblaite states 5,000 and more years ago.

But more important than these great empires were the great civilisations they bequeathed, alongside which our brash Romans must have appeared awkward backwater rustics. Near Eastern civilisation was a very homogeneous one. There was always a thread of cultural continuity making it essentially one civilisation that lasted an incredibly long time from its origins in the still little understood fifth millennium BC until its eventual transformation and dissemination by the Romans. Indeed, these events marking the end of this Near Eastern continuum are nearer to our own times than the shadowy events over 7,000 years ago that marked its beginning. It was into this – ultimately to be transformed by it – that the Romans came.

By the year AD 116 a Spaniard who was one of Rome's greatest emperors – Trajan – stood on the shores of the Persian Gulf: the first time that a European potentate had stood by the waters of both the Atlantic and Indian Oceans. By the year 200, most of the antique lands of the Near East – from the Black Sea in the north to the Red Sea in the south, from the Mediterranean in the west to the foothills of Iran in the east – lay under Rome. At times, Roman arms even penetrated deep into the highlands of Iran and across the deserts of Arabia to Yemen; caravans carried Roman goods even further east to Central Asia, while merchant ships carried them across the seas to India and the Far East. The Atlantic had brought Rome to a full stop in the West, but the East seemed unlimited. Roman influence seemed to spread throughout the East.

Or was it eastern influence spreading to Rome? By the time of Rome's greatest extent, emperors from the East were beginning to rule Rome: the emperors Caracalla and Geta were half Punic, half Syrian, while Elagabalus, Severus Alexander and Philip the Arab were wholly Syrian. Under the priest-emperor Elagabalus, the cult of Syrian Baal was proclaimed supreme in Rome to the horror of the conservative Roman establishment. Of course, the cult of Baal did not catch on, but another 'Syrian cult' was soon triumphant.

Such Near Eastern influence at the heart of the Roman world helped change European history in two fundamental ways. Although not necessarily Christians themselves, such Syrian emperors and their entourages – and their popularisation of eastern cults – nonetheless made the spread of another eastern religion, Christianity, more acceptable. Moreover, from the time of the Syrian emperors Rome increasingly turned its back upon its ramshackle empire in Europe and looked more towards the East. In the end, Rome became more of an Asian than a European power. Rome itself eventually moved to the East, with the foundation of the New Rome at Byzantium ensuring the continuation of the Roman Empire for a further 1,300 years at the cost of ditching Europe to the barbarians. It was finally extinguished in 1453 with the conquest of Constantinople by a people whose origins lay on the borders of China.

Constraints and considerations

Sources, perspectives and evidence

In explaining Rome's fascination with the East, several considerations immediately become apparent. Works that deal with the Roman East are usually written by Classicists. These are necessarily Eurocentric. This work aims to redress the balance by writing from the Near Eastern perspective. Although the Greeks in the East have been written about from a refreshingly eastern standpoint,[2] the Romans in the East are almost universally viewed from an overly western cultural bias.[3] It might be forgivable for Gibbon, writing several hundred years ago, to contrast 'the valour of the west' with the 'decadence of the east' or to write that 'the troops of Europe asserted their usual ascendant over the effeminate natives of Asia'.[4] But such bias still prevails. One recent major work on the Roman Near East, for example, constantly labours the lack of native 'character' – hence civilisation – compared to Graeco-Roman superiority.[5] In a recent admirable collection of source material for the Roman eastern frontier, a reservation is expressed about a major Persian source as 'solely expressing the Persian point of view',[6] a reservation not expressed by the overwhelming amount of Greek and Latin sources (which, of course, express the Roman point of view). Elsewhere in the same work,[7] the western campaigns of Shapur I are dismissed as plundering raids and 'razzias', an archaic and derogatory term with overtones of raids by mere semi-civilised nomads. No Classicist would ever dismiss, for example, Trajan's campaigns into Mesopotamia as 'razzias'. In another work, reservations are expressed about the one major non-Roman source that we do have, Josephus, as 'one-sided',[8] reservations which are rarely expressed about Roman sources (usually one-sided) when dealing with Near Eastern events. Elsewhere, ritual prostitution is assumed to have taken place in the temple at Heliopolis merely because Eusebius (hardly the most unbiased source for paganism!) says so,[9] whereas Tacitus' account of ritual cannibalism on the part of the early Christians has long been rejected. Western bias in the sources is accepted uncritically; criticism is only applied, it seems, to those that give the eastern viewpoint. Today, the words may be different from Gibbon's, but the bias is the same.

To some extent, a western perspective is attributed to the lack of native literary sources for the East. This is exaggerated. One of the greatest Roman historians, Josephus, was a native of Palestine, whilst Ammianus Marcellinus, described as 'the last great Roman historian, whose writings stand comparison with those of Livy and Tacitus',[10] was a native of Antioch. Herodian, Libanius and John Malalas were also from Antioch, Dio Cassius and Strabo were from Anatolia, Procopius and Eusebius were from Caesarea, to name but a few of the more important native historians of the Near East. The eastern Roman world boasted as great a literary pedigree as European Rome did. Classical literary and historical traditions generally can be traced back to Herodotus and Homer – both, it must be noted, natives of Asia, not Europe – and the Phoenician historical traditions of the end of the second millennium. The historian Sanchuniathon (or Sakkunnyaton), for example, wrote an eight-book history of the Phoenicians which survived in summary form.[11] Sanchuniathon was a part of a long tradition of Phoenician historiography that probably had its origins in Ugaritic literature much earlier and in Mesopotamian historiography earlier still. The 'Classical' Levantine historians, such as Josephus, Ammianus and Eusebius, were as much a part of these eastern traditions as western.

Epigraphy is the source of much of the history of the Roman East. It is equally the source of much modern prejudice. The evidence of Greek inscriptions in the East has in many ways created more problems than it has solved. It has resulted in a tendency to load far too much on the evidence of a single Greek inscription – and distort the result. For example, an enquiry that was recorded in Greek on an inscription at Dmayr near Damascus has been taken as evidence that everybody concerned actually spoke it.[12] It does not necessarily follow that anyone, apart from the person who carved the inscription, actually spoke it. Other Greek inscriptions in the Near East are regarded as evidence for the Greek 'character' and culture of an entire city or region. But the converse, Palmyrene inscriptions in Britain, Numidia or Dacia, is merely taken as evidence that 'such soldiers could (at least) have access to persons who could compose brief texts in Palmyrene, and then have them inscribed'.[13] Apart from the implied prejudice (most Greeks by definition were literate, a mere Palmyrene needed a scribe?) the fact that Greek inscriptions in the Near East might equally have been written by a small minority of 'persons who could compose brief texts . . . and then have them inscribed' is never even considered. A mere mention of Ana on the Euphrates in a Greek document from Dura prompts the statement that 'it is probable that Greek was also used, at least as an official language, at Anath(a) itself', while western Mesopotamia is confidently stated as 'bilingual and bicultural' on the evidence of a *single* inscription.[14] On the evidence of a few scraps of parchment and graffiti, the Jewish community at Dura Europos is pronounced as 'fully bilingual'.[15]

But the inscriptions merely show that Greek was used as a *lingua franca* throughout an area where other languages were spoken, such as Nabataean, Arabic, Palmyrene, Aramaic, Phoenician, Hebrew, and doubtless many others which have left no trace. To administer such an area, an acceptable *lingua franca* would have been essential; Aramaic, the former *lingua franca*, would have been unacceptable to the administrators themselves. In any case, a native *lingua franca* would have been unacceptable to rival regions (the Hebrews, for example, would never have countenanced Nabataean). The situation is comparable to post-independence India, where English is both a *lingua franca* and a unifier of diverse linguistic rivalries. In the Roman East, the use of Greek was nothing more than this. It in no way implies any Greek 'character' or even much Greek culture in the region, let alone the extinction of native languages.

Ultimately, what does the evidence of just a handful of Greek documents amount to? The answer has to be a very little. After all, the actual quantity of documents – inscriptions, some graffiti, a few parchments – that have come down to us through the accident of survival is tiny. It does not remotely compare, either in quantity or quality, to the amount of documentation that has survived, for example, from the ancient Mesopotamian civilisations. Here, in the cuneiform documents, we have virtually entire state archives and a mass of other documentation at our disposal, from census records and epic literature to business transactions, private correspondence and school exercises. Indeed, even much of the Hellenistic history of the Near East is preserved in cuneiform documents, offering an important contrast to the Greek documents.[16] When compared to other periods and other places in Near Eastern history, therefore, the Greek documents are not even remotely adequate to enable such bold statements of language, culture or character to be made.

In this context, it is worth comparing the situation of the over-used Greek inscriptions in the Near East with that of the lesser known native inscriptions for the same period: Aramaic, Palmyrene, Safaitic and Thamudic. The Safaitic inscriptions alone, numbering a remarkable 18,000 or so, are found mainly in the deserts of southern Syria and northern Jordan, with occasional finds as far away as Dura Europos, the Lebanese coast, western Iraq and even Pompeii.[17] They cover a broad date roughly between 500 BC and AD 500, with the bulk between the first and the fourth centuries AD. They are found almost entirely in the desert areas and only rarely in settled parts.[18] Their content is almost entirely related to nomadism, so it is difficult to escape from the conclusion that they must have been written by nomads.[19] A large number are graffiti, mainly giving onomastic and tribal information that sheds considerable light on personal genealogies, tribal treaties and religious invocations.[20] Many give information on pasturing, animal husbandry and migrations. For quality of information they can be compared with the information from the Greek inscriptions. In quantity, they greatly outnumber the extant Greek and Latin inscriptions from the Near East.

Classical epigraphic and literary sources have been used, therefore, not only too uncritically, but too exclusively. This has distorted the true picture. One authority, for example, emphasises: '. . . how far our understanding is limited by what our sources happen to be interested in saying' and that 'Above all, the notion that there was a "Syrian" culture, embracing equally the zone of Syriac literature and Roman Syria, goes beyond our evidence'.[21] But the bulk of 'our evidence' is neither epigraphic nor literary sources. It is the material remains. Nowhere is this more so than in the Roman East, which has more material remains than any other part of the empire, with the possible exception of North Africa. Material remains have all too often been relegated to mere illustrative material by historians. But they reflect a far more accurate picture of a society as a whole – and can often considerably alter the historical picture provided by the more conventional sources.

The need, first, for an eastern viewpoint and second, to use the material remains as a source, therefore, has never been greater. These are the two prime considerations in writing the present work. Only in this way can the main objective be achieved: to examine Rome's involvement in the East and its ultimate transformation.

Terminology

Terminology is both a source and a manifestation of cultural confusion. In particular, the terms 'Greek' versus 'Macedonian', 'Persian' versus 'Iranian', and 'Byzantine' versus 'Roman' require clarification.

The term 'Greek' is often used to describe both the Seleucid Empire and much of the character of the Roman period in the East as well.[22] Hence, the term 'Graeco-Roman' has rapidly gained almost universal acceptance to describe the Near East from Alexander to Muhammad. To begin with, such assumptions minimise the Macedonian element: 'Macedonian' soon becomes equated with 'Greek' in a haste to trace civilisation back to a semi-mythic Athens. To continually characterise the resulting Seleucid successor state, as well as Roman rule in the East, as 'Greek' and 'Graeco-Roman' does an injustice both to Greek and Macedonian culture (not to mention Roman and Near Eastern). Even 'Hellenistic' is little better: it is a moot point whether the initial Macedonian conquests can be described as 'Hellenic', and the ensuing Seleucid state is characterised as much by Persian elements as Hellenic.[23] Hence, the terms 'Seleucid' or 'Macedonian' are preferred.

The terms 'Parthia' and 'Persia' are also problematic. Adopting the usage of the sources, most modern histories refer to Iran during the period we are dealing with successively as 'Parthia' and 'Persia'. From an eastern standpoint, both terms are unsatisfactory. 'Parthia', strictly speaking, corresponds only to the region east and south-east of the Caspian; to an Iranologist – or an Iranian – referring to parts of Mesopotamia as 'Parthia' (as most of our Classical sources do) is misleading. Similarly, 'Persia' is just that part of Iran which corresponds to the region adjacent to the Persian Gulf: modern Fars Province. The empires of both the Parthian and Persian (Sasanian) dynasties were multinational, and neither dynasty used 'Parthian' or 'Persian' in a supra-national sense in the way that 'Rome' and 'Roman Empire' were used. To the Iranians, their empire was Eranshahr, 'Land of Iran', whilst to the Romans their empire was 'Rome'. For the Romans, the capital was everything; for the Iranians, the capital mattered little, the land was everything.[24] In addition, there was a strong element of continuity between the Parthian and Sasanian dynasties. Both used the royal title Shahinshah, 'King of Kings', both were Iranian nationalist in character, and both claimed continuity from the ancient Achaemenid kings.[25] Both 'Parthia' and 'Persia' are western appellations; for the Iranians themselves the country has always been 'Iran' or 'Eranshahr'.[26] For these reasons, the term 'Iran' is generally preferred.

5

The terms 'Byzantium', 'Byzantine' and 'Byzantine Empire' also pose problems. The term 'Byzantine Empire' was coined comparatively late in European history to describe the eastern Roman Empire ruled from Constantinople as distinct and separate from the western Roman Empire ruled from Rome.[27] Scholars have debated about when the Roman Empire became 'Byzantine' ever since. In this way, the 'Byzantine Empire' was disinherited from the Roman legacy and mainstream European history, the origins of which are identified so much with Rome. The reasons were mainly religious, to assert the primacy of the Roman Church over Constantinople. 'Byzantine' rapidly came to stand for everything that was degenerate, corrupt, 'oriental' – in other words, the perceived antithesis of 'Roman'. But it is important to remember that the Byzantine Empire never existed as an institution: it was always officially the 'Roman Empire' right down until the fifteenth century, ruled by Roman emperors in an unbroken institutional line from Augustus to Constantine Dragases. Of course, it cannot be denied that long before the fifteenth century the character of the Roman Empire had changed fundamentally, but both the area and the period covered in this book is marked by continuity. Any division between 'Roman' and 'Byzantine' empires would introduce a note of artificiality. 'Roman Empire', therefore, is used.

There are a few more minor points of terminology that need to be noted. Generally, native versions of Near Eastern personal names are preferred to the Greek or Latin. This is to underline their essentially Near Eastern character, which the Greek or Latin versions of their names have tended to obscure or to deny. Hence, Palmyrene 'Udaynath and Wahballath instead of Odaenathus and Vaballathus; Nabataean Maliku and 'Obaydath, instead of Malichus and Obodas; Arab Mawiyya and al-Mundhir instead of Mavia and Alamoundaros, etc. However, when a Near Eastern name is far more familiar under its Latin version, I have used this. Hence, Zenobia instead of Zabba, Domna instead of Dumayma, Herod instead of Hairan, etc.

Geographical limits

Strictly speaking, the 'Roman East' includes everywhere east of the Bosphorus, particularly Anatolia, one of the most important regions in the empire. For the purposes of this work, however, only the Near East is included – roughly the Arab countries of today – corresponding broadly to the Roman provinces of Syria, Palestine, Arabia and (briefly) Mesopotamia. Somewhat reluctantly, Anatolia is excluded (apart from occasional references). But limits must be imposed somewhere: such is the wealth of Roman remains in Anatolia that including it here would make this work impossibly long and would better form the subject of a separate study. The Near East forms a fairly self-contained unit, as much in modern terms as ancient. Herodian, for example, puts the dividing line between East and West not so much at the Bosphorus but at the Taurus Mountains.[28] Egypt is also not included for much the same reasons.

Objectives

This book is a work of synthesis, a general study of the history, architecture and archaeology of the Near Eastern provinces of the Roman Empire, of Roman penetration beyond the frontiers, and of the ensuing eastern influences that brought about Rome's own transformation. The period covered is from the conquest of the Near East by

Pompey in 63 BC to its loss by Heraclius in AD 636. The actual historical process is first traced to provide a basic framework upon which the remainder of the book can be hung.

Much of the East that Rome entered comprised a patchwork of client kingdoms that were only indirectly ruled by Rome, a system of proxy rule (and occasionally proxy war) that proved very effective. The main ones were Emesa, Judaea, Nabataea, Palmyra, Edessa and later the tribal confederations of the Tanukhids and Ghassanids. All these states, whilst very different from each other, were in separate ways to have a profound effect upon Rome. Whilst usually tiny and invariably subservient to Rome, many were ruled from glittering capitals whose monuments were some of the greatest in the empire: Jerusalem, Petra and Palmyra, for example. The power of Rome was felt east of the frontiers too, through military campaigns, trade, or artistic influences. Hence, the book also incorporates material from as far away as Yemen, Iran, Afghanistan, Central Asia, India and China.

Outside the client states, Roman rule was exercised most directly through the towns and cities, most notably the capital of Antioch. These cities contain some of the most spectacular remains in the entire Roman world: Apamaea, Rasafa, Caesarea, Tyre, Jerash. The pattern of settlement, rule and influence in the cities is contrasted with that observed in the countryside. Impressive though the remains of cities are, the countryside of the Roman East probably contains a greater concentration of ancient remains than anywhere else in the Mediterranean.

Finally, the resurgence of the East under Roman rule and the gradual domination of the East over Rome is examined. Much of this is apparent from a closer study of the material remains. This reveals fundamentally eastern influences at work that can be traced back deep into the cultural traditions of the ancient Near East, Iran and even India. In analysing eastern Roman architecture from within its eastern context, the nature of much of imperial Roman architecture as a whole is called into question. Ultimately, the Roman cultural presence in the East is demonstrated to be far more superficial than is usually realised.

In understanding the strengths and domination of native culture under Roman rule, the gradual extension of Near Eastern culture into Europe becomes more explicable. The movement of peoples – and with it their ideas – from East to West is viewed as a part of this process, and the rise of Arab emperors of Rome a logical outcome. This culminated in an oriental revolution in the Roman Empire: the adoption of an oriental religion and the move of the capital to the East. This 'oriental revolution' is one of the central facts of European history: it laid the foundations for the ensuing development of a 'European' culture and 'European' identity. The entire book can be viewed as the background to this central fact.

2

HISTORICAL BACKGROUND

To the Euphrates

The ghost of Alexander seems always to lie heavily upon those who venture east, the Romans no less than the Crusaders no less than Napoleon.[1] The Romans too felt heirs to Hellenism. But they also suffered an inferiority complex. It was towards the east that conquerors cut their teeth: Alexander had, as it were, defined the very concept of conquest and empire. After the Punic Wars an empire almost by definition had to be eastern. From Pompey to Heraclius the road to glory lay eastwards, some like Pompey or Trajan achieving it, others like Crassus or Julian coming to grief. The East was also the source of wealth above all others, and the endless round of civil wars in the Roman Republic was costing money that only the eastern coffers could recoup. Above all, the East was the only area which held another great power that could match Rome: Iran.

Rome and Iran

The history of Rome in the East was dominated by Iran more than any other single factor. Iran was the greatest power to oppose Rome, so there is understandable preoccupation with eastern policies. But the same was probably not as true for Iran, which – particularly under the Sasanians – faced great powers to the east as well, where it actually conquered a great empire: the Kushans. Sasanian–Kushan relations, therefore, where we have scarcely any documentary sources, were probably just as important a preoccupation for them as Sasanian–Roman relations are to us, where we have copious sources. The East was probably of far more concern to Iran than Rome ever was: the Parthians established relations with China, for example, before they did with Rome. All the information that we have about the history of pre-Islamic Iran shows an overwhelming concern for the East – 'Turan' of the epics – rather than for the West.[2] Much of the ancient Iranian perception of the Romans has survived in the imagery of medieval poetry. Here, 'Rome' – *Rum* in Persian – is merely a stock image for the exotic, for distance, for the barbaric, occasionally for mystery. In other words, it is virtually identical to the medieval and later European imagery for the 'Orient'.[3] The foundation of Constantinople was seen as a direct consequence of Roman defeats by the Iranians.[4] When Roman emperors are mentioned, it is usually in relation either to Jewish history (for example, Vespasian and Hadrian, who destroyed Jerusalem) or to Islamic history (for example, Heraclius, who lost the East to Islam). In both al-Tabari and al-Biruni the whole of the history of the Roman Empire from Tiberius to Heraclius is summarised in just a king-list, as little more than a footnote to the story of Christ and a preface to the coming of Muhammad.[5] One is left with the impression that, for Iran, Rome was simply a minor – even tributary – power.[6]

The Romans may have had no 'grand strategy'.[7] But there were 'grand preoccupations' that, at times, were even obsessive, and strategic considerations would follow from these. The East was the greatest of these preoccupations. For Iran was the only nation in the ancient world that matched Roman power, defeating Rome on a number of occasions. Several authorities emphasise that in the never-ending Rome–Iran struggle, it was almost invariably Rome that was the aggressor. Indeed, the earliest Parthian overtures to Rome were peaceful.[8] But apart from being a preoccupation that often amounted to an aggressive obsession, Rome never showed any curiosity towards its great neighbour (as the Greeks did – Herodotus or Xenophon, for example). No attempts were made at gaining worthwhile intelligence:[9] Mark Antony's disastrous campaign into Iran is a prime example, while Julius Caesar's 'grand strategy' for an invasion of Iran displayed such colossal ignorance that, had it been implemented, it would have been as disastrous as Antony's.

With the notable exception of Strabo and one or two other natives of the East, the Romans on the whole display ignorance of Iran. They are, for example, often indiscriminately called Persians, Parthians or Medes regardless of which dynasty is in power, or there is frequent confusion between the Aral, Caspian and Black Seas. Ammianus Marcellinus, who is otherwise one of the main Roman authorities on the East, seems to make no differentiation between Mede, Persian or Parthian. The *Chronicon Paschale* in the seventh century refers to Shapur as 'Pharaoh' and even as late as the eleventh century, Michael Psellus was still referring to Iran under the Seljuks as 'Parthia', while the Abbasids of the tenth century were called the 'Assyrians' and the Caliph at-Taʾiʾ is referred to as 'Chosroes' the 'Babylonian'. Nor did Rome ever develop any sound, consistent policy towards Iran other than the vague notion that one must clobber it every now and then when opportunism came its way. Even those attacks when they came – distinguished as often by disastrous defeats as by inconclusive victories – were markedly lacking any soundly thought-out strategy or war aims, let alone a policy to follow in the event of a total victory (i.e., what would one do on suddenly annexing territory that stretched to the Jaxartes and the Indus?)[10]

Hannibal and Antiochus the Great

The first act in Rome's eastern involvement was also the last in its wars against Carthage. For it was Hannibal who, in encouraging the Seleucid Empire to defeat his sworn enemy, unwittingly brought Rome to the East for the first time – with his own and the Seleucid's ultimate downfall as the outcome. In itself, it may be of minimal historical relevance, but it does at least serve to illustrate how entwined Rome and the East were from the very beginning of Rome's imperial expansion.[11]

Asia's expansion into Europe began much earlier than Europe's into Asia. During the course of this Asian expansion we see Phoenician merchant venturers charting the coast of Britain and Phoenician scribes bequeathing to Europe what is arguably one of the greatest single assets of its civilisation: the alphabet. Hannibal's campaigns in Spain and Italy were the last episode in this long history. Rome's Punic Wars first thrust Rome onto the broader Mediterranean stage and the eventual road to eastern expansion. With his armies routed and his capital occupied, Hannibal was forced to flee eastwards. He sought sanctuary at the court of the only other major power in the Mediterranean that could resist Rome: the Seleucid kingdom of Antiochus III.

Antiochus III, known as the Great, was a descendant of Seleucus Nicator, the Macedonian warlord who founded the Seleucid Empire following the death of Alexander. In many ways, Antiochus' achievements were not far short of those of Alexander himself. The mighty army that he built up, developed from both Macedonian and Persian models, was one of the first in the West to make cavalry a significant element. He campaigned as far as India in 209 BC, and in 204 he turned his war machine against the Seleucid kingdom's old rivals and fellow Macedonians, the Ptolemaic dynasty of Egypt, and inflicted a crushing defeat on them at the Battle of Paneas at the headwaters of the Jordan. Antiochus was proclaimed conqueror of the East, the new Alexander and defender of Hellenism. Hannibal could find no truer champion against his own enemy. He warned Antiochus of the new threat from the West and urged him to turn his might against Italy. The combination of two of the ancient world's great generals together – the victor of Cannae and the conqueror of India[12] – was a heady one that seemed to spell doom for the brash new power of Rome.

It was not to be. Despite Antiochus' dynamic efforts to restore Seleucid fortunes, the Seleucid kingdom was an old one that had long begun its decline. Antiochus, despite Hannibal's urgings, was cautious: he had no wish to set his sights beyond mainland Greece. Rome had already been making inroads into Greece, defeating Antiochus' forces at the historic battlefield of Thermopylae in 191 BC, and occupying most of Greece with little effort. Then in 190 Roman soldiers for the first time set foot in Asia. An army commanded by Rome's two greatest generals, the legendary Scipio brothers, crossed the Dardanelles. With foes of the calibre of Antiochus and Hannibal, Rome put its greatest into the field. The two armies met at the Battle of Magnesia in Asia Minor in 189 BC, the Seleucid army of 75,000 strong opposed by a Roman army numbering only some 30,000. It was an historic battle between new and old legends: Roman legion met Macedonian phalanx. Both sides also fielded elephants: Rome's African versus the Macedonians' Asiatic. Despite the odds and some brilliant cavalry tactics by Antiochus, the Seleucid army was completely routed, with the Romans slaughtering the Macedonians on a massive scale.[13] Rome had arrived in Asia.

Pompey the Great[14]

Pompey has always been overshadowed by his rival and eventual destroyer, Caesar. Caesar, it is true, added an important province to Rome, but Pompey added a sophisticated empire. Caesar's rustic tribes from the north could not be compared to the roll-call of nations that were inscribed on Pompey's triumph, the greatest that Rome had ever seen up until then: 'Pontus, Armenia, Cappadocia, Paphlagonia, Media, Colchis, the Iberians, the Albanians, Syria, Cilicia, and Mesopotamia, together with Phoenicia and Palestine, Judaea, Arabia, and all the power of the pirates subdued by sea and land.'[15] In the days when the writing was on the wall for Republicanism in Rome, it was Pompey who pointed the way forward: Empire. Rome conquered an eastern empire; as a result the eastern concept of empire conquered Rome. Pompey, likened to no less a hero than Alexander, was hailed 'Imperator' by his army and proclaimed 'King of Kings', the ancient Persian title for an emperor. Ultimately, it was Pompey who was awarded the epithet 'the Great',[16] not Caesar.

It was Pontus and Armenia that brought Pompey eastwards. Adopting the old Iranian royal title – as well as much of its mantle – of 'King of Kings',[17] King Tigranes of Armenia had expanded his kingdom over much of Anatolia and Syria at the expense of the declining Seleucids after 95 BC. As well as a challenge to Rome's new presence in the region following the Battle of Magnesia, Armenia – and the neighbouring kingdom of Pontus under Tigranes' father-in-law Mithradates – offered refuge for disaffected elements. Pontus and Armenia encouraged piracy on a large scale, and 'pirate' raids from Armenian and Pontic bases in Anatolia extended as far as Ostia (although they are only referred to as pirates by the Roman authors: when the Romans did it, it was, of course, legitimate maritime business and naval expeditions!).

At first, Rome sent Lucullus, 'the first Roman to cross the Taurus with an army for warfare',[18] to face this new challenge. He defeated Mithradates in 72 BC in a battle on the Granicus (where much was made of its being the site of an earlier defeat of Asiatics by Europeans, being Alexander's first victory over the Persians) when the Romans are said to have slaughtered some 300,000 soldiers and camp followers. He then defeated Tigranes in 69 BC in battle near the Armenian capital of Tigranocerta amidst further slaughter (and perhaps the world's first use of chemical warfare).[19] Lucullus defeated the Armenians again in 68 BC in a bid to capture the other Armenian capital of Artaxata. Indeed, it seems possible that this greatly underrated general might have completely overrun Anatolia and forestalled Pompey's later conquest of Syria – he even briefly contemplated Iran – if he had not been recalled to Rome the following year.

Lucullus' recall was possibly at the jealous instigation of Pompey (or at least the Roman moneylenders whose rapacious activities he had curtailed in Anatolia), who succeeded Lucullus as commander of the East. Pompey was invested with such power ('Never did any man before Pompey set forth with so great authority conferred upon him by the Romans')[20] that his position was tantamount to that of an absolute monarch – the demands of the East had already embedded the idea of emperor in the Roman consciousness. With a massive force at his disposal, his first task was to sweep the seas of the pirates. This he achieved with astonishing success and without a fight (perhaps due partly to a deal struck with the pirates). Lucullus accused Pompey of simply being a bird of prey coming upon the carcass when others had slain the dead. Indeed, when the two rivals met in Galatia, Lucullus stooped to open personal abuse.[21] Pompey swept on to defeat Mithradates, first in a night-time battle and then, more decisively, in 66 BC. Tigranes surrendered to Pompey, but the humiliation forced him to commit suicide three years later – a sad end for a king who, more than any other, established a sense of Armenian nationhood which still survives to this day.

Syria was the next plum to fall. It was not difficult for Pompey. Tigranes' previous conquest had rendered the Seleucid state largely meaningless. The Maccabaean revolt and the subsequent Hasmonaean kings had robbed it of Palestine; the rise of the Nabataean kingdom in the south had robbed it of its trade; claims for the throne by rival members of the Seleucid family had robbed it of any leadership; local Arab dynasties asserted independence in Edessa, Chalcis and Emesa. In the end, Pompey did not even extend token recognition to the last Seleucid claimant, Antiochus XIII, as a client king. The rump Seleucid Empire became the Roman province of Syria overnight. 'In this way the Romans, without fighting, came into possession of Cilicia, inland Syria and Coele-Syria, Phoenicia, Palestine, and all the other countries bearing the Syrian name from the Euphrates to Egypt and the sea.'[22] What was arguably the greatest single conquest in

Rome's history fell without even a blow. Nor did it attract much notice: neither Dio nor Plutarch devote more than a single line to write of it, mentioning the annexation simply as a footnote to Pompey's Anatolian campaigns.[23] Judaea was added the following year. Thus, Pompey's arrival in Antioch in the summer of 64 BC marked the end of one empire and the beginning of another. The end of an empire that had once stretched all the way to India founded by the ancient world's greatest hero, Alexander. The remainder of Alexander's successor states soon also crumbled: Ptolemaic Egypt fell to Octavian in 30 BC and the last Greek kingdom in India fell to the Indo-Parthians in about 28 BC. But of all the successor states, the Seleucid kingdom was the one that incorporated the bulk of Alexander's conquests. With its end, the Romans became the direct heirs of Alexander.

Crassus, Carrhae and the Parthians[24]

In the heady first days after acquiring a great eastern empire, blinded by the spectacular great wealth that it brought in, Rome ignored the great new power that loomed beyond it: Iran. For it was no longer the emasculated, humiliated Iran that Alexander left behind in the ashes of Persepolis, but a new power dominated by the last of the great Indo-Iranian tribal confederations to migrate westwards from Central Asia. These were the Parthians, ruled by the Arsacid dynasty.

Like the Medes and Persians before them, the Parthians were initially little more than a tribal confederation, until in about 238 BC they seized control of the trans-Caspian territories of the Seleucid Empire. Building up a power-base in what is now Turkmenistan and Khorasan, they were at first a Central Asian power. By the middle of the second century the Parthians were ready to launch a full-scale invasion of Seleucid-held Iran. This culminated in Mithradates I being crowned King of Kings of a new Iranian empire in the old Iranian capital of Babylon in 141 BC. An Iranian renaissance was dawning.

The Parthian Empire is a very shadowy one. We know surprisingly little about it – surprising for an empire that lasted for nearly 500 years, the longest dynasty in Iranian history, and the only serious challenger to the Romans. The Parthian period has been long neglected: scholarship has always favoured the more flamboyant Sasanians – even the modern Iranians have tended to look upon the Parthian period as merely an interregnum between the Achaemenids and Sasanians. There is, of course, a serious lack of documents, not only Iranian but also Roman. The little Roman documentary evidence we have is heavily biased, without even the exuberant curiosity that the Iranians aroused in Herodotus or the admiration in Xenophon. But the Romans by no means had a monopoly of anti-Parthian bias: the Sasanians themselves suppressed Parthian history in their efforts to identify with a pre-Parthian past. The Parthians, therefore, are lost behind centuries of bias from both sides. To some extent we have inherited the Romans' prejudices, and tend to look on the Parthian Empire only in terms of its relations with Rome. But for the Parthians themselves, the Romans were probably their least concern. Parthia was in origin a Central Asian power, and Central Asia remained in many ways both its heartland and its prime concern, even after the capital was transferred to Ctesiphon in Mesopotamia. For most of Iranian history, the greatest threats came from the east, not the west. The Iranians were probably more concerned with relations further east than with Rome.

It may have been a shadowy empire, but it was also a very vigorous one. Whilst it has left us with few historical sources, it has left us with a wealth of art which can be just as revealing. Parthian sculptures convey an aggressive image: proud-looking warriors, barely removed from their Central Asian steppe roots, sporting beards and long hair, very masculinely clad in trousers and armed with broadswords.[25] Such an art conjures up images of warlords and campfires rather than the poetry and rose-gardens more often associated with Iranian culture. Such vigour re-established the self-confidence of Iranian civilisation after its humiliating setback at the hands of the Macedonians.

The achievements of the Parthian state were very impressive. They soon re-established most of the old Persian Empire and even extended their rule deep into India. Members of the Parthian royal house set up separate dynasties elsewhere in the East: in Seistan, from which the Rustam cycle of the Persian epic poem the *Shahnameh* emerged; in India, where they ousted the Scythian successors to the Greek kingdom in Gandhara; and most notably in Armenia (hence the cause of endless confrontation with Rome) where they long outlasted the parent dynasty in Iran itself. The Parthians successfully fended off several Seleucid attempts to regain their lost territories, most notably that by Antiochus III in the second century BC, whose gains the Parthians recovered after his death. It was Mithradates II – called Mithradates the Great – more than any other Parthian king who established the Parthian Empire on a firm footing. He was the first king of Iran since the Achaemenids to resurrect the ancient Persian title of King of Kings, or *Shahinshah*, he re-established Iranian rule in Babylonia and Seistan following revolts after the death of Mithradates I, and he established direct relations with the Chinese Empire.

Mithradates also sent his special envoy, Orobazes, to establish relations with the Roman Empire and offer an alliance. Orobazes met Sulla in Cilicia in 92 BC. It was an historic meeting, the very first between Roman and Iranian. The Chinese emperor had had the wisdom to send Iranian envoys back to Mithradates with messages of friendship and gifts of silk. Sulla treated Orobazes with contempt and sent him back offering Iran merely vassal status to Rome. The affront sowed the seed of centuries of discord between the two powers.

Thus, with power, prestige, wealth – and hurt pride – it was a new Iran that faced Rome. Two brand new superpowers flexing their outward muscles, one claiming the mantle of Alexander, the other the mantle of Cyrus, both meeting face-to-face at the Euphrates which formed their border. It only required a spark to ignite the inevitable. This was provided by the arrival in Syria of the avaricious Crassus, the Roman triumvir who was appointed proconsul of Syria in 55 BC. A combination of greed and a desire to emulate Caesar's conquests in Gaul prompted Crassus to set his sights on Iranian conquest. Ignoring both a treaty of friendship recently signed between Rome and Iran and the true strength of the Iranians, Crassus crossed the Euphrates and entered Mesopotamia.[26]

Opposing Crassus was the Parthian King Orodes' great general Suren, a commander of high calibre as well as one of the most remarkable men to dominate the period. Suren was a general who could choose his own ground, recognise the weaknesses of his enemy and use the peculiar tactics of his Iranian cavalry to complete advantage. But despite the personal description of Suren that has survived in Plutarch, he remains an enigma: we do not even know his name. 'Suren' (or 'Surenas') was the family name of a dynasty of great princes from Seistan in south-eastern Iran, not a personal name. It has been suggested that the 'Suren' of Carrhae was none other than the greatest of all Iranian heroes: the legendary Rustam, hero of the *Shahnameh*, who also originated from Seistan. Such an explanation might explain the otherwise complete absence of Suren in Iranian sources, an astonishing lacuna for one of ancient Iran's greatest generals. The figure of Suren and his family certainly cast a long shadow over the subsequent centuries in the Near East: St Gregory the Illuminator, patron saint of Armenia, was supposedly a descendant, and many of the noble families of medieval Armenia traced their descent from him.[27]

Rome and Iran collided head-on in 53 BC, only eleven years after the Romans had entered Syria, at the open plains of Carrhae (modern Harran in south-eastern Turkey). Here, Iranian intelligence, through its agent the Arab king Ariamnes,[28] had lured the Romans out of the protective covering of the hills into tailor-made cavalry country.[29] Plutarch has left us with a vivid – and harrowing – account of the battle, where we first learn of the famous 'Parthian shot' which has since passed into our language. Suren had a thousand heavy cavalry and several thousand light cavalry as well as a thousand baggage camels, altogether a force of some ten thousand. Crassus' army, at 40,000 strong, easily outnumbered Suren's. But despite numerical superiority, the Roman army was mainly infantry, with little cavalry. This could little withstand both the merciless hail of arrows and the repeated cavalry charges of the Iranians when full combat came. The Roman army was annihilated, suffering its greatest defeat since Hannibal's wars. Crassus himself was killed in the mopping up operations[30] along with 20,000 of his army. Ten thousand were taken off into captivity deep into the eastern fringes of the Iranian Empire. Iran had won its greatest victory since the great days of Darius.

King Orodes' son, Pakores, ruled Mesopotamia on his father's behalf and later succeeded Suren as army commander. Pakores had the longer-term strategic vision that Suren lacked, being able to follow up military victory with political consolidation, taking most of Syria from the Romans two years later. Crassus was succeeded in Syria by Cassius, who withdrew to Antioch. But Pakores' success excited suspicion from his jealous father, and Orodes withdrew Pakores back to Mesopotamia. The Romans, for their part, were by then distracted by the Civil War between the two surviving triumvirs, Pompey and Caesar.

Carrhae may have been the end of Crassus and tens of thousands of Roman lives, but it was not the end of the Parthian War. Rome had to respond – to retrieve captured standards as much as wounded pride. With Pompey now dead, it was left to the third triumvir, Julius Caesar. He came through Syria in 47 BC, following his Egyptian campaign. Apart from conferring a few administrative changes, he returned to Rome. From there Caesar pondered his own deification and proposed the grandly ambitious idea in 45 BC to invade Iran through Armenia, sweeping on past the Caspian to the Caucasus up through southern Russia and so back to Rome picking off Germany and Gaul on the way. His assassination put paid to such an unrealistic plan. In the ensuing Civil War, there was even an extraordinary suggestion that, after Antony and Cleopatra's defeat at Actium, Antony might shift the theatre of operations from the eastern Mediterranean to the Persian Gulf. Cleopatra had actually assembled a fleet in the Red Sea ready to transport her forces there, only for it to be burnt by the Nabataeans at the request of the governor of Syria.[31]

In the meantime, the Iranians returned in force to Syria under the joint command of Pakores – now reinstated in his father's favour – and a Roman renegade Labienus, a former associate of Brutus and Cassius. Iranian rule in the west was on the whole a benevolent one, contrasting with the early years of Rome's rule. The Syrians, smarting under Roman taxes and still remembering Persian generosity towards subject countries centuries before under Cyrus, welcomed the Parthians as deliverers. They thrived under Pakores' wise rule, feeling 'unusual affection for Pakores on account of his justness and mildness, an affection as great as they had felt for the best kings that had ever ruled them'.[32] Such accommodation from the population made Pakores' campaign an easy one. Whilst Labienus' division was easily defeated by a force dispatched from Rome, Pakores was able to capture most of Syria, all of Palestine and large parts of Anatolia. Just as Orodes was proclaiming his son conqueror of the Romans, however, Pakores was killed in 37 BC in a trap set for him by the Roman general Ventidius, perhaps in alliance with the Judaeans.[33]

Orodes abdicated in favour of his son Phraates IV, who consolidated his reign by promptly murdering his father and thirty of his brothers – as well as his own eldest son and a few leading families – thus plunging Iran into civil war. Mark Antony's subsequent disastrous campaign in 36 BC quickly reversed any advantage the Romans might have gained from Pakores' death and the ensuing Iranian weakness.[34] However, Phraates IV returned the Roman standards captured from Carrhae to Augustus in 20 BC, together with as many Roman prisoners of war from Crassus' and Antony's debacles as could be rounded up.

Peace was established at a great ceremony on an island in the Euphrates in AD 1. The Iranian delegation was led by the half-Italian King Phraates V,[35] the son of Phraates IV. The Roman delegation was led by Augustus' nominated successor and adoptive son, Gaius. Watched by the two armies drawn up on either bank, the two imperial delegations crossed over to the island in no-man's land and formally ended over half a century of war between the two powers. Thus, fifty-four years and tens of thousands of lives after Carrhae, the frontier between the Roman and Iranian empires reverted to where it had been in the first place: the Euphrates. It was as though Carrhae had never happened.[36]

Beyond the Euphrates

After the Augustan peace, Roman borders in the Near East remained more or less static for over a century as Rome and Iran enjoyed a period of stable, even friendly, relations. We even read of the Iranian ambassador to Rome urging Nero to change his capital. Whilst there is only a single source for this anecdote,[37] the story is a believable one, for the Iranians frequently changed theirs. In the end, the capital stayed at Rome and Nero simply burnt it down, but in the long term, the Iranians' recommendations were to prevail. Subsequent years were to see many more battles and some major wars fought in the East. It was in the East that Octavian brought to a final end the round of civil wars that had marked the last years of the republic. In the course of this we see Octavian, the republican general, both extinguishing some eastern monarchies and confirming others: the house of Ptolemy in Egypt, for example, came to an end, while that of Herod the Great in Judaea was given a new lease of life. In doing so, he returned home an emperor. Other major wars were to be fought, most notably the Jewish War fought by Vespasian and Titus.[38] But there was no expansion of any significance until the time of Trajan at the beginning of the second century.

Trajan and the ghost of Alexander

Annexing Arabia was perhaps made inevitable after the annexation of Palestine. For the secret of Palestine's security lay not in controlling the coasts – Rome's initial reason for entering Palestine – but in the control of its hinterland beyond the Jordan. Control of the lands beyond the Jordan had a powerful economic as well as strategic attraction too, for beyond lay the immensely wealthy Nabataean state with all the trans-Arabian trade routes that it controlled.[39]

Trajan also wanted to safeguard his rear before embarking upon a far more ambitious campaign. For Trajan set his sights on Iran. Up until AD 114, the Romans were content to leave the Euphrates as the boundary between Iran and Rome. After 114 this policy changed. The main reason – apart, of course, from aggression[40] – was the need to preserve a friendly client kingdom of Armenia as a buffer state. Whenever the balance in Armenia was upset – or looked like being upset – Rome advanced eastwards. Armenia was Rome's Afghanistan in this second- and third-century 'Great Game'.

Iran's replacement of an Armenian king by one more sympathetic to its interests in 113 first brought Trajan eastwards, and he fought several campaigns in Armenia and Adiabene in 114 and 115.[41] He marched down the Euphrates in AD 116, capturing Ctesiphon. Here, he placed a puppet Parthian king on the throne, then continued down the Euphrates to the shores of the Persian Gulf. Gazing yearningly at a merchant ship about to embark for India, he thought enviously of Alexander's opportunities and youth. Trajan reluctantly turned back, pausing to gaze at the ruins of Babylon and to offer sacrifice to Alexander's memory in the supposed room where he died. Trajan thus laid the ghost of Alexander, and turned his face westwards, leaving behind two new Roman provinces in upper Mesopotamia.[42]

Although Trajan's advance into Iranian territory was one of the most successful campaigns by a European in the East since Alexander, it achieved little in the short term. His eastern conquests – apart from Arabia – were handed back by his successor Hadrian in the face of instability elsewhere. Or perhaps, given the inadequacy of our sources for the reign of Hadrian,[43] the Romans were simply forced out of Mesopotamia by the Iranians. After all, Iran's client remained on the Armenian throne, and the Iranians themselves bounced back as just as large a threat to Roman supremacy as they had been before. For whilst Rome could annex vast tracts of Iranian territory and even occupy the capital of Ctesiphon, the roots of Iran's power lay further to the east, deep in the plateau of Iran proper and beyond to the original Parthian homeland east of the Caspian. The Iranians could always absorb the loss of their capital: they had several more to retire to. Trajan's occupation of Mesopotamia made little difference to Iranian power, therefore. Trajan himself probably realised, when he thought longingly of emulating Alexander whilst standing by the warm waters of the Persian Gulf, that to conquer Iran it had to be all the way to India or nothing. Sensibly, Trajan turned back.

Although it achieved little in the short term, there were major longer-term ramifications. To begin with, it created a precedent: in removing the Euphrates as a barrier in the Roman mind – far more a psychological than a physical barrier[44] – it made the eastern boundaries of the empire effectively unlimited. To the west, the Atlantic halted further expansion, whilst the forests of the north and deserts of the south made further expansion in those directions pointless. The Euphrates formed a useful line on the map; its removal meant that the East remained open.

Trajan's campaigns also brought a Roman emperor to the East on a semi-permanent basis, 'marking an important stage in the beginning of the cultural shift towards the East'.[45] Trajan resided in the East for three years, administering the rest of the empire quite effectively during the time. Antioch was his main imperial residence, and in effect it became the second capital of the Roman Empire. Successive emperors, both real and pretender, proclaimed themselves in Antioch.[46] This first happened following Trajan's death when his successor Hadrian was proclaimed emperor there. After Trajan, therefore, Rome looked increasingly to the East: as the only place where real expansion still lay open, as a natural heart of their own empire, as an alternative to Rome as the capital. The eventual transformation of Rome into an oriental empire had begun.

After Trajan, there were more and more incursions across the Euphrates, and even the establishment of short-lived Roman provinces. There was another war with Iran in AD 161–5 after the accession of Marcus Aurelius, again caused by the Romans refusing to accept a pro-Iranian king on the Armenian throne. This time Marcus Aurelius' co-emperor, Lucius Verus, took charge in the East, basing himself at Antioch for four years. For the first time Rome had an emperor for the East, ruling from an eastern capital. Once again Ctesiphon was taken, Seleucia on the Tigris was sacked, and Iranian territory was laid waste.[47] But the apparent completeness of this and other Roman victories against Iran must be questioned somewhat as exaggerated: after all they appeared to have had very little effect on real Iranian power and they resulted in few permanent gains for the Romans. In the end, we have only the Roman word for their victories – and the very vagueness and spuriousness of many Roman accounts of these campaigns leave much to be questioned.[48]

The real hero of the Parthian war was Avidius Cassius, a native Syrian from Cyrrhus, rather than the indolent Emperor Lucius Verus.[49] The career of Avidius Cassius was to have important later ramifications. After the end of the Parthian War he was proclaimed emperor in 175 following premature reports of Marcus Aurelius' death. Avidius Cassius lasted only three months and his murder appears to mark the end of what seems to be only a footnote (although, significantly, he gained the allegiance of both Syria and Egypt and was immensely popular in Antioch).[50] But the matter did not end there: Lucius Verus had set the precedent for a Roman eastern emperor; Avidius Cassius set the precedent for a native of the East to become emperor of Rome.[51]

Septimius Severus and Mesopotamia[52]

Pescennius Niger in 193 was the next to be proclaimed emperor from Antioch by the Roman army in Syria. Again, Antioch became an imperial capital, and Niger received delegations from all over the East, including Iran.[53] Unlike Avidius Cassius, Pescennius Niger was not a native of the East,[54] but the man who eventually put him down had the strongest associations of any emperor yet with the East. This was the North African of Phoenician descent, Septimius Severus, the Phoenician connection being reaffirmed with his marriage to a Syrian princess (Plate 151).[55] He had already served in Syria as a rising young officer in the Roman army, and it was Niger's proclamation as emperor in 193 which brought Septimius Severus back to Syria the following year. Now emperor himself, Septimius Severus was quick to suppress Niger's revolt. The two armies met first at Nicaea then more decisively at the historic battlefield of Issus. Herodian describes the outcome as the same as when Alexander defeated Darius there half a millennium before: 'the West defeated the East.'[56] Herodian's dramatic ironies aside, it seems clear that the idea of eastern and western empires was already beginning to form in the Roman consciousness. Syria was definitely characterised as 'eastern' rather than 'western', even when the 'West' was commanded by a Libyan and the 'East' by an Italian. Indeed, remnants of Niger's defeated army fled to Iran, where they were able to teach some Roman military expertise which was quickly put to good use in new Iranian battle techniques.[57]

Septimius Severus stayed on in Antioch to begin his long-cherished invasion of Mesopotamia on the pretext that Iran had supported Niger. 'It was commonly said that Septimius Severus' motive for the Parthian War was a desire for glory, and that it was not launched out of any necessity.'[58] After suppressing another rival emperor in Britain (Clodius Albinus) he launched his invasion in 197. Like Trajan before him, Septimius Severus failed to capture Hatra in a near disastrous siege the following year.[59] But he did capture Ctesiphon, taking the Parthian king completely by surprise – implying perhaps that there was a truce at the time. The city was looted and plundered by the Romans following their surprise attack, and Herodian writes, 'Thus, more by luck than good judgement, Septimius Severus won the glory of a Parthian victory.'[60] Rome had arrived on the banks of the Tigris to stay.

Septimius Severus established his new conquests as the Roman province of Mesopotamia with its capital at Nisibis. In addition, he divided the old large province of Syria into two: Coele Syria and Syria Phoenice. Contrary to what one is led to expect by these new provincial names (Syria Phoenice refers to the coast and Coele or 'Hollow' Syria presumably refers to the rift valley inland), the divisions were north–south rather than east–west, with Coele Syria to the north. The reasons for this division were not so much administrative as strategic, the need to limit the forces available to any single provincial commander.[61] For with so many real and would-be emperors, from Vespasian to Niger, being proclaimed from a Syrian power-base, Septimius Severus wanted to ensure that no threats would arise to his own rule. He finally left Antioch in 202 after having spent in the East seven of the ten years he had reigned so far.

With the establishment of the limits of the empire on the Tigris, we see for the first time the beginnings of substantial Roman material remains east of Aleppo. Remains of the Roman garrison town at Singara (modern Sinjar in northern Iraq) are still extant, and more remains have been found further east. These include a military camp at ʿAin Sinu and a milestone of Alexander Severus between Singara and the river, while remains at Seh Qubba on a bluff overlooking the Tigris probably represent the remains of the outpost of Castra Maurorum (Plate 1), the easternmost Roman site so far excavated.[62] More substantial Roman military remains have been excavated at Dura Europos (Figure 29, Plate 37), and the vast semi-desert areas that make up the present borderlands of Syria, Jordan and Iraq are covered with a complex system of Roman roads, frontier forts and border settlements (Figure 86).[63] Whilst most of these date from the later years of Roman rule there – especially the military reforms of Diocletian – it is clear that with the crossing of the Euphrates by Septimius Severus, the Romans had come to stay.

Septimius Severus' Mesopotamian conquests were followed up in 216 by his son Caracalla, who defeated the unsuspecting Parthian king, Artabanus, outside Ctesiphon whilst pretending do be a suitor for his daughter.[64] Artabanus, having been twice tricked by both father and son, was determined not to be caught unawares again, and he launched a massive invasion. The subsequent murder of Caracalla, however, deprived Artabanus of his satisfaction. In the face of the advancing threat from the wrathful Artabanus and his huge army, the Roman army hastily proclaimed the ill-prepared lawyer Macrinus as emperor.[65]

There followed a second great battle between Romans and Iranians on the fateful battlefield of Carrhae, with a result almost the same as the first, and the Romans looked like facing certain defeat once more at Carrhae.[66] Doubtless the fate of Crassus and his lost army were very much on Macrinus' mind, so he hastily sued for peace. Macrinus

Plate 1 Seh Qubba overlooking the Euphrates in northern Iraq, probably the site
of the Roman fort of Castra Maurorum, the easternmost Roman site excavated

pointed out that Artabanus' grudge was a personal one against Caracalla, who was now
dead, rather than the Roman Empire as a whole. Artabanus accepted the truce.

Thus, both sides retired from the second Battle of Carrhae. Two Roman leaders had
met their end there, Crassus and Caracalla. It was the site of the first battle that the
Parthians had fought against the Romans – and the last. Within a few years Artabanus and
the Parthians were to be overthrown by a vigorous new Persian dynasty from the same
heartland of ancient Persia whence hailed the Achaemenids: the Sasanians under their
founder Ardeshir.

The end of the beginning

One should not, of course, view Rome's acquisition of its eastern empire too strongly in terms of the personalities involved and it is perhaps a mistake to condemn the vacuous Crassus or the unscrupulous Orodes too harshly. Rome's pursuit of its vendetta against Hannibal no doubt played its part, but Rome would still have come east without Hannibal. Personal ambition by the conquering founders – Lucullus, Pompey, Crassus, *et al.* – no doubt played a part too. But so did the importance of maintaining and ruling the growing Roman state sensibly. Pompey's extinction of the house of Seleucus without allowing it even the grace of client status was not so much Pompey's personal aggrandisement but sound policy in not allowing a token Seleucid court to act as a magnet for disaffected factions. Crassus may have been old and venal and Suren young and energetic, but at the end of the day it was better arms, better supplies, better tactics, better intelligence and better command that won Carrhae. Lucullus may have been a far better military commander than either Pompey or Crassus, but Lucullus lacked one thing that both the others possessed: status. Pompey and Crassus were triumvirs – effectively co-emperors (or rather 'proto-co-emperors'). Hence, Pompey's appointment to the eastern command right at the very beginning of the eastern empire set a precedent that marked its end: so important did the eastern empire become that it needed an eastern emperor, eventually culminating in the division of the Roman Empire. In a sense, Pompey anticipated the eastern emperors. Similarly, Crassus' appointment as proconsul of Syria was more than mere avarice. The importance of Rome's eastern frontier was such that nobody of lower status than a triumvir and proconsul could fill the post. Rome may have blundered over Carrhae, but both initial and long-term policy in Syria did not lack wisdom or foresight: its strategic position and wealth were too important to entrust to mere client kings or field commanders: only Rome's highest citizens would do.

For Iran's part, the pragmatic Orodes was right to concentrate more on tying a major land power like Armenia to his empire than a seaboard province like Syria – and to withdraw back behind the Euphrates after his headstrong son took Syria.[67] Syria would have been too far out on a limb for a people whose heartland lay east of the Caspian. For a land power, the Syrian deserts made a more defensible frontier than the Mediterranean. Most of all, from the Iranian point of view the Roman war was merely an incident, probably perceived as nothing more than raids by barbarians on their western borders. Iranian sources are entirely silent about Carrhae. Parthian sources were suppressed, it is true, by the Sasanians, but the little that has indirectly survived shows concern almost wholly with their eastern and northern borders, not the west.[68] The Parthians had little conception of the Romans as a great power, even less as a civilised one, and any perception they had of them would simply have been as raiders from across the distant western sea. Wars with the Parthians' own nomadic brethren of Central Asia were seen to be of utmost importance; a war with the West, even a victory such as Carrhae, would barely rate a mention.

When compared to the massive expansion of Roman building activity from the second century onwards, Rome has left surprisingly little trace of the first century and a half of its rule there.[69] Few monuments survive and the archaeological evidence suggests a general decline, even depression, in the Near East for this period. In assessing the initial impact of Rome in the East in these early years, therefore, one must be wary of overestimating its importance, such as the literary sources imply. Rome played a large part, it is true, but it probably had very little effect on either the character or the culture of the region. Rome's initial rule was characterised by exploitation, rapaciousness and avarice. The Romans came as conquerors, not civilisers, and their occupation was brutal and unpopular. True, the Jews were the only people of the East to revolt on a large scale in this period, but the resentment was very real, and the Iranians as we have seen were hailed as liberators. Roman economic prosperity and cultural wealth, and with it the material remains, was not to come until much later. The first period of Roman rule in the East down to about the time of Trajan or even Hadrian, therefore, appears to have been a material decline.

Pompey had brought back from the East more than an empire: he brought the idea of an emperor. The West had no counterpart to the eastern concept of emperor. Hitherto the West had only kings, there was no precedent for any status above that, a 'super-king' or 'king of kings'. Iran had bequeathed to the East its ancient royal title of *shahinshah* or 'king of kings', as well as the tradition of royal purple. In the East, furthermore, the title went even beyond the concept of a mere king of kings, for he was a god as well: emperors were deified (a lesson not lost on Alexander some three centuries previously). Both the colour purple and the title that went with it was taken over by the Parthian royal house as well as by Tigranes of Armenia, Pompey's main adversary.[70] The observation was not lost on the Romans. One of the first Romans to be actually hailed as 'Imperator' by his troops, Pompey was soon also to be hailed 'a king of kings' and the purple was to become synonymous with Roman imperium.[71] Herod's courting of Octavian after the Battle of Actium may have been mere sycophancy, but it emphasised an important message to Octavian: Herod was one of the most opulent and glittering of the monarchs of the East. Even though it was republican Rome that had made him king, the message of royalty was not lost on Octavian. There would be no more Marii, Sullas or Gracchi: henceforth, Rome too had to have a monarch, an emperor to rule an empire, and the emperors were to become gods.[72]

Following the death of Caracalla and the second Battle of Carrhae, Macrinus remained in Antioch, which he used as his capital to rule the empire. In taking up residence in the East, Macrinus also became more oriental, adopting oriental dress with studded cummerbunds and other eastern trappings that filled his entourage with misgivings.[73] Thus, Rome's first period of expansion into the East began with a Republican dictator bringing back the eastern concept of emperor; it ended with an emperor adopting a fashion that was ultimately to prove addictive.

The long retreat

The campaigns of Septimius Severus near the end of the second century represented the last great eastward expansion of the Roman Empire. Whilst there would still be the occasional Roman gains at the expense of the Iranians and even some great victories, the beginning of the third century was the beginning of a slow retraction of Rome's eastern empire. The next four centuries were to be a long retreat that culminated in the final evacuation of Rome's Near Eastern provinces in the face of the advancing Muslim Arabs in the seventh century.

But the victorious Muslims merely delivered the death blow to an eastern empire that was diminishing long before. For the intervening centuries saw the rise and fall of a great new dynasty in Iran that did even more than the Parthians had to restore Iranian might. This was the Sasanian.

Iran restored: Severus Alexander and Artaxerxes[74]

Parthian vigour and Parthian victories against the West's greatest superpower re-established the self-confidence of Iranian civilisation, paving the way for a new dynasty of Iranian kings. These were the Sasanians. Members of the Parthian royal family lived on as rulers of Armenia in the west and Seistan in the east,[75] but it was the Sasanian royal family who, originating from the same heartland of Persia as the ancient Achaemenid kings, consciously proclaimed a renaissance of the Achaemenid glories of old. Their first ruler was Ardeshir I. He is often referred to in the sources as Artaxerxes (of which the name Ardeshir is a later variation), almost as a conscious archaism in referring back to the ancient kings of the Achaemenid Empire.[76] Although the Sasanians were a dynasty of warrior kings, their foundation was religious: Ardeshir-Artaxerxes hailed from a line of high-priests who were hereditary guardians of the great temple at Istakhr in southern Iran[77] – a tradition of religious leaders assuming secular power in Iran that is still alive today. Ardeshir overthrew the last Parthian king, Artabanus V, in 224, to proclaim a new empire that was to last for the next 430 years. The event sent shock-waves to the very heart of Rome.

Ardeshir was not the only emperor to hail from a long line of eastern high-priests. So did his counterpart in Rome. For the Syrian emperor, Severus Alexander, was descended from the high-priests of Baal at Emesa, a family that had been brought to the forefront of Roman politics by his grandmother Julia Maesa and her sister Julia Domna (Plate 156).[78] The wars of the previous generations between the Romans and the Iranians had brought the two sides to stalemate, resulting in a truce between Macrinus and Artabanus following the second Battle of Carrhae. But the truce meant nothing to Artabanus' usurper, and the Romans meant even less. Ardeshir viewed the Romans merely as upstart occupiers of lands that were Iranian by historic right. Accordingly, he overran the Roman province of Mesopotamia and demanded the return of all of Rome's Near Eastern possessions.[79]

Rome was stunned. In an impassioned speech in Rome Severus Alexander emphasised the threat to be one of the most serious that a Roman emperor ever had to face. Rome was in an uproar as it bade goodbye to its beloved emperor – one of the mildest that Rome had had the good fortune to experience since the Antonine golden age. He took leave of his adoptive city expecting never to see it again. The Roman Emperor Alexander sailed home to Syria to answer the new Iranian challenge.

Thus, two emperors faced each other, a new Artaxerxes facing a new Alexander,[80] both of them natives of the East, both descendants of priests. Severus Alexander planned a major, three-pronged invasion of Iran. It was disastrous. One army 'suffered a staggering disaster; it is not easy to recall another like it, one in which a great army was destroyed', another was 'almost totally destroyed in the mountains; a great many soldiers suffered mutilation in the frigid country, and only a handful of the large numbers of troops who started the march managed to reach Antioch' whilst the third did not engage the enemy.[81] Having triumphed, Ardeshir disbanded his army. Severus Alexander eventually paid the ultimate price for his defeat, when a disaffected army faction killed him on campaign on the Rhine and proclaimed a Thracian, Maximinus, emperor in his place.

Shapur I, Valerian and the disaster of Edessa[82]

The war between Severus Alexander and Ardeshir was a dress rehearsal for the wars fought by Ardeshir's successor, Shapur I, the greatest of the Sasanian emperors (Plate 27).

Shapur saw himself as the heir to Cyrus the Great: he re-established much of the ancient borders of the Persian Empire, he reformed and reorganised the administration, he encouraged religious toleration but at the same time reaffirmed Zoroastrianism as the state religion. But it was Rome, not Iran, that renewed the war with the aggression of the Emperor Gordian III in 243, although both he and his army were wiped out by the Sasanians in a battle in northern Mesopotamia in 244.[83] The army hurriedly elected an Arab officer, Philip, as emperor, who requested Shapur for terms. An enormous indemnity was imposed, and a shaky peace returned to the Near East.

It did not last long. Citing Roman meddling in Armenia as an excuse, Shapur invaded Syria once more in 252, renewing the war that was to last for almost another ten years. Antioch was captured twice, in 256 and again in 260.[84] Large numbers of its citizens, particularly those with technical expertise, were deported to Iran to the new city of Gundishapur.[85] But despite the sacking and deportations, the Syrians still remembered the first time Iranians had occupied Roman Syria under Pakores and under Cyrus before that. The account by Peter Patricius of the occupation of Antioch implies that the common folk – the native Syrian population – welcomed the Iranians as deliverers once more.[86] This seems to suggest that the Syrian founders of Gundishapur followed their captors willingly – they were certainly allowed full religious freedom in Iran and Shapur's toleration and mildness encouraged a minor Syrian 'renaissance' at Gundishapur.

The war brought a Roman emperor eastwards once more, this time the Emperor Valerian. Again, the armies of Rome and Iran met in a momentous battle, at Edessa in 260 – ironically not far from the site of the Battle of Carrhae some 300 years earlier. Again, a Roman army was utterly defeated: 60,000 Roman prisoners of war were taken into Persia, including the greatest prize of all: the Roman Emperor Valerian himself, who was captured and brought in chains to kneel before Shapur. The event is celebrated in a series of rock-reliefs in southern Iran that depict the humiliated Valerian (Plates 25–7).[87]

Never before had Iran been greater, and the subsequent centuries of Sasanian history would see success after success for Iran, often at Rome's expense. In contrast, Rome never seemed weaker. For in addition to Shapur's invasion there had been massive Gothic invasions. With the Goths to the west and Iranians to the east, Rome seemed caught in the middle.

Shapur II, Constantius and the disaster of Amida

But fortunately for Rome, the great Shapur died in 272 and the Emperor Aurelian was able to restore order to the empire.[88] Towards the end of the century the decline was halted by the administrative and military reforms of Diocletian. In Iran, the great warrior king Bahram II or Bahram Gur (276–93) might well have continued Iran's western expansion, but he was distracted by problems in the eastern borderlands – always of more concern to Iran than its western borders. Seizing their chance, the Romans invaded Mesopotamia under Emperor Carus in 283.[89] They advanced to the gates of Ctesiphon and Rome regained the province of Mesopotamia for a short time, but both Carus and his son Numerianus lost their lives during this campaign.[90] Bahram's successor, Narseh, was able to retake Mesopotamia and defeat Diocletian's co-emperor Galerius. A peace – the so-called 'Forty year Peace' – was finally re-established in 298 by Diocletian and the entire eastern defences reorganised.[91]

In 309 an infant ascended the Sasanian throne.[92] This was Shapur II, whose victories against Rome were destined to almost match those of his great namesake, and his reign of seventy years was the longest in Iranian history. But it was a new Rome that faced Iran, a Rome that now had far more of a vested interest in the Near East. With Constantine adopting an eastern religion, Rome itself had come east, turning its back upon Europe and founding a new, Christian Rome at Constantinople. For the first time Rome and Iran now faced each other in their own mutual back yard. After a few brief indecisive campaigns, Constantine gathered together a huge army to invade Iran but died in 337 before the invasion had got properly under way. It was left to his successor Constantius to answer the Iranian threat.[93]

Neither side emerged as absolute victor, but Constantius felt the situation secure enough to garrison Syria and return to the west in 350. There followed a few years of relative peace, a peace that was as inconclusive as the war had been. Shapur resumed hostilities once more in 359. This time the Iranians launched a massive invasion along the Euphrates, turning northwards towards the Anatolian foothills. The Roman forces sent against Shapur's mighty war-machine could not withstand the onslaught. They were forced to retreat to the stronghold of Amida – modern Diyarbakir – at the foothills of the Taurus Mountains. Ammianus Marcellinus has left us with a harrowing eyewitness account of the Iranian capture of Amida, one of Shapur's more spectacular victories. Amida fell and a general massacre ensued (Ammianus only just managing a hair-raising escape) after a siege that had lasted 73 days with many tens of thousands of losses.[94]

Julian and the loss of the Tigris provinces

Constantius died in Cilicia in 361. He was succeeded by the last of Constantine's house and one of the more interesting of Rome's emperors, Julian the Apostate.[95] As well as trying to bring back paganism, Julian was another who, like Caracalla and other emperors, took Alexander as his role model – at least in the view of his admirers.[96] But emulating Alexander entails invading Iran, and this time, Iran was to be dealt with once and for all. Contemporaries viewed Julian's war as East against West, the Trojan Wars, the ancient Persian Wars of the Greeks, and Alexander all rolled into one.[97]

After ten months in Constantinople consolidating his home position Julian moved on to Antioch, symbolically camping at Alexander's great battlefield at Issus on the way.[98] There he rejected an Iranian request for peace, despite a plea from the citizens of Antioch. The Syrians were rather more realistic about war with Iran after their experience a generation previously – and had a long tradition of sympathies with the Iranians, as we have seen. Julian set out from Antioch in the spring of 361, proceeding down the Euphrates to Carrhae. At the historic battlefield of Carrhae Julian halted, and drew up his entire army numbering 65,000 in a grand review. Such stage-managements, like Hitler and the railway carriage in the woods of Compiègne, have all the hallmarks of a propaganda exercise. To a scholar like Julian the historical irony of reviewing his army at Carrhae cannot have been lost, and was doubtless devised as a message both to his troops and to Shapur. He cited the former campaigns of Lucullus, Pompey, Mark Antony, Trajan, Verus and Septimius Severus and the need to overthrow Iran once and for all as their Roman ancestors had overthrown Carthage. But ominously, unlike Hitler, Julian did not yet hold the trump card, and the emperor and his 'Grande Armée' left Carrhae with little more than a morale boost.[99]

Initially, the invasion went tolerably well. The 'army whose numbers had never been surpassed under any previous emperor'[100] proceeded down the Euphrates on a fleet of 1,150 boats, with supplies, siege engines and the heavy cavalry following on land. They then entered lower Mesopotamia, much of which had been flooded by breaching the canals to hinder the Roman advance. The army floundered through endless mud, but still succeeded in taking several towns and gaining a stunning victory against the Iranians on the banks of the Nahr al-Malik canal. On crossing the Tigris Julian made the fateful decision to burn his boats: there was to be no turning back, the defeat of Iran was to be pursued to the end. Julian was not the only one, however, to burn his assets, for the Romans from then on encountered the scorched earth policy that Shapur had commanded. Julian pushed on to the scene of Alexander's great victory at Gaugamela, even making plans for the future Roman administration of Hyrcania and Panjab.[101] But the scorched earth kept the army hungry, even threatening mutiny at one point,[102] while Iranian skirmishers kept the Roman army constantly on the defensive.

During one of these skirmishes, Julian himself was struck in the side by a spear and the Emperor Julian – last of the pagan emperors,[103] last of the house of Constantine, last of the scholar-hero emperors – died.[104] With him died a whole era of Rome's history as well as the dream of resurrecting Alexander's empire. Libanius, his greatest admirer, lamented, 'The Persian empire should now lie in ruins, and Roman governors instead of satraps now be administering their territory under our laws: our temples here should be adorned with booty got from them, while the victor in this contest should be seated on his imperial throne, receiving the orations composed in honour of his exploits. Such, I am sure, would be right and proper. . . . We expected the whole empire of Persia to form part of that of Rome.'[105] The next day a pitched battle left the Romans badly mauled.[106]

The chaotic retreat that ensued could not have been in greater contrast to the heroic overtones of the advance. Leaderless, the army hurriedly elected the lacklustre Jovian as emperor. Heavy losses were suffered and the retreat rapidly become a panic-stricken debacle, with lack of provisions threatening famine. The remnants of Julian's 'Grande Armée', one of the most ambitious and vaunted invasions of Asia since Alexander, was reduced to a shambles.

Jovian received Shapur's emissaries in his tent[107] and a bilateral thirty-year peace was agreed. Jovian ceded all the trans-Tigris possessions, as well as Nisibis, and most of Armenia to Iran. In return, the Romans were granted safe conduct back to Syria. Julian's stage-managed attempt to lay the ghost of Carrhae had backfired, for Zosimus describes Jovian's humiliation in 363 as greater than either Crassus' or Antony's debacles and the beginning of the end of Rome's Near Eastern empire.[108] In particular, the surrender of the frontier city of Nisibis to the Iranians without a fight was a bitter pill for Rome to swallow. It was even worse for the citizens of the city itself, for under the terms of Iran's 'diktat', the city had to be evacuated. They understandably felt betrayed by Jovian and contemporary accounts paint a vivid picture of the agony of an entire people streaming out of their homes with whatever possessions they could grab, to end up as refugees. The betrayal was felt equally by many of Jovian's soldiers with the unenviable job of having to enforce the eviction. Jovian's name became reviled. No mention now of any military defeat, and there were mutterings by the army of a stab in the back. Jovian returned through the towns of the East, dispatching Julian's body to Tarsus for burial. Fortunately, illness got to him before a dissatisfied army could. The humiliated Jovian died in Bithynia after only an eight-month reign and a Roman legacy in the East in shambles.[109]

Jovian is almost universally reviled by ancient historians for the humiliating handover of Nisibis. He may have been an incompetent emperor, but one suspects that behind the welter of criticisms and 'stab in the back' accusations, his agreement to this peace probably saved the Roman army and Roman prestige from a disaster that might have cost it the entire Near East. To modern observers he appears particularly lacklustre under the shadow of his flamboyant and quixotic predecessor. No doubt he was, but when all is said and done the fact remains that it was Julian, not Jovian, who was responsible for the disaster in the East, and Jovian who saved what he could from Julian's debacle. Even without his restoration of Christianity, Jovian deserves a kinder press.

Justinian the peasant's son and Khusrau of the Immortal Soul[110]

Subsequent years saw a number of Persian Wars and Roman reversals, though it is not intended to detail all of them here. By and large, however, it was a period of peace on the Near Eastern frontier, as both superpowers were distracted for once by invasions from the north rather than by each other. Hence, many of the frontier defences in the Near East were allowed to deteriorate.[111] But such threats nonetheless forced Rome's wealth more and more into its defence, so that by the end of the fourth century Rome had a standing army estimated to number an astonishing 635,000 men.[112] In 395–7 the Near East saw an invasion by a completely new enemy whose name both Rome and Iran had cause to shudder at, when the Huns broke through the Caucasian passes and entered the Near East for the first time. Although the Huns were new to the Near East and to the Roman Empire (apart from a brief encounter under the walls of Amida), Iran already had some experience of these incredibly mobile – and ruthless – steppe nomads in their wars with them in the previous century. Shapur II had managed to halt their depredations in Central Asia, but it merely served to deflect them around the Caspian Sea to their north-west frontier in the Caucasus. Iranian–Roman relations were subsequently dominated by the need for Iran to maintain the Caucasian defences against the Huns. Hence, Constantinople contributed to the upkeep of the defence of the passes in the form of regular payments made to Ctesiphon; safeguarding the passes stopped the Huns from coming into Roman possessions as much as into Persian. The great defences at Darband in Daghestan still stand today as mute evidence of the importance of this policy.[113] Roman defaulting on these payments contributed more than anything else to the gradual deterioration of relations between the two powers throughout the fifth century. Ultimately, however, even halting the Huns at the Caucasus passes merely deflected them around the Black Sea to the Roman West.[114]

The state of uneasy but stable equilibrium between Iran and Rome was shattered in the early sixth century in a series of wars lasting almost a hundred years. These wars ended up exhausting both powers. The sixth century also saw two of their greatest kings emerge: the Emperor Justinian of Rome and the Great King Khusrau I Anushirvan of Iran.

In 527 a peasant's son from Thrace ascended the Roman throne in Constantinople who was able, for a short time, to reinstate the ancient glory of the Roman Empire. This was Justinian. Two years after Justinian ascended his throne, the Sasanian Emperor Kavadh sent an army of 30,000 into eastern Anatolia. The Iranians attacked Roman positions at Dara with a force of 70,000 but were defeated and forced to retreat to Nisibis. A peace treaty was duly negotiated – the 'Endless Peace' of 532 – but the endless war continued intermittently nonetheless with several battles being fought.

Meanwhile, in 531 a new emperor had ascended the throne in Iran after Kavadh's death, the legendary Khusrau I Anushirvan ('of the Immortal Soul'). For the Iranians, Khusrau Anushirvan has gone down in history as one of their greatest kings. Often referred to as 'the Just King', his long reign remained a model for kingship, lordly virtues and wise rule that was used as a mirror for subsequent rulers of Iran down to the Islamic Middle Ages.[115] Khusrau certainly had considerable gall: he demanded, and got, from Justinian a share of the spoils from the North African reconquest on the grounds that it would never have been possible for the Romans without a peaceful Iran![116] He may also have conquered Ceylon in a naval campaign, and certainly mounted a successful naval invasion and occupation of Yemen, possibly a part of a pincer movement to block Rome's access to the lucrative Indian Ocean trade through both the Persian Gulf and the Red Sea.[117] Peace was soon broken with a surrogate war fought by both empires' Arab allies, the Lakhm and the Ghassan (see Chapter 3). In the end, it broke out into direct war when Khusrau accused Justinian of provoking the Huns into invading Iran. Accordingly, taking advantage of Constantinople's preoccupation in the west, Khusrau invaded the Roman Empire in 540.

His triumphal progress through Syria was made easy for him by many mass desertions to his side from the Roman army. The archaeological evidence from the Syrian countryside, furthermore, suggests Iranian support for the local economy and protection of the villages, quite contrary to the picture of destruction that the western sources imply.[118] Apamaea surrendered peacefully, and Khusrau's subsequent capture of Antioch was a foregone conclusion. He went on to the port of Seleucia by the Mediterranean, the dream of Iran's emperors ever since they lost the Mediterranean seaboard to Alexander some eight and a half centuries previously. Emulating Shapur's precedent three centuries before, Khusrau founded a new city settled by captured prisoners from Antioch, triumphantly naming it *Veh Antiok Khusrau* or 'Khusrau's Better than Antioch'.

Justinian's great general Belisarius had some success in recapturing Syria for the empire, but he failed to recapture Nisibis and was recalled to Constantinople in 543. In the end, the two sides fought themselves to exhaustion and Iran was faced with the new threat from the Turkish Kaghanate on its eastern frontier. Accordingly, a Fifty-Year Peace was finally declared in 561 to end a war that had lasted thirty-one years.[119] But war was resumed under Justin II in 571. Khusrau responded by invading Syria, following it up with an invasion of Armenia in 575. Both sides suffered defeats, Rome in Syria and Iran in Armenia, and so a peace between the two exhausted powers was negotiated in 576 and renewed two years later. The following year, Khusrau I Anushirvan died after a reign of forty-eight years.

Endgame: Heraclius, Khusrau Parviz and Muhammad

An intermittent and indecisive war of attrition resumed in 579 and continued until a new peace was negotiated in 591. Meanwhile, a vigorous new king had ascended the throne in Iran. This was Khusrau II Parviz, who was destined to outshine his namesake and become one of Iran's greatest kings. In 603 Khusrau Parviz resumed the war against the historic enemy to the west. This time, Iran not only finally realised its age-old dream of reinstating the ancient borders of the Achaemenid kings, but came close to capturing Constantinople itself.

Khusrau Parviz's successes were nothing short of spectacular – not since the heady days of Cyrus and Darius had the world witnessed such conquests by a Persian king.[120] The initial pretext for Khusrau was the overthrow of the pro-Iranian Emperor Maurice by Phocas. The Roman Empire's great Anatolian fortress-cities fell to the victorious Iranians one by one, and by 606 Khusrau's armies had entered Cappadocia. The way to Constantinople lay open and virtually unguarded. In Constantinople itself the city was undergoing one of its periodic bouts of blood-letting, as the rival political factions, the Greens and Blues, fought each other in pitched street battles. Out of the rivalry the unpopular Emperor Phocas was deposed in 610. He was replaced by Heraclius, the disastrous seventh century's most capable emperor – but the one who tragically was to end up losing the most. In the meantime, the mighty Iranian army under Khusrau's general Shahrbaraz was able to advance virtually unopposed to Constantinople, pitching their tents on the Asiatic shores of the Bosphorus opposite the capital in 615.[121]

The final outcome of seven hundred years of on–off war between Romans and Iranians seemed about to be decided. Elsewhere in the Middle East Khusrau's victories had been equally impressive. Tarsus and Damascus were taken in 613, then in the following year, like Cyrus the Great over a thousand years previously, Cyrus the Last (the name 'Khusrau' is a later version of the name 'Cyrus') entered Jerusalem. Perhaps, like the first Cyrus before him, Khusrau was hoping to restore the city and its temple to the Jews and be hailed as a liberator and a prophet, for the Christian buildings of the city were ransacked and the holy relics taken off as loot deep into Iran. Khusrau then swept on to the greatest of all his conquests: in 619 he took Alexandria. Thus, in Alexander the Great's city Khusrau II Parviz, Great King and King of Kings, finally laid to rest the ghost of the 'Demon King', Alexander. The shadow of Alexander always lay heavily on all who had felt it. For the Iranians, it had haunted their consciousness for a millennium as a constant reminder of their humiliating defeat by an invader whose victory the Iranians had looked upon more than any other single event as the source of their misfortunes, as well as their grievances and rage towards the West. Egypt was soon occupied by Khusrau's forces. It must have been a great moment for Khusrau: Cyrus the Last could certainly gaze eastwards and see all of Asia from the Nile to the Indus once more under the Persians. Cyrus the Great could finally rest in peace: 'Sleep well, O Cyrus, for we are awake.'

But like the Iranian king who actually uttered those words,[122] the last Cyrus too was asleep, and in the end Khusrau was no Cyrus. Cyrus the Great had entered Jerusalem and restored it out of respect for its religion; Khusrau arrogantly flouted it. For Jerusalem's religion had changed since Cyrus' day, and the great Christian Empire of Rome felt this even more keenly than they felt the swords of the conquerors themselves. This was Khusrau's cardinal mistake. More than anything else it galvanised Constantinople into a response. In 622 Heraclius was accordingly able to unite Constantinople's quarrelling factions behind him. He used the occupation of Jerusalem and the loss of its holy relics to set a precedent that altered the subsequent history of the European Middle Ages and whose effect is still felt today: Heraclius declared Holy War.

Armed with religious zeal, these first Crusaders were able to penetrate deep into Iran in 622 where they plundered the Iranian holy city of Shiz (Plate 21), partly to seize back the holy relics which the Iranians had taken from Jerusalem, and partly as revenge for the plunder of Jerusalem itself.[123] Heraclius advanced to the historic battlefield of Nineveh in 627, whose capture by the Medes in 612 BC had first signalled the arrival of the Iranians upon the Near Eastern scene. This time the Iranians were defeated and the following year Khusrau II Parviz was murdered. His successor, Kavadh II, sued for peace. In 634

Heraclius recaptured Antioch, which became his headquarters and the imperial Roman seat once more. Heraclius was able to negotiate a withdrawal back to previous borders. Peace, like countless previous ones, was established once more.

Heraclius' retaliation against Iran was one of the most spectacular revivals in Roman history. Indeed, Heraclius was one of Rome's greatest generals, deserving far greater prominence than history has granted him, for he was able to save an empire brought to within an ace of extinction by the Iranians. He rallied the empire's tottering resources and was able to instil personal motivation in his troops by declaring that those who died would be martyrs and go directly to heaven. Heraclius' proclamation of holy war has its exact counterpart in the Islamic concept of *jihad*, first traditionally articulated by Muhammad in the very same year – 622 – that Heraclius formulated his.[124] The irony for Heraclius was that his revolutionary new concept of war would be taken up by others; the tragedy was that it was used to take away everything that he had won in the East.

For it was the last time that Antioch would host a Roman emperor. It appeared that out of this increasingly bitter conflict one or other of the powers would fall. In the end it was both, at the hands of an entirely new power from an entirely unexpected quarter of the Near East: the Arabs of the Hijaz. The Iranian–Roman wars had made conquest easy for the Arabs, and less than a century later, these unknown Arabs with their revolutionary new religion ruled an empire that stretched from the borders of China to the Atlantic, an empire far greater than Cyrus or Shapur, Caesar or Alexander, could ever have conceived. A renaissance of Semitic civilisation, dormant since the Iranians ended the Assyrian Empire at the sack of Nineveh nearly 1,300 years previously, was dawning. The age of Islam had arrived.

3

THE PRINCELY STATES
Near Eastern kingdoms under Roman protection

On arriving in the East, republican Rome came into direct contact with kings. The East was a patchwork of small but glittering princely states. The bluff, republican Roman administrators and soldiers were blinded and seduced by royalty (literally so in Egypt). They were kings, furthermore, who became Roman citizens. The contact was a heady and ultimately addictive one, a contact which republican Rome could not withstand. Rome thereafter became a monarchy.

If there was one difference more than any other between Rome's European and Near Eastern empires, it was that Rome came to the Near East as a brash newcomer entering civilisations far older than its own. Some of the nations it annexed had histories of nationhood far older than Rome's, and as nations continued far longer (Armenia, for example). Many of these remained as distinct units ruled by their own kings as clients of Rome – the so-called 'Friendly Kings'[1] – long after Rome had extended its empire there. Roman rule was exercised only indirectly through its client king, often with just a small Roman garrison to protect Roman interests. By and large these client kingdoms were left to their own affairs so long as they behaved themselves. In this way the system resembled the system of Princely States through which Britain ruled its Indian Empire. If they did not behave themselves, they would be annexed and ruled directly, although very occasionally client status could be restored (as in the case of Judaea). Not all were 'kingdoms' in the traditional sense: Herod was only created a 'king' by the Roman Senate, Palmyra never had any kings until its client status became open to question, and the Tanukhid and Ghassanid 'kingdoms' were really tribal confederations ruled by their shaikhs who were appointed as 'phylarchs' by the Romans.

The system of 'Princely States' was a constant feature of Roman history in the East, right down until the end of its empire there. They are normally associated only with the early years, with the independence of most of them coming to an end during the course of the late first and beginning of the second century. The system of client states in the East was ended by Caracalla in the early third century with his abolition of the Edessan monarchy. To some extent, it represents a system of 'creeping conquest'. On arrival in the Near East, the Romans would recognise the 'independence' of a state with mutual exchanges between both – but as a client of Rome. Soon, the client state would be tied increasingly closer, both politically and economically. Inevitably, its independence would be put to an end on a pretext and it would be quietly – and bloodlessly – absorbed directly into the empire. The system of client states represented Rome's most effective means of conquest. There was a revival of the system – albeit modified – with the *foederati* or federated tribal allies of the fourth century, the most notable of whom were the Tanukhid and Ghassanid confederations.

To some extent, the system was a feature of Iran as well, under both the Parthian and the Sasanian dynasties. On its western borders a string of client kingdoms were maintained as buffers against the Roman Empire. Hira, Characene, Adiabene and Hatra[2] were the main ones that affect the present history, with Armenia the constant bone of contention between both empires. Indeed, the royal families of the client kingdoms on both sides of the border were often closely bound up in various intermarriages and complex relationships.[3]

Some of Rome's client kingdoms in Anatolia represented Iranian enclaves within Roman territory. Armenia always had a considerable Iranian element, both cultural and dynastic. Its kings were often drawn from Iranian royal houses, most notably the Parthian Arsacids, who continued to rule in Armenia long after they had been supplanted in Iran itself. Two other kingdoms, Cappadocia and Commagene, were ruled by the descendants of former Persian satraps who claimed descent from the Achaemenid kings and remained as pockets of Iranian culture within the Roman Empire. Whilst any Iranian culture of Cappadocia and Commagene might have been tenuous – particularly when compared to their Hellenism – it was nonetheless to have important repercussions in Roman history as we shall see.[4] But important – indeed crucial – though Armenia is to any history of Rome in the East, this and other client kingdoms in the mountainous regions of Anatolia are beyond the scope of the present work (although reference will be made to them throughout),[5] which is concerned chiefly with the client kingdoms of the lowland areas of the Near East. The main ones are Emesa, Judaea, Nabataea, Palmyra, Edessa, and the Tanukhid and Ghassanid confederations. In addition there were numerous minor client states – probably more than twenty – such as Chalcis and Anthemusia, often just principalities or even small towns or tribes,[6] but these are not treated separately. All of them differed very considerably, both from each other and in their relations to Rome. Yet there are common threads that run through them, despite those differences. Most of all, each in very different ways were to affect the history of Rome fundamentally, in some cases having a permanent effect on the subsequent history of European civilisation.

Rome and the Arabs

Before describing the different client states of the Near East, it is worth digressing to consider the one element that most of them had in common. This was their Arab make-up. With the exception of Judaea, all were to a greater or lesser extent 'Arab'.[7] Whilst the term must not be viewed in its rather emotive modern nationalistic sense, it is nonetheless important to emphasise the Arab population that so much of the pre-Islamic Near East shared, if only to counterbalance the 'Greek character' which is so often imparted to the region throughout the Roman period by modern scholarship.[8]

History has an impression of the Arabs bursting, like Athena fully armed, out of the deserts for the first time in the seventh century to inundate the Near East in a tide of Islam. Hence, there is a frequent tendency to associate Arab civilisation exclusively with Islamic. But before Islam, Arab civilisation had a long history in the Near East and the Mediterranean, with Arabs even becoming emperors of Rome itself.[9] The East which Rome inherited was largely a legacy of the Seleucid Empire, but the actual native populations were Aramaic and Arab. The Roman period was one of increasing reassertion by the Arabs culminating in the great Arab empires of early Islam, so that 'by the time of the [Muslim] conquest, Arab forces had centuries of experience of warfare as allies of the two empires [Rome and Iran]'.[10] They also had centuries of experience as a distinctive culture. This was to have as profound an effect on Rome and Europe as Arab Islamic civilisation later did on the rest of the world. Rome's early client states, Emesa, Chalcis and Nabataea, for example, were described by contemporaries as 'Arab', as were later states such as Palmyra or Edessa. The rise of the Arab tribal confederations throughout the third to sixth centuries – the Lakhm, the Tanukh, the Salih, and the Ghassan are the main ones – is also an essential part of this story.[11] When viewing the spectacular ruins of Petra or Palmyra, therefore, or unravelling the history of the early years of Christendom, or even explaining much of the pagan religion of ancient Rome itself, it is not often appreciated that one is examining Arab civilisation as much as if one were examining Islamic Damascus or Baghdad.

There are actually five regions called 'Arabia' in the Roman sources, three of them quite distinct.[12] This has led to some confusion. Within the empire were the 'Arabia' of the eastern delta of Egypt, the 'Arabia' of northern Mesopotamia and – most commonly – Nabataea or Arabia Petraea. Outside the empire there was also Arabia Deserta (central Arabia) and Arabia Felix (southern Arabia or Yemen). Only one was an officially designated Roman province: the Provincia Arabia, corresponding to the old Nabataean kingdom. The term 'Arab', however, had a far wider meaning beyond the inhabitants of the specific 'Arabias', and was applied fairly loosely to many outside these areas as well, particularly the Bedouin. History's attitudes to the Bedouin Arab range from uncivilised barbarians of the desert fringes, constantly threatening the civilisation of the Fertile Crescent, to the European Romantic era's adulation of the Bedouin as the ultimate embodiment of nobility and environmental harmony.[13] Much conventional history preserves the myth of the perpetual conflict between 'the desert and sown', with the nomads of the desert a constant threat to the sedentary civilisations on its rim. But Near Eastern history demonstrates more than anything else the constant interdependence of nomad and sedentary: Near Eastern civilisation was a product of both. Any threat was largely illusory.[14] The perennial threat to Rome was Iran, not the Arabs, despite the myth of the desert raids. Roman relations with the Arabs, therefore, only make sense in the context of Roman relations with Iran, not the Arabs.[15] Rome mainly used the Arabs in its wars against Iran, and only rarely to exert its control over the larger area of Arabia. This became increasingly apparent towards the end, as we shall see.

The nomad Arabs were hardly less literate than the settled Graeco-Roman-Aramaic population under Roman rule, graphically demonstrated by the vast number of Safaitic and Thamudic inscriptions they have left.[16] There is no evidence from these that they were brigands or in any way posed a threat to Roman stability. 'Indeed, they show that the vast majority of their authors were for the most part entirely concerned with their own pursuits and were largely indifferent to the imperium' . . . 'We are thus faced with the curious paradox of a non-literate society in which large numbers of people could read and write. A society in which literacy, having apparently no useful place, seems largely to have been used as a pastime.'[17] Small wonder that when these desert Arabs finally did achieve power, after Islam, the importance of the written word was one of their greatest contributions, and the beauty of the written word for its own sake remains one of the Arabs' greatest contributions to civilisation. Clearly, therefore, the defence of the Roman East against the Arab nomads was no mere simple case of defending the borders of civilisation against barbaric hordes of nomads. One is left wondering who were defending whom against what.

Emesa and the Sun Kings[18]

Emesa corresponds to modern Homs in Syria. The actual boundaries of the kingdom are difficult to define (Figure 2). It certainly comprised the Homs Basin of the middle Orontes region. This area also included the ancient towns of Laodicaea ad Libanum to

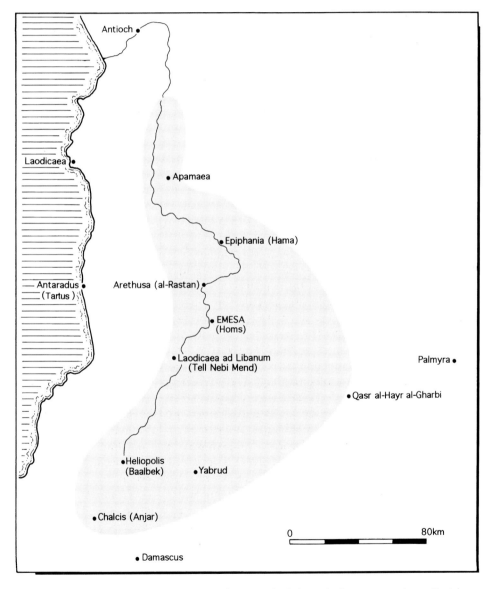

Figure 2 Map to illustrate the Kingdom of Emesa. Shaded area indicates approximate limits at greatest extent

the south and Arethusa to the north (modern Tell Nebi Mend and al-Rastan respectively). The history of the Emesenes is also intimately bound up with the Orontes Valley to the south and north as well: southwards to Yabrud near Damascus and into the Baqʻa Valley as far as Heliopolis (modern Baalbek), and northwards down the central Orontes Basin – the Ghab – around Apamaea. To the west, the so-called 'Homs Gap' – dominated in the Middle Ages by the castle of Crac des Chevaliers – provided access to the Mediterranean at Antaradus (modern Tartus). To the east, it extended into the desert as far as Qasr al-Hayr al-Gharbi, where a boundary stone[19] marks its 'border' with the territory of Palmyra – the histories of the two kingdoms of Emesa and Palmyra were closely tied. Emesa was thus at the centre of communications between the Syrian desert and the sea, as well as between Arabia and northern Syria.[20]

The kings of Emesa

The first mention of the Emesenes occurs in the Seleucid period in the mid-second century BC, when the Seleucid pretender Alexander Balas entrusted his son in 151 BC to the care of Iamblichus (Yamlikel),[21] the shaikh of the Emesene tribe around Apamaea. It is implied that the Emesenes were a nomadic Arab tribe in the region, rather than the inhabitants of a city called Emesa, which only emerges in the first century BC – presumably so named after they eventually settled there (see below). Another shaikh, Aziz, is recorded in the Aleppo region around 94 BC, but it is uncertain what – if any – relation Aziz had to the tribe of the Emesenoi. The greatest of the shaikhs from the tribal days was Samsigeramus (Shamshigeram), who became embroiled in the rival claims to the Seleucid throne between Philip II and Antiochus XIII in 69 BC. On Pompey's incorporation of the Seleucid state into the Roman Empire in 64 BC, the Emesenes were made vassals to the Romans. Their chief Samsigeramus was confirmed by Pompey as phylarch, or king, of the Emesenes, with their capital at Arethusa, a town founded by Seleucus I on the Orontes just to the north of Emesa. Arethusa thus became the first capital of the Emesenes, and Samsigeramus I is usually credited with being the founder of the dynasty (Family tree 1).

Samsigeramus' 'kingdom' was the first of Rome's Arab clients on the desert fringes. These were established to exert indirect control over the desert tribes of the interior. As soon as they became settled the Emesenes began to accumulate riches from their control of the trading caravans – a far more profitable business than merely raiding them. It is presumably as result of this new-found wealth that Samsigeramus I and the Emesenes became more settled and founded a new capital that would carry their name. This was Emesa, governed at first by Iamblichus, the son of Samsigeramus (who remained in Arethusa). By the fourth century AD, the city of Emesa had grown to rank with Tyre, Sidon, Beirut and Damascus,[22] probably exceeding them in splendour due to its famous Temple of the Sun.

Allying Samsigeramus and the Emesenes to Rome was a wise move by Pompey, for in the Parthian invasion of Syria following the disaster of Carrhae ten years later, the Emesenes remained loyal to Rome. The king by now was Iamblichus I,[23] son of Samsigeramus I. Iamblichus, together with Ptolemaus and Sohaemus (Suhaym), two other princes from the Baqʻa Valley who were probably related to the Emesene royal house,[24] sent detachments to Egypt in 41 BC to aid Caesar in his siege of Alexandria. The family subsequently became embroiled in the civil war between Antony and Octavian. On Antony's encouragement, Alexas, the brother of Iamblichus I, usurped the throne and put

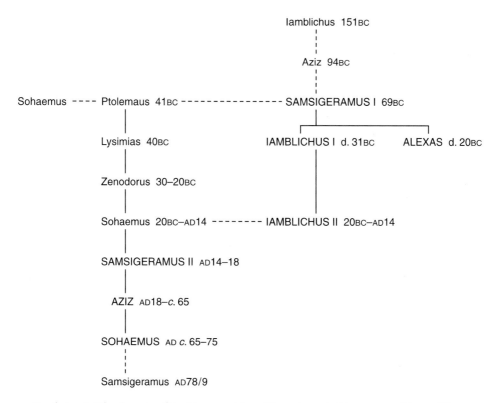

Family tree 1 The dynasty of the Emesene kings. Those in capital letters were kings of Emesa. Dotted lines imply an uncertain connection.

Iamblichus to death on the eve of the Battle of Actium in 31 BC, throwing in his lot with Antony. Alexas, however, never came to terms with Octavian and so was put to death in 20 BC for his support of Antony and complicity in his brother's murder. The throne of Emesa then reverted to the direct royal line under Iamblichus II, son of Iamblichus I.[25]

The principality of Chalcis ad Libanum in the Baq'a Valley seems to have been closely associated with Emesa. Chalcis is located at the modern town of Anjar, to the south of Baalbek, where there are impressive remains (Plate 79). These, however, are of the Umayyad period, despite their Roman appearance. Its line of princes are described as 'Arabs' in the sources and, like the Emesene kings, occupied the dual function of king and high-priest. The raids by one of its princes, Ptolemaus, against Damascus prompted a brief annexation of that city by the Nabataeans in the middle of the first century BC. He was succeeded by his son Lysimias in 40 BC but was soon put to death by Mark Antony, who proclaimed Cleopatra as Queen of Chalcis. On her death in 30 BC Lysimias' son Zenodorus became prince. He reigned until about 20 BC when he was succeeded by Sohaemus, whose son was destined to become the greatest of Emesa's kings (see below).[26]

The Augustan Peace was a golden age for Emesa under the stable rule of Iamblichus II (20 BC–AD 14) and his successor Samsigeramus II (AD 14–48) – literally so, if their gold funerary masks discovered at the Emesene royal tombs at Tell Abu Sabun outside Emesa are any indication.[27] Iamblichus II was the first of his family to gain Roman citizenship. A branch of the family under Sohaemus ruled from 20 BC to AD 14 in Chalcis as vassals of Iamblichus. This Sohaemus was presumably a descendant of the Sohaemus who supplied troops to Caesar a generation before. The two branches of the Emesene royal house came together, for it was the son of Sohaemus of Chalcis, Samsigeramus II, who became Emesa's greatest king after the death of Iamblichus II in AD 14. Inscriptions at both Baalbek and Palmyra commemorate Samsigeramus as 'the great king',[28] a title that recalls ancient Persian protocol. Whilst this might not necessarily imply any jurisdiction over Palmyra by Samsigeramus, it does at least indicate very close relations between Emesa and Palmyra, as well as between Emesa and Chalcis. This was reinforced when Samsigeramus acted as an official intermediary in Tiberius' embassy to Palmyra in AD 32. Baalbek and the Baqʻa Valley, however, the traditional homeland of Sohaemus's branch of the royal family, were drawn under the direct rule of Emesa, as the first-century inscription there also honours Samsigeramus. Towards the end of his reign, Samsigeramus's old seat of Chalcis was given as a principality for a brief while to Herod the Younger between 44 and 48.[29] Samsigeramus was succeeded by his son King Aziz.

The family also consolidated its position amongst Rome's other client kingdoms in the Near East by marriage alliances with the royal houses of both Commagene and Judaea. A Sohaemus is recorded as King of Armenia for a while in 163, although it is unclear whether this was a connection.[30] Under King Sohaemus of Emesa, who succeeded Aziz, relations with Rome became very close, with Emesa supplying a regular levy of archers – the Hemeseni – as auxiliaries. King Sohaemus also sent special contingents of Emesenes to assist in the siege of Jerusalem in 66 as well as to suppress his own distant relatives, the kings of Commagene, in 72. But his loyalty did him little good. For reasons that are not entirely clear, Sohaemus and the independence of Emesa disappeared in about 75, when it was incorporated directly into the Roman Empire. It has been assumed that Sohaemus abdicated,[31] but he may have simply died without a direct heir, prompting Roman annexation. In 78/9 an impressive Palmyrene-style tomb tower was erected at Emesa commemorating 'Gaius Julius Samsigeramus . . . son of Gaius Julius Alexios'[32] who may have been connected to the royal family. There are various historical and epigraphical references to people bearing the names Samsigeramus and Sohaemus – the most famous being Julia Sohaemias, mother of Emperor Elagabalus – over the next century or so. But the names were presumably popular Emesene ones generally, and may not necessarily refer to the royal family as such, despite the names' close associations with both the ruling dynasty and the Emesene Sun cult.[33] Otherwise, the family does not re-emerge until the late second century with its assumed connection to the family of Julia Domna (Chapter 8).

This brief survey shows Emesa to be one of the more obscure client kingdoms, particularly in comparison to famous neighbours. It never held the balance of power between Rome and Iran, as Armenia did, it never rose in spectacular revolt against Rome, as Judaea or Palmyra did, it boasts no spectacular remains, no great battles or beautiful queens. Indeed, the history of Emesa and its kings would form little more than a footnote were it not for two important factors, both related. The first is the religion that was practised at Emesa, the Sun cult. And the second was the Emesene family who became one of Rome's imperial dynasties. Both were to have important ramifications for Rome's history, as we shall see.[34]

The religion of Emesa

The dynasty no longer ruled as kings after its incorporation into the Roman Empire, but remained as hereditary high-priests of the temple of the Emesene Sun god, or the 'Baal of the Emesenes'. This temple was associated with the cult of Elah Gabal, later to achieve fame – or notoriety – when one of the temple priests, the Emperor Elagabalus, tried to enforce it upon an unwilling Rome. The emperor's name is actually the name of the deity itself, a Latinised form of *Elah Gabal*, which literally means 'God of the Mountain' (the modern Arabic words *Allah*, 'God', and *jabal*, 'mountain', are the same). Like other eastern abstract concepts of deity – such as the Jewish – the cult of Elagabal baffled the prosaic Romans, for 'no statue made by man in the likeness of the god stands in this temple, as in Greek and Roman temples'.[35] Instead, the cult object was a large black stone, presumably volcanic or meteoric. This is a relatively common type of cult object amongst the Semites – one recalls the similar pre-Islamic cult object at the Ka'ba at Mecca, as well as numerous sacred *baetyls* elsewhere.[36] The huge temple to this deity was one of the most lavish in the East, being amply endowed by neighbouring rulers with sumptuous gold, silver and precious stone ornamentation, so that Emesa became 'the Jerusalem of the Sun god',[37] with its kings both patrons and high-priests. The names of the Emesene kings were theophoric: Samsigeramus derives from *Shams*, the Mesopotamian name of the Sun god, and *geram* is from the Arabic root *k.r.m.* meaning 'decide' or 'venerate'. The name thus means 'the Sun god had decided' or 'the Sun god is venerated'.[38] Sohaemus derives from the root *Suhaym* which has been explained as meaning 'black' or 'precious stone',[39] either of which can be taken to refer to the black stone of Elah Gabal. Iamblichus is more problematical, with the root *Yamlik-El* being postulated,[40] *Yamlik* deriving from the root *mlk* meaning 'king' or 'reign', *El* being the same well-known Semitic root that is found in Elah Gabal meaning 'god' (e.g., El, Ba'al, Allah, etc.). The name occurs at Palmyra as *Yamlichu*. Iamblichus, therefore, may mean 'the rule of god'.[41]

The great Temple of Emesene Baal

The temple of the Emesene Sun god was one of the greatest in the East. Of the various local deities depicted on Emesene coins, Sol-Elagabalus predominates. These depict a peripteral Corinthian temple with 6 × 11 columns, standing on a podium approached by steps up the middle, of a style that looks typically Antonine – and could apply to any number of temples throughout the Roman East (Figure 3). The sacred stone of Elahgabal is depicted on the earlier coins as standing free in the temple sanctuary, surrounded by a balustrade. The altar is depicted as a rectangular stone block – again recalling the Ka'ba.[42] Herodian has the most complete description of the temple. He describes it as a huge building, lavishly decorated with gold, silver and gemstones. It was richly endowed both by the Emesene and other Near Eastern kings. The image was not in man's likeness, but was just a black stone. The temple – and cult – is called 'Phoenician' throughout.[43]

The great temple of the Sun god at Emesa, one of the greatest of the East rivalling those at Jerusalem, Palmyra and Damascus, is also one of the East's greatest mysteries. For no trace survives – there is not a shred of material evidence showing where it stood or, indeed, whether it even existed. It has been supposed that it stood on the site of the relatively recent Mosque of Nuri at Homs, which incorporates a few antique columns,[44]

Figure 3 The Temple of Emesene Baal, taken from a coin of the 'Emperor Uranius'

but this is highly unlikely. These columns were probably from a Christian church on the site, not the Sun Temple. In any case, even the most ambitious of mosques or churches built on the site of such a great temple would still be dominated by its pagan remains, as the Temple of Jupiter-Hadad still dominates (architecturally speaking) the Great Mosque of Damascus. Even the much more modest Temple of Jupiter-Malik of Yabrud in Emesene territory to the south still survives in part in the cathedral built on the site.[45] It seems unlikely – and to no purpose – that alone amongst the great Near Eastern temples, the Temple of Sun would be so thoroughly eradicated that no trace of it would remain in Emesa. No ancient source even hints at such a destruction. If such a temple did exist, therefore, it cannot have been in Emesa itself.

But the temple did exist – the evidence of the coins and Herodian's description leaves no doubt. Herodian's description does provide one clue, albeit a negative one: nowhere does he state that the temple was actually *in* Emesa itself.[46] Indeed, it is surely significant that the temple is almost invariably called the 'Temple of the *Emesenes*' or of '*Emesene* Baal' rather than the Temple of *Emesa* specifically, implying that it may not necessarily have been in the city, merely Emesene territory.[47] The difference between the 'Emesenes' and 'Emesa' has already been emphasised, the former not necessarily presupposing the existence of the latter, and the temple might be as little associated with Emesa as the Emesenes originally were.

One authority has postulated, on numismatic grounds, an 'annual cycle of worship' for Sol Elagabalus, the god migrating between summer and winter 'quarters' or temples.[48] This receives some support in the description of Elagabalus' ritual when he took the cult to Rome, where the black stone of Elah Gabal would be placed in a chariot for ritual procession.[49] In other words, there is the distinct possibility that there were two temples, one in lowland bordering the desert (presumably in Emesa itself or the older capital of Arethusa) and the other elsewhere higher up, presumably in an elevated position like so many temples in the region. Given the nomadic origins of the Emesenes, this is entirely plausible – the ancient Persians, for example, similarly nomadic in origin, maintained migrations between seasonal capitals for many centuries after becoming sedentary. It receives added support in the name of the Sun god itself, *Elah-gabal* which means 'god of the mountain'.[50] In view of this, it seems almost unthinkable that the main temple of the Emesene Baal could be situated in a lowland depression such as Emesa; it must be found in higher, mountainous terrain.

Accordingly, any temple in Emesa itself, such as the one in which Aurelian sacrificed after his victory over Zenobia,[51] may have been a secondary one leaving little trace today; the main temple described by the coins and Herodian would be located in the mountains. The only temple answering such a description in Emesene territory is Baalbek, ancient Heliopolis (Figures 4 and 5).

Heliopolis was first so-named by the Ptolemaic dynasty of Egypt in the third century BC, possibly after the better known Heliopolis in Egypt. It was made a Roman veteran colony after 15 BC as part of Augustus' foundation of Beirut, and made an independent city by Septimius Severus. One should not assume, however, that the population consisted solely of Roman veterans and their descendants, nor that they would even have formed a majority.[52] Such a colony – as elsewhere throughout the East – would merely have been grafted on to an existing population. There was a much older Phoenician settlement there, according to excavations, associated with the Temple of Baal-Hadad.[53] It is for this temple, rather than as a minor Roman colony, that Baalbek is famous. The architecture of the temple is discussed in Chapter 7. For the moment, it is only necessary to recall some of its more salient points.

Historically, the temple is fraught with problems. The sources are curiously silent about it – indeed, there are no contemporary accounts at all. Apart from depictions on some of the coins of the Syrian emperors, the first historical mentions do not occur until the seventh century, by John Malalas and the *Chronicon Paschale*.[54] For one of the most ambitious building projects ever undertaken in the Roman world, this lack of literary evidence is curious to say the least – and in direct contrast to the Temple of Emesene Baal, which has contemporary descriptions as we have noted. Both the historical references – or lack of them – and the site itself are also silent as to the date. Apart from some dated inscriptions ranging from AD 60 to 211–17, the main dating evidence is stylistic. Taken together, they suggests that the building was begun in the early first century AD with the main work carried out during the later first century, with a further spurt in the third century. The main planning and early construction corresponds, therefore, with the period of the Emesene kings, and the second spurt with their descendants, the 'Syrian' emperors.

The identity of the cult is also problematical.[55] The historical evidence – flimsy though it is – suggests a triad of Jupiter, Venus and Mercury. Such a triad is an odd combination: Jupiter was equated with Hadad and Venus with Atargatis, both familiar Semitic deities, but Mercury had no Semitic counterpart and seems to be the sole wholly Roman member of the 'triad'. The complex is generally attributed to Baal-Hadad – 'Balanius' according to one of the few historical mentions.[56] *Baal* is a generic name meaning simply 'lord' or 'chief deity' rather than any specific deity, but Hadad was a storm god, often equated with Jupiter (such as at Damascus). Upon Romanisation, Hadad of Baalbek becomes

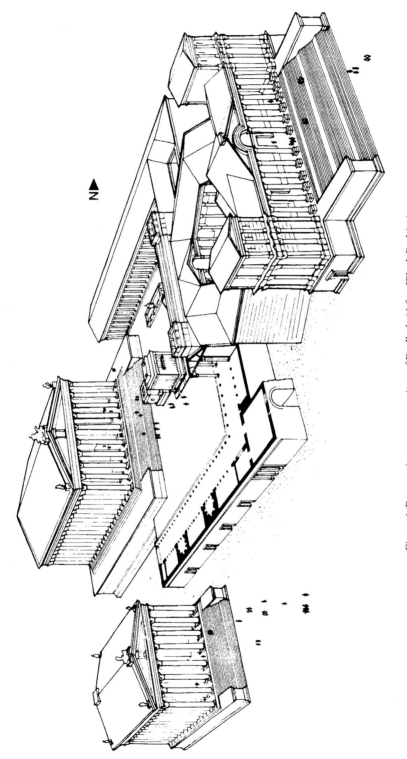

Figure 4 Perspective reconstruction of Baalbek (After Ward–Perkins)

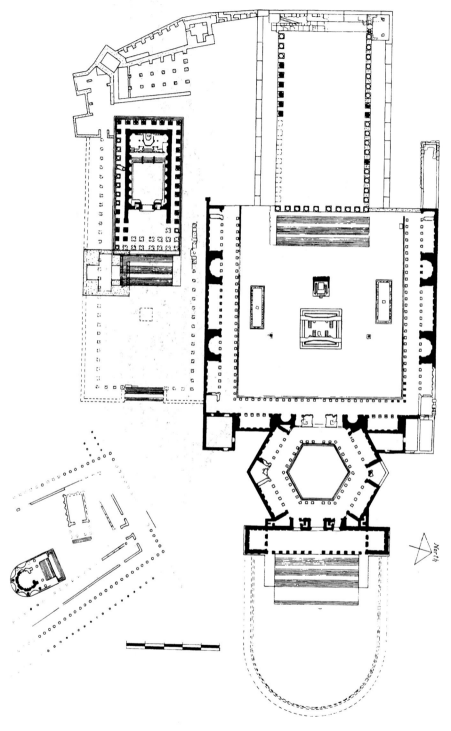

Figure 5 Plan of the temple complex at Baalbek (After Ragette)

Jupiter Heliopolitanus and inscriptions on the site commemorate IOMH: 'Iupiter Optimus Maximus Heliopolitanus'. The centre of the Phoenician cult of Hadad was at Ptolemais (Akka), and the Jupiter of Ptolemais became assimilated to Jupiter Heliopolitanus of Baalbek. It is significant that the religious ties of Ptolemais with Heliopolis were reinforced by Rome's 'Syrian' emperors, from Caracalla onwards.[57] To add to the complication, all three deities at Baalbek were assimilated with the Sun cult. For whatever Baalbek's other affiliations, there is little doubt that its main cult was the Sun god or 'Helios', as the name Heliopolis implies[58] – it is significant that the temple, like the first Christian churches, faced the rising sun. The cult stuck tenaciously to Baalbek: in 269 it was sufficient simply for an actor to declare himself a Christian there for him to be stoned to death, and Baalbek's fame as a centre sacred to the Sun lasted well into the Islamic period when it was still remembered as far away as Central Asia.[59] In other words, the cult was a variation of, or the same as, the Sun-god cult at Emesa.

If such a pantheon appears complicated, so do the physical remains (Figure 5). At first sight the arrangement of the temples appear to confirm a triad: a main temple (Plates 2 and 3), a smaller temple alongside (the 'Temple of Bacchus', Plate 4), with a small third temple (the 'Temple of Venus') just in front. But these do not match the triad. The main temple was dedicated to Jupiter-Hadad, or perhaps to the triad itself. The smaller temple alongside is of unknown dedication, the only agreement being that it was *not* Bacchus, as its popular designation implies. Neither is there any evidence that it was dedicated to Venus-Atargatis, Hadad's 'consort'. It has been suggested[60] that this too was dedicated to the triad, the larger temple for public use and the smaller one for private mysteries. The third temple of the architectural 'triad', the 'Temple of Venus' is also a misnomer. It was dedicated neither to Venus, nor to Mercury, the third member of the triad, but probably to Tyche. Mercury had an entirely separate temple on top of Shaikh Abdullah Hill overlooking Baalbek. This has entirely disappeared apart from parts of the monumental staircase that ascended the hill, but depictions of the temple have been preserved on coins. Once again, Mercury appears the 'odd man out', being the only member of the triad to have its own temple in addition to a 'shared' temple in the main complex. And whilst Mercury is a wholly Graeco-Roman deity, the temple is expressed solely in Semitic terms in the form of its location on a sacred 'high place'.[61] To complicate matters further, remains of a Temple to the Muses have been excavated adjacent to the Temple of Venus/ Tyche, and evidence for the worship of Sabazius, an obscure Phrygio-Thracian cult, has also been found.[62]

To summarise, there is evidence for at least eight cults at Baalbek: Baal, the Sun, Jupiter-Hadad, Venus-Atargatis, Mercury, Tyche, the Muses and Sabazius. The physical remains include traces of five temples, none of which correspond neatly with what we know of the cults, nor are conclusively identified. Clearly, Baalbek is a cult above all of syncretism and assimilation, presumably all assimilated to the supreme Sun cult. Such syncretism accords with much of what we know of the Emesene Sun cult: Emperor Elagabalus attempted to syncretise the cult in Rome with Pallas and Uranius, as well as Judaism and Christianity.

Perhaps the main point that needs emphasising in the present discussion is the sheer scale of the temple complex (Plates 2 and 5). It has been fashionable both to emphasise and disparage the size of Baalbek.[63] For any visitor today the scale is certainly overwhelming, and must have been even more so in antiquity: the greatest temple in the East, indeed one of the most ambitious building works ever undertaken in the Roman world. Money was no object in its construction: if colossal monolithic columns were required, nothing but the best would do and great columns of pink Egyptian granite were imported all the way from Aswan – not just one or two, but dozens. Stones weighing up to a thousand tons – the largest monoliths in the world – were cut and dragged into place to construct the immense platforms (Plate 5).[64] The raking cornices of the entablature alone, standing over a hundred feet up in the air, weighed over 75 tons. Nothing was too good, too big, or too expensive – and nothing like it stood anywhere else, not even in Rome itself. But what impresses even more than its sheer size is the temple's colossal arrogance: it pushes both engineering and cost to their extreme limits. Whatever it is, Baalbek is one gigantic architectural boast.

So much for what Baalbek was. But this is only worth emphasising in order to contrast it with what it was *not*. For despite boasting one of the greatest buildings of antiquity, Baalbek was no great capital or the centre of any great dynasty. It was not a Roman provincial capital nor even a town of any significance. Nor did it lie on any major route of communication or command any wealth carried in by great caravans *en route* to Mediterranean markets. In the list of cities represented at the Council of Nicaea in 325, Heliopolis is not even mentioned, although Emesa is. Similarly, in the roll-call of the eastern empire given by Ammianus, Heliopolis does not rate a mention – although once again, Emesa significantly does.[65] Capitals, dynastic seats, provincial administrative centres, market towns, trade entrepôts, all lay elsewhere. Baalbek in antiquity was nothing more than it is today: a minor provincial town of little more than local significance. What it *was* is an historical enigma that matches that of the Temple of the Sun of the Emesenes.

Heliopolis/Baalbek is not, of course, Emesa. But was it Emesene? The close links between Emesa and Heliopolis have already been emphasised. Whilst for much of its history it seems to have come under Beirut (at least since 15 BC), its associations were closer with Emesa, under which it also came at different times. The whole region, incorporating both Emesa and Heliopolis, was in any case usually viewed as a single 'Phoenician' entity with exotic Phoenician cults regardless of official political boundaries.[66] Such confusions of both boundaries and political responsibilities seem common in the Roman East.[67] In other words, the fact that Heliopolis was considered a part of Beirut does not exclude its belonging to Emesa at the same time, and it seems possible that there was shared administration at various times, that territoriality was not as crucial a factor as is often assumed.

Hence, many features at Baalbek correspond with what we know of the Temple of Emesene Baal. Its sheer size, opulence and extravagance to begin with. The arrangement of a large temple and a smaller one alongside might have been for public services and private mysteries as was suggested;[68] equally it might have been for a ritual 'migration' of the cult object, as postulated for Elahgabal – indeed we know that the cult object of Baalbek was also paraded on a litter.[69] Either explanations are consistent with the Emesene temple. The arrangement of two adjacent temples recalls that of Siʿ. It has been suggested that the panels in the peristyle ceiling of the smaller temple record dedications from different cities in the East,[70] which again accords with Herodian's description of the Emesene temple. The altar of the Temple of Emesene Baal is depicted on coins as a rectangular block or cube, and the altar in the great court at Baalbek is also cuboid, the only such altar known in any of the eastern Roman temples (Figure 4).

It was at Heliopolis that an inscription was found honouring the Emesene 'great king' Sohaemus, son of 'the great king' Samsigeramus.[71] There is no way that an otherwise

Plate 2 The columns of the Temple of Jupiter at Baalbek, with part of the
fallen cornice in the foreground

insignificant, small country town like Baalbek could ever have undertaken a building
project on such a scale. Rome itself might, but would hardly waste its resources on a
minor veterans' colony in a distant corner of the empire when projects closer to home
demanded higher priority. It has been suggested[72] that Baalbek was a conscious Roman
effort to implant its own cultural domination of the Near East by attempting to outshine
the Near Eastern temples and cults, such as those of Damascus or Jerusalem. But if this
were so, the imperial cults of the Capitoline Triad or Rome and Augustus would have
been chosen, not the cults that we have observed at Baalbek. The architecture of Baalbek
– the great temenos, the high places, and other features – in any case follows Near Eastern

Plate 3 The courtyard and sanctuary stairs of the main temple at Baalbek

Plate 4 The 'Temple of Bacchus' at Baalbek

Plate 5 The quarry at Baalbek, with one of the monoliths used in construction. The six columns of the Temple of Jupiter in the background

forms, not Roman (see Chapter 7). In addition, 'it is noteworthy that not a single emperor has taken the credit that he alone was responsible for the cost of the great temple complex at Baalbek'.[73]

However, Baalbek can be explained by the Sun Kings of Emesa, enriched by the lucrative caravan traffic they controlled, and the Syrian emperors of Rome, both royal dynasties endowing their main temple: *the* Sun Temple. It was, after all, Septimius Severus who made Heliopolis an independent city, and awarded it the name 'Colonia Julia Augusta Felix Heliopolitanus'. It is surely significant that Septimius chose to rename it after his wife Julia Domna – the 'Julia Augusta' of the title – a descendant of the Sun Temple's priest-kings. The wealth of the Emesene kingdom was proverbial, as was the wealth of the descendants of the Emesene royal family who became emperors under the Severan dynasty. Members of this family were able to command massive sums of money on demand – a major reason for the family's success. It is noteworthy that the coins of the Severan dynasty are virtually the only ones which depict Baalbek: Septimius Severus, Caracalla and (significantly) Julia Domna. Jupiter Heliopolitanus is depicted on the cuirass of a statue of Severus Alexander at Carnuntum near Vienna, where there was a Temple of Jupiter Heliopolitanus.[74] The only other coins which depict Baalbek are those of Philip and his wife Ocatilia, both, significantly, native Syrians. The cult of Baalbek was also worshipped at Arca in Lebanon, the birthplace of the Emperor Severus Alexander.

The cult image of Elahgabal is depicted (on coins) and described as a conical stone, whilst the cult image of Heliopolitan Jupiter is a personified image in accordance with Graeco-Roman religious practice. But this is not as contradictory as it seems, reflecting merely two views of the one god, not two separate deities. The Baalbek cult object was also known to have been a stone *baetyl* like Elahgabal.[75] Dushara, for example, was similarly depicted in two ways: as an abstract square by the Nabataeans and a personified image by the Hellenisers. The Emesene coins depict a peripteral temple for Emesene Baal of 6 × 11 columns rather than the 10 × 19 columns of Baalbek's gigantic proportions. But it must be borne in mind that these are only coins, not architectural drawings. It is also significant that descriptions and coin depictions of the (now vanished) temple that Emperor Elagabalus built on the Palatine in Rome reveal a complex startlingly similar to the main temple at Baalbek: it too was entered through a monumental propylaeum approached by a flight of stairs, it too had high places of worship (known from descriptions), it too had a large colonnaded temenos, the sanctuary too was located at the end of the temenos, it was also peripteral, it was also on a podium approached by another flight of stairs. In other words, the Emesene Temple in Rome is virtually a copy of Baalbek (Figure 6 – compare with Figure 4).[76] The one certainty of Baalbek is that descendants of a small group of Roman veterans living off army pensions *could not* have built it. Neither could it have been the temple of the very insignificant Kingdom of Chalcis in the Baqʿa Valley.

Judaea, Herod the Great and the Jewish Revolt

Adding Judaea (Figure 7) to Roman rule was hardly more difficult for Pompey than his acquisition of Syria the year previously – and was prompted by much the same circumstances. Like the declining Seleucid royal house, the last members of the once vigorous Hasmonaean house of Judaea had spent the previous decades fighting each other. Eventually one of the claimants, Hyrcanus, appealed to Pompey for support against his brother. Pompey used the opportunity to march into Judaea in 63 BC, taking Jerusalem after a

Figure 6 The Temple of Elahgabal in Rome, taken from a medallion of
Severus Alexander

47

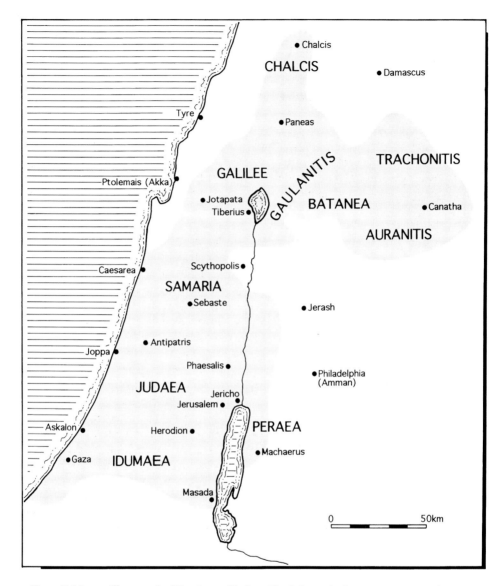

Figure 7 Map to illustrate the Kingdom of Judaea. Shaded area indicates approximate limits at greatest extent

three-month siege. The capture was facilitated by making his final offensive on the Sabbath. Not having any equivalent day of rest themselves (a weekly day of rest is perhaps the Jews' greatest gift to mankind), the attacking Romans were baffled at this 'most peculiar observance'[77] of the Jews, with priests calmly carrying on the performance of religious ritual as they were being killed.[78]

The acquisition of Judaea[79] and the adjacent coastal strip of Palestine was more than mere opportunism by Pompey or land lust by Rome. Rome was obsessed by pirates[80] – or maritime threats generally – so that extending its rule along the remaining parts of the eastern Mediterranean littoral was dictated by sound policy. Indeed, the greatest threat to Rome's existence had come from a maritime power, the Carthaginians. The original home of the Carthaginians was not North Africa, but the Phoenician homelands of the Levant. The eventual annexation of Palestine, therefore, was vital to Rome once it had established its foothold on the north Levantine coast.[81]

Inevitably, in solving one problem the Romans had to face another: Judaea's volatile population with its peculiar religion. The Jews arrived under Roman control with a tradition of nationalist revolt. For the Jews, religion was indissoluble from politics – a bond reaffirmed by Judaism's most recent offshoot, Islam, after Christianity imposed the clear division between what was God's and what was Caesar's. This was to create a major dilemma for the Romans, committed as they became to allowing Jewish religious freedom on the one hand but suppressing nationalist movements on the other: for the Jews, religion *was* nationalism.

The Maccabaean Revolt against Rome's predecessors in the region, the Seleucids in 171 BC, is one of the more important events in Jewish history. It would not normally form a part of this story but for several significant points. First, it formed a precedent for the far more devastating Jewish revolts under Roman rule. But second – and more important – the underlying reasons that caused it were to have immense ramifications for Roman history. Antiochus IV, whose mishandling of Jewish religious sentiment had sparked off the revolt, may have been an arch-Helleniser and religious bigot, and the Jewish religion by its nature may have been exclusive and zealous. But the clash of two such opposite peoples was not the real reason. The real culprits were the Hellenisers *within* Judaism, not the Hellenisers among the Seleucids; it was the Hellenised Jews who provoked a reaction amongst their more conservative compatriots. Jewish insurrections in antiquity had a strong element of civil war in them: the outbreak of the Jewish Revolt against Rome was marked as much by pleas from moderates and pragmatists as by anti-Roman jingoism from the hotheads.[82] Jew fought Jew as much as Gentile in these revolts. It is a mistake, furthermore, to write off these Hellenisers as merely Jewish renegades seduced by Hellenism who betrayed the fundamental nature of the religion of Moses.[83] Judaism by its very nature – its revolutionary idea of a single god – was one of the most powerful religious ideas of the ancient world. And the Hellenising – or westernising – element among the Jews recognised that the only way for such a message to spread beyond the inwardness of Judaism was to open itself up to the outside world.

The Rise of Herod[84]

Pompey did not immediately annex Judaea outright, allowing a puppet Hasmonaean king to remain. But the days of the dynasty were numbered. Under the Hasmonaeans, Judaea had been an independent Jewish state – but exclusively Jewish. Roman rule allowed Hellenised Syrians as well as other religious and ethnic minorities to flourish – the suppressed Samaritan religion, for example, was recognised. Caesar subsequently granted religious autonomy and exempted Jews from army service. This emphasised the kingdom's semi-independent status. But whilst Pompey restored the Hasmonaean family's traditional rights as high-priests of the Temple, he reduced their powers considerably. Eventually, caught between a client king wielding no real power and Roman rule that could only be exercised indirectly, Rome needed a local strong man who could keep the

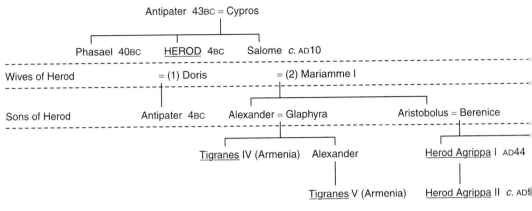

Family tree 2 The family of Herod the Great. Those underlined were reigning kings. Dates refer to dates of death

different factions in Judaea under firm control. Real power, therefore, was invested in Antipater, who was made procurator answerable directly to Rome.

Antipater had made himself a force to reckon with in the previous decades in the internecine fighting between rival branches of the Hasmonaean family, with Antipater playing off one side against the other. In the appointment of Antipater, Rome was also exercising a 'divide and rule' policy, for Antipater was no Judaean. He was an Idumaean, a member of a minority people of southern Judaea whom the Jews despised, despite – or perhaps because of – their forced conversion to Judaism in the late second century BC. The Idumaeans were descended from the reviled Edomites of the Old Testament, who had been displaced and forced to migrate by the Nabataeans. Indeed, Antipater cemented his ties with the land of his Edomite forbears by his marriage to Cypros, a member of the Nabataean royal family. From this union was born a son, Herod (Family tree 2).[85]

Antipater made Herod governor of Galilee. Galilee has always been one of the wealthier provinces in Palestine, where successive leaders, from Jesus of Nazareth soon after Herod, to Josephus during the Jewish Revolt, to Tancred during the First Crusade, have built up considerable prestige. From Galilee, Herod was able to challenge the Hasmonaean king, Hyrcanus, directly. He was also able to build good relations with the Romans just next door in Syria, relations that were to serve him well. Antipater was poisoned by a rival in 43 BC, leaving Herod the most powerful figure in Palestine. He later consolidated this power through friendship (backed up by bribes) with Mark Antony, then courting Cleopatra. Antony responded by making him and his brother joint rulers of Judaea above King Hyrcanus in 38 BC.

Following the Iranian occupation of Judaea in 40 BC, an anti-Roman member of the Hasmonaean family, Antigonus, was installed on the throne. Herod was forced to flee, at first to the court of Maliku (Malchus) II at Petra and then to Cleopatra's court in Egypt. Both eastern monarchs had little time for the dispossessed Idumaean wanderer,[86] so he went to Rome later the same year where he renewed friendship with Mark Antony. The Romans were still smarting under the loss of Palestine to Iran. In siding with the Iranians the Hasmonaeans had forfeited all Roman support for even nominal recognition. This was Herod's great chance: Antony saw in Herod a leader who might win Palestine back

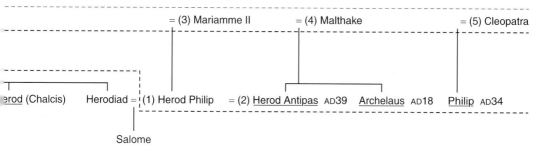

for him. The Senate proclaimed him King of the Jews (in a ceremony in the Temple of Jupiter!) and awarded him a splendid coronation in Rome.

Armed with a new title – and a Roman army to give it teeth – Herod was sent out in 39 BC to regain his kingdom. It took two years' of hard fighting simply to get from Galilee to Jerusalem, as the Hasmonaeans still enjoyed widespread support. After a tough four-month siege, he finally captured the city in 37 BC. Herod then proceeded to liquidate all members of the Hasmonaean family and its supporters, as well as make the usual obligatory war against the Arabs across the Jordan. But his revenge on the Hasmonaeans did not last long, for the Battle of Actium in 31 BC removed his Roman benefactor, Mark Antony. Hastily, Herod set sail for Rhodes to submit to the new Roman strong man, Octavian, who confirmed his appointment as King of Judaea under Roman protection. Octavian also enlarged Herod's kingdom as recognition for services rendered to the Roman state. Thus, a plebeian, born half Idumaean half Nabataean, proclaimed king in a republican ceremony in a pagan temple, armed with a Roman army, became King of the Jews.

Herod realised more than most that in the confused power struggles under way in Rome's civil wars in the first century BC, the 'vital question became one of loyalty not to Rome but to the right individual Roman'.[87] He even quietly hedged his bets with the appointment of a Babylonian Jew to the high-priesthood of the Temple, just in case the Iranians returned. Having few allies among his fellow-countrymen, much of Herod's life was spent in forming alliances outside, at first with Maliku and Cleopatra, later with Antony and Octavian. Antony proved true. Not only did he obtain for Herod his kingship in the first place, he even resisted Cleopatra's subsequent pressures to take it all away again when she requested Palestine as a wedding present following their nuptials in 36 BC. Herod, in return, was loyal, dedicating the main monuments in his kingdom to leading Romans or his own family: the citadel of Antonia in Jerusalem he named after Mark Antony, his palace named Agrippaeum after Agrippa, a tower at Caesarea named Drusium after Augustus' stepson Drusus, the towns of Antipatris named after his father and Phaeselis named after his brother. His greatest dedications, however, were named in honour of Octavian (Caesar): another palace in Jerusalem called Caesareum, and two entirely new cities, one in Samaria called Sebaste (Greek for Augustus) (Figure 31, Plate 39) and a complete new port for Palestine named Caesarea (Figure 31).[88]

As well as embellishing Jerusalem and the rest of his kingdom, Herod endowed monuments throughout the eastern Mediterranean. An aqueduct at Laodicaea, for example, a colonnaded street at Antioch (Figure 23), theatres and gymnasia at Damascus and Tripoli, the temple to Apollo at Rhodes, various endowments at Athens and Sparta, to name but a few. His lavishness even extended to rescuing the declining Olympic Games, which he presided over in great pomp in 16 BC, being rewarded with the title of perpetual president of the Games. But his greatest building project was begun in 18 BC, when he rebuilt the Temple in Jerusalem on a scale intended to outshine Solomon's original structure (Figure 8, Plate 6). It was a massive undertaking, taking eight years before it was dedicated in 10 BC, although construction continued sporadically for a further seventy years. The Haram ash-Sharif today represents Herod's much enlarged Temple enclosure, which surrounded the sanctuary itself in the centre.[89] He also greatly enlarged and embellished the city itself,[90] he rebuilt the city walls, he restored the city water supply, he added a theatre and a hippodrome. When he died in 4 BC Herod left behind a city that was one of the greatest in the East, a city that in many ways had the standard trappings of a Graeco-Roman city (Figure 9). But Herod's main emphasis on the Temple had made Jerusalem above all a *Jewish* city once more. Ultimately, what Judas Maccabaeus and his arch-Jewish followers failed to do, it took a Romanised Idumaean to do.

Herod the Great[91] ruled for over thirty years – a long time for the period and the place – and he brought wealth, stability and prosperity to his kingdom. Few dynasties matched Herod's in sheer ostentatious magnificence. Judaea under Herod must have been immensely wealthy – the scale and lavishness of Herod's building activities far beyond his own borders are alone evidence for that. The construction and dedication of Caesarea, for example, was on a 'money no object' basis. These endowments were far out of proportion to the size or wealth of a small kingdom like Judaea.[92] Such wealth was due not so much to any inherent wealth in Judaea itself – its lands never produced particularly significant contributions to the Roman coffers. The source for this wealth was Herod's restored Temple, the scale of which was deliberately planned to attract remissions from the Jewish Diaspora. By far the largest and wealthiest Diaspora community at the time was in Iran. The wealth of Herod's kingdom, therefore, reflects the wealth of both Rome and Iran as a whole, a one-way flow of wealth between the two rival empires.[93]

Herod's kingdom was divided into a number of provinces on both sides of the river Jordan (Figure 7). The western provinces were Galilee, Samaria, Judaea and Idumaea. To the east were Gaulanitis (Golan) and Batanea, Auranitis and Trachonitis, corresponding broadly to the Hauran in southern Syria, as well as Peraea to the east of the Dead Sea. Under Herod, Judaea and Judaism reached its greatest glory. Money was no object for Herod to lavish on the Jewish capital, the Jewish Temple, and Jewish communities around the eastern Mediterranean: Herod's endowments outside his country were possibly directed not so much at the Graeco-Roman cities he endowed as the Jewish communities who lived in them.[94] As an Idumaean, Herod was plagued by hard-line doubts of his Jewishness, so had to resort to buying it. Thus, Herod the Idumaean had to court the Jews by rebuilding their temple on a magnificent scale.

At the same time Herod was a Helleniser and a Romanophile. Jerusalem, it is true, was embellished to a degree intended to outshine David's and Solomon's city. But they were Hellenistic and Roman embellishments, while the new cities of Sebaste and Caesarea were essentially Roman implants on Palestinian soil.[95] The buildings in his kingdom honoured Romans, not Jews; he sent his sons to Rome for their education; he himself went consistently out of his way to curry favour with the Romans. Herod's Romanisation may be seen as a betrayal of the Jews, or at least ambivalence towards them. But Herod was a pragmatist who had the vision to realise that the only way for a small kingdom like Palestine to survive was to accommodate Rome, not oppose it, and that the only way for an unusual religion like Judaism to survive was to come to terms with foreign elements, not exclude them. The subsequent tragedy of the Jewish Revolt was to prove him entirely right.

But Herod himself was hated, hated because he was an Idumaean, hated because he was a Romanophile, hated because he was a tyrant. He rebuilt the Temple, it is true, but its opulence was based on pagan models – yet too glorious to condemn either. He married into the Hasmonaean royal family – through Mariamme – to curry favour with his subjects, but ruined it by butchering every male Hasmonaean he could. Despite loving his Hasmonaean wife with a passion matched only by Mariamme's hatred for him, he had her executed in a fit of jealous rage – and went mad with remorse immediately after. Her death certainly seems to have left him unhinged, and the remainder of his life alternated between bouts of blind suspicion and bitter remorse. His relations with his own sons – from various marriages (nine to be exact; Jewish law still allowed ten) – were fraught with savage suspicion. Herod's hatred of the Hasmonaean line even went as far as having his two sons by Mariamme strangled, thus extinguishing the Hasmonaean line for good[96] (he had enough other sons not to be endangering his own!). As he lay dying he gave orders for a blood-bath to be carried out in the event of his death to ensure national mourning.[97] One of his last acts was to have his eldest son and original favourite and heir, Antipater, executed as well. Herod survived his son's murder by only five days, finally succumbing just before Passover in 4 BC.

The successors of Herod

There had been intense fraternal discord between Herod's numerous sons by various marriages. Only three survived to succeeded him: Philip, Antipas and Archelaus.[98] Archelaus was made king in Herod's will, despite opposing claims by Antipas. Beginning his reign with a massacre, the Romans divided the kingdom into three to minimise his excesses. Philip was given the north-eastern provinces of Gaulanitis, Trachonitis, Batanea and the city of Paneas (renamed Caesarea Philippi), while Antipas was given Galilee and the south-eastern province of Peraea. Archelaus (demoted from 'king' to 'prince') was left to rule the core provinces of the kingdom, Samaria, Idumaea and Judaea itself, from Jerusalem. Under his reign there were sporadic outbursts of revolt, the resulting instability representing a real threat to Rome's position. In the end, his rule was so inept, cruel and unstable, that the Romans responded to popular demand and deposed him in AD 6 when, after only ten years in power, Archelaus was exiled to Gaul.

Judaea passed to direct Roman rule, represented by a prefect (a title soon changed to procurator) appointed from Rome, supported by auxiliary troops drawn largely from the local non-Jewish population. No Roman legions were stationed in Judaea until after Vespasian. The seat of Roman government from AD 6 was Caesarea, which remained a westward-looking enclave in Palestine throughout antiquity.[99] A secondary garrison was maintained in Jerusalem, where the procurator would make regular visits to attend to local matters. Philip and Antipas continued to rule as princes in their respective domains.

Plate 6 Herod's Temple (A model in the Holy Land Hotel, Jerusalem)

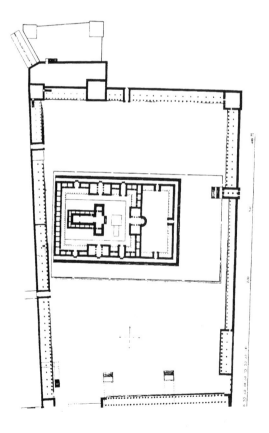

Figure 8 Herod's Temple (After Busink)

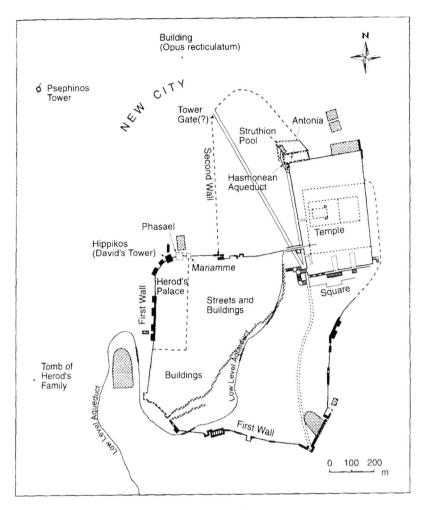

Figure 9 Jerusalem at the time of Herod (After Roller)

Philip's rule over Gaulanitis was exemplary, unmarred by any upheavals, and his capital of Caesarea Philippi embellished along Hellenistic lines. Antipas' rule from Tiberias, the capital of Galilee which he created by the Sea of Galilee, was similarly uneventful and inoffensive. There was a brief restoration of the Judaean kingdom under Herod's grandson, Agrippa I, from 41 to 44. Returning from Rome at the completion of his education, Agrippa eventually succeeded to his uncle Philip's kingdom in AD 37 and took over Antipas' kingdom shortly afterwards through intrigue. Finally, in return for favours instrumental in bringing his childhood friend, the Emperor Claudius, to the throne, he was granted Judaea as well. Agrippa thus ended up with a kingdom that was larger than Herod the Great's. But all of Palestine, from Galilee in the north to Idumaea in the south, passed back under direct Roman rule with the death of Agrippa I.

Agrippa's nephew, Agrippa II, was given the token 'kingdom' of Chalcis in the Beq'a Valley[100] by Claudius in AD 50. Although the kingdom of Chalcis was so small as to be largely meaningless, the title carried with it the important responsibility for the Temple in Jerusalem, including the appointment of its high-priests. Agrippa II also had the power to summon the Sanhedrin, and made frequent visits to Jerusalem, where he maintained a palace. More real power followed three years later when he was 'transferred' to the much larger kingship of southern Syria: Herod the Great's former provinces of Gaulanitis, Batanaea, Trachonitis and Auranitis. Nero added parts of Galilee and Peraea to Agrippa's kingdom in AD 54. Agrippa's kingdom was soon thought powerful enough for the Romans to call upon it for levies to assist in operations in Armenia; later it was also able to dispatch 2,000 cavalry to assist Titus in his siege of Jerusalem in 66. The seat of his kingdom was the city of Caesarea Philippi at the foot of Mt Hermon. King Agrippa II's by then not inconsiderable territories finally passed to the Romans at his death in about 93 – a rule of forty years, longer than that of Herod the Great himself and ruling a territory not much smaller. And his powers amongst the priesthood and elders in Jerusalem meant that his powers were more than token. But with his death, the Herodian line as rulers seems to have come to an end.

The Jewish Revolt[101]

But before that, one of the most important events in the history of Judaism shook Palestine, ultimately to change its ethnic character. Although Herod the Great was an Idumaean, not a Judaean, he was at least a native king who rebuilt the ancient Temple of the Jews on an unprecedented scale. The more extreme elements in Judaea therefore felt few threats in the first century of Roman control. Indeed, the Romans respected the sanctity of the Temple, with the death penalty – even for Roman citizens – rigidly enforced by the Roman authorities themselves upon transgressors. In the middle of the first century AD, however, events combined to seriously upset the delicate balance between extreme Judaism and creeping westernisation.

After the death of King Agrippa I in 44, Judaea came under direct Roman rule. It was benevolent enough, but the Jewish religion baffled the Romans, and tension was caused by lack of understanding in far-off Rome for Jewish repugnance at performing worship of the official cult of Rome and Augustus as Roman law required.[102] Earlier Roman representatives, such as Pilate or Petronius, ended up giving way to Jewish sentiments, but later ones were not so tolerant, and Roman rule was increasingly marked by arrogance, suppression and deteriorating relations with the Jews as the first century wore on. This was matched by increasing Jewish resistance, and there was an unusually large outburst of 'messiahs' in the middle of the first century. Whilst these were presumably false, the powerful Jewish belief in ultimate deliverance from oppression by a messiah probably lent much support to Jewish self-confidence. This was bolstered up by a current Jewish prophecy that out of Judaea would come the ruler of the world. The Jews doubtless took the prophecy to mean their Messiah, forgetting that prophecies, like Delphic oracles, have a nasty habit of working in reverse: the Romans (later on) simply took it as confirmation of Vespasian's candidacy for the purple when he was proclaimed emperor in the East.

The situation was exacerbated by about AD 60 when Herod's great building project, the rebuilding of the Temple, finally came to an end, suddenly releasing 18,000 workmen onto the streets. Many of these may have taken to the hills, as we read of new problems in Judaea from roaming groups of bandits. These had to be put down with increasing force by the Romans. The combination of ensuing instability, a large unemployed mob, and the threats – real or perceived – felt by the conservative elements in Judaea was the stuff of insurrection. The situation was exacerbated by the inept procurator of Judaea, Gessius Florus, in his tactless handling of the different factions. Insurrection broke out in Caesarea with a clash between the rival Jewish and Greek populations of the city in 66. This led to full-scale revolt in Jerusalem a short while after and the abolition of the mandatory sacrifices to Rome and Augustus. This latter insult to Rome's prestige made war inevitable.

There were leaders to the revolt, but none with the charisma of Maccabaeus or – later – Bar Kochba. This contributed to its ultimate failure. Much of the real leadership lay with the commanders in the field, such as the future historian Josephus. Josephus, the commander in Galilee, was a Pharisee who traced his ancestry back to the Hasmonaeans. But much of the leadership was tainted by the brush of 'westernisation' – either of the older Hellenistic or the new, Roman kind (even Josephus the Pharisee had been to Rome several years previously). The real force behind the revolt lay with the far more conservative non-Hellenised proletariat. The intense, religious belief in their god sending a messiah to throw off Roman rule had a conviction that was far more real to them than the common-sense reality of taking on a power like Rome. When this intense belief failed them, it was replaced by an equally intense – albeit forlorn – belief that their Jewish brethren in exile around the Mediterranean would rise against the Romans in support, together with the far greater Jewish communities in Iran who would bring a mighty oriental host with them. In the end, even this hope failed them, and all they had left to fight with was their despair.

But the more westernised leaders such as Josephus certainly had common-sense doubts, particularly when the religious zeal which accounted for the initial success of the revolt had faltered somewhat after the Romans were able to move over to the offensive. The year 67 saw the arrival in Palestine of the general Vespasian to take over the command of the Jewish War. Josephus, who formed his army along Roman lines, managed to hold off the Roman advance into Palestine in a heroic defence at Jotapata, when even Vespasian sustained injury. When Jotapata eventually fell, rather than continue in a cause he saw to be lost, Josephus surrendered to the Romans.[103] On his capture Josephus used his priestly knowledge to prophesy Vespasian's rise to the imperial purple.[104] Vespasian, befriending Josephus in gratitude, set his eyes on horizons beyond Palestine.

Vespasian was for a while distracted from the Judaean campaign in the chaos following Nero's death. However, the campaign had proved the crowning asset to Vespasian's qualifications: he was recalled to Rome in 69 to assume the purple himself. He left the command of the campaign to his son Titus. To the Fifth, Tenth and Fifteenth Legions that had been left Titus by his father, Titus added the Twelfth from Syria and the Twenty-Second and the Third from Alexandria. Units were also contributed by Agrippa II and the kings of Commagene, Emesa and Nabataea. This was nearly a fifth of the entire forces of the Roman Empire – altogether one of the most formidable forces so far assembled by the Romans. This was an acknowledgement not so much of the seriousness of the Revolt as of the importance of an eastern empire where the much larger threat of Iran loomed just beyond the horizon. It laid siege to Jerusalem the following year. Inside, the city was defended by a mixed bag of different private armies representing the various factions, altogether totalling 23,400 fighting men.

Titus launched a general assault in February AD 70. The siege took nearly six months of hard fighting, with extraordinary acts of courage on both sides, before it finally fell with the destruction of the Temple and much of the city on 28 August, AD 70. Titus then proceeded to raze the Temple, as well as most of the surrounding city, so completely as to provide no rallying point for future Jewish insurrection. Many of the survivors were executed or enslaved (although many too were reprieved at the personal intervention of Josephus). Of the prisoners, many were disposed of in the arenas during Titus' triumphal progression back to Rome; many more were spared to be paraded through Rome at the great triumphal procession held to celebrate Titus' victory, only later to perish in the arena also. The sacred books of the Temple as well as the great Menorah were taken off in triumph to Rome (where it is still illustrated on the victory arch erected to commemorate Titus' triumph). It would be nearly five hundred years before it would be returned to Jerusalem.[105] The number killed in the siege probably amounted to some 220,000, with over 19,000 taken prisoner.[106] The Temple never rose again.[107]

There was not, however, any active suppression of Judaism: the Romans did not alter their policy of religious tolerance. But there was an aftermath that in Jewish national consciousness has since assumed almost the same proportions as the Revolt itself. This was the siege and capture of Masada in 74 by the new governor of Palestine, Flavius Silva (Plate 105). Masada was little more than a footnote to the main story of the Jewish Revolt, but it has come to assume a significance far higher. For the defence of Masada had all the unambiguous, heroic qualities that the defence of Jerusalem lacked. Masada was heroism and self-sacrifice pure and simple; Jerusalem, whilst undoubtedly heroic, was at the same time tainted by internal dissension, questionable motives, shameful acts, pointless sacrifice. Small wonder that Masada has come to rank almost as much as Jerusalem itself as a Jewish national shrine.

Jewish insurrection returned, first in the uprising of Diaspora communities in Alexandria, Cyrenaica and Cyprus in AD 115–17 (not a part of the present story – although significantly it was triggered by Trajan's Parthian campaign and included the Jews of Roman-occupied Mesopotamia),[108] then more seriously in Palestine again in 132–5. The last Jewish revolt in Palestine occurred in 351–2.[109] The revolt of 132–5 was once again in response to the threat of Westernisation. This time, the threat was Hadrian's plan in AD 130 to Romanise the site of Jerusalem completely as the new Roman colony of Aelia Capitolina – in today's terminology, Jerusalem was to be Rome's own strategic settlement on occupied territory.[110] Insurrection was led by Simon Bar Kochba who, in 132, proclaimed the independence of a Jewish state. Bar Kochba was initially very successful, but the insurrection came to an end in 135 soon after his death.[111]

Hadrian immediately proceeded with his plans for Aelia Capitolina, a city that was to be so thoroughly Roman that no Jews were allowed in or near it. A new Roman temple dedicated to Jupiter Capitolinus was built on the site of the old Temple. In actual fact, Hadrian's rebuilding of Jerusalem probably did not amount to much: there is not a single Hadrianic building inscription in Jerusalem and, apart from the 'Ecce Homo' Arch, archaeological excavations have shown very few structures built between Titus' destruction and Constantine.[112] Jerusalem only really recovered from Titus when it became a Christian pilgrimage centre after Constantine. But Hadrian did hasten Jerusalem's decline as a Jewish city: after the creation of Aelia Capitolina the Jewish population of Palestine slowly diminished, becoming a minority, eventually to disperse throughout the world. Only then did the Jews finally assume the international, cosmopolitan characteristics that they had resisted so long. In doing so, they survived.

The undoubted heroism of Jewish defence, the emotional issues related to the subsequent Jewish Diaspora and the special place that Jerusalem has in our minds have tended to obscure the real reasons behind Titus' destruction of Jerusalem. In fact it had little to do with the Jews, the Diaspora or even Jerusalem itself. The Jews did not figure greatly in Roman politics, Judaea was not a granary essential for Rome's economy, the Diaspora had begun many centuries before, Jerusalem had little strategic importance.[113] As always with Rome's eastern policies, the threat of Iran – real or perceived – was the predominating reason. The Jewish Revolt, whilst not related directly to events in Iran, had to be suppressed so completely so as to leave no focus for future insurrection or disaffected elements that might bring the Iranians back to the Mediterranean. After all, only a threat from Iran could prompt Rome into putting such a massive force into the field – nearly a fifth of the entire forces of the Roman Empire – into suppressing what was, after all, a provincial revolt.

So brutal a suppression has been cited as incipient anti-Semitism. This was not necessarily the case. Roman rule in Judaea was inept rather than racially prejudiced, and Rome was no more intolerant of Judaism than of other religions, so long as it remained outside politics. Pompey's initial reaction to the Temple – apart from puzzlement – was respect (even though the Jews themselves may not have seen it that way). But more important, Rome's policies in the East were dictated by the highest strategic considerations that were vital for Rome's security. Anti-Semitism or particular intolerance against the Jews – even if it did exist – had nothing to do with it.

Palestine was vitally important to Rome's security. Threats from 'pirates', real or perceived, was one of them – and after Rome controlled the entire Mediterranean littoral trouble from pirates virtually ceased. But more important was Iran, which posed a real threat. Although Palestine did not share common borders with Iran, in some ways it figured higher in the 'Iranian question' than Syria or Armenia, which do. For Palestine shared a common people: the Jews. The largest population of Jews outside Judaea itself was in Iran. These were descendants of the Jews who had been exiled by Nebuchadnezzar in 587 BC but who had chosen not to return, even after Judaea was restored to them by Cyrus the Great in 538.[114] Indeed, during the Jewish Revolt the Jews were hoping for substantial support from their compatriots there.[115] Given the traditional sympathy between Jews and Iranians following Cyrus' restoration of the Temple (a bond doubtless reinforced by mutual monotheism), a threat from Judaea was perceived by Rome as a potential threat from Iran itself. Furthermore, Josephus writes that 'there is not a region in the world without its Jewish colony',[116] particularly in the vital – and often volatile – second and third cities of the Roman Empire, Alexandria and Antioch. The reason why Rome had to put down any Jewish revolt so thoroughly, therefore, was not incipient anti-Semitism, nor intolerance of their strange religion, nor even that they posed any real threat. It was because the large numbers of Jewish communities throughout the Mediterranean represented a perceived 'fifth column' in the heart of the Roman Empire – as well as potential oriental hordes at the gates of the empire. Never mind that such threats were not real, it was the *perceived* threat that mattered to the Romans rather than any reality, rather as modern great powers might overreact to threats that are more imagined than real, such as Communism or Islamic fundamentalism.

Josephus, in apparently betraying the Jews and befriending Vespasian, has been almost universally condemned. But Josephus was no renegade Jew; on the contrary, he shows every sign of being an arch-Judophile, and his actions cannot be dismissed so simply. The Jewish Revolt was undoubtedly nationalist in overtone (although it is dangerous to apply modern notions of nationalism to ancient history). But equally it did not enjoy total Jewish support: the appeal to the Jews of Iran, for example, went unanswered as we have noted, nor did it spread to Jewish communities outside Palestine, and the Jewish 'king', Agrippa II, supported Rome. All Jewish revolts were tempered by a strong element of civil war; of internal divisions as much as cohesiveness, of deeply conflicting Judaising and westernising elements. Events in Israel to this day still underline this.[117] Josephus himself states that the real tragedy of his country was that it 'was destroyed by internal dissensions' rather than by the Romans, and 'for our misfortunes we have only ourselves to blame'.[118] One cannot, therefore, simply condemn Josephus as a traitor. Josephus at least had the vision to foresee the inevitability of Roman victory. Moreover, in supporting Vespasian perhaps he was hoping to return to Palestine as a governor or even client king under Roman protection. This is not as unlikely as it sounds: after all, this is exactly what happened to Josephus' illustrious predecessor as governor of Galilee, Herod, in befriending Antony and Octavian. It hardly needs reiterating that Herod's actions in supporting Antony and Octavian did far more for the Jews than any insurrection did – a lesson not lost on Josephus. Josephus' descent was hardly less illustrious than Herod's, and just as Herod displaced the Hasmonaean line, Josephus may have hoped to replace the Herodian. His surrender in Galilee might be seen as treachery, but in doing so he saved many Jewish lives – and bequeathed to his own people and posterity at large one of the greatest accounts of courage and heroism from antiquity.

There is no sign that Josephus ever renounced Judaism. On the contrary, he was ultimately vindicated as a great Jewish patriot, not only by his *Jewish War* and *Jewish Antiquities*, but with the publication towards the end of his life of the great defence of Judaism *In Apionem*, 'an impassioned but well-written and well-argued comprehensive *apologia* for the Jews and Judaism, a defence of his people, their religion, their law and their customs against the malicious and often ill-informed attacks made on them'.[119] In the end, Josephus, the priest turned general, as well as a great historian was a great patriot, a passionate Judophile, and – who knows – a man who would be king?

Arabia and the Nabataeans

Although there were many 'Arabias',[120] only one was an officially designated Roman Province: the Provincia Arabia, corresponding to the old Nabataean kingdom.[121] This comprised much of the present area of Jordan together with Sinai and the Negev (including Gaza), northern Hijaz and parts of southern Syria up to and including (for a short while) Damascus (Figure 10). The Decapolis in the northern part of the kingdom comprised in the first century a Roman enclave in the Nabataean kingdom, although boundaries and even responsibilities were often blurred.[122] The Nabataean kingdom was of considerable strategic importance to Rome as a link between the Mediterranean and the Red Sea, hence Africa and the Indian Ocean.

The rise of the Nabataeans

The first known inhabitants of southern Jordan around Petra were the Edomites. The Nabataeans are known from Hebrew and Assyrian sources as early as the seventh century BC as a nomadic tribe inhabiting the desert regions of north-western Arabia,[123] who may originally have migrated from southern Arabia. They spoke a dialect akin to modern

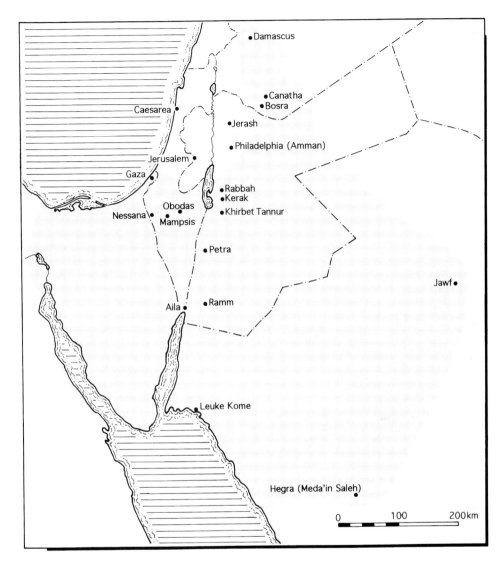

Figure 10 Map illustrating the Nabataean Kingdom. Shaded area indicates approximate limits at greatest extent

Arabic – indeed, the Nabataean script is a forerunner of the Arabic. Even more than the other 'Princely States', therefore, it must be emphasised that in any examination of the civilisation of the Nabataeans, they form as much a part of the broader spectrum of Arab civilisation as, say, the Umayyads, Abbasids or Fatimids do.

There was no sudden invasion of southern Jordan, but a long process of usually peaceful infiltration and gradual displacement of the Edomite inhabitants between the sixth and the fourth centuries BC, assimilating many Edomite cultural ideas in the process and absorbing much of the population.[124] By the end of the fourth century they had established a base at Petra which gradually grew in wealth from its location alongside several important trade routes. The incense trade from south Arabia was the main source of this prosperity, but they also harvested asphalt from the Dead Sea, an important (and much neglected) commodity in the ancient world. At about this time we read of their first contact with the Macedonian rulers of Syria, who tried unsuccessfully to take over Petra when even the legendary general Demetrius Poliorcetes, 'the Besieger', failed in a campaign of 312 BC. From the first century BC onwards they appear to have become a sedentary people. Historical references to the Nabataeans then become more plentiful, allowing a fairly accurate reconstruction of their history.

Under its kings, Nabataea gradually expanded over much of southern Palestine and most of Jordan. King Harithath (al-Harith, Aretas) II in particular was very energetic, coming into conflict with Alexander Jannaeus of Judaea in about 100 BC. In 87 BC during the reign of his son and successor, ʿObaydath (al-ʿUbaydah, Obodas, Avdat) I, Antiochus XII of the Seleucid kingdom invaded but was decisively beaten at the Battle of Cana by ʿObaydath, when Antiochus himself was slain. As a result, the Nabataean kingdom was able to expand greatly at the expense of the Seleucids. ʿObaydath's son Harithath III, who reigned from 86 to 62 BC, took advantage of a conflict between the Hasmonaeans of Judaea and the Seleucids of Syria to extend his borders as far as Damascus in 84 BC, probably incorporating the cities later known as the Decapolis at the same time. Intermittent warfare continued with Judaea for much of this period. Damascus was taken from the Nabataeans in 72 BC by Tigranes of Armenia. Pompey's creation of the Roman Province of Syria in 64 BC recognised the autonomy of the Decapolis and limited the northward expansion of the Nabataeans, but appears to have had no effect on their expanding trade.

The first Roman incursion into Nabataea was in 63 BC following the incorporation of Judaea.[125] This was the campaign by Pompey's lieutenant, Scaurus, but he only got as far as Pella before circumstances turned him back. This was followed up by another inconclusive campaign in 55 BC by Gabinius. From this time onwards Nabataea seems to have become a client kingdom of Rome, but the sources are unclear: nowhere is this specifically stated, it is simply implied.[126] It is certainly true that Nabataean kings from Maliku (al-Malik, Malichus) I onwards appear to be more answerable to Rome. Maliku, who became king in about 54 BC,[127] fought an indecisive war with Herod the Great. Like Herod, Maliku was careful to preserve good relations with Octavian after Actium.

Maliku was succeeded in 30 BC by ʿObaydath II. Aelius Gallus' expedition to southern Arabia in 26 BC[128] implies some form of link between Rome and the Nabataean kingdom, as 1,000 Nabataean auxiliaries were attached to it. The machinations of Gallus' Nabataean 'guide' for this campaign, Syllaeus, later led to another war with Herod until Rome intervened in 9 BC. Then in 8 BC King Harithath IV, surnamed 'the lover of his people', ascended the throne, reigning until AD 40. During this long reign the Nabataean kingdom reached the height of its prosperity: like Palmyra later on, with Rome seeing to external security, the Nabataeans could get on with the more important business of making money. It also reached its greatest extent, covering all of Sinai, the southern Negev, Jordan, the Hauran, the Wadi Sirhan as far as Jawf, and the Red Sea coast as far as Hegra (Figure 10). It has been argued, mainly on numismatic grounds, that Nabataea was briefly annexed by Rome between 3 BC and AD 1 due to instability in the region following Herod's death. This is precisely the period which sees the rise of Hegra (modern Madaʾin Saleh in Saudi Arabia), one of the few accurately dated Nabataean sites. It is argued that this was deliberately created as a Nabataean capital in exile by Harithath IV after his supposed deposition by Augustus. Augustus sent his grandson, Gaius Caesar, on a fact-finding mission to both the Judaean and Nabataean kingdoms in AD 1 to investigate the state of affairs in the East following the unsatisfactory situation after Herod's death. The mission went as far as the Gulf of Aqaba and – presumably as a result of Gaius' recommendations – Harithath was reinstated as a client king, while Judaea was in due course annexed. Nabataea then retained that status until its annexation by Trajan.[129]

Thus restored, Harithath IV was able to resume building work at Petra, as well as the age-old confrontation with the enemy across the Jordan river. Harithath fought a war in alliance with Abgar V of Edessa against Antipas,[130] who was defeated. After this victory the Nabataeans may even have won back Damascus for a short while, as they seem to have been the occupying power at the time of Paul's celebrated basket escape in AD 37.[131] Tiberius contemplated chastening Harithath on seeing the balance upset and instructed the governor of Syria, Vitellius, to prepare an expeditionary force. But the Nabataeans received a reprieve with Tiberius' death, and the invasion was called off.

Perhaps Damascus was returned by negotiation, for we hear no further word of any Nabataean occupation. But the Nabataeans certainly continued to consolidate the northern borderlands of their kingdom under Harithath's successors, Maliku II (AD 40–70) and Rabbel II (70–106). Indeed, the focus shifted northwards to such an extent that the capital of the kingdom itself was transferred from Petra to Bosra in 93.[132] Rabbel II continued the expansion of the kingdom's activities that were begun by Harithath IV, and his equally long reign saw increased irrigation, agriculture and urbanisation, as well as the construction and embellishment of Bosra, the new capital (Figure 41). The move to Bosra possibly corresponds with a shift in the Arabian trade routes from the Red Sea to the Wadi Sirhan.[133] Certainly Roman Egypt was taking over more of the Red Sea trade during this period at the expense of the Nabataeans. But whatever the reasons, the shift of focus from Petra and the south, in the heart of Arabia, to Bosra in the more Hellenised climate of Syria certainly ensured the importance of Bosra as an urban and religious centre for many centuries after. Hitherto, the Nabataean kingdom had been an essentially Arabian power, looking to the east. With this shift of focus, the Nabataeans seemed poised to become more of a power – both politically and economically – in the mainstream of the Near East and the eastern Mediterranean. In the end, it was to be another Arab power, Palmyra, which took advantage of this trade shift, not Nabataea.

Perhaps it was for this reason that Trajan annexed the kingdom on the death of King Rabbel in 106: its expansion, not to mention earlier successes in its wars against Judaea, might have been perceived by Trajan as a threat to the status quo in the East. Presumably the death of Rabbel II provided a convenient excuse (although he did have a son and heir, 'Obaydath). There is little or no source material for the 'noiseless'[134] annexation of Nabataea and the creation of the Roman Province of Arabia in its place, so the reasons are speculative. It has been argued that Trajan was simply safeguarding his rear prior to his Parthian campaign.[135] But for two centuries – from Trajan's annexation to Diocletian's reorganisation – Arabia was a single-legion province (the Third Cyrenaican). This minimal strength of Arabia's defence surely argues *against* its being annexed by Trajan as part of his Parthian campaign. After all, it was never the scene of uprisings, as Judaea was, nor did it border Iran making annexation a strategic necessity, so never posed any threat to Rome's security.[136] Perhaps simple land-grabbing for personal glory was the overriding consideration. Indeed, it is rather the *lack* of any threat or difficulties that is the real explanation for Nabataea's annexation: it simply provided an easy conquest with little effort for Trajan to feather his cap with – not to mention his nest, given the money

Nabataea's lucrative trade would bring in. Whatever the reason, it was a peaceful annexation with no force required.[137] Thus, in 106 the area of the Nabataean state became the new Roman province of Arabia with its capital at Bosra.

The Nabataean achievement

There had been over a hundred years of prosperity and stability for the Nabataean kingdom, despite occasional minor wars with Judaea and its possible brief loss of independence under Harithath IV. For it was a period which saw unusually long reigns of just three kings: Harithath IV ruled for 48 years and the reigns of Maliku II and Rabbel II were an impressive 30 and 46 years respectively. Furthermore, the transition from one reign to the next appears to have been entirely smooth, without the endless rounds of fratricides, civil strife and general bloodletting that characterised so many Near Eastern monarchies (or Rome itself for that matter). Indeed, Strabo's words that the kingdom was 'exceedingly well-governed . . ., that none of the natives prosecuted one another, and that they in every way kept peace with one another'[138] has a very true ring. Strabo's description of the structure of Nabataean society is essentially of a tribal one, with the king ruling as a shaikh supported by tribal elders[139] – hardly the Hellenistic society that many see Nabataea to be. This stability allowed for an astonishing upsurge in building activity and creativity. Nabataean skills in water management and rock cutting were famous even by the fourth century BC.[140] Accordingly, by the first century AD areas of the desert which had never before seen cultivation – and in some cases never since – flourished, water resources were conserved and harnessed with an efficiency that anticipated our own era's environmental revolution,[141] and one of the most magnificent cities of the ancient world was built whose fame today has become a byword for all that is exotic and spectacular (Figure 11, Plates 7, 8, 10–14). Impressive achievements indeed for a kingdom that was, in fact, really on the sidelines of the great civilisations of the ancient Near East.

Nabataean control of the trade from south Arabia had in fact declined in this period: advances in maritime technology made the sea routes more feasible than the land routes, which Petra controlled, and much of the trade was usurped by Roman Egypt. This is reflected in south Arabia, where a major shift in the pattern occurred from the old trading kingdoms of Ma'an, Saba (Sheba) and Qataban on the inland desert fringes, to the new kingdom of Himyar on the highlands, reflecting a shift in emphasis from the overland routes of the desert to the new sea routes of the Red Sea.[142] However, despite the decline in trade, the substantial developments that the Nabataeans had made in hydrology, water management and agriculture ensured that Petra continued to flourish and even expand. The city was massively embellished, with its most famous monuments – the theatre, the Temple of Dushara (Qasr al-Bint) (Figure 89c) and probably the Khazneh (Plate 8) – dating from the reign of Harithath.[143] As well as being impressive monuments, the buildings at Petra have an eclecticism rare amongst ancient civilisations, combining elements of Hellenistic, Roman, Egyptian, Assyrian and Persian architecture bonded by the strong cement of their own Arabian forms. In addition to reflecting the Nabataeans' own accomplishment, therefore, Petra reflects much of the ancient Near Eastern and Mediterranean achievement as a whole.[144]

Virtually all of the major building work at Petra was completed before the Roman annexation in AD 106. This not only included the more Nabataean and non-Classical types of building – most notably the majority of the tomb façades and the temples – but

1: Deir.
2: Turkmaniyah Tomb.
3: Conway Tower.
4: Moghar an-Nassara.
5: Tomb of Sextus Florentinus.
6: Palace Tomb.
7: Corinthian Tomb.
8: Silk Tomb.
9: Urn Tomb.
10: Khubtha High Places.
11: Temple of the Winged Lions.
12: Qasr al-Bint.
13: Temenos Arch.
14: Unfinished Tomb.
15: Great Temple.
16: Colonnaded street.
17: Nymphaeum.
18: Pharaoh's Pillar.
19: Umm al-Biyara Summit.
20: Broken Pediment Tomb.
21: Renaissance Tomb.
22: Roman Soldier Triclinium.
23: Roman Soldier Tomb.
24: Garden Temple.
25: Lion Fountain.
26: Madhbah High Place.
27: Theatre.
28: Street of façades.
29: Tomb of Unaishu.
30: Khazneh.
31: Siq.
32: Arch.
33: Obelisk Tomb.
34: God Blocks.

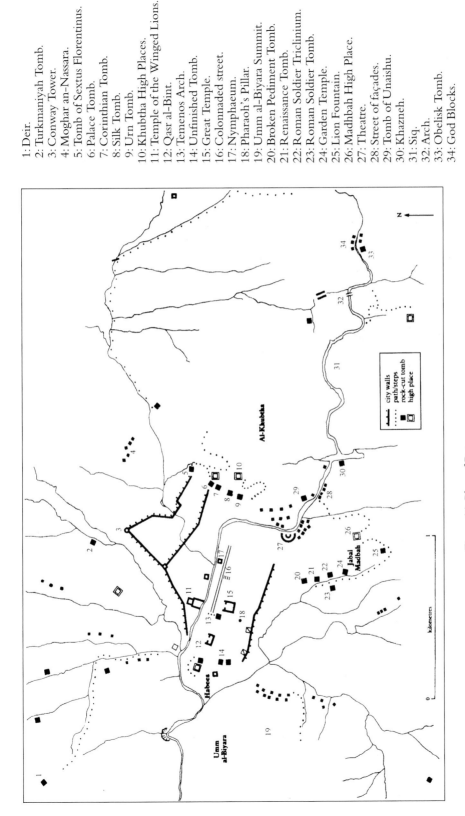

Figure 11 Plan of Petra

Plate 8 The Khazneh at Petra

Plate 7 Petra: the main colonnaded street towards the 'Royal Tombs'

also the more 'Roman' styles of building, such as the theatre and the colonnaded street.[145] Technically speaking, therefore, the architecture of Petra must be described as Nabataean rather than Roman.

The embellishment did not stop with its annexation. Despite the reaffirmation of Bosra as the capital of the new province, the pre-eminence of Petra as the historic Nabataean centre ensured that it too did not lag behind any of the other cities of the Roman East, particularly in the lavish monumentalisation that took place throughout the region during the course of the second century. Indeed, the transformation from client kingdom to province is not marked by any discernible break in continuity in the archaeological record. Nabataean cities elsewhere in the province also grew to their greatest extent in the Roman period, such as Mampsis in the Negev and Rabbah in Moab (Plate 9). Trajan's great road network, the Via Nova Trajan from the Gulf of Aqaba to Bosra, was constructed in 111. Petra's eventual decline was a gradual one. An earthquake in the fourth century left major devastation, and during the fourth, fifth and sixth centuries, Petra slowly contracted in size as the area of southern Jordan became more of a backwater.

Nabataean religion

Religion is one of the least known aspects of Nabataean culture, despite religious buildings being their most familiar legacy. The ramifications of Nabataean religion are more widespread than is immediately apparent. For example, the Nabataean abstract representation of their main deity, Dushara, is a simple, square block of stone. This is seen

Plate 9 The Nabataean Temple at al-Qasr

throughout Petra, either as simple squares, as cubic stones (the 'god-blocks') or in the form of a 'cuboid' architecture generally. The affinities with the square block of the Ka'ba (itself of pre-Islamic origins) in Mecca, forming a focal point for Arab identity as well as the Islamic faith, are obvious. This is not to suggest that the pre-Islamic Ka'ba was a Nabataean Temple of Dushara. But the Islamic abstract concept of deity certainly owes a debt to Nabataean religion.[146]

Even more ubiquitous at Petra than the cubic blocks are the sacred high places.[147] They are usually described as places of sacrifice, often human, with the altar interpreted for the sacrificial victim, the channels for the blood, etc. One authority on the Nabataeans, for example, writes that 'it is probable . . . that it [the Madhbah high place] served for blood sacrifice' *solely* because there is a channel. Thereafter the altar automatically becomes a 'blood altar' and the idea that 'Dushara must have had blood sacrifices offered to him' becomes fact.[148] There is a Nabataean inscription from Meda'in Saleh in Saudi Arabia which refers explicitly to a young man being consecrated 'to be immolated to Dhu Dubat', that is often quoted as confirmation of Nabataean human sacrifice.[149] This hardly suffices as evidence: it may have been no more than a ritual gesture that was purely symbolic, perhaps involving the entry of a young man into the priesthood. Of course, some sort of sacrifice may have been involved at the high place, but it may have been purely symbolic, as we have suggested, or perhaps merely with a goat as victim (such as is sacrificed in the Id al-Fitr celebrations of Muslims today).

The architecture of Nabataean high places may offer a different explanation. The Nabataeans almost certainly held water to be sacred: they were, after all, masters in the science of water technology.[150] The high places invariably have tanks associated with them, and channels for run-off from the altars. The very location of their places of worship high up in the air also implies some form of sky worship. Indeed, Strabo writes that 'They worship the sun, building an altar on top of the house, and pouring libations on it daily.' His description hints at another explanation with the extraordinary remark that their kings are left on refuse heaps after death.[151] Strabo's comments on Nabataean disposal of the dead have been compared to other Classical descriptions of exposure in the Iranian world to suggest that the Nabataeans also practised exposure. The pro-Parthian leanings of Maliku I (50–30 BC), as well as the strong links between Nabataean and Iranian temple plans,[152] are cited in support. With this in mind, many of the rock-cut 'high places' at Petra have been reinterpreted as exposure platforms (*dakhmas* in Persian), based on comparisons with similar places of exposure in Iran, such as Kuh-i Shahrak in Fars.[153]

Since this interpretation was first proposed in the 1960s, it has received a mixed reaction, usually negative.[154] But it has no less to commend it than blood sacrifice and deserves a reappraisal. Iran has a very rich tradition of high-place architecture.[155] A new study of both the exposure platforms and fire altars of Sasanian Iran, including the one at Kuh-i Shahrak, has reinterpreted most of them as *astadans* or ossuaries for secondary burial after exposure.[156] Hence, many of the 'fittings' associated with Nabataean high places might be explained in this way. The circular 'washing basin' at the main high place of al-Madhbah, for example, is surrounded by a lip as if to take a cover (Figure 12) – an arrangement almost identical to the classic Iranian *astadan*. Some evidence for secondary burial has been found at other Nabataean sites: at Mampsis, for example, while the inner sanctuary of Khirbet Tannur contained a number of small underground 'offering boxes' of an unknown nature.[157] In the third phase of its construction, Khirbet Tannur has a

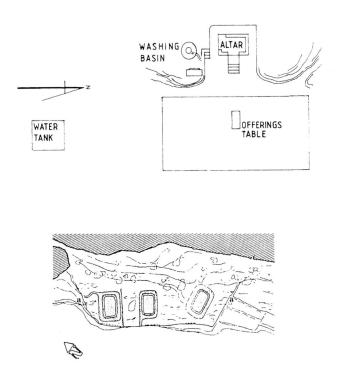

Figure 12 The al-Madhbah high place at Petra (top, after Browning) compared
to the Kuh-i Rahmat *astadans* in Iran (bottom, after Huff). Not to scale

small staircase on the exterior of the inner shrine leading to the altar proper on top, so
there exists at Khirbet Tannur the same arrangement as exposure platforms and ossuary
complexes in Iran.

Part of the explanation might lie in there being more than one method of disposal of
the dead. It has been suggested that at Petra, slab-lined graves were used for ordinary
people, shaft tombs for the middle classes, and façade tombs for the upper classes.[158] If, as
the interpretation of Strabo's controversial passage has suggested, the Nabataean rulers did
practice exposure, then the greatest of the 'tomb façades' might well fit such an explanation. High up in the façades of the Urn Tomb and the Palace Tomb are several small
openings (Plates 10 and 11). There are three in the Urn Tomb which, when investigated,
contained some textile fragments, while in one of the lateral walls of its rock-cut forecourt there are five more, now empty (Plate 12). Those in the Palace Tomb are shallow
niches (one opening into a tunnel).[159] It is tempting to interpret these openings as ossuaries. The Corinthian Tomb is too eroded to determine whether it had similar openings or
not. These three façades are generally interpreted as royal tombs – the façades, in other
words, could function as monumental royal ossuaries, rather like the Achaemenid royal
tombs at Naqsh-i Rustam were. But the two other great façades at Petra, the Khazneh and
the Deir, have defied attempts at explanation, being interpreted variously as shrines,
tombs, temples or temple-tombs.[160] The reason for the controversy is that no obvious
function is apparent: their internal arrangements are different from known Nabataean
temples, neither do they incorporate any obvious places for receiving burials. However,
they *could* receive ossuary caskets: the Khazneh has an opening just above its door (Plate

Plate 10 The Urn Tomb at Petra. Note openings in upper façade

13), while the Deir has five deeply recessed niches in its façade, three on the upper storey and two on the lower, all plainly designed to contain something (Plate 14). They would certainly function as appropriate settings if they were to receive royal ossuaries. All five of the great façades – the Khazneh, the Urn Tomb, the Corinthian Tomb, the Palace Tomb and the Deir – also have another feature in common. None of them contain shaft burials, as many of the smaller tomb façades do (such as the recently excavated Tomb of Unaishu), but all contain arcosolia for sarcophagi (Figure 13). However, no sarcophagi have been found at Petra: if these arcosolia were to contain something, they were probably not

Plate 11 The Palace Tomb at Petra. Note openings in upper façade

Plate 12 Openings in the forecourt wall of the Urn Tomb

Plate 13 The Khazneh. Note opening above the inner door

Plate 14 The Deir

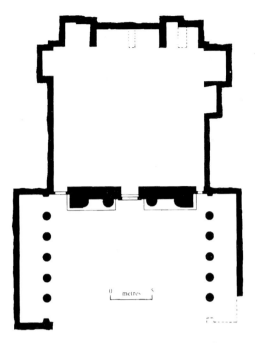

Figure 13 Plan of the Urn Tomb at Petra showing
the arcosolia (After Khouri/Qsus)

sarcophagi. In this way, all of the 'grand façades' at Petra, which clearly belong together aesthetically, would also belong together functionally.

The tomb façades at Petra are argued elsewhere[161] as nothing more than just façades, settings. In other words, what happened behind them was less important than what happened in front or within the façades themselves. Some of the other tombs contain similar openings high up in their façades. The most notable is the Roman Soldier Tomb, where the openings are blocked by reliefs of soldiers. Again, the interior has arcosolia where sarcophagi are conspicuously absent.

It must be emphasised that explaining Nabataean high places as exposure platforms and *some* (at least) of the façades as monumental ossuaries must of necessity remain speculative. It also does not necessarily imply any form of Zoroastrianism practised by the Nabataeans (although it is important to stress that Nabataean rock burial generally was consistent with the Zoroastrian practice forbidding the pollution of the sacred earth).[162] It must also be emphasised that whether or not exposure was practised, Nabataean burials also 'appear to have included almost every variation in the treatment of the body, including ordinary burial, burial with lime, possibly burial after exposure, partial cremation, and cremation'.[163] Exposure would apply, furthermore, only to some of the Nabataean high places at Petra. The high places incorporated into the Roman-period temples elsewhere in Syria did not function in this way.

Palmyra and Queen Zenobia[164]

Origins of Palmyra

A permanent settlement was established at Palmyra by the end of the third millennium BC. The first written references (under its Semitic name of Tadmor) occur in Assyrian and Mari records of the early second millennium. The Biblical reference to Tadmor as a foundation of Solomon's is now located elsewhere, and Palmyrene 'Tadmor' is thought to derive from the Arabic *tamar* meaning 'date' [palm], from which its Latin name of 'Palmyra' also derives.

In the vacuum left by the decline of Seleucid power, many small Arab principalities sprang up all over Syria. Palmyra was founded as a confederation of four Arab tribes: the Komare, Battabol, Maazin, and the ʿAmlaqi or ʿAmalaqi.[165] This may be reflected in the four main cults of the Palmyrene pantheon: Baal-Shamin, Aglibol-Malakbel, Arsu and Atargatis.[166] The first Roman conflict with Palmyra was Mark Antony's campaign in 41 BC.[167] But Palmyra remained little more than a desert shaikhdom and a watering hole for nomads and occasional caravans off the normal route, until early in the second century AD two events occurred that were to change its fortunes. The first was the decline of Emesa, which had previously been in charge of the desert routes. But the main wealth lay in the routes controlled by the Nabataeans rather than the Emesenes. The second, therefore, was the collapse of the Nabataean control of the trade routes at the end of the first century AD, when Palmyra's geographical position gave it a major advantage. The trade routes moved further north, a move dictated as much by the increasing importance of Roman Antioch as by the decline of trade controlled by Petra. Parallel to these events was the rise of the new Parthian Empire of Iran in the east. Between the two, Rome and Iran, lay Palmyra, acting both as middleman and buffer state. The Palmyrenes were able to exploit the situation to the fullest.

It would be a mistake, however, to overstate Palmyra's geographical advantage in controlling trade routes. A glance at the map (Figure 14) shows that the natural trade route goes up the Euphrates to just east of Aleppo, before branching off directly to Antioch (which was after all the main market and entrepôt). Diverting from the Euphrates to cross the desert to Palmyra and thence to Emesa or Damascus, whence the nearest ports were relatively minor ones (e.g., Aradus), was certainly neither natural nor logical. Palmyra is the only example in history when such a route was the main one; at nearly all other times, the Euphrates–Aleppo–Antioch route was used. Crossing the desert via Palmyra makes little sense. The point that needs emphasising is that the Palmyrenes *made* this the trade route. Hence, there were Palmyrene agents from Dura Europos and Babylon on the Euphrates through to the Persian Gulf and mouth of the Indus to ensure that the trade went their way. This is why, rarely amongst Rome's clients in the East, Palmyra always had a standing army: if the merchants could not persuade the trade to come their way, a little further encouragement might.

Opinion as to when Palmyra became a part of the Roman Empire varies. It presumably must have been by AD 75 or earlier, when a dated Roman milestone east of Palmyra was erected. It was certainly no later than 114, perhaps as a part of Trajan's annexation of Nabataea. But it was not a Roman province in the same way that the rest of Syria was. The Romans instead were satisfied with merely installing a garrison there to counter Parthian influence. This left the Palmyrenes free to concentrate on trade.

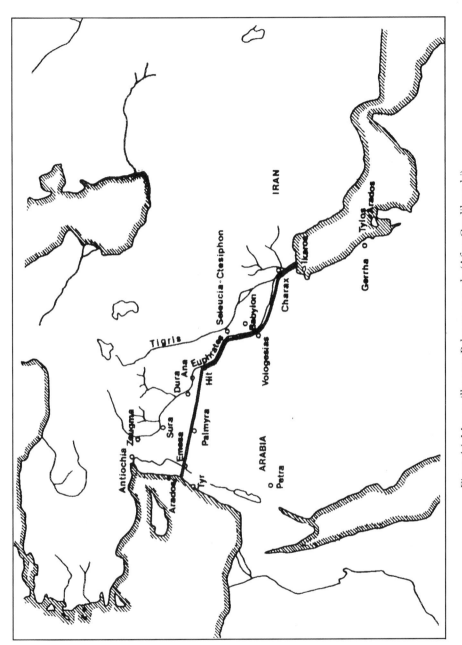

Figure 14 Map to illustrate Palmyrene trade (After Gawlikowski)

Palmyra was not a 'kingdom' in the conventional sense, as the other Roman client states were. Palmyra does not seem to have had a dynasty of kings: the first royal titles of 'Udaynath and members of his family are not native but Roman ones awarded for good service to the empire. The evidence seems to suggest that Palmyra was a state ruled by a council of elders, either tribal or mercantile or both.[168] Before 'Udaynath and Zenobia, there does not appear to have been a monarchy or a royal family like those at Emesa or Edessa or even Judaea (where neither the Maccabaean nor Herodian 'royal house' were traditional dynasties; both were artificial creations). There has not been any royal palace definitely recognised in the remains.[169] The western terms 'republic' or 'oligarchy' do not fit. It was more simply a gigantic business enterprise![170] However, the system of rule by a council of elders was familiar enough in traditional Arabian society.

Palmyrene trade

Whilst not extending its territories much outside the Syrian desert, the Palmyrenes organised a trade network spanning much of western Asia and the Mediterranean that channelled merchandise through Palmyra. A stele discovered at Palmyra records slaves and salt, dried foods and dyed purple cloth, perfumes and prostitutes as coming through Palmyra by AD 137. Evidence from excavations has added silk, jade, muslin, spices, ebony, incense, ivory, precious stones and glass to the list. The entire city revolved around trade. A caravan would be financed and organised by a single merchant, by a consortium of merchants, or by the city itself, depending upon the size. The city treasurer was one of the highest offices in the state, taxes were clearly – and fairly – regulated and collected, the revenues being used either to invest in further trade ventures or – more usually – to embellish the city. Indeed, the latter was given particularly high priority by both state and industry: by the second century AD many of the monuments were privately endowed by merchants with a lavishness and ostentation (some might say vulgarity!) rarely seen elsewhere. As befitted an architecture of private enterprise, the emphasis was more on show and display than on strict forms of Classical aesthetics. This was designed to reflect the credit of the merchants paying for it all, who in turn had statues of themselves on the columns lining the city's thoroughfares. The rebuilding of the greatest of the city's monuments, the Temple of Bel, was entirely financed in AD 139 by a leading merchant, Male Agrippa, who also paid for the visit to Palmyra by the Emperor Hadrian ten years earlier.

The Palmyrene trade route immediately east has been carefully researched.[171] It was not a link in any supposed trans-Asian caravan network – the largely spurious 'Silk Route' – but formed virtually as much a part of the sea network as any sea port did. Palmyrene merchants travelled directly across the desert to the Euphrates, whence they would sail down to the Persian Gulf (Figure 14). From there, the trade became a part of the sea routes to India examined below,[172] with Palmyrene agents established in ports of call on the way. In this way the Palmyrenes established a commercial empire that reached throughout the known world. Today, evidence for Palmyrene merchant houses has been found as far apart as Bahrain, the Indus Delta, Merv, Rome and Newcastle-upon-Tyne in England.[173]

The rise of ʿUdaynath

The background of the family of ʿUdaynath (modern Arabic ʿUday, Latin Odaenathus) and its rise to supreme power in Palmyra is very shadowy. It can be assumed that ʿUdaynath's family belonged to the tribal elite who ruled Palmyra, but it is by no means certain. During the second and third centuries AD there were a number of Palmyrene individuals whose wealth brought both power and the notice of Rome. Such recognition would be marked by bestowing Roman rank and titles, but this never implied the existence of a king or even a royal family.[174] One such individual may have been Hayran (Latin Herodes), the son of Wahballath Nasor, who had a son in about 220. This was ʿUdaynath, whose rise to prominence during the third century forms the background to Palmyra's supposed revolt against Rome. Inscriptions in the 250s refer to him only under the title *raʾs*, 'chief' or shaikh – probably by election rather than inheritance. He may have been shaikh of one of the four tribes of Palmyra, as inscriptions also refer to other Palmyrenes of similar rank and power at the time, but more likely belonged to Palmyra's mercantile elite rather than a desert tribe.[175] One can only speculate as to what events led ʿUdaynath to become the supreme chief over the others. His marriage to Zenobia, head of one of the most powerful of the desert tribes (see below), undoubtedly strengthened his position. Presumably the increasing unreliability of the Pax Romana in the face of Gothic and Iranian invasions had forced the Palmyrenes to be more self-reliant for their defence. This would necessitate both the raising of an army and the election from their elite of somebody to command it.

In the aftermath of Valerian's humiliation at Edessa in 260, it was ʿUdaynath who rallied against the threat from Iran rather than Valerian's vacillating successor the Emperor Gallienus. ʿUdaynath first put down several pretenders to the purple at Emesa and elsewhere, before continuing the war against Iran in a campaign of 262–6. Nisibis was successfully retaken and the Palmyrenes advanced towards Ctesiphon, supposedly defeating an Iranian force. This, however, is almost certainly exaggeration. It seems unlikely that the kind of desert force that Palmyra had at its disposal could have inflicted a defeat on an empire at the height of its power, and it does not appear to have affected Iran in any way. There was presumably a successful raid and Rome, anxious to snatch any crumb of comfort from so momentous a defeat as Edessa, would have been swift to embroider it into a great victory. It certainly worked to ʿUdaynath's advantage, for in gratitude the Emperor Gallienus bestowed the titles 'Corrector' or 'Commander-in-chief of the East' and 'Augustus' on ʿUdaynath.

In 267, however, at the height of his glory ʿUdaynath was murdered in Emesa, together with his favourite son Hayran (Latin Herodes). The murder was probably a family affair, but it was never made clear. Whether his ambitious wife Zenobia was involved was also never ascertained. Hayran was ʿUdaynath's son by a different wife, and Zenobia naturally favoured her own son by ʿUdaynath, Wahballath (Palmyrene for 'Gift of Allath', Latin Vaballathus), so she certainly had a powerful enough motive. Either way, Zenobia was quick to execute a scapegoat and take up the reins of power as Regent for Wahballath, who was a minor.[176]

Zenobia

History can never resist a warrior queen. Since ancient times the names of Semiramis, Cleopatra and Boadicaea have been favourite heroines. Invariably beautiful, warlike yet nubile, and usually tragic, they are written about by both contemporary and later writers with a lasciviousness equal only to their disregard for truth. Zenobia was no exception, and her image varies 'from a shameless virago to a paragon of beauty and valour, from a model of chastity to a tyrant, from a Christian to a debauchee'.[177] The Romance of Zenobia reached its peak in the middle of the nineteenth century with Lady Hester Stanhope's extraordinary claim to have emulated her, riding in triumph into Palmyra to a tumultuous reception of singing and dancing Bedouin warriors and nymphettes standing on the statue brackets. The desert extravaganza culminated in nothing less than an attempted resurrection of Zenobia herself: 'I have been crowned Queen of the Desert under the triumphal arch of Palmyra . . . I am the sun, the star, the pearl, the lion, the light from Heaven . . . all Syria is in astonishment at my courage and success.'[178] We have only Lady Hester's own word for her entry into Palmyra, but such is the power of myths like that of Zenobia, that few question her extravagant claims.

Attempts in the Classical sources to trace Zenobia's (Arabic al-Zabba or Zainab) ancestry back via the Seleucids to the Ptolemies of Egypt, hence providing a tenuous link with Cleopatra, appear as apocryphal as the Arab tradition which links her with the Queen of Sheba.[179] But Cleopatra was certainly a role model, as was Julia Domna, both of whom Zenobia claimed to emulate. Epigraphic and Western sources are silent about Zenobia's immediate family origins, apart from the references to remote Seleucid and Ptolemaic connections, but Arab sources are clearer. According to al-Tabari she belonged to the same tribe as ʿUdaynath, the ʿAmlaqi, probably one of the original four tribes of Palmyra. Her father was ʿAmr Ibn Zarib, the shaikh of the ʿAmlaqi who was killed in a war with their tribal rivals, the Tanukh (later to achieve considerable prominence as Roman allies).[180] ʿAmr had two daughters, Zenobia (also called Naʾilah) and Zabibah. After his death, Zenobia became head of the tribe and continued a nomadic lifestyle, leading the tribe between summer and winter pastures.[181] However, she was no mere desert shepherdess for she was undoubtedly wealthy and educated. As well as her native Palmyrene dialect of Aramaic, she reputedly spoke Egyptian and Greek fluently, but Latin only hesitantly. At some point she married ʿUdaynath, a member of the Palmyrene mercantile elite, forming an alliance between the desert tribes and the city. After this she probably spent more time in Palmyra, although she maintained her tribal links at all times. Her court combined both Persian and Roman ceremonial, and there is some evidence that she was a Manichee.[182] In the *Augustan History* 'her face was dark and of a swarthy hue, her eyes were black and powerful beyond the usual wont, . . . and her beauty incredible'[183] which – embroidering aside – is certainly in keeping with the complexion of the Syrian desert Arabs. Sources claimed her the most beautiful woman in the East, a true a heir to Cleopatra's legacy, although there the resemblance ended for her reputation for extreme chastity was such that it is little wonder that her husband fathered children by other women.[184] Both Classical and Arabic sources concur that she carried herself as a man, riding, hunting and drinking on occasions with her officers. Palmyrene art is famed for its portraiture, but no portraits of Zenobia survive (apart from some coins which tell us little) – although even if any had, it is doubtful if the wooden, almost sightless expressions that characterise Palmyrene portraits would tell us much about either her personality or her appearance.

As well as accrediting her with great beauty, tradition has surrounded Zenobia with a glittering salon of poets, rhetoricians and philosophers. The most celebrated is Cassius Longinus. Longinus came to Palmyra when he was about sixty, but the presence of a philosopher or two hardly makes the place into an Athens of the desert – academics can be bought as easily as mercenaries, and Longinus was not the first (and would hardly be the last) to hasten to some well-endowed provincial sinecure simply because the pay and perks were good. Gothic hordes beating at the gates of Athens would also have removed all doubt of dallying at the Academy. Certainly when he got to Palmyra, apart from finding the climate pleasant enough, he bemoans the lack of any decent library or publishing facilities[185] – hardly an intellectual centre overflowing with royal endowment for the arts. Apart from Longinus, no other scholar of any note is definitely attested at Zenobia's 'court'; Palmyra did not compare with other eastern centres of learning, such as Edessa or Tyre or Gadara, let alone Antioch or Alexandria.[186] Tradition has also embroidered the Zenobia image as a great builder with, at times, even the great monuments at Palmyra ascribed to her. But nearly all were built before Zenobia, with those later ones mainly ascribed to Diocletian. Even efforts by archaeologists to locate Zenobia's 'palace' have never gone beyond the theoretical stage; the fact remains that not a single building can be definitely ascribed to her.[187] This is not as surprising as one may think, for the period from the time of her assumption of power after the death of 'Udaynath until her capture by Aurelian was a mere five years, a period when she was mainly taken up with campaigning. This left little time either for building works or a court salon. The image of Zenobia 'housed in a palace that was just one of the many splendours of one of the most magnificent cities of the East, surrounded by a court of philosophers and writers'[188] simply does not stand.

The revolt

Palmyra's revolt against Rome is plagued by a paucity of sources (one longs for a Josephus – although our copious documentation for the Jewish Revolt has perhaps resulted in an exaggeration of its importance). Our main Classical sources are Zosimus and the extremely unreliable *Augustan History*, supplemented by some Arabic and Manichaean sources.[189] Aurelius Victor writes the entire episode off with merely a passing indirect reference to 'bandits, or more accurately a woman [who] controlled the east' without even mentioning her name.[190] The Arabic sources add several important details not known from the Classical, but more important than the details is the different perspective offered. This is discussed more fully below.

It was the combination of two unrelated events that prompted Zenobia's war. The first was Zenobia's assumption of supreme power in Palmyra following 'Udaynath's murder, and the second was Rome's distractions – indeed, near 'annihilation'[191] – by the Gothic invasions. Thus, the rare opportunism presented by Rome's distraction fed Zenobia's ambition. It was a combination that might never be repeated, and Zenobia was quick to realise it.

Initially, Zenobia's war was not directed against Rome but against Palmyra's tribal enemies, the Tanukh, who had been responsible for the death of Zenobia's father. Hence, her first campaign was to Arabia in about 269. But the campaign was unexpectedly successful, despite divisions in the tribal support suggested by the Safaitic inscriptions,[192] not only because of her victory over the hated Tanukh, but because of the new possibilities that it opened up. For in the course of the campaign the Roman provincial capital of Bostra fell to the Palmyrenes – whether by accident or design – along with a Roman force.[193] The victory resulted in much of Roman Syria and Arabia falling under Palmyrene control. It added fuel to Zenobia's ambitions and she set her sights beyond Syria.

Accordingly, the following year an army said to number 70,000 invaded Egypt, possibly accompanied by Zenobia herself to enact out her own wish to be seen as a true latter-day Cleopatra.[194] A battle against the Roman garrison resulted in victory for the Palmyrenes. The Romans counter-attacked under the general Probus, who was eventually defeated. Thus, Zenobia became Egypt's first queen since Cleopatra.[195] Another Palmyrene force had advanced into Asia Minor as far as Ancyra (Ankara). This was destined to be the furthest limit for Zenobia's army, for in 271 the empire struck back under Emperor Aurelian.

Aurelian had succeeded to the purple the previous year after a series of weak emperors and a civil war had left the empire in all but ruins. Aurelian was of a different stamp altogether from his immediate predecessors. He was renowned both for his quick temper and for his cruelty, which could well have turned him into another Caracalla.[196] But Aurelian was a veteran soldier before he became emperor, so that his volatile personality was tempered by sound pragmatism and common sense – as well as by a ruthless sense of mission to save the tottering empire from the brink of collapse. Raking up a rag-tag army from whoever would supply recruits, he first managed to push the Goths back with immense energy. Then, crossing the Bosphorus into Anatolia, he retook Tyana in Cappadocia from the Palmyrenes and went on to recapture Ancyra, pursuing the Palmyrenes back to Syria. Outside Antioch the two armies faced each other, the Palmyrenes commanded by Zenobia herself. The Palmyrenes were armed in the Iranian style: heavier armour and better cavalry than the Romans. When battle commenced Aurelian was careful, therefore, to avoid Zenobia's heavy cavalry, resulting in Zenobia's defeat and withdrawal to Emesa. Aurelian in the meantime entered Antioch in triumph, sparing the city and showing leniency to its citizens despite their pro-Palmyrene sentiments.[197] He then advanced to Emesa, where he again defeated Zenobia with considerable slaughter of her army. His victory was attributed to the divine intervention of the Emesene Sun god. Aurelian entered Emesa where he was well received, but making sure all the same to placate the Emesenes – traditional allies of the Palmyrenes – by sacrificing in their great Temple of the Sun.[198]

Zenobia and the remnants of her troops fled back to Palmyra. The neighbouring tribes rallied to provide food for the population and Zenobia hastily fortified the city. Aurelian set out across the desert, his army suffering from continual raids by the Arabs when even Aurelian was wounded. Weary from the desert march and Bedouin depredations, Aurelian first attempted negotiation with Zenobia, sending her a conciliatory letter offering terms. The city, together with herself and the lives of her children, were to be spared in return for handing over all 'your jewels, gold, silver, silks, horses, and camels'. But Aurelian also demanded the person of Zenobia herself. To this Zenobia predictably sent a stinging refusal, citing Cleopatra as her model, and threatening Iranian reinforcements.

Aurelian then laid siege to Zenobia's city. The Iranian threat was no idle boast by Zenobia, for Aurelian took it seriously. Accordingly, his first action was to cut off any line of reinforcements, an act which was to clinch his victory. He then managed to buy over Zenobia's Armenian and Bedouin allies. In particular, Palmyra's traditional tribal enemies, the Tanukh under their great leader ʿAmr Ibn ʿAdi, rallied to Aurelian's banner at the prospect of seeing their enemy humbled.[199] This was Aurelian's greatest coup, for Zenobia was then left isolated, with only her loyal city behind her. Palmyra still resisted and Zenobia, seeing the inevitability of Roman triumph, tried to escape eastwards by camel to enlist the Iranian help she had threatened the Romans with, but she was captured whilst attempting to cross the Euphrates.[200] The citizens of Palmyra continued resistance for a short while, but the city elders requested terms from Aurelian and capitulated. Aurelian accordingly spared the city, retiring to Emesa with Zenobia and her son.

He took the two captives back to Europe, but opinion differs as to Zenobia's fate. She probably died soon afterwards, either from an unstated illness or – emulating Julia Domna to the end – by fasting to death. According to other versions, however, she was first displayed in Antioch and Rome as 'Queen of the barbarian Saracens', then beheaded, although other sources refer to her being married off and living in retirement outside Rome, where her descendants were still supposedly pointed out a century later.[201]

Aurelian treated Palmyra itself leniently, content with taking only their queen and infant king, executing a few of the leading citizens (including the philosopher Longinus) and leaving in their place a Roman garrison. Being ruled, however, by a military garrison did not compare with their own previous status. A year later Palmyra revolted under Achilleus, a relative of Zenobia. Aurelian was quick to return, and this time he was to show his true colours. Aurelian is described as 'a brutal sort of person and bloodthirsty . . . much inclined towards cruelty'.[202] After a brief siege Palmyra fell and Aurelian turned the city, one of the most splendid in the entire empire, over to his troops. Aurelian himself and many of the regular officers may well have appreciated the true value of the monuments and works of art that Palmyra boasted, and the finest were carefully removed to later adorn Aurelian's new Temple to the Sun in Rome. But the bulk of the troops of Aurelian's army were only semi-Romanised auxiliaries from the fringes of the empire: Celts, Goths, Moors, Arabs, and others.[203] Buildings were smashed, citizens were clubbed and cudgelled, the great Temple of Bel – one of the wonders of the East – was pillaged. As well as its great monuments, Palmyra boasted treasures and rare works of art from as far off as India and China.[204] All that were not taken off to embellish Aurelian's triumph in Rome were destroyed in the rampage. After a few days, Zenobia's lovely city lay shattered.[205]

Aftermath of the revolt

The Revolt of Palmyra and its sack by Rome have prompted comparisons with the only other revolt in the East on the same scale: the Jewish Revolt and sack of Jerusalem. But the one point to emphasise in such a comparison is that the Palmyrenes were not revolting against Rome as the Jews were. The Jewish Revolt was largely nationalist in character; in contrast, Zenobia's ultimate prize was not Palmyrene independence, but Rome itself.

Palmyra is often regarded as some form of 'Arab revolt', an independence movement from Rome or a 'unilateral declaration of independence'.[206] Zenobia's self-conscious emulation of Cleopatra is cited in support of this.[207] But the Cleopatra analogy can be stretched too far: it must be remembered that Cleopatra wanted to be Queen of Rome rather than Egypt – and was a Macedonian in any case, not an Egyptian or Arab nationalist. Such notions apply nineteenth-century nationalist and liberal – even romantic – ideas to the ancient world which are untenable. Zenobia was not splitting the empire but aimed as much as Aurelian did to unify it. Hers was no Palmyrene Empire, just as Septimius' was no Libyan Empire – or Constantine's revolt in Britain against Maxentius was in any way an incipient British Empire. Palmyra had no history of revolt or resentment against Rome: Rome had not trampled on Palmyrene sentiments as the Procurator Florus did on Jewish, it had not insulted its religion as Pompey did Judaism, it had never enslaved Palmyrene citizens nor (until 273) sacked its cities. Quite the contrary. Palmyra did extremely well indeed out of belonging to the Roman club, and the Palmyrenes were far too astute as businessmen to be bothered with any nonsense about independence or religious niceties, let alone incipient ideas of Arab nationalism. In other words, Palmyra had not the slightest reasons for revolt.

Consequently, the rise of 'Udaynath represented no challenge to Rome. On the contrary, whilst his rise to strong local power may have been a response to the weakness of Roman central rule, his subsequent use of that power was entirely in Rome's interests: he fought Roman enemies, he restored Roman borders, he put down pretenders to the Roman purple, he remained a loyal servant of Rome to the end. The aim of 'Udaynath was to restore Roman power and prestige, as any good servant of Rome would, not to challenge it. As a result, Rome itself rewarded him with Roman titles: he was made an 'Augustus'. On the death of 'Udaynath, there was no reason why his successor should not continue in that aim.[208]

Accordingly, the subsequent career of Zenobia was a continuation of 'Udaynath's aim: to restore Rome. The stakes had simply changed. The far more ambitious Zenobia instead sought to restore Rome by making her own family's claim for the imperial purple, just as other 'Augustuses' had done in the past, both successfully and unsuccessfully. Coins struck in Antioch in 270 depicted both Aurelian and Wahballath. Further issues in Antioch and Alexandria in 271 depict Wahballath as Augustus and Zenobia as Augusta – all assertions of Roman pretensions, not of Palmyrene independence.[209] Zenobia was merely one in a long line since Vespasian who had made bids for the purple from a Syrian power base. All men, it is true, but Julia Domna and her female relatives had set the precedent of making the way open for women of the East to promote their own families to rule Rome as well. The rise of the Emesene royal family, as well as that of Philip of Shahba, were valid precedents for Zenobia's own imperial ambitions. Zenobia, as well as consciously and openly modelling herself on Cleopatra, also modelled herself on Julia Domna.[210] The aims of Julia Domna and Zenobia were identical; the only difference was method – and Zenobia's ultimate failure. Her success would have meant a united empire – not an independent 'Palmyrene Empire' nor a divided Roman one.

Aurelian's destruction of one of Rome's own cities had few precedents since Titus' destruction of Jerusalem. For Palmyra was not an enemy, foreign city but was an integral part of the Roman Empire – it had been a Roman Colony since 211. True, it had revolted and supported a pretender, but so too had other cities of the Roman provinces (such as Antioch) on a number of occasions. No other Roman city since Jerusalem had had such punishment meted out to it. As in the case of Jerusalem and the Jewish Revolt, therefore, one must look for reasons beyond the revolt itself.

The reasons probably lie in the background of the calamitous third century. The Iranian and Gothic invasions had brought Rome to the brink of collapse, and a succession of weak emperors had dissipated its funds. Increasingly, Rome had to buy mercenaries for its defence. The empire was bankrupt. Aurelian had done more than most of his immediate predecessors to restore the empire's fortunes, but these efforts had to be paid for. In particular, Aurelian had bought the co-operation of the Near East's desert tribes, without whose compliance no victory over Palmyra's desert kingdom would have been possible. Aurelian had only just been able to hold his troops back from plundering Antioch,[211] but they were baying for blood – or at least loot. Faced with empty coffers back home, a large standing army in the field, desert tribes whose allegiance Aurelian had bought at the eleventh hour, and mercenaries from all over the empire demanding the fulfilment of promises, the rich plum of Palmyra offered Aurelian at one stroke the only short-term solution that seemed possible. In the light of Rome's recent history, nobody realised more than Aurelian that a fickle army that supported an emperor one day might turn against him the next. And Aurelian's first demand to Palmyra, it will be recalled, was for all 'your jewels, gold, silver, silks, horses, and camels' – in other words, for hard cash. So, Aurelian gave Palmyra and its citizens to his army to do with as they pleased – indeed, Palmyra's second revolt in 273 was such a god-given opportunity for Aurelian that it might almost have been engineered by the garrison he installed there the previous year.

Alas, Aurelian's master-stroke and Palmyra's agony saved neither the empire nor its emperor. Aurelian went the same way after all as so many other emperors of the third century when a group of officers murdered him in Thrace just a few years later. But more than that, in destroying Palmyra Aurelian had unwittingly done more than most emperors to destroy the very empire he tried to restore. Aurelian simply destroyed the means by which it indirectly exerted control over the desert frontier. Without Palmyra, the last buffer was removed and the eastern frontier was wide open.

But of far greater importance, Palmyra's commercial empire had brought wealth into Rome. To give them their due the Romans made some attempt at restitution for Aurelian's destruction. The city and its principal monuments were tacked back together and there were even some major new monuments built during the reign of Diocletian who, more than most emperors, was far-sighted enough to see beyond immediate material gains. But Diocletian's efforts were too late. After its sack Palmyra had neither the heart nor – more important – the capital to start from scratch again. Palmyra's commercial empire rapidly declined, and with it went the wealth it had brought to Rome.[212] The real tragedy of Aurelian is that in doing so much to restore Rome's greatness, he simply did more than most to hasten its decline.

Palmyrene civilisation

A western visitor today to the ruins that Aurelian left behind at Palmyra is immediately confronted not so much with the strange, but the familiar (Figure 15, Plates 15–17, 77, 86, 98, 100, 112, 125). Here, in the heart of an eastern desert in a foreign country a long way from home, one finds a civilisation with which it is immediately possible to relate. Here are long lines of columns exhibiting all the standard forms of Graeco-Roman architecture that have formed the basis of western architectural vocabulary for over two thousand years. It is very easy to see why Palmyra is traditionally viewed through western, particularly Classical, spectacles as 'this greatest assemblage of Roman architecture at its artistic crest' and 'the most conspicuous expression of the Roman character of the city is its magnificent architecture'.[213] Hence, Palmyra is often seen as essentially 'Greek' in terms of character, layout, institutions and architecture. Even when it is at least (grudgingly?) conceded as native, it is merely taken as sophisticated enough to recognise the

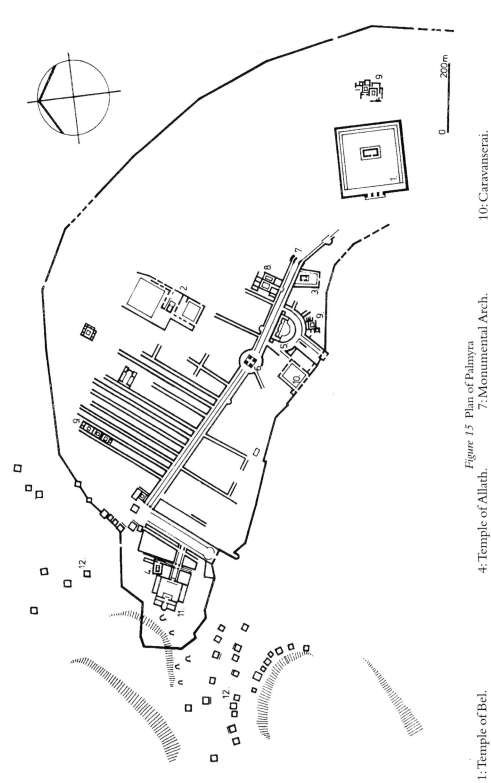

Figure 15 Plan of Palmyra

1: Temple of Bel.
2: Temple of Baal-Shamin.
3: Temple of Nabu.

4: Temple of Allath.
5: Theatre.
6: Tetrapylon.

7: Monumental Arch.
8: Baths of Diocletian.
9: Houses.

10: Caravanserai.
11: Diocletian Camp.
12: Tombs. (After Mikhailowski)

Plate 15 The monumental arch and main colonnaded street at Palmyra

superiority of Graeco-Roman culture and receive it gratefully.[214] This has obscured the overriding Semitic and other oriental elements of its character.

Al-Tabari and the Arab sources unwittingly raise an important issue when they give sole credit to the Tanukh and their leader, ʿAmr Ibn ʿAdi, for the defeat of Zenobia and the destruction of Palmyra. Aurelian and the Romans are not even mentioned: Palmyra's war was an entirely Arab affair.[215] Which are right, the Classical sources which do not mention ʿAmr or the Arabic which do not mention Aurelian? Of course, that is hardly the point: it was a coalition between Aurelian and ʿAmr that defeated Zenobia. But the real issue here is that, in addition to shedding considerable light on the destruction of Palmyra, the Arabic sources are a salutary lesson in just how much we accept our own sources for a one-sided view of events. It is important to recognise, therefore, these other, non-western elements of Palmyra to achieve a correct perspective.

Both ʿUdaynath and Zenobia are specifically described in the sources as Saracens,[216] i.e., Arabs, and there was certainly widespread sympathy for her amongst many of the Arabs.[217] One authority in fact sees the collapse of Palmyra as crucial to the eventual rise of Mecca and Islam;[218] of course, the origins of Islam are complex and need not concern us here, but it does nonetheless serve to emphasise Palmyra from the Arab perspective; and the 'Roman' architecture of Palmyra on analysis is essentially Semitic, not Classical (this is discussed at length in Chapter 7).

There was also a considerable Iranian element. A dedication to Zenobia and her son of 268/9 combines both Roman and Iranian imperial titles, with Wahballath given the ancient Iranian title of 'King of Kings' as well as the Roman one of 'Corrector of all the East'.[219] There is also the suggestion that Zenobia (or her sister) converted to Manichaeism, an Iranian religion.[220] Palmyra's art, furthermore, depicts Palmyrene dress as Iranian. Court ceremonial, when a Palmyrene 'monarchy' was established by 'Udaynath and Zenobia, was Iranian, and the Palmyrene army followed Iranian arms and tactics as we have seen. There are Iranian overtones in the love of the hunt, so beloved by the Palmyrene upper classes, and the threat of a Palmyrene–Iranian alliance was taken seriously by Aurelian.[221]

Palmyrene religion sheds further light on its character. The two main deities, Baal-Shamin and Bel, belong to two different religious traditions which may reflect two ethnic groups in the foundation of Palmyra. Baal-Shamin had many manifestations, including the Arabian Allat or the 'Anonymous God', whose temple has recently been found at Palmyra[222] and who also belonged in the Nabataean pantheon. Baal-Shamin was Syro-Phoenician in origin, while Bel was Mesopotamian, related to Bel Marduk, the supreme deity of the Babylonian pantheon.[223] The Mesopotamian connection is further reinforced by the cult of Nebo or Nabu at Palmyra (Plate 16), also Babylonian in origin, closely associated with Marduk. The most important element of ritual in Babylon associated with the worship of Marduk was the sacred New Year Festival.[224] It was for the New Year Festival that Babylon's famous processional way was built, and it is tempting to see Palmyra's great colonnaded street that terminates in the Temple of Bel simply as Marduk's processional way at Babylon transposed to Palmyra (Plate 17). Certainly Palmyra's trading links were strongest with the middle and lower Tigris-Euphrates.[225] But whilst Palmyra's colonnaded street may have formed in part a processional way, it is explained architecturally elsewhere as belonging to a different – albeit Semitic – tradition.[226] Nothing in the religion of Palmyra betrays Graeco-Roman influence, despite the Corinthian

Plate 16 The Temple of Nabu at Palmyra

Plate 17 The Temple of Bel at Palmyra. Note foundations of the altar in the middle distance

and other orders which embellished the temples or the 'off-the-hook' Athena statue brought in to personify Allat. Palmyrene religion was cosmopolitan in character, but with mainly Semitic elements.

Edessa and the coming of Christendom[227]

Geographically the Kingdom of Edessa straddles the Mesopotamian plains and the Anatolian foothills (Figure 16), and the city is located at the point where the foothills meet the plains. Its geography has thus marked Edessa as both a meeting place and a buffer state throughout its history. The boundaries of the kingdom are not specifically defined in the various Roman accounts. The western boundary was presumably the Euphrates, although Mambij, on the west bank, was closely associated with Edessa. The eastern boundaries are more uncertain, with sites as far as the Church of St Thaddeus in the mountains of Iranian Azerbaijan traditionally associated with Edessa (see below). Indeed, there were strong connections between the two ruling houses of Edessa and the Jewish client kingdom of Adiabene in western Iran. The armies of both, for example, were allied in a joint siege of Nisibis in AD 194, and Jewish elements were particularly strong in both kingdoms.[228] Just to the south-west, between Edessa and the Euphrates, was Batnae, the capital of the minor Arab kingdom of Anthemusia, which was annexed by Rome (with Edessan encouragement) in 115.[229] Nisibis to the south-east was also closely associated with Edessa throughout its history – indeed Nisibis may have been the capital of the kingdom before Edessa itself. The city which was most closely associated with Edessa – often as its arch rival – was Harran, or Carrhae, on the plains just to the south.

The region has always occupied a singular place in Near Eastern political history. Harran saw the last stand of both the Assyrian and Babylonian Empires: a rump Assyrian kingdom under Ashur-uballit managed to hold out against the Medes and Babylonians for a further seven years after the sack of Nineveh in 612 BC. It was also in Harran that the

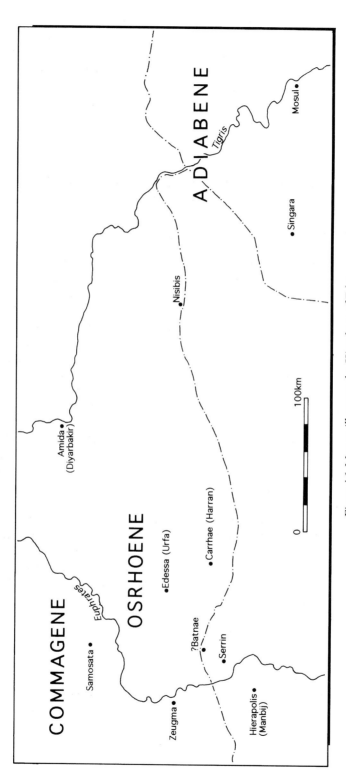

Figure 16 Map to illustrate the Kingdom of Edessa

aged King Nabu-na'id (Nabonidus), last of the Babylonians, succumbed in 546 BC to the new Persian conquests of Cyrus the Great.[230] The original 'Arabia', the 'Arabistan' of the Persians, was also located in this region rather than in the Arabian peninsula.[231] Edessa, along with Harran and Nisibis, became some of the most important cities on the ancient thoroughfare linking Syria with Mesopotamia. There were particularly close trading links with Palmyra as well, as tomb towers and inscriptions of Palmyrene type have been found in and around Edessa.[232]

Origins

As well as possessing a variety of ethnic affiliations, the origins of Edessa are tied up in several historical traditions. The Edessans identified their city with Biblical Erech, founded by the mythical Nimrod and associated with Abraham of Ur. Just a short time ago one could justifiably dismiss such traditions as 'untenable', writing that 'we need not take these learned theologians too literally'.[233] While an identification with Biblical Erech may indeed be untenable (Erech is identified with Uruk, modern Warka in southern Iraq), recent archaeological investigations have revealed links between the area of Edessa and the southern Mesopotamian Uruk culture in the fourth millennium.[234] Furthermore, the name Orhai/Urfa may well be linguistically linked to the name Ur. Perhaps King Nabu-na'id, the last king of Babylon, well-known for his interests both in southern Mesopotamian antiquarian research and in the great temple of Harran,[235] transferred the names 'Uruk' and 'Ur' to Edessa – the foundation of a 'New Erech' after the loss of the old one to the Persians? Of course, such links may be illusory (and the 'Uruk' culture of the archaeologists may have nothing to do with the city of Uruk/Erech itself). But ancient Edessan tradition certainly arrived at these links thousands of years before modern archaeologists did.

Edessa was one of several military colonies founded at the older city of Orhai by Seleucus Nicator in 303/2 BC, who renamed it Edessa after the capital of Macedonia.[236] Seleucid Edessa was described as following the regular Macedonian military plan: a grid plan dominated by four intersecting streets with four city gates, with its citadel outside the walls.[237] It was renamed 'Antioch by the Callirhoe' in 163 BC, but with the plethora of 'Antiochs' around at the time (including an 'Antioch Mygdonia' nearby at Nisibis), the name Edessa was the one that stuck until the older Semitic name of Orhai resurfaced as Urfa on the Islamic conquest. This initial Macedonian colonisation imparted a superficial Hellenistic overlay to the city that was reinforced with the later westernisation of such kings as Abgar the Great. But this Hellenisation, like the name Edessa itself, was never more than skin deep, and the city and region remained fundamentally Semitic in character throughout, as we shall see.[238]

With the decline of the Seleucids in the second century BC, Edessa became the seat of an Arab dynasty allied to the Parthians in about 132 BC. This dynasty was originally based at Nisibis, before transferring its capital – along with all its idols – to Edessa.[239] According to Armenian sources, however, Edessa formed a part of the broader Armenian historical tradition.[240] Its earliest kings certainly have Armenian (or Parthian) names (e.g., Aryu, Fradhasht, Ezad), rather than Arab, so the dynastic origins may well be Armenian. There was also a strong Iranian element both in the titles of the state officials and the style of dress they wore.[241] But most of the names of the kings are either Nabataean (Ma'nu, Bakru, Gebar'u) or Arabic (Abgar, Maz'ur, Wa'el, 'Amr), and Classical sources describe the inhabitants almost invariably as Arabs.[242] The history of Edessa is further confused by most of its kings being called by the name of 'Abgar', but the name is presumably a title rather than a personal name (although, like 'Caesar', probably originating as a personal name). Hence, the dynasty is often referred to as the Abgarids. The kings ruled much as Arab shaikhs, through a council of tribal elders, even until the end of the monarchy after it had undergone superficial Romanisation. Whatever their origins, therefore, the dynasty soon became Arabised, perhaps after the first century BC when it ceased to belong to Armenia.

The kings

One of its early kings, Abgar I Piqa, was killed by the Romans in 69 BC during Lucullus' war against Tigranes of Armenia. At this time, Osrhoene was still a part of Armenia, but after Abgar I's death the kingdom of Edessa (called 'Armenia' by Moses Khorenats'i) was divided into two, perhaps as a result of Armenia's defeat by Lucullus: Edessa and Armenia proper.[243] Its history then becomes quite distinct from that of Armenia. Abgar II (68–53 BC) maintained Edessa's independence from Rome during Pompey's subsequent campaign against Armenia, who confirmed Abgar as king of Edessa. After the Battle of Carrhae, Iranian influence became stronger, possibly because of the support by Abgar II for Iran. Abgar II is identified with the 'Ariamnes' of Plutarch, whose support of the Iranians is held responsible by the Romans for Crassus' defeat, although the Syriac sources imply that Abgar supported the Romans at Carrhae.[244] Subsequently, Edessa maintained a balance between the two. At times it actually held the balance of power, with its early kings strong enough to impose dynastic settlements on the Parthian kings on occasion.[245]

The first Edessan king to achieve prominence was Abgar V Ukkama bar Ma'nu (4 BC–AD 7). He established the kingdom on a strong footing, sending an army abroad on one occasion to aid Harithath of Petra in his war against Antipas.[246] But Abgar V is most remembered for the events that record his supposed conversion to Christianity. This is discussed more below.

Edessa's aloofness from Roman affairs came inevitably to an end in the late first century. Abgar VII (109–16) supported Trajan's campaign into Mesopotamia, entertaining him sumptuously at court. But he later revolted, resulting in the Roman capture and destruction of Edessa and the death of Abgar VII.[247] Hadrian installed a puppet Parthian prince, Parthamaspat, on the Edessan throne in 117, but the native dynasty was restored in 123 with the establishment of King Ma'nu VII, who remained loyal to the Romans until his death in 139. During the Parthian War of Lucius Verus the Parthians captured Edessa and placed a puppet king, Wa'el bar Sharu, on the throne in 163. The legitimate king Ma'nu VIII bar Ma'nu, took refuge with the Romans. Avidius Cassius was able to retake Edessa in 165 and restore Ma'nu VIII to his kingdom. But Ma'nu VIII and the city of Edessa had to pay the price for its restoration: Osrhoene became a client kingdom of Rome in 166.

Ma'nu was succeeded in 177 by Abgar VIII, the Great, who ruled until 212. Abgar the Great[248] supported Pescennius Niger in his civil war with Septimius Severus, with the result that Septimius Severus reduced Osrhoene to Roman provincial status and Abgar was left with just the city of Edessa as a rump kingdom. Despite such vicissitudes, Abgar VIII is considered the greatest of the kings of Edessa: a cultured king, a wise administrator, and a patron of learning that made Edessa one of the main intellectual centres of the East. As a client of Rome with only the city to look after, Abgar could afford to retire from international politics and become one of the Near East's greatest patrons of the arts and learning. Then one night in 201 the city of Edessa suffered a great calamity that was also a golden opportunity for Abgar: it was almost wiped out in a devastating flood. A graphic, eyewitness account of this survives in the *Chronicle of Edessa*.[249] Over 2,000 people perished and much of the city and palace was destroyed, with Abgar and his officials just managing to make a dramatic night-time escape.

But the flood provided an opportunity for King Abgar to rebuild his city anew. He ordered a massive new building programme to begin immediately, with remission of taxes for all those affected by the flood. The city was rebuilt following the earlier Seleucid town plan. Whilst the flood-damaged palace was rebuilt by the river, Abgar was careful to build new winter residences for himself and many of his nobles on higher ground. Many new monuments were built including the magnificent Cathedral of St Sophia,[250] but nothing of these is left today apart from the famous 'Fish pools of Abraham', possibly a part of Abgar the Great's summer palace.[251] The two columns on the citadel also formed a part of Abgar's rebuilding (Plate 18). The eastern column has a Syriac dedication to Abgar's Queen, Shalmath, and they possibly formed a part of his winter palace.[252] Otherwise, the only remains of Abgar's today are about a hundred pagan, Jewish and Christian cave tombs – some decorated with fine mosaics – in the hills surrounding Edessa.

As well as rebuilding Edessa, Abgar the Great managed to rebuild relations with Septimius Severus to such an extent that Abgar's state visit to Rome in 204 was the most lavish that even Rome had witnessed in 150 years. But Abgar the Great is remembered not so much for his lavishness or even his ambitious building programme, as for his reputed conversion to Christianity in about 200. If true, this makes his kingdom the world's first Christian state. This is discussed further below.

Abgar the Great was succeeded by Abgar IX, surnamed Severus to pander to the current Romanising climate. It did him little good, for he was summoned with his son to Rome in 213 and murdered at Caracalla's orders. Caracalla ended even token independence when he made Edessa into a Roman colony the following year. There seems to be a poetic justice that this emperor was himself was done to death at Carrhae near Edessa in 217. There is some evidence from a Syriac chronicle of a nominal king after Edessa became a Roman Colony, Ma'nu IX, son of Abgar IX, who reigned without note until 240. The only event worth remark is the account of the Indian embassy to Elagabalus that passed through his court in about 218,[253] one of many Edessan links with the East, as we shall see. There is also some evidence of a restoration of the Edessan monarchy during the time of Gordian III (238–44) under a King Abgar X, who was finally expelled in 248 by Philip the Arab because of a revolt by Edessa.[254] It was occupied briefly by Shapur in 259 following the Battle of Edessa, but was soon recaptured by the Romans. The dynasty may have been restored yet again, however, by the Iranians, as a King ʿAmr the Abgarid is referred to in Iranian sources as a vassal of the Sasanians in 293.[255] This is the last we hear of the dynasty.

Religion at Edessa

Edessa is important as a buffer state between Rome and Iran. Its character was formed by an Aramaic substratum with a superficial Hellenistic overlay, into which also came a considerable Iranian element. But it is the Semitic element that predominates. One authority[256] emphasises the importance of Edessa as a great cultural centre for the Semitic East, a counterbalance of the Hellenic culture of Antioch. It was the birthplace of Syriac literature and the kings and inhabitants of Edessa were usually called 'Arab' throughout by the Classical sources.[257] Whilst the Armenian sources prefer an Armenian slant to Edessa's character, most Edessan names – including its kings – confirm the predominantly Arab and Semitic element. This alone makes Edessa a major historical factor in the rise of the Arabs to pre-eminence. But it is religion where Edessa made its main mark.

Edessa was one of the main religious melting pots of the ancient Near East.[258] Nebo and Bel were the main cults, belonging to the oldest traditions. Bel was also the main cult at Palmyra, where the Nebo cult was also practised. In origin, the cult of Nebo – or Nabu – originated in Borsippa in Mesopotamia and was subsequently adopted by the Babylonians where it became assimilated to the cult of the Babylonian deity, Marduk. The cult was probably brought to Harran in the sixth century BC by the last Babylonian king, Nabu-na'id, an adherent to the cult as his name implies, as well as a devotee of cults in Harran, as we have seen. The cult of Nebo became quite popular in the Near East: it was from a Mt Nebo that Moses looked out over the promised land, and there is a temple, built in 224, at Kafr Nabu in the Dead Cities region.[259]

Many more cults flourished at Edessa. There was the cult of the Moon and Sun of Harran – known as the Sabian religion – as well as the rather gruesome cult of Atargatis of Mambij, both cult centres lying fairly close to Edessa. The Sabians believed in spiritual intermediaries between man and the heavenly bodies, with prayer only possible through the intermediaries. All life – human, plant, animal – was regarded as inherently evil and as the result of the activities of the intermediaries. Hence, nobody – not even a prophet – could mediate with the deities represented by the heavenly bodies. Creation was supposedly renewed every 26,425 years. The importance accorded by the Sabians to the Sun and Moon, as well as the belief in the inherently evil nature of living matter, survived in Manichaeism.[260] The Sabians and many of the other pagan religions of Edessa survived until well into the Islamic era – the Sabians even claimed the right to be recognised by the Muslims as fellow 'peoples of the book'. Al-Biruni, the great medieval Islamic scholar from Khwarazm in Central Asia, whilst recognising the sun and moon elements of the Sabians, describes them as descendants of the 'pseudo-prophet . . . Budhasaf [i.e., Buddha] who came forward in India' and adds that 'in former times . . . the country up to the frontier of Syria was Buddhistic'.[261] Whilst such a claim is exaggerated, it must be recalled that the Mauryan emperor of India, Ashoka, sent Buddhist missions to the Hellenistic kingdoms of the area as early as the third century BC, and an Indian embassy made a point of stopping off at Edessa in the third century AD.[262]

The Atargatis cult was centred at Hierapolis/Mambij, part of the Edessan state (for much of its history). It attracted considerable notoriety throughout the Roman world, mainly because of its practice of self-emasculation, until the practice was outlawed by Abgar the Great. The cult also incorporated tame animals and eagles. Its most important festival was the first day of spring, which suggests links with the ancient Iranian Nauruz festival on the Spring equinox. The festival was marked by ritual circumambulation of images and immolation of offerings. Another ritual centred around two wooden columns 60 feet high at the entrance to the temple, which a holy man would ascend twice a year to spend seven days in contemplation. This anticipates the Christian stylite practice which became particularly popular through northern Syria, most famously with St Simeon

Stylites. Indeed, it is noteworthy that not only was the father of St Simeon from Edessa, but the golden emblem that stood between the two deities in the inner sanctuary of the Temple of Atargatis at Mambij was known as a 'Simeion'. Two similar such columns at the temple of Mushairfeh on top of the Jebel Wastani in northern Syria might be associated with the Atargatis cult. The two columns still standing on top of the citadel at Edessa may be the remains of such a temple rather than Abgar's winter palace (Plate 18), just as the tank of sacred carp at its foot – still surviving in Urfa today as sacred to Abraham – may originally have been a part of a Temple of Atargatis rather than Abgar's summer palace.[263]

Indeed, water and sacred fish played a significant role in virtually all cults practised in Edessa and adjacent regions – the Atargatis cult is probably the origin of the Pisces sign in the Zodiac. In addition to the pools of sacred fish at Mambij and Edessa, others were known at the sources to the Balikh and Khabur rivers, the former still extant.[264] From further away came the Nabataean cult of Dushara, as well as Ishtar from Mesopotamia, who was equated with Venus. Another was Sin, the ancient Mesopotamian moon god, whose cult has been found in the hills south-east of Urfa. Another important cult at Edessa was that of the virgin mother and child, which became fairly common all over northern Syria before Christianity – with obvious implications for the development of Christianity itself. Women in fact traditionally held a high position at Edessa.[265]

Judaism was also very strong,[266] with the Jewish community still significant as late as the fourth century. The historical links between the kingdom of Edessa and the Jewish kingdom of Adiabene have already been noted, and one of the largest Jewish communities in the Near East was at Nisibis, which had a Jewish academy and a Jerusalem

Plate 18 Modern Urfa, ancient Edessa, with the two columns on the citadel, possibly forming a part of Abgar's palace

93

Temple treasury. The Jewish community in the kingdom were mainly merchants. When Edessa formed part of the trade network that linked the Persian Gulf with the Mediterranean, many of the Jewish community were involved in the trade in precious fabrics. Traditionally, the Jews in the East were pro-Iranian and anti-Roman, which partly accounts for Edessa's shifts in policy throughout its history. The rapid progress made by Christianity at Edessa was probably through the Jewish community – one recalls that the Apostle Thaddeus stayed at the house of the Jew Tobias (see below).

Edessa and Christianity

King Abgar V is best remembered for the events recorded in the *Doctrina Addai*, a fourth-century Edessan tradition that is also recorded by Eusebius. This tradition relates the legendary story of the apostle Addai, or St Thaddeus, who preached Christianity in Edessa after Christ's death. It revolves around the supposed correspondence between Abgar V and Christ, the original letters of which were still preserved in the state archives of Edessa as late as the fourth century when they were recorded and translated into Greek by Eusebius.[267]

Abgar V followed up his letter to Christ by writing to Emperor Tiberius, Narseh the 'king of Assyria', and 'Artashes of Persia' (probably Artaxias of Armenia), spreading the Christian message. Tiberius purportedly replied, after due consideration by the Senate, but no record survives of other replies.[268] The overall tone and nature of Abgar's proselytising messages recalls the Emperor Ashoka's messages to various Hellenistic kings in the eastern Mediterranean in the third century BC on his adoption of the new-found religion of Buddhism.[269] Indirect references to Ashoka's edicts occurred elsewhere in Edessa, as we have seen.

After the crucifixion, the apostle Addai (St Thaddeus) was accordingly sent to Edessa by the Apostle Thomas, staying in the house of Tobias the Jew. On converting Abgar through a miraculous cure, St Thaddeus was encouraged to preach openly throughout the kingdom and converted many of its citizens.[270] His teachings took him into the neighbouring kingdom of Adiabene, where the spectacular Armenian monastery church of St Thaddeus in north-western Iran, supposedly founded by the apostle on the site of a pagan temple, marks the place of his martyrdom in AD 66.[271]

The story of St Thaddeus and the conversion of Abgar V received wide credence in the ancient world, particularly through the authority of a theologian of Eusebius' stature. But the Mar Addai of Syriac tradition may not be the same person as St Thaddeus of Greek tradition, and the entire story of the *Doctrina Addai* and Christ's correspondence is extremely doubtful. It has even been condemned as 'one of the most successful frauds of history'.[272] The veracity of the story, however, is not important here. What is important is the unique blend of religions in Edessa which forms the background to the story, as well as the undoubted importance of Edessa subsequently in the history of Christianity: the *Doctrina Addai* was meant to establish the orthodoxy, purity and primogeniture of Edessan Christianity as stemming from Christ himself.

Further events in the development of Edessan Christianity occurred almost two centuries later in the era of Abgar the Great, who displayed a remarkable and liberal attitude to religion and learning. One of the most important philosophers of the Semitic East to emerge was the teacher Bardaisan, who was patronised by Abgar. Bardaisan was born in about 154 in Mambij and educated by a priest of the Atargatis temple there. On moving to Edessa as an adult he was converted to Christianity by Bishop Hystaspes (an Iranian name), but was expelled from the church by his successor because of non-conformist views. He founded his own religious sect towards the end of his life, dying in the year 222. But the sect he founded far outlasted him, surviving in Edessa despite the predominance of mainstream Christianity until the eighth–ninth century. Adherents were still recorded in Iraq, Khorasan and even Chinese Turkestan as late as the tenth century according to Muslim sources. As well as being a theologian of immense reputation, Bardaisan was a prodigious writer of hymns, religious, philosophical and astronomical works, in addition to histories of Armenia and India. His main work to have survived is the *Book of the Laws of Countries* (probably compiled by his disciple, Philip).[273]

More significant than Bardaisan's conversion to Christianity was the conversion – reported by Bardaisan – of Abgar the Great himself.[274] The conversion is controversial,[275] but whether or not he became a Christian, Abgar had the wisdom to recognise the inherent order and stability in Christianity a century before Constantine did. He encouraged it as essential for maintaining Edessa's precarious balance between Rome and Iran. Thus, it is Abgar the Great who lays claim to being the world's first Christian monarch and Edessa the first Christian state. More than anything else, a major precedent had been set for the conversion of Rome itself.

The stories of the conversions of both Abgar V and Abgar VIII may not be true, and have been doubted by a number of Western authorities (with more than a hint at unwillingness to relinquish Rome's and St Peter's own primogeniture?). But whether true or not, the stories did establish Edessa as one of the more important centres for early Christendom. This resulted in the establishment of a line of bishops in the early fourth century lasting a thousand years, which included such major theologians as St Ephraim in the later fourth century. By the fifth century Edessa had become one of the main centres of Christian learning in the East.

With such a complex religious background it could be argued that Christianity might have found stern resistance in Edessa. On the contrary, Edessa's religions provided Christianity with fertile ground, for 'it was the belief . . . in a single divinity of cosmic proportions that must already have provided the monotheism of the Jews with a ready hearing. The motif of a divine trinity was familiar in this region of the ancient East, and the hope of the life after death was, as we have seen, widespread at Edessa. The idea of a human divine mediator won an immediate response. In this environment Christianity could not fail to appeal'.[276]

Christianity in Edessa merely added an additional overlay – or several additional overlays – to the older religions and in no way replaced them. Indeed, Christianity and paganism coexisted quite amicably at Edessa – and added to the Edessans' traditional delight in their 'pick and mix' religious experimentation. The last century of the monarchy was an era of considerable religious ferment, with the Marcionites, Gnostics and Manichees rubbing shoulders happily with the Christians, Jews and pagans. The Edessan Gnostic belief in five basic elements was incorporated into Manichaeism as well as into the philosophy of Bardaisan. The spread of Manichaeism throughout Edessa was associated with two disciples of the prophet Mani called Addai and Thomas, and remained strong in Edessa until the fifth century. The former was also supposedly responsible for the conversion of Zenobia.[277] The coincidence with the two Christian apostles of the same name has obvious implications for the spread of Christianity to Edessa.[278] Out of the melting pot emerged several, uniquely Edessan, syncretic religions. The Bardaisanites have already been commented upon. The Elkesaites were another. Their sect was founded by their prophet Elkesai, who was supposedly a reincarnation of Jesus. Indeed, the Elkesaite belief in reincarnation recalls the possible Edessan links with Buddhism already mentioned.[279] It was a monotheistic religion combining elements of Judaism, Christianity and paganism. It rejected the earlier prophets but venerated Christ and the Holy Spirit, in addition to water and male and female elements. The prophet Mani was an Elkesaite before he founded his new religion, which drew heavily upon Elkesaism.[280] Being essentially a syncretic religion, Manichaeism also found ready ground in Edessa. Indeed, the main importance of religion at Edessa was not so much its Christianity, nor its Judaism, Sabianism or any of the other cults tolerated amongst its broad-minded tradition. The real importance was its syncretic, composite nature, incorporating Babylonian, Aramaean, Arab, Jewish, Iranian, Indian and Hellenistic elements.

The Tanukh and Queen Mawiyya

The system of client states in the East came to an end with Caracalla's annexation of Edessa. The confederations of the Tanukh, Ghassan and other Arab tribes in the fourth to sixth centuries were, strictly speaking, *foederati*, or allies. The system of allied tribes consisted of one main confederation, whose shaikh would be recognised by the Romans as *phylarch*, or 'king', being given subsidies by the Romans to defend the frontier, both against the Iranians and against raids by non-allied tribes.[281] This was different from the former relationship between Rome and its client kingdoms. To take the parallel with British India further, it resembled the Tribal Territories of the North-West Frontier. But there were similarities nonetheless, and the system still forms an integral part of Rome's position in the East and her relationship with its native people.

Whilst the 'Arab' identity of the earlier client kingdoms – Emesa, Nabataea, Palmyra and Edessa – may be questioned, there can be little doubt about the *foederati*, who maintained an Arab identity far more than the more settled 'Arab' states.[282] The role of the Arabs as allies of Rome began under the early empire. At first this just involved establishing relations with the desert Arabs and incorporating nomad auxiliaries into the army. More specifically, the job of the desert *foederati* was to contribute highly mobile professional cavalry units to the Roman army. In contrast to the sedentary Arabs, these semi-nomadic Arabs were professional fighters whose techniques were based on the tradition of the raid. As such, the *foederati* comprised a mobile defence, as opposed to the static defensive line of the Roman frontier. Their favourite weapon was the long cavalry lance. This both recalls the *sarissa* of the Macedonian phalanx and anticipates the cavalry lance of medieval Europe. In contrast to the Macedonian *sarissa*, the Arab lance was more like the lance of the Iranian cavalry – or the traditional lance of mounted Afghan tribesmen until recently[283] – which, properly handled by a disciplined, mobile strike force, was deadly.

Several tribal confederations were formed which entered into more formal relations with Rome. The Emesene was probably the first, before it evolved into the kingdom of Emesa, and there were others during the early empire. The first on the desert fringes was the Thamud confederation, whose temple inscription in Nabataean, dated 167–9 at Ruwwafa in the Hijaz, honours Marcus Aurelius and Lucius Verus.[284] Although beyond the actual boundary of the Roman Empire, it is the first evidence of a form of alliance with the Bedouin Arabs.

'King of the Arabs'

The third and early fourth century saw the rise of far more powerful confederations of Arab tribes in northern Arabia. These were the Lakhmid and Tanukhid confederations,[285] whose inscriptions have been found at Umm al-Jimal in Jordan and Namara in Syria. Both were closely interrelated. Indeed, there is often considerable confusion between the two in the literature on the subject, mainly because – like tribal groups everywhere – the genealogies are extremely complex.

The Tanukh were a fairly loosely connected tribal grouping, originating probably in south Arabia. In the early third century they started migrating northwards, eventually settling in two main areas: southern Mesopotamia and northern Syria. Both areas formed the bases of important Tanukh vassals to Iran and Rome respectively. At first, both Rome and Iran tried to woo the desert tribes to use them as pawns against each other. Being courted by both sides, the Tanukh felt able to form alliances with either, neither or occasionally both. Owing no particular allegiance to either great power in the early days, the Tanukh were able to follow their own inclination – or rather the loot, as in their participation in the Roman sack of Palmyra.

The Syrian branch of the Tanukh were allied to the Romans, forming a desert shield around Aleppo. Indeed, the Tanukh were instrumental as allies in bringing about the fall of Palmyra to Aurelian, as we have seen. But they also partly inherited the mantle of the Palmyrenes. This was in more ways than one. With Palmyra gone, the Tanukh stepped into the vacuum as Rome's main desert shield against Iran. Moreover the Tanukh also produced another desert queen in the person of Mawiyya who, like Zenobia before her, was eventually to challenge Rome. But that is to anticipate events. Whatever else it was, Palmyra was a watershed for the Tanukh, for as victors they emerged as a force to be reckoned with by the Romans. Henceforth, they were to be feted by both sides, and with their victory came the trappings of power and wider political responsibility.

The first shaikh of the Tanukh that we read about was Jadhima al-Abrash Ibn Malik who is referred to in an inscription at Umm al-Jimal as 'king of the Tanukh'. Jadhima was responsible for the death of Zenobia's father, thus sparking off her war and prompting the Tanukh to side with the Romans. The Tanukh confederation in Syria remained firm allies of the Romans throughout the later third and early fourth centuries.

The leader of the southern Mesopotamian branch of the tribe was a nephew of 'King' Jadhima, ʿAmr Ibn ʿAdi, who had been Aurelian's ally in his defeat of Zenobia. An earlier family alliance had also connected ʿAmr's family to the Edessan kings.[286] Thus, with wide Tanukh marriage connections, ʿAmr Ibn ʿAdi founded a new kingdom at Hira in the fourth century, under his own branch of the Tanukh, the Lakhmid dynasty. Hira (which means 'camp') is near Kufa, well within the Sasanian sphere of influence over the border tribes. Hence, the Lakhmids of Hira – as this branch of the Tanukh became known – became vassals of Sasanian Iran.

ʿAmr was succeeded by his illustrious son, Imruʾl-Qays. Imruʾl-Qays was one of the greatest of pre-Islamic Arab kings, celebrated in romance.[287] He has even been tentatively identified in the sources with the legendary Arab prince Dhuʾl-Qarnayn, who was usually identified with Alexander the Great.[288] He campaigned widely, reaching as far as Najran in south Arabia.[289] But sometime in the early fourth century an event occurred which called into question his entire relationship with Zoroastrian Iran: Imruʾl-Qays became a Christian. The dynastic connections of the Lakhmid family with Abgar VIII, the great

Christian monarch of Edessa, was probably the reason for the conversion, but his father, 'Amr Ibn 'Adi, had already upset the Zoroastrian establishment by his protection of the Manichaeans fleeing persecution in Iran.[290] Shapur II's Arabian campaign in 326 may have been partly directed against the Tanukh – it would have at least interfered with Tanukhid/Lakhmid interests there. For various reasons, therefore, Imru'l-Qays decided to leave Mesopotamia and join his Tanukh cousins in Roman Syria.

Imru'l-Qays took over the leadership of the western Tanukhid confederation. Whether this was by force – and he would have brought a considerable tribal force with him – or by sheer prestige we do not know. But the defection to the West of so important a shaikh – an Iranian client king no less – must have been a considerable coup for Rome. As well as bringing the allegiance of the desert tribes, it would have seriously weakened Iran's own border policies. It also dramatically extended Rome's influence throughout Arabia – one recalls that Imru'l-Qays' campaigns stretched all the way to Yemen. Small wonder that Constantine added the name 'Arabicus' to his title.[291] When Imru'l-Qays died in 328 the inscription on his tomb at Namara in the Syrian desert proclaimed 'This is the tomb of Imru'l-Qays, the son of 'Amr, king of all the Arabs.' For the first time in a century, Rome had a client king on its eastern borders once more.[292]

Queen Mawiyya's revolt

The Syrian branch of the Tanukh remained more or less loyal to the Romans. They settled in northern Syria, which became their base. This was generally in the semi-desert fringes to the east and south-east of Aleppo, where evidence – mainly linguistic – for Tanukh settlement has been found. The main Tanukh centre was Chalcis (Qinnesrin), south of Aleppo. Some fortifications in the area have been associated specifically with the *foederati*.[293] They were probably the main Tanukh bases in the fourth and fifth centuries, but it is probable that a large element of the tribe remained nomadic, albeit centred upon the same region. As such the Tanukh bases formed a part of Diocletian's line of desert defences protecting Antioch, being responsible for the desert defence in the fourth century in the same way as the Palmyrenes were in the third. But towards the end of the fourth century, the relationship with Rome started to sour.

It probably started to go wrong during Julian's Iranian campaign in 363. Although in many ways one of Rome's more brilliant emperors, Julian's political and military background was from the Roman West, and he never did show a sound grasp of eastern politics. Accordingly, one of his first mistakes on coming east was to withdraw the privileges from the Arab allies. The mistake probably cost Julian his life, as well as many years of strife and military reverses for Rome in the Near East, for Julian's murder has been blamed on one of the Arab auxiliaries of his campaign.[294] The motive may have been religious, for the staunchly Christian Arabs would have been as horrified at Julian's apostasy as many others were. Alternatively, the murder may have been political, as a reprisal for withdrawing the privileges from the Arabs.

Religion certainly played a significant part, for it was religion that sparked off an Arab revolt against Rome soon afterwards. The 'king of the Saracens' who headed the Arab allies of Rome is anonymous in the Classical sources, but might be the last Tanukhid king known from Arabic sources as al-Hawari, possibly a grandson of Imru'l-Qays.[295] The king died in about 375 leaving no heir. The Emperor Valens took advantage of the old shaikh's death to abrogate Rome's treaty with the Tanukh. Valens' motives may have been political, blaming the Arabs for Julian's death, but Constantinople's private attitude to the embarrassing apostate's murder is more likely to have been a good riddance – hence a quiet handshake to the Arabs, rather than an open diplomatic breach. The real reasons were religious, for Valens was a heterodox Arian while the Arabs were staunch Mono-physite Christians. Valens' insistence on imposing an Arian bishop on the Arabs was unacceptable. The result was revolt.

With the death of the Tanukh shaikh without an heir, Valens might have thought the time opportune and his job an easy one. But Valens did not reckon – and who would? – on the shaikh's wife, the extraordinary Queen Mawiyya, who took over the leadership of the confederation on her husband's death.[296] Leaving the Tanukh-settled areas around Aleppo, she withdrew into the desert. Soon all the desert Arabs and much of Arabia and Syria had gathered to her side.

Mawiyya then proceeded to strike hard at the vulnerable Roman positions. Her raids extended deep into Palestine and even Egypt as far as the Nile. They had a deadly effect on the Romans, who had little defence against the guerrilla warfare of Mawiyya's highly mobile units. The defence of the Roman East was geared towards the Iranian steamroller: of ponderous army meeting ponderous army, of hitting back at finite targets. Even the Zenobian revolt had presented Rome with the target of Palmyra, but Mawiyya was able to withdraw from the Tanukh-settled positions around Aleppo and use only the desert as her base – and her strength. The Romans had nothing to strike against. After a century of depending too heavily upon the Arabs for their desert defence, the Romans found that without them they were entirely lost in a desert war which could be fought on Mawiyya's terms.

But it was not only in desert warfare that Mawiyya's forces were able to better the Romans. A century of fighting alongside them as allies had proved the Arabs good students as well, and an initial force sent against them, commanded by the Roman governor of Phoenicia and Palestine, was defeated. Victorious in the desert and in open battle, Mawiyya met success in the towns as well. For in a war fought along religious lines, Mawiyya's cause against an Arian emperor aroused sympathy amongst the Monophysite townspeople, smarting from Valens' insensitive attempt at imposing Arianism. It was beginning to look as if the whole East might break away under Queen Mawiyya and her Arabs.

Accordingly, Constantinople sent another force, this time led by the Roman military commander of the East himself: a second defeat could not be countenanced. The two forces met in battle with Queen Mawiyya taking command in person. Mawiyya proved herself as good a field tactician as she was a political leader. The Arab forces, too, proved themselves masters of both Roman battle technique and their own traditional fighting methods. The combination of strong discipline, the swift manoeuvrability of their cavalry and the long lances that they wielded proved deadly. The last time the Romans had encountered these long, *sarissa*-like lances had been at the Battle of Magnesia over five and a half centuries before. Then, the lances held by Seleucid infantry phalanxes were no match for a disciplined Roman legion. But now, in the hands of rapidly mobile cavalry units, the lances had a devastating effect on the Romans. The result was a Roman defeat. Once more, Rome in the East faced humiliation at the hands of a woman.

This time, Rome had no Aurelian to rally a strong counter-attack. It must be remembered, too, that Aurelian was only able to put down Zenobia's revolt with the aid of the Tanukh: this time, the Tanukh were arrayed against Rome. Faced with the mounting pressure of a looming Gothic war on his western borders, the blundering Valens had no alternative but to sue for peace.

Having fought the war on her own terms, Mawiyya was able to dictate the peace. The choice of bishop – the cause of the revolt in the first place – fell entirely to Queen Mawiyya. To underline both her religious and ethnic stance she chose one whose moral credentials were above reproach, who was both a Monophysite and an Arab. This was the ascetic Moses who, like his great namesake, had spent many years wandering in the wilderness. The choice was a brilliant one, for Moses' life of preaching had attracted a considerable following amongst the eastern Monophysites in general and the Arabs in particular. The Arian Valens had no choice but to accept, and Moses was duly ordained as the first Arab bishop of the Arabs. An incipient Arab Church seemed in the making, attracting many leading Tanukh figures from Mesopotamia to settle in the Roman Empire.[297] Mawiyya's demand for a reinstatement of allied status was also met, and they returned to the privileges that they had enjoyed before Julian. To cement the new alliance and mark the conclusion of the war, Queen Mawiyya's daughter Princess Chasidat[298] was married to a senior Roman officer, Victor. As well as being a senior officer of long standing (he was a veteran of Julian's eastern campaign), Victor was zealously Monophysite. Under their Queen, the Arabs had achieved a 'just and lasting peace'.

Aftermath

Just, it may have been; lasting it was not. The seeds of the next revolt were sown in the peace of the last. In accordance with the terms of the peace, Mawiyya provided Constantinople with Arab auxiliaries to fight alongside the Romans in its disastrous Gothic War that broke out immediately on the conclusion of its Arab War. On their own ground the Arabs had been unbeatable, but in Thrace they were in unfamiliar territory – and the ferocity of the Goths they encountered had no counterpart in the desert. Valens himself was killed at the Battle of Adrianople in 378 and the Goths pushed the Romans back to the walls of Constantinople. Here, we read of the heroic defence of Constantinople by Mawiyya's Arabs – indeed, virtually saving the city from the Goths, according to Ammianus Marcellinus.[299] But they had been badly bruised in the war, so that it was a depleted force that eventually made its way back to the East. The new emperor, Theodosius, showed sympathy to the Goths at the expense of the Arabs. Soon Goths were increasingly incorporated into the Roman army and administration.

The situation was exacerbated by the Antioch demagogue Libanius, who stirred up feelings against the Arabs. Libanius had been a great friend of the Emperor Julian, and used the old argument of Arab culpability in Julian's death. Julian's paganism, of course, had to be minimised in an increasingly ecclesiastical world. But Julian, for all his paganism, was after all the last of the line of Constantine, and Libanius played this for all it was worth. Whether the Arabs were blamed in any way for the disasters of the Gothic War seems doubtful, but Libanius' anti-Arab crusade played into Theodosius' increasingly pro-Gothic camp, and privileges were withdrawn from the Tanukh once again. The Arabs, feeling that they had demonstrated their loyalty to the Romans in the defence of Constantinople, felt betrayed and broke out into open revolt once more in 383. This time, the Romans were better prepared, and the second Arab revolt was quickly put down within the same year. It spelt the end of Rome's relationship with the Tanukh, and Rome switched its attention to a new Arab tribe, the Salih from the southern Arabian marches.

By the end of the fourth century the Salih had replaced the Tanukh as Rome's chief Arab ally.

We do not know what part Mawiyya took in the second revolt. She presumably led it again – although the sources give no clue – as there were no other known leaders of the Tanukh at this time (although equally, it may have been the lack of her leadership that was the cause of its failure). At least she fared better than Zenobia. It seems that she lived to a ripe old age, retiring to the town of Anasartha on the desert fringes east of Aleppo in the heart of Tanukh tribal territory, where an inscription records her death in 425.[300]

The Romans had ultimately won against Mawiyya and her desert Arabs. But the lesson had not been lost on the Arabs. For Mawiyya's astonishing victories had, for the Romans, an ominous note. They revealed first just how quickly the native populations in the towns and cities of the Roman Near East would desert the Romans and join the Arab side in time of war. But far more importantly, they demonstrated just how effective a disciplined, well-armed but highly mobile desert force of Bedouin cavalry could be against conventional Roman forces. The next time this was to happen, the Arabs would be triumphant.

The Ghassan and the coming of Islam

There was not so great a need during the late fourth and fifth centuries for strong allied Arab tribes to defend the frontier, as the period was one of unusual peace between Rome and Iran – they were too busy fighting off respective barbarian invasions to bother much with each other. Hence, many of the desert fortifications, dating mainly from the time of Diocletian, fell into disrepair.[301] However, some new alliances were made, if only to use one tribe to keep the others from encroaching. With the decline of the Tanukh, a new Arab tribe was favoured with allied status. This was the Salih during the reign of Arcadius (395–408). Other Arab tribes also enjoyed allied status, including the Tanukh (albeit on a much reduced status) during the course of the fifth century, but the Salih were the main one.

The Salih were centred mainly in Jordan, i.e., well to the south of the Tanukh tribal lands in northern Syria, although evidence for them is found in the north as well. The Salih had been allies of the 'Amlaqi, Zenobia's tribe, hence enemies of the Tanukh.[302] The best known Salihid 'king' was Dawud, who built the Monastery of Dawud (between Rasafa and Isriya south-east of Aleppo).[303] In 468 the Emperor Leo incorporated a large contingent of Salihid allies in his disastrous North African campaign against the Vandals, when the contingent was almost wiped out. The resulting loss of manpower resulted in the weakening of the Salih and the rise of an Arab tribe to replace them as Rome's ally. This was the Ghassan, originally tributary to the Salih but destined to become the most powerful of Rome's tribal allies.[304]

The Ghassan were originally a nomadic tribe from further south in Arabia.[305] They started moving northwards in a series of tribal migrations after the end of the first century AD, their diaspora prompted, according to tradition, by the bursting of the Mareb Dam in Yemen. Many Arab tribes trace their diaspora from the same event.[306] The founder of the tribe was Jafnah Ibn 'Amr Muzayqiya', but both his date and the number and names of his successors are uncertain. They eventually arrived in the western deserts of Syria and Jordan around the end of the fifth century. After that date they began to challenge the supremacy of the Salih by gaining control of the trans-Arabian trade routes to Bosra. One of their shaikhs, known in Byzantine sources as Amorkesos, like ʿAmr Ibn ʿAdi of the Tanukh before him, was originally a defector from Iran and was well received by the Emperor Leo in 473. In 502–3 the Emperor Anastasius recognised the Ghassan under their chief al-Harith I as supreme over their rivals, the Salih, who fell increasingly out of favour. In about 528 Justinian awarded his son, al-Harith II Ibn Jabalah, the titles of Patricius as well as supreme Phylarch, or head, over all the other tribes.[307] In Arabic sources he has the title *malik* or 'king'.

Although probably not related to the earlier Nabataean tribes, the Ghassanids may have traced a traditional, if spurious, genealogy to the Nabataean kings. Thus, the name 'al-Harith' might have been a conscious revival of the Nabataean 'Harithath' (Aretas) in an attempt at continuity of Arab tradition in the region. Al-Harith II remained as both Roman phylarch and Arab king until his death in 569.

This renewed emphasis on courting one of the tribal confederations by Justinian was in response to new threats from Iran. The eastern frontier, having been relatively peaceful for so long, was changing with the rise of Khusrau I Anushirvan (see Chapter 2). Forming a strong alliance with a strong tribe was essential. Making the Ghassan supreme had a distinct advantage: the Ghassan, unlike the Tanukh, had no blood ties with Rome's enemies in the Arab world, the Lakhm of Hira. For the Sasanians of Iran made increasing use of their Lakhmid allies to strike deep at Rome's Near Eastern possessions. Since they were just allies, rather than a full part of the Sasanian Empire, excuses could always be made that they were outside Sasanian control if these strikes came when there was sup-posedly peace between the two empires. The Romans used their Arabs in much the same way in a surrogate war. The Lakhm under their king al-Mundhir raided as far as Antioch in 531. Harith Ibn Jabala was victorious, but the Lakhm soon returned with 15,000 additional troops supplied by the Sasanian Emperor Kavadh the same year. Whilst such raids ultimately failed, they demonstrated that Rome had to turn more and more to the Arabs for its eastern defence, as well as how effective the Arab lightning tactics were against Roman conventional forces.[308] Against such a force even the legendary Belisarius was defeated in a battle at Callinicum, although the Ghassan under al-Harith Ibn Jabala acquitted themselves with distinction.[309]

However, al-Harith was ultimately victorious over Mundhir at a battle near Chalcis in 554, when Mundhir himself was killed. Over the following years al-Harith consolidated his position amongst the desert tribes, building up his Ghassanid followers as the main force in the Near East. In 563 he visited Constantinople, leaving a powerful and long-lasting impression. The Emperor Justinian awarded him all the pomp and ceremony that befitted a visiting king. He died in 569 and was succeeded by his son Mundhir, who reigned until 581/2.

The Emperor Justin II (565–78), however, did not inherit the personal relationship that existed between his predecessor and al-Harith, and was suspicious of al-Mundhir – or rather of the Ghassan's growing power. The Ghassanid 'kingdom' by now comprised virtually all of the eastern areas of the provinces of Arabia and Syria, ruled with little reference to Constantinople. In addition, the increasing Monophysitism espoused by the Ghassan (see below) and the subsequent virtual independence of the Syrian Church alienated Orthodox Constantinople. Justin II accordingly ordered the Roman governor of Syria to have Mundhir killed. However, Ghassanid agents intercepted the letter. This action itself demonstrates just how powerful they had become in Syria, where even official imperial communications between Constantinople and Antioch were subject to scrutiny by Ghassanid 'intelligence'. Mundhir responded by abrogating the alliance and allowing the Lakhmids to raid Roman territory once more. Without Arab support, all of the Roman Near East was vulnerable, so a reconciliation was hastily concluded in a treaty drawn up in Rasafa in 575, and the Ghassan returned to halting Lakhmid raids. After a major victory when even the Lakhmid capital of al-Hira in Iraq was sacked, a rapprochement was made and al-Mundhir was awarded a state visit to Constantinople in 580 by the Emperor Tiberius II, who personally placed a crown on al-Mundhir's head.

But the rapprochement with Constantinople was short-lived. Tiberius' lieutenant, the Caesar Maurice, was badly mauled in an abortive invasion of Mesopotamia and blamed Mundhir for the debacle. Tiberius accordingly had Mundhir exiled to Sicily and tried to force the Ghassanid tribe – staunch Monophysites – to become Orthodox. The four sons of Mundhir raised the banner of revolt. Maurice hastily called for negotiations with the eldest son Nu'man, but tricked him into going to Constantinople and thence into joining his father in exile. After this, the Ghassanid federation began to break up. Their shaikh was still accorded the title of 'Phylarch' by Constantinople, but their power was considerably reduced after 586. The remaining Ghassanid princes were left to lead a life of considerable extravagance but little real power.

There was some reinstatement of the Ghassan by Heraclius in 629 after his successful campaign against Iran. The last Ghassanid king, Jabalah Ibn Ayhan, was made supreme over the other tribes once more. As a result the Ghassan remained with the Romans to the bitter end, joining Heraclius in resisting the Arab Muslim invasion. The Ghassan, however, fell to Muslim rule after the Battle of Yarmuk and submitted to Umar in 637. But they never surrendered their religion to Islam, so revolted again soon after. Jabalah and the last members of the house eventually retreated to Constantinople, where one of his descendants even became emperor in the ninth century (Nicephorus I, 802–11).

The principal Ghassanid 'encampment' – although it was more a town – was Jabiyah in the Golan where there was a sanctuary to St Sergius. Other encampments were near Damascus and Adr'a (at Saida). But they were courts of opulent luxury all the same, attracting a considerable literary circle. Indeed, the Ghassanid courts were the most important centres for Arabic poetry before the rise of the Caliphal courts under Islam. The luxury of their courts and the patronage of poets, musicians and artists by the Ghassanid princes formed an immediate model for the Umayyad courts in Damascus and anticipated their own desert 'palaces'.

Various buildings have been attributed to the Ghassan, mainly churches and towers, such as the towers at Dmayr and Qasr al-Hayr al-Gharbi, the latter built by Harith in 559 according to an inscription. Ghassanid family tombs are known from Jabiya and Adr'a. Other important Ghassanid centres were Rasafa, Bosra and Amman. The 'church' outside the north gate at Rasafa – probably in fact a Roman-type praetorium or assembly hall – has an inscription to al-Mundhir in it.[310] The city of Rasafa itself is to some extent a Ghassanid creation, due mainly to the popularity of the cult of St Sergius that was spread by the Ghassan amongst the Arabs. The huge cisterns in Rasafa are generally attributed to the Ghassan, and the massive wealth generated by the pilgrimage traffic to Rasafa reached its height under them, used to embellish the city to an extent that rivalled Palmyra in an earlier era (Plate 19). The extraordinary desert palace complex of Qasr Ibn Wardan in northern Syria, built probably by architects from Constantinople on the imperial (as opposed to Syrian) model, may have been built by Justinian for the Ghassanid princes (Plate 20).[311] But the real architectural legacy of the Ghassan must surely be the vast

Plate 19 The North Gate at Rasafa

Plate 20 The church and palace at Qasr Ibn Wardan. The remains of a barracks in the foreground

numbers of remains that can be found in northern Syria, the Dead Cities and the desert areas (Figure 44). The huge expansion of settlements, as well as their undoubted prosperity and ecclesiasticism, is a true testament to the stability brought to the area by the Ghassanid federation. These remains are discussed in detail in Chapter 6. It has become conventional in scholarly works to call this remarkable series of ruins – one of the most remarkable in the world – as well as Rasafa, 'Roman' or 'Byzantine'. Might they not better be described 'Ghassanid'?[312]

The Ghassan, particularly under al-Harith II, reinvigorated Monophysitism in Syria. Several Monophysite bishops were ordained, including the famous Jacob Baradaeus, who in turn ordained eighty-nine bishops and an astonishing 100,000 priests. This number sounds unbelievable, but the sheer quantity of ecclesiastical remains, particularly in northern Syria (some 1,200 churches – see Chapter 6), is graphic evidence of Baradaeus' activities. As a result, the Syrian Church achieved virtual independence from Constantinople. Ghassanid missionary activity extended deep into Arabia as well as across the Red Sea to Ethiopia. Although the Ghassanid tribe remained staunch Christians after Islam, it is nonetheless true that the rigorous Monophysitism that they promulgated, with its emphasis on the single nature of Christ and its simpler version of Christianity compared to Byzantine orthodoxy, made the rapid spread of Islam much easier when it did come. Most of all, it imparted a specifically 'Arab' character to Christianity, again anticipating Islam.

Bosra was an important caravan and religious centre during the Ghassanid ascendancy. Indeed, both the Christianity of Bosra and its important Christian buildings must be seen as much – or more – a product of Ghassanid culture as Roman. A part of Bosra's religious importance stemmed from its being the residence of a famous monk and teacher, Bahira. Bahira – the name is a Syriac title that simply means 'reverend' – was an anchorite monk. According to Islamic tradition, Bosra was frequented at that time by a leading merchant from Mecca, Abu Talib, who brought his still unknown nephew with him on his trade missions. This was Muhammad, and conversations between the elderly Christian monk and the young Meccan caravan leader were believed to influence the last great religious movement in the Near East.[313] Whether or not such traditions are true is not relevant. What is important is that by the time of the Ghassanid ascendancy, the Arabs had become a major factor on the Near Eastern stage and monotheism had become a major factor for the Arabs. In the words of Philip Hitti, 'they served as a pre-view of the gigantic show to come'.[314] When it did come, Islam was as much a new beginning for Arab civilisation as a culmination: a culmination of the gradual rise of Arab civilisation over the past seven centuries of Roman rule. 'The clients of Byzantium had become its rivals.'[315]

4

ROME EAST OF THE FRONTIERS

The Tigris may have been Rome's eastern frontier for much of its history, but the presence of so great a power as Rome was felt far beyond.[1] Direct and indirect traces of Rome are encountered throughout Asia, from chance remarks in ancient Chinese annals to chance finds on remote Indian beaches. The very images of Roman soldiers form a dramatic backdrop to passing tribal migrations in the valleys of southern Persia (Plate 26), while the portrait busts that look at us from Buddhist monuments in India are of Romans rather than Indians (Plate 29). These traces generally fall into four main categories: direct military campaigns, Roman prisoners of war, Roman trade and Roman artistic influence.

Military campaigns

The history of Roman military expansion in the East was overshadowed by the memory of Alexander of Macedon throughout. The first (and, surprisingly, the only) emperor in the ancient world to be named after the great conqueror was the Syrian-born Emperor Severus Alexander in the third century. But before that, Mark Antony called his son by Cleopatra after Alexander in his own ludicrous claim to Alexander's legacy. Equally ludicrous was the emulation of him by Emperor Caracalla. Trajan's and Julian's fascination with Alexander, although less ludicrous, was hardly more successful than Caracalla's. In the heady days after first acquiring an eastern empire, thoughts of Alexander were uppermost. Augustus supposedly dreamt of a 'universal empire' with the addition of Iran and India to Rome's domains (never mind that this was not so much Alexander's vision but Cyrus' reality),[2] Nero planned an invasion of Iran spearheaded by a specially raised legion named 'The Phalanx of Alexander the Great'[3] and Trajan, as we have seen, was very much in Alexander's shadow. But despite breaching eastern – mainly Iranian – defences on numerous occasions, Iran and any long-term conquests of Asia lay permanently beyond Rome's grasp.

Sources recount the capture of the Iranian 'capital' of Ctesiphon with such tedious regularity that one is left doubting their veracity. These occasions need not concern us here. Of more interest are the rare occasions when Roman arms penetrated deep beyond the frontiers. The two main ones – both disasters occurring within the first decades of Rome's eastern empire, before it had learnt enough about its eastern frontier to know better – were Mark Antony's campaign into Iran in 36 BC and Aelius Gallus' campaign into south Arabia in 25–24 BC.

Mark Antony and Iran (Figure 17)[4]

The bloodbath which marked the accession of Phraates IV to the Parthian throne in 37 BC forced many Parthian nobles to flee westwards.[5] Many ended up in Antioch where Mark Antony had just arrived from Rome, mainly to deal with Iran (although this did not prevent him from holding court with Cleopatra whom he had just sent for). Here in oriental Antioch, Antony, the republican soldier from Rome, was feeling every bit the eastern potentate as he basked in the Egyptian queen's easy attentions, so was easy prey to the aristocratic Parthian exiles. Anxious to prove himself to Cleopatra – who in any case was never one to turn down an opportunity to meddle in foreign politics[6] – Mark Antony casually made her a gift of Cyprus as well as half of Syria, Palestine and Arabia. Hardly his to give – the Senate took poorly to Antony's high-handed largesse – but no matter: all he needed as icing to the cake was to add Iran to Cleopatra's booty. Convinced by the Parthian exiles that an Iranian campaign would be made easy by the local support of a population anxious to rise against their tyrant, Antony decided on invasion.

All the same, the memory of Carrhae still lay heavily upon Roman minds – the loss of its standards as much as the loss of its legions. Antony, therefore, made sure that it would not be done by halves. He set out for Armenia, where he proceeded to raise an army with the help of his ally, King Artavasdes. As well as his own army of 70,000 Romans, there was a massive arsenal of 300 wagonloads of siege engines and weapons. On top of this were an additional 30,000 troops contributed by various Near Eastern client kings, of which the largest number was 13,000 lent by Artavasdes. Altogether, Antony was able to muster a grand army of 100,000 well-armed men, sending ripples of alarm – according to Plutarch – as far off as Bactria and India. The invasion was launched early the following year – the largest force to invade Iran from the west since Alexander (Figure 17).

Despite setting off before winter was over, the campaign initially went quite well and Antony penetrated deep into western Iran. He first besieged the Parthian winter palace of Vera, to the south-east of Lake Urmia in Azerbaijan. There, Antony made his first cardinal mistake: in his haste he decided to leave behind his heavy baggage, which included the all-important 300 wagonloads of siege engines and weapons. At this point it seems that the Armenians, seeing which way the wind was blowing, also withdrew their support.[7] Accordingly, when Antony went on to lay siege of the Parthian royal residence of Praaspa deep in the mountains, it went off half-cocked. Without either their siege equipment, or their Armenian allies who were used to mountain warfare, the Romans were useless against the strong walls of Praaspa. With winter coming on, bands of Iranian irregulars in the countryside prevented Roman foragers from obtaining adequate supplies. Famine started to take its toll amongst the Roman besiegers far more than amongst the besieged. From the security of their walls, the defenders were able to pick off the Romans with ease. Faced with the problem of no siege engines, dwindling supplies and a dwindling army, Antony decided upon that most classic of all military blunders: a winter retreat. A retreat, moreover, through enemy territory and the mountain passes of Azerbaijan and Armenia.

The retreat was a colossal disaster. The Iranians were able to ambush the weakened Romans with ease from the hillsides. Local guides engaged by the Romans deliberately led them astray into the ambushes of the waiting Iranian archers. Without adequate supplies, hunger continued to kill as many as the Iranians did. What hunger and the archers left, the extreme cold took away. In the end the battered army that returned to

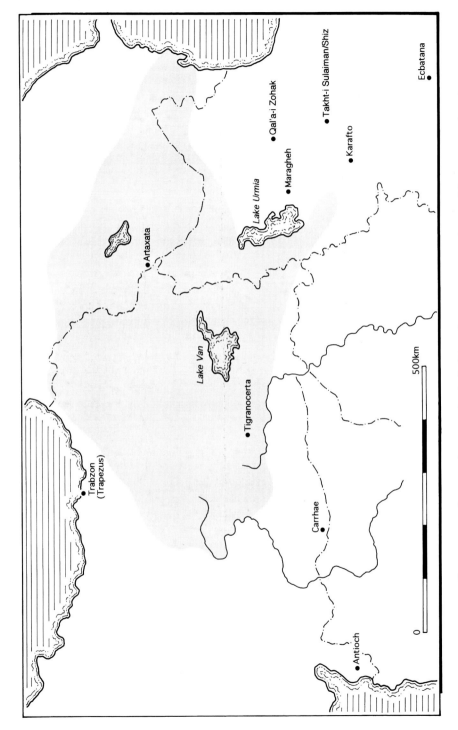

Figure 17 Map illustrating Mark Antony's campaign. Shaded area shows approximate limits of the Armenian kingdom

Armenia in the winter of 36 BC was but a fraction of the 'Grande Armée' that had set off so confidently the previous year.

Antony's troubles were still not over. The Armenian king, friendly enough when Antony had an army behind him, was less than welcoming to the tattered remnants that crept back into his kingdom. It took all of Antony's powers of persuasion to keep Artavasdes friendly. An eleventh-hour reprieve only came in the form of funds sent by Cleopatra, with which he was able to pay off his troops and return to Alexandria – albeit kidnapping Artavasdes at the last minute as a scapegoat. He presented the Armenian king to Cleopatra as a war trophy. Cleopatra had Artavasdes, as well as his queen and two of his sons, brutally tortured to death.[8] So disastrous was Antony's eastern venture that word of it was carefully concealed back at Rome.[9] Some two years later Antony casually – and unrealistically – awarded all of Iran 'as far as India' to his son by Cleopatra – whom he grandly named Alexander. But the reality had cost Rome the loss of an army, a loss that rivalled Crassus' debacle, and achieved nothing.

The news of Antony's massive Parthian disaster, when it eventually did trickle back to Rome, was decisive in Octavian's bid to assume absolute power. Absolutism – monarchy – was by then inevitable for Rome in any case, as Antony's assumption of royal pomp in Alexandria made plain. But Antony's failure in Iran decided that it would be Octavian and his successors, not Antony, who made it so.

The location of Praaspa and the exact route of Antony's retreat remains problematical. A tantalising Greek inscription in the artificial caves of Karafto near Takab in Azerbaijan reads 'Here resides Herakles; nothing evil may enter.' This, however, probably refers to a local cult of Herakles in the region that is mentioned by Tacitus rather than to the passage of Antony's army.[10] Praaspa might be identified with the spectacular walled Sasanian holy city of Shiz, modern Takht-i Sulaiman, deep in the remote mountains of north-west Iran (Plate 21).[11] Most authorities, however, have doubted this, favouring Maragheh at the south-eastern corner of Lake Urmia, citing the lack of substantial Parthian remains at Takht-i Sulaiman.[12] But there are no Parthian remains at Maragheh either, and certainly no ancient ramparts, while substantial Parthian remains have been found at Takht-i

Plate 21 The walled city of Takht-i Sulaiman in Iran, possibly identified with ancient Praaspa which was besieged by Mark Antony in 36 BC

Sulaiman. A more recent suggestion for Praaspa was made following the discovery of the Parthian pavilion of Qal'a-i Zohak near Miyaneh (77D).[13] The remains are certainly impressive enough, but here too no traces of the walls which Antony invested exist. It is true that the ramparts at Takht-i Sulaiman are Sasanian in date, but they may well have replaced Parthian ones. Most important, Takht-i Sulaiman, as ancient Shiz, was a great religious centre (at least later on during the Sasanian period). This would make it an obvious site for keeping war trophies such as the Carrhae standards, the main object of Antony's campaign.

The same area of Azerbaijan was the scene of another major Roman military disaster in 233, when Severus Alexander's ill-fated army was cut to pieces in the mountains during a winter retreat after attacking Ardeshir I.[14] The holy city of Shiz/Takht-i Sulaiman was also invested by a Roman army over 600 years after Antony. This was the campaign of the Emperor Heraclius into Iran following the Sasanian sack of Jerusalem by Khusrau Parviz in 613. Like Antony, Heraclius was in pursuit of captured booty. This time it was the holy relics which Khusrau had taken from Jerusalem. Unlike Antony, however, Heraclius was entirely successful and managed to capture the city (although legends of the Holy Grail still cling to Takht-i Sulaiman).[15]

Aelius Gallus and Yemen (Figure 18)[16]

The Arabian peninsula beyond the present-day kingdom of Jordan was the one area of the ancient Near East least penetrated by the Romans. There is a temple with a dedicatory inscription in Greek and Nabataean to Marcus Aurelius and Lucius Verus at Ruwwafa, north-west of Mada'in Salih in Hijaz, but this area formed a part of the Roman Province of Arabia in the second century. Some inscriptions down the Wadi Sirhan as far as Jawf also imply some form of Roman presence, but it seems doubtful whether Rome extended much beyond Ruwwafa.[17] The main reason why Roman arms never stretched further was the disastrous campaign of Aelius Gallus in 25–24 BC.

Strabo refers to Yemen – Arabia Felix, or 'Blessed Arabia' – as being extremely wealthy but only comprising a very small part of Arabia. Other such reports of legendary wealth in aromatics and precious stones reached Rome – and were themselves echoes of earlier reports in Egyptian and Biblical records.[18] Furthermore, unlike Iran, Arabia did not have a great empire to guard its wealth: it was simply there for the taking. Accordingly, Augustus sent an expedition under Aelius Gallus, the governor of Egypt, to explore Arabia and Ethiopia and adjacent coasts with the purpose of conquest. The Romans were also urged on by the Nabataeans with promises of assistance and co-operation – doubtless for motives of their own as we shall see.

The expedition seemed doomed from the start: by poor leadership, poor planning and poor guides. When all was ready, Aelius Gallus set sail with a force consisting of about 10,000 infantry drawn from the Roman garrisons in Egypt. With it came an auxiliary force of 500 Judaeans and 1,000 Nabataeans under their own commander, Syllaeus, who was to act as guide. But Syllaeus, acting under orders from the Nabataean king 'Ubaydath II, had other priorities. He apparently set out deliberately to mislead the expedition: the Nabataeans wished to safeguard the lucrative Arabian trade for themselves. They saw Gallus' expedition as the perfect opportunity both to extend their own influence into Arabia, the Nabataeans' traditional source of wealth, and to weaken Rome's new-found position in Egypt, the Nabataeans' most lucrative market. To begin with, Syllaeus made

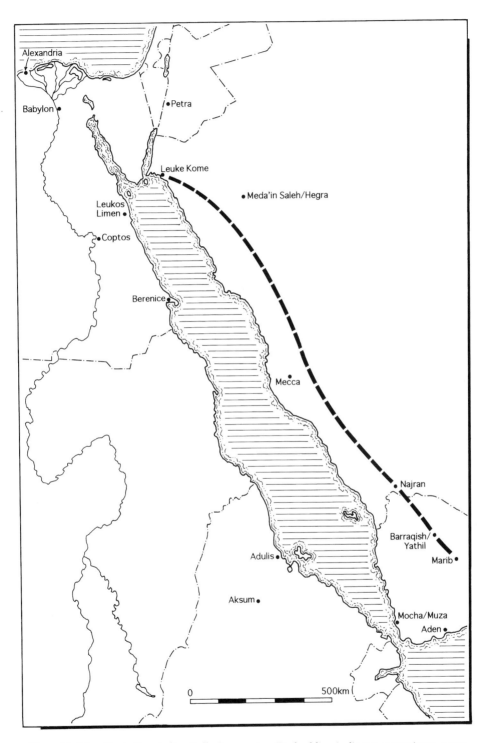

Figure 18 Map illustrating Aelius Gallus' campaign. Dashed line indicates approximate route

111

sure that the sea crossing was as difficult as possible, landing only on the rockiest shores most devoid of provisions, water or safe anchorages. By the time they arrived at Leuce Come, the main Nabataean trade emporium at the northern end of the Red Sea,[19] many of the boats and crew had already been lost and many of the men were suffering from scurvy and paralysis.

So depleted was his force that Gallus had to spend the summer and all of the winter at Leuce Come to recover. On proceeding by land, Syllaeus then led them through long, circuitous routes that avoided wells and provisions, hoping to deplete the Romans by hunger, disease and general fatigue rather than by enemy action. After crossing a desert devoid of water, the Romans finally arrived at the Minnaean city of Negrana, modern Najran in Saudi Arabia, the beginning of the fertile mountainous areas of south Arabia. The king had fled Negrana, so the Romans occupied it with ease. But from then on, the Romans did face armed opposition. Depleted by disease, hunger and treachery though they were, superior Roman military training proved effective and they were able to defeat the south Arabians with few losses. They advanced deeper into south Arabia towards the legendary kingdom of Sheba, the most powerful of the south Arabian kingdoms. They occupied and garrisoned the Minnaean religious capital of Yathil, modern Barraqish in Yemen,[20] using it as a base for operations against Sheba just to the south-east (Plate 22). From Yathil Aelius Gallus then advanced to its capital of Marib, which he besieged.

Marib was the capital of the most powerful and wealthiest of the south Arabian

Plate 22 The site of Barraqish in Yemen, ancient Yathil, captured by the Romans in Aelius Gallus' campaign in 24 BC

kingdoms and the key to the incense trade which the Romans sought to control. It lay in the middle of a fertile plain watered by its famous dam, one of the greatest engineering marvels of the ancient world. On one side the mountains that form the highlands of Yemen rise dramatically up to the south, while on the other side immense sand dunes stretch off into the Empty Quarter. The city of Marib itself was formidably fortified. The ancient south Arabians had a mastery of stone masonry second to none, and Marib was surrounded by great limestone ramparts that were a credit to the military engineer's art: 6-metre-thick walls constructed of superbly dressed, close-fitting basalt and limestone blocks, strengthened by regularly spaced bastions and pierced by eight well-defended gateways.[21] These walls must have formed a formidable obstacle, even to superior Roman siege tactics. The Romans assaulted the city, but after only six days withdrew. The reasons given were lack of water, but the Marib oasis was well watered with canals and the city was surrounded by productive villages. Furthermore, unlimited supplies of water lay only a few kilometres to the south at the great dam. More likely, the Romans were by then far too demoralised by illness, exhaustion and treachery, and their lines of communication and supply far too extended, for any effective action against Marib's defences.

The Roman army would have known something of deserts from their duties in Egypt. But the harsh desert environment around Marib was something altogether beyond their experience. This was not the 'Blessed Arabia' – Arabia Felix – of repute. The green, lush highlands of Yemen, watered by the monsoons of the Indian Ocean, were well beyond the haze of the mountains that rise abruptly behind Marib and would have lain beyond their knowledge and reach. The reality of the Arabia that confronted them must have appeared an alien world altogether, particularly for those soldiers drawn from Gaul and northern Italy. Many of them succumbed. One of them, the Equestrian Publius Cornelius, was commemorated by an inscribed gravestone found recently at Barraqish.[22]

Aelius Gallus then turned his army back. Having finally realised the unreliability of Syllaeus he engaged new guides. Whilst the outward journey had taken six months, he achieved the return journey in only two, obtaining adequate water and provisions on the way. Gallus eventually reached Alexandria with the tattered remnants of his army. He had lost most of his men: only seven by enemy action, the rest by treachery and incompetence. The whole episode had achieved nothing.

Much is made of Syllaeus' duplicitous role in the entire episode, with the accusations – by both ancient and modern authors – of the untrustworthy, treacherous oriental having more than just a hint of good old-fashioned cultural prejudice. But Syllaeus can hardly be reviled for holding his own country's interests first, especially against such a bare-faced attempt by Rome to subvert the Nabataeans' livelihood. He was simply seized upon by the Romans as the most convenient foreigner to make into a scapegoat for their own blunders. After this episode, Syllaeus seems to have risen high in the Nabataean hierarchy, becoming a major power behind the throne of 'Ubaydath II and a sort of roving Nabataean ambassador at large both to Judaea (where he had a much publicised affair with Herod's sister, Salome) and to Rome itself.[23] Blaming the Nabataeans for the Roman failure to extend its empire to Arabia Felix was largely a face-saving device to explain a military disaster. Even without treachery such a desert expedition is difficult, today as much as then. The harshness of the terrain, the extended lines of communication, the inexperience of the Romans in desert travel, would have made such a conquest unrealistic even with the best guides in the world. The Romans never made any further attempts at conquest deep into the Arabian peninsula.[24]

Roman prisoners of war

Roman soldiers were to penetrate much further east than either Azerbaijan or Yemen, not by military campaigns, however, but as prisoners of war. Both Rome and Iran took innumerable prisoners in all of their wars, but the largest numbers were those taken by Iran at its two greatest victories against Rome: Carrhae in 53 BC and Edessa in AD 260. The Near East had for thousands of years a well-established tradition of transporting populations: Tiglath-Pileser I and his successors of the Assyrian Empire transported populations around on a massive – and brutal – scale. Captive Romans have formed a part of this Near Eastern tradition ranging from the Jewish exile to Saddam's transportation of the Kurds. Survivors of the Battle of Edessa have left their traces very visibly in Iran. The fate of the survivors of Carrhae requires some comment, if only because of the interest and controversy it has aroused.

Crassus' lost legions?

Of the Romans who survived the carnage of Carrhae in 53 BC, ten thousand managed to straggle back to Antioch. Another ten thousand fell to the Iranians as prisoners of war.[25] Never before did Iran have to cope with such a huge influx of prisoners. They could not be imprisoned anywhere in their western borderlands, within reach of any rescue attempt such as that which Mark Antony attempted in 36 BC. There was also always the danger that so large a body of prisoners so close to Roman territory might break free and fight their way back home – the lesson of Xenophon's Ten Thousand under an earlier Persian Empire would not have been lost on their successors.

But the earlier Persian Empire did supply precedents of what to do with prisoners from the troublesome West: deport them to the remote East. Such had been the fate of many of the Ionians who revolted under Darius, and Iran's vast hinterland in Central Asia has always been a convenient dumping-ground for unwanted deportees.[26] The Iranians were settling Greeks there long before Alexander did, legends of Israel's lost tribes still cling to the region,[27] and Stalin's mass deportations there of peoples as diverse as Germans and Koreans simply continued a tradition thousands of years old.

Accordingly, the Roman Ten Thousand were taken to Margiana on the north-eastern fringes of the Parthian Empire.[28] Margiana and the regions east of the Caspian were the original heartland of the Parthian tribes themselves: nothing demonstrated more clearly just how far they had come from their tribal origins than decorating their homeland with so visible a sign of their victory. There, they were put to good works, presumably forming a convenient source of cheap labour mainly in agriculture and construction. Some Parthian documents excavated at Nisa, to the south of Ashkhabad, have been interpreted as referring to Roman legionary commanders engaged in agricultural work. Several Roman inscriptions, one in Greek and two in Latin, have also been discovered on the Surkhan River of southern Uzbekistan. One of them has been interpreted as possibly referring to the Fifteenth Pannonian Legion. Since this was only formed in AD 62, the inscriptions would have been made by Roman prisoners captured in another war, but the interpretation is by no means certain.[29] There has also been speculation that the prisoners were used in the construction of the immense Parthian-period ramparts at Marga (Merv) itself, but archaeological investigations have not substantiated this.[30]

Doubtless many of the legionaries would have become resigned to their new surroundings and settled down, taking wives from amongst the local Iranian population – the western character of some elements in the population of Merv still survived in the fourth century AD.[31] But the purported fate of one group of Roman prisoners was pieced together in the 1950s by a Sinologist, H. H. Dubs, from some references in the Chinese sources that were taken to refer to Romans. According to Dubs, some Roman legionaries escaped and entered the service of the nomadic Hun Empire, where they were employed as mercenaries in a war against the Chinese in 36 BC. The Chinese sources appear to refer to Roman-type military manoeuvres – most notably the *testudo* formation – with reference to these mercenaries. Descriptions of the Chinese pictorial representation of this campaign have also been interpreted as in keeping with Roman rather than Chinese art, and subsequent Chinese sources have been interpreted as referring to groups of Romans being settled on their western borderlands between Gansu and Lop Nor.

The entire story, based as it is on the concurrence of the flimsiest of mentions in both Chinese and Classical sources, has since aroused considerable controversy, and most authorities now doubt Dubs' interpretation of the Chinese sources.[32] It must be borne in mind that there is not a single shred of material evidence to support it (although the interpretation of some of the Parthian documents from Nisa has been taken as indirect confirmation of Romans serving with the Huns).[33]

Survivors of Edessa (Figure 19)

Following the Battle of Edessa in AD 260, 60,000 Roman prisoners of war were captured with Emperor Valerian and settled in Assyria, Susiana, Persia and elsewhere. Shapur founded four cities peopled by the prisoners of war and named after himself: Sod Shapur in Mesene, Bishapur in Fars, Buzurg Shapur on the Tigris and Gundishapur (a corruption of *Veh Antioch Shapur* or 'Better than Antioch Shapur') in Susiana.[34] The prisoners were put to good works, particularly in construction. Dams and bridges were built in Susiana, and Gundeshapur, the main centre for Roman deportees, was built along the lines of a Roman military camp.

Gundeshapur (or Jundeshapur) was to have a long and illustrious history. It evolved into a major city, later likened to Constantinople itself, doubtless a reference to its Roman origins. It became a major religious and intellectual centre, attracting some of the greatest minds of both the Roman and Iranian worlds. Iran's most important centre of Christianity was there, its bishop one of the most senior in the East. Gundeshapur became one of the foremost academic towns of the East, with a famous observatory and medical school that lasted well into the Islamic period. By the sixth century it had become a centre of learning where Roman, Greek and Syrian scholars were able to meet their Iranian counterparts in an atmosphere of religious and intellectual toleration not known in the Roman world at the time. When Justinian closed down Plato's ancient Academy at Athens, it was, significantly, to Gundeshapur that the heirs to the Greek philosophers moved.[35] The glory that was Gundeshapur is a tribute to both of the civilisations that produced it.

There is very little left today of Gundeshapur (modern Shahabad). Only a few mounds mark its position, and excavations revealed few traces of its remarkable past.[36] The city that showed most the physical imprint of the Roman deportees was Shapur's new royal city of Bishapur, founded as a victory city to celebrate his great triumph over the Romans. The city itself was laid out on a square plan, in accordance with standard

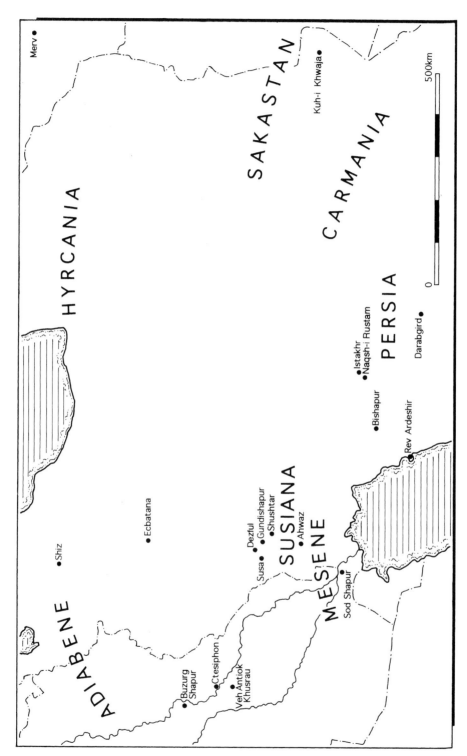

Figure 19 Map illustrating Roman traces in Iran

Roman practice, rather than the circular plan more usual of Iran.[37] Shapur's palace at Bishapur, although conforming to a standard cruciform plan of other Sasanian architecture, was decorated with mosaics which depict reclining, standing and dancing women, garlanded and playing music. These are clearly Roman of the Antioch school, almost certainly made by deportees from Antioch. The construction of this palace is of the conventional rubble and mortar of Sasanian buildings elsewhere in Iran. But the Temple of Anahita, adjacent to it, is far more clearly of Roman Syrian workmanship: large, well-masoned, ashlar block walls, with trapezoid-shaped doorways (Plate 23). Valerian himself was housed in a specially built palace at Bishapur. At the intersection of the two main transverse streets at Bishapur – typical Roman Cardo and Decumanus – stands a dedicatory Corinthian column with an inscription dated 263 honouring Shapur. Such a monument is also seen to be of Roman inspiration, being quite atypical of Sasanian monuments – indeed, the arrangement has its counterpart at Apamaea in Syria.[38]

Equally graphic reminders of these prisoners can still be seen today in Khuzistan, ancient Susiana. Here, the Romans were made to build a massive dam and bridge over the river at Shushtar. Like its British counterpart on the River Kwai in Burma, the Roman POW bridge survives today, still known as the *Band-i Qaysar* or 'Caesar's Dam' (albeit after many later restorations and modifications). It is 516 metres long and the 41 piers which support it are of typical Roman workmanship. More bridges, which still survive or partly survive, were built by the prisoners at Ahwaz (ancient Hormizd Shahr), Pa-i Pul near Karkha (Greek Choaspes) and Dizful (Greek Coprates). The latter, like Shushtar a

Plate 23 The Temple of Anahita at Bishapur in Iran, probably built by
Roman prisoners

117

combination of bridge and dam, is also reasonably well preserved, the piers still forming the base of a modern bridge carrying heavy traffic (Plate 24). Other 'wondrous Roman-type structures' were built by the prisoners at Istakhr and on the Khorasan road.[39]

But the greatest visible signs of captive Romans and their emperors are to be seen in a number of victory reliefs that Shapur had cut into the cliff faces of his homeland in Fars. Five depict Roman captives, some depicting no fewer than three Roman emperors humbled by the great equestrian figure of Shapur. Of these, two are at Bishapur (numbered Bishapur 2 and 3, Plates 25 and 26) and one at Darabgird. Two others – another at Bishapur (Bishapur 1) and the famous one at Naqsh–i Rustam (Naqsh–i Rustam 4, Plate 27) – depict just two Roman emperors. All show one or more Romans in acts of supplication, typically one kneeling in front of the mounted figure of Shapur and another standing in the background. Those depicting three Romans have the third lying prostrate under the hooves of Shapur's horse (e.g., Plate 26). The relief at Darabgird, for example, has two Romans facing the mounted figure of Shapur, the one in the foreground standing and holding out his hands in supplication, the one in the background with one hand raised aloft and with Shapur's head resting on his head. There is a prostrate Roman under the king's horse, and a crowd of Romans in the background. A crowd of Persian retainers flank the king. The most famous – and most intact – of the reliefs is that at Naqsh–i Rustam, famous not least because of its close association with Persepolis (an association not lost on the Sasanians themselves). Here, a Roman is kneeling in front of Shapur while another stands in the background with one arm raised to Shapur (Plate 27).[40]

The figures of the Romans have been interpreted differently. Formerly, it was thought that the suppliant in all reliefs was Valerian with the standing figure either Mariades (the Antiochene who led Shapur to Antioch) or Philip the Arab, and the prostrate figure an

Plate 24 The bridge at Ahwaz, on piers probably built by Roman prisoners

Plate 25 Shapur's great victory relief at Bishapur (no. 3), depicting Roman prisoners and the Emperors Valerian, Philip and Gordian

anonymous Roman.[41] Whilst the identification with Valerian appears obvious, there is no evidence that the standing figure would be Mariades. That the prostrate figure would be an anonymous Roman does not accord with Sasanian iconography, where reliefs of the emperor depict him trampling somebody of equivalent but opposite rank. Investiture scenes of Ardeshir I, for example, depict Ardeshir trampling the deposed Parthian king Artabanus IV opposite the god Ahuramazda trampling the god of darkness, Ahriman. The great Shapur would hardly be depicted trampling a mere unknown soldier.

A more recent interpretation is now favoured.[42] This seems to accord most closely with Shapur's own account of his victories. The relevant passages concerning three Roman emperors are as follows:

> Gordian Caesar raised in all of the Roman Empire a force from the Goth and German realms and marched on Babylonia against the Empire of Iran and against us. On the border of Babylonia . . . a great battle occurred. Gordian Caesar was killed and the Roman force was destroyed. And the Romans made Philip Caesar. Then Philip Caesar came to us for terms, and to ransom their lives, gave us 500,000 *denars*, and became tributary to us. . . . And Caesar lied again and did wrong to Armenia. Then we attacked the Roman Empire . . . In the third campaign, when we attacked Carrhae and Urhai [Edessa] and were besieging Carrhae and Edessa Valerian Caesar marched against us. He had with him a force of 70,000 . . . And beyond Carrhae and Edessa we had a great battle with Valerian Caesar. We made prisoner with our own hands Valerian Caesar and the others, chiefs of that army . . .[43]

Plate 26 The Emperor Philip the Arab kneeling before the mounted figure of Shapur at Bishapur (no. 1). The Emperor Gordian lies trampled underneath Shapur's horse

The prostrate figure on one of the Bishapur reliefs was wearing a wreath, so must be an emperor. This could only be Gordian III: the beardless and youthful features in the Bishapur relief moreover correspond to coin portraits of Gordian III, who, after all, was only nineteen when he was killed. The suppliant figure is identified with Philip the Arab, who was forced to make terms with Shapur. The resemblance of the suppliant figure, particularly in the Naqsh-i Rustam relief, to known portraits of Philip, such as the Vatican bust, supports this identification (Plate 157). This would make the third, standing, figure Valerian. Shapur's own reference to his capture 'with our hands' is a formulaic phrase going back to Assyrian annals which means taking credit for the capture rather than any literal meaning. This is depicted symbolically in the reliefs, where in all cases Shapur is shown placing hands on the standing figure. The depiction of all three emperors in the one scene, despite a gap of seventeen years (Gordian III was killed in 243, Philip the Arab made terms in 244, Valerian was captured in 260), is symbolically consistent with a triumphal scene. The only inconsistency are those two reliefs depicting just the two Roman emperors. Since all reliefs must have been carved after 260 – if the standing figure is indeed Valerian – there is no reason for leaving out the prostrate figure of Gordian III, the first of Shapur's clutch of emperors. If a relief was to depict only two emperors, therefore, it would be Gordian and Philip, not Philip and Valerian. But despite this inconsistency, the present identification is the most plausible.

The only other Sasanian relief that depicts a Roman is a later jousting scene at Naqsh-i Rustam that has been interpreted as Emperor Bahram II vanquishing the Roman

Plate 27 The Emperor Philip the Arab kneeling before the mounted figure of Shapur at Naqsh-i Rustam near Persepolis. The Emperor Valerian stands in the background

Emperor Carus.[44] Perhaps the most impressive and intriguing of all of Shapur's victory reliefs is the large one at Bishapur, curved like a cinerama screen, that depicts his victory in a series of five sequential panels, one above the other (Plate 25).[45] Here, we see virtually the full triumph: not only Shapur himself with the two Roman emperors discussed above, but long lines of both Persian soldiers and Roman prisoners. One authority emphasises the implicit non-violence and magnanimity depicted here of Shapur's victory: unlike Roman triumphs, which generally culminate in a blood-bath in the arena, Shapur's captives are depicted unchained, still allowed to bear arms, with dignity.[46] Included are horses, elephants and a Roman chariot.

But despite this being the most graphic representation of his victory, it is also the most curious. For it is atypical of Sasanian relief sculpture, which is almost invariably in the form of just single large panels. The technique of sequential panels, however, is typically Roman – used, for example, in the Column of Trajan. It also depicts a typical 'Roman' triumph; we have no idea whether the Sasanians held triumphs in this way. Furthermore, the sculptural details, although of poor quality, exhibit more of the characteristics of Roman than Persian craftsmanship. In other words, this relief was carved by the prisoners themselves to depict their own humiliation, the poorer quality in keeping with work carried out by soldiers rather than trained craftsmen.

Large numbers of Christians were also taken during Shapur's campaigns, adding greatly to the spread of Christianity through Iran.[47] Many might well have been voluntary exiles fleeing Valerian's persecutions. In fact the life of a Christian taken from the Roman Empire in Iran was not too bad: there was no persecution and no oppressive taxation, on the contrary the deportees were given grants of land. Even if the initial deportations were enforced, it seems likely that there would have been many more voluntary exiles following in their wake. Accordingly, many prospered. The Christians were the most organised of the Roman exiles and soon became the most prosperous, rising in the Sasanian Empire in ways that they could not have dreamt of in the Roman. For the pagan captives, Christianity would have been an attractive way of retaining their 'Roman' identity. Christians, therefore, flourished under Shapur's tolerant rule – a bishop from Iran was later to attend the Council of Nicaea. Syriac was the predominant language, but some Greek still survived into the fifth century. Two churches were built at Rev Ardeshir, one for Romans and one for native Iranians. Many Iranian Christians were presumably converts from Manichaeism, as Manichaeism incorporates Christianity and – unlike Christianity – was savagely persecuted by the Iranians as heterodox (from Zoroastrianism). The conversion of Armenia to Christianity was probably as much due to the Christians of Iran as to any impetus from the West. Later Armenian sources refer to the immense success of Iranian Christianity, spreading to the Kushan Empire and even down into India, where it still survives (in Kerala). There was some persecution of the Christians in Iran following the edict of persecution against the Manichaeans by the high-priest Kartir in the 280s, with whom the Zoroastrian clergy often confused the Christians. (Indeed many Manichaeans pretended to be Christians to escape persecution.)

One Christian deportee, Bar Saba, rose at the court of Shapur II as a physician. He became very influential and converted the Shah's sister, Princess Siraram, to Christianity. Alarmed, Shapur sent her away as far as he could, marrying her off to the provincial governor of Merv. Far from vanquishing Christianity, however, she took her faith with her where it found fertile ground in the Merv oasis as many of the inhabitants considered themselves 'Greek' descendants of Alexander.[48] Princess Siraram built a church, inviting Bar Saba to follow her and become Bishop of Merv. There followed the evangelisation of Central Asia. Christian buildings have been excavated by archaeologists at Merv, and a Christian church was still noted north of Herat as late as the tenth century.[49] But the Christianity of many of the Roman deportees is probably greatly exaggerated, as most of our sources are later Christian ones with vested interests.

Khusrau Anushirvan in the sixth century continued Shapur's policy of deportation and resettlement, when he founded a new city south of Ctesiphon named 'Better Antioch of Khusrau' with the captives from Antioch. It was constructed along standard Roman lines with baths, a hippodrome and other familiar amenities, being modelled as closely as possible after Antioch so that captives could even resettle in their own 'neighbourhoods' and enjoy the same pastimes as they did before. His new 'Better Antioch' was made a free city in the Persian Empire and awarded favourable status, so that by the end of the century its population had risen to 30,000.[50]

The Romans also deported prisoners captured in their Iranian campaigns, but unlike the Iranians, they had no coherent policy of resettlement. They would simply be used for their propaganda value, to be paraded and displayed at triumphs before being disposed of either in the arenas or the slave markets. Occasionally, Iranian soldiers would be incorporated into the Roman army as special units, particularly when the Romans had much to learn from specific Iranian military skills (such as cavalry techniques, or the use of heavy armour). But there was never any effort to create small Iranian enclaves nor to protect and encourage the separate identity and culture of their captives, as the Iranians did (although Newcastle-upon-Tyne seems to have been settled partially by Arabs).[51] On the whole, the captives of Rome were destined for public spectacle and eventual slaughter. The idea of actually encouraging their native culture and self-expression would never even have occurred to the Rome's. Rome's treatment of its captives could not stand in greater contrast to the Iranians' mild treatment of theirs.[52]

Roman trade

Rome in India (Figures 20 and 21)[53]

The presence of Rome in India rests upon a number of dramatic – indeed, spectacular – pieces of evidence: literary, numismatic and archaeological. Such is the dramatic quality of the evidence that it was once even thought that southern India formed a part of the Roman monetary system – a sort of early form of the sterling area – controlled through a series of colonies. This view seemed to decline with the passing of British India,[54] but the evidence for Roman expansion is certainly impressive.

One of the most important maps preserved from the ancient world is the Peutinger Table, a medieval copy of a fourth-century version of a Roman map of the world from the Augustan period. It shows the existence of a 'Temple to Augustus' at Muziris, one of the main ports for the Roman trade on the south-west coast of India.[55] This has been supplemented by references to the sea trade in Book 6 of Pliny's *Natural History* and descriptions in a number of other Classical works, such as the first-century AD *Periplus of the Erythraean Sea* and the sixth-century *Christian Topography* of Cosmas Indicopleustes.[56] But the number of actual named trading missions from the Roman world to India are extremely few. In the time of Claudius, a trader in Somalia called Iamblos (probably a Syrian) sailed to Ceylon and spent several years there before continuing on to 'Palibothra' (Pataliputra, modern Patna in north-eastern India) and returning overland. Pliny also recounts how a freedman of Annius Plocamus at about the same time sailed to Ceylon, returning with gifts from its ruler. To these can be added a handful of references to named traders mentioned on documents – mainly ostraca and graffiti – found at some of the Red Sea ports themselves. These refer to Egyptians, Greeks, Romans, Arabs and Indians resident in the Red Sea ports controlling the India trade.[57]

In a much discussed passage, Pliny estimates that some 100 million sesterces annually went eastwards from Rome during the time of Nero to pay for this trade. This figure has been questioned by many modern authorities. But if it is taken as referring to the actual value of the trade, rather than the amount of coinage as such, it becomes more believable. For example, just one documented consignment from Muziris to Alexandria consisted of 700–1,700 pounds of nard (an aromatic balsam), over 4,700 pounds of ivory and almost 790 pounds of textiles. This has been calculated as worth a total value of 131 talents, enough to purchase 2,400 acres of the best farmland in Egypt. When it is borne in mind that an average Roman cargo ship would have held about 150 such consignments, Pliny's figure becomes entirely plausible.[58] With such staggering profits it is little wonder that the Roman government in Egypt actively encouraged – and profited by! – the trade: a 25 per cent tax on all goods from India was levied by the Romans at the Red Sea port of Leuce Come. Small wonder that Pliny's protests went unnoticed by those in power.[59]

The most remarkable of the Classical sources for the trade is the mid-first-century AD *Periplus of the Erythraean Sea*. It is an anonymous maritime manual and navigational aid written by an Egyptian Greek for merchants sailing from the Red Sea to trade with east Africa, south Arabia and India. Most of the information it contains appears to be from personal experience. The importance of the *Periplus* as a document has been rated as

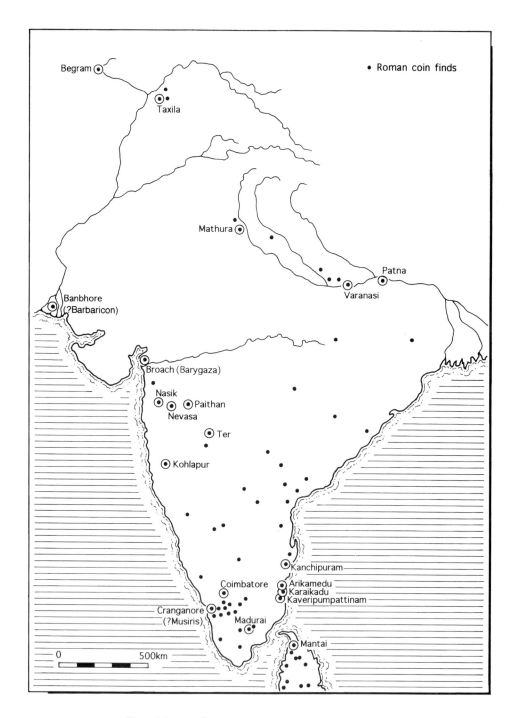

Figure 20 Map illustrating Roman-related sites in India

Begram

Taxila

• Roman coin finds

Mathura

Patna

Varanasi

Banbhore
(?Barbaricon)

Broach (Barygaza)

Nasik
Nevasa
Paithan

Ter

Kohlapur

Kanchipuram

Coimbatore

Arikamedu
Karaikadu
Kaveripumpattinam

Cranganore
(?Musiris)
Madurai

Mantai

0   500km

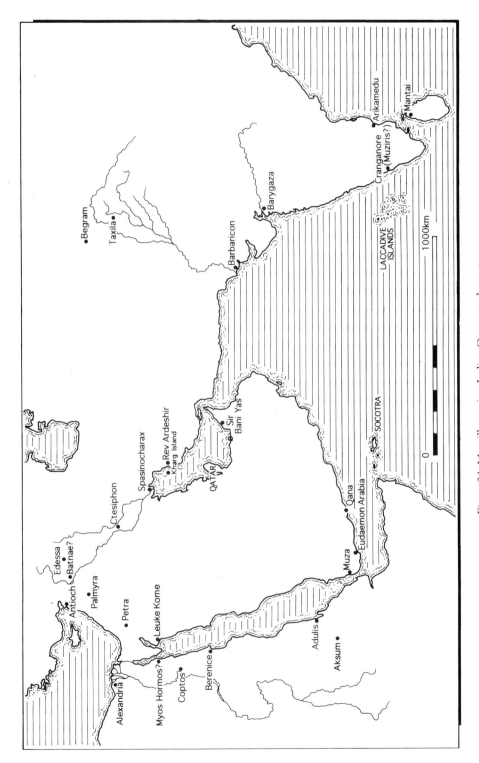

Figure 21 Map illustrating Indian Ocean trade routes

highly in the history of exploration as the accounts of Marco Polo or Columbus. It describes the sea route to India from the Red Sea ports of Myos Hormos and Berenice, thence to the ports of Mouza, Ocelis and Qana in south Arabia, thence either to Barbaricon and Barygaza in north-western India or to Muziris in southern India. The journey time averaged about six months. The routes into the Persian Gulf and down the east coast of Africa are also indicated, and information about the ports for much of the western and northern Indian Ocean as a whole is given. Some of the mainland routes are also out-lined, particularly into the interior of India from its west coast ports and into Central Asia from the mouth of the Indus. There is much information that would naturally be of concern to a navigator: supplies, safe anchorages and prevailing winds (in particular the monsoons). The *Periplus* is also a mine of information of prime importance for the economic historian: the products of particular lands, trade opportunities in particular ports, the movements of particular products, the peculiarities of the natives, etc. Altogether, it ranks with Strabo's *Geography* as one of the most important sources of the ancient historical geography of Asia that has come down to us.[60]

The Classical accounts are complemented in Indian literature to some extent by a number of references to foreigners known as the 'Yavanas'.[61] There has been much writ-ten – and speculated – upon the Yavanas. The word *Yavana* is derived from 'Ionia', from which nearly all eastern languages derive their word for 'Greek' or 'Greece': Old Persian *Yauna*, Hebrew *Yawan*, Arabic *Yunan*, Chinese *Ye-meï-ni*, etc.[62] The term – and its variations *Yona* and *Yonaka* – came into Indian languages as early as the third century BC following contact with Greeks after Alexander. Later, however, the meaning broadened to mean just 'westerner' generally rather than 'Greek' specifically. In this way, the Indian 'Yavana' can be likened to our own term 'Indian', which has been used to cover 'natives' broadly from the Far East to North America – or the term 'Feringhi', deriving from 'Frank', used throughout the East to designate any European, rather than Frenchman specifically.[63] Hence, when 'Yavana' occurs in contexts associated with Roman trade, it has often been taken as meaning 'Roman'.

In general, the Yavanas are associated with the western coast of India, so are consistent with a 'western' identification. Tamil literature of the second century AD has several such references. References are made, for example, to the wealthy houses of a 'Yavana' mer-chant colony at Puhar near Pondicherry and to 'Yavana' ships arriving with gold and leaving with pepper. Yavana merchants are also mentioned in association with the ancient trading centre of Tagara (modern Ter in Maharashthra) where many Roman and Roman-derived objects have been excavated.[64] Other Tamil texts describe the Yavanas as being in demand as carpenters, traders and craftsmen at Pumpahar in the Chola kingdom and elsewhere (where a possible Roman presence has been detected from excavations), as well as mercenaries and private bodyguards at Madurai, the capital of the Pandya kingdom. This latter reference might be the origin of a surprising passage in Plautus, referring to a Roman mercenary campaign in India. There are also some Indian art representations of Yavana bodyguards. Since both the Roman and Indian sources refer to the export of slaves from the Roman Empire to India, where they are known as Yavanas, the mercenar-ies might be the half-caste descendants of these slaves. In some Buddhist caves inland from Bombay there are votive inscriptions recording religious gifts by Yavanas. One of the more important of these caves, at Nasik, has a second-century inscription referring to the *Raumakas*, which some have identified with the Romans. Nasik also has dedicatory inscriptions by Yavanas and some Roman-derived objects (discussed below). Another

Tamil text refers to the excellence of the wines brought by the Yavanas, which suggests a Mediterranean origin.

Apart from literary sources, much of the evidence rests on various coin finds, mostly sporadic (Figure 20).[65] Many are hoards, such as the 1,531 *denarii* found at Akkampalle. Altogether, the Roman coin finds from southern India total some 5,400 *denarii* and 800 gold *aurei*. To these can be added 700 Roman coins found in the Laccadive Islands.[66] Of these, very few are republican. Most are Julio-Claudian, particularly of Augustus and Tiberius. This, however, does not reflect the date of the trade, as they were probably deposited long after the minting judging from the wear on them. The Julio-Claudian coins, as well as the few republican coins found, were of much higher quality than those issued after Nero, so were probably reserved for the trade. The evidence of the coins, therefore, must be hedged with many a caveat. After Nero's coin reform Roman coins virtually disappear, with payment either in gold bullion or the higher quality 'antique' Julio-Claudian coins, although some of the gold *aurei* continued and were even copied locally. The slump in the number of Roman coins reaching India in the third century has been interpreted as corresponding to Valerian's capture by Shapur in 260, although it is probably more symptomatic of a decline in wealth and trade generally. There is an increase again in the fourth century with a revival in the fifth with the establishment of the Byzantine gold *solidus*. The last coin finds are of Justinian.

The distribution of the coin finds appears to reflect the main trade routes in the broadest sense, with most of them – particularly the coin hoards – found within a 30-kilometre radius of the beryl mines at Coimbatore in southern India. Very few are found in northwestern India, despite the evidence for Roman trade there from literary sources, perhaps because the trade there was paid for in goods rather than money. Even coin finds in the south were probably not derived from trade in the monetary – modern – sense as the evidence might initially suggest, as the coins more likely represent a trade in metal rather than actual face value. However, the coins were often imitated on bullae for their decorative use (mainly jewellery), which suggests that Roman coins did nonetheless enjoy a certain amount of status. It must also be remembered that any perceived pattern derived from archaeological distribution is so often merely a reflection of current research rather than historical actuality.[67]

The numismatic evidence is complemented by the archaeological, although much of this is indirect. Roman amphorae – including Indian imitations – have been found near the coasts of Gujerat and Tamil Nadu. This confirms the importance of Broach and the site of Arikamedu (discussed below) respectively in the trade with the West, although the only complete amphora stamp (probably from Pompeii) was found at Mathura. The amphorae, most of which were found at Arikamedu, almost all derived from the wine trade, possibly Greek wine from Cos, but garum from Greece and olive oil from Spain were also exported to India in amphorae.[68] Southern Gallic and northern Italian Arretine ware of the first century BC to fifth century AD has also been found, again mainly at Arikamedu and Gujerat. The bulk of the Arikamedu Arretine ware has been dated precisely to 10–30 AD. The existence of Arretine ware in India has prompted speculation that it inspired a similar ceramic, Indian red-polished ware, produced in Gujerat. But despite Gujerat figuring highly in the Roman trade, the production of Indian red-polished ware begins before the rise of trade with Rome, so it more likely evolved out of native styles with the resemblance to Mediterranean wares illusory.[69] Another Indian ceramic, however, Rouletted ware, probably does derive from Roman prototypes. Rouletted ware is found mainly on the east coast, although none found to date are demonstrably Roman originals. But both red-polished ware and Rouletted ware are essentially local ceramics, local to the west and east coasts respectively. Other Roman objects, such as terracotta heads and statuettes, were widely imitated in the Deccan.[70]

Roman glass has been found in considerable quantities in southern and western India, again mainly at Arikamedu, where the discovery of glass ingots and wasters suggest a production centre, perhaps from raw glass transported from the Mediterranean as ballast.[71] Other Roman and Roman-related finds, such as the occasional Samian sherd, imitation 'Megarian' bowls, glass, intaglios, mirrors and other bronzes, have been recovered from excavations at the sites of Nasik, Ter, Paithan, Nevasa and Kanchipuram in central and southern India. Nasik is the site of important Buddhist caves that contained dedications by Yavanas (discussed above). Ter, ancient Tagara, was an important inland trading station in Maharashthra. Paithan (ancient Pratishthana near Aurangabad) was the capital of the ancient Satavahana kingdom. Amongst the most impressive Roman finds were a series of 102 bronzes from Kohlapur in Maharashthra, consisting of vessels, statuettes (including a fine Poseidon), lamps, mirrors, stands and tools. Most were Indian imitations, but at least ten were genuine Roman imports, probably from Campania.[72]

The most extensive evidence for Roman trade has been found, as would be expected, at a number of sites at the southern coast tip of India. At Kaveripumpattinam (ancient Pumpahar on the Coromandel coast) a brick wharf was excavated associated with Rouletted ware and Roman coins. Probably the most important site for the Indo-Roman trade after Arikamedu is Karaikadu (or Kudikadu) near Cuddalore, also on the Coromandel coast, about 30 kilometres south of Arikamedu. Roman and Roman imitation wares were found there, as well as more evidence for glass and bead manufacture, probably Roman in origin. Fragments of Mediterranean amphorae and other related finds have been found at several other coastal sites, including Alagankulam on the Coromandel coast nearest Sri Lanka (currently the scene of new excavations) and Kanchipuram, just inland between Pondicherry and Madras.[73]

The most dramatic archaeological evidence for the Roman trade was revealed by the excavations at Arikamedu, a small coastal settlement on the Coromandel coast just to the south of Pondicherry.[74] The revelations of Mortimer Wheeler's excavations there in the 1940s are best described in his own words:

> This village, like its modern equivalents in the neighbourhood, doubtless consisted of simple fisher-folk who caught the gullible fish of the region from the shore or from small outriggers, gathered the fruits and juices of the palms, cultivated rice-patches, and lived in a leisurely and unenterprising fashion just above subsistence level. To it suddenly, from unthought of lands 5,000 miles away, came strange wines, table-wares far beyond the local skill, lamps of a strange sort, glass, cut gems. . . . A small foreign quarter like that of Puhar came into being, and finally the village was replaced by a brick-built town, spreading northwards to the sea.[75]

Wheeler's and later excavations here have brought to light what appears to be a Roman trading colony, identified with the port of Poduke mentioned in the *Periplus*. The date was from the early first century AD to about 200. A warehouse and industrial area was found, as well as some possible dying vats. No houses or monumental buildings were found. Arikamedu is the only site where Arretine *terra siggilata* has been excavated; it does not appear to have been imported elsewhere in India. This has prompted the suggestion that it might have been imported just as personal table ware by the Roman expatriate community.[76]

Wheeler sums up the excitement that was felt at this astonishing discovery when he writes that 'the imagination of the modern enquirer kindles as he lifts from the alluvium of the Bay of Bengal sherds bearing the names of craftsmen whose kilns lay on the outskirts of Arezzo. From the woods of Hertfordshire to the palm-groves of the Coromandel, these red-glazed cups and dishes symbolise the routine adventures of tradesmen whose story may be set only a little below that of King Alexander himself.'[77] But a more cautionary note is provided by David Whitehouse, himself an excavator of the ancient trading ports of the Indian Ocean:

> The question, of course, is: do 150 fragments of Mediterranean amphorae, 50 fragments of Arretine ware, a handful of Roman glass, two pieces of Roman lamps, one engraved gem, and what may be a Roman stylus, deposited over a period of more than 200 years, really add up to a 'colony of Westerners'? The answer, I suspect, is no. The Roman finds from pre-Claudian Colchester in southern England are not wholly dissimilar from the Roman finds from Arikamedu (fragments of at least 13 amphorae, 26 Arretine vessels, and 3 glass objects, deposited in less than 40 years) – and there is no reason to suppose that the population included a community of resident aliens. Until we find distinctive 'colonial' architecture or a Greek or Latin inscription, I think we would do well to regard the possibility of a Roman community at Arikamedu as a hypothesis that cannot at present be tested.[78]

Or, as an Indian historian writes more bluntly: 'The results of these early excavations at Arikamedu continue to maintain a stranglehold on Indian historical writing. . . . An elementary calculation of the few hundred amphorae sherds representing a span of four centuries at Arikamedu would make it obvious that they do not translate into the flourishing [Mediterranean] wine trade that Wheeler made out.'[79]

Such 'colonial' architecture as the Peutinger Table's Temple of Augustus is still beyond our grasp, and much else of 'Roman India' must of necessity be highly speculative. From the above combination of literary, numismatic and archaeological evidence, the history of the maritime trade to India can be summed up. The existence of maritime trade between the ancient Near East and India hardly requires the *Periplus* and other sources to demonstrate: such a trade was in place thousands of years before they were written.[80] But it was revolutionised with the exploitation of the monsoons about AD 40–50 and the increasing demand for luxury goods – particularly spices – by Rome. The two most important ports in India for the Roman trade were Barygaza and Muziris. Barygaza is the modern city of Broach in Gujerat. Muziris – and its supposed Temple of Augustus – has never been identified. It was probably near Cannanore on the north coast of Kerala, where pepper is, and was, the main product, or perhaps further south at Karur near Cranganore, where a Roman coin hoard was recently found.[81] Small scale excavations at Cranganore itself, however, revealed no evidence for Roman trade.[82] Up until the second century AD, the trade was mainly with the Buddhist Tamil kingdoms of southern India, the Cheras on the south-west coast, the Cholas on the south-east and the Pandyas at the southern tip. A secondary sea route reached the Indo-Scythian and later Kushan kingdoms at the mouth of the Indus at Barbaricon in north-western India. Both of these kingdoms stretched into Central Asia. There was a decline after Marcus Aurelius, reflecting a decline in the Empire generally. Ethiopians and Arabians most likely became the middlemen rather than the Alexandrians, and barter replaced gold, hence showing up less in the archaeological record. With the revival of the trade after the fourth century, Ceylon was the main trade mart.

After the fifth century the Nestorian Church became prominent in the trade. The Nestorians were a Christian sect centred in Syria who were savagely persecuted by the Orthodox court in Constantinople, being forced to flee progressively further eastwards. Rome's loss not only reinvigorated intellectual life in Iran but also stimulated much of the trade of Asia, both overland and maritime. Their role in the China trade is reviewed separately below. In the Persian Gulf and Indian Ocean regions the Nestorians established a number of communities, with bishoprics throughout southern Iran, southern Mesopotamia, northern Arabia and western and southern India. Metropolitans were established in Charax, Rev Ardeshir (Bushehr) and Qatar, and descendants of these Nestorians form the Christian population of Kerala in India today. Nestorian church complexes have been excavated on a number of islands in the Gulf, notably Kharg Island off Iran and Sir Bani Yas off Abu Dhabi, and smaller Christian remains have been excavated elsewhere on the Gulf. Many of the pilots were Nestorians, and there seems little doubt that much of the actual mechanism of the trade was in the hands of Nestorian seafarers operating under the protection of Sasanian Iran. One of our main sources for the Indian Ocean trade, the *Christian Topography* of Cosmas Indicopleustes, was Nestorian. Being mainly Syrian in origin, the Nestorians were simply inheriting a tradition that had begun by the Palmyrenes.[83]

The Nestorian connections must be seen against the background of early Christian proselytising in the East. The most famous is the supposed journey of the Apostle Thomas. He travelled to the court of the Indo-Parthian king Gondophares at Taxila in the middle of the first century BC and supposedly converted the people of Malabar in southern India, who preserve the tradition to this day. The apocryphal Gospel of Thomas was fundamental to the development of Gnosticism and Manichaeism. The story, like so many of the early spread of Christianity, was probably compiled at Edessa in about 250. Another such mission was of the Sicilian-born Christian, Pantaenus, who left Alexandria in about 180 and sailed to India. Here, he found native Christians who had been converted by St Bartholomew and showed him Matthew's gospel in the original Hebrew. It is possible that there is considerable confusion between the Bartholomew–Thomas–Pantaenus traditions – not to mention the journey of the pagan philosopher Apollonius of Tyana to northern India, paralleled so closely by the Thomas story.[84]

By the sixth century Iran ruled the waves from naval bases throughout the Gulf as well as in south Arabia, the mouth of the Indus and possibly Ceylon, with mercantile colonies stretching from the East African coast to the South China Sea. The Indian Ocean was becoming an Iranian lake and the trade dominated, to a lesser extent, by the Indians and Ethiopians as well; no Roman ships are mentioned at all. In the sixth century the Emperor Anastasius, and later Justinian, made efforts in Arabia and the Red Sea to try and circumvent Iran's control of Asian trade, but to no avail. Mantai in Ceylon had replaced the southern Indian ports as the main trade entrepôt for this time. It may, in part, have even been controlled by the Sasanians.[85]

Items imported from India were mainly luxury goods, for only their high retail value in western markets could justify the high cost of transporting them across such distances. They included silk, pearls, precious woods, ivory, precious stones and spices such as cinnamon, nard, cassia, cardamom and pepper. Occasionally, exotic animals such as tigers and leopards would be imported. There may also have been occasional female Indian slaves. Pearls figured highly, and precious stones were entirely from the East (amber was the only one from Europe). Above all, spices were the main import from the East, especially pepper – Warmington details every stage of the movement of pepper from the forests of Kerala to the Roman middle-class table. Silk (which mainly came via India rather than direct from China – see below) was never the main commodity, despite the high profile given to it in modern accounts.[86]

Recent archaeological studies have tended to focus attention almost entirely on the Red Sea, and hence on the primary role of Roman Egypt, in the trade to India. Because of the admittedly spectacular finds of Roman coins and pottery, more attention has also been focused on southern rather than north-western India. But this has diverted attention from the Persian Gulf, which probably played just as big or bigger a part. The Gulf, furthermore, was dominated by Palmyrenes, Arabs and Iranians rather than Romans, and was pre-eminent in the India trade long before the Roman period. According to Chinese sources the Indian trade with the Roman Empire went via the Gulf rather than the Red Sea and recent discoveries of a large amount of Roman glassware of the first century BC to the first century AD in the Emirates have confirmed a Roman involvement in this trade. This was, after all, the Palmyrene route and Indian and Chinese merchants themselves would sail up the Euphrates to the Palmyrene-controlled trade fair at Batnae. Moreover, the bulk of the Chinese trade with the Roman Empire would have been transhipped through north-western India and the Gulf.[87] This is discussed more below, and the part played by the Indians themselves in this trade is discussed further in Chapter 8. But for the moment, it is worth remembering that our picture of the expansion of Roman trade into southern India built up from the Peutinger Table, the *Periplus*, the coins and Arikamedu is only a part of the whole picture, and perhaps the lesser part at that.

In the long history of this extraordinary interaction between two such widely different ancient civilisations, the role of the Romans has been much exaggerated. This is partly because of cultural bias, and partly because we simply know more about the Roman side.[88] The Yavanas were not necessarily Romans or even Greeks, but might just as easily be Arabs or Ethiopians or even Iranians. The *Periplus*, important though it undoubtedly may be, is after all just an isolated document hardly longer than the modern reviews of its latest edition. The much vaunted 'Temple of Augustus' at Muziris was probably merely a temple to a local cult *approximated* with the Augustus cult, much as non-Roman temples and cults everywhere outside the direct Roman world were. Despite the well-established knowledge of the sea routes implicit in the *Periplus*, the Romans seemed totally unaware of the origin of many main trade items they supposedly controlled. Cardamom, for example, was described as originating in Armenia, Media or Assyria, never Ceylon; cinnamon and many other commodities were thought to be from south Arabia or north-east Africa, never Malaya; rice was thought to be from Ethiopia rather than the Far East, etc. This suggests that the Romans neither controlled nor even knew about the sea routes as much as we think. Indeed, the highly effective policy of misinformation about the origin of such products, mainly by the south Arabians, at the height of the supposed 'Roman' trade suggests a domination of the trade routes by the Arabians and Indians at the expense of the Romans.[89]

The discoveries of Roman coin hoards in India are certainly dramatic. But coin deposits are notoriously unreliable as archaeological evidence, and numismatic conclusions often a little too glib. Coins and coin hoards with their ready answers can so often be almost as much a problem in archaeology as an asset. Archaeological discoveries in the future, for example, of hoards of nineteenth-century Maria-Theresa dollars in twentieth-century Yemen would in no way imply any Austrian colonies there. Similarly with any 'discovery' of hoards of US dollars almost anywhere in the world today (not least in the hands of countries, such as Iran or Iraq, most outside America's sphere of influence). The occurrence of most of the Roman coin hoards within a 30-kilometre radius of the beryl mines, for example, ostensibly appears to be a very satisfying (and certainly often quoted) bit of evidence – until one recalls that beryl was one of the least important items of export.[90] Coin hoards closer to Arikamedu, where nearly all discussion of Roman trade and colonies focus, are conspicuous by their absence. Clearly it is a mistake to pin too much on these coins – far more Roman coin hoards have been found, for example, in Poland and Germany.[91] One must remember above all that the sum total of *all* Roman coin finds in India is still only 5,400 *denarii* and 800 *aurei*, totalling perhaps some 100,000 *sestercii* – or a mere .01 per cent of just the annual flow of cash according to Pliny's figures that we have reviewed above. Even in making generous allowances for Pliny's exaggeration (which, as we have seen above, is quite likely accurate), this still represents only a negligible amount of the evidence.

Similarly, the archaeological evidence for Roman trade in southern India is not quite as positive as it seems, as the cautionary remarks quoted above imply. Archaeological evidence has a nasty habit of reflecting patterns of modern research opportunities rather than patterns of ancient trade. The Roman finds from Arikamedu might suggest a colony of 'Romans' (more likely Syrians or Alexandrians, and certainly not the 'convincing evidence' for a Roman colony as one major authority supposes).[92] But contrast this with Taxila in north-western India, a site which in theory would be far more likely to contain a Roman merchant colony, where Roman and Roman-related finds are very few. The finds of gems and intaglios in India with Classical motifs, which are often indiscriminately labelled 'Roman', more likely derive from Indo-Greek prototypes and are not the evidence for Roman trade they seem to be.[93] The discovery of objects brought from a long distance do not in any case presuppose the existence of an organised trade 'system' as such: the finds of cloves, for example, in the second-millennium BC city of Terqa on the Euphrates in no way implies direct trade with Indonesia at that time.[94]

It is highly unlikely that the Roman bulk cargo vessels, used for transporting grain and other bulk cargoes across the Mediterranean, could have sailed the Indian Ocean as is assumed.[95] They would not have stood up to the heavy wear and their square rig was too primitive for the sophisticated navigation that deep ocean sailing demanded. India had a long ship-building tradition, with ocean-going boats being built in Gujerat from the second century BC. These were large enough to carry between 500 and 700 passengers according to Indian sources, or 3,000 amphorae (corresponding to 75 tons) according to Pliny.[96] The traditional vessel of the Indian Ocean, the Arab stitched vessel or *sambuq*, was far more seaworthy, as tests have shown, and probably the only type of vessel that would have made the crossing in ancient times.[97] This in itself suggests a greater role in the trade for the Arabs and the Indians (where the stitched dhows probably originated) than the texts suggest, although this does not, of course, exclude Roman merchants sailing on Arab and Indian vessels. In this context it must be borne in mind that the *Periplus* is a handbook aimed at merchants rather than navigators.

The Iranians – at least after Ardeshir I – made a deliberate effort to exert control over the Persian Gulf and the India trade which, by the fifth and sixth centuries, resulted in Iran probably being the major maritime power in the western Indian Ocean.[98] The Arabs, too, were after all as actively involved in the Mediterranean sea trade as they were in the Indian Ocean, a role they inherited from the Phoenicians.[99] This and the movement westwards of Indians and Indian ideas into the Roman Empire is reviewed separately in Chapter 8.

Rome in Central Asia and China[100]

Nowhere has the presence of Rome in Asia fired more speculation, excitement and imagination than in China and Central Asia. The reason can be summed up in two words: the Silk Road. The Silk Road is one of the most romantic of images known to history. Images amongst the most evocative we know that found their echoes in the poetry of Flecker and Coleridge, not to mention a vast array of travel writing. It has conjured up an image of a great international and multinational highway where Romans, Chinese, Indians and Tartars freely met and intermingled. The evidence for the 'Silk Road' and Roman trade to China, therefore, requires very careful examination. Again, the evidence rests on a combination of literary references and archaeological remains.

Just as the sea route to India is documented by an extraordinary ancient text, the *Periplus of the Erythraean Sea*, so too is the land route through western Asia. This is the *Parthian Stations*, a handbook written by a Greek native of lower Mesopotamia, Isidore of Charax. Charax, or Characene, lay at the head of the Persian Gulf. It became a major trading partner with Palmyra during the first few centuries AD, enjoying a similar semi-independent status under Iran that Palmyra did under Rome. Both were able, therefore, to dominate the Rome–Iran trade disproportionate to the small size of the two kingdoms. Characene had the additional advantage of its strategic location at the head of the Gulf, thereby being in a favourable position to control sea routes to the east.[101] Isidore of Charax lived in the first century AD, although both his date and his identity is subject to dispute. His *Parthian Stations* is probably just a fragment of a larger work, now lost. It describes one specific route, from Mesopotamia through Iran to Arachosia (Kandahar in Afghanistan), listing the stopping places, main cities and distances along the way.[102]

To this main source can be added the other main western sources for Asia mentioned above in relation to India: Ptolemy, Pliny, Strabo and parts of the *Periplus*, together with Ammianus Marcellinus in the third century. As we have seen, they are mainly concerned with the maritime routes, only describing overland routes where they relate to the Indian Ocean ports. In particular, a major overland route connected ports in north-western India with Bactria in Central Asia through Kushan territory (centred on present-day Afghanistan). This route is where the most archaeological evidence has been found (see below). A minor route, mentioned by Pliny and Strabo, ran via the Black and Caspian seas, thence the Oxus River upstream to Bactria (the Oxus having emptied into the Caspian in that period rather than into the Aral Sea as it does today).[103] Some archaeological evidence for a 'steppe route' to the north of this has also been detected,[104] although it is unlikely that this was regularly used.

From occasional such references, we obtain a glimmer of some Roman overland trade, although nothing comparable to the quantity or quality that relates to the Indian Ocean trade. In the time of Hadrian, for example, agents of the Syrian merchant Maes Titianus travelled eastwards as far as the Chinese border at 'Stone Tower', possibly identified with Tashkurghan (Turkish for 'stone fort' or 'tower') in the Pamir mountains and Ptolemy refers to trade in the second–third centuries as far as Cattigora (Canton).[105] There is little more. Even the *Parthian Stations*, on closer examination, proves to provide far less information on Roman trade than might initially be expected – and certainly far less than the *Periplus*. For the *Parthian Stations* is little more than the title implies: a record of just one of several official routes *within* Iran, relating to Parthian administration rather than trade, and even less to Rome. It makes no reference to any supposed connections beyond, neither to the Mediterranean nor to China. As evidence for Roman overland trade, therefore, it is practically valueless.

Some evidence of a Roman presence of a very indirect kind through Asia is found in a number of recurring place names relating to the Emperor Decius (AD 249–51). This is the name *Daqianus* or *Shahr-i Daqianus* ('City of Decius') that can be found associated with a number of archaeological sites from Turkey to China. The name is applied, for example, to the ruins of the medieval city of Jiruft in south-eastern Iran, an area of low mounds covered in pottery that stretches for many miles.[106] The name is also applied to the site of Karakhoja or Khocho (Chinese Gaochang), the main ancient city of the Turfan Oasis in Xinjiang between the fifth and ninth centuries. Its remains include Buddhist, Zoroastrian, Manichaean and Nestorian Christian religious buildings. In addition to the name Shahr-i Daqianus, it is also known locally as *Apsus* or 'Ephesus'. In the neighbouring valley of Toyuq is a famous Islamic cave shrine, replacing an earlier Buddhist shrine, that attracts pilgrims from throughout Islamic China known as the 'Cave of the Seven Sleepers [of Ephesus]'.[107] The same association of Daqianus, Ephesus and the Cave of the Seven Sleepers is found in northern Iraq as well as in north-western Afghanistan, several places in Turkey and elsewhere in central and western Asia. In north-western Afghanistan, for example, the cave of Ashab al-Kahf near Maimana is locally supposed to be the resting place of the Seven Sleepers and is associated with Daqianus, as well as a nearby ruined city called *Shahr-i Afsuz* or 'Ephesus'.[108] All relate, of course, to the persecution of the Christians by the Emperor Decius which entered into legend in the story of the Seven Sleepers of Ephesus. Its occurrence throughout Asia, however, is probably due to traditions that arrived with Islam rather than the Romans, for the tradition is preserved in the ʾQurʾan (18: 9–27).

Whilst hardly 'Roman', one aspect of Roman Syria was to have a profound effect upon Central Asia for over a thousand years. This was Nestorian Christianity. We have already observed above ('Rome in India') how the Nestorian Syrians, following their persecution in the Roman Empire, became active after the fifth century in operation of the sea trade with the East. They were similarly active inland. The combination of Christian missionary activity and the Sasanian deportations from Syria had already made Christianity an important minority religion in Iran by the third century, with missionaries reaching Merv in Central Asia by AD 200 or earlier.[109] In 410–15 Syrian sources describe the establishment of a Metropolitan See in Samarkand. In 635 Chinese sources mention a Nestorian missionary from Syria establishing a church in Xinjiang, with further missions taking Nestorian Christianity to China after the early eighth century.[110] It certainly took root in Central Asia as early as the fifth century, becoming one of the main religions of the Soghdians after the sixth century and of the Uighur Empire of Xinjiang after the eighth century. Many archaeological discoveries, in both the former Soviet Union and in China, attest to its importance. These have included the churches themselves as well as paintings and manuscripts still written in Aramaic as late as the twelfth century. From the Uighurs, Nestorianism passed to the Mongols, forming an important element – not to mention a strong Christian lobby – in the Mongol aristocracy following the conquests of Chingiz Khan. Nestorianism in Central Asia was the main origin of the medieval European legends of Prester John, the oriental Christian Empire which would join forces with western Christendom to drive the Muslims from the Holy Land. One Nestorian priest from Peking even performed mass for Edward I of England at his court in 1297.[111]

Chinese sources have little more to offer. Later Han annals refer to the arrival of Romans: an envoy representing 'the King of Da-tsin, An-tun' in 166. Da-tsin is the later Chinese name for Rome and 'An-tun' is presumably Marcus Aurelius Antoninus. This 'envoy' landed at Annam and was probably a Syrian – or Palmyrene – and is thought to have been a private merchant rather than an official representative of Marcus Aurelius. In 226 another Roman merchant called Ts'in Lun (probably another Syrian) reached Vietnam and China, being received by the Emperor Wu at Nanking, and in 284 another trade delegation from Roman Egypt presented the emperor of China with goods. Chinese sources also mention jugglers coming from Syria between the second century BC and second century AD. Syria was certainly famous for its jugglers in the Classical sources.[112] All of these chance remarks, however, are not evidence of any overland 'Silk Route', but merely of sea trade.[113]

In contrast to the Roman lack of interest in lands to the east of their borders, the first great Chinese imperial expansion in the first few centuries BC was marked by a distinct drive to the west, together with efforts to gain first-hand intelligence. The most energetic of the Han emperors, Wu Ti (141–87 BC), sent his general Chang Chi'en on two major diplomatic missions westwards. Chang himself travelled as far west as Ferghana (in present-day Uzbekistan), gathering intelligence on all the lands he passed through, as well as on Bactria, India and Iran. This resulted in Wu Ti establishing direct relations with Mithradates the Great of Iran in about 113 BC as we have seen. At the end of the first century BC another mission was sent to Iran under Kan Ying. Although Kan Ying was apparently treated to some deliberate misinformation about the trade routes further west by the Iranians anxious to keep it to themselves, some information about the western lands and the Roman Empire was brought back. The Emperor Yang Ti (605–17) tried unsuccessfully to establish direct relations with Constantinople, and there was a resurgence of Chinese interest in the Roman Empire after the establishment of the Tang dynasty in 618, when a fairly detailed Chinese description of Constantinople was produced.[114]

Archaeological remains, despite their occasionally spectacular nature, add surprisingly little to the picture derived from literature. In the Far East, Roman or Roman-inspired Antonine intaglios were excavated at the site of Oc-Eo, a trading station in the Mekong Delta just inland from the Gulf of Thailand. At another Mekong site, P'ong Tuk, a Roman bronze lamp was found, and a coin of Maximian was found in the Tonkin region. But it must be emphasised that such chance remains – and even the mentions in the Chinese sources – are no more than odd snippets. Any evidence for Roman trade with south-east Asia is largely illusory, more likely to have arrived through Indian middlemen rather than directly, and in any case is evidence for sea trade, not overland.[115] In Central Asia there have been occasional Roman coin finds, from Tiberius through to

Justinian, as well as a few other Roman and Roman-derived objects: vessels, terracottas, glass, bronze, jewellery, etc.[116] Most of the coin finds, however, are from stupa deposits, so are questionable as evidence for trade, and none of these finds compare in quantity with those found in India.

Perhaps the most spectacular archaeological evidence for a Roman cultural presence in Central Asia is the discoveries at Begram. Begram was one of the royal cities of the Kushan Empire in the first–third centuries AD. Two rooms excavated in the palace contained an astonishing treasure that comprised an eclectic collection of works of art from all over Asia. It included stuccoes, bronzes, ivories from India, lacquers from China and – most important for the present discussion – among the most impressive collections of Roman glassware that have ever been discovered (Plate 28). The treasure has been interpreted variously, but mostly as either a private royal collection by the Kushan kings for aesthetic purposes – an ancient 'museum' – or as tax in kind of the luxury goods which were traded through Begram, with the rooms in which they were found some sort of bonded warehouse. Either way, it is graphic evidence indeed for both the trade between China, India and the Roman world, and the nature of the goods traded.[117]

Controversy, however, has centred on the date of the treasure. There are many archaeological and stratigraphical problems relating to the excavations in the 1930s and 1940s, so that dating has had to be dependent almost entirely upon stylistic analyses of the treasure itself. The objects range over a long period, making any date for their deposition difficult. Most opinion favours a mid-third-century AD deposition,[118] but an important recent study has re-examined the glass in the light of current knowledge of Roman glassware. The glass is seen to be fundamentally different from the Roman glass of Syria and

Plate 28 Glass beaker with a gladiator: part of the Roman glassware from Begram, Afghanistan, now in the Musée Guimet. (Photo: © Agence Photographique de la Réunion des Musées Nationaux, Paris)

Palestine, the closest similarities being with Egyptian glass. Some might even have originated in Yemen. The glass is now re-dated to between 50 and 125 AD, favouring an early second-century AD date for the concealment of the treasure.[119]

The artistic implications of this are discussed more below ('Romano-Buddhist' art). More important for the present discussion are the Egyptian and Red Sea origins of the glassware. This implies that the glass reached Begram by sea via the Red Sea and India, thence by land to the Hindu Kush, following the route described above (Roman trade with India) and in the *Periplus*. If the route was directly overland, it is far more likely that the objects would be from Syrian workshops rather than Egyptian and Yemeni. The Begram treasures, therefore, support a sea route from the Mediterranean to Central Asia, rather than the land route initially implied.[120]

The Roman Empire could provide little that China wanted. Glass was important, and the Begram glass might have been such imports en route to China, but most glass found in Xinjiang is probably of local manufacture, not Mediterranean. Silk, the most publicised item of the China trade, in fact only arrived indirectly via India, rather than on any purported 'Silk Route' overland through Asia.[121] Despite its glamour, the import of silk into the Roman Empire was never the main commodity from the East, but was far exceeded by spices and other commodities. With little to trade in return, the silk had to be paid for in gold coinage. This makes the almost complete absence of Roman coins in China all the more surprising, especially when compared to India. Apart from a few isolated finds the only hoard was one consisting of sixteen coins from Tiberius to Aurelian found at Xian, and some Byzantine gold coins found in Xinjiang. Once again, this paucity suggests that the China trade was largely indirect, coming via India rather than overland through Iran.[122] The real question that must be posed concerning Roman trade with China, therefore, is not what *Roman* objects are found in China, but what Indian?

The route to China from the Mediterranean was, therefore, at best indirect. It was mainly just a part of the India trade and the sea routes; there were never any direct overland routes established with China. The overland trade that did exist went from either the Red Sea or the Persian Gulf to Barygaza (Broach) in north-western India; in other words it was indistinguishable from the India trade reviewed above. As for Palmyra's much vaunted part in this 'Silk Road', it formed more a part of the sea routes, for Palmyra's trade went down the Euphrates and thence to the Persian Gulf.[123] From Barygaza the trade went northwards through the Kushan Empire that straddled north-western India and Central Asia, and eventually to China, with much of the mechanism of the trade probably in the hands of Soghdian merchants from the environs of Samarkand.[124]

From the Chinese end, any drive towards the west was motivated above all by the problem of the Hsiung-nu and other warlike nomadic nations on their north-west frontier, not by any interest in the Roman Empire and even less by what goods they had to offer. The nomad problem dominated Chinese politics almost obsessively for many centuries – as the Great Wall today bears mute testimony – and Chinese policies in Central Asia were invariably diplomatic and military efforts at out-manoeuvring the steppe nations. Trade and economy was only secondary. When it did figure, it was aimed at gaining control over the sources of raw material – such as jade – and livestock in the Tien Shan Mountains.[125] Trade further west was of negligible interest, and efforts by the Han Chinese to 'link up' with some hypothetical trans-Asian caravan routes entirely myth. Political contacts further west – such as those established with the Parthians – were solely to diplomatically outflank the Hsiung-nu rather than for trade.

None of the routes, therefore, were part of any concerted overland trade mechanism aimed at linking China and the West. Of the few bits of both archaeological and literary evidence that we have, by far the bulk supports a mainly sea route from the Persian Gulf and Red Sea to north-western India, thence through the Kushan Empire. Other overland routes were almost negligible in terms of Roman trade links with Central Asia. In reviewing the evidence for these routes, one senses that we have inherited a little of our Victorian forebears' obsession with routes, dominated as it is by concerns with wheeled transport. In actual fact, established routes – lines drawn with such confidence across maps – were largely non-existent in ancient times, the itineraries of Isadore of Charax (or the ninth-century Arab geographers) notwithstanding. There were rarely ever 'roads' or even trade mechanisms in the organisational sense, with all the associated paraphernalia that define roads and trade routes in more recent history. Ancient 'routes' were nothing more than amorphous networks, with many minor branches and offshoots subject to endless fluctuations and variations. They even varied from journey to journey as well as from period to period, depending upon the myriad factors of supplies, water, trading opportunities, political circumstances and security. In the days before wheeled transport a route need not even be a track: for animal transport, anywhere barring high mountains would qualify as a route – and even many high mountainous regions qualified. The greatest mountain barrier in the world, for example, the Pamir and Karakorum 'knot', may appear impenetrable but was honeycombed with routes in antiquity where only one exists now.[126] It seems ironic that in such terrain the motor car and twentieth-century technology creates far more barriers than it conquers. Any ancient 'route', therefore, was at best simply a broad channel of communications across a region for the movement of people, goods and ideas. It rarely followed any fixed pathway. It was never transcontinental.

In reviewing the vast literature on the subject, one gains the strong impression that the whole story of the Rome–China trade has been vastly exaggerated by the myth of the Silk Route. The images it evokes now could not be further from the truth. Such is the power of the Silk Road today that few realise that the whole thing is a modern fabrication. The term was only coined in the mid-nineteenth century by the Baron von Richtofen, a German geographer of Central Asia, to describe the largely imagined silk trade with China in Roman–Han times.[127] Even then the term did not come into common usage until the twentieth century. The person now probably associated with the 'Silk Road' more than anybody else, Marco Polo, would never have heard of the term. It was not until 1938 that a book was first published entitled *The Silk Road*, by Sven Hedin, himself one of the main explorers of the region. Another of the same title was published in 1966.[128] Since then the term has not only gained credence, but has caught both popular and academic imagination with an enthusiasm bordering mania proportions. Any number of spurious tracks throughout most countries between the Mediterranean and China are confidently pointed out as 'the Silk Road' – not only by tourist guides but by academics who should know better. Modern scholarship has become almost obsessed with the idea and virtually all discussion of Roman trade with the East revolves around it, with the 'Silk Road' being the glib answer to all questions of trade and communication. It is significant that Edward Gibbon, writing of Roman trade with the East before this contemporary obsession, makes no reference to any purported 'Silk Road' or route nor even any reference to China. Eastern trade was seen – correctly – solely in terms of Arabia and India, China is not mentioned, and silk only referred to in passing in reference to India and the spice trade.[129] Today, there seem to be few references to the history or geography of the inner Asian countries without some reference to it. The fall of the Iron Curtain in 1989 prompted a virtual 'Silk Road' mania. Its 'reopening' has been formally announced on several occasions, even by heads of state,[130] and there is a rash of 'Silk Road' conferences, projects, exhibitions, institutions and publications of every description at highest academic level. The 'Silk Road', in other words, has now been elevated to historic fact.[131]

But the fact remains that the existence of the 'Silk Road' is not based on a single shred of historical or material evidence. There was never any such 'road' or even a route in the organisational sense, there was no free movement of goods between China and the West until the Mongol Empire in the Middle Ages,[132] silk was by no means the main commodity in trade with the East, and there is not a single ancient historical record, neither Chinese nor Classical, that even hints at the existence of such a road. The arrival of silk in the West was more the result of a series of accidents rather than organised trade. Chinese monopoly and protectionism of sericulture is largely myth.[133] Despite technology existing in ancient China far in advance of anything in the West, most of it did not reach the West until the Middle Ages (usually via the Mongols) when much of it was already up to a thousand years old.[134] Both ancient Rome and China had only the haziest notions of each other's existence and even less interest, and the little relationship that did exist between East and West in the broadest sense was usually one-sided, with the stimulus coming mainly from the Chinese. The greatest value of the Silk Road to history is as a lesson – and an important one at that – at how quickly and how thoroughly a myth can become enshrined as unquestioned academic fact.

'Romano–Buddhist' art

If one were to place a second-century AD portrait bust from a Buddhist monument in Afghanistan next to a Roman portrait bust from Europe of the same period, the differences would be indistinguishable to anybody but an expert (e.g., Plate 29). The undoubted 'Roman' appearance of much of the Buddhist art of north-western India – Gandharan art – and Central Asia in the first few centuries AD is the most dramatic and most graphic evidence of Rome beyond its frontiers. Not surprisingly, it has prompted wide speculation.[135]

The region known as Gandhara straddles the borderland of northern Pakistan and eastern Afghanistan, centred around Peshawar and Charsadda. Other centres were Taxila, near Rawalpindi, to the east, the Swat Valley to the north, and Hadda, near Jalalabad in Afghanistan, to the west. This was the heart of the ancient Greek kingdom of India, founded by the Greeks of Bactria in the middle of the third century BC.[136] Indo-Greek civilisation was hybrid, a mix of Greek and Indian as well as Central Asian and Iranian elements. Its predominant elements were the Buddhist religion and Classical art. The fusion of these two completely foreign elements eventually produced the art style known Gandharan.

Gandharan art evolved between the first century BC and the first century AD. Politically, this was a confused period, for the old Indo-Greek kingdom had collapsed in the face of successive Scythian, Parthian and Kushan invasions from the north. The latter were originally a nomadic nation from the western Chinese borderlands. The Kushans carved out an empire centred on Gandhara that straddled the Indo-Iranian and Central Asian borderlands. It lasted until its overthrow by Sasanian Iran in the middle of the third

Plate 29 Bust of a bodhisattva from Hadda, Afghanistan, now in the Musée Guimet. (Photo: © Agence Photographique de la Réunion des Musées Nationaux, Paris)

century AD. With few artistic traditions of their own, the Kushans adopted both the Hellenistic art and the Buddhist religion of the lands they conquered, providing Gandharan art with political expression.

Gandharan art – usually sculpture – is almost entirely Buddhist in subject matter but essentially Classical in style. The term 'Romano-Buddhist' was first coined to describe this in 1876. The characteristic style consists of relief panels adorning virtually every wall surface around the exteriors of stupas (Buddhist shrines), as well as the interiors of associated chapels and monasteries (Figure 22). These wall surfaces are often divided horizontally by Classical entablatures, with relief panels separated by pilasters, usually in the Corinthian order. Both the entablatures and the Corinthian capitals are often heavily debased and in themselves may not reflect strong Roman influence.

Far more 'Roman' in style, however, is the sculpture itself. Its characteristic technique of depicting a story in relief as a series of episodic panels is thought to be derived from Roman models (e.g., the Column of Trajan), rather than Indian, where continuous narrative was the norm. A far more important iconographical element purported to be from the West is the Buddha image itself. Previous to about AD 100 (the date is subject to dispute), the Buddha was depicted in Indian art only in the abstract, e.g., as a footprint. The first Buddha images, which appeared after this date, are thought to have been modelled after statues of the Roman emperors: iconographically, the authority of the Founder, i.e., Buddha, in Buddhist art is linked to the Roman cult of the emperor. This is one of the most predominant themes in Buddhist art. The closest similarities are with the Roman art of the mid-second century.

But the strongest links lie not so much in iconographic concepts but the actual appearance of the sculpture itself. The resemblance is quite astonishing. The similarity of a standing Buddha found at Mardan to Roman emperor statues, for example, is one of the most famous and frequently cited examples.[137] There are many others. The British Museum relief of the Indian goddess Hairiti would not be out of place in a western church depicting the Virgin and Child, for example, while another extraordinary relief depicting a balcony scene might be straight from a Roman triumphal arch or sarcophagus (Plates 30 and 31). Indeed, the sarcophagi art of the Roman world probably provides the closest similarities to Gandharan art. Other recurring motifs include: mythical beings from Greek mythology, such as ichthyocentaurs, tritons, gryphons, etc.; Atlas figures, often depicted holding up Classical entablatures; cupids; garlanding and other details of Classical ornament, such as tendrils, bead and reels, egg and darts, palmettes, etc.; the almost universal use of the Corinthian order. Many Indian deities are depicted in well-known Classical guise: Vajrapani, for example, is depicted as Heracles, Hairiti as Tyche, and Dionysiac imagery constantly recurs. There is even a very puzzling Trojan horse relief that could only have been inspired by Virgil, rather than Homer. Such works bear almost no relation to contemporary or earlier Indian sculpture, and almost as little with the Hellenised art of Palmyra or Parthia.[138]

Perhaps the most striking are the large numbers of portrait busts in Gandharan sculpture, particularly the stucco sculpture from Hadda in Afghanistan (Plate 29). Some, such as the Heracles relief from Tepe Shotor, appear almost identical to Roman art in Asia Minor or Syria of the first–second centuries AD. Most of the Hadda stuccoes are generally thought to be later, occurring after the third century, although there are problems with dating. One authority sees these stuccoes as 'essentially Greek figures, executed by artists fully conversant with far more than the externals of the classical style'.[139] They are usually heads of Buddhas or Bodhisattvas which form part of a relief narrative, but now occur mainly in isolation in museum collections. Such busts closely resemble Roman portrait sculpture – the resemblance of one Bodhisattva to the 'Antinous' sculptures of the Hadrianic period is a particularly famous example (Plate 29).[140] These stucco busts are thought to be the result of mass-production, the stucco medium lending itself more easily than stone to imitative workshops. The dominance of Alexandrian stucco workshops is emphasised in this context. Much of the Roman style of Hadda appears to anticipate

Figure 22 A votive stupa from Taxila (After Marshall)

Plate 30 Gandharan relief of the Indian goddess Hairiti with
children from northern Pakistan, now in the British Museum.
(Photo: © British Museum)

European Gothic art a thousand years later: just as late Roman art in the West evolved
into Gothic, late Romano-Buddhist art in the East evolved into the 'so-called Gothic art
of Hadda'.[141]

There are three channels from which this 'Roman' art might be derived. First, as a
natural evolution of the Hellenistic art of the same area (Bactrian Greek), a parallel
evolution to the development of Roman art itself in the West. Second, as direct influence
by itinerant groups of artists from the Roman Empire. And third, as indirect influence
stemming from Romanising elements in Iranian art.[142]

Its evolution from Greek art of the same region – the Hellenistic successor states of

Plate 31 Gandharan relief depicting a scene from Buddhist mythology, now in the British Museum.
(Photo: © British Museum)

Bactria and India – at first appears the most plausible. After all, the Hellenism was
undoubtedly there, and the Roman appearance of the later art seems as logical an evolution as Roman art in the West, which evolved similarly from Hellenistic art. It has
certainly won eminent supporters, including the scholar who, perhaps more than most,
rediscovered Gandharan art, Alfred Foucher.[143] The main objection, however, is that the
Greek kingdoms disappeared long before the appearance of the first syncretic Gandharan
art style, with the Hellenism of Bactria dwindling almost to 'vanishing point'; there seems
no smooth, artistic transition such as occurred between Hellenistic and Roman art in the
West. Consequently, there are too many missing links to enable a convincing evolution to
be documented, and that only the arrival of entirely new contacts with the West can
explain the style. There is almost no Buddhist art, for example, at Taxila before about

144

AD 50. Argument, therefore, has revolved around efforts to date many of the pieces with demonstrable western influence as early as possible.

After the initial discovery of Gandharan art, these arguments gradually gave way to those who favoured a more direct Roman origin for the style. But the argument still has much to recommend it. To begin with, the post-Hellenistic invasions – Scythian, Parthian, Kushan – which brought the Hellenistic kingdoms to an end were probably neither a 'dark age' nor a material break. The archaeological record indicates far stronger continuity in the region than previously thought, with the invaders promoting and continuing Hellenism rather than extinguishing it. The absence of artistic links, therefore, does not mean that such links never existed. They may yet be found – indeed, our knowledge of the archaeology of Afghanistan is notoriously inadequate. The discovery and excavation in the 1960s and 1970s of the Greek city of Ai Khanum on the Oxus has demonstrated beyond doubt that Greek art did take root in the region, fusing with local elements. Finally, relatively recent studies have focused on a hitherto neglected aspect of Gandharan art. These are the so-called palettes or 'toilet trays', dated between the late second century BC and the first century AD, belonging to a Hellenistic tradition that originated in Anatolia or Alexandria. The art of these stone palettes has done much towards filling gaps in the evolution.[144]

Most discussion, however, has centred on the second hypothesis, that the art must have been a product of 'journeymen craftsmen from the Roman east'[145] – and the schools which they founded – working in north-western India after the first century AD.[146] Only such direct influence can explain such close similarities. Hence, anonymous Roman sculptors have been postulated as arriving in India, either forming entourages in official diplomatic delegations or arriving independently. Whilst no such delegations are known, the reverse is attested, such as the 'embassy' to Antoninus mentioned by Aurelius Victor. This is interpreted as coming from one of the Kushan emperors, either Kanishka or Vasishka.[147] It is suggested that such a delegation might have returned from Rome with sculptors with the specific intention of lending an appropriately 'imperial tone' to Kushan sculpture, our worthy Kushan rustics having doubtless been bowled over with the glories they saw in Rome itself. A sculptor in the wake of such a delegation might have trained an assistant who was responsible, for example, for the undoubted Roman influence in the Calcutta frieze.[148] Support for such hypothetical Roman sculptors roaming the East is seen in the 'Yavana' (i.e., Greek, presumed Roman) artisans mentioned in southern Indian literature at the time, or the apocryphal story of the journey of St Thomas – a carpenter – to Taxila in the first century AD. The collection of such a travelling artist's stock of finished and unfinished Graeco-Persian gems was found at Taxila.[149] The spectacular discovery of the hoard of Roman glass at Begram[150] in Afghanistan certainly demonstrated links with the art of the Roman world (Plate 28). Whilst these were merely trade items, and not Roman works of art produced locally, Begram and the other trade links reviewed above in this chapter may provide a background for the possibilities of artists arriving in the wake of the objects.

An important recent study has re-examined the Roman glassware and other Roman-related objects at Begram, re-dating them to the first and early second centuries AD rather than the mid-third century as previously thought. Thus, the Roman objects at Begram now provide us with the required Roman 'missing link' before the formative period of Gandharan art. Indeed, the Roman-inspired plaster palettes from Begram might well have formed a part of samplers of a western craftsman at the Kushan court.[151] Against this, it must be borne in mind that such efforts to re-date the Begram treasure have centred almost exclusively on the Roman glass; equally exhaustive studies of the Indian ivories and Chinese lacquers that also make up the treasure need to be incorporated before a conclusive date for Begram can be arrived at.

Other speculation has emphasised the importance of Hellenistic elements in Iranian art of the same period. The sculpture at Palmyra, Hatra and Shami in south-western Iran, as well as the paintings at Dura Europos, belong to this 'Irano-Hellenistic' style. Here, the frontality of the art, as well as the dress, the ornament and the framing of the reliefs are seen to be essentially Iranian variations on an underlying Hellenistic theme. Many of these elements, however, especially frontality, more likely originate in Arabian funerary architecture.[152] These variations are also found in the Gandharan art of north-western India, and are therefore seen to be an extension. In this context the precarious nature of Greek art in Bactria has been emphasised as well as, perhaps, its shallowness, in contrast to the remarkably more durable arts of Iran.[153] The stucco medium of, for example, the Hadda busts, which are generally late, is also thought to be inspired by Iranian art which favoured the stucco medium, particularly after the Sasanian occupation of Gandhara in 241.[154] But whilst such connections undoubtedly exist, the Roman element in Gandharan art is far more pronounced than the Parthian – or even Palmyrene – calling for more complex explanations which suggest more direct links.

In Central Asia, artistically an extension of the Gandharan art of north-west India, many more Classical elements have been recognised. Third-century AD 'Greek' seal impressions depicting Eros, Hermes, Pallas, Heracles, Zeus and other mythological figures were found at Niya in Xinjiang.[155] An important group of wall paintings were recovered from Miran on the southern rim of the Takla Makan Desert in Xinjiang which show astonishing western influence. They have been dated broadly to the third–fourth century AD – the site itself was abandoned in the fourth century. The group betrays specifically Roman rather than Hellenistic characteristics: Roman techniques of portraiture, the treatment of the drapery and the use of chiaroscuro (a clear coat of paint laid over the highlights that was to become popular in Byzantine art). One of the paintings is actually signed by the artist, Tita, presumed a variation of the name Titus, which suggests a Roman origin. All the stylistically related paintings from Miran appear to be by the same hand so it is suggested that Titus might have been a master heading a group of itinerant artists. Other paintings from the caves at Qizil, on the opposite side of the Takla Makan Desert to Miran, have Classical friezes in perspective that 'might easily have graced a Roman wall'. The figures themselves, however, are more Indian in style.[156] It might be that the borders, which depict the friezes, were painted by different artists from those who painted the figures, i.e., local and foreign artists (from the West?), a common technique of wall painting. The Miran paintings – those by Titus and his 'school'? – have been related stylistically to a group of sculptures of the same date from Swat. How a Roman artist came so far east, let alone practised so widely over an area almost as large as the Roman Empire itself, must be a matter of pure speculation, but too much must not be pinned onto what are, after all, stylistic interpretations.[157]

At the Soghdian site of Qal'a-i Kahkaha in the western foothills of the Tien Shan a seventh-century wall painting of a she-wolf suckling two infants – Romulus and Remus? – suggests Roman derivation, but it is probably too far distant for the resemblance to be other than coincidental.[158] Distant Classical derivatives, such as debased Corinthian capitals and Classical decorative motifs, are also found in the paintings of Xinjiang, but derived via Gandhara rather than directly from the West. In Central Asian art as a whole, the emphasis given to the human form has been viewed as a western element.[159] Overall, however, the Xinjiang paintings are more Irano-Indian than Romano-Indian (with the notable exception of Miran). One authority concludes his examination of this region by commenting on the tenaciousness of earlier Persian art forms on the Eurasian steppes, found in objects as far away as Siberia to the east and the Ukrainian steppes to the west, that were never matched by Classical forms.[160]

The real problem lies in the state of Gandharan art itself. The story of its rediscovery since the nineteenth century is sad tale of despoliation of sites, looting and accidental discoveries. By far the majority of objects in museum collections are divorced from their contexts, with very few from controlled excavations. It is a problem that continues today more than ever before: the recent destruction and looting of the National Museum in Kabul is merely the latest episode in a long and ongoing story.[161] Consequently, it is impossible to date much of the sculpture closer than first century BC to sixth century AD, and chronology is the biggest problem that continues to plague the study of Gandharan art. Most is divorced both from its sculptural and archaeological contexts, as well as the broader social and historical contexts that might provide us with the information to fill the many gaps in its evolution. Gandharan art and the academic questions which surround it, perhaps more than most other art styles, is a victim of its own collectability and intrinsic value.

Much discussion has concerned the conceptual origins of the Buddha image. In particular, it has been argued that this was directly inspired by the Roman cult of the emperor, central to the Buddhist iconographical cult of the authority of Buddha. The origins of such a cult, however, whether of the Roman emperor or the Buddha authority, lie not in Roman art but in Persian. The cult of the Great King is one of the most predominant themes of Achaemenid art, emphasised so strongly at Persepolis and continuing as a major Iranian artistic theme down to the great rock reliefs of the Sasanian emperors (Plate 27). Recently, it has been argued that the development of the Buddha image occurred entirely within the religious development of Buddhism in India, and not as a response to any western ruler concepts.[162] The episodic style of Gandharan reliefs, thought to derive from Roman art, also occurs far earlier in the Persepolis reliefs.

In postulating how Roman artisans might have arrived in India, speculation has centred around the various delegations to Rome from 'Bactria' and elsewhere in the East which the historical sources mention, such as those which came to Augustus.[163] It is suggested that such delegations might have brought back groups of artists with them. But the central point of these delegations is that, if anything, they are evidence of an *east to west* movement, not the reverse: we have virtually no evidence that such delegations were reciprocated by Rome, our only evidence is for Indians coming to Rome. Other speculations on the artistic links have looked to the Roman trade with southern India, reviewed above, for an explanation. Ancient southern Indian sources certainly mention 'Yavana' artisans working in southern India. But even if the Yavanas were Romans (and it is unlikely the term was so precise, as we have seen), no 'Romano-Indian' art has been found in the south, where all the archaeological evidence, such as it is, suggests that it would be. It is all in the north-west, which had few links with the south – and even fewer links, apart from artistic, with the Roman world. Indian literature furthermore makes no mention of Yavanas – craftsmen or otherwise – in the north at this time.

The similarities between Roman and Gandharan sculpture are self-evident – and overwhelmingly persuasive enough to be convincing of artistic links. But the 'missing links' that have been put forward – a hoard of Roman glass here, an unexplained series of stuccoes there, the occasional intaglio elsewhere – are not enough. What is lacking are sculptures themselves to provide missing links, as it is in sculptural art that the similarities exist, not glassware or other objects. What is more lacking, however, is any convincing historical framework that would have allowed such links to form. Central to the argument is the existence of 'journeymen craftsmen' from the Roman world. The idea that a hypothetical sculptor in an entirely hypothetical entourage of an equally hypothetical Roman delegation to the Kushan court might have trained local craftsmen in Roman sculpture to influence a subcontinent is so ridiculously tenuous as to appear unworthy of serious consideration. The picture of itinerant groups of Roman sculptors – swags of samplers, patterns and tools over their backs, wandering around from court to court in parts of remotest Asia that few of even the best educated Romans had ever heard of, teaching the natives how to sculpt in languages mutually incomprehensible, heads brimful of abstruse iconographical concepts – somehow lacks conviction! Even more lacking is any cast iron archaeological or social context in which the hypothesis might be placed.

Most of all, it must be pointed out that the controversies over Graeco-Bactrian versus direct Roman versus Irano-Hellenistic origins for Gandharan art not in conflict: *all* hypotheses must be substantially correct. None of the hypotheses so far argued can by themselves account for the unquestionably western character of the style. But the combination of *all* forces and influences is the only possible explanation for perhaps the most extraordinary syncretism in art history. To argue for one hypothesis over the others is to miss the point.

5

THE TOWNS AND CITIES

Much is made of the Hellenistic and subsequent Roman urbanisation of the East, of how cities were both the cornerstone of Roman rule there and their main legacy, that the 'Roman government consciously encouraged the development of settlements into cities'.[1] Yet the fact remains that the Romans did not found a *single* new city in the East. All were refoundations of existing cities, some of them Seleucid foundations but most of them cities that had existed thousands of years before. Beirut, the one city often cited as a new Roman foundation in contrast to the others, was a Phoenician city long before, as current excavations are revealing. Even the Macedonian 'foundations' were hardly the 'Greek' cities that we imagine them to be. They were probably Semitic, in terms both of the majority of their population and their character, for after the Battle of Magnesia in 191 BC, which cut off the supply of settlers from Greece, 'we can be sure that the foundation of cities means not colonisation but the grants of autonomy to native towns'.[2]

To some extent, the impression of Roman urbanisation is distorted by inscriptions and definitions, and the surviving inscriptions have been interpreted as a 'conscious disassociation' by the Roman cities from their Semitic past.[3] But the inscriptions were only written by the colonisers or by westernised natives, and cannot be taken as representative of a city's 'consciousness'.[4] Furthermore, Roman definitions of city status or otherwise are not so much evidence for urbanisation as imperial whim: a minor settlement, such as Shahba, might be promoted to the rank of city merely because an emperor was born there, whilst a major city, such as Antioch, might be demoted to the rank of village because another emperor was insulted there. 'Roman foundation' of a city in the East or its definition otherwise of its status was usually nothing more than a bureaucratic matter that had only minimal effect on the city concerned. But the Romans neither defined nor founded cities in the East. The East had great cities long before and could always teach the Romans a thing or two about cities and urbanisation.

Perhaps nothing demonstrates more thoroughly the essential shallowness of 'Roman' cities than the rapidity by which their Greek names reverted to the older Semitic ones on the Arab conquest in the seventh century. Philadelphia reverted to Amman, Scythopolis to Beit Shan, Epiphania to Hama, Beroea to Aleppo, Hierapolis to Mambij, to name just a few. Virtually the only places which retained their Greek names were those which were wholly Macedonian in foundation in the first place, such as Antioch (Antakya) or Laodicaea (Lattaqiya). The only other exceptions, surprisingly, were some of the cities of Palestine: Neopolis remained as Nablus instead of reverting to Shechem, Sebaste remained Sabastiya instead of Samaria, for example. Even Jerusalem retained its Roman name of Aelia, as Arabic Iliya, until the Middle Ages. Elsewhere, the Greek names were swept away

149

and the ancient names revived – or probably retained, for such was the rapidity and thoroughness of the revivals that it seems likely that they remained in common usage all the way through the Macedonian–Roman 'interregnum'.[5] If the names are anything to go by, it was as if nine centuries of Graeco-Roman cities disappeared overnight.

But the cities were certainly the centres of Roman rule, however 'un-Roman' they might have been in origin, composition or character. In the following overview, the main cities and groups of cities are outlined, with a view to assessing the impact of Rome.[6]

Antioch the imperial city[7]

Origins

Antioch was born out of the chaos following the division of the spoils after the death of Alexander the Great. The bulk of the Asiatic portions of Alexander's empire fell to Seleucus Nicator, one of Alexander's main generals. His first capital was Seleucia on the Tigris, appropriately close to Babylon where Alexander had died. But Babylon had also been a capital of the Persian Empire before. Associating a new capital too closely with a city that saw the death of two empires – not to mention the perennial threat of an Iranian revival on his doorstep – prompted Seleucus to look further west. It was a wise move, for this is exactly what did happen with the establishment of the Parthian Empire in the third century BC.

Seleucus' choice fell on Seleucia-ad-Pieria, founded within a year after his victory over Antigonus at the Battle of Ipsus in 301 BC. It was located on the north Syrian coast, appropriately sited with a view to the Macedonians' all-important life-line to the Mediterranean. In April 300, a month after its foundation, Seleucus founded another city in Seleucia's agricultural hinterland some thirty kilometres upstream on the Orontes, naming it after his father Antiochus (Figure 23, Plate 32). Antioch, however, was not the first Hellenistic foundation in that locality: in 307 BC Antigonus had founded his own city, Antigoneia, several kilometres north of the site of the future Antioch.[8] Seleucus' foundation of Antioch, therefore, was both to proclaim his victory over and obliterate the memory of his rival. Thus, out of chaos on one hand and spite on the other, Antioch was born.

Seleucia remained the capital until the accession of Antiochus I Soter, Seleucus' son, in 281 BC. But Seleucia's lifeline to the sea was also its potential death-knell, for the Seleucids' bitter rivals, the Ptolemies of Egypt, occupied Seleucia from the sea on several occasions. Hence, Antiochus moved the capital to Antioch, where it remained. It expanded rapidly. Antioch was settled initially by Greeks and Macedonians, but it was soon to have a considerable population of Jews as well as, of course, a large native Syrian population.[9] When Pompey conquered it in 64 BC it was the most populous city of Syria, and the natural choice as capital for Rome's new province.

It was a Roman provincial capital rather than Seleucid royal capital that the city's main urban embellishments celebrate. In the first century BC Caesar endowed a basilica, the 'Kaisarion', as well as the rebuilding of the Pantheon, a new theatre, an amphitheatre, an aqueduct and a bath. The amphitheatre was one of the earliest in the Roman world. The Antioch 'Olympic Games' instigated at this time eventually became one of the most famous festivals of the Roman world. Agrippa endowed some new baths, and enlarged the theatre and restored the hippodrome.[10]

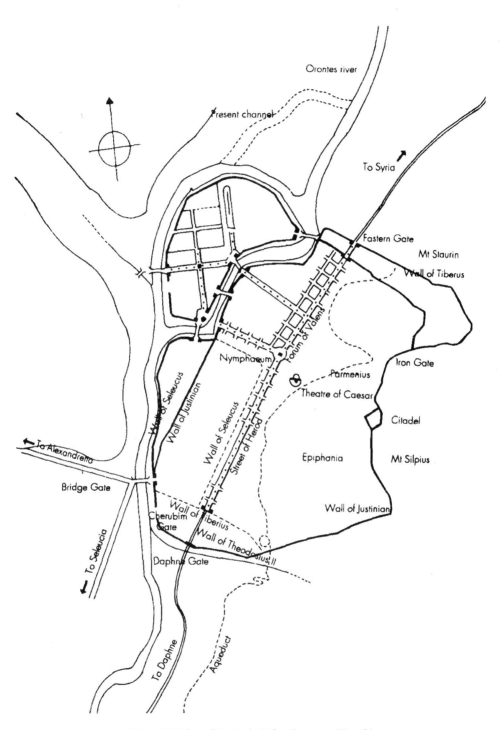

Figure 23 Plan of Antioch (After Downey/Cimak)

Plate 32 Antioch today. The Orontes is in the foreground, Mt Silpius in the background

In the first century AD there was a new wave of embellishment. A great colonnaded street was laid out, two Roman miles in length, with tetrapyla at the main intersections. Herod and Tiberius paid for the paving and the colonnading respectively. Midway along was an oval plaza with a column and statue of Tiberius adorning the centre and a nymphaeum to one side. From this plaza a secondary colonnaded street led off to the west. Tiberius also completed the Epiphania quarter and endowed a number of temples, including one to Jupiter Capitolinus, and the East Gate was surmounted with a statue of Romulus and Remus with the she-wolf. With the addition of the Temple of Jupiter Capitolinus and the Romulus and Remus Gate, Antioch was given the trappings of a Roman city.[11]

Over the following century, more baths, temples, aqueducts and a theatre, together with further embellishments and restorations of existing monuments (particularly following the earthquake of 115) were endowed by Gaius Caligula, Claudius, Titus, Trajan and Hadrian.[12] Following the city's support for the pretender Niger, Septimius Severus (no lover of the Antiochenes who made him the butt of their humour!) demoted the city to village status, elevating Laodicaea to provincial capital over Antioch – punishment indeed, coming as the culmination of a tradition of rivalry between the two cities.[13]

After the mid-third century, there was increasing disaffection at Antioch. Although its status as capital was soon restored, Antioch's humiliation caused many other resentments to surface. Philip the Arab's heavy taxes and levies led to discontent in 248, after which there was increasing support for a pro-Iranian faction led by Mariades (Aramaic Maryad), a member of the senatorial class. Pro-Roman accounts not surprisingly describe Mariades variously as a thief and embezzler. However, there seems little doubt that his sentiment was not only genuine but reflected popular pro-Iranian feelings amongst the native Syrian population.[14] The traditional Iranophilism of the Syrians dated back to the time of Pakores' occupation of Syria in the first century BC, and probably preserved an earlier memory of the great days of the Achaemenid Empire. Whilst content enough with Roman rule, pro-Iranian feelings were quick to re-emerge at times of Roman oppression. Mariades defected to Iran, coming back with the army of Shapur II in 256.[15]

After the Iranian occupation, much was rebuilt by Valerian, who began the fort that later became Diocletian's palace. Diocletian's palace anticipated his one at Split in both size and layout, and is depicted on his triumphal arch at Salonica. It had pillared galleries overlooking the river, and had a colonnaded street running from the centre of the island to the palace with a tetrapylon in the middle. He also carried out an extensive rebuilding programme in both Antioch and Daphne. After Rome moved to Constantinople, Antioch came in for renewed embellishments, albeit with an increasing Christian flavour. Constantine's octagonal church was one of the greatest of the early churches, and further extensive embellishments were carried out by Constantius, Julian, Valens, Theodosius I and Theodosius II.[16]

The calamitous sixth century saw the beginning of the end. A major fire in 525 followed by earthquakes in 526, when a quarter of a million were said to have perished, and another in 528 destroyed most that had been rebuilt after the sack by Shapur II nearly two centuries previously. This was followed by another Iranian occupation under Khusrau Anushirvan in 540. Justinian's attempt at restoration was aimed mainly at refortification and the city utilities. A great plague devastated the population again in 542, with minor outbreaks recurring for the rest of the century, and there were more earthquakes in the middle of the century. The Iranians occupied Antioch once again in 611 under Khusrau Parviz, but Heraclius regained Antioch in 628. However, when the Muslim Arabs appeared on the scene soon after, the citizens no longer had the heart to defend what was left of their once great city, and opened its gate to them without resistance – one almost senses with relief.

Eastern city or foreign implant?

It is a common fallacy that Antioch was founded by the Macedonians (and Greeks) in a vacuum; that Greek civilisation brought urbanisation to a region of the Near East which hitherto had not known it, and remained a Greek/Hellenistic enclave since. Long before Seleucus, the Iranians had founded a temple on the site of the future city, and the Iranian element was a constant feature of its subsequent history down until the seventh century as we have seen.[17] But our own obsession with Greek civilisation often obscures historical reality. To begin with, such assumptions minimise the Macedonian element: 'Macedonian' soon becomes equated with 'Greek' in a haste to trace all progress back to a semi-mythic Athens, forgetting that the Macedonians – at least at first – were not only quite distinct from the Greeks but bitter enemies of them as well.

More important, it leaves out the local element. For despite its original Macedonian foundation, its subsequent rise as the third city of the Roman world, its gloss of Graeco-Roman monumental architecture, and the Graeco-Roman trappings of its organisation and administration, it was a *Syrian* city above all: in population and character. Antioch never existed in any vacuum, nor did it exist without earlier, native Syrian roots. Antioch lies at the southern end of the Amuq Plain, a finite area which has a long and continuous sequence of ancient settlement (Figure 24).[18] Antioch forms as much a part of this cultural continuum as, for example, Tell Achana (Alalakh) or any other settlement in the vicinity does.

The third-century historian Herodian – a native of Antioch – leaves little doubt of this when he emphasises the people of Antioch as Syrians rather than as Greeks and Romans. 'The fact is that those who live in the East, separated from the West by a great continent

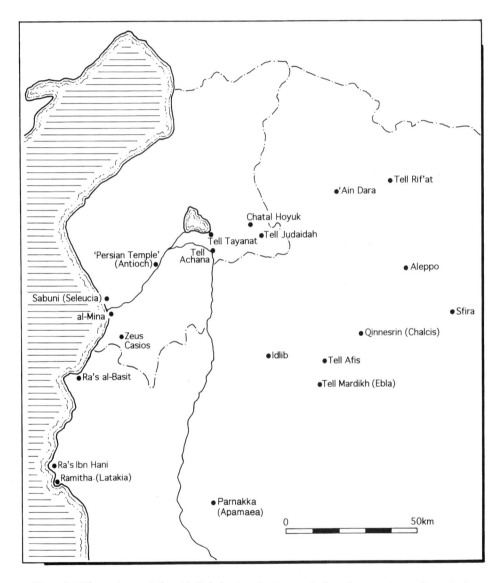

Figure 24 The main pre-Seleucid (Babylonian–Persian period) settlements in northern Syria. Given the state of our archaeological knowledge for this period, the real number of settlements is probably much higher

and broad sea, scarcely ever hear of Italy.' Syrians may have written in Greek, much as intellectuals in Europe were still writing in Latin until the eighteenth century or educated Indians writing in Persian until the nineteenth (or English in the twentieth). But that did not detract from their Syrian character. Literacy in Greek after all belonged only to a small elite who could hardly be taken as representative of overall 'character': Aramaic was the language of everyday use, spoken by the majority. Herodian's descriptions are, admittedly, fairly deprecating about his fellow-Syrians. But whilst a staunch Romanophile, Herodian still referred to the Romans as 'them', not 'us'.[19] The architecture of Antioch belongs within the eastern forms of Roman architecture rather than western.[20] The question of what language the inscriptions carved on them were in is hardly important.

Antioch as an imperial city[21]

Nonetheless, a major Roman cultural element still existed − it was, after all, Roman for seven centuries and only Seleucid for less than two-and-a-half. With Antioch becoming Roman it soon became one of the great cities of the empire, along with Alexandria, Ephesus and Carthage. The Roman element may have been little more than a superficial veneer thinly covering the native Syrian majority. But Antioch had one attribute which made it distinct, not only from other cities of the East but from those elsewhere in the empire. For it became an imperial city, the seat of emperors like no other apart from Rome itself and, later, Constantinople.

This began very soon after its incorporation into the rapidly growing Roman Empire by Pompey in 63 BC. It was as if the Romans were very aware, not only of its strategic value but of its imperial associations with the Seleucid kings and its links − albeit largely spurious − to an empire ultimately founded by Alexander. Thereafter, it rapidly became a favoured seat for Roman emperors and power base for their proclamations of power, becoming the virtual capital of the empire on numerous occasions. Vespasian was the first emperor to be proclaimed there, and it formed Trajan's headquarters during his eastern campaigns. Trajan resided there for three years, and his successor Hadrian was proclaimed from there. When Marcus Aurelius deputed his co-emperor Lucius Verus to take charge of the Parthian campaigns, Verus used Antioch as an eastern imperial capital, ruled by an eastern emperor, for four years, deputing Avidius Cassius to actually lead the Parthian campaigns while he remained in Antioch and Daphne. Following this, Avidius Cassius himself was proclaimed emperor in Antioch, as was Pescennius Niger a short time after, both enjoying the support of the Antiochenes.

The Severan dynasty, dominated as it was by Julia Domna's Syrian family, formed the closest associations of any emperors with Antioch. Septimius Severus spent seven of his first ten years in office there, probably more than he did in either Rome or in his birthplace of Lepcis Magna. His son Caracalla used it as headquarters for his own eastern campaigns, with Julia Domna staying on in Antioch to carry out the actual business of government of the Empire during her son's absence. Following Caracalla's death, the Emperor Macrinus' brief period of office was solely at Antioch, and Elagabalus went there directly after his proclamation to consolidate his position. His cousin and successor Emperor Alexander in turn used it as his headquarters during his eastern campaign.

In the later third century Valerian also made Antioch his headquarters. Afterwards, Macrianus and his son Quietus were proclaimed emperors in Antioch and recognised by the Syrians, until their defeat by Gallienus. Antioch figured highly in the civil war between Aurelian and Zenobia, with both claiming it as their imperial seat at different times. In about 280 Julius Saturninus was proclaimed emperor in Antioch, even issuing coins, until he was killed by Probus.[22] When Diocletian came to Antioch for the Iranian campaign he remained there while deputing his Caesar Maximian to carry out the campaign. He remained in Antioch on a semi-permanent basis, celebrating a joint triumph with Galerius and entering his seventh consulship in 299.[23]

When Constantine made the momentous decision to move the capital of the empire to the East, Antioch was thus considered to be the natural choice. However, Antioch, like Rome itself, was weighed down by its pagan past, prompting Constantine to choose the less important but less sullied city of Byzantium instead. But this did not alter Antioch's status as second Roman capital. Constantius was made Augustus of the East with Antioch as his capital between 338 and 350, and Julian preferred pagan Antioch to Christian Constantinople, perhaps even considering moving the capital there.[24] Indeed, Julian might well have made Antioch sole Roman capital if it had not been for his premature death. Paganism certainly remained as potent a symbol for Antioch as its imperial status was: the rival Emperor Leontius used it as his own capital, attempting to revive paganism in the process, from 484 to 488 during the time of Emperor Zeno. Antioch's position as imperial Roman city did not quite end with the Muslim conquest, for another rival emperor (to Michael II), Thomas the Slav, went through a Byzantine coronation in 821 in Muslim Antioch. Emperor Nicephoras Phocas' recapture of the city in 969 represents almost as much a Roman triumph as Justinian's recapture of the city of Rome itself over four centuries earlier had been.[25] For the Romans, Antioch was an imperial city when they first entered it. It remained so for the rest of their history.

The Macedonian heartland of the north[26]

North Syria is often seen as the heart of western influence, at first Graeco-Macedonian and then Roman, comprising as it does the core cities of Seleucia, Antioch, Laodicaea and Apamaea. These four cities were occasionally referred to as the 'Seleukiad' or the 'Tetrapolis', all founded in the initial period of Macedonian colonisation after Alexander. With this core were a number of other Macedonian foundations, such as Beroea (Aleppo), Chalcis (Qinnesrin), Cyrrhus, Larissa (Shaizar) and Dura Europos, all named after founding members of the Seleucid dynasty or cities in Macedon. As such, they form a distinctive Macedonian – and later Roman – cultural bloc in the East, often regarded as culturally isolated from the Semitic world around them.[27]

To a large extent, this area has 'suffered' more than most from both Classical prejudice and Near Eastern archaeological fashion, which have focussed on specific periods to the detriment of others. From the Classical viewpoint it is often described as essentially unurbanised until the Seleucid period,[28] with cities there being a mark of Classical civilisation only. Equally, Near Eastern archaeological research interests have focused almost exclusively on earlier periods, especially the periods of ancient urbanism in the area of the third and second millennia. Hence, a spurious gap between the early first millennium and the Macedonian conquest has 'appeared' in the archaeological continuum that has become compounded in discussions of the area.[29]

To begin with, this region had some of the most important cities of the ancient Near East: Aleppo, Ebla, Carchemish, Tell Achana, to name a few (Figure 24). Aleppo in particular is one of the Near East's perennial cities, disputing with Damascus (and now a whole host of others) the distinction of being the world's oldest continuously inhabited city. Most of the urban settlements in the area had unbroken sequences into the Macedonian and Roman periods. For example, ʿAin Dara and Tell Rifʿat (ancient Arpad), north of Aleppo, have continuous settlement from the Neo-Hittite period to Roman.[30] Although Carchemish itself was unoccupied after the Babylonian invasion, the nearby site of Deve Hüyük appears to have been a cemetery for an unlocated Achaemenid garrison in the area, perhaps at Jerablus-Tahtani just downstream, which appears to have been reoccupied after the destruction of Carchemish.[31] At Ebla, in the understandable attention focused on its third and second millennia remains it is often forgotten that it was inhabited continuously down to the Hellenistic period.[32] Indeed, all of the Macedonian Tetrapolis cities, far from being new foundations, were grafted on to older settlements with continuous histories going back hundreds, if not thousands, of years before the Macedonians supposedly 'invented' cities in the region, as we shall see. The only exception to this is Antioch (so far as we know: massive overburden at the site would obscure any earlier remains in any case). But even Antioch must be viewed as a part of the cultural continuum of the Antioch Plain, a sequence where Antioch is linked through Tell Tayanat and Tell Achana to a Near Eastern urban tradition many thousands of years old.[33] To suggest that the Macedonian – hence Roman – cities in the region were either new or apart from their cultural environment is absurd.

Seleucia and Laodicaea

Seleucia[34] was founded slightly earlier than Antioch, and formed the Seleucid capital until 289 BC as we have seen. However, it was on, or near, the site of earlier settlement, as excavations at the ancient Phoenician sites of al-Mina and Sabuni have demonstrated. Another Phoenician port lay a little further down the coast at Raʾs al-Basit, becoming the Seleucid port of Posidonium.[35] Seleucia was, moreover, dominated – literally – by a famous oracle of Zeus Casios on top of the mountain that overlooks the bay of Seleucia. Like all such sacred high places, this was a native religious feature,[36] and was presumably sacred to Semitic Baal or Hadad long before Greek Zeus. Without doubting its Hellenistic and Roman overlay, therefore, an underlying Phoenician element provided the cultural identity and continuity.

Subsequently the prosperity of Seleucia rose with that of Antioch, becoming the main port for that city throughout the Roman period. Seleucia was, however, subject to considerable flooding by the Orontes River. This has resulted in practically no extant remains today. But it also resulted in Seleucia's most impressive monument, a massive underground rock-cut water channel constructed to divert floodwaters from the city, begun under the Flavians and completed under the Antonines. There are also several impressive rock-cut tombs, both underground hypogea and rock façades. Otherwise, there is little evidence to suggest what form or layout the city took.

Laodicaea[37] (modern Lattaqiya) was named by Seleucus I Nicator after his mother, Laodice. It was the main harbour for Apamaea with which it was linked by a road across the Nusayri Mountains. Laodicaea had an ancient history long before Alexander. In the second millennium BC it was the Canaanite port of Ramitha, part of the kingdom of Ugarit only a few miles further north. Between Ugarit and Latakia, at Raʾs Ibn Hani, was another ancient settlement known as Diospolis in the Macedonian–Roman period (its Phoenician name is not known). Excavations have shown continuous occupation here

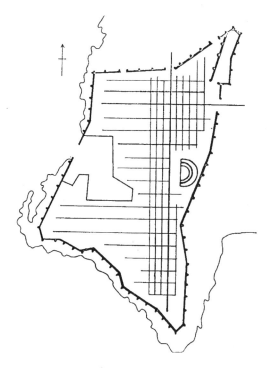

Figure 25 Plan of Roman Latakia (After Sauvaget)

Plate 33 The Tetrapylon at Latakia

from the late Bronze Age in the second millennium BC to the beginning of the Islamic period.[38] As Ugarit declined at the end of the second millennium BC the better natural harbour facilities at Ramitha/Laodicaea increased its importance. Thus, Macedonian–Roman Laodicaea represents a Syro-Phoenician cultural continuum rather than any new 'western' implant.

Laodicaea became a major port second to Seleucia. It flourished under the Romans: the slopes behind the city were covered with gardens and vines (Laodicaea's wines were famous), Herod the Great endowed the city with an aqueduct and Septimius Severus endowed the colonnaded streets. Very few Roman remains survive, but the basic street plan has been recognised as essentially Hellenistic or Roman (Figure 25). There is a fragmentary Corinthian colonnade, probably a part of a Temple of Adonis. Nearby is the impressive Tetrapylon that would have marked the intersection of two colonnaded streets (Plate 33). Elsewhere, occasional reused Classical fragments or part-buried columns attest to further remains below ground, whilst parks and roundabouts in the modern city are adorned with re-erected colonnades discovered in the course of building work.

Apamaea[39]

Apamaea lies at the foot of a high, partly artificial mound with a commanding position overlooking the very fertile Orontes Valley, where occupation has been traced back to the Chalcolithic period. It was the site of the Persian town of Parnakka or Pharnake,[40] renamed Pella by the Macedonians after Philip's capital in Macedon. It was again renamed Apamaea by Seleucus Nicator (one of three cities he so named) after his wife Apama, daughter of the Bactrian Prince Spitamenes, and became the Seleucid army headquarters. With such excellent pasturage in the surrounding valley, Apamaea was ideally situated for a stud farm, training area and supply centre generally for the army: 30,000 mares, 300 stallions and some 500 elephants are recorded as being bred and trained there. Virtually nothing survives of the Seleucid city, although the actual gridded layout consisting of an immense walled enclosure over a mile long is presumably Seleucid (Figure 26). Pompey destroyed its citadel in 64 BC, but the town continued as a prosperous, albeit less military, centre for many more centuries: its population was recorded as numbering 117,000 free inhabitants shortly after his conquest.[41] Its oracle and Temple of Bel were famous and its wealth and continued prosperity seemed assured.

On 3 December in AD 115 it all seemed to come to an end when a massive earthquake hit Syria. Antioch was severely damaged – Trajan himself had to camp out in the hippodrome – but Apamaea was completely destroyed. However, Apamaea's agony was an architect's dream: it was a blank slate to rebuild the city. This began almost immediately. A local philanthropist, Julius Agrippa, endowed much of the initial work. The great Cardo colonnade, today Apamaea's most outstanding feature (largely restored), was rebuilt on an unsurpassed scale (Figures 26 and 67, Plates 34, 35, 80, 136 and 137). Work continued all throughout the second century, progressing from north to south, eventually reaching two kilometres in length. It was enlarged from 30 metres to 37 metres in width and the smaller, east-west Decumanus enlarged from 16 to 22 metres. The intersections are marked by single columns on elaborate plinths, rather than the more usual tetrapylons (Plate 35). In every way – length, breadth, ornamentation and general opulence – the

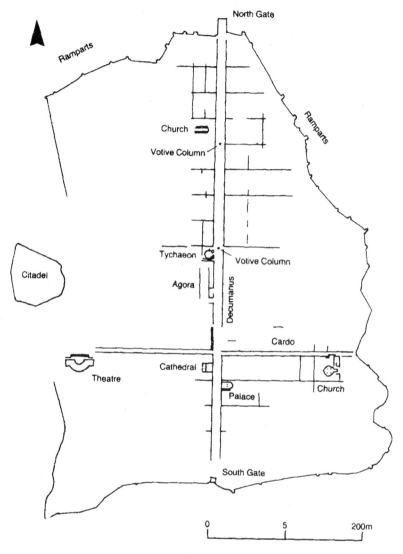

Figure 26 Plan of Apamaea (After Balty)

Apamaea Cardo is one of the most magnificent monumental avenues ever made.[42] Reconstruction in the centre around the Agora was completed in the middle of the second century. Inscriptions record the local families who endowed this new work. By the end of the second century the 'baroque' nymphaeum, the magnificent new theatre – the largest in the East and one of the largest ever built in the Roman world –and the rebuilt Temple of Zeus Belos were completed. This was a famous oracle that later figured highly in the growth of the Neoplatonic school of Apamaea under Iamblichus. Virtually no trace of it survives now, having been completely destroyed by Bishop Marcellus at the end of the fourth century.

Plate 34 The main colonnaded street at Apamaea

After the beginning of the third century there was a revival of Apamaea's position as an army town, when it became winter quarters of the Second Parthian Legion.[43] Its prosperity continued into the fourth century, when it became the centre of an important bishopric. The main Christian monument is a sixth-century church with a distinctive, and architecturally important, quatrefoil plan (Figure 110H). It all ended dramatically in AD 540 however, with the invasion of Khusrau I Parviz of Persia, who destroyed Apamaea. Ironically, both its beginning and its end were linked with the Iranians.

The sheer opulence and ostentation of second- and third-century Apamaea stands out even in the East, where opulence was the norm. But Apamaea was no provincial capital, nor was it the capital of any of the glittering local client kingdoms. Perhaps the explanation lies in its close association with the third century's greatest imperial dynasty, the Severi. Whilst Julia Domna and her female relatives, who dominated the dynasty, were from Emesa, the early history of the Emesenes was intimately tied to the Orontes Valley around Apamaea as we have seen.[44] The father of Emperor Elagabalus was from Apamaea, and it was at the oracle of Zeus Belos at Apamaea that the young Septimius Severus first received intimations of his own imperial destiny. The family's wealth was proverbial. Small wonder that the city found almost as much favour with the family as Lepcis Magna.

Plate 35 Votive column at Apamaea, marking the intersection of two streets

Aleppo[45]

Aleppo is ideally located for a great city. Lying midway between the Mediterranean coast and the great bend in the Euphrates, it was a northern pivot for much of the ancient world's trade for many thousands of years. Like Damascus, its origins are very ancient, and we first read about it in the third millennium. In the early second millennium it was the capital of the Amorite kingdom of Yamhad and following the collapse of the Hittite Empire in about 1200 BC, Aleppo re-emerged as one of the more important Neo–Hittite city-states in northern Syria. The Seleucid 'foundation' of Beroea at Aleppo, therefore, named after a city in Macedon, marks continuation rather than any new beginning. With the trade routes from the Seleucid East coming up the Euphrates via Dura Europos and across to Antioch, Aleppo profited enormously. This prosperity continued throughout the Roman period.

Such continuity has meant that there is little remaining of the Roman city today. The citadel, built only partly on a natural elevation, represents thousands of years of this continuum. This tell continued as the religious and military centre of the city throughout the Seleucid and Roman periods when it was heavily fortified, for it withstood the siege by Khusrau I Anushirvan in AD 540. Only the foundations and parts of the base of the walls might be Roman. The old street plan between the citadel and the Antioch Gate

162

follow the original Macedonian plan, the main souq occupying the Cardo Maximus of the Roman city (Figure 27). The Great Mosque was built in the courtyard of the cathedral, which in turn was on the site of a Roman temple temenos or perhaps the Seleucid agora. Parts of the original cathedral are still standing, incorporated into the Madrasa Halawiya next door to the Great Mosque. The oldest mosque in Aleppo, the Tutah Mosque founded in the mid-seventh century just inside the Antioch Gate, incorporates parts of a Roman monumental arch on its west façade.

Cyrrhus and Chalcis

Cyrrhus (modern Nabi Khouri),[46] was founded by the Seleucids as a fortified post guarding Antioch's north-eastern flank. Almost alone amongst Seleucid foundations, there seems to be no earlier settlement at Cyrrhus. It was rejuvenated and embellished after the Roman conquest as both a military and a commercial centre. Cyrrhus was the birthplace of the pretender Avidius Cassius, who was proclaimed emperor in Antioch following the false report of the death of Marcus Aurelius. It was badly damaged in the Iranian invasions of the mid-third century, but revived after the fourth century when it became the capital of the newly created Roman province of Euphratensis. For a time it was known as Hagiopolis ('City of the Saints'), mainly because of its relics of SS Damian and Cosmas.

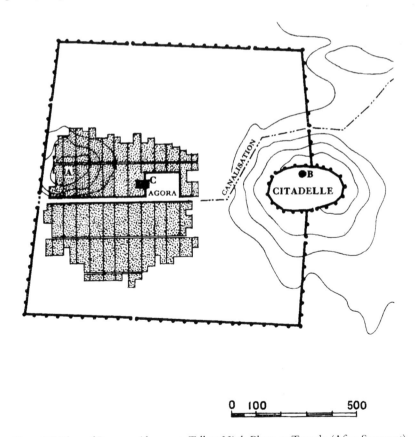

Figure 27 Plan of Roman Aleppo. A: Tell. B: High Place. C: Temple (After Sauvaget)

After the Arab conquest it slowly declined, and by the end of the twelfth century it had largely disappeared.

The city forms a rough, walled triangle along the banks of the Sabun River. The outline of the city walls and acropolis still exist, but inside much is indistinct. The city was bisected by a colonnaded street, but the most intact building is the second-century theatre in the centre of the city (Plate 36). At the northern end of the Cardo a large enclosure, entered through a propylaeum, probably marks the site of a former temple temenos. The remains of several churches can still be identified, and outside the city to the east is a fine hexagonal mausoleum with a pyramid roof (Plate 123).

Qinnesrin, to the south of Aleppo, is the site of the city of Chalcis[47] founded by Seleucus Nicator in the late fourth century BC. During the Roman period it became one of the main centres in northern Syria, surpassing Aleppo for a time, as it stood in the centre of a very fertile plain and lay at the hub of the Roman road network in north Syria. Its pre-eminence led to it becoming the capital of the Tanukh confederation in the sixth century. It was fortified in the mid-sixth century by Justinian, but destroyed in about 637 in the Muslim invasions. There is not a great deal surviving, although the acropolis, the outline of the city ramparts, and the street pattern are fairly easily discernible. Outside is a vast necropolis and quarry area, in which are numerous impressive hypogea.

Plate 36 Cyrrhus, with the theatre in the foreground

The Euphrates and Mesopotamia[48]

This region was a frontier region throughout, even when the empire extended beyond the Tigris. Hence, settlements tended to be defensive in nature, particularly after the fourth century when cities were equipped with some of the most formidable urban defences outside Constantinople. It was also dominated by Iran at different times in its history. Hence, in progressing across the vast plains of north-eastern Syria and into Iraq – the Jazira – one crosses a cultural watershed. Stone construction gives way to the traditional mud-brick of Mesopotamia and Iran and both people and cultural traditions become more Mesopotamian than Levantine.

The Euphrates was a frontier for the early part of the empire. More important, it was a channel for communications. Hence, more cities in the Roman period are to be found on its banks than in the fertile plains that stretch to its north. For much of its history, the great garrison town of Zeugma was Rome's main stronghold, frontier town and river crossing on the Euphrates. The site is located at Balqis on the right bank just upstream from Birecik in Turkey. The name is an ancient corruption of Seleucia-on-the-Euphrates, founded by Seleucus Nicator with another Apamaea on the opposite bank. Recently, Zeugma has been identified with the far older Persian and earlier city of Thapsacus, mentioned first in the Bible. The remains of Zeugma, however, are so scant that the very whereabouts of it were uncertain until recently.[49] At Raqqa, further downstream on the north bank of the Euphrates, a town was first founded by the Macedonians, called successively Nicephorium, Callinicum and Leontopolis.[50] Both remained important frontier towns.

Halabiya[51]

A far more important stronghold lay further downstream. This was Halabiya, ancient Zenobia, one of the greatest Roman fortifications on the eastern frontier. Again, it is an older site, guarding an important ford across the Euphrates. It became a Palmyrene post in the third century AD (hence the name's association with Queen Zenobia – it might have formed one of her tribal lands) guarding the routes along the Euphrates and across the desert. The Romans took it over after their destruction of Palmyra, and it subsequently assumed major importance as one of the empire's main frontier defences against the Iranians. The emperor Justinian in the sixth century provided it with massive defences, but despite such precautions, the Iranians stormed it in 540 and again in 610. The town never recovered and was slowly abandoned.

The ramparts are pierced by five gateways, three facing the river reflecting its importance. The main south gate leads onto the main north–south street. The interior is very ruined, and includes two churches. Other remains have been identified as a possible market place, a praetorium from the time of Justinian with vaulted rooms still surviving up to three storeys high, a bath house, and a very ruined keep. Parts of the town spread outside the walls as well. Just to the north is the necropolis where there are tower tombs and hypogea in the Palmyrene tradition. On the opposite bank some three kilometres downstream are the ruins of Zalabiya, a large rectangular enclosure reinforced with square towers after the same style of Halabiya.

Rasafa[52]

The immense walled city of Rasafa, ancient Sergiopolis, was a minor desert settlement going back to the second millennium, but the martyrdom in about 303 of St Sergius, a Christian officer in the Roman army, brought Rasafa into prominence. A shrine was built over his tomb at Rasafa which quickly attracted a wide following amongst the Arabs as a pilgrimage centre, and the name accordingly changed to Sergiopolis. Under Emperor Anastasius (491–518) and the Ghassanid federation of the sixth century, Sergiopolis was massively embellished, both as a religious centre and a frontier fortification. Its great walls withstood the Iranian invasion of Syria in 540, but were taken in the next invasion by Khusrau II.

The walls enclose a vast rectangle, pierced by four gateways in the middle of each side (Figure 28). The main entrance today is through the north gate, a richly decorated triple entrance framed by Corinthian columns supporting a graceful arcaded pediment that is one of the finest intact gateways in the world of Byzantine architecture (Plate 19). This belongs within the Near Eastern architectural tradition of sacred processional ways and propylaea reviewed in Chapter 7. Inside is the Cathedral of St Sergius (or Cathedral of the Holy Cross), one of the most impressive churches in Syria built in the early years of the sixth century. Other buildings include an elaborate quatrefoil martyrium and a series of immense underground cisterns, probably built by the Ghassanid princes. Rasafa/ Sergiopolis thus reflects native Syrian Christianity, a native dynasty and native architectural elements.

Dura Europos[53]

Dura Europos was founded as a Macedonian military colony in about 300 BC by Seleucus I to guard the Euphrates route from Mesopotamia, roughly midway between the two Seleucid capitals of Seleucia-ad-Pieria and Seleucia-on-the-Tigris. It was named after Seleucus' native town of Europos in Macedon (*dur* is an ancient Semitic prefix meaning 'fort' or 'city'). Unusually, therefore, it has no pre-Seleucid origins (although one must remember the name is part Semitic). With the loss of the Seleucid eastern provinces to Iran in the late second century BC it came under Iran. But it remained an autonomous city-state acting as commercial go-between for both empires, occupying a similar position to Palmyra. This role increased when the Romans replaced the Seleucids in Syria. Rome only occupied it during the Severan period, when it became an important forward position on their eastern frontier. For most of its history it had maintained its semi-independence under a loose Iranian overlordship, becoming increasingly orientalised in the process as the links with Macedon became more tenuous. In the third century AD the sack of the city by the Iranians in 256 and the sack of Palmyra by the Romans in 271 brought about a collapse. It quickly declined, so that by the fourth century it was practically deserted.

The site is an easily defensible one on a plateau overlooking the Euphrates, protected by the river escarpment on one side and deep gorges on two others (Figure 29, Plate 37). The fourth side, facing the open desert, is defended by impressive ramparts. It was laid out with the regular trappings of a Macedonian military encampment: a street plan following a strict grid pattern dominated in the centre by an open agora, surrounded by commercial buildings on one side and temples to Artemis, Apollo and Zeus to the south. Apart from

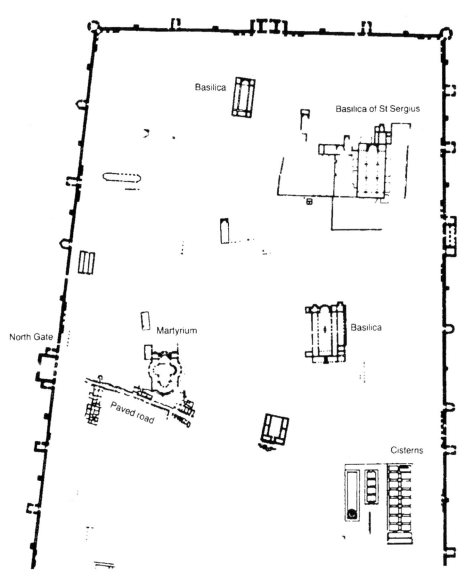

Basilica

Basilica of St Sergius

Martyrium

North Gate

Paved road

Basilica

Cisterns

Figure 28 Plan of Rasafa (After Karnapp)

167

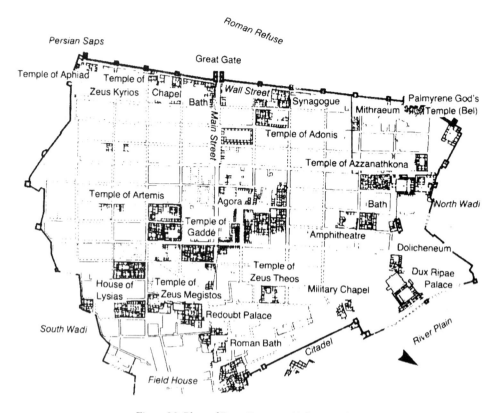

Figure 29 Plan of Dura Europos (After Hopkins)

the actual layout and some fragments of a Doric colonnade in the Temple of Artemis, practically nothing remains of Macedonian Dura, and most of the monuments date from the Partho-Roman period of the first centuries AD.

With its position on the borders of both Rome and Iran, it comes as no surprise that its inhabitants practised a great diversity of religions, and monuments of the Palmyrene, Iranian, Syrian, Jewish, Christian and ancient Greek religions have been found. A Temple of the Palmyrene Gods was built into an angle of the city walls, under-going several modifications over the first three centuries AD. Just outside the temple is a Mithraeum. Although Mithraism was an Iranian religion – and frescos inside depicted Zoroaster and other figures – it was erected by Roman soldiers, Mithraism being one of the army's most popular cults.[54] The most intact religious buildings were a Jewish syn-agogue and a Christian 'church' (more correctly a meeting house),[55] both resembling the conventional, private courtyard houses of the day rather than great public monuments, as befitted religious minorities. The synagogue is particularly impressive for the series of frescos depicting scenes from the Old Testament – the oldest such cycle surviving. The church also contained wall paintings, depicting scenes from the miracles of Christ and other Christian symbols. It also contained a bishop's 'throne' and a font. It is accurately dated by a graffiti of AD 231/2, making it the oldest dated church in the world. Both buildings owe their remarkable state of preservation to their situation alongside the city

Plate 37 Dura Europos, overlooking the Euphrates. The citadel is in the foreground

walls: apart from the protection afforded by the greater bulk of the ramparts behind, the walls were widened in AD 256 and strengthened by filling all adjacent houses – including the synagogue and church – with sand, the house walls forming casemates.

If the Jewish and Christian buildings of Dura had to be hidden away in the back-streets, monuments of the Graeco-Macedonian religion were appropriately situated in the centre by the agora. These were the temples of Artemis, Apollo and Zeus. But the religion of Dura very soon acquired a Semitic transformation. Artemis became Nanaia, an ancient Mesopotamian deity, and temples to two other goddesses were built alongside: Atargatis, a deity popular elsewhere in Syria, and Azzanathkona, a deity found only at Dura (although she too was occasionally equated with Artemis). The Temple of Artemis-Nanaia, after its reconstruction in the first century AD, resembled Mesopotamian temple styles rather than the peripteral Doric temple first laid out by the Macedonians. This and the Temples of Atargatis and Azzanathkona followed the eastern design of a sanctuary set within a large enclosure.

To the already cosmopolitan pantheon of Dura Europos can be added temples to more obscure Arab gods such as Arsu, A'shera and Sa'ad, as well as gods from the Roman occupation such as Jupiter. But equally important were the civic monuments. The agora formed a large open square in the centre of the city. As the city became more orientalised so did its architecture, and the agora gradually became transformed into covered souqs and street-side shops. The houses, too, resemble the traditional eastern courtyard houses. The Romans left their mark with the construction of a large praetorium complex taking up nearly a quarter of the walled city. As well as a governor's palace consisting of two colonnaded courtyard buildings, there were barracks, a small amphitheatre, several baths and a parade ground. These were the last major buildings to be erected before the city's destruction by the Iranians. Unlike all of the other monuments at Dura, they are entirely western in style, with the Roman foot being used as the standard measurement rather than the local cubit.[56] Overlooking the Euphrates is the citadel, originally laid out by the Macedonians but in its present form largely Parthian (Plate 37). Outside the ramparts a necropolis included underground chambers and occasional tomb towers in the Palmyrene style.

In the physical remains at Dura Europos, one of the few cities whose development has been nearly all recovered through archaeology, we thus see a city that could almost form a model for the 'Graeco-Roman' urbanisation of the East: an initial Macedonian foundation that gradually merged with the Semitic and other eastern cultures that surrounded it. In the end, it was practically indistinguishable from the Near Eastern environment in which it was initially implanted. The oriental artistic and architectural forms are even more unambiguous than at Palmyra. Despite this it is stated that 'Dura always remained a Greek, or in the end a Graeco-Roman, city. The traces . . . of Semitic . . . and Iranian languages do not serve to refute this proposition'.[57] The material remains at Dura refute that proposition very strongly indeed. The most that one can say is that Dura was a city of mixed elements, with the non-Hellenistic elements predominating.

Mesopotamia

Further north on the great plains between the middle reaches of the Euphrates and Tigris Rivers, the main cities outside the Kingdom of Edessa were frontier cities, dating mainly from the later empire. Nisibis,[58] modern Nusaybin, had a very ancient history, figuring prominently in the second and first millennia BC, but Constantina,[59] modern Viransehir to the north-west, appears to date from the fourth century AD. Nisibis was of great strategic importance in the later Roman wars with Iran, becoming a major bone of contention on both the battlefield and the negotiating table. It changed hands a number of times, most notoriously in the settlement of the Emperor Jovian following Julian's death in the fourth century.[60] Apart from a very ruined Roman arch and the remains of a fourth-century church, very little of it survives today. Constantina, however, still preserves much of its massive basalt ramparts that were built in the time of Justinian. Dara was another massively fortified Roman site, with impressive cisterns still surviving today.[61]

Further east, the garrison town of Circesium formed an important link in the chain of fortified posts of the eastern frontier during the time of Diocletian.[62] It was strategically located near the confluence of the Khabur and Euphrates rivers and formed the head-quarters of the Third Parthian Legion in the fourth century. It is on the site of a former Assyrian post but virtually nothing remains of the Roman period today. More survives of the legionary headquarters of Singara, modern Sinjar in northern Iraq.[63] This was the headquarters of the First Flavian and First Parthian Legions after Septimius Severus incorporated the area into the empire at the end of the second century, and today much of its city walls and a gateway are still standing.

The Phoenician Coast[64]

This region was urbanised long before the Macedonian-Roman period and retained its 'native' (in this case Phoenician) character throughout. The main cities, Aradus, Byblos, Sidon, Tyre, Akka (Ptolemais) and Gaza, had enjoyed venerable histories, with Tyre long anticipating Rome in controlling most of the Mediterranean as its own commercial 'lake' in the early and middle first millennium BC. Even the main Roman 'enclave' on the coast, Beirut, was a settlement long before and presumably retained its native population during the Roman period. The one city to retain its Graeco-Roman name was Tripoli (the Phoenician name, however, is not known).[65]

The northern Levantine coast was dominated by Seleucia and Laodicaea, as well as a few minor ports such as Posidonium and Diospolis. All of these largely incorporated and continued older Phoenician ports as we have seen. Further down the Levantine coast, continuity from the Phoenician past is far stronger: like Beirut today, even their western gloss remained firmly rooted in Near Eastern traditions.

Macedonian and subsequent Roman conquest did, however, result – indirectly – in bringing one fundamental change to the ancient Phoenician ports. This was the foundation and rapid rise of Alexandria, creating a direct Hellenistic challenge to the Phoenician maritime and commercial supremacy in the Mediterranean. To some extent this was offset during the Hellenistic period by the north–south division of the eastern Mediterranean into the two rival Macedonian dynasties, the Seleucids protecting the Phoenicians' older supremacy against the Ptolemies encouraging Alexandria's rise. But the destruction of Carthage by Rome further exacerbated the position, a Phoenician loss that was Alexandria's gain. With Alexandria and all of the Phoenician city-states passing to the Romans in the first century BC, Alexandria's monopoly of the seas was assured.

Ultimately, perhaps the Phoenicians gained the most. For the Phoenician creative energies and intellectual talents, hitherto absorbed by trade, could be redirected elsewhere. Hence, the Phoenicians enjoyed a renaissance under the Romans. Historiography figured prominently, and Philo of Byblos (probably late second century AD) made available the ancient Phoenician historical works to the world of Classical learning. Chief of these were the writings of Sanchuniathon, who lived in the seventh century BC or earlier.[66] Josephus, although a Judaean, together with Eusebius and Procopius of Caesarea as well as Herodian, Ammianus Marcellinus, Libanius, John Malalas and other historians of the Antioch 'school', must ultimately be considered a part of this Phoenician historiographical tradition. In geography the Phoenician achievement in the Roman period was no less impressive. Marinus of Tyre (early second century AD) drew upon ancient Phoenician traditions of navigation, not to mention their nautical charts and other geographical records, to lay the foundations of scientific geography. He was the first to allocate localities to specific latitude and longitude using mathematically based maps rather than merely descriptive itineraries. His work forms the foundation of Ptolemy's geography. Other areas where Phoenician intellectual activity excelled included philosophy, particularly the Neo-Platonists Porphyry of Tyre and Iamblichus of Chalcis, and law, explored in more detail in the section on Beirut below.

Aradus, Antaradus and Marathus[67]

Roman Aradus was just one of a closely linked group of three originally distinct Phoenician settlements: Aradus, Antaradus and Marathus. The name Aradus initially applied only to the island two kilometres offshore. Its main colony on the mainland was known as Antaradus, both evolving to Arwad (or Ruwad) and Tartus (or Tortosa) respectively. Of the two, Arwad is probably the more ancient. A few kilometres south of Tartus is the site of another Aradian colony: Marathus (modern Amrit). Indeed, Arwad is about

equidistant from both Amrit and Tartus. Amrit tried to break free from Arwad's domination in 219 BC, which probably explains why it declined in the Hellenistic–Roman
period while Tartus rose.

The island of Arwad passed peacefully to Alexander the Great, having the wisdom to
submit rather than try to match the famous siege – and spectacular defeat – that the other
Phoenician island-city of Tyre underwent. Because of this, it enjoyed new-found prosperity, but in the Roman period its fortunes passed to Tartus on the mainland. Under the
Pax Romana the natural defences of an island were no longer necessary, whilst the
mainland had room for expansion, so Tartus grew at the expense of Arwad. It underwent
a major programme of rebuilding in 346 under Constantine, probably because of its
ancient shrine dedicated to the Virgin Mary. This shine itself replaced and incorporated
an older Phoenician fertility cult, probably Astarte.

Neither city, however, preserves many remains from either their Phoenician or their
Roman past (although Arwad still has foundations of its Phoenician ramparts). But
Marathus, which escaped later overbuilding, has many. These include some of the most
important Phoenician monuments on the entire coast, consisting of a temple and a
number of funerary monuments of considerable importance for the evolution of Near
Eastern architecture in the Roman period (Plates 116, 128 and 129).[68] There are also
traces of a stadium, possibly from the Macedonian period (the only one in the Near East
apart from Sebaste).

Further down the coast was the important Phoenician cult centre of Arqa (located just
inland).[69] It was a place of some importance in the second millennium BC, mentioned in
both Assyrian and Egyptian sources. In the Roman period it was known as Caesarea ad-
Libanum when its temples of Atargatis and Astarte achieved considerable fame. But it was
as the birthplace of the Emperor Severus Alexander that Arqa was best known. In spite of
this, Arqa never became a Lepcis Magna or even a Shahba,[70] and only a tell and a few
modest columns now mark the site. These belong either to one of the temples or to a
palace that Alexander supposedly built here.

Tripoli was founded as a joint colony of Aradus, Tyre and Sidon in about 800 BC.[71]
Hence its Greek name, but uniquely of the more important Phoenician cities, the original
Phoenician name is lost. Its location was at the modern port of al-Mina rather than the
present city of Tripoli itself. It was considerably embellished during both the Macedonian
and Roman periods, but apart from a few columns and other fragments, all of this has
either been lost through earthquakes and other destruction or obscured by almost
continuous over-building since antiquity.

Byblos[72]

Byblos, modern Jubayl, was one of the greatest Phoenician city-states, with a long – and
archaeologically well-documented – history before the Romans. Civic buildings from the
Roman period include street colonnades, a baths, a theatre, a basilica, a nymphaeum and
an extensive drainage system. Along with the other Phoenician city-states it was a major
trade centre, but Byblos specialised in two commodities. Its chief import was papyrus,
imported from Egypt and trans-shipped throughout the Greek-speaking world and elsewhere in the Mediterranean (hence the word for book – bible – derived from Byblos). Its
chief export was cedar wood, as Byblos was the nearest port to the great cedar forests
inland. In the area of these former forests, over eighty Latin inscriptions from the time of

Hadrian have been recorded. This suggests that the lucrative forestry of Byblos was a monopoly of the Roman emperors. Of equal importance to the cedars, but less emphasised, was the plentiful supply of other timber which Byblos also had ready access to, mostly cypress and Aleppo pine. These were probably more in demand for ship-building than cedar. Apart from masts and keels, cedar was used more for monumental building, particularly as roof beams to span the enormous distances that temple roofs demanded. In addition, linen from Egypt was trans-shipped through Byblos, and vintage wine was a popular export.

Byblos was renowned for its religion at least as much as for its trade, and many of its ancient kings bore theophoric names. Central to the pantheon was the cult and famous temple of Baalat Gabal, 'Our Lady of the Mountain'. Hence, the city was occasionally referred to as 'Holy Byblos', one of many such holy cities in the Near East that rivalled Jerusalem. Its temple was completely rebuilt in the Roman period on the same position as the Bronze Age one and a colonnaded approach added. The colossal Bronze Age stone images were reused in this reconstruction, but contemporary coins depict a large *baetyl*, rather like the sacred stone of Elagabal, as the cult object.

Baalat-Gabal was the patron goddess, but many other deities were worshiped in 'Holy Byblos' as well. Another large temple to an unidentified male deity was built in the Roman period. The Adonis cult with its important annual festival was also centred on Byblos, where it was almost as important as Baalat-Gabal. The annual blood-red discolor-ation of the nearby Adonis River (the Nahr Ibrahim) was central to this cult. Egyptian Isis and Osiris were also popular, probably because of their close links with the Adonis cult, and the theme of rebirth and resurrection common to the two cults both anticipated and paved the way for Christianity.[73] Hellenisation might have been a major element at Byblos along with the other Phoenician cities, but when it came to religion it was the older traditions that prevailed.

Beirut[74]

Beirut's origins are very ancient, and recent excavations in the centre of the city have brought to light a Bronze Age settlement defended by ramparts that resemble those of Byblos.[75] As such it was one of many similar Phoenician trading cities up and down the Levantine coast, but it achieved neither the fame nor the commercial domination of its better known neighbours – it was beneath Alexander the Great's notice in his rampage down the coast – remaining one of the more insignificant ports until the Roman period.

In 15 BC Augustus founded a veteran colony at Beirut. This rapidly became Rome's only Latin-speaking enclave in the Near East, 'an isle of Romanism in a sea of Hellen-ism',[76] remaining western in outlook to the present day. It rapidly gained all the trappings of a Roman city: two forums, a baths, a theatre, an amphitheatre and a circus.[77] Few traces of these have been recovered in modern excavations, so it is not possible to check whether such buildings were simply a Roman gloss, thinly disguising stronger native elements, as in other Roman cities (see Chapter 7). But if these most Roman of all buildings do not display its Latin and western character, the description of the inaugural games held in the amphitheatre removes all doubt: seven hundred pairs of criminals forced to slaughter each other until none were left alive.

At the beginning of the third century the Emperor Septimius Severus founded Beirut's most famous institution. This was the Law School, the first such institution in the Roman world, and it was enthusiastically supported by the Severan emperors. The Beirut Law School was to have a profound effect on Roman civilisation. It represents the birth of Roman – hence European – jurisprudence, of which Justinian's monumental *Digest* was the first great achievement. It attracted many prominent legal minds, mostly drawn from the Phoenician population of the Levant itself. The most famous were Papinian, a native of Emesa, and his contemporary Ulpian, a native of Tyre. Both were patronised by the Severan dynasty (although Caracalla had Papinian murdered for his association with Geta) and both are acknowledged in Justinian's *Digest* as forming the basis of Roman Law. This subsequently formed the basis of legal systems throughout Europe, and in much of the rest of the world as well.

Beirut and its justly famous law school, and with it its profound legacy, is regarded as a 'western' and Roman enclave in the Near East. But it was founded and promoted by emperors whose origins and destinies were intimately bound to Phoenician culture.[78] Above all, it must be emphasised that, Latin enclave though it might have been, the environment of Beirut and its law school is the Near East, not Italy. Many of the great scholars who dominated it were natives of the Near East, however Romanised, notably Papinian and Ulpian. It drew upon literary traditions that stretched back to Sanchunia-thon of Beirut in the seventh century BC and legal traditions that stretched back even further to the Judaic traditions of the early first millennium and the Mesopotamian law codes of the early second millennium. Ultimately, therefore, should we be viewing Beirut in the context of Rome or of Babylon?

Sidon and Tyre[79]

The greatest of the Phoenician maritime cities in the late second and early first millennia BC were Sidon and Tyre, both rivals for commercial and colonial supremacy. Out of this rivalry it was the island city of Tyre that emerged uppermost, although Sidon gained revenge by joining forces with Alexander in his attack on Tyre, with its subsequent destruction of the city and its population. Accordingly, Sidon enjoyed a glittering revival in the Hellenistic period, if the lavish sarcophagi of its princes, today forming the centre-piece of the Istanbul Archaeological Museum, are anything to go by. Tyre's main trade was the famous purple dye – Tyrian purple – derived from the murex sea-snails found on its coast – a commodity exploited by Tyre more than the other Phoenician coastal cities. Sidon's main commodity was glass – again a product of the sea, for good glass-producing sands occurred around Sidon.

Alexander's destruction of Tyre unwittingly sowed the seeds of its revival. Razing the city not only created a new building site, but the mole he constructed to bring Dunsinane Wood to Cawdor – the mainland to the island in this case – created virgin building land. Hence, this mole was to become the heart of the new Roman city, and Tyre preserves more Roman imperial remains than any other city of the Levantine coast. Another factor was the civil war between Septimius Severus and Pescennius Niger, when Tyre had the good sense to support the former – it did not make the mistake of opposing a winner for the second time. Although Niger plundered the city, Septimius rewarded its loyalty by elevating it to Colony in 201. Its renewed prosperity was assured. A magnificent colon-naded Decumanus and a hippodrome, one of the largest in the Roman world, were built on the isthmus (Figure 30). The eastern end of the Decumanus is marked by a monumental arch (Plate 38). To the west, on the site of the former island, the Decumanus was some 21

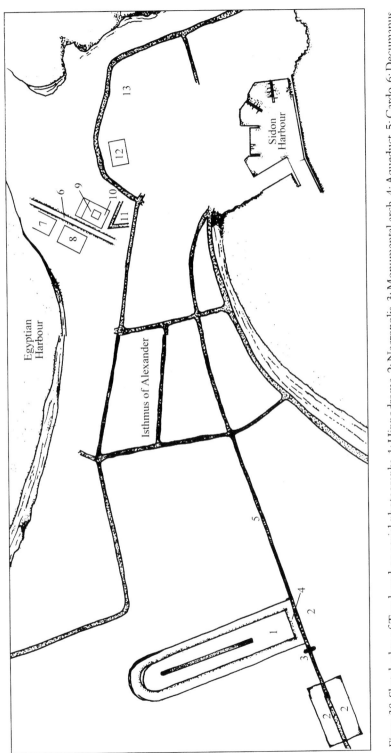

Figure 30 Sketch plan of Tyre based on aerial photographs. 1: Hippodrome. 2: Necropolis. 3: Monumental arch. 4: Aqueduct. 5: Cardo. 6: Decumanus. 7: Palaestra. 8: Baths. 9: Square arena. 10: Cisterns (under). 11: Colonnaded street. 12: Crusader cathedral. 13: Houses.

Plate 38 The monumental arch at Tyre

metres in width and paved originally with mosaic, replaced in the early third century by marble slabs. The columns are of imported cipollino from Greece. Baths and gymnasia have also been excavated to the south of the street. To the north is a unique rectangular building with seating around all four of its sides resembling a rectangular amphitheatre, possibly used for religious spectacle. Outside the city stretches a vast necropolis on either side of the paved road that is an extension of the colonnaded Decumanus. As well as underground hypogea decorated with some of the finest paintings in the Roman East, there are large numbers of particularly elaborate sarcophagi.

The main cult of Tyre was Phoenician Melqart.[80] Although Melqart was considered an aspect of Baal in the Phoenician pantheon, the Greeks and Romans equated him with Heracles. The cult was taken with the Tyrian colonists to the western Mediterranean, where it achieved great popularity in Carthage, as well as Cadiz and other Phoenician centres in Spain. Hence, the Straits of Gibraltar were known as the 'Pillars of Hercules', a direct reference to the popularity of the Melqart cult there. The lack of figural representation of the 'Temple of Hercules' at Cadiz later baffled the Romans, and the concept of rebirth and resurrection, central to the cult, prepared the way for the later popularity of Christianity in North Africa and Spain.[81] Astarte was also popular at Tyre, as was Baal-Shamin, thus forming a possible trinity with Melqart. The Temple of Astarte is depicted on Roman coins from Tyre, but excavations have so far revealed no traces.

Caesarea

South of Tyre the next main city was Akka, renamed Ptolemais in the third century BC by Ptolemy II Philadelphus of Egypt to offset Seleucid influence in the region. Ptolemy renamed Amman Philadelphia for the same reason. Akka-Ptolemais was the centre of the Phoenician cult of Hadad, equated by the Romans with Jupiter. Surprisingly, the Ptolemaic Hadad cult was assimilated to that of Jupiter Heliopolitanus of Baalbek, rather than to Jupiter-Hadad of Damascus. However, very little is known of Ptolemais in the Roman period, and virtually no remains have come to light.

Caesarea[82] is the only city of the coast where no pre-Macedonian traces have been discovered. It was founded in the fourth century BC by King Strato of Sidon, becoming known as Strato's Tower. It remained, however, only a minor settlement throughout the Macedonian period, although it has traces of second-century BC ramparts. But Strato's Tower was probably little more than a watering station on Sidon's trade with Egypt until it became one of the main objects of King Herod's ambitious building programme at the end of the first century BC. Herod founded a new city on the site between 22 and 10 BC, renaming it Caesarea in a deliberate attempt to curry favour with Augustus (Caesar). In addition to its Roman name, Herod endowed Caesarea Maritima (as it came to be known, to distinguish it from other 'Caesareas' elsewhere) with buildings that were a deliberate attempt at Romanisation: a Temple to Rome and Augustus, a forum, baths, a theatre and an amphitheatre (Figure 31). Much of the building technique followed Roman rather than Near Eastern patterns: for example, archaeological investigations have shown that cast concrete, almost certainly imported from Italy, was used extensively. Concrete was rarely used in the East, stone being more popular, so it seems that even some of the builders of Caesarea came from the West. Herod also built a palace and massively enlarged the harbour, possibly in an attempt to rival Alexandria. Large areas of good agricultural land inland were allocated for the city's income. Caesarea was settled with a mixed population of Greek-speakers and Jews, which was to remain a source of friction in the events leading up to the Jewish Revolt.

Herod consciously sought to make Caesarea a *Roman* city above all, bringing 'Roman entertainment, Roman gods, and even Roman concrete',[83] imparting a western veneer which he could not possibly attempt at holy Jerusalem. Hence, the emphasis on such Roman trappings as the Temple to Rome and Augustus and the amphitheatre. Caesarea must have superficially resembled similar port cities of the western Mediterranean quite closely. Herod founded Sebaste for much the same reasons, and it too was dominated by a Temple of Rome and Augustus, as well as a forum with a basilica alongside (Figure 32), both features highly unusual in the Near East.[84] But at Sebaste the Roman veneer is more superficial: the streets were colonnaded in the eastern fashion, unlike Caesarea (Plate 39), while the Temple of Rome and Augustus was built in the Near Eastern style, despite its dedication.[85] The material remains, therefore, demonstrate that Herod's efforts to implant Romanisation in his kingdom found considerable resistance in the more conservative inland. But Caesarea, facing the sea, could look to the West and wear its Roman airs with far more confidence.

Hence, Caesarea was the natural choice as capital of Roman Palestine. This accelerated the city's Romanisation and Caesarea remained a Roman enclave. Following the Jewish Revolt, the Caesarea arena was the natural choice for the execution of 2,500 Jewish prisoners by Titus. The destruction of the former Jewish capital also meant that greater

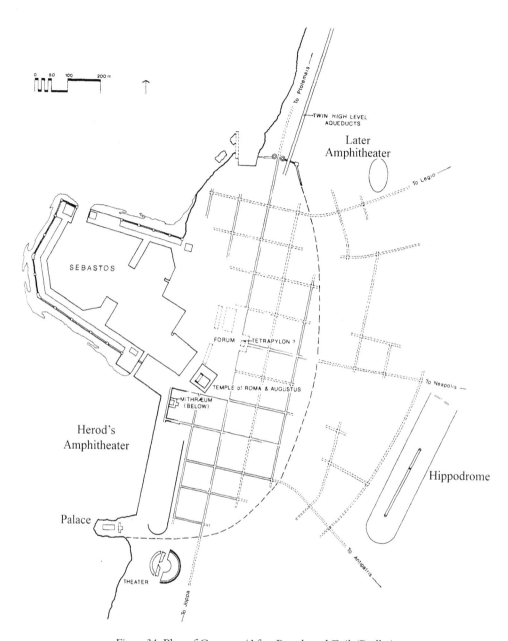

Figure 31 Plan of Caesarea (After Porath and Zeik/Roller)

prosperity flowed into Caesarea. Accordingly, with both Roman confidence and Herod's initial endowments behind it, Caesarea grew rapidly in the first two centuries of Roman rule. A magnificent double aqueduct, now one of Caesarea's more prominent landmarks (Plate 40), was constructed during the time of Hadrian. The same emperor endowed a magnificent new temple dedicated to himself, and a superb colossal porphyry statue of the emperor that recently came to light probably belongs to this. Other temples were

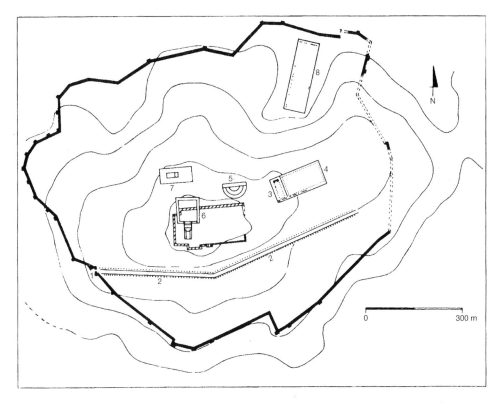

Figure 32 Plan of Sebaste. 1: West Gate. 2: Colonnaded street. 3: Basilica. 4: Forum. 5: Theatre. 6: Temple of Augustus. 7: Temple of Kore. 8: Stadium. (After Segal/Crowfoot)

built and existing ones embellished. Traces of the cults of Mithras, Osiris, Tyche, Apollo, Demeter and Ephesian Artemis have been found in the excavations; native Semitic cults are almost entirely absent.

But the third century also saw the introduction of a new Semitic element into Caesarea's western fabric. This was Christianity, which became particularly prominent at Caesarea when the great Alexandrian theologian, Origen, turned Caesarea into a centre for Christian learning. By the end of the third century a native of Caesarea and the greatest of the early Christian historians, Eusebius, set the seal on the city's transformation. In this way Caesarea participated in what can only be termed the 'Phoenician renaissance'. This immense upsurge of intellectual activity in the later Roman period encompassed the religious, philosophical, historiographical and legal traditions of Antioch, Byblos, Beirut, Sidon, Tyre and Gaza, in addition to Caesarea. It represented the last flowering in antiquity of the cities of the Phoenician coast. To say that these Phoenician cities were 'characterised . . . above all by a recognised identity within Graeco-Roman culture'[86] is to miss the obvious. Ultimately, Caesarea formed a part of the culture on which it was founded.

179

Plate 39 The colonnaded street at Sebaste

Plate 40 The aqueduct at Caesarea

The Decapolis[87]

The Decapolis was a loose confederation of former Macedonian cities under indirect Roman rule between the first century BC and the first century AD. It covered the present borderland region of Jordan, Israel and Syria, stretching roughly from Amman to Damascus (Figure 33). Consisting originally of ten cities (hence its name), the number eventually grew to some twelve or fifteen (the exact figure is disputed) by the end of the first century AD. Philadelphia (Amman), Gerasa (Jerash), Pella (Tabaqat Fahl in the Jordan Valley), Capitolias (Bait Ra's near Irbid), Gadara (Umm Qais), Abila (the last two near the Yarmuk ravine), Raphana and probably Dion are within the present borders of Jordan. The whereabouts of the latter two are uncertain, but they may have been names for the same place. Arbela (modern Irbid) may also have 'belonged' to the Decapolis although it is more likely that it came under neighbouring Capitolias. The only one on the west bank of the Jordan was Scythopolis (Beth Shean in Israel). Hippos overlooked the eastern shores of the Sea of Galilee on the Golan Heights, and Adra (Der'a) and Canatha (Qanawat) are in the Hauran in Syria. Damascus was also briefly included in the first century AD.

It would be a mistake to view the Decapolis as somehow Hellenistic. Vague an administrative unit though it was, all evidence suggests that it was a creation of Pompey's annexation of Syria, and should not be seen as either Seleucid in foundation or Hellenistic in nature.[88] There is certainly no evidence that the Decapolis was a fully fledged League in the same way that Greek city-states were elsewhere in the eastern Mediterranean. At best, it was simply a loose geographical term, reflecting perhaps the Macedonian foundations (or re-foundations) of the cities in an earlier period, together with some form of economic link. The use of the term may even have been simply propagandistic, an effort to emphasise a Roman presence in an area otherwise almost wholly Arab. It is doubtful, after all, if the Nabataeans used the term. Hence, the extreme vagueness in the sources of the exact number of cities in the Decapolis: it simply did not matter.

The Decapolis has been regarded as a sort of Hellenic alliance against the increasingly powerful Semitic states of Judaea and Nabataea respectively. But all three regions – Judaea, Nabataea and the Decapolis – were in any case indirectly under Rome so that any such 'alliance' would have been neither necessary nor tolerated. Furthermore, there was no contiguous union in the territorial sense: both Judaea and Nabataea extended into the area of the Decapolis. Even after the Decapolis was 'formed', some Decapolis cities were transferred to Judaean and Nabataean administration and vice versa at various times, while the actual capital of the Nabataean kingdom itself was moved in the first century AD from Petra to Bosra, within the Decapolis 'enclave'. Nabataean influence in particular was considerable. From a cultural and ethnic point of view the populations of the Decapolis cities were mixed Graeco-Macedonian, Arab and Jewish (particularly in Scythopolis). The Arabs probably formed the bulk of the population with Greeks and Macedonians – or Hellenised Arabs – forming the upper echelons of the administration.[89] The old Semitic names of the cities were either retained or lay just below the surface throughout, resurfacing the moment Roman rule ended. The architecture is oriental, the temples and the cults were to local Semitic deities.[90] To view the Decapolis as an 'island of Hellenism'[91] or as 'unambiguously Greek' in 'public character'[92] is untenable.

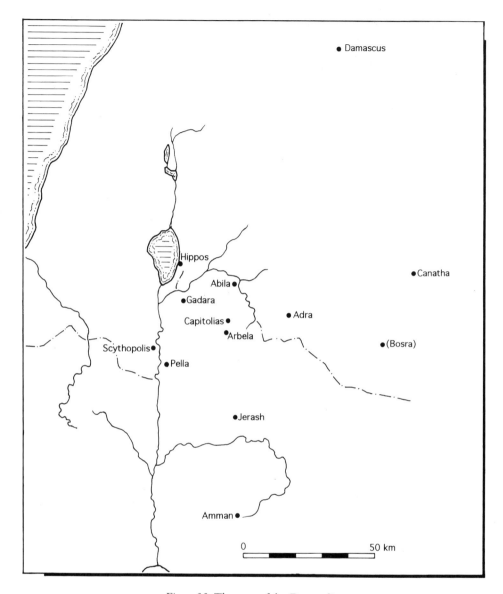

Figure 33 The area of the Decapolis

With the end of most of the Near Eastern client kingdoms and the imposition of direct Roman rule – the Judaean kingdom came to an end in AD 94, followed soon by the Nabataean kingdom in 106 – the Decapolis seems to disappear. It was all now a part of the Roman Empire, so any propaganda value in the term Decapolis was no longer valid. With the subsequent administrative reorganisation, all of the Decapolis cities were divided between the new provinces of Syria, Arabia and Palestine. But informal 'membership' still remained an empty honour long afterwards – much as the Hanseatic League continued in the Baltic.[93]

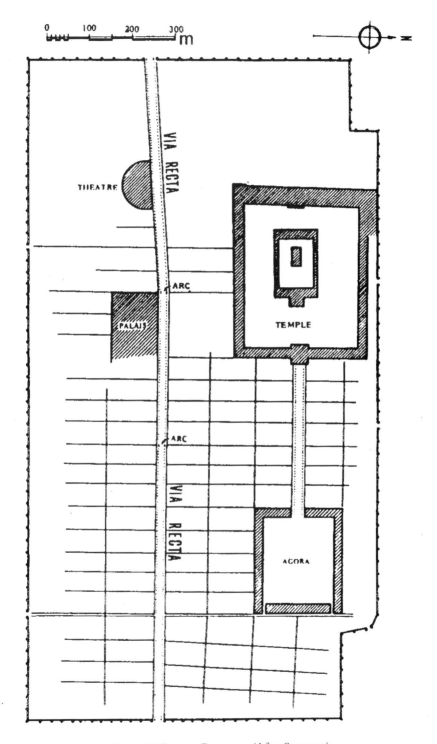

Figure 34 Roman Damascus (After Sauvaget)

183

Plate 41 The East Gate at Damascus

Damascus[94]

Written testimonies to Damascus begin in the third millennium. In the Aramaean period of the early first millennium BC Damascus first emerged as a major regional centre, and has maintained this status ever since. Following the Roman conquest of Syria it seems to have been at different times under Roman and Nabataean administration. Its naturally pre-eminent role was recognised by Hadrian, who elevated it to the status of metropolis. It was further elevated to the status of Roman colony by Septimius Severus.

Much of the gridded street pattern of Damascus today is presumed to be third century BC, although with such a long history before and continual over-building since, this cannot be certain. When originally laid out by the Romans the ramparts enclosed a rectangular area measuring approximately 1,340 by 750 metres, and they follow much the same line today (Figure 34). They have however, been continually rebuilt, so that only the foundations or small stretches (particularly along the north side) are thought to be Roman. The Bab Sharqi (Eastern Gate) is the only original Roman gate still standing (Plate 41). It is a standard Roman triple entrance and the central arch is aligned on the Roman Decumanus (the Biblical 'Street Called Straight'). Laid out in Roman times, the Decumanus cut across the older grid pattern from east to west. Like other cities of the Roman East, it was originally colonnaded, and a fragment of the original colonnade still stands just inside the Bab Sharqi. Unusually, it was arcaded and in the Doric order.

Halfway along the Decumanus are the remains of a Roman monumental arch, probably marking the intersection of two streets (re-erected on present street level, the original being some 5 metres lower).

The greatest building of Roman Damascus was its gigantic temple of Jupiter Damascenus (Figure 35).[95] The Umayyad Mosque is set in the inner temenos of this temple, itself replacing – and largely incorporating – the earlier temple to Hadad (with whom the Romans equated Jupiter). It was built in the first century AD, although much of the present enclosure wall probably dates from the third or fourth century (Plate 42). But it was a far older sacred site, as a ninth-century BC basalt orthostat, probably belonging to the original Aramaean Temple of Hadad, was discovered in the north-eastern corner of the temenos. The temenos wall, built of fine ashlar blocks, originally had a square tower at each corner. Each side was originally pierced by triple entrances. The one on the east, with a propylaeum in front of it, was the main gate to the Roman temple and still forms

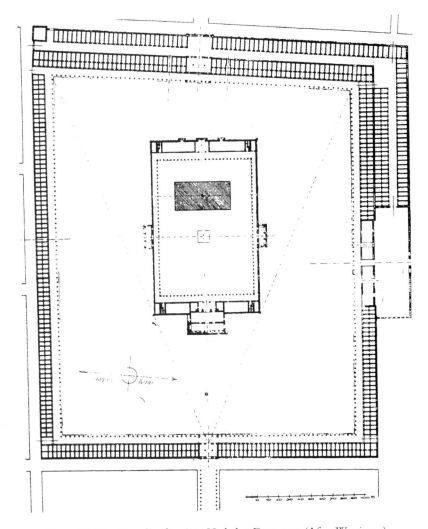

Figure 35 The Temple of Jupiter-Hadad at Damascus (After Watzinger)

Plate 42 The enclosure wall and corner tower of the Temple
of Jupiter-Hadad at Damascus

the main entrance to the mosque. The original sanctuary would have been placed in the centre of the enclosure, but this was destroyed when the enclosure was used for a basilica dedicated to John the Baptist. To the east of the enclosure are the remains of the Roman propylaeum consisting of part of an elaborately decorated pediment resting on four Corinthian columns. This formed the entrance to a gigantic outer enclosure, originally measuring some 315 by 360 metres, or approximately 113,400 square metres in area, that has now largely disappeared. This makes the temple one of the largest in the Roman East.

This temple belongs firmly within Near Eastern, rather than Roman, architectural traditions,[96] and the cult worshipped there was a Semitic one.[97] As such, the vast temple marks Damascus as another of the East's holy cities, in this case the centre of the Hadad cult. It seems possible that Herod's great building programme at Jerusalem, marking a conscious effort at making his temple the grandest in the East and its religion pre-eminent, sparked off a religious competition with rival cults. Damascene Hadad – in addition to Emesene Baal, Palmyrene Bel and perhaps even Hierapolitan Atargatis, Tyrian Melqart, Bibline Baalat and numerous other cults – felt prompted to respond with building programmes intended to offset that of Jerusalem.

Qanawat and Si'[98]

Since Bosra was never a part of the Decapolis, Qanawat (Roman Canatha) was the main Decapolis city of the Hauran in the first century BC. In all of the Decapolis cities, the Nabataean element was uppermost and the Hellenistic least. This was because of the important Nabataean cult centre at Si'.

Inside Qanawat itself, the main surviving monuments are also religious. The main concentration is a complex known as the 'Seraglio', a series of buildings with a rather complex architectural history. It consists of two apsidal structures, probably a temple complex, on the south and east sides of a colonnaded courtyard, the southern one second century AD and the eastern temple late third or early fourth century. Other buildings include a possible hall, dated by an inscription to AD 124, a small theatre and the remains of a nymphaeum. To the south-east of the Seraglio there are the remains of a peripteral temple, probably dedicated to the sun god, Helios, and a prostyle temple dedicated to Zeus (or the local equivalent).

The sacred site of Si' (Seia) lies further up the slopes to the south-east of Qanawat. Si' was not a separate town but forms an integral part of ancient Qanawat. The two are connected by a paved road that winds up to Si', probably a processional way. Si' was sacred to the Semitic gods Baal-Shamin and Dushara, the latter the main deity of the Nabataean pantheon. The worship of Baal-Shamin was practised here long before the Roman period, though the cult of Dushara probably arrived with the Nabataean conquest in the early first century BC. Both temples date to the late first century BC, when the Nabataeans ruled the area.

The temple complex at Si' was excavated and studied in great detail at the beginning of the century by an American expedition, which was able to reconstruct the buildings by a careful study of the surviving fragments. It consisted of a sacred precinct entered through a propylaeum, surrounded by three temples to the south, west and north (Figure 36). The small temple to the south is a simple, prostyle temple of fairly conventional design, but the other two are highly unusual. That on the west is the Temple of Dushara, which

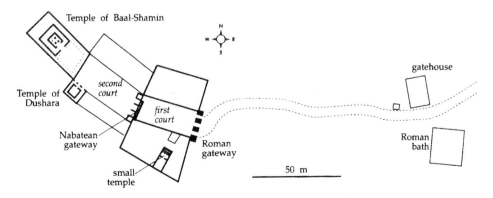

Figure 36 Plan of the Si' temples (After Burns/Butler)

187

originally had an arched entablature over the columns forming its entrance. That on the north is the Temple of Baal-Shamin, dedicated in 33 BC, entered through a very elaborately decorated entrance (Figure 108A).[99] Its façade consisted of a pedimented colonnade flanked by two square towers. The sanctuaries of both main temples consist of two enclosed squares which in turn enclose a third square formed by four columns.

Siʿ is an important part of Syrian architectural history, for it contains many important elements from a variety of cultural traditions. Both deities place it firmly in the Semitic tradition. This tradition is given architectural expression by the twin towers that flanked the Baal-Shamin façade, related to the ancient Semitic worship of high places. The fondness for complex and rich decoration owes much to Nabataean architecture, as at the Temple of Khirbet Tannur in southern Jordan, but the overall 'language' of the decoration – the Classical orders (or modified versions of it) and much of the actual decorative patterns – belongs to the Hellenistic tradition. Another element however, comes from a third direction altogether. This is the 'square in square' arrangement of the sanctuaries, which belong to an Iranian tradition. This and the other architectural features are analysed in more detail in Chapter 7. Suffice to observe here that the Siʿ religious complex places this part of the Decapolis firmly in the Semitic tradition.

Jerash[100]

The origins of Jerash (Roman Gerasa) lie in the, as yet poorly documented, Bronze and Iron Ages. The first major evidence for the pre-Roman settlement comes from remains on 'Camp Hill' and the Temple of Zeus temenos, where traces of a Macedonian settlement have been recorded. At the end of the fourth century BC it was re-founded as a city for settling veterans, supposedly by Perdiccas, one of Alexander's generals, under the name Antioch-of-the-Chrysoroas ('of the Golden River'). Fragments of an elaborate Hellenistic temple have recently been found in the Zeus temenos under the Roman-period altar. Subsequent centuries saw substantial and rapid expansion (Figure 37, Plate 43). The Cardo was laid out at the end of the first century AD and was soon adorned with colonnades in the Ionic order (Plate 78), and a theatre was built next to the Zeus Temple. Decorated archways were erected at the northern and southern ends of the Cardo in the early second century AD (Plate 91), with a monumental commemorative arch outside the city to the south to mark the state visit by the Emperor Hadrian (Plate 90). The most dramatic expansion occurred after the middle of the second century, when the two Decumani were laid out and colonnaded, the Cardo was widened and recolonnaded in the Corinthian order (Plate 74; the older Ionic capitals being re-used for the Decumani), the hippodrome (Plate 104) and a second theatre were constructed, and the gigantic Artemis Temple complex with its elaborate propylaeum and processional way were built (Figure 65, Plates 75, 110 and 115). These merely mark the city's more ambitious building programmes. Numerous lesser buildings were constructed and more streets were laid out. The Cardo continued northwards outside the city, past an unlocated Temple of Nemesis and several mausolea, to the suburb of Birkatayn some two kilometres away. A small theatre and tanks were built here, connected to the Maiumas festival held in sacred groves at Birkatayn.[101] By the beginning of the fourth century Jerash had reached its maximum extent on both sides of the river, and was surrounded by ramparts. It never expanded, however, as far as the Arch of Hadrian, and the Temple of Artemis remained unfinished, suggesting that the city had overreached itself.

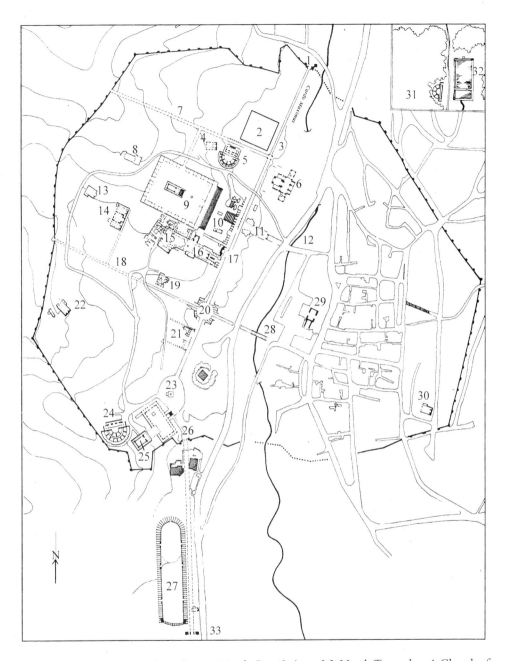

Figure 37 Plan of Jerash (After Pillen). 1: North Gate. 2: Agora? 3: North Tetrapylon. 4: Church of Bishop Isiah. 5: North Theatre. 6: West Baths. 7: North Decumanus. 8: Synagogue Church. 9: Artemis Propylaeum. 10: Temple of Artemis. 11: Artemis Processional Way. 12: North Bridge. 13: Church of Bishop Genesius. 14: Church of St John Complex. 15: Church of St Theodore. 16: Cathedral. 17: Nymphaeum. 18: South Decumanus. 19: Ummayyad houses. 20: South Tetrapylon. 21: Macellum. 22: Church of SS Peter and Paul. 23: Oval Plaza. 24: South Theatre. 25: Temple of Zeus. 26: South Gate. 27: Hippodrome. 28: South Bridge. 29: East Baths. 30: Church of Procopius. 31: Festival Theatre. 32: Tanks. 33: Arch of Hadrian.

Plate 43 Jerash from the Temple of Zeus. The Oval Plaza is in the foreground

Being probably the best preserved of all Roman cities in the East, Jerash has received almost an excess of attention. But the undoubtedly impressive nature of its Roman remains, together with the overt 'Roman-ness' of the architecture, has diverted attention from the real issues at Jerash. On the surface it appears to be an entirely Roman town – indeed, almost overbearingly so, a completely foreign transplant that architecturally has more in common with the West than the Near Eastern world in which it was implanted. The architectural forms, styles and details are immediately familiar to the westerner, from its massive Corinthian temples to the carvings that decorate them. On closer examination, however, this obvious 'Roman-ness' recedes, being merely a veneer that hides an essentially oriental city built with familiar oriental architectural forms. This is explored in greater detail in Chapter 7.

It must also be emphasised that whilst Jerash is deservedly one of the most spectacular towns in the entire Roman world, it was in its own day nothing more than Jerash is today: a minor provincial town. In the Decapolis alone, Scythopolis was larger, and outside it were numerous other more splendid cities. Splendid though the remains undoubtedly are, it was no great capital embellished by successive emperors, nor was it a wealthy city-state controlling major caravan routes throughout the East. Even the region's main artery in Roman times, the Via Trajana from Bosra to the Gulf of Aqaba, bypassed Jerash. It was just a minor market town, made unique today only by the accident of its preservation.

Jerash thus provides us with a glimpse of the spectacular nature and immense wealth of these Roman cities in the East in their heyday in the second and third centuries. But the size and ambition of its monuments are rather more than a mere accident of preservation. The Temple of Artemis is, after all, one of the largest in the East, rivalling Jerusalem, Damascus, Baalbek and Palmyra. It boasts a magnificent Arch of Hadrian. Never mind that the city itself could not expand to meet this arch, it remains the only monumental Roman arch in the East that approaches the great triumphal arches in Rome itself. The other embellishments, too, mark Jerash as exceptional: the Temple of Zeus only slightly smaller than that of Artemis; the oval plaza, one of the finest Roman architectural ensembles to survive antiquity; together with the colonnaded streets, theatres and other trappings, all add up to something rather more than a minor provincial city. Yet Jerash was not the capital of a Near Eastern kingdom, nor the centre of a major cult, nor astride major trade routes. Why, therefore, the paradox?

Perhaps much of the explanation of Jerash lies in its name: Antioch-on-the-Chrysoroas, the result of a dynastic tug-of-war. The whole region became a bitterly squabbled over area between the rival royal houses of Seleucid Syria and Ptolemaic Egypt. Hence, the name 'Antioch' is a Seleucid dynastic name, to stake a Seleucid claim in the Ptolemaic borderlands. Conversely, Amman was renamed 'Philadelphia' and Akka 'Ptolemais' after Ptolemy Philadelphus of Egypt, staking his claim.

And here perhaps is the key to Jerash's grandeur. Although the name 'Gerasa' seems to have been more commonly used, the name 'Antioch' gave it an image which it felt compelled to live up to, the image of its better-known namesake in north Syria. Of course, the Near East in the Seleucid period was littered with 'Antiochs', many of them little more than small towns. But Antioch-on-the-Chrysoroas, confronting Ptolemaic Egypt, had a political statement to make. Even after this no longer became necessary when both states became Roman, Jerash tried consciously to model itself on Antioch-on-the-Orontes: the magnificent colonnaded streets (some of the earliest in the Near East after Antioch itself), the circular plazas, the tetrapylons and nymphaeum appear conscious – albeit paler – imitations of their grander counterparts at Antioch. Jerash even had its processional way out to the cult centre at Birkatayn, an exact counterpart to Antioch and Daphne. The other monuments, such as the over-ambitious temples or the Arch of Hadrian or the hippodrome, would certainly make sense if Jerash was the centre of a major cult, as Damascus was, or the capital of a local dynasty, as Bosra was, or a Roman provincial capital, as Caesarea was, or the centre of a web of trade routes, as Palmyra was. But Jerash was none of these. Such grandioseness does, however, find an explanation as a conscious attempt to be another 'Antioch'.

Jerash and its monuments are certainly magnificent. But it is a magnificence that it could never quite achieve, an ambition it could never quite fulfil, monuments that it could never quite finish. The Artemis Temple is a stupendous complex, but it was never finished; the hippodrome is magnificent, but it is the smallest in the East; the Arch of Hadrian proclaims a city that never quite made it. The overriding feeling one has of them is of an empty boast, a pale imitation, an inferiority complex. In the end, Jerash was not so much Semitic 'Gerasa' and even less Hellenistic 'Antioch-on-the-Chrysoroas', but merely 'Antioch-not-on-the-Orontes'.

Amman[102]

Like so many Hellenistic 'foundations', Amman is a far older city, the Iron Age city of Ammon. Indeed, it is one of the very few cities in the region still to preserve major Iron Age monumental remains. The region east of the Jordan became a hotly disputed frontier zone between the rival Seleucid and Ptolemaic dynasties. This resulted in a dramatic increase in the strategic importance of Amman, with the obvious natural defences of its citadel. Under the energetic leadership of Ptolemy II Philadelphus of Egypt, much of southern Syria was won from the Seleucids in the 270s BC. An upsurge in building activity and cultural assertiveness by the Ptolemaic dynasty ensued, and the strategically important but hitherto minor city of Amman was refounded in about 255 BC as the new Ptolemaic city of Philadelphia, named after the king. The older name, however, still survived as the region of Ammanitis, corresponding roughly to the Biblical kingdom of Ammon. Indeed, some of the sources continued to call the city itself by its old name of Rabbath-Ammon, or 'Rabbatammana' – clearly the change of name was regarded as of little significance.[103] The city too continued to be ruled for the Ptolemies by the same local dynasty who ruled it on behalf of the Iranians, the Jewish Tobiad house.

Antiochus the Great managed to capture Philadelphia from the Ptolemies by siege in 218 BC, bringing most of Jordan under Seleucid control. The rise of the Nabataean kingdom further south, however, meant that Amman remained in a border zone. It is not clear exactly whose writ ran in Amman – the Nabataeans probably exerted some form of control after Seleucid decline at the end of the third century – but the uncertainty allowed the Jewish Tobiad family to rule virtually independently. The Roman annexation of Syria in 64 BC meant that Philadelphia became one of the cities of the Decapolis, being the southernmost of the confederation, a 'gateway', as it were, to Nabataea and Arabia. With the creation of the province of Arabia by Trajan, Philadelphia assumed additional importance on the Via Nova Trajana. Traces of this road – consisting mostly of milestones – have been found to the north of Amman. As a result, the second century AD brought great prosperity and embellishment. It acquired a theatre, an odeon, a public square or forum, baths, a nymphaeum, colonnaded streets and temple complexes (Figure 38, Plate 44). To these were added, after the third century, the standard quota of churches, but the Christian period as a whole appears to be one of obscurity, if not decline, for Philadelphia. The colonnaded streets and

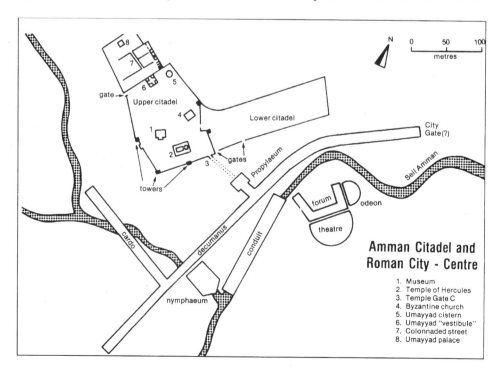

Figure 38 Plan of Roman Amman (After Politis)

Plate 44 The Theatre and Forum at Amman

the temple belong within the Near Eastern architectural traditions, with the nymphaeum in particular probably a *kalybe*, a specifically Nabataean type of monument.[104] The perceived 'unambiguously Greek' element of Philadelphia/Amman,[105] therefore, recedes against an overall background of both cultural continuity and Semitic assertiveness.

Other Decapolis cities

Capitolias,[106] modern Bayt Ra's in north Jordan, was founded in AD 97/8 by Nerva or Trajan and named after Jupiter Capitolinus. Its height was in the latter half of the second and first half of the third centuries, when it minted its own coins. Both Greek and Nabataean inscriptions of the second and third century show a mixed population. Located only five kilometres from Arbela (Irbid), it is likely that the two 'cities' formed a single agglomeration – or at least were closely interconnected. Arbela was the older city, with continuous occupation from the Middle Bronze Age or earlier. Arbela, however, does not seem to have appeared in any of the lists of Decapolis cities, so was presumably subordinate to Capitolias.[107] From the point of view of continuity from a Semitic past, Capitolias and Arbela can be regarded as the one urban area.

Scythopolis was the largest of the Decapolis cities according to Josephus, and current Israeli excavations there appear to be confirming this as more and more monumental buildings are revealed (Figure 39).[108] The city is liberally bestrewn with colonnaded

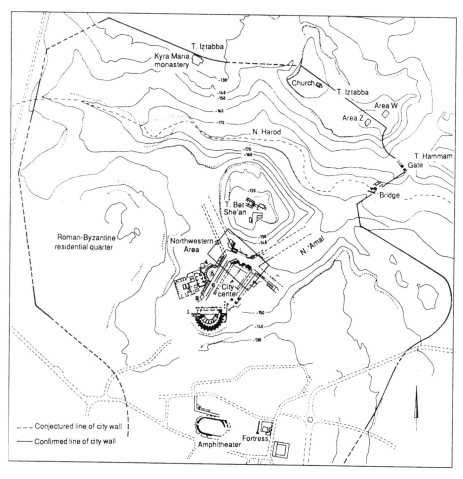

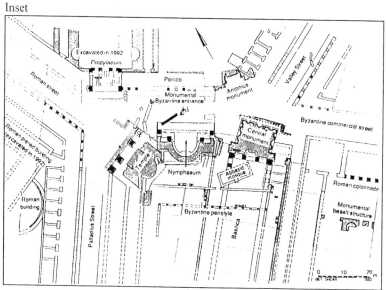

Figure 39 Plan of Beth Shean, with the monumental centre inset. (After Foerster and Tsafrir)

Plate 45 View along 'Valley Street' at Beth Shean, towards the
monumental centre

streets, although there is no overall grid pattern. Four of these streets converge upon a
monumental centre marked by an impressive nymphaeum, a propylaeum leading to an
unexcavated temple on top of the tell, as well as a further temple and several unidentified
ornate monuments (Figure 39, Plate 45). Other major buildings include a large theatre, a
baths complex, an amphitheatre and a large exedra facing one of the colonnaded streets.
Occupation has been recorded on the Tell of Beth Shean (Biblical Beisan) at least since
the Bronze Age. The name 'Scythopolis' represents a renaming, reverting to Beth Shean
(or variants) with the Islamic conquest. The origin of the name Scythopolis is unknown,
as there are no known associations of Scythians with Palestine.[109] The term 'Scythian'
does, however, have close associations with Jews, as the name 'Ashkenaz' is derived from
the Old Persian term for 'Scythian',[110] and Scythopolis alone of the Decapolis cities
probably had a majority Jewish population in the Roman period. In support of an argument for Greek character, it has been written that Scythopolis 'describes itself' as a Greek
city.[111] This is to put the cart before the horse: *Scythopolis* 'describes' no such thing, an
inscription at Scythopolis did, which is something quite different. The current programme
of excavations and restorations looks set to 'create' a monumental Roman city that could
well rival Jerash.

Pella, modern Tabaqat Fahl, lay on the opposite side of the Jordan Valley to Scythopolis
and has also been subject to extensive excavations.[112] These have revealed almost uninter-
rupted occupation since the fourth millennium BC. It became a walled town, having an

extensive trade with neighbouring countries in the Bronze Age, when Egyptian texts record its name as Pahel, of which the modern name, Fahl, is a derivation. Following the Macedonian conquest in the fourth century BC a new Seleucid settlement was founded, centred on the main mound of Tell Hosn. It was 'renamed' Pella after the city in Macedon, but the name Pella equally represents a Macedonian approximation of its native name. In the Roman period, Pella shared in the general expansion and wealth of the other Decapolis cities. Coins depict an impressive temple on top of Tell Hosn, as well as a monumental nymphaeum. Remains include a recently discovered portion of the possible temenos wall of this temple and fragments of a civic complex that included an odeon (Plate 46). However, the general scarcity of Roman monumental building stands in marked contrast to the other cities of the Decapolis. No traces, for example, have been found of colonnaded streets.

Far more survives of ancient Gadara,[113] modern Umm Qays in northern Jordan, where remains include a colonnaded Decumanus, a baths, a nymphaeum, a theatre, an odeon, a hippodrome and a monumental arch (Figure 40). Associated with the town is the thermal baths complex of Hammat Gadar in the Jordan Valley below Gadara. Gadara is certainly the most spectacularly sited of all Decapolis towns, with views over the Sea of Galilee, the Jordan River, the Yarmuk River and the Golan Heights. Perhaps this setting proved inspirational in ancient times, for Gadara was an important centre of learning throughout

Plate 46 The civic centre and excavations at Pella, from Tell Hosn

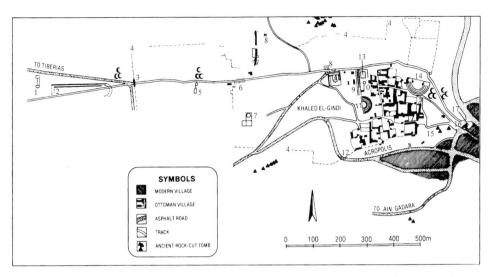

Figure 40 Plan of Umm Qays (After Bablick, Hagen, Reidel). 1: Monumental Arch. 2: Hippodrome.
3: West Gate. 4: City walls. 5: Mausoleum. 6: Decumanus. 7: Al-Qasr. 8: Nymphaeum. 9: Shops.
10: Church. 11: West Theatre. 12: Tower. 13: Church. 14: East Theatre. 15: Tomb of Chaireas.
16: Tomb of Modestus. 17: Tomb of the Germani.

both the Macedonian and Roman periods. A number of noted philosophers, poets and rhetoricians were associated with Gadara. However, it did not match Edessa, Antioch, Beirut or Tyre, for example. The 'school' of Gadarene learning appears to belong entirely in the Hellenistic traditions, and there is no trace of any settlement prior to the establishment of a Macedonian military settlement there. But the name 'Gadara' is a Semitic one, presumably pre-Macedonian, and Nabataean influence is known to have been strong, while the colonnaded street and other elements of its architecture belong within Near Eastern traditions. It would be a mistake, therefore, to overstate either its Hellenistic nature or its intellectual achievement.

At Abila (modern Qweilbeh),[114] located in the fertile hilly region of northern Jordan just south of the Yarmuk River, the Roman-period settlement once again appears to have been the culmination of continuous settlement from at least the Middle Bronze Age. By the second century AD it was adorned with the normal trappings of a Decapolis city, albeit on a more modest scale than Jerash or Damascus, divided by a Cardo and Decumanus and overlooked by an acropolis. It has received only limited excavations. These and associated surveys have recorded a temple (incorporated into the sixth-century church), a theatre, a market or palaestra, some subterranean aqueducts and possibly a baths and a nymphaeum. The population of the city in the Roman period has been estimated at between 8,000 and 10,000. It had a vigorous economy based on its rich agricultural hinterland, which created enough surplus for the importation of luxury items.

Susita (Hippos), located in the foothills of the Golan Heights, remains the least investigated of the Decapolis towns.[115] The town plan is bisected by a colonnaded Decumanus, and a monumental nymphaeum and a church have been identified.

'Roman' Arabia: Bosra and Shahba

Bosra[116]

For standing remains, Bosra compares with Palmyra and Jerash in the Roman East, although it lies heavily obscured under the modern town. With more of the ancient city being exposed by the current programme of relocation, clearance and archaeological investigation, Bosra will probably be the most intact Roman town of the East. Like both Jerash and Palmyra, the Roman nature of the architecture – hence character of the city – appears almost overwhelming, so must be carefully considered.

Bosra had a continuous history of development as a Near Eastern settlement since the Bronze Age. This culminated in the later part of the first century AD when Rabbel II moved the capital of the Nabataean kingdom there from Petra. From then until the final annexation of the Nabataean kingdom in AD 107, the city is inextricably bound up with the Decapolis cities which lay around it: inextricably since the Decapolis was (nominally at least) under Roman administration, whilst Bosra was the Nabataean capital. There must have been considerable overlap, and certainly no neat 'border lines', during this period.

Bosra was made the capital of the Roman province of Arabia, as well as the garrison town of the Third Cyrenaica Legion, under the name Nova Trajana Bostra. It continued to be a major trade entrepôt, taking over much of the trade that Petra previously controlled, forming the head of the new road that the Romans built down to the Gulf of Aqaba, the Via Trajana, successor to the Biblical King's Highway. Bosra remained an important centre in the Christian period, when it became successively a bishopric then archbishopric. During the period of Ghassanid ascendancy in the sixth century, Bosra formed one of the main Ghassanid centres, and a major cathedral was built – in its day, one of the greatest of the East. It remained a centre of considerable importance down to the Middle Ages as an important stopping place on the pilgrimage route to Mecca.

Most of the layout of the city, and many of the monuments, are in fact Nabataean rather than Roman (Figure 41). The eastern layout has long been recognised as Nabataean, even though the original settlement was at the western side. Within this eastern area was a large temple enclosure, of which only a few columns of its colonnaded temenos survive. This was entered through a monumental propylaeum, the East Gate or Nabataean Gate, so-called because of the Nabataean style of the capitals which adorn it, dated to the late first century AD (Plate 47).[117] The area of the temenos is now occupied by the Old Cathedral, presumably the reason for the temple's demolition. To the south of the temenos are the remains of a palace, still standing in parts up to its first floor (Figure 42). This was originally thought to be the palace of the Roman governor of Arabia, but is now generally believed to have been the palace of Rabbel II (although it was doubtless reused by the Roman governors following the annexation – and in fact is no more opulent than some of the larger houses in the Dead Cities). It has a two-storeyed portico surrounding three sides of a courtyard. A series of rooms opened onto the courtyard, those on the main central block being reception rooms, with each wing being domestic and administrative quarters respectively. Recently, it has been argued that the main transverse street, the 'Roman' Decumanus, was in fact a part of the Nabataean layout from the time of Rabbel II. In this way it formed a processional way to the temple similar to the same arrangement at Petra. The West Gate, or Bab al-Hawa, would thus form a part of the whole religious ensemble leading to the temple (Plate 48). The northern transverse

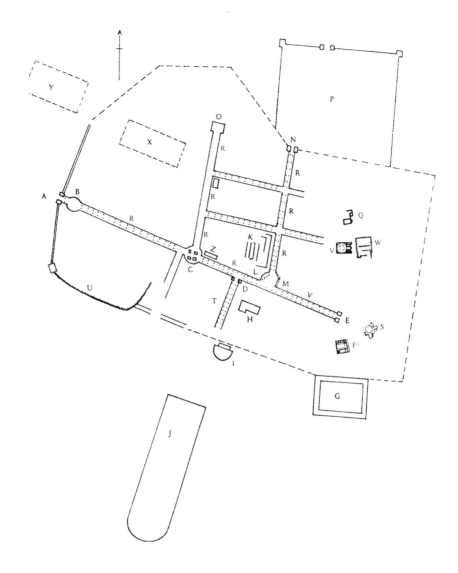

Figure 41 Nabataean and Roman Bosra (After Meinecke/Peters).

A: Bab al-Hawa.
B: Oval Plaza.
C: Tetrapylon.
D: Bab Qandil.
E: Nabataean Arch.
F: Palace.
G: Reservoir.
H: South Baths.
I: Theatre.
J: Hippodrome.
K: Caravanserai.
L: Nymphaeum.
M: *Kalybe*.

N: North Gate.
O: Spring.
P: Legionary Headquarters.
Q: Basilica.
R: Nabataean streets.
S: South Cathedral.
T: Roman street.
U: City walls.
V: North Cathedral.
W: Bishop's Palace.
X: Depression.
Y: Enclosure.

199

Plate 47 The Nabataean Arch at Bosra

streets were also a part of this Nabataean monumental layout.[118] The colonnades of these streets are consistent with an earlier, pre-Roman date, as they are in the Ionic order rather than the Corinthian that was more favoured by the Romans. The replacement of first-century Ionic colonnades by Corinthian in the second century is well attested at Jerash.

On closer examination, therefore, much of the 'Roman' city of Bosra – and most of its layout – turns out to be Nabataean. The Roman contribution to the urban layout probably only consisted of the addition of the colonnaded street from the theatre to the Central Arch ('Theatre Street') and the insertion of focal points at major street junctions: the Tetrapylon at the junction of the Decumanus with the first transverse street, the Central Arch at its junction with the second, and the Nymphaeum and possibly *kalybe* at the junction with the third. The *kalybe* is argued to be a Nabataean type of monument in Chapter 7, and the Tetrapylon, too, is argued to belong more to eastern architecture. The Oval Plaza, just inside the West Gate, might also have been another Roman insertion. However, it is consistent with the processional nature of the street, and oval plazas in general are argued (in Chapter 7) to be more in keeping with Near Eastern than Roman forms of architecture, so might also be Nabataean.

The 'Theatre Street' formed a part of a single architectural ensemble of the second century that included the theatre, the South Baths and the Central Arch. This and the southern parts of Bosra around it can, therefore, be viewed as the 'Roman cantonnment' (Figure 41). The theatre is one of the largest and most intact in the Roman world,

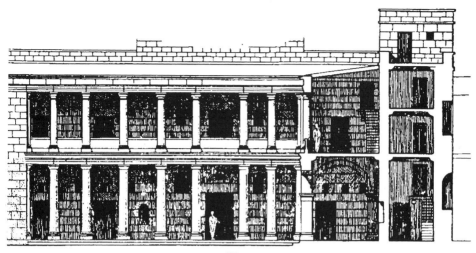

SECTION AB RESTORED·

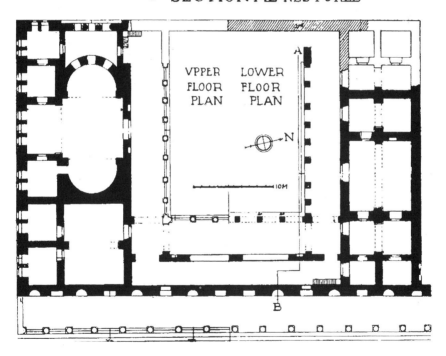

UPPER FLOOR PLAN   LOWER FLOOR PLAN

N

10M

A

B

Figure 42 The Palace at Bosra (After Butler)

preserved almost perfectly by being incorporated into a castle in the twelfth century (Plate 49). It was built in the second century AD, possibly on the site of an earlier Nabataean citadel. It has a diameter of over 100 metres, and with at least 35 tiers it would have seated some 15,000 spectators. Around the top of the auditorium a colonnade still stands almost in its entirety. The *scenae frons*, or stage backdrop, has three stage entrances set in deep recesses and was adorned with three storeys of elaborate white limestone colonnades in

Plate 48 The West Gate at Bosra

Plate 49 The Theatre at Bosra

dramatic contrast to the black basalt of the rest of the theatre. Behind the stage are two colonnaded courtyards and an immense vault. The Central Arch – Bab Qandil or 'Arch of the Lantern' – is a standard Roman triple arch, commemorating the IIIrd Cyrenaican legion. Building material throughout, both in the Nabataean and Roman periods, was the incredibly durable black volcanic basalt, which is plentifully available locally.[119] To the Romans posted to this outpost, the unrelenting black of the Hauran basalt must have appeared depressingly grim. Hence, the white limestone used for the colonnades of the new 'Theatre Street' comes as welcome relief.[120]

To this quarter were added other trappings of Roman urban life: the South Baths, which follow a clear Italian design, to the east of the colonnaded street, a possible small amphitheatre to the west, and a hippodrome to the south. On the opposite side of the city the Romans built the headquarters of the Third Cyrenaican Legion. This consists of a large square enclosure that can only be made out from aerial photographs, but its identification has been confirmed by the discovery of tile stamps in the enclosure.[121] The North Baths probably formed a part of this army camp. To the north of the Cardo is a large courtyard, the Khan al-Dibis, that was probably the market-place. Nearby is the third-century AD pre-Christian Basilica, or Roman public assembly hall (Plate 50), a superbly intact, large hall, well lit by clerestory windows, open at the front and with an apse at its end. The Hippodrome, just outside the city to the south, completes the Roman quarter of Bosra. Thus, we see in the urban layout of Bosra a very similar arrangement to that which characterised Indian cities during the period of the British Raj: a large 'native quarter', comprising the bulk of the city, a 'civil lines' for the administrators which

Plate 50 The Basilica at Bosra

would include the main residential and recreational buildings, and a 'military lines' or cantonments for the army.

Bosra was a major Christian centre and has a number of important early Christian buildings. The main one is the Cathedral of SS Sergius, Bacchus and Leontius just south of the Basilica, built in 512. It is essentially circular, with an octagonal interior colonnade set in a square, originally covered by a dome some 26 metres in diameter. It is thus an important stage in the development of Christian architecture, forming the prototype that culminated in the great domed buildings of Ravenna and Constantinople. The Cathedral at Bosra was also the model for the Dome of the Rock in Jerusalem. There are the remains of a bishop's palace opposite the Cathedral, and another Cathedral, also on a circular plan, has recently been discovered in the area near the Governor's Palace.

This rise in the importance of the Christian community must be a reflection of its prevailing Arab character and continuity from the past, which would naturally respond to a local religion. To see it as a form of 'Greek' influence and character[122] is entirely out of keeping with the background of Bosra's history, ethnic make-up and material remains. Bosra remained a Nabataean/Arab city throughout. Of all the personal names yielded by Greek and Latin inscriptions from Bosra, more than half of them are Semitic. One can assume that the bulk of the population would not record their names in inscriptions, and these must have been overwhelmingly Semitic.[123] Even the presence of Greek personal names implies no more Greek character to Bosra than Greek-derived names (such as Peter) in Britain today.

Shahba[124]

Shahba was the birthplace of the Emperor Philip the Arab (AD 232–7), who renamed his home town Philippopolis and elevated it to the rank of colony. Enjoying imperial patronage it was embellished with some particularly fine monuments in the third century. But Philippopolis never became a Lepcis Magna and does not appear to have ever been more than a small country town, probably not even expanding to fill the 'city' walls which Philip so ambitiously provided it with. It is in the form of a walled rectangle pierced by four gateways, through which pass two paved streets, the Cardo and Decumanus (Figure 43). Their intersection was marked by a Tetrapylon (recorded earlier this century but no trace remains today). The streets were originally colonnaded. Most of the monuments are along or just off the paved street that goes westwards from the central intersection. A little way along is an impressive portico consisting of four large Corinthian columns. This probably led to a now vanished temple, or perhaps was a monumental façade (*kalybe*). Further along, the street opens onto a wide paved square dominated by a magnificent façade on a podium (Plate 51). This is a curious type of building known as a *kalybe*, resembling a nymphaeum. Of possible Nabataean associations, it is discussed in Chapter 7. To the left of the façade is a marvellously preserved prostyle temple, the Philippeion, erected by Philip in memory of his deified father. Behind this is a small theatre, also built in the third century. In the centre, the two main monuments are the House of Mosaics and the baths, which follows the standard Roman arrangement of rooms. There are the remains of an aqueduct adjacent to the baths.

It has been observed that Shahba 'remains the most complete expression of the export to the edge of the [Syrian] steppe of the Graeco-roman ideal of the city'.[125] But where is the forum? Or the amphitheatre? Where in the 'ideal' Graeco-Roman city are the col-

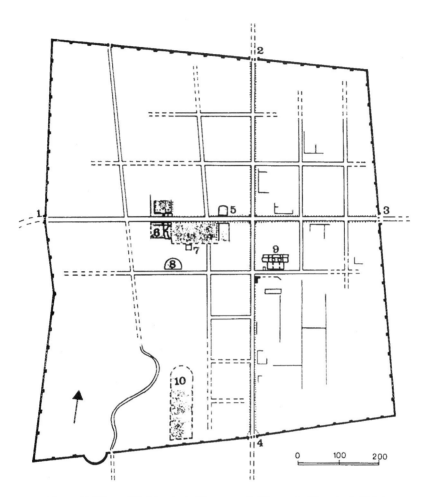

Figure 43 Plan of Shahba. 1–4: City gates. 5: Hexastyle Temple. 6: *Kalybe.*
7: Philippeion. 8: Theatre. 9: Baths. 10: Hippodrome. (After Freyberger)

onnaded streets, which Shahba and other cities of the Roman East abound in, and which do not occur in any cities of the Roman West? These questions and the real 'character' of Shahba and other cities are answered in Chapter 7.

Conclusion

Seven hundred years of Roman rule is certainly a very long period. But it is nothing compared to the immensely long continuum of Near Eastern cities before the Romans came, which was nearer to seven thousand than a mere seven hundred years. If there is one thing that a study of Roman urbanisation of the Near East proves, it is that cities had been flourishing there for hundreds, often thousands, of years before the Romans came, and the Romans merely occupied these cities, usually located on the same sites. The

Plate 51 The *kalybe* façade at Shahba

pottery record recovered from excavations shows continuity into the Roman period, not a break. Since pottery reflects the bulk of the population, the true character of these cities is unambiguously native and Semitic: the Roman element was a veneer. The architectural record (Chapter 7) demonstrates the same. Virtually all of the 'Roman' cities examined in the above brief survey were continuations of cities that had existed in the same positions for hundreds, even thousands, of years. The Romans brought very little that was new in terms of urbanisation. When looked at in the full perspective of towns and cities in the ancient Near East, therefore, the Roman impact was small.

The greatest period of expansion and monumentalisation did not take place until some time after the Romans arrived. If the evidence of the cities and their monuments is anything to go by, the actual conquest and first few centuries of Roman rule in the Near East had little initial impact. There were massive embellishments carried out at places such as Jerusalem, Bosra and Petra, it is true, but these belonged to the client states, not to Rome directly. It was only in the second century AD – particularly after the middle of the century – that we begin to see specifically Roman expansion: the large-scale developments and programmes of monumentalisation at Apamaea and Jerash, for example. The peak of Roman urbanisation in the East seems to be the second and third centuries, when the cities of the Roman East became some of the most impressive and most monumental in the empire.

After the third century there began a decline: little urban expansion, few new monuments being built. The only new monuments were those associated with the new religion: churches and cathedrals. But with few exceptions these did not match the opulence – the sheer ostentatious wealth – of the earlier great building programmes. The focus of expansion, and with it the evidence for continued growth and wealth, seems to shift from the cities to the countryside. We examine this evidence next.

6

THE COUNTRYSIDE

'There is no other country in the world where the architectural monuments of antiquity have been preserved in such large numbers, in such perfection, and in so many varieties as in Northern Central Syria and in the Hauran.' This was written by Howard Crosby Butler, the leader of the American Archaeological Expedition to Syria at the end of the nineteenth century.[1] The region west and south-west of Aleppo is one of the most extraordinary areas of ruins and probably the greatest storehouse of late Roman architecture to be found in the ancient world. This region is known as the Dead Cities, the remains of an astonishing eight hundred[2] deserted towns, villages and monastic settlements in the hill country between Aleppo, Antioch and Apamaea. Buildings are very well preserved and the villages often have the ancient field systems surrounding them intact. In this extraordinary landscape it is still possible to wander along streets, into modest houses or grander villas and churches that in many cases are almost perfectly preserved, with only their roofs missing, to obtain one of the most perfect – and most enchanting! – pictures of the world of late antiquity to be found anywhere (Figure 44, Plates 52 and 53).

The Dead Cities[3]

The term 'Dead Cities' is perhaps a misnomer: 'Dead Towns' or even 'Dead Villages', whilst less dramatic, more accurately reflects the nature of the settlements. There are roughly three groups, corresponding to the low ranges of hills in which they are situated. These are: the Jebel Shaikh Barakat and the Jebel Sim'an to the west and north-west of Aleppo, which include the best known of the Dead Cities comprising the monastery of St Simeon Stylites and associated remains; the Jebel Barisha and Jebel al-'Ala to the west near the present Turkish border, which has the largest concentration of ruins; and the Jebel Zawiya to the south-west towards the Orontes Valley, where settlements are mainly a little earlier (Figures 45 and 46).

The settlements and their setting

Altogether, some 820 rural settlements – country towns, villages and monastic settlements – have been counted covering an area of 5,500 square kilometres. The settlements are very close together, averaging one every 2 square kilometres in the north where settlement is densest. They are wider spaced in the Jebel Zawiya to the south, where the average territory per village is 7 square kilometres. The majority average just twenty to

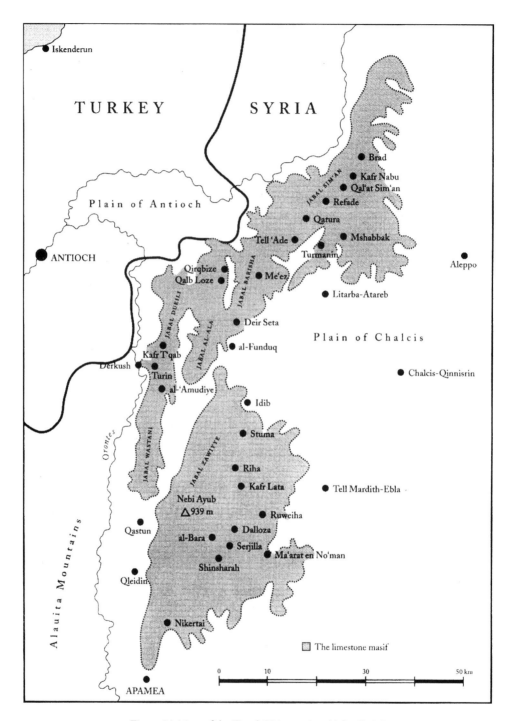

Figure 44 Map of the Dead Cities region (After Peña)

208

Plate 52 View of part of the Dead Cities region from Burj Baqirha, with ruined settlements of Baqirha, Dar Qita and Ba'udeh below

Plate 53 View of part of the Dead Cities region from St Simeon Stylites, with ruined settlements of Deir Sim'an and Rafada below. Note ancient field boundaries

Figure 45 Map of the Jebel Barakat-Jebel Sim'an Dead Cities group

sixty houses, although many of these houses are fairly substantial and probably supported a higher population than the numbers suggest. The rural population for the region (excluding the cities) has been calculated at 300,000.[4] Settlements do not adhere to any overall plan; houses appear fairly randomly scattered. The only exception is the town of Me'ez in the Jebel al-'Ala, which adheres to a grid plan.

Several administrative and market centres have been identified, largely from their size and relatively high number of public buildings. Barad in the Jebel Sim'an, for example, has a public baths, a cathedral, two monastic complexes, five warehouses, and buildings that have been identified as a meeting house and a 'magistrate's residence'. Ba'uda seems to be the market town for the Jebel Barisha. Al-Bara, ancient Kapropera, is the most extensive series of ruins in the Jebel Zawiya, with five churches, six monasteries, many elaborate substantial houses and many satellite villages (Plate 54). Many of the houses are large farmhouses, with olive presses, stables and barns attached to them. The monastery of Dayr Sobat near al-Bara provides a fairly intact picture of the layout of an ancient working monastery. The ruins of al-Bara lie in olive groves, giving an appearance most approximating to the ancient appearance of the Dead Cities in contrast to the harsh, semi-desert appearance that characterises the region today. Serjilla nearby seems to have had a town council and a formal administrative structure, as well as public baths, churches and other public buildings including what has been interpreted as a tavern (Figure 47, Plates 55 and 58).[5]

Figure 46 Map of the Jebel Zawiya Dead Cities group

Plate 54 Al-Bara, ancient Kapropera, in the Jebel Zawiya. Note the olive groves surrounding

211

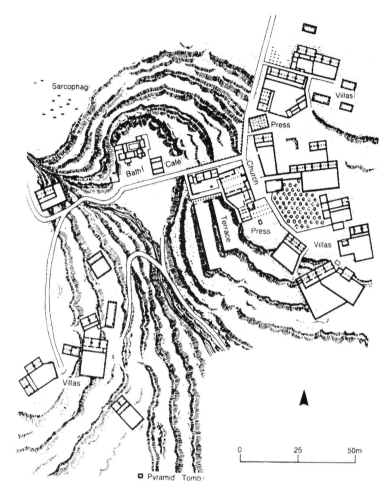

Figure 47 Plan of Serjilla (After Krautheimer/Butler)

None of the settlements are walled, reflecting the high degree of security in the coun-tryside, although houses tend to be surrounded by high walls (Figure 48). Fortifications, when they occur, consist of just single towers, usually on the edges of the villages and surrounding fields, generally guarding the fields rather than the houses. These, however, would only protect against casual raids; they would not deter an army (Figures 48E and 49). The tallest tower at Jarada in the Jebel Zawiya still stands six storeys, nearly 20 metres high. The small projecting balcony near the top here and at other towers in the north was a prototype of the machicolation that later achieved such prominence in Arab and Crusader fortifications (Plate 56).[6]

Apart from the arceate forms of the churches (see below), which are an essentially non-eastern form, the architecture as a whole reflects the Near Eastern predilection for bold, almost cubist, trabeate forms. These are simple slab and lintel construction techniques and long lines of square, almost monolithic pillars supporting porticoes sometimes several storeys high (Figure 48, Plates 57 and 68). These forms appear very distant from the more

Plate 55 Serjilla, with the so-called 'tavern' in the foreground

flowing, rounded forms of Byzantine architecture. Whilst the portico form *might* be seen as Classical in origin, the monolithic almost 'cubist' vocabulary of the porticoes seems to hearken back to a pre-Classical Semitic past.[7] These simple trabeate forms – allied to a Syrian mastery of stone-working – enabled domestic buildings and towers to reach several storeys. This is similar in some respects to the Hauran (see below), although the corbelling techniques and external stone staircases characteristic there are virtually absent in the north.

Ancient field patterns are often still in place. These consist of stone walls marking field boundaries, with occasional cairns that mark field and village boundaries (Plates 53 and 58). These field patterns, however, were also their agricultural death-knell: clearing the stones from the fields and using them to mark their boundaries resulted in the loss of soil cover and consequent erosion. No irrigation channels have been found, nor would they have been necessary. There are occasional field cisterns, but these were to provide water for livestock rather than the fields.

Near Tell Aqibrin is one of the finest stretches of paved road in the Roman world (Plate 59). This was a part of the ancient network that linked Aleppo and Qinnesrin with Antioch, although it was not all paved like this. It is constructed of massive limestone paving slabs up to a metre thick. At Bab al-Hawa ('Gate of Winds') further west, remains include a Roman monumental arch over the ancient road. Other arterial roads connected Antioch, Apamaea and Cyrrhus. Alongside were numerous hostelries, public fountains and way stations built to service them and assist the traveller. In addition, the region was honeycombed by an extensive network of minor roads, largely marked nowadays by the stone walls on either side. Indeed, lines of parallel rubble walls snaking across a hillside is one of the most ubiquitous – not to say picturesque! – features of the landscape today (Plate 58).[8]

213

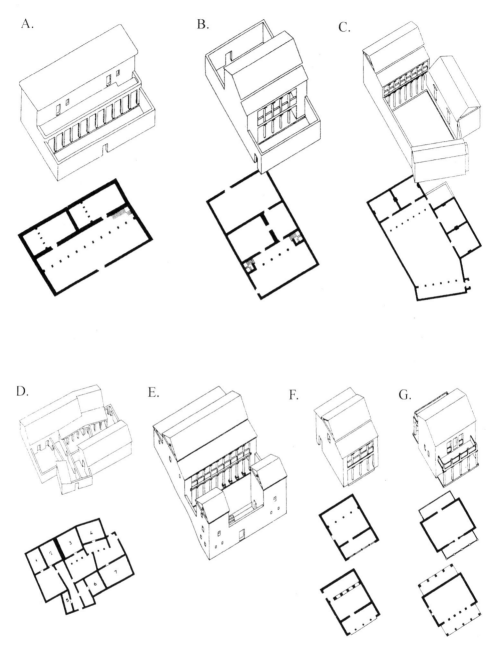

Figure 48 House types in the Dead Cities. A: Taqleh. B: Banaqfur. C: Serjilla. D: Behyo. E: Dalloza. F: Serjilla. G: Ba'uda. (After Tchalenko)

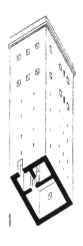
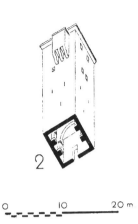
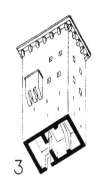

Figure 49 Types of towers in the Dead Cities (After Tchalenko)

Plate 56 One of the towers at Jerada. Note the projecting balconies

The houses

In a representative sample of forty-six villages selected for intensive study,[9] 95 per cent of all the buildings were houses. These were generally simple two-storey dwellings, with the upper storey for living quarters and the lower for animals. Unlike the usual form of

215

Plate 57 The monastery at al–Braijj. Note the 3–storey portico

Plate 58 Ancient field patterns and roads between Serjilla (foreground) and Rabiʿah (distance)

Plate 59 Roman road near Tell Aqibrin

Plate 60 A courtyard house in Jerada. Note the animal trough under the portico

Plate 61 A row of portico houses at Serjilla. The animals in the courtyard reflect its ancient function

housing in the Middle East (which consists of rooms surrounding a central courtyard) courtyards were generally just to one or either side of the rooms, with the house forming a central block. The almost universal use of troughs suggests that the courtyards were used for animals rather than ornament – there is no evidence for fountains, pools, or gardens – with the ground-floor rooms for feeding and storage, again demonstrated by the number of animal fixtures in them (Figure 48, Plates 60 and 61). Roofs were generally gabled, presumably made of timber and tile. Stairs to the upper floors were almost invariably external, usually of wood and incorporated into the external porticoes. Porticoes were an important feature of both domestic and public buildings. Many houses had a portico or veranda along one or two sides, usually on two storeys. Longer porticoes alongside streets would form stables or bazaar shops, a tradition that survives intact today, and are probably the architectural descendants of the colonnaded streets that are such a feature of the cities (Plate 62). Indeed, such 'verandaed' houses must have borne a strong resemblance to European colonial architecture, with the porticoed streets resembling the verandaed streets of the American West and Australian Outback (Plate 81). Like the colonnaded streets of the Roman East, such architectural forms are obviously a response to the demands imposed by climate.

The vivid picture of rural life presented by the ruins is graphically supplemented by the mosaics that have been found in the region.[10] They depict, of course, the hunting and mythological scenes that were popular throughout the Roman world, which here emanate from the styles and workshops of Antioch.[11] The popularity of abstract and geometric designs anticipates Islam, but of more interest are cruder mosaics that appear far distant

Plate 62 View along a porticoed street at Jerada

from Antioch and are presumably local in manufacture. Although lacking in sophistication, they have a naivety and homeliness that provide an intensely endearing picture. We see the ordinary farms themselves, along with the farmers, their chickens, their livestock and their everyday activities. Together with the ruins they conjure up a very vivid and attractive picture that seems far distant from the grandeur of imperial Rome.

Public buildings

Public baths are found in six settlements in the Dead Cities, with particularly fine complexes at Serjilla, Barad and Babisqa (Figure 50) – the latter boasting two. They follow the same general layout of Roman baths elsewhere, but would have catered entirely for a local population, so cannot be taken as evidence for any Latin 'expatriate' population. Thus, they mark the transition from the Roman baths to the Islamic *hammam*.

On top of the Jebel Shaikh Barakat – some 850 metres high – are the remains of a large colonnaded temenos of a Roman prostyle temple of Zeus (Figure 88E). Although there is little standing, its position is spectacular – it is presumably the site of an ancient Semitic sacred high place. At Burj Baqirha, on another mountain on the opposite side of the Dana Plain to Shaikh Barakat, is another Temple of Zeus dated AD 161 (Plate 63). This also probably occupies the site of an earlier Semitic sacred high place. Its monumental entrance and parts of the small prostyle sanctuary are well preserved. One of the best preserved temples is at al-Mushayrfa on the peak of the Jebel Wastani some 700 metres high. Two isolated columns inside the temenos suggest the Mambij pillar cult of Atargatis. Other pagan temples have been recorded at Me'ez, Babisqa, Kafr Nabu, Jebel Srir and at a

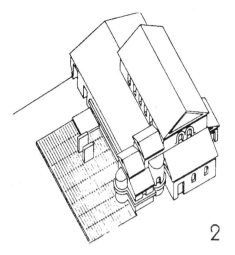
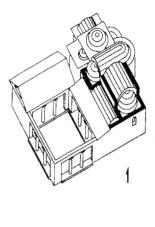

Figure 50 Baths in the Dead Cities. 1: Barad. 2: Serjilla. (After Tchalenko)

Plate 63 Temple of Zeus at Burj Baqirha

few other places in the Dead Cities, but their number never remotely approached that of the churches (even allowing for the better preservation of churches and the destruction of the temples).

There are also several other ancient sacred high places on exposed hill and mountain tops in the region. These usually consist of open-air enclosures containing an altar, channels, grottoes, tanks and other associated paraphernalia. As such, they resemble the Nabataean high places fairly closely. Like their Nabataean counterparts, those in the north are usually interpreted as places for blood sacrifices, but – again like the Nabataean high places – there is no evidence that they were. Fairly intact high-place complexes have been recorded at Umm Taqa, Kfar Daryan, Rabi'a, Barad, Wadi Marthun and Magharat al-Mallaab (Figure 51). That at Kfar Daryan is still known as Ashtarat – presumably Ashtaroth or Astarte. Some of those associated with grottoes, notably Wadi Marthun, have been interpreted as oracles.[12]

Christian buildings

By far the majority of the non-domestic buildings are churches. Indeed, the remains of an astonishing *1,200* churches have been counted in the Dead Cities – approximately one for every 4.5 square kilometres.[13] In the sixty-one settlements of Jebel Barisha alone, for example, twenty-three had one church each, eighteen had two, and five had three – only at fifteen of the settlements have no churches been recorded. This reflects an extremely devout population: at Banqusa, for example, there were three churches in a village of only thirty houses, presumably with a population of only 250–300. Accordingly, it has been

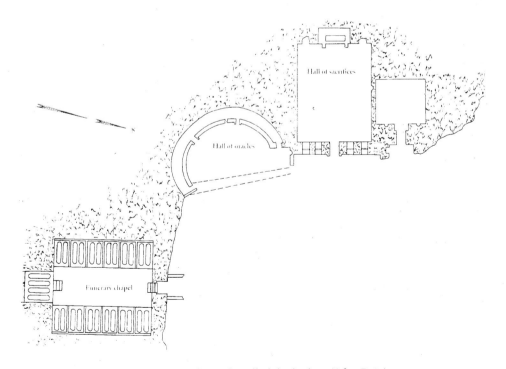

Figure 51 Magharat al-Mallaab high place (After Peña)

Plate 64 The church at Mushabbak

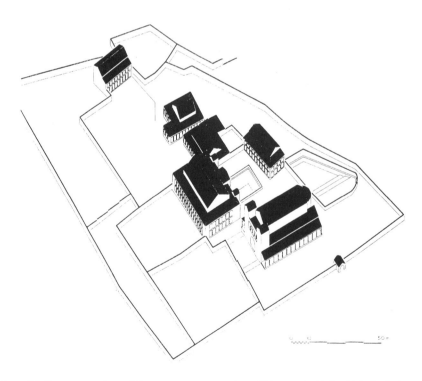

Figure 52 Reconstruction of the monastery complex of Turmanin (After Tchalenko)

estimated that the clergy numbered some 4–6 per cent of the population.[14] Many, such as the late fifth-century hilltop church at Mushabbak, are almost perfectly preserved (Plate 64). Many form the cores of extensive monastery complexes, such as the ruined monastery of Sitt ar-Rum near Rafada. A particularly fine fifth-century monastery church was still standing until quite recently at Turmanin, and its associated monastery – originally a very large complex almost as big as St Simeon – is still extant (Figure 52). Other monastic remains abound in the region.

The greatest of them all – indeed, one of the greatest religious establishments of early Christendom – was the monastery-church of St Simeon Stylites. It was built in about AD 480–90 on a scale and lavishness rarely seen in the East since the era of the great temples. The complex is set within an immense enclosure, built partly on a terrace overlooking the plain, comprising inner and outer courtyards (Figure 53). This seems to recall the great temple enclosures of an earlier era – indeed, it encloses an area approximately a third as large as Herod's Temple at Jerusalem. The main entrance was to the south, up a sacred processional way through a monumental arch leading from the pilgrim town of Telanissos (Dayr Simʿan) below (Plate 65). This led into the outer enclosure next to the magnificent baptistery built at the same time as the main church. The main entrance to the church was through the south wing, one of the most splendid features of the complex (Plate 66). The exterior of the church is particularly graceful: the walls of each wing are pierced by alternating arched windows and doorways, and the junctions of the wings are marked by semicircular exedra; these disparate parts are then pulled together into a harmonious whole by two sharply delineated string courses, the lower one emphasising the graceful curves of the openings (Plate 67). The stump of St Simeon's pillar is surrounded by a large octagonal chamber, possibly originally domed. The octagon is squared off by the four basilical halls on each side, the east one terminating in a triple apse. The church thus combines three separate early church forms: the central 'martyrium' plan, the basilica and the cross (Figure 54). The combination however, does not jar; there are no clumsy transitions nor inherent contradictions, and the three quite separate elements combine most effectively, together forming one of the greatest masterpieces of early Christian architecture. Covering an area of some 5,000 square metres, it was one of the largest churches ever built and could contain some 10,000 worshippers – larger than many of the great churches of medieval Europe, such as Notre Dame in Paris or the gigantic Benedictine abbey church at Cluny.

The monastery buildings are grouped around an inner courtyard, formed in part by the arms of the church itself. The façades consist of an impressive portico, in places surviving to three storeys. The bold slab and lintel technique of these porticoes, with its strong emphasis on simple verticals and horizontals, contrasts starkly with the more graceful curvilinear architecture of the church itself. These two contrasting styles probably represent a meeting – or clash? – of eastern and western forms: the curvilinear representing a western tradition that culminated in the Romanesque, and the trabeate being a much earlier Semitic tradition with its emphasis on simple angular forms.[15] Such was the importance of the monastery that it maintained its independence after the Arab conquest down to the tenth century.[16]

The pilgrimage town of Telannisos (Dayr Simʿan) below St Simeon's contains a large number of religious establishments: churches, monasteries and hospices, many superbly preserved (Plate 68). To the south-east of Qalʿat Simʿan is the town of Taqleh, which has a fine fifth-century church, and at Fafertin, further east, is the second oldest dated church in

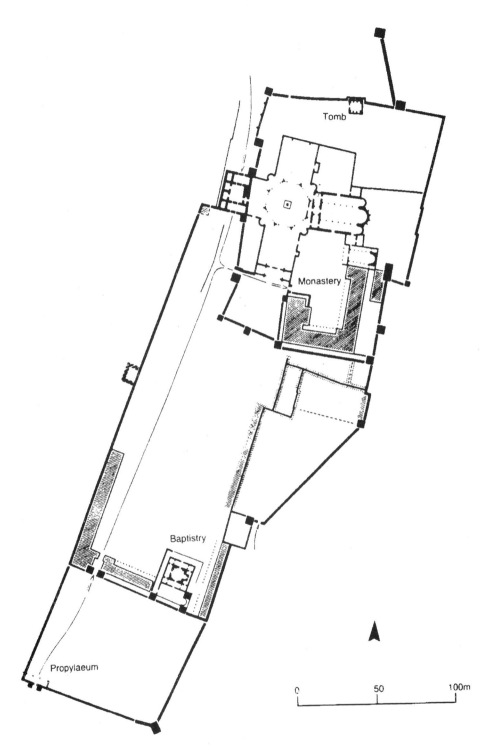

Tomb

Monastery

Baptistry

Propylaeum

0   50   100m

Figure 53 St Simeon Stylites (After Tchalenko)

224

Plate 65 Propylaeum to the sacred way up to St Simeon Stylites

Plate 66 Main entrance to St Simeon Stylites

Plate 67 Exterior of St Simeon Stylites. Note the string course over the windows

Syria (after Dura Europos), a basilica dated AD 372. Earlier dates, however, have been postulated for a number of house-churches in the region. A house-church at Qirqbizeh is probably pre-313, and late fourth-century house-churches have been identified elsewhere, before the canonical basilical form was established in about 390. These house-churches are modest and discreet, being essentially meeting houses, similar to the dated one at Dura Europos.[17]

More ruined churches occur northwards along the Jebel Sim'an. At Barad are the remains of a cathedral dated 399–402 and several other churches, as well as a monastery. Kharaba Shams further east has a particularly well preserved basilica of the late fifth century (Plate 69). At Qasr al-Banat, near the present Syrian–Turkish border, there is an extensive sixth-century complex of monastic ruins dominated by a massive six-storey tower. The churches generally appear to have been architect-designed, and the names of a number of architects and technicians have been preserved. Both this and the evidence for interrelated regional styles suggests schools of architecture.[18]

The Jebel Barisha area further south is astonishingly rich in churches, many villages containing more than one, all with features that make each one unique. Many preserve rich decoration, particularly the flowing string course around windows and doors, an extremely effective technique of binding all elements of a façade together. This technique appears peculiar to the area. Many churches form parts of extensive monastery complexes. At the village of Qalb Lauzah is one of the loveliest and most intact churches in Syria, a mid-fifth-century cathedral probably dedicated to SS Gabriel and Michael (Figure 54B, Plate 70). The entrance is flanked by three-storey towers, a form originating with the temples at Si' and Baalbek. Inside, the aisles are separated from the nave by three arches on thick, square piers. The solidness of these piers is relieved by the rich decoration of the

Plate 68 A religious complex incorporating a hospice and monastery at Deir Sim'an

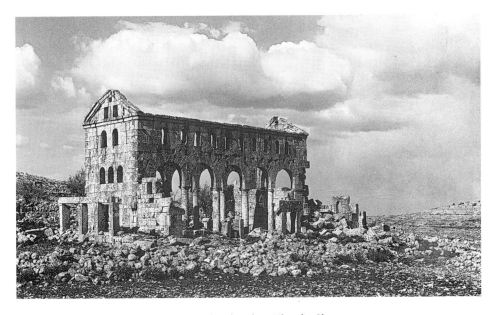

Plate 69 The church at Kharaba Shams

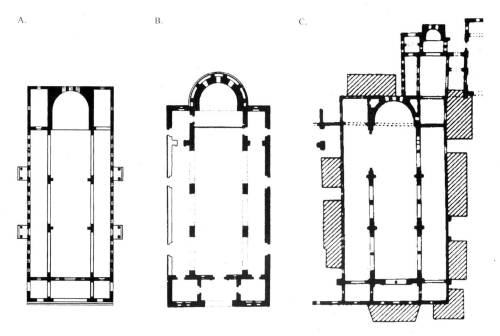

Figure 54 Church plans in north Syria. A: Ruwayha. B: Qalb Lauzah. C: Rasafa.

Plate 70 The church at Qalb Lauzah

capitals and arches, which also surround the doorways leading in from the narthex. The aisles are roofed by a series of ingenious interlocking stone slabs. A similar style of church with three large arches resting on piers to divide nave and aisles is the impressive fourth-century fortified Church of Bizzos at Ruwayha in the Jebel Zawiya, as well as the churches at Rasafa and Cyrrhus. Ruwayha is one of the largest churches in the region and like the similar-sized church at Qalb Lauzah, its façade is framed by two towers.[19]

These probably comprise the largest concentration of churches surviving anywhere in the ancient world. Most were quite small; apart from a few exceptions, such as St Simeon Stylites and Qalb Lauzah, there are few larger churches or cathedrals. Although their architecture generally follows imported forms – they almost invariably follow the conventional basilical form developed in the Roman west – there are a number of local variations. For example, entrances are usually lateral in the south wall opening directly into the south aisle, rather than in the western end opposite the apse (Figure 54, Plate 70). This is thought to derive from a similar practice in synagogues, perhaps reflecting different entrances for lay and clergy. It often meant that the narthex would be omitted. Apses are usually flanked by two small square chambers, opening from the ends of each aisle, perhaps following pre-Christian temple layouts (Figure 54). Apses in the form of small niches would often be found in baptisteries as well, the form probably deriving from the torah-niches of synagogues and ultimately evolving into the mihrabs of mosques. In addition, the centre of the nave would often be occupied by an exedra, or bema, facing the apse, reflecting differing liturgical usages in the north Syrian church where the eastern half of the church would be reserved for clergy in certain services. The bemata, like the lateral southern entrances and the small apses found in baptisteries, are thought to derive from synagogues of the Hellenistic period.[20] If the overall forms of north Syrian churches reflect western architectural styles, the details and the church buildings associated with them were purely local in style: the monastery buildings, for example, are architecturally almost indistinguishable from domestic buildings.

Much of the wealth of the region might have been tied up in church plate.[21] The sheer quantity of churches certainly appears to suggest considerable wealth in the countryside, but it might equally suggest the exact opposite: the number of churches in contemporary Ethiopia, for example, is evidence of rural poverty rather than wealth. Compare the sudden increase of opulent cinemas in Depression America. However, when taken with the evidence of the houses themselves, there seems little doubt that the Dead Cities region was very wealthy indeed. The sheer number of religious buildings might in fact be explained by the rhythm of the olive cultivation, which demands intense activity from October to February, leaving the remainder of the year relatively free – to build churches?[22]

Whereas the settlements in the Dead Cities declined after the seventh century, the monasteries probably survived for several centuries longer – the monastery of St Simeon Stylites, for example, maintained its independence until the tenth century as we have seen. The first Muslims respected the Christian monasteries and the learning they represented, for in addition to being centres of Christianity they were repositories for the Classical learning which the Muslims were as much heirs to as the Christians. Indeed, it has even been suggested that the decline in Islamic civilisation in the Near East in the twelfth and thirteenth centuries was due as much to the extinction of the Christian monasteries as to external factors, such as the Mongol invasions.[23]

Economy

The Dead Cities were dominated by the olive industry, as the limestone terrain of the north Syrian hills is ideally suited for their cultivation. In this context the immense importance of this commodity in the ancient world, far more important than the olive is nowadays, must be emphasised. The olive was the ancient world's sole source of oil. It was used for cooking, anointing, as a base for medicines, aromatics and cosmetics, but most importantly, it was virtually the sole form of lighting. The demand, consequently, was huge. This increased enormously after the North African provinces, traditionally the main source for olive oil in the Roman Empire, were lost in 439. That date corresponds to the height of the Dead Cities' prosperity after 450 (see below).

Accordingly the olive was the main cash crop, and large numbers of olive presses have been found throughout the region – 245 in the 45 villages intensively surveyed by the most recent French mission. The village of Qalb Lauzah, for example, had twenty-three olive presses for an estimated population of 250, Dayhis has forty in a population of 500, Kafr Marays sixty for 300.[24] Such extraordinary quantities can only be explained in terms of export, not domestic consumption. One recalls that Antioch was the only city of the Roman Empire that had public street lighting – a fact solely due to the local availability of plentiful olive oil. From nurturing, harvesting and pressing to packing, marketing and transporting, the entire region revolved around olives. The industry was both very labour intensive and seasonal, demanding regular influxes of itinerant labour, perhaps nomads. The seasonal nature of the industry released a large labour force onto the market at the end of the season in February, which might then have been used in the construction industry until the olive season resumed in October. This might indicate an itinerant, presumably nomadic, labour force, as suggested above. On the other hand, the high cash value of the olive crop would support a high seasonally idle, sedentary population in any case. This has been used to explain the large number of churches in the Dead Cities.

After olives, grapes were the commonest crop, along with cereals, pulses, vegetables and fruit. Stock raising probably figured almost as highly as olives: the courtyards and ground-floor rooms of most houses surveyed contained livestock troughs (Plate 60). Stock raising tended to be more predominant in the north of the region, with cereals more predominant in the south towards the Orontes Valley. Olives were grown throughout, but predominating in the centre of the region, almost to the exclusion of all else.

Nearly all of the pottery recovered, both from excavation and surface collections, was simple in style and locally produced, reinforcing the impression of rustic simplicity.[25] Features previously interpreted as 'bazaar streets' and 'shops' on examination have recently proved to be mainly stables. There was little trace of the hand of imperial Rome, apart from some traces of Roman surveying between the first and third centuries. None of the settlements were veteran colonies, and there was virtually a complete absence of the kind of great landowners – usually absentee Romans – that characterise the rural areas of the North African provinces.[26] The substantial wealth of the region furthermore suggests an absence of crushing imperial taxes or rapacious landlords. There is no evidence of the large slave estates that characterised southern Italy and other parts of the empire. It was all local Syrians, peasants, but peasants who were extremely well off and could afford paid labourers rather than slaves.

Date

The towns are mostly late Roman in date, but are often as representative of earlier countryside architecture since the basic forms did not change much. Indeed, few other areas in the Roman world evoke the life of the provinces as well as the Dead Cities do. The existence of a number of walls of superbly fitted 'Cyclopean' masonry (for example, at Rafada, Bamuqqa, Babisqa and Banqusa) suggests the survival of earlier building techniques. In general the observed pattern is that of continuous growth from the first to the mid-third century. Following a slump in the mid-third century, they continued to grow steadily again between about 270 and 550, particularly after 320, with a noticeable spurt between about 410 and 480. The height was roughly in the thirty years between 450 and 480, after which they declined steadily until about 610. Surprisingly, there seems to be little evidence for substantial decline following the Iranian invasions of the 540s. Rather, there was continued stability. This seems to suggest that the Iranians supported the local infrastructure, presumably to incorporate it into their own empire, and the locals in turn supported the Iranian occupation; there is no evidence for the sort of destruction that the western sources imply.

The great invasions of the seventh century changed the picture. Whilst these invasions were not necessarily destructive, they nonetheless brought about a decline through more indirect – and unwitting – means. The Iranian conquests at the beginning of the century resulted in the closure of the Mediterranean to Syria, hence a loss of the all-important markets – particularly in olive oil – upon which the economy of the region depended. This was reinforced by the Islamic conquest: the demographic and political centre of Syria moved from Antioch to Damascus. Accordingly, the region behind Antioch declined in its wake. Exhaustion of the soils coupled with a loss of ground cover and consequent erosion would have contributed to an agricultural decline. The very agricultural expansion itself, requiring as it did clearing the fields of their protective covering of stones, contributed to the soil loss from the beginning. Whilst Aleppo was a large enough centre to sustain this decline, the towns and villages in the region were not: the populations slowly moved elsewhere, leaving their towns empty. Not being destroyed by invasions or natural disasters, they became simply ghost towns, surviving in some cases almost intact.

Explanation

An explanation was first proposed by the French aristocrat who surveyed them, the Comte Melchior De Voguë. His interpretation provides a romantic image of a rich, elegant, rural aristocracy: of leisured country gentry in their villas surveying their pillared courtyards and the formal gardens that surrounded them and the slaves toiling in the fields beyond from the ornate verandas of their first floors that succumbed to the scourge of Islam[27] – an interpretation heavily influenced by the picture of rural France on the eve of the Revolution. Subsequent surveys, however, did not substantially alter the picture – and with good reason, for the picture of rural idyll presented by the ruins is difficult to resist. Much the same interpretation was confirmed by Howard Crosby Butler half a century later,[28] whose lavishly published American surveys of the beginning of this century still form the basis of much archaeological work in Syria: a rich, highly sophisticated but essentially aristocratic rural elite, although the end was put down more to environmental change (such as loss of vegetal cover) than anti-Christian, anti-aristocratic

Muslims. The definitive survey, again French, of the Dead Cities was the outstanding study in the middle decades of this century by Georges Tchalenko.[29] He interpreted a much more diverse society, but again essentially a 'civilisation rurale' consisting of great estates that gradually broke up into smallholdings.

New French investigations under Georges Tate[30] have dramatically altered the picture. Based on excavations at one village, Dayhis, followed up by an intensive survey of a representative forty-six other villages, the Dead Cities were reappraised as an essentially peasant community of independent smallholdings. Houses were small – albeit often solidly built of fine masonry and richly decorated – consisting of just one or two dwelling rooms above the stables, and generally clustered together in an irregular plan. There was very little evidence for larger estates; the 'villas', on examination, proved to be extended peasant houses for larger families rather than villas. Although very prosperous, the image of leisured country gentry in their villas was completely vanquished: the Dead Cities became a community of workers with the means of production in their own hands enjoying the benefits of their labours – from aristocratic feudalism to workers' paradise. But the sheer quality, quantity, wealth, elegance and sophistication of the Dead Cities could not stand in more contrast to their apparent explanation: of a simple, rustic, peasant and herder community. Clearly, Tate's admirable work poses as many questions as it answers.

Today, the region appears bleached white by the sun and drained of soil by wind and rain so that now it is a harsh, bare terrain of protruding bedrock, stones and sparse vegetation (Plates 53, 58, 71). It might appear strange that this area supported such a large population in the past. But it must be remembered that this was the hinterland of Antioch, one of the greatest cities of the Mediterranean world in Roman times and the natural centre of Syria in late antiquity. Attempts at explaining the settlements concentrate merely on their *rural* aspect, but the true explanation must ultimately be urban, as Antioch's hinterland. They must be viewed, therefore, as much in the context of Antioch as of the countryside.

The massive increase in the countryside after the fourth century, both in terms of

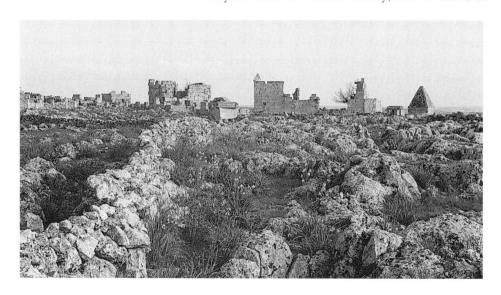

Plate 71 The village of Baudeh between al-Bara and Serjilla. Note protruding bedrock

population and wealth, might well correspond to a decline in the cities. Such a decline has been observed in Chapter 4. The cities in late antiquity were becoming increasingly undesirable places to live. The urban proletariat became more impoverished when the imperial coffers had less money to support them. Inner cities as a consequence became more squalid: we see little quality building after the fourth century, and late Roman urban architecture in the East is characterised by shoddy workmanship, second-hand materials and smaller units – in other words, slums. Mob rule became common, particularly the hooliganism associated with the rival chariot-racing factions, the greens and the blues. Families who could afford it therefore might well have moved to the countryside for a better quality of life. In this context it must be borne in mind that the Dead Cities form as much a hinterland of Antioch as the other cities of north Syria: Apamaea, Laodicaea, Beroea, etc. Having moved out, the rich would have taken to the land, only coming to the depressed cities on occasion for market and other reasons.

It is tempting to see the two extreme rural interpretations as products of French political thought, lying as they do at either end of the political spectrum: the one essentially eighteenth-century pre-Revolutionary aristocratic, the other late twentieth-century fashionable Socialism. But perhaps the new interpretation of ancient Antiochene middle classes discovering rural bliss in the countryside from where they would commute to declining inner cities is as much a child of its time and place: from the perspective of 1990s Britain.

The Near East boasts some of the greatest monuments of the Roman world: gigantic temples such as Baalbek, great monumental cities such as Apamaea or Jerash, long colonnades and a wealth of other buildings and cities. But in many ways the most impressive are not the biggest but the smallest. What makes the Dead Cities so remarkable is not so much their large size but their smallness, their very *ordinariness*, nothing more than unassuming, everyday, small country towns such as can be found the world over. One can see virtually the full layout of modest but prosperous country towns in their entirety: the farmhouses with the labourers' cottages, stables and farm buildings nearby; the parish church and the village shops; the central squares with the modest town public buildings clustered around them; the olive presses and cattle troughs and other workings of small farming; the field boundaries and the roadways to the market towns in the countryside surrounding them. The mosaics provide a vivid picture of the life that was lived there, depicting everyday rural scenes of farming, the hunt, of ordinary life. It all seems so remarkably peaceful and rural, so ordinary and everyday – as indeed it must have been. The picture first projected of the Dead Cities, by De Vogüe and the first explorers, of country gentry and great estates, has now been dismissed. But the picture of country life that the new studies show is hardly less appealing. It is impossible not to be utterly enchanted by the Dead Cities.

Other areas

The real significance of the Dead Cities is that they are only unique *now*, and not necessarily in the past: they are, in other words, a perfect example of the accident of preservation. If they had been built of wood or mud-brick instead of limestone, we would never have heard of the Dead Cities. Explanations have consequently concentrated on them as a unique phenomenon, but such rural wealth may well have been more widespread in the past than present remains indicate. The Dead Cities, therefore, might reflect an overall level of wealth in the Roman East in late antiquity, and not be just an isolated instance.

Elsewhere in north Syria

To some extent, the Dead Cites are a victim of their own impressiveness. The focus of attention on these remains has detracted from studies of the ancient countryside elsewhere. Hence, many observations on ancient settlement in the countryside made on the basis of the Dead Cities might be distorted: the Dead Cities are unique not necessarily because it was the only area so densely populated and wealthy, but merely because it has survived so remarkably due to the limestone construction. An examination of the countryside outside the limestone area, therefore, where standing remains might be less common, is vital in order to place the Dead Cities into their true rural context.

The first areas that must be considered are the non-limestone valleys and plains of the Dead Cities region itself. For it must be remembered that 'Dead Cities' are found almost exclusively in the limestone hills, not on the fertile valleys and plains below them where one would most expect to find settlement – the Dana Plain, for example. But an apparent absence of settlement here only represents an actual absence of recording, not necessarily of remains. In the hills, where even farm sheds were built of limestone, the remains are still extant, whilst in the plains any settlements would have been built of far less permanent mud-brick (as it was until comparatively recently) and have consequently disappeared. No efforts have been made to record such settlement – if they existed – or to determine land-use in the valleys in order to compare them with those observed in the limestone areas. The record is recoverable: the sophisticated, intensive surveying techniques pioneered by Wilkinson and used with such success elsewhere in northern Syria and surrounding regions have recovered a remarkable quantity and quality of information in comparable terrain – and have usually revealed a higher density of settlement than would be apparent from a superficial survey.[31] A similar survey of the plains and valley floors of the Dead Cities region must be considered the highest archaeological priority if ever the Dead Cities are to be fully understood.

When we turn to other regions adjacent to the Dead Cities, the record is revealing – and similarly frustrating. Other regions in north Syria – for example, the Quwayq River, the Antioch Plain, the Orontes Valley – have also been subject to archaeological survey, in some cases quite detailed, but usually attention has been focused on the earlier periods, with Roman and later settlement only of marginal interest. Some details, however, have a bearing on the Dead Cities. In a survey of the Quwayq River basin north of Aleppo, only 9 out of the 88 sites surveyed had early Roman fine wares. There was then a total lack of fine wares from the second to the fourth centuries AD. Settlement picked up again after the fourth century, with late Roman fine and coarse wares recovered from 27 sites and a smooth continuity of occupation into the early Islamic period. The record seems to suggest considerable mobility: sites were abandoned and later reoccupied, with a lack of population and abandonment between the second and fourth centuries. A peak in settlement after the fourth century appears parallel to the pattern observed in the Dead Cities.[32]

In a survey of the Orontes Valley alongside the Jebel Zawiya Dead Cities, large numbers of sites were recorded, but interest was focused almost exclusively on the earlier periods, mainly the Bronze Age. We do not know if there was any absence of Roman sites or merely that they were left unrecorded.[33] In the Plain of Antioch one would expect to find rural settlement even denser than that of the Dead Cities, but interest has similarly focused almost solely on the Bronze and Iron Ages. 'Roman' is recorded in passing as being present, but no other details are given.[34] In the region of the former Kingdom of Edessa (the Roman province of Osrhoene), intensive surveys have once again revealed a dramatic rural increase in the 'late Roman/Byzantine' period, marked not only by an increase in settlements but also in intensive cultivation made possible by artificial field fertilisation.[35]

Thus, the pattern of rural settlement and development is affected not so much by the actual remains but by archaeological fashion. We have already observed in Chapter 5 how academic priorities can distort the received view of urban continuity. The rural surveys, in concentrating too exclusively on specific research interests, have resulted in the true picture being distorted.

The desert fringes

These hold a surprising amount of remains. Their existence in fact belies the term 'desert': although certainly dry and sparse by temperate standards, it holds sufficient water in wadis and wells which can, when properly conserved, support settlement and agriculture.[36] A 'group' of settlements, albeit rather amorphous, comprises a long chain of widely spaced, mainly late Roman ruined desert settlements, cities and fortifications throughout the north-western desert areas of Syria. It includes places as far apart as Qasr Ibn Wardan and al-Anderin towards Hama and Rasafa south of the Euphrates.[37] They are quite different to the Dead Cities: more wide-spaced, as befits the sparser terrain; often defensive in nature, either against nomads or the Iranian invasions of the sixth century; and there is an increasing use of mud-brick, as the sources of good stone become scarcer the further away from the hill country. Because of their wider scatter, they do not form as cohesive a group as the Dead Cities do.

Most stretch in a rough line south-eastwards, crossing the old desert route to Palmyra via the Jebel Khass. From Sfira (ancient Sipri, where there are the remains of a mid-second-millennium fortified city, as well as some Roman remains), two routes branch off, the first following the old route to the east towards Rasafa, and the second to Palmyra via Isriya. Both routes include ruined towns with churches and other remains. Isriya, ancient Seriana, at an important desert junction on the second route roughly halfway between Aleppo and Palmyra, as well as between Hama (Ephiphania) and Rasafa, has a beautifully intact Roman prostyle temple of the third century AD, surrounded by the ruins of the ancient town (Figure 97G).

Isriya is virtually the only third-century monumental building in the region. Remains in the semi-desert area north-east of Hama are generally later, and a survey there confirmed a denser population in the fifth-sixth centuries than in the first to fourth.[38] Salamiya, ancient Salamias, is an extensive area of ruins with continuous occupation down to the tenth century. At al-Andarin the ruins of the ancient fortified town of Androna cover a large area. It was abandoned soon after the Arab conquest. Public buildings are of well-made masonry blocks, but most of the houses are of mud-brick. Another desert fortification, Qasr al-Antar to the south-west, was built in 557–8. The most important of the desert remains is Qasr Ibn Wardan. There are three buildings: a palace, a church, and a barracks (Figure 55, Plate 20), forming an imperial desert outpost built between 561 and 564 during the time of Justinian. Their building style is unique in Syria, built entirely in the imperial style of Constantinople, rather than in the local Syrian style. Hence, construction

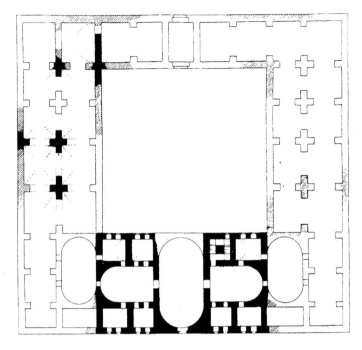

Figure 55 Qasr Ibn Wardan

is of alternating bands of small stone masonry and brick, identical to buildings in Constantinople, rather than the large masonry blocks that were almost universally used in Roman Syria. In a country where even modest domestic buildings were of stone, the use of brick was exceptional – and presumably unnecessary. Indeed, the bricks are identical in size to the standard bricks of Constantinople – presumably the actual moulds were imported. With such a clear disregard of local building practices, the design, the architects and even some of the skilled workmen of Qasr Ibn Wardan were presumably imported. The church plan – probably a chapel or private church to the palace – may also have been imported from Constantinople as it does not copy local Syrian models.[39] The complex at Qasr Ibn Wardan is an anomaly. It has no associated town or religious centre, yet its strong architectural associations with the imperial capital indicate that this was no mere desert outpost under local control. Clearly, its construction must have been of considerable importance to Constantinople. The complex is more in the nature of the desert palaces, such as Qasr al-Hayr or the ones in Jordan, such as appeared much later in the Umayyad period.

Cilicia

The amount of standing Roman remains in Cilicia are scarcely less than in the Dead Cities, although it is less well surveyed. The section of coast between Seleucia (modern Silifke) and Corycos (modern Kiz Kalesi), for example, is almost continuously built up with quite substantial buildings surviving. Remains of extensive towns and cities can also be found at Olba, Tarsus, Pompeiopolis and Hierapolis Castabala.[40] This area forms almost as important a hinterland to Antioch as the Dead Cities do.

The Negev[41]

A surprising number of cities – or at least large settlements, the term is controversial here – exist in areas of the Negev Desert that today appear unproductive or at least peripheral in terms of agriculture. Such settlements exist at Elousa, Nessana, Eboda (Avdat), Sobata (Shivta), Kuraub (Mampsis), Rehovot and Saadi (Soudanon). They are all quite large, generally fourth century and later (although some were Nabataean), and exhibit all signs of comfortable prosperity, with large, opulent churches. Wine presses were common, a surprising feature in view of the aridity of the area today. All except Eboda and Nessana are unfortified. Like the Dead Cities, they declined in the seventh century, becoming deserted by the end of the century.

Outside these 'cities', the countryside presents an equally surprising picture. Large numbers of smaller late Roman sites have been found, mainly along the wadi beds. Most are agricultural – many nothing more than agricultural installations – with threshing floors, wine presses and sheep pens providing evidence for quite intensive sedentary agriculture. Again the sheer quantity seems astonishing: 223 in the Har Nafha region, 170 in Har Hamran, similar numbers throughout the Negev. Their development was a result of a long and gradual process since the Nabataean period in the first few centuries BC. There was a sharp decline in the Umayyad period, with none continuing after the middle of the ninth century.

Jordan

Recent work in and around Madaba has emphasised the richness of the late Roman period: remains of many churches, a palace, and large amounts of mosaics have been recorded, evidence of an obviously very wealthy community. Of the 125 sites around Hesban, 108 (86 per cent) belong to the fourth–seventh centuries, whilst further south, between the Mujib and al-Hasa wadis, over 400 Christian funerary inscriptions have been recorded.[42]

In the region of north Jordan around the Decapolis cities, surveys have revealed traces of some 600 rural sites, 400 of them occupied from the fourth to the seventh centuries (excluding the Decapolis cities themselves).[43] The hinterland of Pella has revealed an astonishingly rich range of agricultural activity that peaked in the 'Byzantine' period (presumably fourth–seventh centuries). Initially, in the Hellenistic period, the area was heavily fortified with quite large-scale defensive systems, indicating considerable rural instability. These gradually gave way to smaller fortified posts in the earlier Roman period and eventually to open farmsteads in the late Roman. The rural area so far surveyed included for this period a large 'villa', several smaller farmsteads and a number of indeterminate structures, at least twenty-two wine presses, water installations (basins, cisterns, reservoirs), several open enclosures (presumably animal pens) and agricultural terraces and field walls scattered over the landscape.[44]

Considerable evidence for the Roman road network has also been recorded, particularly of the Via Nova Trajana. It ran from Bosra, the capital of Roman Arabia, and terminated at Aila, the province's main seaport on the Gulf of Aqaba, linking up the main Roman cities in the province (except, surprisingly, Jerash). Its length was some 430 kilometres (excluding subsidiary roads). Construction probably began in 107, soon after the annexation, and was completed between 111 and 114. It is documented by the Peutinger

Table, and on the ground by numerous inscriptions from the time of Hadrian to Constantine found on some 240 milestones. In addition, there are several well-preserved paved and unpaved stretches visible on the ground, with more visible from the air. Associated with the road network are numerous forts, way stations and settlements. The roads do not represent the creation of new routes by the Romans, but are merely the renewal of older Nabataean routes, themselves probably forming a part of the even older Persian Royal Road system.[45]

The Hauran[46]

The Hauran is dominated by the range of volcanic hills known as the Jebel Arab (Jebel Druze or Jebel Hauran), and the area is covered in black basalt rock and lava flows. The central Hauran is up to 1,800 metres high and is often snow-covered in winter. To the south-east it gives way to the Black Desert of eastern Syria and Jordan. This area of volcanic desolation is interspersed with abundant, rich agricultural land and settlement, and has almost as high a concentration of ancient ruins as the Dead Cities – the remains of some three hundred ancient towns and villages have been recorded (Figure 56). For the volcanic action also produced a highly fertile soil in the valleys and plains not covered by the lava flows, making it a major grain-growing region in antiquity. The basalt, furthermore, is also one of the hardest building materials known, so much is still standing. Virtually all building work in the Hauran until very recently used this readily available material.

There are several factors that make the architecture of the Hauran of particular interest. The first is the black basalt building material which is incredibly durable and rarely weathers or crumbles, so that preservation is unusually high. Its considerable tensile strength allowed for the development of unusual building techniques not normally possible with softer stones. Hence, it was possible to cut long basalt 'beams' and use them in much the same way as timber was used elsewhere, particularly in corbelling and cantilevering techniques to roof considerable areas – 10 metres and more (Figure 116). This gave rise to a distinct, cantilevered 'slab and lintel' architectural style that is peculiar to the black basalt areas of the Hauran. The second factor, which stems directly from the first, is the large quantity of domestic architecture that survives: many of the more humble buildings were built of the basalt as well. The third factor is the Nabataean element. For two centuries before the Roman conquest the area came under the influence of the Nabataeans with their distinctive and vigorous architectural traditions, moving their capital here from Petra in the first century. The architecture of the Hauran thus forms a fusion of Hellenistic, Nabataean and Roman styles.

Villages and their settings

The wealth and stability of the region is reflected in the number and opulence of the public buildings at village level, particularly temples and inns. The villages were essentially self-governing and local, owing little to imperial Rome. The village 'strategos' mentioned in Greek inscriptions was merely the equivalent of the traditional village shaikh, and in no way implies Greek or Roman institutions. Even the settlements described as 'cities' in inscriptions were probably little more than villages: the 'cities' of Dionysias, Canatha, Philippopolis and Maximinianopolis, for example, are located in a compact row 11

Figure 56 Map of the Hauran

kilometres apart, while the concentration of settlements around Dionysias (Suwayda) are less than 5 kilometres apart.[47]

Houses followed a standard pattern of rooms grouped around a courtyard that is common in the Middle East both today and in antiquity, but in the Hauran they differed in one important point. Because of the immense strength of the basalt it was possible to build several storeys, with three and even four storeys still standing in parts (Plate 72).

239

Plate 72 House in Umm al-Jimal. Note cantilevering techniques and exterior stairs

Ground floors were used for storage and stabling, with upper floors for living and sleeping, a pattern that today in the Middle East occurs only in Yemen. Upper floors would often be connected by external stone staircases corbelled out from the walls – good examples occur at Umm al-Jimal (Plate 72). Roofing consisted of long basalt slabs laid across the rooms. Where a space was too wide to be spanned by a single length, two methods would be used: either corbels would be built out at the tops of walls to narrow the space, or a series of arches would span the space and the beams placed from arch to arch, i.e., lengthways to the room. Another peculiarity of the Hauran (although it is occasionally found elsewhere in Syria, e.g., the Palmyra tombs) was the doors, which often consisted of a single upright slab of basalt (sometimes weighing several tons) with stone hinges that would allow it to open and close surprisingly smoothly. Good examples of these building techniques can be seen in most of the ruined towns of the Hauran.

Superbly intact houses survive in many villages, but perhaps the best are at Umm al-Jimal in Jordan. Impressive though these houses are, close examination reveals a very similar picture to that of the Dead Cities: rich peasantry rather than large landowners. Houses generally consisted of a courtyard containing mangers and animal troughs, with stables in the courtyards, and ground-floor rooms were generally small, suggesting animal or storage use.[48]

Elsewhere houses could be quite grand. At Inkhil are the remains of a superb second-century villa (Plate 73). It has a façade with elaborately decorated doorways and conch-head niches. Inside is a large vaulted central hall flanked by smaller rooms, beautifully

Plate 73 Villa at Inkhil

decorated with busts and other sculptures, all carved from the incredibly hard basalt. Further west towards Qunaytra, there are a number of well-preserved houses at Kafr Nasal, including two virtually intact two-storey houses with Doric colonnades in front. They both have some fine decorative treatment, and their layout – a high vaulted central hall flanked by smaller rooms – recalls that of Inkhil. They are second–third century in date.

In the Safa Desert, most of the remains fall into two categories. First are the frontier posts, mainly Roman, that guarded against incursions by nomads. Second are the large numbers of rock-cut inscriptions and petroglyphs pecked onto the iron-hard surfaces of the basalt boulders by the nomads in the first few centuries AD, evidence of a surprisingly high level of literacy – and sophistication – enjoyed by these tribes.[49] They are written in the Safaitic script (which gets its name from the Safa region), derived from the Aramaic.

Settlements have survived from the Bronze Age and even the Chalcolithic period. But the period of greatest prosperity was the early Roman, when the Hauran participated in the 'explosion' of building activity in the second century AD brought about by Roman prosperity and stability. This building activity continued throughout. New surveys in the southern Hauran reveal very dense settlement with a long period of continuous settlement from the Nabataean period through to the Umayyad, which suggests a continuity and stability of rural population that was little affected by the arrival of Rome.[50] In the the Golan, surveys have revealed a well-populated and flourishing rural life of the second–third century, continuing to the sixth and seventh centuries without any discernible break.[51]

Parts of the ancient road network have survived in the Hauran, usually converging upon Bosra. As well as the Via Trajana, part of a Roman road exists at Imtan (ancient Mothana), and guard-posts and milestones that marked the Roman road that crossed the Laijja, as well as parts of the road itself, are still visible. The countryside is also covered with long lines of stone walls marking field boundaries, most of which are probably ancient, similar to the rural landscape of the Dead Cities.

Public buildings

An unusually large number of small rural temples and shrines have survived in the towns and villages of the Hauran, providing a particularly revealing picture of the everyday religion of the countryside. Suwayda (Nabataean Soada) was an important centre for the cult of Dushara. Its name was changed in Roman times to Dionysias, as the Romans identified Dionysius with Dushara. The fine third-century peripteral temple recorded at the beginning of the century is no longer extant, but a few more fragmentary Roman ruins exist elsewhere in the town and current excavations are uncovering more. The important remains of Qanawat, just outside Suwayda, as well as its shrine at Si', have been examined in Chapter 5. To the west of Qanawat are the ruins of a temple at 'Atil, ancient Athila. This is a Roman prostyle temple built in AD 151, with two columns in antis in a curious Corinthian and Ionic composite style. There are the remains of a second temple as well as a church nearby. There is another very fragmentary Roman temple in an Ionic–Corinthian composite order at Suwaylim, ancient Selaema, a short way further north (Plate 138).

More remains can be found in the area to the south and east of Suwayda. At Kafr, ancient Capra, the village contains many reused ancient fragments and parts of ancient houses, but the ruined temple, recorded at the beginning of the century, is no longer extant. Many more remains are found south and east of Salkhad. A prostyle temple dated AD 124 is recorded at Mashquq, and at Miyamas are the remains of two adjacent, small prostyle temples, that were later converted into a single church. At Mushannaf, ancient Nela, on the edges of the desert, is a well-preserved prostyle temple in antis standing in a large colonnaded temenos, as well as other ruins (Figures 89D and 98F). The architecture appears late second century AD, but an inscription on its temenos wall suggests a first-century date.

North and west of Suwayda, temple remains occur at Hayat and Hit, ancient Eitha. More have been recorded at Sur (ancient Saura) and Sahr, the former also containing a very ruined Nabataean temple (Figures 98D and 103G). Sanamayn, ancient Aere, has a magnificently decorated peripteral Temple of Tyche built in 191, one of the finest monuments in the Hauran (Figure 101L). It is a square temple entered through a triple entrance which faces a niche surmounted by conch, flanked by two decorated smaller niches. The interior has a Greek key entablature supported by Corinthian columns standing on pedestals. The rich decoration is all the more remarkable for the extreme hardness of the basalt into which it is carved.

Whilst there are important church and monastic remains in the Hauran, they cannot be compared to the quantity or quality that occur in the Dead Cities – nor, indeed, with the pagan remains in the Hauran. It is possible that the strong Nabataean element here – and Nabataean cult centres – meant that paganism showed greater resistance to Christianity than in the north, at least until the emergence of Bosra as a major Christian centre in the sixth century. Umm al-Qutayn, south of Salkhad, is a ruined Roman town that includes at least three churches and a monastery, the latter quite well preserved. More ruined churches have been recorded at Umm al-Jimal and elsewhere in the southern Hauran. The Church of St George at Ezr'a, the ancient episcopal town of Zorava, built in 515, is in a remarkable state of preservation (Plate 110E). It follows a central plan consisting of an octagon within a square, much the same as the near contemporary Cathedral at Bosra. The circumambulatory plans of these Hauran churches contrast with the basilica and house plans of the north Syrian churches, and might be a survival of the circumambulatory plans of the Nabataean temples of the Hauran.[52] There was another slightly later church at Ezr'a, St Elias, in the form of a cross, a plan that was to gain increasing popularity in later periods.

Shaqqa, ancient Sakkaia or Maximiniopolis, was a Roman town elevated to the rank of colony. In the centre are the remains of a large public building known as the *qaysariya*. There is also a basilica with a square tower, dated AD 176. Like the Bahira basilica at Bosra, this would originally have been a Roman public assembly hall rather than a Christian church. Mismiya, ancient Phaena, had a particularly fine 'praetorium' dating from AD 160 (Figure 57), no longer extant. It consisted of a central chamber of cruciform plan with intact vaulting supported by Corinthian columns.

Conclusions

The general picture now emerging is one of overwhelming rural increase in the Roman Near East from the fourth century onwards: in settlement, population, productivity and wealth. This is demonstrated most of all by the record of the Dead Cities, where most of the standing remains occur. The Hauran is the only other region where a comparable amount of standing remains are to be found. These are generally earlier than those of the Dead Cities, where the rural wealth began in the third century or earlier, but sustaining it throughout the later Roman period as well, so the overall picture is not substantially altered. Whenever the record is examined elsewhere, new archaeological investigations firmly endorse the picture. Whether it is in prime agricultural land such as the hinterlands of Pella and Madaba, or areas of marginal agricultural potential, such as the semi-desert areas of the Negev or north-eastern Syria, the same pattern emerges. The only exception is the borderland areas of eastern Syria and northern Mesopotamia, where the evidence for rural settlement shows a decline after about AD 250, with an increase only becoming apparent after the beginning of Islam in the eighth–ninth centuries. This is presumably because the area was a battleground between Rome and Iran, as the rural decline is paralleled by an increase in fortifications, whether Roman or Sasanian.[53]

The other picture to emerge is that whilst the cities might have been the centres of Romanisation (and even this must be modified – see Chapter 5), the countryside remained firmly a part of the Semitic East. The idea that the villages 'represented their attraction to a Graeco-Roman urban, or sub-urban, style of life and communal organisation'[54] because of the existence of a few Greek inscriptions simply does not hold. On the contrary,

> The theory that villages in the Roman East had an elaborate system of self-government cannot be sustained on the evidence of these inscriptions. It should be discarded. In its place we should instead take the common-sense view that

Figure 57 The 'Praetorium' at Mismiya, drawn in the nineteenth century by De Voguë

villages were ruled by headmen, by informal gatherings of well-respected local men, and by the landowners and their bailiffs. . . . This was the general pattern of village rule in all Iron Age societies, from Assyria to the Industrial Revolution. There is no reason to assume that the Roman East should be any different.[55]

The evidence of the countryside thus presents a picture of substantial wealth in the late Roman period. In many ways, this reflects a far more real wealth than the great temples and urban building projects of the second and third centuries do. Such lavish buildings certainly have an opulence that might reflect wealth, but perhaps only the wealth of a single sector of the society. Indeed, the great temples might just as easily be evidence for impoverishment rather than wealth, the impoverishment of a society bled white in order to build such over-ambitious projects (one recalls, for example, that both the great Temple of Artemis at Jerash and the huge temple complex at Baalbek were never finished). Or, like the glittering opulence of cinemas in the Depression-era United States and the massive, grandiose dams and agricultural schemes in Stalinist Soviet Union, they might even reflect poverty more than wealth, built as a mock façade to shore up an image of wealth by a labour force made cheap from poverty. This may not necessarily be so in the second and third centuries, but it is important to guard against superficial assumptions of wealth. Most of all, it is important to emphasise that the far more modest remains in the country-side reflect a *real* wealth, the wealth of a substantial section – even the majority – of the population.

This pattern of rural increase in the late Roman period is certainly in stark contrast to the cities, which saw their greatest increase and prosperity throughout the second and third centuries. Thus, the wealth of the countryside, Tchalenko's 'civilisation rurale', appears to mark a parallel urban decline. Such patterns of alternating urban and rural development, with the increase of population in one made at the expense of the other, is a familiar pattern in the ancient Near East when observed over a period of many thousands of years.[56]

In the light of this we must revise many of the received notions of the decline of the Roman Empire. The idea that the peasantry and countryside declined, that the cities were 'parasitic centres of consumption' and that landlords and increasing state demands oppressed the countryside, that the Roman Empire was, in short, in a state of decadence, simply no longer holds true. On the contrary, the evidence from the countryside shows an Empire – at least in the East – that was prosperous, confident, stable and anything but declining.[57]

Finally, the evidence shows that the East more than any other region was the source of wealth, *real* wealth, for the Roman Empire. A wealth born of trade further east, but also a wealth born of the thousands of years of continuity of civilisation in the East long before the Romans. A wealth that found its expression in the greatest upsurge of building activity, both in the cities and in the countryside, reflecting a broad prosperity not found elsewhere in the empire. The acquisition of the eastern provinces in the first centuries BC and AD led directly to the rise of Rome and of Roman greatness, the first period of greatness in European history. Their loss after the seventh century led to the European Dark Ages. The East was the real heart of the Roman Empire. Small wonder that Rome itself moved to the East.

7

IMPERIAL VENEER: ARCHITECTURE AND THE RESURGENCE OF THE EAST

Architecture is Rome's most visible legacy. Ever since late antiquity, its colossal ruins have awed all who came under their spell. The vast ruins in Rome inspired Gibbon's equally vast work and a host of others. Architects from all ages, from Renaissance masters to the builders of the great Ottoman mosques, have been in turn inspired and dominated by Roman architecture as they sought to both emulate and surpass it. The basic principles of Roman architecture have become canonical, enshrined in works from Vitruvius to Sir Bannister Fletcher, dictating the forms of virtually all western architecture down until the nineteenth century. Even today, in an age dominated by skyscrapers and technological wonders, many are more overawed by a visit to Rome's great ruin-fields of Pompeii, Lepcis or Jerash than to Manhattan or Tokyo.

Apart from their impressiveness, the reason why Roman ruins overawe is their immediate familiarity. We have all seen the direct descendants of Roman architecture, from nineteenth-century public buildings to minor details in parish churches. Our colonial ancestors took these forms with them to all parts of the world, so that they are almost as familiar in Goa, Sydney or Buenos Aires as they are in Vienna, Berlin or Madrid. Roman architecture, therefore, more than any other single element symbolises western civilisation: its origins, its continuity, its strength. A 'westerner' visiting Lepcis Magna or Baalbek is, as it were, coming home. Roman architecture is nothing if not a gigantic cultural statement: it is 'us'.

With the possible exception of North Africa, more intact Roman monuments survive in the East than any other part of the Roman world, from gigantic temples to entire cities. And here the cultural statement has an additional element: not only are the monuments 'ours', they serve to underline the difference with 'them'. When viewed for the first time, the western visitor feels immediately at home amongst familiar architectural forms: columned porticoes, Corinthian capitals, and standard systems of architectural layout and decorative treatment that have dominated western architecture from the time of the Romans to our own. The long lines of Classical colonnades that stride so confidently across eastern ruin-fields appear to proclaim the superiority of one culture over another in no uncertain terms. Such architectural masterpieces not only 'belong' to 'us', they are used to reaffirm a cultural difference and superiority, a Roman – and by extension western – triumph. In the emotive words of Rose Macaulay:

> Entering some Arab village of squalid hovels, we are in a Roman colony, among temple columns, triumphal arches, traces of theatres and baths which no one has

had the intellect or the cleanliness to use since the Arabs expelled the civilized Graeco-Roman-Syrian inhabitants and squatted among their broken monuments, stabling their horses in the nave of a Christian basilica, their camels in a richly carved pagan temple, their families in mud huts clustering about the proscenium of a theatre: the broken heirlooms of the race that ruled stand like desolate ghosts among the squalor.[1]

Such highly charged descriptions with their overt racism use the Roman buildings to reinforce cultural prejudice, and are unfashionable now (although Rose Macaulay's book remains a popular one). But the sentiments are still alive,[2] and even in academic studies, Roman architecture is often viewed as part of a single, overall pattern because of its superficial homogeneity. It is seen almost as if there was an 'official' Roman architecture suborned to traditions emanating from Rome and Greece, that minimises regionality.[3] One recent study of eastern Roman architecture emphasises the international, 'imperial' style and universality of Roman architecture, drawing upon Greek prototypes but deliberately designed to be a single theme throughout the empire, so that an integrated 'common cultural basis' can be created. Architecture is seen as a manifestation – almost a tool – of Rome consolidating its power over subject nations by a common, imposed vocabulary that was the same in every city of the empire. The only regional differences perceived were in minor decorative details and some construction techniques, otherwise regionality was non-existent.[4] Another recent academic study, when discussing Near Eastern temples, writes that 'the *expression* given to this cult in architectural form belongs, as always, to the Roman Empire' and ' . . . the Near Eastern Greek city of the Imperial period (is) marked above all by its monumental public buildings', i.e., defined in Graeco-Roman terms by the architecture imposed on it.[5] The architecture appears entirely – almost overwhelmingly – Roman (or 'Greek'); a foreign transplant that has more in common with Italy or Greece than with the ancient Near East where the buildings are found. In other words, a symbol of ruler and ruled, an attitude that is merely better disguised than 'them' and 'us' or 'superior' and 'inferior', but not substantially different.

That there is a homogeneity to Roman architecture cannot be denied. But it was never the overriding factor. Nowhere was regionalism more important in Roman architecture than in the East. In the past, this has been minimised, usually because Roman architecture has been viewed almost wholly from the Classical perspective. In the following sections, the architecture of the Roman East is examined from a Near Eastern perspective.

For the purposes of discussion, the architecture is divided into component elements, from broader themes (such as city plans) to minute details (such as decoration). It must be emphasised, however, that these divisions are entirely artificial ones for convenience only. No single type of monument or element existed in isolation, but was a part of a whole. In particular, the division into secular and religious, whilst convenient to describe separate buildings (for example, theatres as opposed to temples), in no way reflects real divisions, either in terms of function or design. A monumental arch, for example, might have both religious and urban functions, whilst theatricality was as much an element in religious buildings as it was in buildings for entertainment. Indeed, religion was – and still is – far more all-embracing in eastern cities than in western ones. Only in the East does one find holy cities, where an entire city's function, purpose and layout (for example Rasafa or Jerusalem) was suborned to religion. To some extent, therefore, not just the temples and churches but all of the architecture described here is religious.

The urban layout

Planned towns

The ordered Graeco-Roman grid system of planned towns is often cited as the most pervasive feature of western domination over native Near Eastern urban forms.[6] It is usually contrasted with the more haphazard native Near Eastern tradition – with all the cultural differences that emotive words such as 'haphazard' versus 'orderly' imply. Grid systems are emphasised as much for their symbol of the superiority of order over disorder, West over East, as for their origins, Greek or otherwise.[7] Even when early forms of Near Eastern grid systems are acknowledged, the Greeks of Asia Minor (Smyrna and Miletus in particular) are emphasised far more[8] – the assumption that the Greeks 'invented' civilisation is a difficult one to shed.

The grid system is often referred to as the 'Hippodamian' town plan after Hippodamos of Miletus, who used it in his rebuilding of the city of Miletus in 479 BC following its destruction by the Iranians. The origins of Greek town planning are seen to go back further to the ordered layouts of Old Smyrna and pre-Hippodamian Miletus in the eighth–seventh centuries BC.[9] Here, however, the layouts are merely ordered rather than truly planned – the difference is important – and were certainly not the planned grids that we see in Near Eastern systems, such as Zerneki Tepe or Tell al-Amarna (see below). Old Smyrna and Miletus in any case appear isolated examples in the Greek world at the time, where town layouts were normally as haphazard as their Near Eastern counterparts. In any case both Old Smyrna and Miletus are in Asia, not Europe, suggesting an Asiatic origin for the planned town.

The first truly planned towns of the Graeco-Roman world are in southern Italy and Sicily rather than around the Aegean. Megara Hyblaea in Sicily had a regular layout, although no overall plan. The first laid-out gridded plan was probably Poseidonia (Paestum) in the sixth century BC, possibly the first properly planned town in the Mediterranean. Several more followed: Metapontum, Selinus and Akragas are those whose plans – and dates – have been ascertained from archaeology. Gridded layouts are seen to be a feature of colonisation, deriving from land allocations essential to the principle of colonisation.[10] Colonies are by their very nature planned artificial creations as opposed to evolved cities, which are more organic. In this context, it is significant that many of the Near Eastern forerunners of the planned town reviewed below were also colonies.

All of these early examples of the gridded town plan are Greek colonies in Sicily and southern Italy of the sixth–fifth centuries BC. This is in striking contrast to the lack of such plans on the Greek mainland, the origin of the colonies themselves. The origins of such plans are presumed to be Old Smyrna and Miletus, but Ionian colonies were usually around the Black Sea and eastern Mediterranean, and do not have gridded layouts. The evidence suggests that the origins of this system, therefore, lie in southern Italy and Sicily, rather than with the Greeks of either the Greek mainland or Asia Minor.

It is significant that southern Italy and Sicily saw colonisation by the Phoenicians long before the arrival of the Greeks.[11] In this context it is worth noting that the only extensively excavated Phoenician city in North Africa not obscured by later overburden is Kerkouane in Tunisia. Founded probably in the sixth century, 'the urban plan shows a well-designed checkerboard pattern with regular crossing streets, but the city blocks (*insulae*) have varying dimensions and adjacent components'.[12] Elsewhere in North Africa, the 'haphazard' plans of Phoenician towns are contrasted with the grid-plans that supposedly characterise Roman towns. Such contrasts are made, for example, at Dougga, Carthage or Sabratha, where Roman 'order' was superimposed over an older Phoenician 'haphazard' or 'un-Roman' plan, with all the implied emotiveness of such terms.[13] However, other cities, such as Lepcis Magna, Sbeitla or Oea were also of Phoenician foundation and have *only* grid plans; their grids are *assumed* to be Roman for no reason other than the assumption that 'grid-plans equals order equals Roman' – an essentially circular argument.

In the Phoenician homeland in the Levant, there is evidence of city planning in the layout of Byblos as early as 2800 BC. Here, 'precautions had been taken in laying out the streets so that access to the city walls from the centre of the city and the residential area would be easy and rapid in the case of attack'.[14] Other Near Eastern planned layouts are discussed below. The Phoenicians, therefore, may have brought town planning from the East long before the Romans arrived to provide us with a glib explanation for the planned elements in the Phoenicio-Roman towns of North Africa. Clearly, the Greek colonial origin of the planned town is more complex than it appears, involving traditions in Italy as well as Asia Minor and Phoenicia – greatly exacerbated by the archaeological difficulties of determining both urban layouts and their dates underneath later overburden.

The rebuilding of Miletus under the Persian Empire after its destruction in 479 BC as a fully planned city on a large scale by Hippodamos marks a new and far more ambitious phase in the history of town planning, for whilst older town plans were based on the street unit, new Miletus was based on the insula unit (Figure 58). Piraeus, Rhodes and Thourioi were also newly laid out at the time, based on mathematical principles.[15] These cities are also attributed to Hippodamos, although the mathematical principle of town planning is Iranian, where it is based on the circle (see below).

Whatever the claims of Hippodamos, the arrival of the Iranians at his home town certainly marks a hallmark in the history of town planning. At the same time, a new concept in town planning appears in the Aegean with the building of Mausolus' new monumental city of Halicarnassus. This 'illustrates the importance of the city as a medium of self-glorification and propaganda'.[16] These new elements involved the introduction of visual priorities: monumental terracing, grand approaches, massive propylaea and a monumentality generally that was to characterise much Hellenistic planning later at places such as Pergamon, Cos, Lindos and Labranda. Once again, Iranian origins can be seen in these new elements, demonstrated so impressively by the monumental royal layouts of Pasargadae, Susa and Persepolis, or perhaps by the earlier Neo-Babylonian ceremonial centre of Babylon. The Iranian royal cities were planned and laid out entities revolving around the king. Once again it is important to bear in mind that the Greek and Hellenistic examples cited are on (or just off) the coast of Asia, not Greece.

From this innovation, the Hippodamian planned system became the standard form of cities throughout the Greek, and subsequently Hellenistic and Roman, worlds. In the East it assumed its greatest popularity following the conquests of Alexander, which instigated one of the greatest spates of city foundations – or refoundations – that the East had seen. Indeed, the conquests of Alexander are usually taken as an urban watershed in most histories of urbanisation in the East. This is mainly because the Hippodamian town plan became a part of the 'standard package' of Hellenisation, with grid systems recognised on Hellenistic sites from as far apart as Dura Europos on the Euphrates to Ai Khanum (Alexandria Oxiana) on the Oxus and Taxila in India, and still discerned in the layouts of

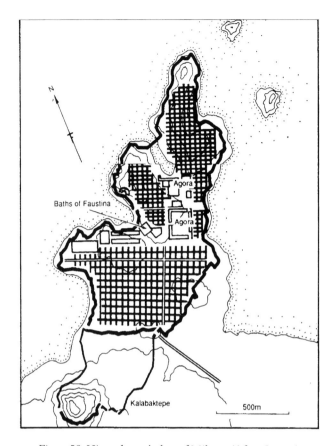

Figure 58 Hippodamos' plan of Miletus (After Owens)

cities such as Latakia, Damascus and Aleppo today. Hence, town planning has become one of the most ubiquitous pieces of evidence for the triumph of West over East.

The grid system of town planning, however, has a far greater pedigree in the East than in the West. The system emerged fully developed in the East long before Alexander or even Hippodamos – indeed, the haphazard nature of early Greek cities is conspicuous in comparison to their later orderliness.[17] In Syria, the seventh-millennium BC settlement of Tell Bouqras on the Euphrates already shows signs of an overall imposed plan,[18] while at the third-millennium BC Sumerian colony of Habuba Kabira on the middle Euphrates in Syria, more careful overall planning is evident. It was laid out in the form of a rectangle, traversed by two north–south and east–west thoroughfares, with the city temple at its intersection (Figure 59).[19] At the early first-millennium BC Neo-Assyrian provincial capital of Dur Katlimmu (Tell Shaikh Hamad) in north-eastern Syria, a systematic plan and layout based on a rectangle, with main north–south and east–west intersecting thoroughfares, becomes more apparent.[20] Such a layout was to characterise the Roman towns of Syria several thousand years later. A more perfect example of the 'classic' grid system has been found at the towns of Kahun and Tell al-Amarna in Egypt, laid out in about 2600 BC as colonies for construction workers.[21]

Despite such examples, it must be conceded that ancient Near Eastern cities generally

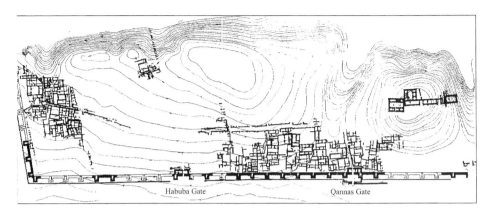

Figure 59 The Sumerian colony of Habuba Kabira on the Euphrates (After Stromenger)

did not adhere to a grid system or any discernible pattern. Their plans were more a product of long evolution and growth rather than new layouts. However, further east, in the Indian subcontinent, the grid system was a feature of both Harappan and early historic city plans.[22] Third-millennium Harappan cities have been noted for their orderly layouts and gridded street plans ever since their rediscovery in the early twentieth century (Figure 60).[23] Whereas ancient Near Eastern grid systems appear to be isolated examples, those of the Indus civilisation are part of a fully developed and general system whose popularity continued long after its collapse. The planned, square layout emerges fully developed at, for example, the early fourth-century BC site of Sisupalgarh in Orissa. Sisupalgarh is dated broadly to about 500–200 BC, with its first rampart – which outlines and defines its gridded town plan – undated, but probably built before 500 BC.[24]

This Indian tradition of laid-out grid systems was written down and formalised in a remarkable late fourth-century BC document from north-eastern India, the *Arthasastra*. This was a treatise covering all aspects of government for the Emperor Chandragupta Maurya, written by Kautilya, his chief minister.[25] In Book 2 Chapter 4, the layout for the ideal fortified city is described in great detail, with arterial roads meeting at right-angles and the royal residence in the centre surrounded by the chief temples and ancillary services (armoury, warehouses, record office, stables, etc.) (Figure 61). Elsewhere in the *Arthasastra* the ideal layout for a fortified military camp is also described in detail. When transcribed graphically, the resemblance to the 'text-book' Roman military camp of centuries later is remarkable (Figure 62).[26]

Nevertheless, remarkable though Kautilya's town planning is, Hippodamos in the early fifth century BC is still earlier than Kautilya in the late fourth. But the Kautilyan form is the culmination of a tradition stretching back several thousand years as we have seen. Of course, Sisupalgarh or Mohenjodaro are a long way from Miletus, and it might appear impossible for an ancient Indian tradition to influence the Mediterranean and that Hippodamos' invention an entirely independent development. But the matrix which bound the two cultures together was the Achaemenid Empire in the sixth to fourth centuries BC – significantly just prior to Hippodamos' 'invention'. Achaemenid civilisation was a true international and eclectic one, where religious, architectural and other ideas were transmitted freely throughout Asia, with Greek ideas travelling east as much as Indian ideas west. The nature of Achaemenid civilisation is well enough known not to

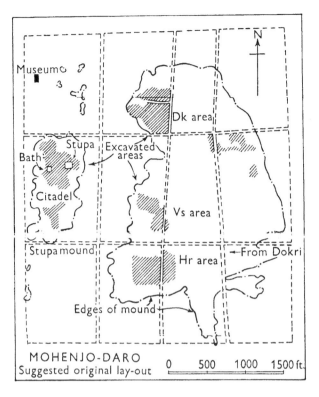

MOHENJO-DARO
Suggested original lay-out

0   500   1000   1500 ft.

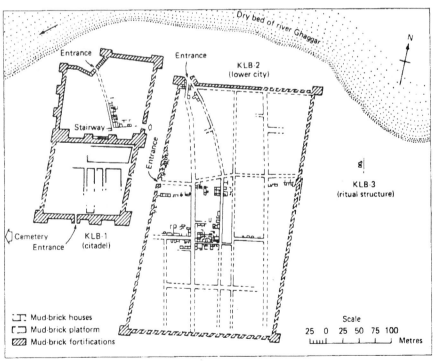

Dry bed of river Ghaggar

N

Entrance

Entrance

KLB-2
(lower city)

Stairway

Entrance

KLB-3
(ritual structure)

Cemetery
Entrance

KLB-1
(citadel)

Mud-brick houses
Mud-brick platform
Mud-brick fortifications

Scale

25   0   25   50   75   100

Metres

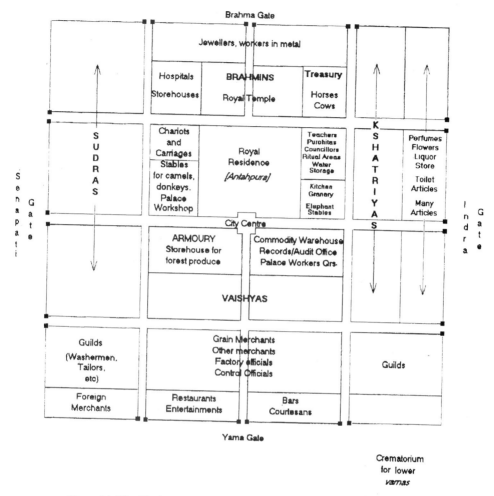

Figure 61 The ideal city according to Kautilya (After Rajarangan/Allchin)

need restating here. Against this background, it is very easy to see how town-planning ideas might have been transmitted, particularly with an urban-based power like the Achaemenids (who ruled from no less than four capital cities). Furthermore, Miletus was better placed for receiving eastern stimuli than most other Greek cities. Not only was it ruled by the Iranians for over two hundred years, but Miletus before that was the greatest of the Greek colonial powers, establishing a maritime and trading network throughout the Black Sea and elsewhere in the East.

The orderly layout of a town or city seems to have been a high priority of the Achaemenids. There can be little doubt, therefore, that Miletus received its idea of town planning from (or via) the Iranians. The native Iranian tradition was probably the circle,

Figure 60 Harappan city plans: Mohenjodaro and Kalibangan (After Wheeler/Thapar)

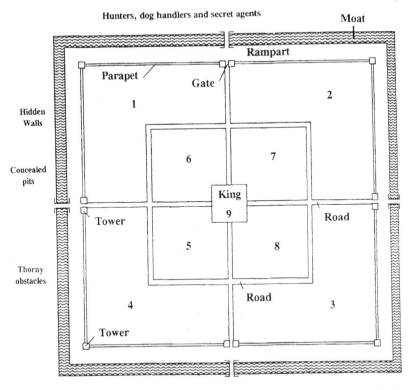

Figure 62 The ideal fortified camp according to Kautilya (After Rajarangan/Allchin)

brought from their original homelands in Central Asia (and it is notable that Plato's 'ideal city' resembled a circle). Achaemenid city plans in Central Asia often follow this, developing upon much older Central Asian circular plans.[27] It is noteworthy that Hellenistic city plans in Central Asia as often followed this circular Iranian plan as their 'own' Hippodamian plan.[28] The circular plan later achieved considerable popularity in Parthian, Sasanian and early Islamic town plans.[29] An alternative origin for the circular plan was the third-millennium BC city of Mari on the middle Euphrates, which was laid out in the form of a circle.[30]

Elsewhere in the Achaemenid Empire little investigation has been carried out on town plans. The grid plan of Zerneki Tepe in eastern Anatolia is virtually 'classic Hippodamian' (Figure 63). When first surveyed, Zerneki Tepe was tentatively thought to be Urartian, but subsequent investigations have favoured an Achaemenid date.[31] A grid plan is also suggested in the lower town of the Urartian site of Karmir-Blur in Armenia.[32] Recent excavations at the Median and Achaemenid capital of Ecbatana (Hamadan) have exposed a very regular grid-plan divided into standardised *insulae*, but the date is uncertain: Seleucid, Parthian, Sasanian and Islamic material having been recovered.[33] The rectangular layout of Achaemenid Kandahar, together with the suggestion of an overall plan that predetermined later development, may suggest a grid system rather than any other form, but this cannot be certain without further excavation.[34] Elsewhere in the Indo-Iranian borderlands Achaemenid garrison towns appear to be similarly ordered and

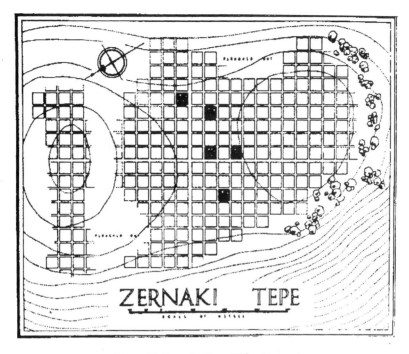

Figure 63 Zerneki Tepe (After Burney)

based on a square plan. Even the new Macedonian city foundations in north Syria have been characterised as adhering to a pattern – viewed as Seleucid – of relatively large acropolis on the edge of a planned town,[35] which is virtually the 'classic' Iranian *qaʿa* and *shahristan* form. It is significant that Hippodamus' famous 'invention' of the town plan came in Miletus *after* it became a part of the Persian Empire, so whatever one says about the 'Hippodamian system', it is as correct to call it Iranian as it is Greek. Suffice to say that the Achaemenids practised town planning, they would have been aware of the Kautilyan system, and they carried many such ideas with them to the West.

The spate of city foundations and refoundations in the East by Macedonians and Romans have nearly all been characterised by the Hippodamian grid-plan, hence often cited as one of many examples of western influence and 'character'. Many of these cities, such as Apamaea or Dura Europos, unambiguously betray these characteristics. But many others do not have an overall grid pattern, even when their Hellenistic antecedents are not in doubt. Examples are Cyrrhus in Syria, Sepphorus and Scythopolis in Palestine and Philadelphia (Amman) in Arabia (Figures 38 and 39). Others are too obscured by over-burden for any layout, grid or otherwise, to be discernible. At other 'Graeco-Roman' cities in the Near East that do have grid plans (e.g., Aleppo, Damascus), there is no actual evidence whether the grid plans are Macedonian or in fact earlier. Establishing a secure date for a city layout when it has been continuously occupied is virtually impossible. Even the planned layouts that are definitely established to be Macedonian–Roman in origin are of a distinctive Syrian variety.[36] At other 'Roman' cities, such as Tripoli in Lebanon, no trace of any grid system survives in the present plan. In other words, the number of *definitely dated*, *definitely established* grid-planned cities in the East of Hellenistic foundation is tiny – and certainly not enough to make any overall statement.[37] To assume such town plans in the East to be evidence of western influence is an oversimplification.[38]

Sacred and processional ways

A feature which differentiates Roman planned towns from the earlier Macedonian ones was the imposition of one or more main thoroughfares. In its classic form (e.g., Figure 37), this consists of an east–west *decumanus* intersecting a north–south *cardo* at right angles. Such intersecting thoroughfares which characterise eastern Roman cities, however, are only assumed to be Roman. They may well have existed before the Roman occupation – indeed, the evidence from Bosra suggests that here at least it was a Nabataean innovation.[39] The evidence reviewed above, too, shows it in Syria as far back as the fourth millennium BC at Habuba Kabira. In Roman Syria, the intersection would often be marked by a monumental arch and the thoroughfares almost invariably colonnaded. These features are discussed separately below.

Some of these thoroughfares have been explained as sacred processional ways.[40] The main colonnaded street at Palmyra, for example, has been interpreted as a *via sacra* from the great Temple of Bel to the main necropolis (Figures 15 and 64D, Plates 15 and 77).[41] The short length of colonnade excavated and re-erected at Byblos probably lined a sacred way leading from the north of the city to the Temple of Baalat-Gabal.[42] The colonnaded streets at both Nabataean capitals of Petra and Bosra have also been interpreted as sacred ways leading from the main city entrances to temple enclosures (Figure 64A and B, Plate 7).[43] This might have formed a Nabataean tradition of sacred ways, with as many as perhaps five such sacred ways at Petra alone (Figure 11). The main Petra high-place complexes of Umm al-Biyara, al-Khubtha and Madhbah have quite magnificent rock-cut ways leading up to them. The way up to the latter from the Wadi Farasa, with its associated paraphernalia of 'way stations', has been likened to a processional way, and the whole summit of the peak on which it was situated was isolated from the rest of the ridge by an artificial, rock-cut chasm, approached through a monumental propylaeum.[44] Another processional way led up to the Deir to the west of Petra. This enigmatic monument is discussed further in the sections on oval plazas and funerary monuments below. For the moment, it need only be noted that, uniquely at Petra, the Deir is an extensive complex of quite elaborate monuments that is completely isolated from other rock façades: the way up, therefore, approaches no other monument. Elsewhere in the Nabataean kingdom, a first-century BC processional way led from Qanawat out to the Shrine of Siʿ (Figure 36),[45] and the sixth-century Madaba Map depicts a colonnaded Cardo at Kerak (ancient Characmoba) terminating in a semi-circular plaza in front of the cathedral (presumably on the site of a former Nabataean temple).[46] Another Nabataean processional way has recently been identified at Sela to the north of Petra, although this might be earlier.[47]

In this context, it must be remembered that Damascus, Shahba, Jerash and Amman, all of them with famous colonnaded streets, were all within the orbit of the Nabataean kingdom (Figure 10).[48] At Jerash the main colonnaded street – the Cardo – is conventionally viewed from its southern, Amman, approach (Figure 37). But if the map were to be turned upside-down and viewed from the north – from the Antioch approach – the Cardo becomes a processional way that leads to the Zeus Temple, with the Oval Plaza aligned on the temple temenos forming the culmination of the procession (Figure 64C, Plate 74). As such, this 'processional way' must include by extension the continuation of

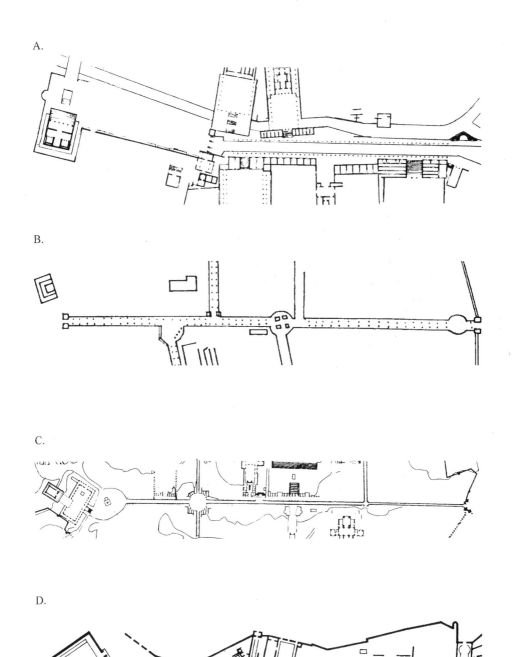

Figure 64 Comparative processional ways (not to scale). A: Petra. B: Bosra. C: Jerash. D: Palmyra

Plate 74 View along the main colonnaded street at Jerash towards the
Temple of Zeus

the Cardo by some two kilometres from the North Gate out of the city past the Temple of Nemesis (known by inscription only) to the sacred area of Birkatayn. This sacred area comprised the (now vanished) Temple of Zeus Epicarpius, the 'Festival Theatre' and a sacred tank.[49] As a sacred extra-mural area, Birkatayn has been likened to Daphne outside Antioch. The sacred way that links it to the city has its exact counterpart with the Nabataean sacred way linking Qanawat with Siʿ. The Jerash colonnaded Cardo, therefore, forms a part of one of the most extensive and monumental sacred ways in the East.

Jerash also boasted another of the most elaborate sacred approaches in Classical architecture. This was the approach to the Artemis Temple (Figure 65, Plate 75). Forming an integral part of the propylaeum is its monumental processional way that includes a small stretch of colonnaded street. The eastern half of the city, on the left bank of the Jerash (Chrysoroas) River, has been obscured by modern housing ever since the first surveys in the nineteenth century. It is not possible, therefore, to trace the Artemis processional way beyond the footings of its bridge. But it can be assumed that it began – and was surely colonnaded? – at the eastern entrance to the city, where we might postulate a third oval plaza at Jerash.

The importance of sacred processional ways in eastern architecture derives from the prominence given to religious procession in eastern ritual. We get some indication of this in the accounts of the Emperor Elagabalus' brief reign in Rome. Being the hereditary high-priest of a major eastern temple, he was naturally obliged to continue upholding the

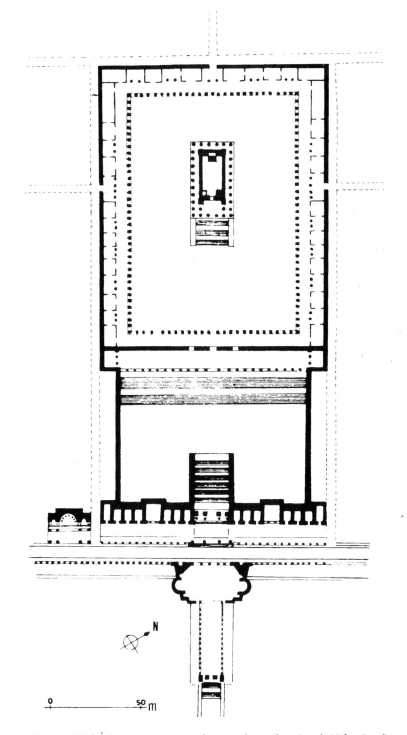

Figure 65 The Artemis processional way and temple at Jerash (After Segal)

Plate 75 The Temple of Artemis processional way and propylaeum at Jerash

ritual even after becoming emperor. The religious procession of Elagabalus' cult was treated with derision by the Romans, but underneath the welter of scorn some important information emerges. The central element of Elagabalus' ritual was a procession in which the cult object – in this case the black stone of Emesa – was drawn along in an elaborate chariot, often with other cult objects. The procession was led by the priest-emperor who walked backwards, facing the chariot, along a processional way that led to the temple. Prominent members of the community – in this case the Senate, much to their acute embarrassment! – were obliged to participate.[50] This ritual, acted out in the unbelieving environment of Rome, was presumably the standard ritual at the Temple of Emesene Baal in Syria. One can assume that the other great temples of the East demanded similar ritual processions. An inscription on the Temple of Zeus at Dumayr north-east of Damascus also makes a reference to religious procession.[51] Of course, religions elsewhere in the Greek and Roman worlds held sacred processions and even had processional ways – the concept is hardly exclusive to the East. But in the East it was accorded greater importance, and was expressed elaborately in architecture.

The eastern tradition of religious procession continued into Christianity, particularly in the East where it remains an important part of ritual to this day. The annual Easter procession along the Via Dolorosa in Jerusalem, for example, is a part of this tradition. And like their pagan counterparts, Christian ritual processions could demand elaborate architecture. At the great pilgrimage church of St Simeon Stylites in northern Syria, for example, the culmination of the pilgrimage was a procession which gathered in an open space flanked by two religious complexes (churches and hospices) in the lower town of Telannisos – the Christian equivalent of the oval plazas of pagan sacred ways. The procession then ascended the hill along a sacred way, passing underneath a monumental arch – equivalent to the temple propylaeum of pagan architecture – and finally into the great enclosure of the monastery-church itself (Figure 53, Plate 65). All of the main elements of a great temple processional way are repeated exactly. Elsewhere in eastern Christian architecture, remains of monumental sacred ways exist at Alahan monastery in Cilicia and the monastic island of Gemili off the coast of Lycia.[52] But perhaps the greatest of the Christian sacred processional ways in the East is that of Rasafa, the ancient pilgrimage centre of Sergiopolis (Figure 28). The entire city revolved around the cult of St Sergius, and its main thoroughfare acted as a sacred way for the pilgrims who flocked there. The magnificent North Gate of Rasafa – probably the finest city gate to survive antiquity – was not defensive in nature but religious: a propylaeum to a sanctuary comparable to the greatest religious propylaea of pagan architecture, with the entire city of Sergiopolis forming the sanctuary (Plate 19). From the North Gate the pilgrim processed along a sacred way (only partially excavated) past the Martyrium of St Sergius, past another church and eventually to the great Church of St Sergius itself, the focus of the entire city.[53]

Sacred ways existed in the Ionian East too. Both Ephesus and Miletus, for example, boasted particularly fine ones leading out to the nearby temples of Artemis and Apollo respectively. An equally impressive one has survived leading to the Temple of Apollo at Cyrene. The eastern context of Ionian architecture has already been emphasised above, so the origins of this feature too probably lie further east. Processions were an integral part of ancient Mesopotamian ritual. The Processional Way and Ishtar Gate built by Nebuchadnezzar at Babylon in the sixth century BC is the best known and one of the most magnificent examples (Plate 76).[54] Equally magnificent was the Gate of All Nations and Processional Way at Persepolis (Plate 92). Whilst not religious, the processional way was at least ritual, being the route that ambassadors from the subject nations would take to pay their respects at the court of the Great King during the Iranian new year festivities.[55] The sacred ways of the Roman East – and with it so much of the layout, structure and function of the eastern Roman city – were a part of this entirely non-western tradition.

Colonnaded streets

In the East the main thoroughfares were almost universally colonnaded. This feature sharply differentiates eastern from western towns. In addition, the arch marking the intersections was often (but not always) a four-way arch or *tetrapylon* (Latin *quadrifons*). Colonnaded streets perhaps form the most ubiquitous element of Roman eastern architecture, sharply defining the difference with the West more than any other feature. They have often been examined from within the broader context of Roman and western architectural traditions, with explanations for them either unsatisfactory, unconvincing or entirely lacking. Surprisingly, nowhere has this uniquely eastern architectural feature been examined in terms of Near Eastern architecture. The tetrapylon is examined separately.

More than any other single architectural feature, the colonnaded streets provided eastern Roman cities with their unique character. A distant view of an eastern Roman city today resembles a veritable forest of columns, in strong contrast to, say, Ostia or Dougga. From end to end and side to side main thoroughfares are lined with well-ordered rows of them providing monumental vistas rarely encountered in the ancient world. These

Plate 76 Model of the Processional Way and Ishtar Gate at Babylon (Photo: © Antikensammlung, Staatliche Museen zu Berlin – Preussischer Kulturbesitz)

colonnaded streets bestow upon the city an architectural unity, a common thread, that brings all the separate parts together to make the whole city a single monument.

Virtually no city of the Roman East was complete without at least one colonnaded street. They survive most famously at Apamaea, Palmyra, Bosra, Jerash and Sebaste, mainly through accidents of survival (Plates 34, 35, 39, 43, 74 and 77).[56] The most magnificent is the Cardo at Apamaea, 37.5 metres wide including its sidewalks (the carriageway alone is 20.5 metres) stretching for a total length of 1. 85 kilometres (Figure 26, Plates 34, 35 and 137). With its commemorative columns marking the intersections, not to mention the occasional flourish made by statue brackets and spiral fluted columns, the Apamaea Cardo offers one of the most splendid unbroken vistas that have survived antiquity (Plate 34).[57] For sheer ostentation, however, probably no street in the Roman world matched the colonnaded street leading to the 'Egyptian Harbour' at Tyre. The columns themselves were of imported Italian *cipollino*, and the surface of the carriageway was paved in the second century with mosaic and covered over in the early third century with marble.[58] Even smaller cities with comparatively few extant remains today, such as Deir al-Qal'a in Lebanon, Shahba or Hammat Gader, were adorned with street colonnades. Whenever new excavations take place, it is the colonnaded streets that appear, as it were, almost to spring from the earth, such as at Scythopolis (Beth-Shean) and Madaba (Plate 45). Only rarely have excavations at a Roman city in the East failed to reveal a colonnaded street, such as at Beirut or Pella. But this is probably because they were either dismantled in antiquity or still lie buried, rather than never existed.[59] Even where the Roman remains have been all but obliterated by later building, such as at Latakia, Damascus or Jerusalem, traces of the street colonnades have survived. Most of the cities depicted on the Madaba

Plate 77 The main colonnaded street at Palmyra. Note the statue brackets

Map contain colonnaded streets, such as at Kerak, Nablus, Lod, Eleutheropolis, Ashdod, Ashkalon, Beersheba, Gaza and Jerusalem. The present city plans of Ashkalon, Gaza and Jerusalem have been found to follow their ancient plans as depicted on the Map, so they are presumably accurate representations.[60] The colonnaded streets of the Roman East, either extant or known from archaeological, literary or graphic evidence, have been listed elsewhere, so there is no need to give a complete catalogue here:[61] suffice to say that they are its most ubiquitous architectural feature.

They are almost as common in Anatolia as well: Ephesus, for example, boasts street colonnades as great as any in Syria.[62] Colonnaded streets become more of a feature nearer to Syria (e.g., at Side), particularly in Cappadocia where good examples exist at Olba, Pompeiopolis and Hierapolis Castabala. Outside the East, colonnaded streets only occur in a few places in North Africa, notably at Luxor in Egypt (the Camp of Diocletian), Lepcis Magna in Libya, and Timgad in Algeria.[63] The Madaba Map also depicts them in the towns of Pelusium and Athribis in the eastern Nile Delta, but these are close enough to Palestine to belong more to a Syrian than an Egyptian tradition.[64] That at Lepcis Magna is explained as a conscious 'orientalism'.[65]

In Europe, there are virtually no colonnaded streets, even in Greece, otherwise the origin of so much of Roman architecture. The streets of Italica in Spain, birthplace of Trajan and Hadrian, were colonnaded in the second and third centuries.[66] The only other major exceptions are from the Tetrarchy in the early fourth century: Diocletian's great palace at Split and Galerius' mausoleum complex at Thessalonike (Figure 66). The former

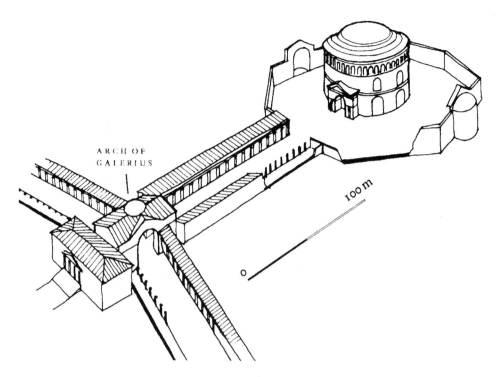

Figure 66 The colonnaded street and tetrapylon at Thessalonike (After Ward-Perkins)

has two colonnaded streets intersecting in the middle.[67] These are not colonnaded streets in the eastern fashion but are arcaded, unlike the trabeate tradition that characterises eastern colonnaded streets.[68] The models for the palace at Split are in any case from the East: Diocletian's camps at Palmyra and Luxor, for example, or his earlier palace at Antioch. Diocletian's great palace at Antioch, judging from contemporary descriptions and its depiction on the triumphal arch of Diocletian at Thessalonike, was very similar to his one at Split. It incorporated a colonnaded street from the centre of the island to the palace, with a Tetrapylon in the middle, very similar to the Diocletian Camp at Palmyra (Figure 82).[69] Galerius' complex at Thessalonike is far closer to the Syrian style. It consists of a colonnaded section of the Via Egnatia intersected by another colonnaded street leading to his mausoleum, the intersection marked by a four-way arch (Figure 66).[70] The eastern associations of this arch are discussed further in the section on Tetrapylons below. The colonnaded streets appear to be a deliberate copy of eastern models, presumably to commemorate Galerius' eastern victories, much as his triumphal arch does. These few examples of colonnaded streets in Europe are, therefore, late in date and (apart from Italica) styled on eastern traditions. It is safe to conclude that colonnaded streets are an eastern innovation, not Roman.

The oldest colonnaded street recorded is the earlier form of the Cardo at Apamaea (recovered from a study of excavated fragments). In its original form, dating from the end of the Seleucid period, the street was lined by two storeyed colonnades in the Doric order. These were replaced when the Cardo was rebuilt and widened to its more familiar and largely Corinthian form, following their destruction in the earthquake of 115 (Figure

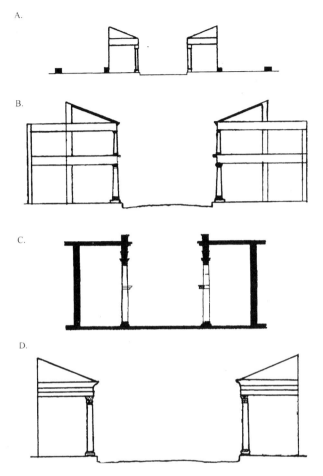

Figure 67 Colonnaded streets. A: Antioch. B: Hellenistic Apamaea.
C: Palmyra. D: Roman Apamaea (After Lassus, Balty, Gabriel)

67B).[71] Otherwise, the earliest was probably at Antioch, laid out soon after the Roman conquest of Syria (Figure 23). It was two Roman miles in length, endowed by Herod and Tiberius who provided the paving, roofing and *tetrapyla* at the main intersections. These were amongst the earliest of their kind in the Roman period, contemporary with other colonnaded streets at Olba and Pompeiopolis in Cilicia. Midway along the street was a plaza, probably with Tiberius' column and statue in the middle, and a nymphaeum. There was another colonnaded street from the Plaza to an unidentified monumental building on the Orontes. Tiberius' colonnades were rebuilt in the time of Claudius after earthquake damage. Trajan restored them again after the earthquake of 115, and Antoninus Pius paved the colonnaded street and all other streets in 'Theban granite'. The devastating earthquake of 458 destroyed the tetrapylon and colonnades, but the Emperor Zeno built two new colonnaded streets with a tetrapylon between them, presumably replacements of the ones destroyed in this earthquake.[72]

The sixth-century Antiochene historian John Malalas has left us with one of the most complete descriptions of a colonnaded street from antiquity:

On his [Tiberius'] return to Rome (from the Persian campaign), he came to Antioch the Great and built outside the city near the mountain known as Silpios two great and very handsome roofed colonnades, with a total length of four miles. He built vaulted *tetrapyla* at the cross-streets, adorning them with mosaic work and marble, and ornamented the street with bronze figurines and statues. He surrounded the colonnades with a wall, enclosing the mountain within it . . . The council and people of Antioch set up a bronze statue in honour of Tiberius Caesar and placed it on a great Theban column in the street in the centre of the colonnades he had built. This place was called the navel of the city, and had a relief of an eye carved in stone. This statue stands to the present day.[73]

The original Apamaea and Antioch colonnaded streets have completely disappeared, although limited excavations have confirmed their layout and their width.[74] Probably the oldest still extant is the northern, Ionic, section of the Cardo at Jerash, completed in the late first century AD (Plate 78) and widened and recolonnaded in the Corinthian order in the second century.[75] The second and third centuries are the date of most of the colonnaded streets, part of a general 'monumentalisation' that characterised all cities of the Roman East during the peak of their prosperity in that period. The construction of colonnaded streets, however, continued to be popular well into late antiquity in the East.

Plate 78 The original Ionic Cardo at Jerash

A late Roman colonnaded street has recently been excavated (and re-erected) at Madaba, and the two transverse streets of the eighth-century Umayyad town of Anjar in Lebanon were colonnaded almost as a conscious archaism (Plate 79).[76] Probably the latest occurrence of a colonnaded street is the eleventh–twelfth-century Ghaznavid bazaar at Lashkari Bazar in southern Afghanistan, where virtually a 'canonical' colonnaded street (albeit in brick, not stone) has been excavated (Figure 68).[77] In late antiquity it is tempting, too, to see the porticoes that characterise many of the 'Dead Cities' of northern Syria[78] as architectural descendants of the colonnaded streets, but this might be illusory. Suffice that the colonnaded streets remained an integral feature of eastern urban architecture down to the Islamic period.

The eastern predominance of the colonnaded street is refuted by some authorities (although convincing examples of an equal western predominance are lacking).[79] Colonnaded streets are seen to be a part of a broader Roman tradition of porticoed streets; engaged pilasters and arcades are included as a part of this tradition. However, architecturally porticoed and arcaded streets, together with streets lined with pilasters or engaged columns, such as those at Ostia or Vasio,[80] belong to an entirely separate tradition architecturally quite distinct from the colonnaded streets of the East.

More usually, the late Hellenistic colonnaded stoas of Greece and Asia Minor are cited as the origins of the eastern colonnaded street.[81] But the stoa and the colonnaded street differ fundamentally in concept, the one a feature of open spaces, the other of thoroughfares. Furthermore, if they had developed out of stoas, one would surely find colonnaded

Plate 79 The Umayyad colonnaded street and tetrapylon at Anjar

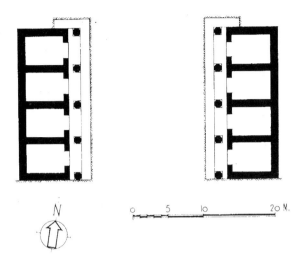

Figure 68 Part of the eleventh-century bazaar at Lashkari Bazar in
Afghanistan (After Le Berre/Schlumberger)

streets in Greece where the stoa originated, rather than in the Near East which had no
tradition of stoas. One must look for an origin, therefore, in eastern urban traditions, not
western.

A possible explanation for their origin might be the sacred processional ways of many
eastern cities, discussed above.[82] But although these seem to be an eastern architectural
tradition and *may* explain Palmyra and some of the other colonnaded streets, it is certainly
not possible to explain all colonnaded streets in terms of religious processions. The colonnaded streets of Antioch, Apamaea, Sebaste and Amman, for example, were not sacred
ways (i.e., they do not lead to temples). In any case, the eastern tradition of sacred and
processional ways simply explains the *way* or route, not its *colonnades* (which formed no
ritual function apart from a suitably gorgeous backdrop). Many of the eastern processional ways were in any case uncolonnaded (e.g., Siʿ). The actual colonnading, therefore,
must belong to a separate tradition.

In contrasting the ubiquitousness of colonnaded streets in the East with their absence
in the West, a reciprocal contrast immediately becomes apparent. This is the ubiquitousness of forums in the West in contrast to their almost complete absence in the East.
Forums do exist in the East, so the contrast is not absolute. They are discussed in more
detail below ('Public squares'); suffice to say here that they are extremely rare. Even when
an occasional open space in an eastern city has been identified as a forum, they do not
compare, in scale, function or quantity, to the forums of Roman Europe and North
Africa where they form virtually a universal feature of every town and city centre. It can
be fairly safely stated, therefore, that where a western Roman town was dominated by its
forum, an eastern one was dominated by its colonnaded street. In other words, the one is
the counterpart of the other.

With this observation, both the origin and the function of colonnaded streets immediately becomes clearer. For one of the most fundamental of eastern urban architectural
concepts is the market street, or bazaar. The bazaar street (Arabic *suq*, Persian *bazar*) forms
the core of most traditional Middle Eastern towns and cities. A bazaar is invariably a

street, usually a single broad avenue or occasionally a series of narrow, winding lanes. But it is never an open place such as the western-style market-square (out of which both the agora and the forum – and ultimately the Italian piazza – evolved). Bazaars are frequently covered and are often just as grand monumental works of architecture, particularly in Iran, as Roman colonnaded streets are (Plate 83). In the first cities of the Near East commerce congregated around specific quarters, but perhaps as early as about 1500 BC the urban concept of a bazaar, or 'street of shops', had emerged.[83] By the first millennium BC it had become commonplace, and has remained an essential part of the eastern urban fabric to this day.

With this in mind, we can view the colonnaded streets of the Roman East in a fresh perspective. For the essential features of these streets were not so much the colonnades themselves but what lay behind them. These were rows of shops (Plate 80). At Palmyra, we often have the names and trades of the proprietors themselves inscribed over the shops, while at Apamaea and Jerash some of the shops behind the colonnades have recently been dramatically – and appropriately – restored. The colonnaded streets of the East, far from being evidence of any Roman character, become on analysis grand oriental bazaars.[84] When the grand colonnade at Palmyra was 'converted' to a souq in the Umayyad period, it was simply continuing the tradition for which the colonnade was built in the first place, while at the eleventh–twelfth-century city of Lashkari Bazar in Afghanistan the colonnaded street/oriental bazaar comes full circle.[85] The eastern colonnaded street thus becomes the counterpart to the western forums and agoras; both originated as markets.

Plate 80 Rows of shops behind the main colonnade at Apamaea

This certainly explains the function of the streets but not necessarily the colonnades themselves: why colonnade a bazaar? There is, of course, the obvious need to embellish, to architecturally emphasise a part of a city that was, after all, its economic mainstay. The great urban bazaars of Iran, for example, are every bit as grand and monumental as a 'Roman' colonnaded street. Of course, the monumental bazaars of Isfahan and Shiraz are a thousand years and more later than those of Palmyra or Petra, but the concept is the same and the strength of tradition wholly eastern. Merely the vocabulary, the veneer, is different: in Syria they are dressed up in Graeco-Roman colonnades instead of Persian vaulting. It must be recalled in any case that in north Syria the idea of a monumental colonnade adorning a public building goes back thousands of years before the Romans, to the third-millennium BC Royal Palace at Ebla, for example, or the early first-millennium BC palace and temple at Tell Tayanat (Figure 69).[86]

But perhaps the real reason for colonnading a bazaar was simply the need for shade. The Iranians vaulted their bazaars, the Syrians colonnaded theirs. In this way it is worth recalling that when European street architecture was transposed to America or Australia, the streets became, in effect, colonnaded (Plate 81). One authority[87] emphasises the naked – albeit photogenic! – impression that colonnaded streets give now, standing in relative isolation and divorced from their covered roofs, adjacent building walls, etc. (e.g., Plate 77). It is easy to forget, therefore, that the prime aim of these colonnades was to provide cover. Hence, the few ancient descriptions of colonnaded streets are of covered buildings, rather

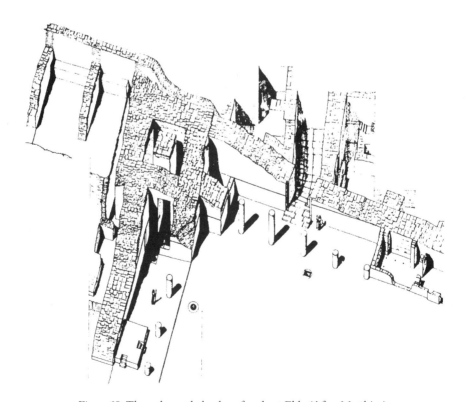

Figure 69 The colonnaded palace façade at Ebla (After Matthiae)

Plate 81 Colonial street in New South Wales, where the streets are traditionally – in effect – colonnaded

than the open monuments they appear today in their ruined state. Antioch's colonnaded streets, for example, are described specifically as roofed,[88] and the collapse of the colonnade at Hierapolis is described with reference to beams and timbers – implying a roof – that were enough to crush fifty soldiers underneath them.[89]

In modern theoretical reconstructions of colonnaded streets, it is almost invariably the sidewalks rather than the carriageways that are shown as roofed (e.g., Figures 67, 70).[90] Doubtless, many of the sidewalks were indeed roofed, and it is certainly true that the main ancient depiction that we have of an eastern colonnaded street – that of Jerusalem in the Madaba map – does show the sidewalks roofed and carriageway open (Figure 71).[91] But a closer examination of the extant remains shows that in some cases, at least, it would have been the carriageways that were roofed, rather than the sidewalks. The Amman colonnaded streets, for example, had no sidewalks (Figure 72),[92] and there is no sidewalk for a long stretch of the Jerash Cardo (Figure 73; see also Figure 37).[93] Even in many cases where there are sidewalks, the flanking walls were too narrow and too flimsy (such as many stretches of the Jerash Cardo or the Petra Decumanus) to have reached either the height or the strength to support a roof at entablature height. Any roof, therefore, would have been over the carriageway rather than the sidewalks. This would have been a far more effective means of providing shade, but at the same time allowing light and air to circulate to the street below through the columns on either side. Such roofed colonnaded streets would have appeared from the outside almost identical to the covered bazaars of eastern tradition (Figure 74).

Even where the colonnaded streets remained open, they may well have been covered

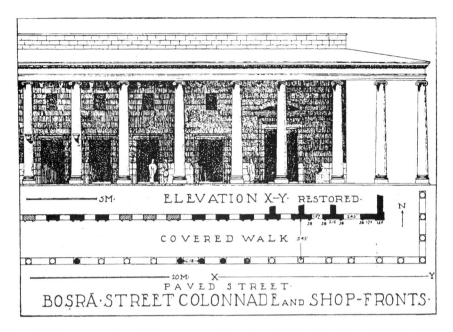

Figure 70 Reconstruction of a Bosra street colonnade, with the sidewalk roofed (After Butler)

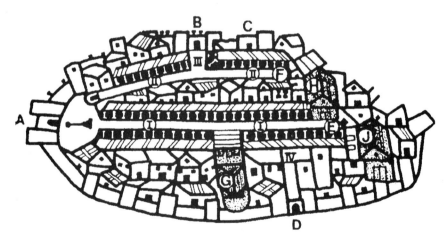

Figure 71 The Jerusalem street colonnades depicted in the Madaba mosaic, with the sidewalks roofed (After Avigad/Segal)

with temporary awnings during the summer months. Columns in this case would be extremely practical for tying such awnings to (and perhaps we can find an additional explanation for the 'statue brackets' of the colonnades at Palmyra and elsewhere in this?). This is, after all, just the case in many unroofed modern eastern bazaar streets where temporary shades are erected during the summer (Plate 82), while the traditional Iranian bazaar is permanently roofed (Plate 83).

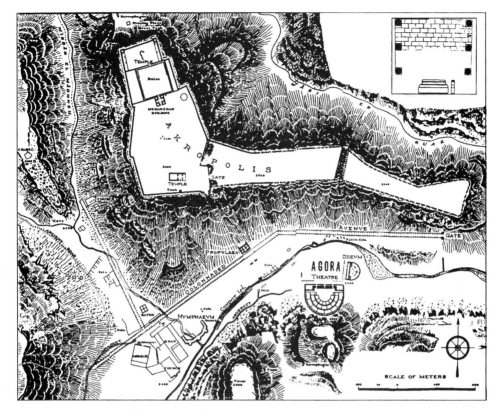

Figure 72 The Amman colonnaded street. Note the absence of a sidewalk

The four-way arch

The study of architecture is, quite literally, the study of arches. Rarely is this more applicable than in Roman architecture, where arches are its most characteristic feature. Arches – particularly the so-called triumphal arch – are one of the most familiar and dominant forms in Roman architecture. Leaving aside the question of the eastern origins of the arch form, Roman monumental arches belong firmly within the architectural traditions of imperial Rome – indeed, they are used to proclaim Roman triumphs, both literally and symbolically as political propaganda – 'the symbols both of Roman rule and Roman cities'.[94] One study of Roman architecture has divided Roman arches into five basic types:[95] (1) free-standing triumphal and commemorative arches astride major roads, often standing outside city walls; (2) town gates forming a part of city walls; (3) propylaea, or monumental entrances to major monuments; (4) civic arches astride major thoroughfares within a city; (5) four-way arches at intersections. The latter type is almost as much a feature of eastern Roman cities as the colonnaded street: Latin *quadrifons* or, more usually, Greek *tetrapylon*.[96] This is analysed here. Other types are discussed elsewhere.

Two types of tetrapylon are generally recognised: the roofed and the unroofed. The former, usually consisting of four arches in a square covered by a dome, is the true tetrapylon. The latter, usually consisting of four free-standing piers or kiosks not

Figure 73 Reconstruction of the Jerash Cardo. Note the absence of a sidewalk on the right

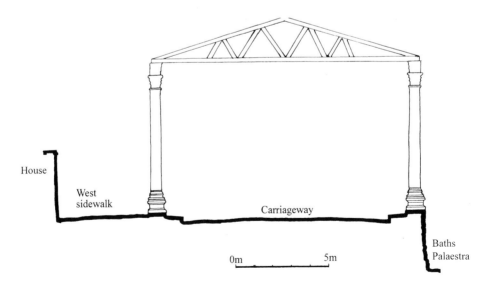

House

West
sidewalk

Carriageway

Baths
Palaestra

0m 5m

Figure 74 Proposed reconstruction of a roofed colonnaded street at Jerash

Plate 82 Traditional bazaar street in Afghanistan. Note the street porticoes and the temporary roof over the carriageway

Plate 83 The traditional Iranian covered bazaar, the equivalent of the roofed colonnaded streets

connected by arches, are more correctly known as a *tetrakionia*. Both typically mark the intersection of two colonnaded streets; only rarely are they found completely isolated from an intersection.

Two further subdivisions can generally be recognised of the former, true tetrapylon, type: funerary and civic monuments. The tetrapylon funerary monuments, usually standing on podia, are found throughout the empire. Their origin has been seen in Greek tetrastyle altars.[97] In the West, examples are the monument of the Julii at Saint Rémy and similar monuments in Italy at Aquileia, Sarsina and Nettuno, all of the early first century.[98] In North Africa such tombs belong more to a Libyo-Phoenician tradition, such as those tetrapylon tombs in the south necropolis at Ghirza.[99] In the East, examples exist at Barad and Dana in north Syria (Figure 112 B and C, Plate 84).[100]

It is the civic tetrapylon and tetrakionion that is our main concern here. They generally appear now free-standing, marking the intersections of streets. Many of these, however, were probably once joined to colonnades now gone, so are not necessarily as free-standing as their present condition might suggest. Many formed the centrepiece of circular plazas.[101]

As with colonnaded streets, tetrapylons tend to be found mainly in the East. Important exceptions are the Arch of Trajan and the Arch of Septimius Severus, both at Lepcis Magna, the Arch of Marcus Aurelius at Oea (Tripoli) and the Arch of Galerius at

Plate 84 A tetrapylon tomb at Dana in north Syria

Thessalonike (Figures 66 and 76, Plate 158).[102] Of these, two have marked eastern associations: the Arch of Septimius at Lepcis, along with its colonnaded street, was a part of a general 'orientalisation' of the Severan city,[103] while the Arch of Galerius was erected to commemorate his victories in the East.

In the East the earliest were probably at Antioch, although none survive. These were the tetrapylons built by Tiberius during the initial laying out of the colonnaded streets, discussed above (Figure 23). Other tetrapylons were built at Latakia, Jerash (the North Tetrapylon), Palmyra (in the Diocletian Camp) and, after the fourth century, in Caesarea (Figures 31, 73, 75 and 76, Plates 33 and 85). The Madaba Map depicts tetrapylons that have now vanished at Nablus, possibly Eleutheropolis, Ashkalon, Gaza and Jerusalem, all of them marking the intersections of colonnaded streets.[104] A four-way arch described as a 'tetrapyrium' has been recorded in the exact centre of the desert settlement of Rasm ar-Ribayt, a stage on the Chalcis-Isriya-Palmyra route in north Syria.[105]

Slightly more common was the variation of the tetrapylon more strictly called a tetrakionion (it is not known which type the Antioch tetrapylons were). These have been found at Palmyra, Jerash (the 'South Tetrapylon'), Bosra, Shahba and Antipatris (Figure 76, Plates 86 and 87).[106] Both types are invariably civic monuments built to provide urban focal points at the intersection of two colonnaded streets (with the exception of Antipatris, where the streets do not appear to have been colonnaded). Typically, the tetrapylon has the colonnades joined to it, while the tetrakionion stands isolated in an (occasionally circular) plaza. Its popularity continued into the Umayyad period, when new tetrapylons

Figure 75 Reconstruction of the North Tetrapylon at Jerash

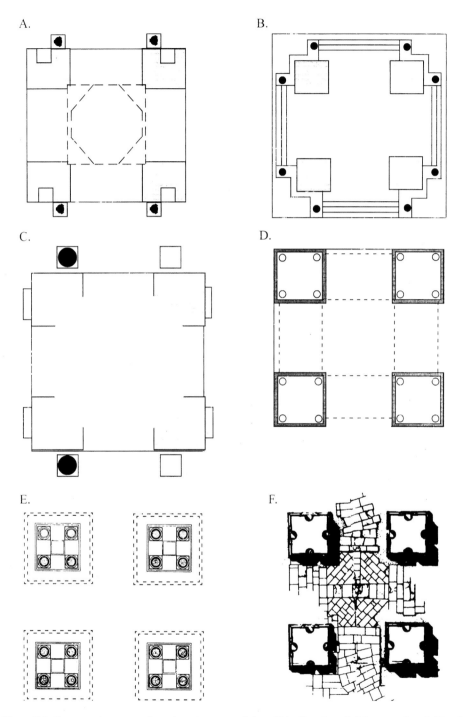

Figure 76 Comparative tetrapylon plans (not to scale). A: Tripoli. B: Lepcis Magna. C: Jerash North Tetrapylon. D: Jerash South Tetrapylon. E: Palmyra. F: Bosra.

Plate 85 The North Tetrapylon at Jerash

Plate 86 The restored tetrapylon at Palmyra

Plate 87 The South Tetrapylon at Jerash

in the ancient style were built at Anjar, Beth-Shean and Damascus.[107] This form of monument, therefore, forms an integral part of the eastern colonnaded street. As such, its origins must also lie in the East.

Once again, the four-way arch is a well-known type of building with a distinguished history when viewed from the eastern perspective. This is the Persian *chahartaq*, literally 'four-way arch', of which the Greek *tetrapylon* is an exact translation. The *chahartaq* is one of the oldest, most fundamental and most ubiquitous 'building-blocks' of Persian architecture, in both religious and secular buildings. Its commonest occurrence, the domed four-way arch, became the standard form of the Zoroastrian fire-temple during the Sasanian period (Figure 77, E–G; Plate 88). It is significant that one of the tetrapylons in Syria, the Rasm ar-Ribayt 'Tetrapyrium' mentioned above, is described as a fire monument. The Pyrtanium of Ephesus – effectively, a fire-temple – also consists of an altar underneath a canopy held up by four columns.[108]

The origins of the form can be traced back to the religious buildings of the Achaemenids. It occurs in their shrines (not necessarily fire-temples) at, for example, Gaga Shahr and Susa (Figure 77 A and B) where they are simply roofs supported by four columns (it is not known what form the roofs took, but they were presumably flat).[109] It had evolved into its canonical form, possibly as a fire-temple, at least as early as the first-century BC Parthian complex at Kuh-i Khwaja in Sistan, where it appears fully developed.[110] A late Parthian domed building, not necessarily a fire-temple (albeit with just two arches, not four), is found much further to the west at Qal'a-i Zohak in Azerbaijan (Figure 77 C and D).[111] By the Sasanian period it had became the main architectural expression of the Zoroastrian religion. These range from very small, isolated dome-chambers on hillsides – the classic *chahartaq*, virtually identical to the tetrapylon – such as Niyasar or Baz-i Khur

281

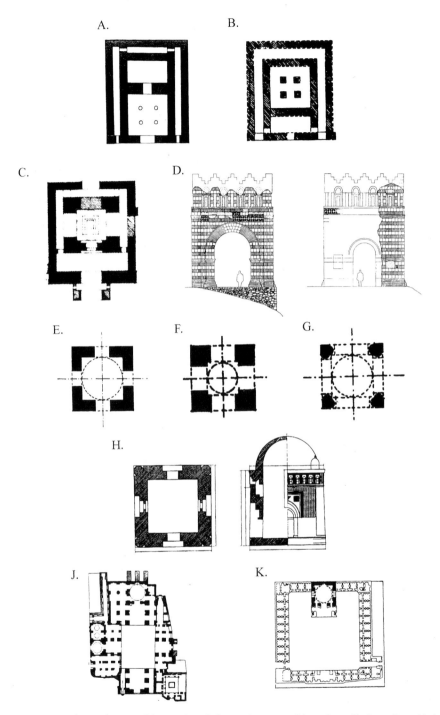

Figure 77 The evolution of the Iranian *chahartaq* (not to scale). A: Gaga Shahr. B: Susa (Achaemenid). C: Kuh-i Khwaja. D: Qal'a-i Zohak (Parthian). E: Qasr-i Shirin. F: Niyasar. G: Ateshkuh (Sasanian). H: Bukhara. J: Ardistan. K: Qazvin (Islamic)

Plate 88 The Sasanian *chahartaq* at Niyasar

(Plate 88), to the focal chambers of large, complex religious establishments such as at Kunar Siah or Takht-i Sulaiman. They range in date from the second century AD to the end of the Sasanian period or later.[112]

The form continued in unbroken transition into Persian Islamic architecture in two types of buildings, the domed mausoleum and the mosque prayer-hall. The key building for this transition is the tenth-century Tomb of Isma'il the Samanid at Bukhara (Figure 77H). One of the greatest masterpieces of Islamic architecture, in form it is a perfect Sasanian *chahartaq*. From this a distinct style of Islamic domed mausolea evolved that culminated in the great royal mausolea of Mughal India, such as the Taj Mahal.[113] The form also occurs in the Iranian style of mosque, presumably originating when the first Muslims converted Sasanian fire-temples. It was enthusiastically incorporated into subsequent mosque architecture, becoming the sanctuary dome chamber in front of the *mihrab*, typical examples occurring in Isfahan, Ardistan and Qazvin (Figure 77 J and K). It has remained an essential feature in Persian Islamic architecture since.[114]

The form enjoys an equally high profile in Persian urban architecture, where it typically marks the intersection of two covered bazaars. As such it is one of the most ubiquitous features of towns and cities throughout Iran today. Shah Abbas' great Qaysariya Bazaar in Isfahan, for example, incorporates at least six *chahartaqs* at its junctions,[115] and equally splendid examples can be seen at Shiraz, Kerman and just about every other covered bazaar in Iran (Plate 89). Thus, we see in the covered bazaar–*chahartaq* combination of Persian architecture the exact counterpart to the colonnaded street–tetrapylon combination of eastern Roman architecture.

Plate 89 The *chahartaq* marking the intersection of two bazaar streets in Kerman

Of course, the quantity of accurately dated, very early domed four-way arches in Iran is still very little. In addition, the oldest accurately dated covered bazaar in Iran is probably the Qaysariya Bazaar of Isfahan, dated 1620. But they are the culmination of a very long period of development, and the strength of the tradition argues for ancient hypothetical prototypes. The impermanent nature of most of Iranian urban architecture when compared to Roman – brick and mud versus stone – not to mention the cataclysmic devastations that have been wreaked on Iranian cities by invaders since the medieval period, have ensured that buildings such as bazaars do not survive.

It must be remembered that domed buildings occur in Roman architecture in the West as well, evolving out of the domed tombs of Etruscan and republican architecture and culminating in such buildings as Nero's Golden House and the Pantheon. Both the Domus Transitoria and Golden House of the Emperor Nero include domes at four-way junctions.[116] But both the strength of tradition and the history of the four-way arch form in general in Iran, when compared to the relative paucity of the tradition in the West, leaves little doubt as to its main origin. The origins of the dome lie in the mud-building traditions of the East, where a dome is the easiest and most natural means of roofing a building in an area where timber is scarce or unavailable. Hence, mud domes have been postulated for the seventh-millennium BC Halaf circular houses of the Syrian steppe, a system of roofing for domestic houses which is still practised in the same region today (see, for example, the conical roofs in Plate 53).[117] The sheer richness and strength of mud-dome traditions in the vernacular architecture of Iran probably argues for an origin there as well.[118]

Other ornamental arches

These belong to the western tradition of Roman architecture, so require little analysis here. One type marked the gateway into a city, another simply marked an important focal point within a city. A third type was a monumental propylaeum to a religious complex. This is discussed in the section on religious architecture, below. From an architectural point of view the two former types can be considered together and indeed could occasionally serve both purposes: the Arch of Hadrian at Jerash, for example, functioned both as an approach to the city and as a commemorative arch (Plate 90). Both types would to all intents and purposes appear the same, with one or three archways, and both might be embellished in the same way with niches, statuary, pilasters, engaged columns, entablatures and attic storeys. The only difference is that a city gateway would usually (but not invariably) be joined to the city walls.

The main extant or partly extant examples of ornamental city gateways include the Antioch Gate at Aleppo, the North Gate at Rasafa (Plate 19), the Bab Sharqi at Damascus (Plate 41), the Bab al-Hawa at Bosra (Plate 48), the North and South Gates at Shahba, the West Gate at Umm Qays, the North Gate at Baalbek, the North and South Gates at Jerash (Plate 91), the Bab as-Siq Gate at Petra and the Damascus Gate at Jerusalem.[119] There were doubtless many more, now no longer extant. Not included here are the many city gateways that were merely simple, unadorned arches, which belong to a separate category of 'ornamental' arches.

The free-standing commemorative arches include the Cardo Arch at Palmyra (Plate 15), the 'Nabataean' Arch and the Arch of the Lantern at Bosra (Plate 47), the Arch of Hadrian at Jerash (Plate 90),[120] the Ecce Homo Arch at Jerusalem, and the Temenos Arch at Petra. Monumental arches occasionally mark an awkward junction, such as the North Gate at Jerash and the monumental arch at Palmyra. Both categories are often erroneously known as 'triumphal' arches. In fact there are no triumphal arches in the East, i.e., arches

Plate 90 The Arch of Hadrian at Jerash

Plate 91 The South Gate at Jerash, a copy of the Arch of Hadrian (compare with Plate 90)

formally commemorating an emperor's triumph, and only three are known to be actual commemorative arches. Those at Jerash and Jerusalem are both dedicated to Hadrian, and the Arch of the Lantern at Bosra honours the Third Cyrenaican Legion, which was based here. Another dedicatory arch, honouring Hadrian, was known to be built by the Third Cyrenaican Legion at Dura Europos in 116.[121]

There might occasionally be minor eastern variations to the 'standard' form of Roman monumental arch. The decoration, for example, often belongs more to eastern styles than western, such as the use of the 'Syrian niche'. This is discussed separately in the section on styles, below. Otherwise, a Roman monumental arch in the East is the one monument that appears unambiguously to be an import from the West. Indeed, more than any other type of Roman monument, the 'triumphal arch' has been used to make a cultural statement in western civilisation generally – Marble Arch in London, the Arc de Triomphe in Paris, or the Brandenburg Gate in Berlin are amongst the best known symbols of modern Europe. Variations of the theme have even been used as symbols of European domination over eastern countries: the Gateway of India in Bombay, for example, built in 1911 to commemorate George V's visit to India for the Delhi Durbar.

Whilst recognising the unambiguously 'western' nature of this type of monument, the origins of the monumental arch in ancient Near Eastern architecture must equally be recognised. Probably the first to use the arch in a monumental, symbolic way were the Assyrians in the early first millennium BC. The great winged-bull gateways to the Assyrian royal capitals and palaces at Khorsabad, Nineveh and Nimrud were built deliberately to impress, to overawe and to proclaim the greatness of the achievements of a monarch and his nation. All of these were drawing upon models already thousands of years old by the time of the Neo-Assyrian Empire. The Neo-Babylonian Ishtar Gate over the processional way built by Nebuchadnezzar in Babylon in the sixth century BC takes the symbolism of a monumental gateway one stage further (Plate 76).[122] None of these are isolated arches in the way that the Roman triumphal arches are, all form a part of walls. But the Gate of All Nations built at Persepolis by Xerxes in the fifth century BC marks a new departure (Plate 92).[123] For the first time this was a gate that had no function as an opening through a wall, but was a single monument in its own right. The massive, monumental second-century BC gates of Sanchi and Sarnath in India are developments from this model.[124] Ultimately, all 'triumphal arches' are descendants of Persepolis.

Dedicatory columns

Votive and monumental columns, like monumental arches, are another feature of Roman urban spaces. The intersections of the colonnaded streets at Apamaea, for example, were marked by votive columns rather than the more usual tetrapylon (Plate 35),[125] the oval plaza that formed the urban heart of Antioch had a column in the centre with a statue of Tiberius on top (Figure 23),[126] the oval plaza just inside the Damascus Gate at Jerusalem also had a column in the centre (Figure 71),[127] and the same arrangement of a votive column in a plaza inside a gate is known from mosaic depictions of Kastron Mefaa in Jordan (Figure 78).[128] Similar single monumental columns are known at Palmyra, Edessa, Yʿat in the Baqʿa Valley, in the temples of Mar Simʿan and Baalbek in Lebanon, and elsewhere.[129] This type of monument became particularly popular with the imperial style of Constantinople, where successive emperors commemorated their

Plate 92 The Gate of All Nations at Persepolis. The Processional Way can be seen leading off to the front

Plate 93 Votive first-century BC Commagene
funerary column at Karakush

Plate 94 Funerary columns at Sarmada in north
Syria. Note entrance to hypogaeum in
foreground

reigns with massive votive columns which dominated the city's skyline as the minarets do today.

The commemorative column became a feature of Roman cities in the West as well, becoming, like the arches, a familiar feature of subsequent European 'triumphal' architecture in general (such as Nelson's Column in Trafalgar Square). The best known is Trajan's column, dominating his forum in Rome as a graphic and visible reminder of the emperor's achievements.[130] However, the Forum of Trajan was designed by an eastern architect, Apollodorus of Damascus. Indeed, some authorities see the Roman idea of mounting a statue on a dedicatory column to be inspired by Syrian prototypes, such as the first-century BC Commagene monuments (Plate 93).[131] Dedicatory and cultic columns certainly have an ancient pedigree in eastern architecture. At Edessa, two such columns still survive, one dedicated to an Edessan queen, although both may have had ritual functions associated with the cult of Atargatis (Plate 18). The Atargatis cult at Edessa involved two columns up which a priest would climb for contemplation during the annual New Year ritual,[132] and evidence for a similar practice has been found at the temple of Mushayrfa at the top of the Jebel Wastani in northern Syria.[133] This found its echo in the later pillar cult of St Simeon Stylites and his many imitators in northern Syria (where forty-four stylite monasteries have been identified),[134] as well as the pillar tombs (either single or paired)

Figure 78 Kastron Mefaa as depicted in the Church of St Stephen mosaic. Note votive column (After Piccirillo)

that feature in the funerary architecture in the same region (Figure 113, Plate 94). A solid square tower at Kastron Mefaa (Umm ar-Rasas) in Jordan has also been interpreted as a stylite tower (Plate 95).[135] The popularity of the Syrian pillar cults has been thought to be the inspiration of the Islamic minaret: the stylite monk addressing devotees from his pillar being replicated by the muezzin calling the faithful to prayer from his minaret.[136]

The intersection of the two main streets of Shapur's 'victory city' at Bishapur in Iran is marked by a dedicatory column on which stood a statue of Shapur.[137] This, however, is seen as Roman in inspiration – the 'Roman' remains at Bishapur are discussed in Chapter 4 ('Survivors of Edessa'). But it might equally have had an earlier Iranian inspiration, for the Mauryan victory pillars of the fourth century BC in India have been seen as Achaemenid influence.[138] Although such influences appear to be of design rather than concept, the concept probably belongs to an older Indian or Indo-Iranian tradition. The idea of a victory pillar or tower certainly continued in Indian architecture, e.g., the fifteenth-century Hindu Victory Tower at Chittorgarh.[139] Whether or not Achaemenid architecture was the source of the votive column, the Achaemenid Empire would still have been the medium for the transmission of the idea from India to the Near East. The idea might also have arrived in the West through the broader Hellenistic world of the first century BC, which included both Commagene and north-western India. The idea survived until well into the Islamic era as the victory tower concept implicit in many minarets in the eastern Islamic world.[140]

Plate 95 Tower at Umm ar-Rasas in Jordan

Nymphaea

Technically, the nymphaeum was originally a religious rather than a secular building, a monument dedicated to the nymphs. However, by the second century AD it had become a civic monument, functioning as an ornamental public drinking fountain. As such it belongs within the broad sphere of Roman architecture, apart from some decorative details (such as 'Syrian niches', discussed below).

Nymphaea were usually in a prominent public location alongside a main colonnaded street or overlooking a public square. Hence, they functioned in much the same way as monumental arches did, providing an urban focal point. Nine nymphaea in the region have been examined in a recent survey: Qanawat, Susita (Hippos), Suwayda, Umm Qays (Gadara), Bosra, Beth-Shean (Scythopolis), Jerash (Plate 96), Amman, and Petra. Two more, at Pella and Akka (Ptolemais), are known from coin depictions but are unlocated,[141] and more were recorded in the sixth-century Madaba mosaic map at Kallirrhoe, Nablus and possibly Eleutheropolis and Gaza.[142] To these can be added the nymphaeum that overlooked the oval plaza at Antioch described by Libanius, and others at Byblos, Apamaea, Temnin al-Foqa in Lebanon and Palmyra.[143] The Amman 'nymphaeum' has since been interpreted as a type of monument known as a *kalybe*, described next.

Plate 96 The nymphaeum at Jerash

The kalybe

One civic building in the East that has no counterpart elsewhere in Roman architecture, despite superficial resemblances, is the *kalybe*. It closely resembles and possibly evolved from the nymphaeum but is quite distinct, serving simply as a public façade or stage-setting, solely for the display of statuary without any fountain. The *kalybe* was first identified as a distinct monument at Bosra (Figure 79A), where it overlooks a square opposite the nymphaeum, the two combining into one of the finer urban ensembles in eastern Roman architecture.[144] Very little of it remains, but at the city of Shahba nearby is a remarkably intact *kalybe* (Figure 79B, Plate 51). This has been interpreted as part of an official imperial cult complex that included the temple opposite honouring the family of Philip the Arab.[145] Another monument at Shahba, usually described as a 'hexastyle temple', was also probably a *kalybe*: its plan has little resemblance to temple plans, but follows the Shahba *kalybe* very closely (Figure 79C).[146] In recent years the Amman nymphaeum has also been reinterpreted as a *kalybe* (Figure 79D). Although now dilapidated and surrounded by the modern commercial buildings of downtown Amman, in its original state it must have been the most magnificent of all the *kalybe* monuments (Figure 80).[147]

Functionally, therefore, the *kalybe* resembles a theatre *scenae frons* or stage backdrop, rather than a nymphaeum. Although now recognised as a distinct building type (rather than just waterless nymphaea), they have never been satisfactorily explained or placed within a broader architectural context. In order to understand this enigmatic type of monument, the following two observations are important. First, whilst a nymphaeum can be situated either alongside a street (e.g., Jerash, Petra, Palmyra, Umm Qays) or overlooking a square (e.g., Antioch, Bosra), a *kalybe* is invariably on a square. Bosra overlooks the 'nymphaeum square', Shahba overlooks the 'Philippeion square', the second one at Shahba (if it is a *kalybe*) is set back from the street overlooking a small enclosure, and Amman is set well back from the decumanus (one might well postulate a square here). And second, they all occur within the former area of the Nabataean state.

The Nabataean element is probably the important one in attempting to relate the *kalybe* to similar works of architecture. The first *kalybe* to be identified was that at Bosra (Figure 79A). Bosra was the Nabataean capital under Rabbel II in the late first century AD, when there was a conscious programme of turning Bosra into a monumental city to closely resemble Petra. The main element in this was the construction of a processional sacred way leading through the city culminating in a large temple temenos, following the arrangement at Petra closely.[148] The *kalybe*, although usually assumed to belong to the Roman embellishments of the second century, forms a part of this ensemble, so might be Nabataean in date. Whatever the date, these enigmatic monuments must be viewed as Nabataean, which forms their geographical and cultural context, rather than Roman architecture simply because of their superficial resemblance to a type of monument (the nymphaeum) from which they so demonstrably differ. In concept, they resemble the best known works of Nabataean architecture, the Petra rock façades. These façades are discussed in more detail in the section on funerary architecture below, where it is argued that they were essentially stage-sets for ritual enacted *in front* of them; whatever functioned *behind* them was secondary. In this way, the *kalybes* might be viewed simply as built-up versions of the Petra rock-cut façades. It is the space in front of them that is the key; the monument itself was nothing more than a backdrop for that. Theatricality was always particularly prominent in eastern architecture, and it is further emphasised below as

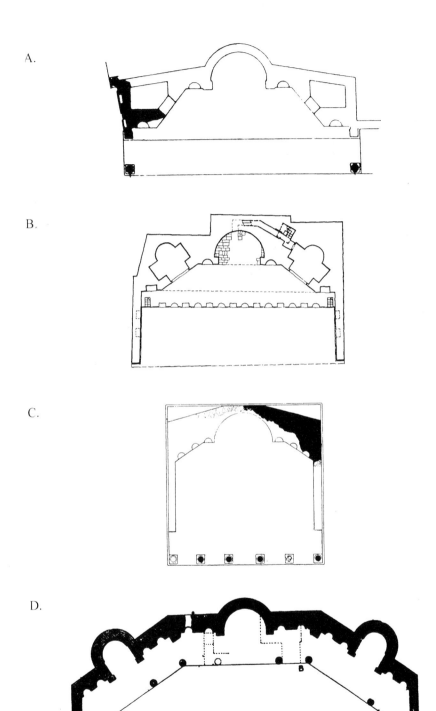

Figure 79 Kalybe-style monuments (not to scale). A: Bosra. B: Shahba. C: Shahba 'hexastyle temple'. D: Amman (After Butler, Segal)

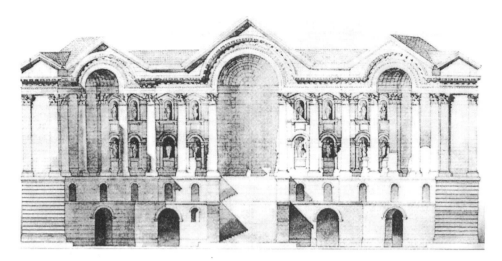

Figure 80 Reconstruction of the *kalybe* at Amman (After Butler)

crucial for the evolution of the Near Eastern temple type. Conceptually, therefore, the temple temenos, the *kalybe* and the Petra façades all belong together.

Forums

Cities in the Roman world had two kinds of public spaces, the forum (or agora), and the public square proper. The marked absence of forums in the East has already been noted above, where it was argued that colonnaded streets took the place of forums. It remains here to examine in more detail the few forums that do occur.

The forum is often regarded simply as an open space, or square. But it is rather more than that, consisting of a combination of open space, buildings and specific functions. The 'typical' Roman forum comprised an open space in the centre of a town which functioned as the market-place and place for public assembly. It would be surrounded by the town's essential public buildings which formed an integral part of the forum. Most important of these was the basilica, or town meeting hall, which would usually be alongside the forum. This functioned almost as an indoor extension of the open space outside: an indoor market place, a meeting hall, an exchange, and occasionally a law court.[149] Almost as important as the basilica would be other public buildings, in particular the temples to Rome's official cults: Rome and Augustus, the deified emperor, or the Capitoline triad (Jupiter, Juno and Minerva). The forum might include other temples as well, but a temple to one of these would be essential, usually incorporating a rostrum at the front for public address. In addition to other temples, a forum often included other civic buildings, such as a curia or council chamber, as well as ornamental buildings such as fountains, monumental arches and displays of statuary. Such forums became virtually the standard trappings of Roman cities and towns throughout the West, as the dozens of largely intact Roman towns in North Africa demonstrate.

It has been necessary to define the 'canonical' Roman forum in some detail if only to underline the fact that this arrangement is almost *entirely* absent in the East. Probably the only city where it existed was Antioch, although even here it has not been established with any certainty. A basilica, called the Kaisarion, was built by Julius Caesar, partly as an official cult building, but the construction of the first true forum at Antioch is not mentioned until the late fourth century in the time of Valens.[150] The only other Near Eastern cities where Forums have been *definitely* established are Beirut, Sebaste, Caesarea and Philadelphia (Amman). At Beirut there seem to have been two forums, an east and a west one, the west forum having a basilica alongside, but there is no sign of any official cult temple. The remains in any case are far too scanty and obscured to be certain.[151] Sebaste, too, had a forum with its basilica alongside, but no cult temples associated with it. Its Temple of Rome and Augustus was in a separate locality and built in a local style (Figure 32).[152] Caesarea had a Temple of Rome and Augustus in its forum, but no trace of a basilica has been found (Figure 31).[153] At Amman the square in front of the theatre and odeon appears to be nothing more than just a public square, similar to that in front of the North Theatre at Jerash (see below) (Figure 38, Plates 44 and 97). However, an inscription has confirmed its identification as a forum, despite the absence of a basilica or official cult temples.[154] A possible forum has been tentatively identified at Antipatris, but the identification is very unclear.[155] A possible forum has also been tentatively postulated at Bosra, on the north side of the Decumanus between the tetrapylon and the nymphaeum, but this too is uncertain.[156]

The famous Oval Plaza at Jerash (Plates 43 and 99), popularly viewed as a forum, has been interpreted variously, the only general agreement being that it was definitely *not* a forum. (This plaza is discussed further below).[157] A forum has been postulated in the

Plate 97 The forum at Amman

angle formed by the North Cardo and the North Decumanus at Jerash (Figure 37), but without excavation this question must remain unanswered.[158] The square in Shahba has been interpreted as a forum. It certainly included a temple to the cult of the Emperor Philip's family as well as a nymphaeum or *kalybe* (discussed above), but the complex was more likely an imperial sanctuary rather than a forum.[159]

With the exception of Amman, those cities with definitely identified forums were deliberate 'western' enclaves or at least imitations. Sebaste and Caesarea were founded by Herod as a deliberate policy to curry favour with the Romans, Caesarea became the Roman capital of Palestine, Antioch's status as imperial residence and third city of the empire hardly needs reiterating, and Beirut was founded by Augustus as a military colony. They can hardly be taken, therefore, as typical of the eastern city, although in all of them the eastern architectural forms predominated to a greater or lesser degree, as we shall see.

The East, therefore, had forums. But there were only very few, they rarely adhered to the canonical form, and were never on the scale, monumentality, lavishness or complexity of the great forums of the West. The reason for this, as has been argued above, was that their place was taken by the colonnaded avenue. The absence of Temples of Rome and Augustus and other official cults is analysed elsewhere (in the section on temples, below). It is also worth observing that in the West, the origins of the forum, according to Vitruvius, were also tied in to the need of a display for gladiatorial shows before the development of the amphitheatre.[160] Whilst the East could not exactly be complacent – cruelty and bloodshed have rarely been absent from any culture – it is nonetheless true that blood sports were held to be abhorrent in the East.

To some extent the Roman forum was a development of the Greek agora. Whilst not an exact equivalent, the agora often took the place of the forum throughout the Hellenised East. But again, the number of *definitely* attested agoras in the East is small. Antioch had two, both dating from Seleucid times,[161] and Damascus, Apamaea and Dura Europos had quite substantial ones.[162] The Apamaea agora, in the form of a long rectangle parallel to the Cardo, might in fact have functioned as the forecourt of the great Temple of Zeus Belos, known from inscriptions but demolished in the fourth century. The present Friday Mosque in Aleppo is generally assumed to be on the site of the agora of ancient Beroea, but neither its size nor a positive identification has been definitely established. The agora at Palmyra probably belongs more to the eastern tradition of caravanserai than to any Hellenistic tradition (Plate 98). The enclosure at Jerash, initially thought to be an agora, has, on excavation, been identified as a market or *macellum*.[163] The identification of an octagonal church at Umm Qays as a macellum merely on its resemblance to that at Jerash seems highly dubious. A building at Bosra is often also identified as a market, but the 'upper, middle and lower markets' at Petra were only labelled as such by the first investigators because of the lack of any other obvious explanation at the time.[164] Recently, these markets or 'agoras' (the one at Bosra in particular) have been more correctly termed *khans*, which is the traditional Arabic term for an enclosed market.[165] This is much more appropriate than either agora or macellum, which imply an imported, Roman type of building. After all, the Greeks and Romans hardly invented buying and selling. Hence, the term 'agora' is largely just another form of negating a Near Eastern character through selective terminology. It must be borne in mind that a Persian, visiting a Graeco-Roman 'agora', would call it a 'caravanserai' or a 'bazaar'. Many 'agoras' in the Near East, therefore, are not so much evidence of Greek institutions as Greek – and hence our own – perceptions of native institutions and monuments.

Plate 98 The 'agora' or caravanserai at Palmyra

Oval and circular plazas

Roman cities in the East had a number of squares which functioned merely as open urban spaces and architectural focal points. The term 'square' is rather a misnomer, for in the East public squares were often round or oval.

Circular and oval spaces are a feature of eastern Roman architecture. There are two distinct types: the completely open, bare oval or circle – a plaza in the full sense – and the roundabout which encloses an arch or similar monument. Of the former, the most famous – and visually the most dramatic, anticipating Bernini's famous piazza in front of St Peter's – is that at Jerash (Plates 43 and 99). It was laid out in the Ionic order during the first major expansion of the city in the mid-first century AD. Visually and architecturally it serves to draw together a number of widely different elements and monuments: the south entrance, the Zeus Temple temenos, the South Theatre and the Cardo. As such it is one of the great masterpieces of ancient urban architecture.[166] Perhaps its most effective function was simply to serve as a dramatic entrance into the city. Hence, the combination of oval plaza and city entrance recurs at the south-western entrance to Palmyra, the western entrance to Bosra and the Damascus Gate at Jerusalem (where it is depicted in the Madaba Map) (Figures 64 and 71). The Madaba Map also depicts an almost identical arrangement to that of Jerusalem at Ashkalon: a plaza just inside the East Gate with two colonnaded streets leading off it (followed by the present town plan), but it is uncertain whether the plaza is square or circular.[167] Perhaps one can include in this category the

297

Plate 99 The Oval Plaza at Jerash

semi-curricular colonnade enclosing the theatre at Palmyra (Figure 15, Plate 100). This is, in a sense, also a plaza, albeit with a theatre inserted into the centre. Like the south-western plaza at Palmyra, it also opens from the short street leading from the South Gate. A semi-circular plaza also exists at Baalbek in front of the Jupiter Propylaeum (Figure 5). No trace of any colonnaded street approaching it survives, although there might well have been one in antiquity. Recent excavations at the North Gate of Apamaea have also revealed a square inside the gate terminating in a semi-circle before it opens onto the colonnaded street.[168] The Madaba Map depicts more possible oval or semicircular plazas at the end of colonnaded streets at Kerak and Lod.[169] All of these plazas functioned, too, as integral parts of the colonnaded streets into which they were incorporated, and all (with the exception of Jerusalem and Baalbek) were colonnaded.

The second type was a circular plaza that also provides a focal point within a city, typically surrounding a tetrapylon. This arrangement occurs at the Jerash South Tetra-pylon, the Palmyra tetrapylon and the Bosra tetrapylon (Figure 76D–F). All mark the intersection of two colonnaded streets. The tetrapylons in the centre in these cases were more strictly speaking tetrakionions, as tetrapylons normally had the colonnades attached directly to them. Hence, these circular plazas are not colonnaded, rather they interrupt the unbroken line of the colonnades of the streets that lead to them. They appear, therefore, to be insertions within the city fabric, interrupting – even jarring – the architectural unity, and are not the masterpieces of urban planning that the entrance plazas are. They are merely traffic roundabouts. At Antioch the main intersection of the colonnaded streets was also marked by an oval plaza, probably colonnaded, but instead of a tetrapylon in the centre there was an honorific column of Tiberius (Figure 23).[170] This arrangement is also known from literary descriptions of Constantinople, where the

Plate 100 Semicircular colonnade around the theatre at Palmyra

Forum of Constantine consisted of a colonnaded oval with an honorific column of Constantine in its centre.

No examples of oval plazas occur in the Roman West, with the exception of the planned (but never completed) oval plaza forming the junction of the colonnaded street with the Baths of Hadrian at Lepcis Magna (Figure 125). Lepcis Magna, however, was a consciously 'orientalised' city in terms of its architecture (as is argued in Chapter 8), so belongs to the eastern tradition. At Dougga in Tunisia a square adjacent to the forum, the 'Place de la Rose des Vents', is semi-circular on its eastern side, but this is hardly in the same category as the oval plazas.[171] The eastern oval open spaces have been viewed as belonging within the western Roman tradition of semicircular exedrae, often paired, such as the Forum of Trajan in Rome.[172] But this appears dubious; such exedrae are very poor cousins to the great sweeps of the eastern plazas. In any case, if there was a connection it would be the other way round, an eastern tradition influencing Rome: the Forum of Trajan was designed by a Syrian architect, Apollodorus of Damascus. The circular designs might, perhaps, relate to the semicircular temples and temple enclosures – often colonnaded – that were built to Phoenician deities in North Africa. Examples are the Temple of Juno Celaestis (Astarte) at Dougga, the Temple of Aesculapius (Eshmoun) at Lambaesis, the Temple of Baal at Thuburbo Majus and the Sanctuary of the Nymphs at Zaghouan.[173] These temple plans have no counterpart in Roman architecture so must be embedded within Phoenician – and hence eastern – traditions.

The few Phoenician temple plans that have survived in the East – such as Amrit – are square. However, oval and semicircular enclosures occur elsewhere in ancient Near Eastern architecture. In south Arabia, both the Temple of ʿIlmuqah at Sirwah, the old capital of Sheba, and the Temple of ʿIlmuqah at Marib, the new capital, have oval enclosures

Plate 101 The oval enclosure of the Temple of ʿIlmuqah at Marib

dating probably from the early sixth century BC (Plate 101).[174] These enclosures probably originated as *hawtah*, sacred enclosures or places of refuge that were neutral territory amongst rival tribes. The existence of similar sacred enclaves in north Arabia in the first millennium cannot be ruled out, particularly in view of the close links between Nabataean and south Arabian cultures.[175] A similar oval sacred enclosure, of uncertain date but presumed pre-Roman, exists near the summit of Mt Hermon.[176]

Perhaps the most elaborate circular enclosure is found in front of the Deir at Petra, dated by association with the Deir façade to the first century AD (Figure 81, Plate 102). Its function is uncertain, but it is presumably religious. It consists of a large circular outline occupying the small plateau in front of the Deir, overlooked on one side by the Deir façade with its associated altar and courtyard. On the other side it is overlooked by an intriguing monument: a high terrace with a double line of columns in front and an unexplained rock-cut room containing an elaborate niche behind (Room 468). Overlooking the circle and in the immediate vicinity are a number of sacred high places.[177] The whole complex, with its component parts of façade, court, altar, circular enclosure, terrace and high places, suggests theatricality: an 'arena', a 'stage backdrop' and a monumental 'grandstand'.[178]

The point to be emphasised here about the Deir plaza is that it is approached by what appears to be a sacred processional way (already discussed above). This brings it much closer, architecturally, to our first type of oval plaza, which are all associated with monumental ways. A religious function for this type of oval plaza, therefore, offers an attractive explanation. It has already been suggested above that some of the colonnaded streets were sacred processional ways: those of Palmyra, Bosra and Jerash, all incorporate the first type

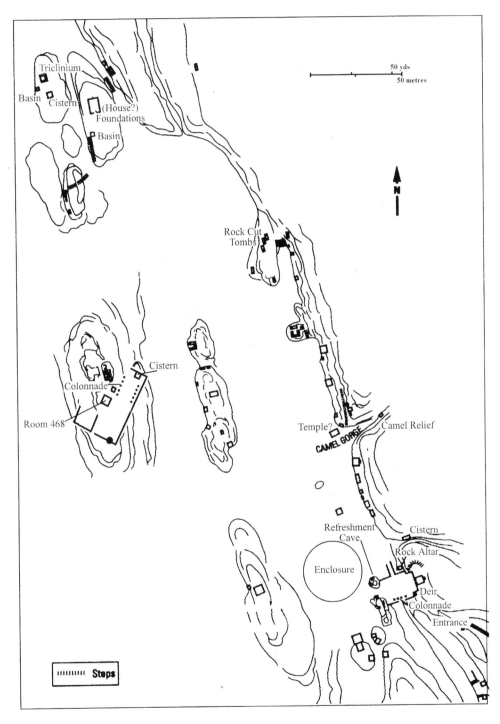

Triclinium

Basin Cistern

(House?)
Foundations

Basin

50 yds

50 metres

N

Rock Cut
Tombs

Cistern

Colonnade

Room 468

Temple?

Camel Relief

CAMEL GORGE

Refreshment
Cave

Cistern

Rock Altar

Enclosure

Deir
Colonnade

Entrance

⁞⁞⁞⁞⁞ Steps

Figure 81 Sketch plan of the Deir complex at Petra

Plate 102 The oval enclosure in front of the Deir at Petra

of open, bare oval plazas. The semicircular plaza at Baalbek forms a part of the temple propylaeum. The possible semicircular plazas depicted on the Madaba Map at Kerak and Lod are similarly associated with religious buildings: at Kerak it appears to be in front of the city's main church (standing, surely, on the site of a former Nabataean temple), and at Lod the colonnade curves around the Church of St George (again, possibly on the site of a former temple).[179] This type of plaza, therefore, might have formed an integral part of the religious processions associated with the sacred way leading to it, perhaps as a place of assembly before proceeding along the sacred way (at Bosra or Palmyra) or immediately prior to the temple (at Jerash and Baalbek). The same combination of semicircular plaza, colonnaded street and temple temenos exists at Jerusalem. The two elements of plaza (Hadrianic) and temple (Herodian) are widely divergent in date, but the arrangement is nonetheless consistent with those at Bosra and Palmyra. Since it is suggested that the Petra colonnaded street was a similar processional way, might an oval plaza be postulated at its eastern end, now eroded by the Wadi Musa? A similar arrangement for the Jerash Artemis temple has also been suggested (above). In such cases, the open type of oval plaza could be considered almost as an additional temenos of the temple it is associated with. The ovals of Marib, Sirwah, the Petra Deir and Mt Hermon certainly function in this way – and Bernini's adoption of the form for St Peter's appears entirely logical. It has been emphasised elsewhere that in the East religion was everything, and that an almost disproportionate part of a city's urban fabric – the gigantic temple compounds, for example – was subordinate to this end.

Against this argument is the suggestion that the oval plazas near the gateways at Palmyra, Jerash and Bosra perhaps functioned as caravanserais, places for the camels to unload their goods on arrival in a city.[180] This would accord with the bazaar explanation of the associated colonnaded streets postulated above. However, if this were the case one would expect to find warehouses and similar places for storage around the plazas, rather than the small shops that we do find. As with so many other features of urban architecture, it is a combination of functions that perhaps offers the best explanation: religious, mercantile and aesthetic.

The only occurrences of round urban spaces in architecture further east is the Iranian tradition of circular planned cities, already discussed. An Iranian origin for the circular plazas, therefore, cannot be ruled out, either as a survival from the Achaemenid occupation in the distant past or arriving through the Hellenistic medium (which included many Iranian elements) in the more recent past. But the connection might be too tenuous and the resemblance too illusory to be certain: plaza plans and city plans are, after all, quite different matters. All that one can say for certain is that circular plazas are entirely within an eastern urban tradition, so is another un-Roman element in the architecture of eastern Roman towns.

The East had more conventionally shaped public spaces as well. These, however, are not basically different from public squares elsewhere, Roman or otherwise, so need only be observed in passing here. Examples are the North Theatre Square at Jerash and the nymphaeum squares at Bosra and Beth-Shean (Figures 37, 39 and 79A).[181]

Buildings for pleasure

Buildings for pleasure belong mainly within the realm of Roman architecture, albeit with local variations. It is not necessary, therefore, to explore them in any detail here, but merely to note any local features. Most of the secular buildings belong to the category of entertainment: baths, theatres, amphitheatres and hippodromes.

Baths

The massive bathing establishments are often the most conspicuous monuments still standing in many Roman sites, both East and West. In the East they range from very modest, local bath-houses such as those at Serjilla, Babisqa or Barad in northern Syria (Figure 50),[182] to elaborate multi-functional complexes that can compare to those in North Africa and Rome. Jerash has two such baths, the East and West Baths (Plate 103), as does Bosra, the South and Central Baths. Other large bath complexes survive at Shahba, Hammat Gader, Beth-Shean, Palmyra and Apamaea.[183] At least five were known to have existed at Antioch.

All of these are on the Italian model and mark unambiguous imports from the West.[184] As such, they have been assumed to be evidence for communities of expatriates – presumably Italians – from the Roman West, with all the unwritten cultural prejudice that this assumption implies ('Romans wash, natives are dirty' etc.). It is certainly true that large bath complexes are entirely absent where the Roman presence was the least, i.e., in the client states: in Palmyra, for example, the baths are associated solely with Diocletian's restoration and not the city of the Palmyrenes, while in Petra the baths next to the Dushara temple are very small in scale. However, it must be remembered that it was the 'dirty East' rather than the 'clean West' that adopted and developed the Roman monumental baths: it evolved into the *hammam* or monumental bath complexes of Islamic

Plate 103 The West Baths at Jerash

architecture, surviving long after public baths had become entirely extinct as an institution in the West.

Perhaps the only difference between baths in the East and the West were that the former never included communal public lavatories. This probably just reflected a difference in attitude rather than cleanliness: in the East the act was a very private one, but in the West it seems to have been far more social, where everyone sat around swapping stories and sponges. In the East much of everyday life may have demanded communal participation, most notably in religious ritual, but this was going too far!

Entertainment

Theatres are another architectural form that is wholly western. All cities, virtually without exception, were supplied with them – indeed, they appear to be a mark of urban status. There is no need to catalogue them here[185] – some, such as Abila, have not even been excavated. Some cities, such as Qanawat, only had an odeon and no theatre. Others had two theatres, although usually the second one would be an odeon. These were Philadelphia, Jerash and Gadara (Figures 37, 38 and 40). Surprisingly, the number of theatres did not appear to be commensurate with the size or status of the city: Antioch, Caesarea and Bosra, for example, all of them provincial capitals, had only one. Most were built into a hillside, although some, such as Palmyra, Bosra, Caesarea and Jebleh, were free-standing. Some of the Syrian theatres were the largest ever built in the entire Roman world: Cyrrhus, Apamaea and Bosra, the latter having the added distinction of probably being the most intact (Plate 49).

A recent survey of Near Eastern theatres has revealed some regional variation on the standard Roman pattern.[186] The most dramatically different of the eastern theatres is the one at Petra which, uniquely in the Roman world, is entirely rock-cut in the local style. The theatre at Batrun in Lebanon is also partly rock-cut.[187] But perhaps the most surprising feature of the Roman theatres of the East is precisely that they are *Roman*, whereas it would be natural to assume that any 'western' cultural life, such as theatre-going, would surely have been Greek, not Roman.[188] This makes it all the more surprising that there is not a single Greek theatre in the East.[189] All conform to the Roman style: semicircular, rather than horseshoe in plan, with a *scenae frons* or stage backdrop, rather than open. The only exception is Byblos, which appears to incorporate some Greek features: it is horseshoe in plan, not semicircular, but otherwise adheres to Roman layout.[190]

Amphitheatres are known at Antioch, Beirut, Caesarea, Scythopolis, Jerusalem, Jericho, Beth Givrin, Dura Europos, and possibly Qanawat and Bosra.[191] The one at Antioch, ordered by Caesar, was one of the earliest in the Roman world.[192] Invariably, amphitheatres would be associated with a resident Latin community, for the East had an abhorrence of the Roman blood sports – Ammianus Marcellinus, a native of Antioch, for example, describes the Emperor Gallus' delight in blood sports in outrage and distaste.[193] Unlike the theatres, all are very small in scale – many in fact smaller than the theatres – in no way comparable to the colossal amphitheatres of Italy, Gaul or North Africa. The unusually large occurrence of amphitheatres in Judaea was probably the result of a deliberate Romanisation of the area following the two great Jewish Revolts.

Caesarea has the remains of a theatre and amphitheatre. The amphitheatre was described by Josephus as the place used by Herod for the inaugural celebrations to mark the foundation of Caesarea, so dates from the very beginning of the city. The existing amphitheatre dates from long after the city's foundation, so cannot be the one described by Josephus. Recent excavations, however, have revealed a second amphitheatre alongside the sea (Figure 31). Despite its 'hippodrome' appearance – its layout and dimensions closely resemble other Near Eastern hippodromes, such as those at Gerasa and Neapolis – it probably corresponds to Herod's 'amphitheatre'. It was built on virgin soil at about the time of the foundation of Caesarea, and inscriptional evidence supports its use for Herod's inauguration of the city. The excavators have interpreted it as a 'multi-purpose mass entertainment complex', rather than either a hippodrome or amphitheatre in the conventional sense, that was used for horse and chariot racing in addition to athletics, blood sports and civic events.[194] Remains of other hippodromes exist at Bosra, Umm Qays, Tyre, Jerash and possibly Shahba, and hippodromes were also known to have existed in Antioch, Laodicaea and Beirut. The Tyre hippodrome was one of the largest in the Roman world, and the Jerash hippodrome, although one of the smallest, is one of the best preserved (Plate 104). Recent excavations at the Jerash hippodrome have uncovered traces of extensive industrial use of the hippodrome, and those at both Jerash and Bosra might also have functioned as caravanserais, or at least as 'corrals' outside the cities where animals would be quartered.[195] The only cities which possessed a Greek-style stadium were Sebaste and possibly Marathus (Amrit).

It appears that, unlike in the Latin West, no clear distinction was made between the use

Plate 104 The Jerash Hippodrome looking towards the *carceres* and the Arch of Hadrian

of an amphitheatre, stadium and hippodrome. Hippodromes, furthermore, had a much greater variety of use than in the West: as places for civic functions, as caravanserais, and as factories, for example. It is noteworthy that the hippodrome at Constantinople came to form the ceremonial heart of the city, functioning as a stage-setting for imperial pageantry and as the city assembly area, in addition to its conventional function as staging chariot races.

Military architecture

It is easy to forget that Rome arrived in the East as a foreign invader and remained as an occupying power throughout the seven hundred years of its presence there. For it left such little evidence of this: the vast majority of the Roman architecture in the East that we are reviewing was not built to house an army or to control the populace. Of course, the East abounds in Roman military architecture – the Syrian desert preserves some of the best military remains in the Roman world – but these were built to *defend* the East from other foreign invaders, not to maintain Rome's hold over the local population, and date largely from the later periods of Rome's rule.

Accordingly, Roman military architecture can be divided into two types: architecture of occupation, of which there are very few extant remains, and architecture of defence, of which there is a large amount. In fact, the two appear much the same, the main difference being merely one of location. In practice, the latter kind was ultimately an architecture of occupation as well, for it defended borders against foreign invaders who were as often as not welcomed as liberators (the Muslim Arabs, for example, or the Iranians on several occasions). Roman military architecture in the East has in recent years come in for a considerable

306

amount of attention: a series of regular international conferences, voluminous subsequent conference proceedings, and numerous worthwhile books.[196] Thankfully, therefore, it would be superfluous to examine either kind in any great detail here.

Occupation

Of the first kind, there is remarkably little to be found in the cities – Roman oppression, such as it was, seems to have kept a remarkably low profile. But a cautionary note has been sounded on the exaggerated view of Roman military remains in the desert merely because they survive better there, as opposed to towns where they are obliterated.[197] Hence, the Fortress of Antonia in Jerusalem exists now largely only in Christian tradition. The very tentatively identified headquarters of the Third Cyrenaican Legion at Bosra exists only in an outline barely discernible from the air. The headquarters of the Third Parthian Legion at Apamaea only survives as inscriptions reused in the city walls. Remains of the great garrison of Zeugma are so scant that the very whereabouts of it were uncertain until recently.[198] Only in three towns have substantial remains of Roman urban military installations survived: the 'praetorium' at Umm al-Jimal, the Camp of

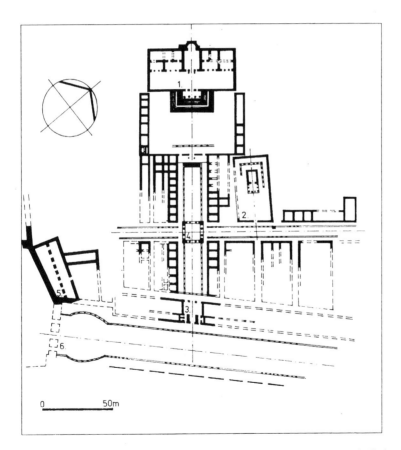

Figure 82 The Camp of Diocletian at Palmyra. 1: Principia. 2: Temple of Allath. 3: Gateway. 4: Tetrapylon. 5: Horraeum. 6: Oval plaza (After Mikhailowski)

Diocletian at Palmyra (Figure 82) and the praetorium and *Dux Ripae* at Dura Europos (Figure 83).[199] Recent studies of the medieval citadel at Damascus have suggested that there was a Roman military installation of an indeterminate nature underneath it.[200] There was also a rather enigmatic building described as a 'praetorium' at Mismiya in the Hauran, although this was demolished last century before it could be properly recorded (Figure 57).[201]

Although not exactly 'military', to this list we can possibly add the Roman Governor's Palace at Bosra, although this is now thought to be Nabataean (Figure 42).[202] Otherwise, the only palaces to have survived are the series of country palaces erected by Herod at Bethlehem (the Herodion), Jericho, Masada and Mukawir (Figure 84).[203] Such royal 'palaces' (more correctly, country residences), located well away from centres of population, are peculiar to Judaea. They may in fact have been a Jewish tradition: the most impressive Hellenistic monument in the Near East is the country palace at 'Araq al-Amir in Jordan built by the otherwise little known Jewish Tobiad dynasty.[204] At the end of the Roman period there was a revival of the tradition with the construction of the so-called 'desert

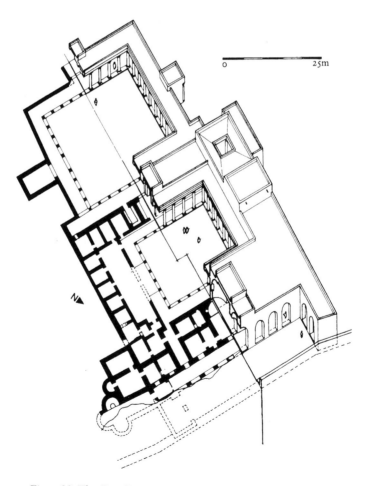

Figure 83 The *Dux Ripae* at Dura Europos (After Ward-Perkins)

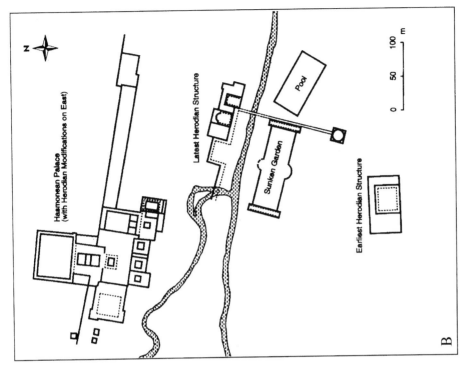

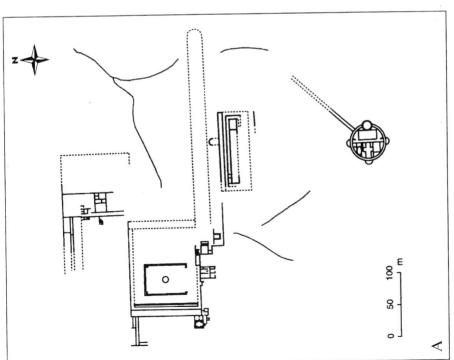

Figure 84 Herod's palaces. A: Herodion. B: Jericho (After Roller)

palaces' by the Umayyad Caliphs, one of them (Khirbet al-Mafjar) built not far from Herod's earlier such palace at Jericho.

Virtually all the cities were enclosed in ramparts, the earliest probably being the walls of Tiberius at Antioch, of which some traces still survive,[205] but it is uncertain whether these were to exert control over the inhabitants or guard them from invaders. Far more vivid evidence for Roman occupation exists in the siege camps and circumvallations that were built during their campaigns against various eastern strongholds. The most famous date from sieges after the Jewish Revolt, such as Masada (Plate 105) and Mukawir, but numerous others are discernible from the air.[206]

Defence

Of the second category, buildings of defence, the East is almost embarrassingly rich in remains. These are to be found mainly in the eastern and southern desert fringes. They range from isolated, almost intact little forts such as Qasr al-Hallabat to textbook fortified legionary camps such as Layjjun and Udhruh (Figure 85) to great fortified frontier cities such as Rasafa and Halabiya (Figure 28, Plate 106).[207] This massive 'system' of frontier defences is conventionally described as a *limes* system, although this recently has been viewed as a modern misconception (Figure 86).[208] Whatever these fortifications were, they stand as mute testimony to the power of Iran as much as of Rome, for this frontier was the most vulnerable of the entire empire. In the end, this massive, costly and constantly

Plate 105 Roman siege camps and circumvallation at Masada

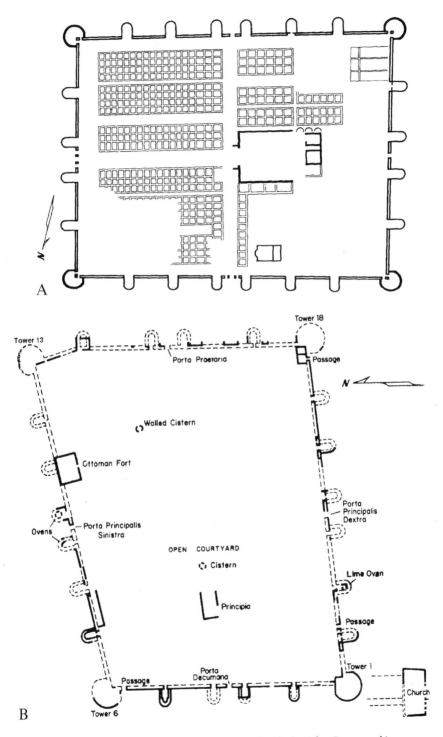

Figure 85 Legionary camps at Layjjun and Udruh (After Bowersock)

Plate 106 The fortifications of Halabiya on the Euphrates

ongoing programme of building work never kept out the very enemy it was designed for, who rendered such defences useless on several occasions. Halabiya, for example, was simply bypassed by the Iranian army in their invasion under Khusrau Anushirvan.

At first sight these defences appear to form a part of the broader spectrum of Roman military architecture, with no regional variation to be found in the East. Recently, however, it has been suggested that the design of the later, square form of Roman fort with outward-projecting towers, as opposed to the earlier round-cornered camp with inward-projecting towers, originated in the East.[209] In this context, it is worth recalling the almost 'textbook' Roman military camp outlined in India in the *Arthasastra* centuries earlier, noted above in the section on 'The urban layout' (Figure 62).

The largest of these building works date from the late Roman period when the threats from the east became more pressing. The immense fortresses of the desert frontier, such as Rasafa and Halabiya, are amongst the most impressive works of military architecture in the ancient world. Roman and 'Byzantine' military architecture is often viewed as a European tradition, emanating from Constantinople. It is certainly true that the city walls of Theodosius at Constantinople are the greatest in the ancient world, and that Qasr Ibn Wardan and Halabiya might have been built by architects from the capital. But there is equally no doubt that such architects would have found in Syria a highly developed and ancient tradition of building great fortifications in stone that have their origin in the ancient urban fortifications of Qatna and Ebla of the second and third millennia BC. The great urban fortifications of Antioch, Rasafa and Halabiya – and perhaps even Constantinople as well? – must be seen as the architectural link between these earlier works and the later great fortresses of the Crusaders, which continued this rich native tradition of military architecture.

There is one type of Roman fortification system which appears to derive from eastern

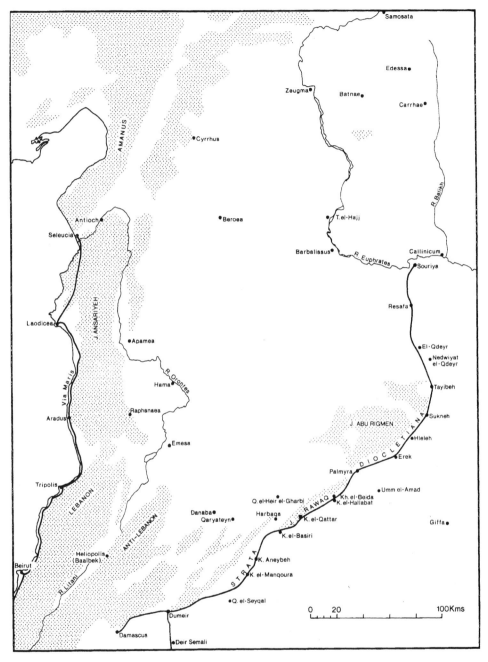

Figure 86 Fortifications system associated with the Strata Diocletiana (After Kennedy and Riley)

Plate 107 Hadrian's Wall at Housesteads

Plate 108 The Antonine Wall at Falkirk

tradition. This is the long walls. Running barriers as defensive systems in the West have been contrasted with the lack of them in the East,[210] but closer investigation shows the opposite to be nearer the truth. There are few from the Roman period in the East, admittedly, and this is the type of fortification that was used for Rome's most famous remains in Britain, Hadrian's Wall, as well as the Antonine Wall further north (Plates 107 and 108). Much later, Justinian had long walls built at Thermopylae and Corinth, while the most impressive were the long walls built by Anastasius across Thrace.[211] But the system of long walls has a very strong tradition in eastern military architecture, where it seems to be Mesopotamian or possibly Central Asian in origin.

The Mesopotamian origins are very ancient. During the reign of King Shu-Suen of Ur (1972–1964 BC), for example, a long defensive wall was constructed running north of Baghdad from the Euphrates to the Tigris and on to the Diyala River to prevent nomadic incursions into the Kingdom of Ur in southern Iraq.[212] In the sixth century BC, Nebuchadnezzar built a long defensive wall north of Babylon, the so-called 'Median Wall' described by Xenophon, that stretched for some 50 kilometres between the Tigris and Euphrates Rivers. The existence and date of this wall have been confirmed by excavation.[213] In the Levant, the long wall built in the third century BC by Alexander Jannaeus in Palestine from Antipatris to Jaffa was in the same tradition, and parts of it have been identified.[214]

The tradition seems more prevalent in Central Asia, although the oldest dated example is only Achaemenid. This is the wall of Kam Pirak, a rammed mud defensive wall that has been traced for about 60 kilometres across northern Afghanistan.[215] Later examples abound, either frontier walls such as Kam Pirak that defended entire territories or giant enclosure walls that encircled entire oases. Of the former, the most famous are the frontier walls between Bactria and Soghdia, dating from the third century BC and later used to mark the northern border of the Kushan Empire.[216] Other examples are known in Daghestan, such as at Darband, one of several built by the Sasanians (with Roman funds!) across the Caucasian passes, as well as in the Kopet Dagh mountains of Turkmenia, to halt Hun incursions.[217] There were also long walls enclosing the oases of Merv, Bukhara, Samarkand and Balkh. These were to keep the nomads at bay and protect the outlying settlements. The Merv oasis is enclosed by two sets of long walls. The inner one, the Giliakin–Chilburj Wall, encloses the inner oasis some 55 square kilometres in area and has been identified as the 'Antiochus Wall' mentioned by Strabo. The outer wall encloses the perimeter of the oasis for some 60 kilometres, and is assumed to be Sasanian.[218] Those around the Bukhara oasis consisted of gates and towers built at half-mile intervals that were completed in 830, but were restorations of earlier walls built in pre-Islamic times. It enclosed an area enclosing approximately 1,300 square kilometres, and remains of it still existed in the early twentieth century.[219]

In Iran, long walls characterised Sasanian systems of defence, particularly along its northern borders most prone to nomadic invasions (and architectural influence from Central Asia).[220] The Darband Wall and other such walls in Daghestan have been mentioned. To this can be added the Walls of Tammisha that crossed the coastal littoral from the Alburz Mountains northwards to the Caspian Sea west of Gurgan.[221] The most famous of these Caspian walls is the so-called 'Alexander's Wall' that stretches eastwards from the Caspian Sea into the Alburz Mountains for at least 190 kilometres (Figure 87). It consists of a curtain wall constructed from brick and mud with (in some places) a ditch on its outside, northern, face and at least thirty-five regularly spaced forts on its southern side. It was formerly thought to be Sasanian in date, but recent investigations have both

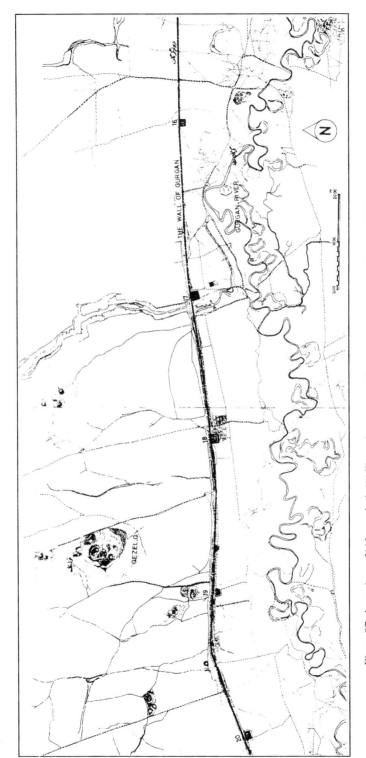

Figure 87 A section of 'Alexander's Wall' on the Gurgan Plain. Note forts on south of wall (After Mehryar/Kiani)

revealed further extensions and dated it to the Parthian period of the later second and early first centuries BC, probably built in the reign of Mithradates II (123–87 BC). It replaced in part an earlier wall dated to the early first millennium BC.[222]

The similarity of Alexander's Wall to Hadrian's Wall has already led to speculation on the possibility of Parthian prisoners of war bringing the tradition westwards with them.[223] The dissimilarity of Hadrian's Wall to Roman defensive systems elsewhere has already been commented upon, so investigating possible eastern links would certainly open up a worthwhile line of enquiry. Asians had been fighting in Europe as auxiliaries in the Roman army ever since the days of Pompey. There were certainly Parthian auxiliaries fighting in the Roman Empire as early as the Dalmatian Wars of AD 6–9 under Tiberius, when an oriental unit was stationed on the Rhine, while later on numbers of Parthian – as well as Armenian and Oshroenian – mercenaries, deserters and prisoners were known to be serving in the Roman army on the Rhine frontier under Alexander and Maximinus.[224] The only literary sources for Hadrian's wall are the *Augustan History*, Eutropius and Aurelius Victor (who both ascribe it to Septimius Severus), so virtually all that we know of it comes from archaeology.[225] The northern frontier of Britain certainly has an unusually high number of archaeological remains of cults, such as Mithraism, connected with resident eastern communities, so an Iranian element is known to have existed.[226] The possible builders of the Wall apart, it was certainly an oriental enclave.[227]

It is further significant that Justinian's long walls at Thermopylae and Corinth were built specifically to keep the Huns out, just as the walls of Daghestan in the Caucasus built by the Iranians were. This in itself suggests that Justinian might have used Iranian architects in their construction.

Pagan architecture

Nowhere is a region's individuality expressed more than in its religion. In the religious architecture of the Roman East we probably see more regional differences from mainstream Roman architecture than in any other area. Indeed, so different are eastern temples from those in the West that the two are really fundamentally different types of building, architecturally, functionally and liturgically. And yet their superficial resemblance to Roman temples in the West has probably done more than anything else to prompt statements on the cultural dominance of the West over the East. In a recent major study of the Roman East, for example, it was written that even temples in the most remote locations were built in the 'Roman' style, and 'occasional perfectly Greek temples in remote locations, high up on the mountain' were cited in the Damascus region as support of the western character of the Near East.[228] In the perceived 'Hellenistic' character of the Graeco-Roman temples of the East, it must be remembered that there are hardly any temples to Greek deities – Apollo or Poseidon or Athena – that characterise Greek settlements elsewhere (southern Italy, Cyrenaica, Ionia, etc.). There are many temples to a 'Zeus' of course, but in all cases the 'Zeus' is merely a thinly disguised Semitic deity, bearing almost no resemblance to the Greek Zeus. Temples of Rome and Augustus are generally conspicuous by their absence in the East, especially when compared to, for example, North Africa.[229] Whilst much is made of the Jewish refusal to have any truck with Rome's official state cult, one is left wondering whether anybody in the East bothered much with it. The different elements of the eastern temple, along with their eastern architectural affiliations, are, therefore, analysed here in detail.

The temenos temple

Cities in the East were usually dominated by single, large temple complexes to the patron god. Religion and holy cities were a major part of the entire urban fabric. Jerusalem, of course, was – and is – the archetypal such holy city, with its temple appropriate to such a status (Plate 6). But it is important to remember that before circumstances made Jerusalem pre-eminent, the East had many such holy cities, sacred to specific cults, all jostling for pre-eminence. Mambij was sacred to Atargatis, Byblos 'the holy' to Baalat-Gabal, Emesa to the Sun god Elagabal, Damascus to Hadad, Qanawat/Siʿ to Dushara, Sebaste to a rival Jehovah, to name but some of the main 'Jerusalems' of the ancient Near East. This is essentially a part of a broader ancient Arabian tradition of the holy city and place of pilgrimage or *haram*: Mecca, Najran, Yathil, Marib and Sanʿa were the main ones in southern Arabia before Islam made Mecca pre-eminent. When a city had more than one temple, there would always be the one to the patron god that outshone all others. It would dwarf the city around it, providing the main focal point around which all of the city's life revolved. It would be built on a massive – one could almost say monolithic – scale, usually much larger than those in the West. Incipient monotheism was never far away in the East, and is amply expressed in architecture. This idea of the single main city temple, with all other temples subservient to it, introduced the concept of the cathedral into European architecture.

The single reason for the massive scale of eastern temples was the temenos or temple compound. Even a remote rural temple far away from any main settlement, such as Husn Sulaiman in the mountains behind Tartus (Figure 88A, Plate 109) or those high up the slopes of Mt Hermon,[230] would be larger than the average Roman temple because of its temenos. The temenos, or temple enclosure, that surrounds the sanctuary (or occasionally in front as a forecourt) perhaps differentiates an eastern temple from its western counterpart more than any other feature.

The temple compound to its patron god usually takes up a major quarter in an eastern city. The Temple of Bel at Palmyra, the Temple of Artemis (probably Atargatis) at Jerash (Plate 110), the Temple of Jupiter-Hadad at Damascus (incorporated in the present Umayyad Mosque), and the Temple at Jerusalem all covered very large areas of a city's total area (Figures 9, 15, 34 and 37). Indeed, Herod's Temple at Jerusalem (Figure 8), covering approximately 151,200 square metres, was the largest temple in the Roman world (although not the largest in the Middle East; the Temple of the Sun at Hatra discussed below, at 156,800 square metres, was larger), with those at Damascus (Figure 35) and Palmyra (Figure 88B) very close behind. Smaller in scale were the Temple of Nebo and the Temple of Baal-Shamin at Palmyra, the Temple of Dushara and the newly excavated 'Great Temple' at Petra, the Temple of Zeus at Jerash, the Temple of Baal-Shamin at Kedesh in Galilee, the Temple to Rome and Augustus at Sebaste and the temple attributed to Heracles (on little evidence) on the acropolis at Amman, all enclosed in a temenos (Figures 88 and 89). The temples of Yammuneh, Labwa, Khirbet al-Knisa, Yanta, Shahim, Masnaqa, Naʾus, Antura, Sfira, Qalʿat Faqra and Nabha al-Qaddan in Lebanon were also all temenos temples.[231] At Pella, a major Roman sanctuary is known from coin depictions to have been situated on Tell Husn. Recent archaeological work here has brought to light the fragmentary remains of a large colonnaded Roman structure, probably a part of the temenos wall of this temple. Coin depictions show similar arrangements at Abila and Capitolias. Another such temple might have existed at Beth-Shean, ancient

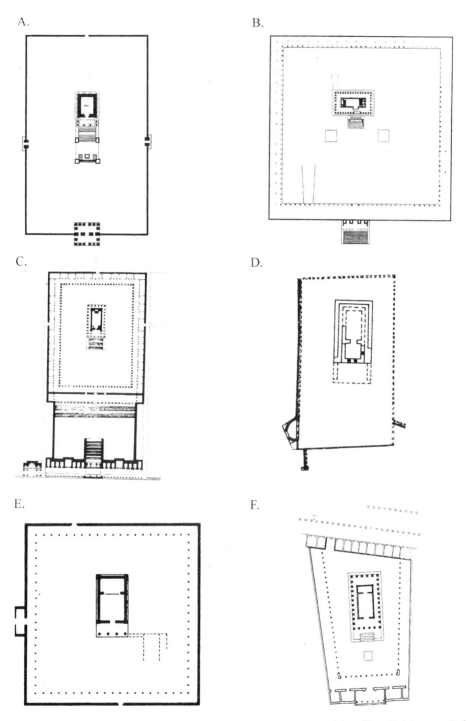

Figure 88 Temenos temples with sanctuaries in the centre (not to scale). A: Husn Sulaiman. B: Bel Temple at Palmyra. C: Artemis Temple at Jerash. D: Heracles Temple at Amman. E: Shaikh Barakat. F: Nabu Temple at Palmyra

Plate 109 Husn Sulaiman

Plate 110 The Temple of Artemis at Jerash

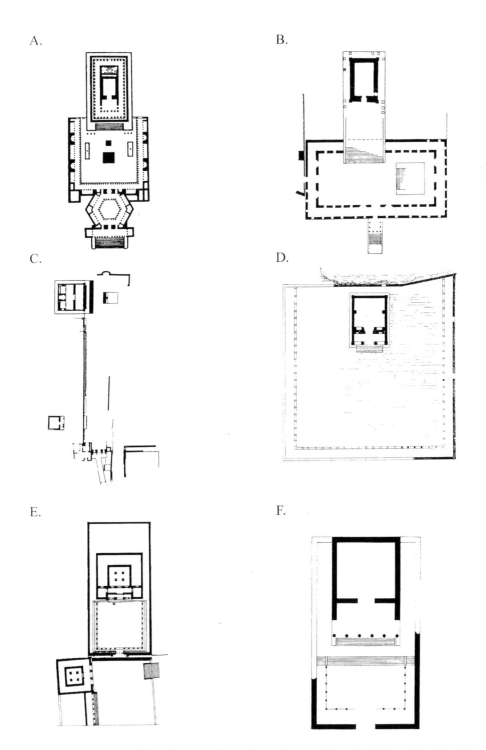

A.　　　　　　　　　　　　B.

C.　　　　　　　　　　　　D.

E.　　　　　　　　　　　　F.

Figure 89 Temenos temples with sanctuaries at the end or one side. A: Baalbek. B: Zeus Temple
at Jerash. C: Dushara Temple at Petra. D: Mushannaf. E: Siʿ. F: Qalʿat Faqra

Scythopolis, where recent excavations uncovered a monumental propylaeum at the foot of the hill (Tell Beth-Shean) suggesting a similar arrangement to Amman and Pella.[232] At Byblos, fragments of the temenos of the Temple of Baalat-Gabal have been found. A large enclosure wall, presumably belonging to a temple, is just discernible on the surface at Cyrrhus. A massive temple complex has been deduced at Bosra, of which the 'Nabataean Arch' is the only part surviving, the remainder probably demolished in the Christian era. Apamaea had a major temple to Zeus Belos, known from inscriptions and literary references, but it has not been excavated. Emesa was known to have one of the greatest temples in the East, the Temple of Elagabal, but no trace of it survives.[233] Although we do not know what form any of these temples that are no longer extant took, it is a safe assumption that they were within temenos enclosures.[234]

The earliest is the Temple at Jerusalem, begun by Herod in 8 BC and finished about AD 60 (Figure 8, Plate 6). Most of the others were begun during the first century AD, but so vast was the undertaking that work on them continued throughout the second century and occasionally into the third. The peak of construction coincided with the great increase in wealth and building activity of the second century. Most were situated on the sites of earlier temples: Hellenistic antecedents to the Temple of Zeus at Jerash and the Temple of Bel at Palmyra are well documented, for example, and fragments of the Temple of Jupiter-Hadad in Damascus date back to the ninth century BC. They often mark, therefore, far more ancient sacred places with histories of continuous religious worship stretching over a very long period of time – in the case of Damascus and Jerusalem, continuing to this day.

All of those temples cited above were urban manifestations, forming integral parts of the social and architectural fabric of great cities. Of equal importance were the massive temple compounds situated *outside* the cities, sometimes in the remote countryside. The most famous of these is the great Temple of Jupiter at Baalbek (Figures 4 and 5, Plates 2–5), one of the greatest temples of the ancient world and one of the most ambitious and lavish works of architecture ever undertaken.[235] It is a gigantic complex that incorporates two sanctuaries, the sanctuary of Jupiter within the temenos and another sanctuary (conventionally, albeit mistakenly, known as the Temple of Bacchus) alongside. As is to be expected with such a gigantic undertaking, it was built over a very long period, beginning in the time of Augustus and continuing sporadically throughout the first, second and third centuries. With the accession of Constantine in the fourth century a halt was finally called, with many details left unfinished. As a sacred site, its origins go back to the late second millennium BC.

It is important to remember above all that Baalbek was in the remote countryside: it was *not* a great city temple as Jerusalem or Damascus or Palmyra were, but only a minor country town otherwise of little significance. Baalbek *was* the temple and the temple Baalbek. Possible reasons why such a great temple existed a long way from any urban centre are given in Chapter 3, where it is suggested that Baalbek might be the great Temple of Emesene Baal. But the question is to some extent unimportant here, for Baalbek is not an isolated example. The Near East had a tradition of major cult shrines outside cities, usually situated on high eminences or otherwise in mountains (the sacred high place is discussed in more detail below), and nowhere more so than in the coastal ranges of Lebanon and Syria. Hence, temple enclosures are often found on mountains. The Temple of Zeus is on the top of Jebel Shaikh Barakat in northern Syria (Figure 88E), the Temple of Zeus Bombos at Burj Baqirha and several others are in similarly elevated

mountain positions nearby (Plate 63), there are several on or near the summit of Mt
Hermon, the Temple of Zeus Kasios on top of a mountain outside Antioch is known
from literary references, and there is a temple on top of Jebel Hardin in Lebanon.[236]
Otherwise, rural temples are usually elevated or in mountainous places. The Baal-
Shamin–Dushara Temple complex at Siʿ on a hillside near Qanawat in the Hauran is a
famous example (Figure 36), while in Lebanon alone nearly sixty such temples have been
recorded. The best known in Lebanon are those at Bziza, Sfira, Niha and Qalʿat Faqra.
There is a particularly high concentration around Mt Hermon (although very few, interestingly, associated with the equally high Mt Saʾuda further north). Another concentration occurs on and around Mt Shaikh Barakat in northern Syria.[237] Exceptionally,
temples are located in lowland areas, such as the temple at Isriya (Figure 97G) between
Palmyra and Rasafa and the temple at Mushannaf east of Jebel Druze (Figure 89D).[238]

Perhaps the most extraordinary in this series is the Temple of Baal Baetococaea at Husn
Sulaiman high up in the mountains inland from Tartus (Plate 109). The dimensions of its
temenos are as vast as many a great city temple, with the size of the stone monoliths used
in its construction comparable to those at Baalbek (Plate 111). In its present form, it was
begun in the first century AD, probably being completed at the end of the second century,

Plate 111 The temenos wall at Husn Sulaiman. Note size of the stones

but the history of the sanctuary as a sacred place goes back to the Achaemenid period in the sixth century BC or earlier. The shrine was dedicated, according to an inscription, to Baetococaean Baal 'the great Thunder god' which, although inconsistent with Baal-Shamin, might be more associated with the cult of Hadad.[239] In both architecture and cult this extraordinary temple complex is entirely consistent with Phoenician and Near Eastern, rather than Roman and western, traditions.[240]

The enclosures usually surrounded the sanctuary, which would be located in or near the centre. At both Palmyra and Jerash Artemis, the sanctuary was in the centre (Plates 110 and 112); at Damascus and Jerusalem, there is no evidence for the location of the sanctuary. Reconstructions of the Jerusalem temple usually have it off centre (Figure 8), but the third-century synagogue fresco at Dura Europos depicts a peripteral temple in the centre of the compound remarkably like Palmyra.[241] Occasionally, the enclosure would be to the front or even the side of the sanctuary, such as at Baalbek, the Dushara Temple at Petra, the Zeus Temple at Jerash (Plate 113), Mushannaf, Si' and Qal'at Faqra (Figure 89).

In many ways, it was the enclosure itself, rather than the sanctuary building inside it, that was the main element of these great temples. The sanctuary was merely the residence of the deity, while outside in the enclosure was where the sacrifices to its honour took place and where mass worship was performed. Hence, the enclosure was more than just a perimeter wall between the city (or country) and the temple: it *was* the temple. It was also an arena, a theatre which provided a setting for elaborate and gorgeous religious spectacle involving mass participation by thousands – 'performances' far more sumptuous than the most ambitious of theatrical productions. This aspect is emphasised architecturally in the temenos of the Temple of Dushara at Petra, which is even provided with seating for

Plate 112 The sanctuary of the Temple of Bel at Palmyra

Plate 113 The Temple of Zeus at Jerash, with the temenos in the foreground

participants to the rituals. In a sense, the only functional difference between a Roman arena and a great eastern temple was that the latter demanded audience participation – and the bloodshed was not gratuitous. The importance of 'stage-settings' in eastern Roman architecture is explored in more detail below. The architecture of these great temple enclosures, therefore, invites some comparison with theatres. Like a stage back-drop, the walls would be lavishly embellished commensurate to the status of the deity itself (Plates 3 and 17). Continuous colonnades, of course, were usual, having the benefit of providing shade in addition to an appropriate setting. The temples of Bel, Nebo and Baal-Shamin at Palmyra, the Artemis Temple at Jerash, the Temple of Baal-Shamin at Si', the Temple of Jerusalem, and the temples at Baalbek, Mushannaf, Shaikh Barakat and Pella all had such colonnades (Figures 88 and 89). The walls would also come in for particularly elaborate decoration, often as elaborate as the sanctuaries themselves. Those of the Temple of Bel at Palmyra, for example, were decorated with repeated 'Syrian niches' (a popular motif for embellishing otherwise blank wall surfaces, discussed in more detail in the section on decoration, below), while the walls of the Baalbek temenos had repeated rows of Syrian niches in addition to exedrae with columns of pink Aswan granite (Plate 114). At Husn Sulaiman the stones used for the construction of its temenos wall were monoliths up to 15 metres long and 2.5 metres high, quite unnecessarily massive for structural or defensive purposes but a testimony to the great importance attached to the enclosure walls (Plate 111).

Plate 114 The temenos wall at Baalbek. Note the Syrian niches

Temple propylaea

It was not just the interiors of the temenos walls that came in for lavish attention, but the exteriors as well. For a temple compound was never exclusive, it never turned its back on the city or community in which it was located. It formed an integral part of it, and the architecture of their exteriors was meant to attract, to draw people in. The walls of the Temple of Bel at Palmyra, for example, are decorated with rows of Corinthian pilasters, but in many other cases – Damascus for example – the exteriors were blank. This was probably because the temples were surrounded by the houses and bazaars of the city itself, rather like a Friday Mosque is today. But more important than the exterior decoration of the walls were the entrances that led to them. Most temple enclosures had elaborate propylaea. These monumental gateways would often come in for more architectural attention than the sanctuaries themselves – and usually far outshone commemorative arches·in sheer elaborate ostentation. The propylaeum to the Dushara Temple temenos at Petra is actually formed by a commemorative arch, and the propylaea to the great temples at Palmyra, Damascus, Jerash and Baalbek are some of the most elaborate in the ancient world. The propylaeum to the so-called Temple of Hercules in Amman was almost as splendid as the Artemis Propylaeum in Jerash, consisting of a gateway to a monumental flight of stairs up to the temple precinct on top of the acropolis. This, however, has now entirely disappeared (Figure 90). The Baalbek Propylaeum consists of a semicircular plaza in front of a flowing bank of stairs (destroyed in the twelfth century) leading to a pedimented and colonnaded portico flanked by the two towers of the temple 'high places' (this curious feature is discussed more below), the whole decorated in pilasters and rows

326

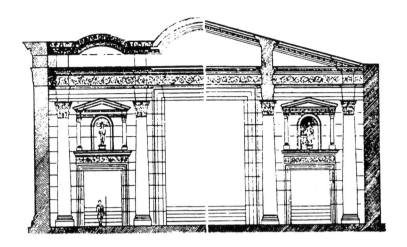

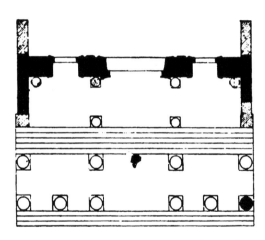

Figure 90 The Amman Propylaeum (After Butler)

of niches that contained statuary (Figure 91). This in turn led into a colonnaded octagonal courtyard, a kind of 'antechamber' to the great courtyard beyond, that architecturally formed a part of the propylaeum complex rather than the temple courtyard itself. One can surely postulate here the existence of a monumental processional way leading to the semicircular plaza, repeating the arrangement found at Jerash and elsewhere.

But the most elaborate propylaeum of all – and surely one of the most elaborate in Classical architecture? – is the Artemis Propylaeum at Jerash (Figure 65, Plate 75).[242] It actually began some distance from the temple itself with a processional way starting at least 300 metres to the east across the Chrysoroas (Jerash) River. This was crossed by a bridge (now gone) and the way then continued up a flight of stairs to the first gateway in the form of a monumental Roman triple arch, embellished with four engaged columns on either side flanking the doorways. It led into a short colonnaded avenue some 40 metres long (converted into a church in the sixth century) which opened out into a

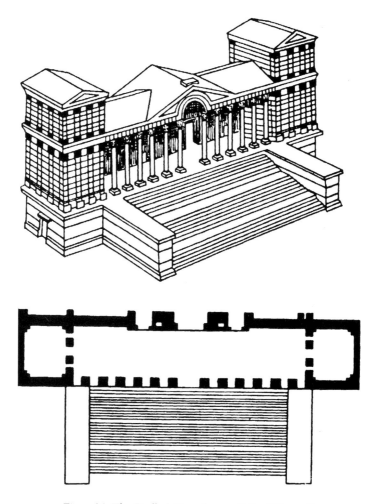

Figure 91 The Baalbek Propylaeum (After Wiegand)

curious courtyard in the form of a trapezium flanked by two semicircular exedrae. The processional way then crossed the Cardo, the east Cardo colonnade stopping short either side of the trapezium courtyard – the columns parting, as it were, for the procession. Dominating the west side of the Cardo was the second gateway, the main propylaeum itself (Plate 115). Four gigantic columns supported a massive pediment and behind it was another triple entrance, its façade adorned with four engaged columns supporting an entablature with two 'Syrian niches' above each lateral doorway. Beyond, a great flowing bank of stairs led up to a broad terrace that extended the full width of the temenos. In the middle of the terrace was an altar, and along its western side was another flight of stairs, almost as broad as the massive temenos above, that led in three flights up to the third and final gateway into the temenos itself. This final gateway, like the Baalbek Propylaeum, consisted of a colonnaded portico flanked by two towers and capped by a pediment. The worshipper would then pass through another triple entrance into the great courtyard beyond. Surely, few more awe-inspiring monumental approaches exist anywhere?

Plate 115 The Artemis Propylaeum at Jerash

It has been suggested above that the main colonnaded streets of Byblos, Palmyra, Petra, Bosra and possibly Jerash were similar processional ways, so perhaps the colonnaded street–oval plaza combinations at some of these cities should also be considered as parts of their temple propylaea – or as extensions to them.

Eastern temple origins

Numerous comparisons have been drawn between eastern Roman temples and those in the West. There are obvious comparisons of detail, of style, even occasionally of evolution and layout, and they are generally discussed within the broader framework of Roman imperial architecture. Indeed, some buildings such as Baalbek or the Artemis Propylaeum of Jerash have featured on the front covers or in otherwise prominent positions in general studies of Roman architecture, as if these buildings epitomised or typified Roman architecture as a whole. There are resemblances, admittedly, and it would be folly to overlook them. But the resemblances are purely superficial. In terms of function, liturgy, antecedents and overall concept, these massive temple enclosures with their elaborate entrances have no counterpart in Roman architecture of the West. Temples might be surrounded by an enclosure wall in the West, but not comparable to the scale of eastern enclosures. More usually a temple would open directly off a street or a forum, without intervening propylaea or enclosures. It is significant that one of the few temenos temples in Rome itself was Aurelian's Temple of the Sun, which was a transference of the cult of

329

Emesene Elagabal.[243] The temenos temples, apart from superficial decorative details, belong wholly within an eastern tradition. Any explanation of them must lie, therefore, in an eastern architectural context.[244]

Two of the greatest works of Parthian architecture immediately spring to mind in considering the eastern Roman temple form. These are the Temple of the Sun at Hatra in northern Iraq and the Temple of Anahita at Kangavar in western Iran. A possible third is the temple at Khurha, south of Tehran.[245] In both major temples the architectural emphasis is on vast enclosed spaces, the temenos. The Hatra temple, lying in the centre of a circular walled city, occupies – like those at Palmyra or Jerusalem – a significant percentage of the total area of the city (Figure 92). At approximately 156,800 square metres it is larger than the Temple at Jerusalem, making it probably the largest single ancient temple complex west of India. About two-thirds of this area is the outer courtyard, with most of the remaining third taken up by the inner courtyard. There is a Hellenistic style peripteral temple at the end of the outer courtyard opposite the main entrance. This is flanked by two inner gateways leading to the inner courtyard, in the centre of which is the main sanctuary. Unlike the peripteral temple, the layout of this inner sanctuary consists of a series of *iwans* (vaulted halls) and an inner circumambulatory (discussed further below). This has no counterpart in Graeco-Roman architecture, belonging wholly within the Iranian tradition.

The Temple of Anahita at Kangavar is only marginally smaller, and again the emphasis is on a great courtyard (Figure 93). Two lateral stairways ascend a massive stone platform recalling Achaemenid traditions. The perimeter of this platform is surrounded on all four sides by a triple colonnade in a debased Doric order. This colonnade is open to both the

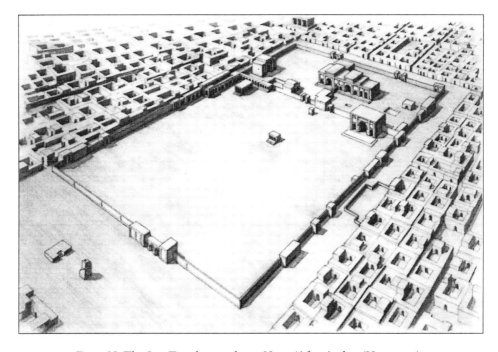

Figure 92 The Sun Temple complex at Hatra (After Andrae/Herrmann)

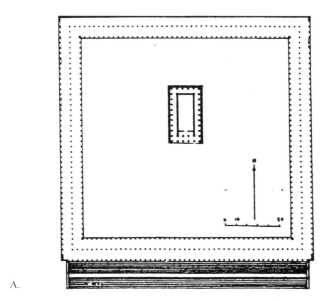

A.

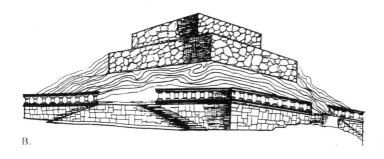

B.

Figure 93 The Temple of Anahita at Kangavar. A: former interpretation (according to Herzfeld). B: new interpretation (according to Kambakhsh Fard)

exterior and interior. The colonnades, furthermore, appear neither to have been roofed nor even joined along the tops: no architraves or similar beams were found in the rubble (unless it was roofed by timber and mud, in the local tradition). One at least of the fallen columns, however, incorporates the springing of an arch,[246] so some of the columns may have been arcaded, perhaps over the entrances. Inside, a vast open space surrounds a sanctuary building. Earlier studies of this monument reconstructed a Hellenistic-style peripteral temple for the sanctuary, based on little more than supposition. Recent archaeological investigations, however, favour two massive superimposed platforms for the sanctuary reconstruction, belonging more to a Mesopotamian tradition.[247]

Another Iranian temple in this tradition is at Khurha, south of Tehran. Very little survives apart from two standing columns in a debased Ionic order. The short length of its stylobate visible today suggests, however, that it too might have formed a part of a temple temenos.

The Hatra temple is generally thought to be second century AD. Dates for Kangavar have been far more divergent. Earlier studies favoured a Seleucid date, with some suggesting an Achaemenid date for the platform. A date in the Parthian period has since been more generally favoured on stylistic grounds, but recent excavations found evidence for major Sasanian construction.[248] However, the colonnaded temenos is close to the style of the great colonnaded temples of Syria and different in almost every respect to Sasanian architecture. Probably, the temple underwent numerous major reconstruction periods, with perhaps a second-century AD date for the temenos colonnade and major Sasanian reconstruction of the sanctuary building inside. Khurha is broadly dated to the Seleucid–Parthian period.

There are obvious Graeco-Roman derivatives in the architecture of these three temples: for example, the peripteral temple and decorative details such as Corinthian pilasters at Hatra, the use of colonnades and Greek orders at all three. These resemblances, however, are superficial. With the overriding emphasis on the temenos and the vast enclosed spaces, these temples clearly belong within the same architectural tradition as those in the Roman East.[249]

This tradition however is not Iranian, Hatra and Kangavar notwithstanding. There are important Iranian elements at both Hatra and Kangavar, the Parthian-style iwans and circumambulatory at Hatra, for example, or the Achaemenid-style platform and staircases at Kangavar. But these, like the Doric and Ionic columns, are not the main element. The vast temenos areas appear as alien to Iranian styles as they are to Graeco-Roman – Iranian religious architecture is more typified by small, enclosed spaces, such as (for the Parthian period) the fire temple at Kuh-i Khwaja.[250] Elsewhere in the Iranian world the only fire temples that are within large enclosures are the sixth-century Soghdian temples, such as the North and South Temples at Panjikent. Both of these are enclosed in colonnaded courtyards, the latter having an additional outer courtyard as a part of a monumental approach that includes inner and outer propylaea and a staircase up to the temple sanctuary.[251] The Soghdian fire-temples, however, whilst firmly a part of an Iranian religious tradition, are probably too far distant (in both time and place) for any architectural connections to be made to Hatra and Kangavar; Iranian fire-temples further west are architecturally quite different.[252] It seems more likely that both the Iranian and the eastern Roman temenos temples belong within a Mesopotamian and Semitic tradition (and one recalls that both Hatra and Kangavar were on the western – Semitic – fringes of the Parthian Empire).

The large temple enclosure has an immensely long history in ancient Near Eastern architecture, particularly in Mesopotamia where the tradition originates in Sumerian architecture.[253] Here, temples are characterised by large courtyards, either surrounding the sanctuary or in front of them. The fourth-millennium 'painted temple' at Tell 'Uqair and the Eanna Temple complex at Uruk, the early third-millennium Oval Temple at Khafaje, the late third-millennium Ur-Nammu Temple precinct at Ur, the early second-millennium Temple of Ishtar-Kititum at Ishchali, the mid-first-millennium Marduk shrine at Babylon, are just some examples (Figure 94). Those at Ur and Babylon are ziggurat complexes.[254] Temple enclosures for sanctuaries have also already been noted in south Arabian architecture.[255]

In Syria and the Levant, most of the earlier large temple enclosures disappeared – or were obscured – under Roman monumentalisation, as they were on sites that were sacred long before the Romans and remained sacred afterwards. The great antiquity of the

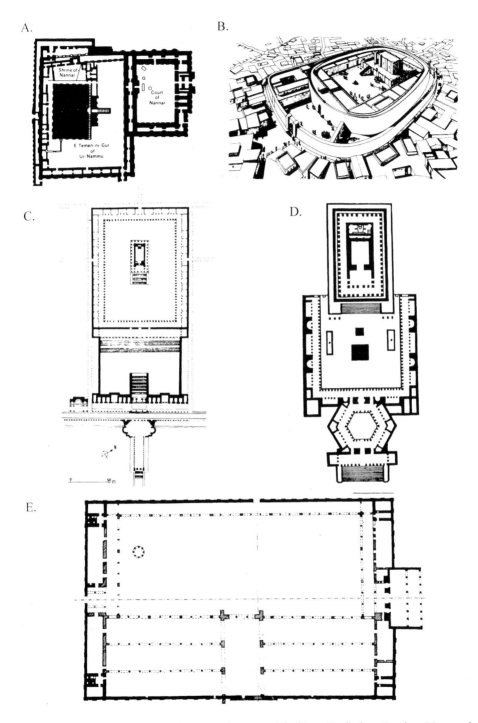

Figure 94 The evolution of the sacred courtyard. A: Ur. B: Khafaje. C: Baalbek. D: Jerash. E: Umayyad
Mosque at Damascus. Not to scale (After Darby, Hawkes, Ragette, Segal, Creswell)

Damascus and Jerusalem temple enclosures has already been noted. The one Levantine temple that has preserved its pre-Roman form is the Temple of Melqart at Amrit, dating from the sixth–fourth centuries BC (Plate 116). Although on a far smaller scale than most of the large temples of the Roman period discussed above, the central element once again is the 'colonnaded' courtyard surrounding a central sanctuary.[256] The great temple enclosures of eastern Roman architecture thus mark the culmination of a very ancient and continuous Near Eastern tradition that is alien to Roman architecture.

The reason for their development was liturgical. In the Graeco-Roman West, a temple needed only to be large enough to house the image of the god (albeit in appropriate splendour) as well as some associated priestly functions. It did not need to accommodate or even to relate much to the public as a whole. In the East, however, participation by the public – a congregation – was as important as housing the image. Virtually all Semitic religions demanded that the entire community gather together on an appointed day for communal worship at the main city temple, a ritual that again goes back to ancient Mesopotamia.[257] Hence, the need for a huge space to house such large numbers. The concept of a congregation is both fundamental and universal to ancient Semitic religion. This demand by Semitic religious ritual for a congregation influenced European architecture with the spread of Christianity, dictating the development of church architecture.[258] When the latest Semitic religion emerged in the Near East at the end of the Roman period with the arrival of Islam, the congregation element remained as one of the new religion's main outward manifestations. It continued to dictate the form that mosque

Plate 116 The Temple of Melqart at Amrit

architecture must take, just as it had dictated the form of the pagan temples. For the central element of the mosque is the courtyard. No building better illustrates both the concept and the development than the Umayyad Mosque at Damascus (Figure 94E). Beginning life as a temple of Hadad in the first millennium BC, it became successively a temple of Jupiter in the early Roman period and a cathedral to John the Baptist in the Christian, before becoming Islam's first great mosque. Throughout, it was the ability of its great courtyard to accommodate large numbers of worshippers that made it entirely appropriate for all four of its incarnations. The enclosure walls of many of the great pilgrimage churches of northern Syria, such as St Simeon Stylites or Qalb Lauzah, also mark a smooth transition into Christian practice of the same tradition.[259]

There was another religious element which might have demanded the evolution of the temple courtyard. This was the Semitic tradition of inviolability. We read, for example, that the sanctuary of Baetococaea (Husn Sulaiman) was made inviolable by both the Seleucids and Ptolemies, and its associated village granted many privileges and exemptions (including tax).[260] This element of inviolability was a very important and ancient one in Arabian religious tradition. It recalls the Arabian tradition of the *haram* or *hawtah* such as existed in pre-Islamic Arabia: Mecca, Najran, Sanʿa, Marib and others.[261] These were sacred enclaves, expressed architecturally as walled enclosures, which acted as neutral, inviolable havens amongst rival tribes or nations (Plate 101). As neutral territory between often warring tribes, these *hawtah* would also act as market-places, where all factions could trade and carry out commerce. Accordingly, it comes as no surprise to learn that inscriptions at the 'inviolable' sacred place of the Temple of Husn Sulaiman also record that it was made a neutral, tax-free market-place.[262] Southern Arabia might seem culturally very distant from the Roman Near East but, before the Macedonian and Roman conquests imparted an east–west political division on the Near East, the entire area was culturally far more unified than the brief, superficial appearance of a few Graeco-Roman art forms might imply. South Arabia is in any case closer than Greece or Rome. Ancient religious and architectural traditions were – and still are – extraordinarily tenacious in this region. The tradition of an inviolate sacred space continued into Christianity: many of the sacred enclosures surrounding some of the pilgrimage churches of north Syria, such as the Church of Bizzos at Ruwayha, were known to be inviolate and places of protection.[263]

Exterior altars

Much of the emphasis on open spaces was linked to the place of altars in eastern temples. They were usually situated in the middle of the temenos, opposite the sanctuary entrance. Indeed, altars often formed as much a focal point to the complex as the sanctuary itself did. Once again this was for mass participation in the worship. The altars often came in for elaborate embellishment and reached monumental proportions: those at the Temple of Bel at Palmyra (Plate 17), the Temple of Zeus at Jerash, and the Temple of Dushara at Petra, for example. The great altar in the temenos at Baalbek was particularly elaborate, built in the form of a tower several storeys high, the exterior decorated with pilasters and the interior having finely coffered ceilings (Figure 95). This altar had the additional function as a sacred high place (discussed below).[264] Qalʿat Faqra has an isolated altar outside the temenos (Plate 117).

Figure 95 The great altar at Baalbek (After Collart and Coupel)

Temple sanctuaries

The sanctuaries would usually be situated in or near the centre of the temenos, such as at the Temples of Bel and Nabu at Palmyra, the Temple of Artemis at Jerash, and the temples at Husn Sulaiman, Sebaste and Amman (Figure 88). Almost as often they would be situated at or near the end of the temenos, such as the 'Great Temple' and Temple of the Winged Lions at Petra, and the temples at Siʿ, Qalʿat Faqra, Mushannaf and Baalbek (Figure 89). This arrangement seems more favoured in Nabataean temples (the first three are Nabataean). At the Temple of Dushara at Petra the sanctuary is to one side of the temenos, at the Temple of Zeus at Jerash the sanctuary is at the centre of the lateral side, and at the Temple of Baal-Shamin at Palmyra the sanctuary has two temenoses on either side. These arrangements are unusual.

The sanctuary buildings themselves would often bear a superficial external resemblance to Roman temple types. Hence, many were peripteral temples: Bel and Nabu at Palmyra, the sanctuaries of Jupiter and 'Bacchus' at Baalbek, the 'Great Temple' at Petra, the sanctuary of Zeus at Jerash, the Helios Temple at Qanawat, and the now vanished temples at Jerusalem, Suwayda and Nablus (Figure 96).[265] Prostyle temples were more popular, in accordance with the general popularity of this form throughout imperial Roman architecture. The Temple of Baal-Shamin at Palmyra, the Temple of Artemis at Jerash, the Temple of Zeus at Qanawat, and the temples at Husn Sulaiman, Qalʿat Faqra, Siʿ, Isriya, Shaikh Barakat, Burj Baqirha and Amman are all prostyle (Figure 97), with the Temple of Dushara at Petra and those at Qasr Rabbah, Diban, Sur, Slim, ʿAtil and

Plate 117 Qal'at Faqra, with the altar in the foreground and tower in the
background

Mushannaf all prostyle *in antis* (Figure 98). Occasionally, temples would have no colonnades, but have only pilasters on the outside. Such are the Philippeion at Shahba and the
temples at Dmayr and Sanamayn (Figure 99).[266]

But there the resemblance with western Roman temples would stop. In many cases,
additional elements were inserted into the sanctuary façades that had no counterpart in
western architecture – indeed, elements that completely affronted the purer Classical forms.
For example, the Temple of Bel at Palmyra had a monumental portal inserted off-centre in
one of its lateral sides, a feature that may derive from Egypt,[267] while the façades of many of
the southern Syrian sanctuaries would be framed with towers or have towers at their tops
(Figure 108). This very un-Classical feature is explored in more detail below ('High places').

More than the exteriors, however, the interiors differed fundamentally from Roman
temples in the West. Many were in the form of circumambulatories, a feature explored in
more detail below. Otherwise, sanctuaries were dominated by a raised platform at one (or
occasionally at either) end, usually approached by a flight of stairs covered by a canopy,
often elaborately decorated. The Temples of Bel at Palmyra (Plate 118), 'Bacchus' at
Baalbek (Figure 100), and the temple at Niha in Lebanon (Plate 119) are particularly
outstanding in this respect. Others with similar elaborate adytons are at Qasr Neba and
Sfira in Lebanon.[268] The reason for such elaboration is that interiors were the throne
room of the deity, and platforms his throne where he received his worshippers in audience, unlike the simpler interiors of Greek or Roman temples which were merely rooms

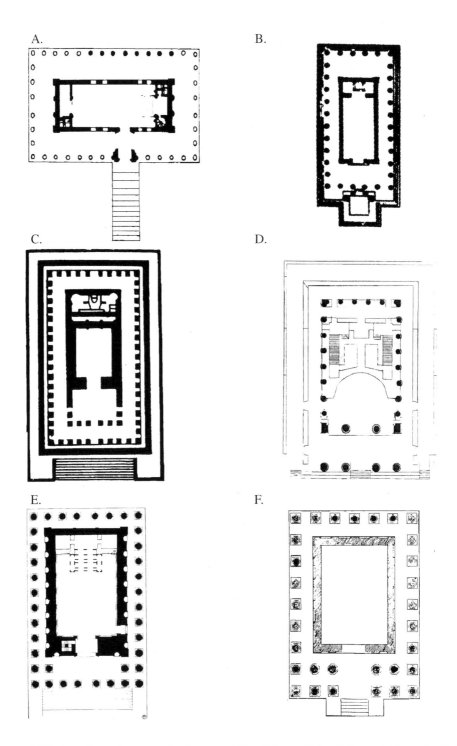

Figure 96 Peripteral temple sanctuaries (not to scale). A: Palmyra-Bel. B: Palmyra-Nabu. C: Baalbek. D: Petra-Great Temple. E: Jerash-Zeus. F: Qanawat-Helios

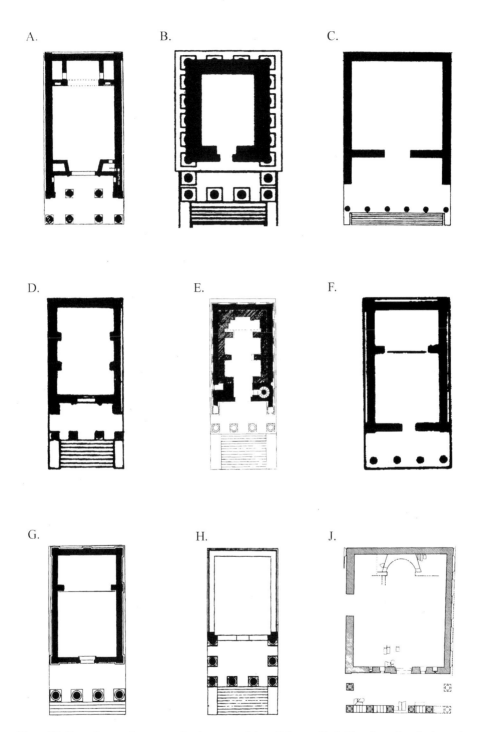

Figure 97 Prostyle temple sanctuaries (not to scale). A: Palmyra-Baal-Shamin. B: Jerash-Artemis.
c: Qanawat-Zeus. D: Husn Sulaiman. E: Qal'at Faqra. F: Si'. G: Isriya. H: Shaikh Barakat.
j: Burj Baqirha

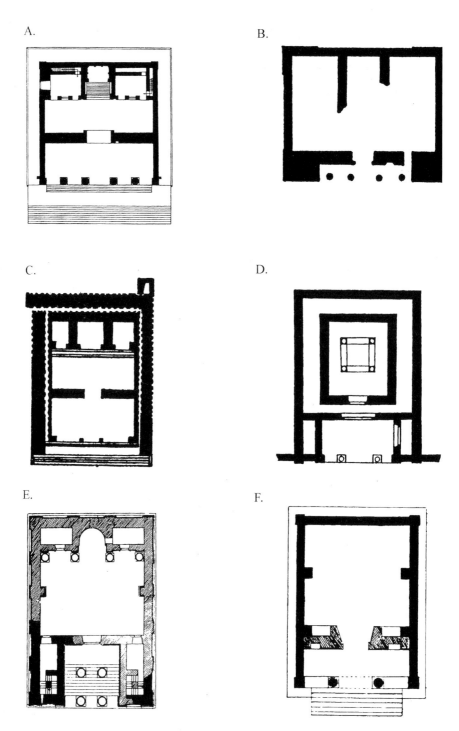

Figure 98 Prostyle *in antis* temple sanctuaries (not to scale). A: Petra-Dushara. B: Rabbah.
C: Diban. D: Sur. E: Slim. F: Mushannaf

A.

B.

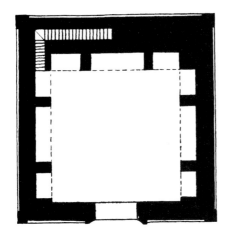

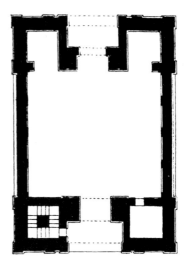

Figure 99 Uncolonnaded temple sanctuaries. A: Shahba. B: Dmayr

Plate 118 The interior adyton of the Temple of Bel at Palmyra

to house his image.[269] For the origins of this we must once more turn to the temple architecture of ancient Mesopotamia. Here, the centre wall or the end of the cella is typically dominated by a dais or platform, exactly like a throne room. Examples exist at Tell Asmar, Khafaja, Tell Agab, Ishchali, Ur, Nimrud and Babylon, ranging from the late fourth to the mid-first millennium BC (Plate 120).[270]

Figure 100 Interior of the 'Bacchus' Temple at Baalbek (After Wiegand)

Many of the cellas were arranged in a tripartite division at their end. Examples can be seen at the Temples of Dushara at Petra, Zeus at Jerash, Baal-Shamin at Palmyra, Zeus at Qanawat, and others at Kedesh, Niha, Tawwan, Qasr Rabbah, Diban, Dmayr, Slim and Sanamayn (Figure 101).[271] Again, the origins of this arrangement lie in ancient Syrian and Mesopotamian prototypes, such as the temples at Tell Achana, Eshnunna, Tell Asmar and Ur (Figure 102).[272] The 'apsidal' arrangement of many of these plans continued in a virtually unbroken tradition into the early Christian architecture of Syria. The cellas of the Temples of Tyche at Sanamayn and Baal-Shamin at Kedesh are remarkably 'church-like' in this respect. Examples are particularly common amongst the churches of north Syria, while church plans in Mesopotamia adhered more closely to the Mesopotamian temple prototypes.[273]

Circumambulatories

There is another, more unusual, sanctuary arrangement in eastern Roman architecture that seems to characterise many Nabataean temples. This consists of an inner chamber surrounded by an outer circumambulatory corridor. This arrangement is neither universal nor exclusive to Nabataean temples – the Temple of Dushara at Petra cited above,

Plate 119 Interior of the temple at Niha

for example, has a tripartite arrangement, and circumambulatories are found in the Roman East outside the Nabataean area. Nevertheless, the arrangement does appear to be a mainly Nabataean type. Examples are the Temples of Baal-Shamin and Dushara at Siʿ, the 'Temple of the Winged Lions' and the 'Great Temple' at Petra, and temples at Khirbet Tannur, Sur, Sahr, Sahir, Khirbet adh-Dharih and Wadi Ramm (Figure 103).[274] Outside the Nabataean area, the sanctuary of 'Temple A' at Hasan Madhur in the desert north-west of Palmyra is in the form of a circumambulatory.[275]

This arrangement has been recognised as Iranian in origin.[276] Comparisons can be drawn with many Parthian-period temples, such as the Temple of the Sun at Hatra, the 'Parthian' Temple at Takht-i Sulaiman in Azerbaijan, Bard-i Nishandeh and Masjid-i Sulaiman in Khuzistan and Kuh-Khwaja in Sistan (Figure 104). It remained a popular form in Sasanian architecture as well. Examples are the Imamzadeh Sayyid Husain fire temple near Bishapur, the Temple of Anahita also at Bishapur, Damghan (Tepe Hisar), Kunar Siah in Fars, Chahar Deh in Khuzistan, Tall-i Ghangi (Farashband 2) in Fars and elsewhere in the Parthian and Sasanian architecture of the Iranian world (Figure 105). The origin might lie in Achaemenid or even Urartian architecture, with examples of the form at Susa in Khuzistan and Altintepe in eastern Anatolia, the latter reused in the Achaemenid period (Figure 106).[277] Virtually all of the Sasanian and many of the Parthian circumambulatories have been interpreted as fire temples, although too little is known about Parthian religion for any attribution to be certain. The reason why such a layout is best suited for fire-temples lies in the ritual of the Zoroastrian religion. The sacred fire is

Plate 120 Interior dais of the Nabu Temple at Nimrud

subject not only to ritual circumambulation, but in some cases must also be hidden from public view, either by a series of baffles or by concentric walls. This is not to imply any form of Iranian Zoroastrianism in Nabataean religion,[278] as a circumambulatory is not solely for fire-worship. Some of the more important Iranian circumambulatory temples did not involve fire-worship, for example the Temple of the Sun at Hatra and the Temple of Anahita at Bishapur. But the architectural influences of this Iranian type of temple on Nabataean architecture are nonetheless convincing. The influence of circumambulatory plans on early Christian architecture is discussed separately below.

High places

A distinctive, but universal, feature of eastern Roman temples with no counterpart in western Roman architecture is the sacred high place. It can take four forms: (1) a staircase to the roof within the sanctuary, (2) one or more towers incorporated into the temple layout, (3) the location of a temple in a naturally elevated position, and (4) an open-air sacred area on top of a naturally elevated position. As often as not, a temple might incorporate more than one form of high place.

The first form, a roof staircase, is found in virtually all extant temples in the Roman East. The only temples where it appears to be absent are those where too little has remained to be certain. Because they are so ubiquitous there is no need to give a complete catalogue here: one study analysed thirty-nine temple plans in Syria, Lebanon and Jordan which have square staircase towers to ritual high places on the roofs. None are

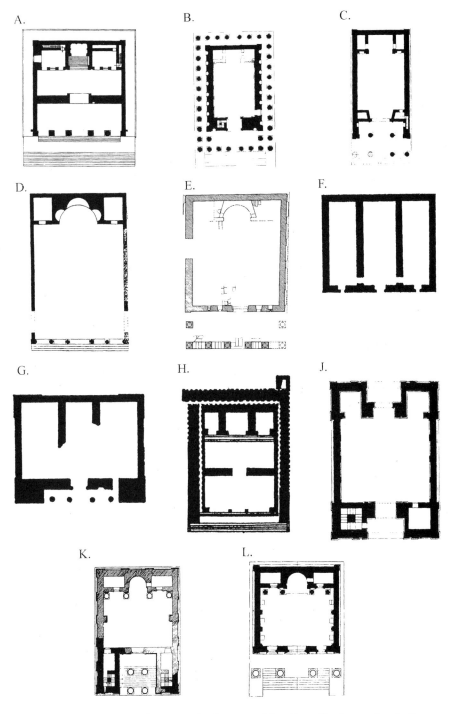

Figure 101 Tripartite temple sanctuaries (not to scale). A: Petra-Dushara. B: Jerash-Zeus.
C: Qanawat-Zeus. D: Qanawat-Seraglio. E: Kedesh. F: Tawwan. G: Rabbah. H: Diban.
J: Dmayr. K: Slim. L: Sanamayn

A.

B.

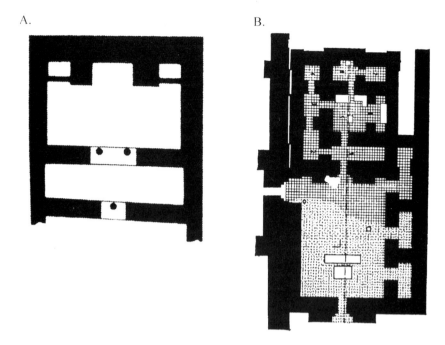

Figure 102 Bronze Age tripartite temple sanctuaries (not to scale). A: Tell Achana. B: Ur.

earlier than the first century BC, and most are second–third centuries AD (Figure 107).[279] To these can be added Nabataean temples at Dat Ra's, Khirbet Tannur, Rabbah, Mhai and Ramm.[280] This need for a high place gave temples a fundamentally different appearance to those in the West: roofs had to be flat (at least in part), unlike the pitched roofs that characterised western temples.[281]

An architecturally far more pleasing effect was provided by the second form of high place, the tower. In temples where roofs remained pitched in accordance with usual Roman architectural practice, the high place would be in the form of a tower rather than a flat area on the roof. The tower might be incorporated either into the sanctuary or the temenos wall. In either case, for aesthetic reasons two towers would be provided, flanking the façade to achieve a highly effective balance – and introduce an entirely new style of building into architecture, as we shall see. Temples with towers incorporated into their sanctuary façades are the Temple of Baal-Shamin at Si' and the temples at Dmayr, Sur and Qasr Rabbah, while those with towers in their temenos façades are Damascus, Baalbek and the Artemis Temple at Jerash (Figure 108).[282]

A temple high place might also simply be implicit in its location on top of a natural eminence. This has already been noted in the discussion on the siting of temples, above. Thus, the temples of Burj Baqirha, Shaikh Barakat, Mt Hermon and Zeus Kasios outside Antioch are located on mountains.[283] Both the Temples of Zeus and Artemis at Jerash are situated on the highest parts of the site, as were the temples at Amman and Pella. Other temples, such as Baalbek, Qal'at Faqra, Husn Sulaiman and Si', are situated in high areas. The monumental approach stairs of many eastern Roman temples, such as the Temple of Artemis at Jerash, have been seen as a part of an overall Roman architectural pattern,[284] but here at least such stairways fit more into the local tradition of high places.

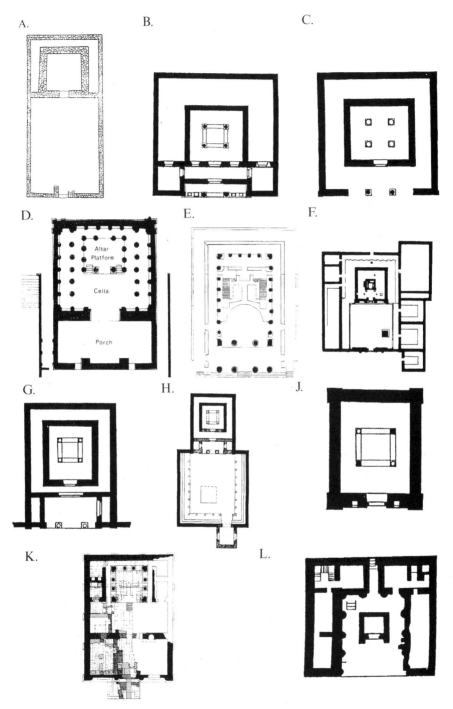

Figure 103 Circumambulatory temples (not to scale). A: Hasan Madbur. B: Siʿ Baal-Shamin.
C: Siʿ Dushara. D: Petra Winged Lions. E: Petra Great Temple. F: Khirbet Tannur. G: Sur.
H: Sahr. J: Sahir. K: Khirbet edh-Dharih. L: Rumm.

A.

B.

C.

D.

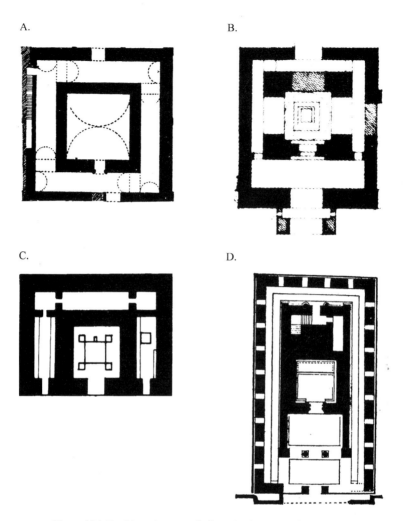

Figure 104 Parthian circumambulatories (not to scale). A: Hatra.
B: Kuh-i Khwaja. C: Surkh Kotal. D: Taxila-Jaulian

The final category are the open-air high places. They are a particular feature at Petra and other Nabataean sites, but they are also common in the limestone terrain around Antioch and the Dead Cities of the north.[285] There are hundreds of them in and around Petra situated on anything from a minor eminence or rock to the peaks of the mountains themselves. These high places are invariably rock-cut and generally consist of an altar table, together with channels and a tank. More elaborate ones might have an additional table and other paraphernalia (Figure 12; Plate 121). Such high places, although open-air, can occasionally have all of the trappings of a major temple complex. The main Petra high place complexes of Umm al-Biyara, al-Khubtha and Jebel Madhbah had quite magnificent rock-cut ways leading up to them. The way up to the latter from the Wadi Farasa has been likened to a processional way, and the whole summit of the peak on which it was situated was isolated from the rest of the ridge by an artificial, rock-cut chasm, approached

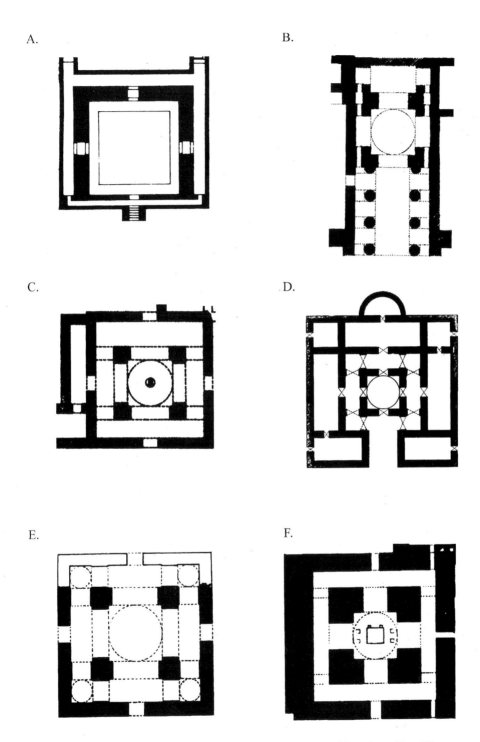

A.

B.

C.

D.

E.

F.

Figure 105 Sasanian circumambulatories. A: Bishapur. B: Sayyid Husain. C: Tepe Hisar.
D: Kunar Siah. E: Chahardeh. F: Farashband 2

A. B.

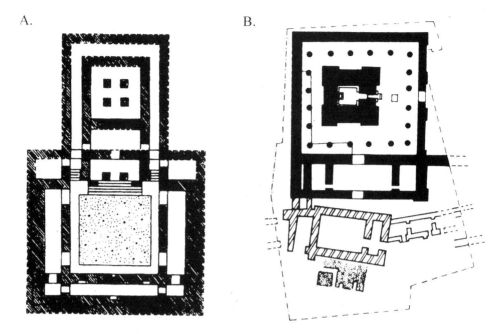

Figure 106 Achaemenid and Urartian circumambulatories. A: Susa. B: Altintepe

through a monumental propylaeum.[286] In the city below, a rather enigmatic monument known as the 'Conway Tower' has been variously interpreted as a fortification and a high place. If it is the latter, it is the only artificial, independent high place so far discovered that is not attached to a temple.[287]

Perhaps the building that most embodies the Nabataean concept of a sacred high place is the temple at Khirbet Tannur.[288] Huge amounts of sculpture were recovered, most of it religious, depicting virtually the entire Nabataean pantheon. The main deity is Atargatis. It is on a commanding position, probably approached by a staircase, overlooking the confluence of two gorges, completely isolated on top of a high hill in the Wadi Hasa (Biblical Zered), without any associated town or settlement. It is even well off the Via Trajana. Khirbet Tannur may have been a Nabataean national shrine, of more than purely local significance. It was in use over several hundred years, undergoing modifications and adaptations in the process, beginning late second or early first century BC. The very elaborate Period II (end of the first century BC) altar in the inner shrine, although subject to Graeco-Roman architectural decoration, was in the form of a cube, hearkening back to the simpler, more basic forms of Nabataean religious architecture. In Period III (first quarter of second century AD) the inner shrine was rebuilt, still in the form of a cube, but with the altar placed on the roof approached by a staircase on the side of the shrine. This altar again was cuboid. The whole complex was probably open to the sky; no evidence was found that it was roofed over. The apparent Hellenism of the sculptures and the deities that they depict is only superficial.

The sacred high place is, therefore, a feature of ancient Syrian and Arabian religious ritual. Whilst it enjoys a particularly high profile in Nabataean religious architecture, the prevalence of high places elsewhere as far north as Antioch indicates that it was both

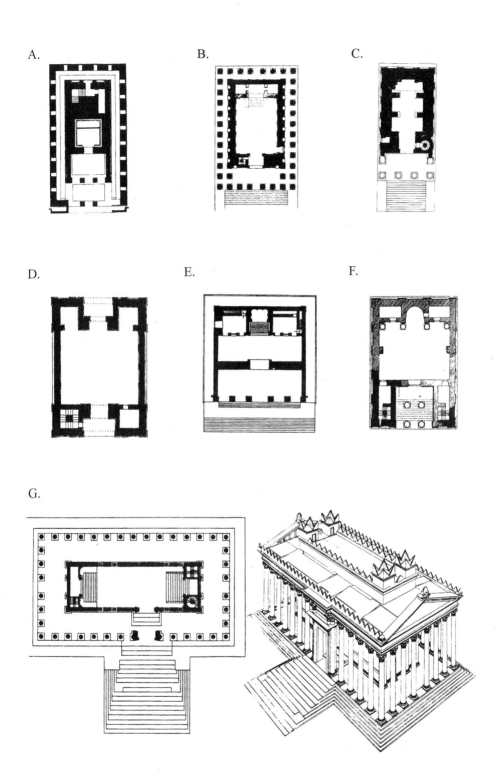

Figure 107 Temple sanctuaries with spiral staircases (not to scale). A: Taxila. B: Jerash-zeus. C: Isriya.
D: Dmayr. E: Petra–Dushara. F: Slim. G: Palmyra–Bel (with reconstruction)

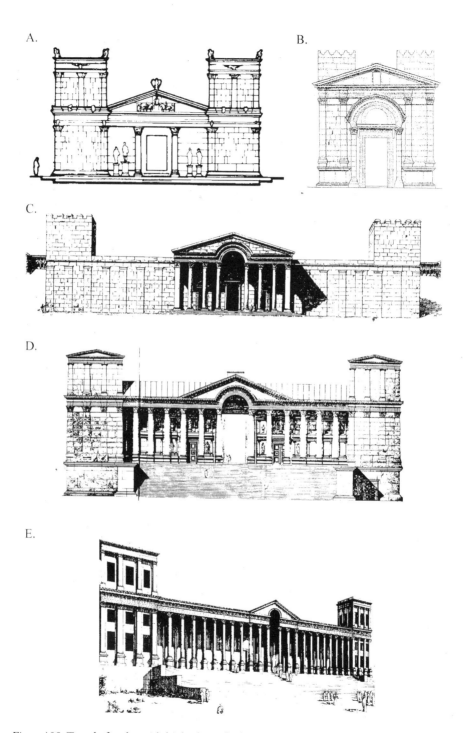

Figure 108 Temple façades with high places flanking a pediment (not to scale). A: Siʿ. B: Dmayr. C: Damascus. D: Baalbek. E: Jerash (After Butler, Klimkott, Dussaud, Wiegand, Browning)

Plate 121 The Madhbah high place at Petra

essential and universal to the non-Judaeo-Christian religious architecture of the Near East. The origin of the high place in religious architecture has been traced to Taxila,[289] but one authority sees it as originating in the Hellenistic architecture of Judaea.[290] Iran has a rich tradition of ancient sacred high-place architecture related to Zoroastrianism, but this might be entirely separate from the Near Eastern tradition.[291] As with so many of the other architectural peculiarities we have reviewed, the origin is probably in ancient Mesopotamia. Here, the importance of sacred high places was almost as prevalent as in Syria. It was given architectural expression in the ziggurat. Ziggurats developed as early as about 5000 BC from temples situated on artificial platforms, which over the millennia grew in both height and elaboration until by about 2100 BC they had achieved the familiar stepped pyramid form of Ur and elsewhere (Plate 122). The largest known ziggurat was the thirteenth-century BC Elamite one at Chogha Zanbil in south-western Iran.[292] Syria and the Levant received so many basic cultural stimuli from Mesopotamia (the use of the cuneiform script, for example) that other links between the two regions appear self-evident. It must be pointed out, of course, that no ziggurats have been identified further west than Tell Leilan and Mari, both in the far east of Syria.[293] But artificial high places, such as ziggurats, would be unnecessary in the Levantine area, amply endowed as it is with mountains and hills.

The ritual associations of high places, particularly in Nabataean architecture where they are most prevalent, have been examined elsewhere here.[294] Whatever their associations, the symbolic importance of high places in ancient Semitic religious architecture proved tenacious, as elements survived in both Christian and Muslim architecture. Many of the temples incorporated two high-place towers on either side of their façades as we

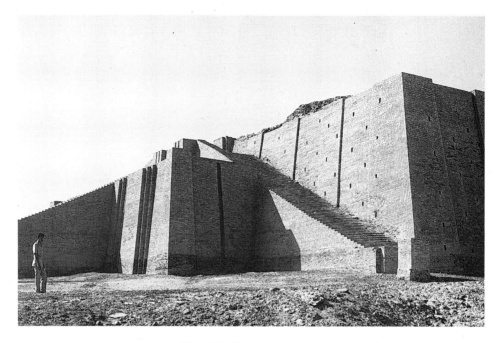

Plate 122 The ziggurat at Ur

have seen, with a Classical pediment between them above the entrance (Figure 108). The Temple of Baal-Shamin at Si˚ and the Baalbek propylaeum are good examples of this aesthetically very pleasing arrangement. In the early Christian architecture of Syria, the arrangement was incorporated into church façades. For example, the churches at Ruwayha, Ma'rata, Turmanin, Karratin, Qalb Lauzah, al-Bara, Behyo and the St Simeon Stylites Baptistery had two towers flanking their entrances.[295] The arrangement seems to have been equally popular in the pre-sixth-century churches of Palestine, as many such churches are depicted on the Madaba Map, for example at St Elisha, St Jonah and Mampsis.[296] The same arrangement is depicted in mosaics at Umm Qays and Khirbet Mukhayyat in Jordan.[297] The façades of the Church of Bizzos at Ruwayha and the church at Qalb Lauzah are particularly fine examples of this arrangement, incorporating also the triangular pediment between them as at Baalbek and Si˚. It has been tentatively suggested that the adoption of these towers in the church architecture of the East was for the rite of *incubatio*, where a pilgrim might sleep in the presence of a saint's relics to acquire healing or holiness.[298] Whatever the function, the form was in turn incorporated into medieval European church architecture, where the arrangement defined the façades of many of Europe's greatest cathedrals for over a thousand years (Figure 109). The thousands of pilgrims who flocked each year to the holy sites of the Near East easily explains the transference back to Europe.

Another major Syrian temple which incorporated high place towers at the corners of its temenos was the Temple of Jupiter-Hadad at Damascus (Figure 35, Plate 42). We have already seen how this became one of the more pivotal buildings of Middle Eastern architecture as a whole, with the temenos becoming the mosque courtyard so essential to Islamic architecture. When this ancient temenos was incorporated into Islam's first great

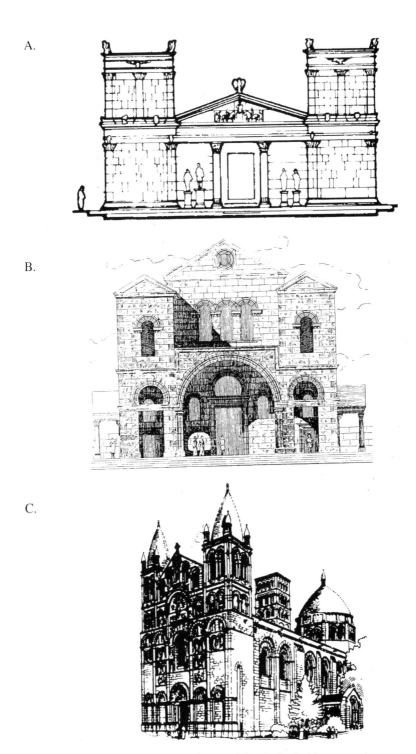

A.

B.

C.

Figure 109 The evolution of the pedimented façade flanked by towers (not to scale). A: Siʿ. B: Ruwayha. C: Angoulême (After Butler, Bannister Fletcher)

mosque by the Caliph al-Walid in 711, there were no minarets in Islamic architecture. Formerly, the call to prayer had been given from roofs or other convenient high places. The four towers of the temenos, former sacred high places of the pagan temple, accordingly became the very first minarets of Islamic architecture.[299] Thus, the latest Semitic religion's most conspicuous architectural feature marks an unbroken continuity of the use of the ancient Semitic high place down to the present.

Early Christian architecture

The basilica[300]

Of all standing remains in the area of the ancient Roman East today, churches probably outnumber all other types of public building – some 1,200 have been counted in the Dead Cities region alone.[301] There are a number of reasons for this. The late Roman period was an ecclesiastical age above all, with all the arrogance of a new-found religion adopted by the world's greatest power. This resulted in an explosion of Christian building throughout the empire. But in the East there was an added dimension: it was the birthplace of this new world religion. Little wonder that it left so many buildings behind to remind us of this.

Apart from religious architecture, the advent of Christianity is not marked by the need for any new types of public buildings, styles of architecture or even administrative centres: the old cities and towns merely continued. Yet there are a number of subtle but significant changes in tone between pagan and Christian architecture. Pagan architecture has a grandioseness – a scale and a massiveness – that Christian architecture, for all its new-found religious certainties, never approaches (except in Constantinople itself). The architecture of the pagan period – the great temple complexes, the ordered streets, the massive baths, the forests of columns – states an arrogant self-confidence, an unquestioning belief in the superiority of its own culture in a way that Christian architecture cannot match. The greatest of cathedrals in the Near East never approached in scale or concept the great pagan temple enclosures. Even much of the building materials they used were second-hand, taken from the earlier pagan buildings; construction was often second-rate, even shoddy.

There is, therefore, a paradox in the Christian architecture of the East. On the one hand we have a new religion, a new Christian civilisation with all of the vigour, certainties and confidence of its infancy. There was at least as much wealth as there had been in the pagan period – the evidence from the countryside reviewed in Chapter 6 demonstrates that – so mere money was no object. There was also ample patronage – indeed, the monolithic, universal Church of the Roman Empire was in a far stronger position as patron than the individual cities which patronised the building of the great temples. On the other hand, we have the shoddy buildings. Why?

In fact Christian architecture quite simply *did* match pagan architecture, but in quantity rather than quality. Previously, only the major cities and the occasional smaller towns could afford a large religious complex: the number of temple remains in the Roman East today, whilst impressive, is still less than a hundred, and probably never numbered much more, Christian and Muslim destruction notwithstanding. But the remains of churches number in the thousands. With the new Christian civilisation, every town had not merely one religious building but many. And not only the major towns but virtually every village could boast a church, sometimes several. The pagans never matched that. This reflects the more even dissemination of wealth throughout the region, rather than simply being concentrated in the cities, that we have noted in our review of the countryside in Chapter 6. It also reflects the greater emphasis that Christianity makes on mass participation. Both factors are manifestations of a greater 'democratisation' that occurred in the civilisation of the Roman East after the fourth century.

There is a further difference between pagan and Christian architecture, subtle but again important – and again revealing a paradox. Underneath the Roman architectural veneer of the great pagan buildings, native Near Eastern forms emerged, as we have seen. But in Christian architecture, these elements seem to recede once more. The bold, probably native, trabeate forms that feature so prominently in the temple architecture of the Roman East give way to the very non-Eastern, rounded arceate forms of Byzantine church architecture; the great open spaces of the temple complexes give way to the equally non-eastern enclosed, internal spaces of the basilicas that appear almost poky in comparison. Despite the eastern origins of the religion, the architecture of Christianity seems to lie uneasily beneath eastern skies.[302]

Why, therefore, if the religion was so eastern, was its architecture so very western? The reasons for this apparent paradox probably lie in the nature of Christianity and Christendom itself. Paganism by its very nature could allow for many alien beliefs: Roman gods were simply equated with native ones, and Roman architectural vocabulary could coexist with non-Roman architectural concepts quite harmoniously. But the monotheistic nature of Christianity was by definition far more exclusive: other religions – and religious forms – could not be embraced. With the adoption of Christianity by the Roman emperors, the temporal capital of Christendom would no longer be Jerusalem or even Damascus or Antioch, but Rome and Constantinople. The architectural forms of Christendom henceforth emanated from the West, not the East.

To trace this process, it is necessary to understand the nature of religion in the Roman world. This is explored more fully below.[303] For the moment, it is sufficient to understand that Roman religion had two quite distinct parts: the public religion of the state and the private religion of individuals.[304] It was for the former that the great temples were built: in the West, the temples to Rome and Augustus, the Capitoline Triad, or the deified emperor; in the East, to the city patron deities. For private religion, small chapels were all that were required, as they did not demand any state function. These might only be a special room in a house put aside for the purpose, or even just an altar in a part of the room. At most, such 'chapels' would simply be modest buildings within a community that hardly differed from the ordinary domestic buildings around them. They stood in direct contrast to the great temples of public religion. To this 'private religious sector' belonged all of the non-public religions of the Roman world: private and professional deities, mystery cults, oriental cults such as those of Isis or Mithras, and so forth. Christianity entered this latter category merely as one of many such cults, in direct contrast – and eventual conflict – with the public religion.

Initially, therefore, before its adoption as the official religion of the empire, Christianity hardly needed a formal 'architecture', but belonged within the domestic vernacular of the other cults. But Christianity differed from the others in one essential respect: it demanded that all members of its community participate in communal, and not merely individual, worship. The introduction of the concept of a congregation posed new demands upon religious architecture: henceforward a religious building had to be a meeting place in addition to a cultic building. At first, when Christianity was just a small, minority religion, this did not demand large buildings. Rather like a modern small group – be it religious, political or social – the first Christians met in the private house of a member of their community. The first 'church architecture', therefore, would simply have been a private house or even just a room in a private house. A little later, when Christian architecture became more formalised, the first churches resembled private houses. Indeed, the world's very first definitely identified 'church' is almost indistinguishable from the ordinary houses of the neighbourhood: the Dura Europos church, dated AD 231.[305] In the Dead Cities region a number of other similar house-churches have been identified, the earliest probably early fourth century.[306]

With the growth in Christianity and consequent growth in the demand for a meeting place, the congregation did exactly what a similar modern group would do when its membership increased: it moved out of the home and into the local hall. The almost universal form of local hall or meeting place in the Roman world was the basilica.

It was this wholly eastern demand for a meeting place – a place of congregation – that first shaped the more monumental forms of Christian architecture. Such a concept was a completely alien one to western religious architecture up until that time, but was fundamental and almost universal to Semitic religions – the religious concept of the congregation dictated the great temple enclosures of the East, as we have seen. Hence, pagan temples in the West (at least at first) could not be converted to Christian use. Apart from the natural abhorrence the first Christians would have felt for the temples of their oppressors, there would have been strong resistance from the still influential pagan establishment, even after Christianity was tolerated. But more importantly, the demands of a pagan temple were quite different from those of a Christian church. A temple was merely the earthly house of a god, requiring only a cella to house the image and associated ritual functions: quite simply, it was *too small*. The only public building in Roman cities that met this requirement was the basilica. The basilical form then became the standard, virtually universal form of Christian religious architecture.

The form of these Christian basilicas adhered to a fairly strict layout with little variation. Thus, the 'standard' basilica consisted of a nave flanked by two aisles with an apse facing east at one end and an entrance room or narthex at the other. Outside there would usually be a small courtyard or atrium and the interior would often be lit by clerestory windows, formed by the greater height of the nave above its flanking aisles. This basic layout formed the standard pattern of churches for many hundreds of years, in some cases – particularly in the East – to this day. But these 'rules' only became set in about the fourth century. Before then the earliest basilicas did not adhere so rigidly to these forms, and displayed a refreshing experimentation.[307] But the Church, as soon as it became established, seemed to impose as rigid an interpretation on its architectural forms as it did on its dogma, so that by the end of the fourth century most churches followed the same general pattern, with even cathedrals differing from small country churches only in scale. The basilica assumed its conventional form, subject only to minor local variations largely dictated by liturgical custom.

The basilical form, therefore, originated in the West and developed into the architectural expression of a universal religion. But even in this most 'western' of buildings, it was solely the demands made by the practice of an eastern religion that affected both the decision to adopt such western architectural forms and its subsequent development. If architecture can be defined as an expression of concept, demand and function, the basilica is a product of eastern as much as western architecture.

The martyrium

If basilicas appear to conform to as rigid a layout as the dogma which dominated them, there was another type of religious building in the Christian East that was less staid. This is the martyrium. With the founder of the religion being martyred – not to mention the many who subsequently suffered a similar fate during the persecutions – buildings that commemorated martyrdom naturally assumed considerable importance as a separate type. In architectural and functional terms this represented an entirely new departure that, unlike the demand for meeting halls and the evolution of the basilica, had no precedents in either the secular or religious architecture of the pagan past: entirely new forms could be developed. Hence, martyria are often architecturally far more refreshing than the basilicas, representing new ideas and experimentation. Since they marked a holy place, rather than merely a convenient area to assemble, the place itself became the focal point, i.e., martyria usually followed a central plan. This allowed far greater innovation. Eventually, this central plan was adopted for many churches, providing a welcome variation on the more conventional basilical theme. They were often – indeed usually – domed, which in itself called for the development of new concepts and techniques culminating in the immense domed structures of Constantinople. Plans could be a simple circle or more elaborate variations: octagonal, quatrefoil, square, or even combinations of all three. The quatrefoil plan became especially popular in the sixth century, and survives at Bosra, Ezra'a, Apamaea, Aleppo (the Madrasa Halawiya), and Rasafa (Figure 110). Combinations were particularly popular: inner and outer octagons such as St George's at Ezra'a have exedrae on four sides of the outer octagon to give a quatrefoil impression; the cathedral at Bosra has an inner octagonal colonnade in an outer circular plan with four exedrae to provide a quatrefoil, the whole encased in a square; the Church of St Simeon Stylites is based on an octagon in a square with small exedrae at each corner to form a quatrefoil, in turn surrounded by four basilicas to form an immense cross (Figure 53).[308]

The tradition of inner and outer central plans for martyria seems to have developed in late antique Syria. Its derivation from the Nabataean circumambulatory temple plan – in turn derived from an Iranian type of plan – that has been reviewed above seems plausible. Once again, the comparisons with Indian circumambulatories are very striking. Many circular *chaitya* halls of early Buddhist architecture appear virtual 'classic' Christian martyria. The excavated fourth–third century BC Mauryan Buddhist shrine at Bairat, for example, consisting of a circular hall enclosing an inner colonnaded circumambulatory, bears a startling (if superficial) resemblance to many early Christian martyria in the east, such as the Constantinian rotunda in the Church of the Holy Sepulchre in Jerusalem (Figure 111).[309] The resemblance is not as illusory as the comparison between two buildings so far apart in space, time and culture might initially suggest.[310] The reverence of relics and ritual circumambulation – of both relics and images – are features of the practice of both religions, and the Iranian–Nabataean medium for the transmission a real one. Such an emphasis on circumambulation naturally creates a demand for centrally planned buildings. The plan of the eighth-century Dome of the Rock in Jerusalem is directly inspired by the martyria plans of Christian architecture in Syria, although this building is an exception in Islamic architecture.[311]

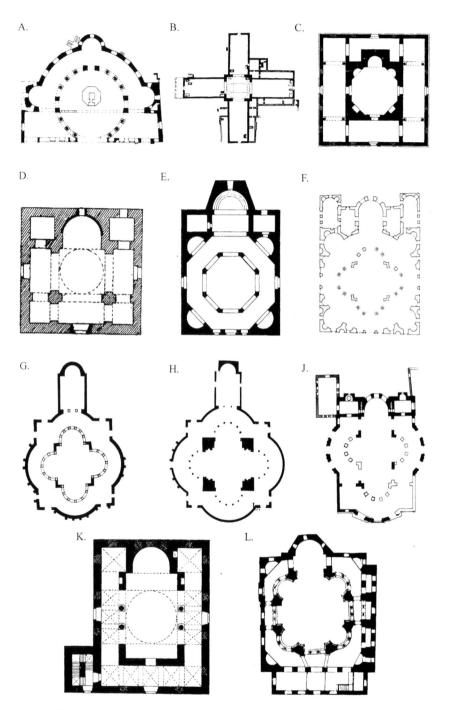

Figure 110 Centrally planned churches (not to scale). A: The Anastasius Rotunda in Jerusalem.
B: Antioch St Babylas. C: St Simeon Baptistry. D: al-Andarin. E: Ezra'a. F: Bosra.
G: Seleucia. H: Apamaea. J: Rasafa martyrium. K: Qasr Ibn Wardan.
L: Constantinople SS Sergius and Bacchus.

A.

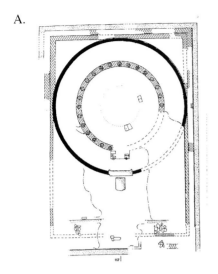

B.

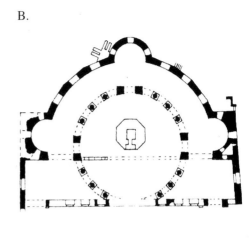

Figure 111 The third-century BC Buddhist *caitya* hall at Bairat in India (after Piggot) compared to the fourth-century AD rotunda at the Church of the Holy Sepulchre (not to scale) (After Corbo/Krautheimer).

Funerary architecture

An immense diversity of tombs survive in the East reflecting a variety of influences. In the north, columns in the Classical style were popular, either singly, in pairs or as a tetrapylon, as were pyramids recalling Egyptian styles. Domes were also fairly common, whilst gabled mausolea sitting on the tops of high plinths are reminiscent of Anatolian forms. Palmyra and the desert areas produced the tomb-tower, one of the most distinctive of funerary buildings. In all areas, rock-cut tombs were popular, either as underground hypogea or as façades, the latter form reaching its height in Petra. Greek, Roman, Anatolian, Assyrian, Persian, Egyptian and ancient Arabian styles were intermingled freely, almost indiscriminately. More than any other type of building, funerary architecture reflected both individuality and regionalism as well as syncretism and internationalism.

Pyramids, temples and columns

The pyramid form has obvious Egyptian derivations but, unlike in Egypt, it was used as a canopy to a tomb rather than for the tomb itself. Surprisingly, they occur mostly in the north of Syria, and are virtually absent in the south and the Nabataean areas where Egyptian influence might otherwise be more expected. Pyramid-roofs characterise the monumental tombs of al-Bara in north Syria, dating mainly from the fifth and sixth centuries (Figure 112, Plates 54, 71, 123 and 124). These are often of considerable proportions and magnificently decorated, and often well preserved. Two more can be seen in the nearby ruined towns of Bauda and Serjilla and there are two more at Kokanaya. At Khirbet Hass there is a particularly fine one that was surrounded by a two-storeyed peripteral colonnade, and a similar one dated to the end of the first century BC/beginning of the first century AD has recently been discovered at Jerash. The one at Jerash and another (now destroyed) at Suwayda are the only pyramid-roofed tombs known outside

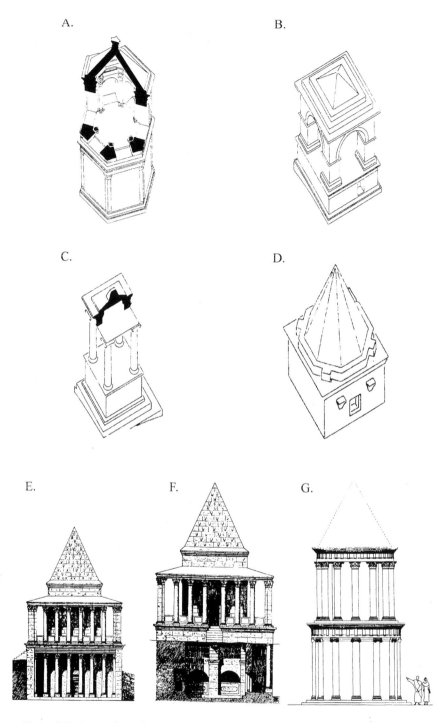

A.   B.

C.   D.

E.   F.   G.

Figure 112 Pyramid-roof tombs (not to scale). A: Cyrrhus. B: Barad. C: Dana (north).
D: Qal'at Kalota. E: Khirbet Khass. F: Dana (south). G: Jerash. (After Tchalenko,
Butler, Seigne)

Plate 123 Octagonal tomb with a pyramid roof at Cyrrhus

northern Syria. Another pyramid-roofed tomb dated 324 at Dana (south) has a columned portico on one side. Related to the pyramid canopies are the polygonal roofs. These are used on a second–third century hexagonal tomb at Cyrrhus and a sixth-century square Tomb of Mariam at Qal'at Kalota. Pyramid-roofs also occur on top of tetrapylon tombs. That at Dana (north) is second century, Barad is seventh century, Dana (south – the Tomb of Olympian) is third or fourth century.[312]

The Barad tetrapylon tomb, apart from its pyramid, more closely follows the urban tetrapylon reviewed above, consisting of four arches springing from piers. At the other two the canopies are supported on four columns rather than piers. Columns were popular to mark tombs elsewhere in north Syria, usually in pairs. Examples are the Tomb of Isodotos dated AD 152 at Sitt ar-Rum, the Tomb of Aemilius Reginus dated AD 195 at Qatura, a second-century AD tomb at Benabil and the mid-second-century AD tomb of Alexandros at Sarmada in the same area (Figure 113, Plate 94). The Tomb of Sosandros dated AD 134 at Beshindlaya is marked by a single column. Significantly, all of these column tombs are close to the later column-cult centre of St Simeon Stylites. All of the column tombs form markers for underground hypogea.[313]

Plate 124 Pyramid roof tomb at al-Bara

Tombs in the form of houses or temples feature throughout Syria. The grandest is the funerary temple in the form of a prostyle temple, with a crypt underneath, that marks the western terminus of the main colonnaded street at Palmyra (Plate 125). Elsewhere at Palmyra there is a particularly fine house tomb, the Qasr al-Abyath ('White Palace'), beyond the end of the valley, and an almost perfectly intact one, the Tomb of Marona, just to the north of the city walls. This latter was built by Julius Aelius Marona in AD 236 and is more consistent with Roman funerary practice.[314] At Ruwayha there is a perfectly preserved tomb in the form of a distyle temple (Plate 126).[315]

Tower tombs

The tower tombs are a feature of Palmyra[316] having no parallel with the Roman architecture of the West. They form the earliest type of funerary monument at Palmyra, so that by the mid-second century AD they had generally gone out of fashion, being replaced by underground tombs, or hypogea. The earlier popularity of such an unusual custom as burying one's dead in towers is perhaps related to the ancient Semitic practice of sacred high places. A tower tomb would be built just for a specific family (albeit an extended family, the largest holding up to 400 burials). Typically, it would be several storeys in height, each storey consisting of tiers of loculi ranged around the room, each loculus sealed by a stone slab usually depicting the occupant in relief. The interiors would usually

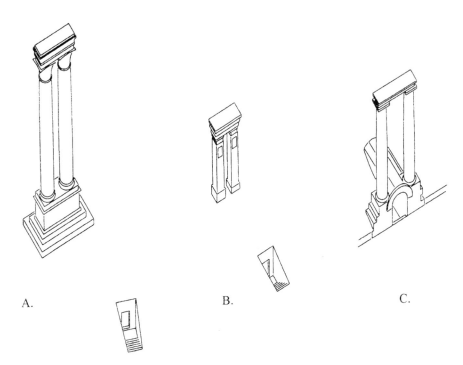

A.   B.   C.

Figure 113 Pillar tombs. A: Sarmada. B: Sitt ar-Rum. C: Qatura (After Tchalenko)

Plate 125 The temple tomb at Palmyra

Plate 126 Temple tomb at Ruwayha

be lavishly decorated in carved relief, and often painted as well, demonstrating in death as much as in life the wealth of a particular family.

The best tower tombs are along the foot of Umm al-Bilqis hill in Palmyra (Plate 127). They are all tombs of notable Palmyrene families, identified by inscriptions. The tallest, a four-storey tower with an exceptionally fine interior, is known as the Tomb of Iamlichu (Iamblichus) from an inscription dated AD 83. At the end of the valley is one of the best preserved, the Tomb of Elahbel dated AD 103, housing the prominent Maani family.

Tower tombs can also be found on the fringes of Palmyrene territory: at Hatra, Halabiya, Dura Europos, Edessa, Sirrin and Emesa. At the religious complex at Qalʿat Faqra in Mt Lebanon, one of the buildings has been interpreted as a tomb tower (Plate 117). The *Chronicle of Edessa* refers to a funerary tower being built in AD 88/9 by King Abgar VI, and the existence of several tomb towers around Urfa today attest to the tradition in Edessan territory.[317] One of the rock-cut 'god-blocks' at the entrance to Petra has been interpreted as a tomb tower because of a grave shaft cut into the top of it (Plate 133).[318] However, there are no other examples of tomb towers in Nabataean territory; they seem to form a distinctly Palmyrene type.

Although no tomb towers are found along or near the coast (apart from the one cited above at Qalʿat Faqra), it is possible that the tower form derives from Phoenician funerary architecture. Amrit, one of the few Phoenician sites which escaped the Romanisation that all but eclipsed Phoenician remains elsewhere, preserves some of the most important Phoenician monuments on the Levantine coast. Amrit, therefore, is remarkable for preserving pre-Classical forms of Semitic religious architecture, without the Classical veneer that nearly all Semitic monuments were subsequently subjected to. Chief of these are two fourth-century BC funerary monuments, known as *al-Maghazil* or 'the spindles'. They consist of square pedestals surmounted by monolithic cylinders, 4 and 7 metres high

Plate 127 Tower tombs at Palmyra

respectively, each further surmounted by a pyramid on the smaller one and a hemisphere on the larger (Plate 128). The area is surrounded by ancient quarries and more funerary monuments. They include a free-standing monolithic mausoleum carved entirely out of the bedrock and containing several chambers, and another cube-shaped mausoleum surmounted by a pyramid. Another tower, the *Burj al-Bazzaq* or 'Tower of the Snails', consists of a black mausoleum in the shape of a cube. It has two superimposed burial chambers and was originally surmounted by an obelisk, the remains of which have fallen below (Plate 129). Another cubic block is nearby, and another fallen obelisk lies further to the south.[319]

The immensely rich and varied funerary architecture of North Africa derives from the Amrit style, for this type of monument was taken by the Phoenicians to their North African colonies. Here, a vast range of tower-like Libyan, Punic and Roman funerary monuments were built over a period of many centuries. Particularly fine examples survive at Dougga, Maktar and Haidra, and another has recently been restored at Sabratha. The most extraordinary are to be found in the necropoleis surrounding the desert settlement of Ghirza in Libya, where a variety of tombs survive.[320]

Underground tombs

The main category of tomb in the Roman East is the underground hypogeum. These have been found associated with virtually every Roman town in the Near East, often in considerable numbers. Many, such as those at Pella, have been found still intact and it has been possible to record the tombs and their contents fully. Some particularly fine underground tombs decorated with superb wall paintings depicting mythological and other scenes have been found at Tyre.[321] Many of the other tomb types enumerated above – column tombs, for example – are associated with underground hypogea. There are far too many to describe here, and they do not differ substantially from Roman hypogea in the

Plate 128 The *al-maghazil* tombs at Amrit

Plate 129 The *burj al-bazzaq* tomb at Amrit

West, so it is not necessary to go into any detail. They do, however, have a very ancient native pedigree, so do not necessarily represent the Roman tradition that they appear to.[322]

The Palmyrene hypogea form a special category.[323] They are generally later than the tower tombs, and are usually cross-shaped or T-shaped, entered from one end by a staircase descending into the ground. One of the finest is the Hypogeum of the Yarhai, now reconstructed in the Damascus Museum. The most impressive is the Hypogeum of the Three Brothers, dating from the middle of the second century (Figure 114), in the southwestern necropolis. On descending a staircase, the tomb is entered through a beautifully carved stone door with inscriptions of the three brothers Male, Saadai and Naamain. Inside are sixty-five recesses, each containing six loculi – a burial capacity totalling an astonishing 360. It is constructed from brick barrel vaults, which are plastered over and painted with frescos. These depict various Greek mythological scenes that combine Hellenistic and Parthian styles. In the right arm of the tomb are three particularly fine sarcophagi with reclining figures on top of them.[324]

Indeed, an immense wealth of the distinctive art of Palmyra has been preserved in the funerary architecture: frescos, fabrics, portrait reliefs, and sculptures of entire families. We

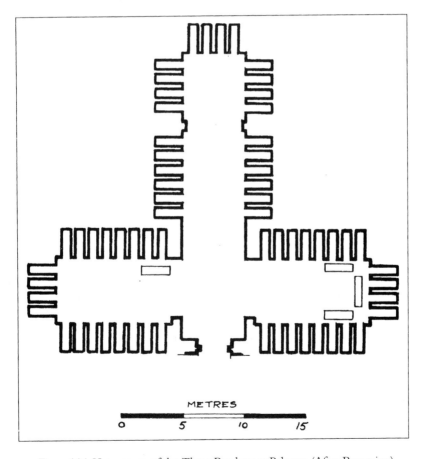

METRES

Figure 114 Hypogeum of the Three Brothers at Palmyra (After Browning)

369

not only know the names of the people who built and lived in Palmyra, but their appearance as well. The sculptures depict a lifestyle that was as happy and as urbane as anywhere in the world – it is certainly not a desert art depicting a provincial backwater away from the mainstreams of culture. The remarkable state of preservation of Palmyrene art is due to the stable conditions of the underground tombs.[325]

Tomb façades

Rock-cut tomb façades had a long history in the East before the Romans. They are particularly prevalent in Anatolia, especially on the Lycian coast where they form the most characteristic type of tomb (along with the house tomb). The most famous are at Fethiye, ancient Termessos, and others exist at Pinara, Xanthos, Kas and elsewhere.[326] Rock-cut façades also characterise the funerary architecture of Phrygia, most notably at Midas Sehri.[327] Elsewhere in Anatolia, the royal tombs of the Pontic kings at Amasya are carved from a cliff face. The Pontic kings were Iranian, so their tombs may be related to the rock-cut tombs of the Achaemenid kings at Naqsh-i Rustam near Persepolis, from whom the Pontic kings traced their descent. But both the Pontic and the Persian royal tombs are probably related ultimately to the Lycian style, one of the strongest and most pervasive forms of funerary architecture in the East.

Anatolia, however, lies generally outside the scope of this book, and its funerary architecture is only cited for its influence elsewhere. In the area under discussion, rock-cut tomb façades are (with one outstanding exception) comparatively rare. There are a few third-century tombs cut into the rock face at Yabrud north of Damascus. The necropolis of the town of Rafada, west of Aleppo, consists of many tombs cut into a rock face at the nearby village of Qatura.[328] Elsewhere in the Dead Cities and the Lebanon mountains, rock-cut tombs tend to be in the form of underground hypogea rather than cliff façades, despite a very vigorous tradition of carving from bedrock.

The 'outstanding exception' is, of course, Petra, which probably boasts the most famous rock façades in the world. More Nabataean rock-cut tomb façades are at Medain Saleh, ancient Hegra, now in Saudi Arabia. They are well enough known not to require describing in any detail here.[329] Very broadly, they can be divided into two categories for present purposes (although they have been subdivided into many more for the purposes of chronological and architectural analysis). The first comprise by far the bulk of the tombs at Petra and all at Medain Saleh. These are the simpler façades, usually exhibiting predominantly native Semitic architectural features. 'Assyrian'-style crow-step merlons, either repeated in a single or double line across the top of a façade or simply as a pair delineating the top, are universal. Flaring 'Egyptian'-style cornices are also common, as are Nabataean pilasters framing the façade and supporting a simplified entablature or flaring cornice or both. Occasionally, the façades were topped by an arch, supported by pilasters. Doorways are often capped by a Classical-style pediment (Figure 115, Plate 130).

In the second, and smaller, category, Classical elements predominate although many native Nabataean and other Semitic elements are still retained. The façades are usually dominated by Classical entablatures and pediments, but subject to immense variations that are usually described as 'baroque'. Entablatures can flow, be curved, and alternatively break forward and recess; pediments can be triangular or semicircular, can be broken, break forward, or interrupted to frame a tholos. To this category belong the most elaborate of the Petra façades: the Tomb of the Roman Soldier, the Broken Pediment Tomb, the

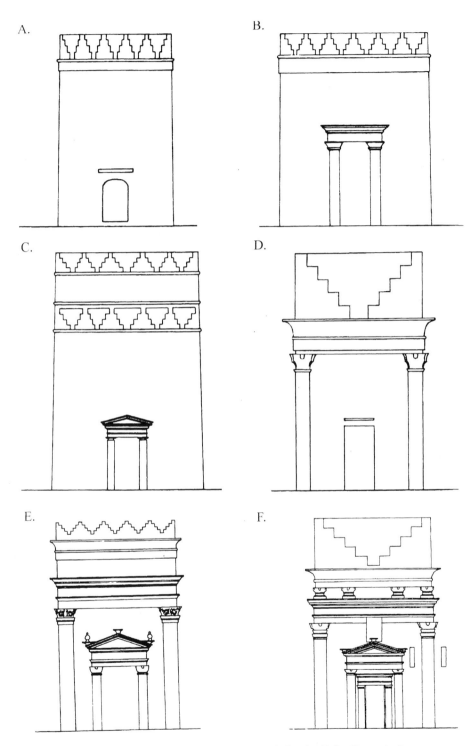

A.

B.

C.

D.

E.

F.

Figure 115 First category of Nabataean tomb façades (After Browning)

Plate 130 First category of tomb façades at Petra

Renaissance Tomb (Plate 131), the Bab as-Siq Triclinium (Plate 132) and the Tomb of Sextus Florentinus. The five largest and most famous of the façades also belong to this category: the Palace Tomb, the Corinthian Tomb, the Urn Tomb, the Khazneh, and the Deir (Plates 8, 10, 11 and 14). The latter two may not be tombs[330] and a variety of explanations have been offered for the function, including tomb, temple, temple-tomb and triclinium.

To a large extent, the Petra façades are the victim of their own fame. They have been the subject of detailed scrutiny, classification and architectural analysis since the nineteenth century in a number of admirable works.[331] But all such works have been blinded by the façades themselves, by the admittedly extraordinary nature of their embellishment, in efforts to understand what happened behind and within them. In other words, they are invariably treated as standing buildings rather than the sculptures which – quite literally – they are: they have a front, a façade, therefore they must have an explicable interior just like any other building (such as a temple) with similarly elaborate façades. Admittedly, such a view of the Petra façades has sufficed to explain nearly all of them as tombs and tomb related triclinia. But this only explains a part of the story – and probably only a small part. It has never sufficed to explain the most famous of the tomb façades, the Khazneh and the Deir (Plates 8 and 14).

If, on the other hand, one regards the Petra façades not so much as the front of something but as the *back*, then their function immediately becomes more explicable. What happened behind them (which was nothing much, at least in the cases of the

Plate 131 The 'Renaissance' Tomb at Petra

Khazneh and the Deir) was less important than what happened in *front* of them. The Petra façades have been likened elsewhere here to theatre backdrops (the *scenae frons*), but only in terms of architectural comparison rather than function. But the comparison becomes a literal one when the façades are regarded as backdrops. This has already been pointed out above, in discussing the *kalybe*, which was seen as a built-up version of the Petra façade. Indeed, theatricality has already been emphasised as an important element – perhaps the most important element – in Near Eastern religious architecture, when discussing the temple temenos above. The Petra façades, therefore, must also be regarded in this light, as a backdrop for religious – presumably funerary – ritual in front of them.

This in fact receives support from the only tomb at Petra where an inscription has survived, the Turkmaniyah Tomb. Here, the inscription describes in some detail not only the ritual of burial but also the paraphernalia of a tomb. The inscription is worth quoting at some length, for the description includes, in addition to the tomb façade and burial behind it, references to

Plate 132 The Bab as-Siq Triclinium and Obelisk Tomb at Petra

the courtyard in front of them and in addition the openings and constructions which are in it, namely the benches and triclinium, water wells, rock walls and retaining walls; as well as the rest of the structures that are in the area: these are a sacred [place] and [a place] consecrated to Dushara, god [and] our lord, his throne Harisa and all the gods by acts of consecration as commanded therein. Dushara and his throne and all the gods watch over the acts of consecration so they will be observed and there will be no change or division of whatever is enclosed in them.[332]

It is clearly stated that the tomb façade which survives today was only a small part – and the minor part – of a much larger complex where elaborate ritual was performed. This involved some form of performance ('acts of consecration') that demanded an audience of gods and perhaps others (who 'watch over' and 'observe' the acts). The ritual furthermore demanded considerably more ancillary buildings: ablution areas ('water wells'), seating for audience and participants ('benches', 'triclinia', 'thrones'), sacred (presumably high) places, and most of all a suitable stage setting for the ritual (a 'courtyard' and 'retaining walls'). The tomb façade itself was merely the stage backdrop, a setting for the pomp, the ritual and the architecture. In a sense, therefore, the great façades at Petra are merely incidental to their function as tombs.

Thus, the Petra façades pass out of the realm of the architectural historian and into that of the archaeologist. The only tombs which still retain fragments of their associated complexes in front are the Tomb of the Roman Soldier, the Unaishu Tomb and the Urn Tomb.[333] Elsewhere, the primary focus of the façades still lies buried under the soil, particularly for the greatest of the façades, the Khazneh, the Corinthian Tomb and the Palace Tomb. Opposite the Khazneh, on the other side of the ravine, the excavation of a minor tomb façade has revealed some 2–3 metres of overburden that covers all of the original surface in front of the Khazneh, thus obscuring any associated buildings that might contribute to a more complete understanding of this enigmatic monument. Similar amounts of overburden exist in front of the main Royal Tombs cut into the eastern cliff face at Petra, as well as the smaller tombs at the foot of Umm al-Biyara, all similarly unexcavated.

Yet we know that the larger façades at least must have been associated with extensive complexes from surface traces in front of the Deir, a monument that is as unsatisfactorily explained as the Khazneh (Figure 81, Plate 102). Whilst this is generally not thought to have been a tomb, most of the component parts of a tomb complex as described in the Turkmaniyah inscription are still extant. It is approached by the processional way implied by the inscription – the ritual, calling for 'acts of consecration' that would involve priests and participants surely calls for a procession. This culminates with a monumental colonnaded propylaeum, traces of which still survive in front of the façade. The remains of these columns might alternatively be a part of a colonnaded square forecourt. Either this or the outline of a circular plaza, visible on the surface a little further away, is the 'courtyard' that formed an arena for the ritual, overlooked on one side by the Deir façade. Between the façade and the circle is the altar required for the 'acts of consecration'. Beyond is perhaps the most interesting monument of all in the Deir complex that has no other counterpart at Petra. This appears to be a monumental colonnaded 'grand stand' overlooking the circular arena, almost surely the 'thrones' from which to 'watch over' and 'observe' the rituals. Behind it is a room (Room 468) containing an elaborately decorated niche. Surrounding and overlooking the entire complex are several sacred high places, the 'sacred places' demanded in the ritual.[334] Together, these tantalising hints make the entire Deir complex the most intriguing – and potentially the most explicable – in Petra. It seems almost certain, therefore, that none of the larger, more monumental façades at Petra existed in the isolation they appear in today, either on the ground or in their voluminous publications. They were merely incidental to larger religious and funerary complexes, the main focal points of which still remain hidden beneath the ground.

Finally, it must be emphasised that whilst these great tomb façades are regarded as characteristic of Nabataean architecture – indeed, many now regard the Nabataeans solely in terms of their deservedly famous rock-cut architecture – they are not typical of the Nabataeans. For they only exist at two Nabataean sites, Petra and Meda'in Saleh: not a *single* other Nabataean site has such remains, either in Jordan, the Hauran or the Negev (unless we regard the *kalybes* of Bosra, Shahba and Amman as masonry versions of the rock-cut façades, as postulated above). Even the supposed tomb of King Ubaydath at the Nabataean site of Avdat (Oboda) in the Negev follows a conventional Roman pattern. Like so much of Nabataean civilisation, these extraordinary façades are ultimately an enigma.

Fabric and styles

Building material

The greatest superficial difference between eastern and western Roman architecture lies in the building material. In the West, brick and mortar was the main material. Poured concrete was increasingly used after the first century, either forming a core to brick-faced walls or as vaults. Stone was used of course – Augustus' boast about transforming Rome into marble was no idle one – but mainly just for cladding on a brick base, as well as for elements of adornment: columns, entablatures, pediments, etc. Buildings that were wholly of stone were relatively rare.

In contrast, the people of the East were masters of a stone building tradition than went back thousands of years.[335] Brick and concrete were almost never used; even stone walls were dry-bonded. The few extant examples of brick building, such as the late palace and church of Qasr Ibn Wardan (Figure 55, Plate 20), were probably made from western designs and supervised by architects from the West. Stone was easily and plentifully available in the Near East. Along the Lebanese coastal ranges and in northern Syria, the bedrock was limestone. Hence, not only civic and religious monuments but ordinary houses and other domestic buildings were constructed of dressed limestone blocks. This has resulted in the extraordinary durability of the architecture here: the phenomenon of the 'Dead Cities' reviewed in Chapter 6.

In the Hauran and the Arabian borderlands in the south, the local building material is the black volcanic basalt which liberally bestrews the countryside. This basalt gave rise to the distinct, cantilevered 'slab and lintel' architectural style that is peculiar to the areas of the Hauran and north-eastern Jordan, described in Chapter 6 (Figure 116). Because of the immense strength of the basalt, domestic architecture evolved along highly distinctive lines, it being possible to build several storeys, with three and even four storeys still standing in parts (Plate 72).

Further south in Arabia, the far softer sandstone made it possible to carve entire monuments out of the living bedrock. These are the famous rock façades of Petra. The theatre was also rock-cut, and in and around Petra ordinary houses were occasionally carved from the bedrock. Elsewhere, some temple sanctuaries were cut from bedrock, such as one of the sanctuaries on Mt Hermon and the partially rock-cut temple at Amrit in Lebanon (Plate 116). Otherwise, carving from the bedrock was used mainly in funerary architecture.

Further east, the scarcity of suitable building stone demanded different techniques, mainly dominated by the mud-brick traditions of Mesopotamia. At Dura Europos and other sites down the Euphrates, the very friable nature of the local stone meant that it was not possible to obtain the large masonry blocks that characterised buildings further west in Syria (Plate 37). Mud and mud-brick was increasingly used, and when stone was used, the blocks were smaller and often bonded in mud mortar.

In the East one gets the sense that there is almost an arrogance in the utter confidence that was felt in the mastery of stone construction. The massive, almost unseemly mono-liths – estimated to weigh over a thousand tons – used in the construction of the Temple of Jupiter at Baalbek were completely unnecessary from a structural point of view, and represent both a boast and a challenge. Similar giganticism for its own sake exists in the stones used in the temenos walls at Husn Sulaiman and elsewhere (Plates 5 and 111).

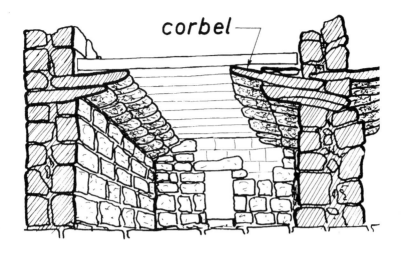

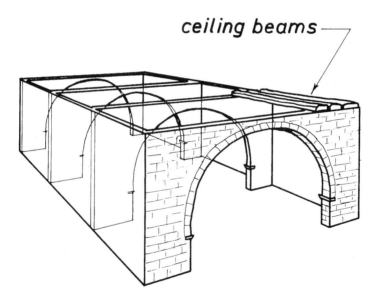

Figure 116 Cantilevering techniques at Umm al-Jimal (After De Vries)

The trabeate style

The Near Eastern mastery of stone masonry led to the development of different styles from those of the West. In the West, the use of bricks and concrete naturally lent itself to the evolution of a more arceate architecture. This contrasted with the East, where the architecture is generally trabeate, with bold slab and lintel techniques predominating – a natural manifestation of stone. The eastern emphasis on long colonnades – particularly the street colonnades – was to some extent a result of this trabeate tradition. Arceate styles did not appear until the importation of the basilica as the standard form of Christian architecture much later on, and this appears very alien in the East as we have observed (Plate 67).[336] One authority remarks that

> while it is certainly true that it was the architects in Rome who first realised the exciting potentialities of building in concrete . . . it appears that throughout the first two centuries of Imperial rule it was the architects of the eastern provinces of the Empire who remained pre-eminent in the evolution and exploitation of the traditional column-and-lintel style. To such an extent is this true that, for many of the more grandiose trabeated buildings erected in Rome under the emperors, workmen trained in the eastern provinces appear to have been brought to Rome.[337]

The mastery of stonemasonry was only one element that contributed to the trabeate style of the East. The other was an ancient Semitic predilection for bold, abstract, cuboid forms. It is a constantly recurring theme, for example, at Petra. A distant view of groups of the smaller façades resembles almost abstract, cubist sculpture. Similarly, the lines of severely rectilinear façades that cluster around the Outer Siq: the rows of regularly repeated square façades, divided by bold horizontal and vertical lines, capped by equally square crow-step gables and merlons, has an overwhelmingly cubist appearance (Plate 130). Such tomb façades belong to the earlier type, before the façades were submerged in Classical baroque embellishment. Hence, they belong more to an older Arabian tradition rather than Classical – all of the Nabataean façades at Medain Saleh belong to this category.

Elsewhere at Petra the cubic motif constantly recurs, either in completely abstract form or as highly stylised deities.[338] The enigmatic 'god-blocks' at the entrance to the Siq are the most perfect example (Plate 133). Carved squares and cubes in relief abound

Plate 133 'God-blocks' at the entrance to Petra

throughout Petra: the *baetyl* in the Siq consists of a cube with two squares carved into the face of one side and two further squares carved onto the larger one (Figure 117). Such rectangular carvings of squares or blocks at Petra are interpreted as abstract representations of Dushara, the main Nabataean deity.[339]

Abstract representation of deity in the form of a square or cube was common throughout the Semitic Near East before Hellenism personified the gods and goes back to Bronze Age traditions.[340] This was the *baetyl*, or stone cult object, the focal point of so many temples not subject to Classicising influences (e.g., Figure 117, Plate 133).[341] The Phoenicians took the concept westwards with them in their expansion in the first half of the first millennium BC. The Carthaginian *tophet* or sacrificial memorial, for example, is marked by a *baetyl* or cube or cubic stele.[342] Occasionally, the motif would be translated into architecture. We have seen this transformation at Petra, but it occurred elsewhere as well. The best example is at the Phoenician site of Amrit on the coast, which preserves some of the pre-Classical forms of Semitic religious architecture without the Classical veneer that nearly all Semitic monuments were subsequently subjected to. The central temple consists of a large court measuring some 65 metres square with a small cella in the centre

Figure 117 Baetyls carved into a cube in the Siq at Petra
(After McKenzie)

raised on a high, rock-cut cube surmounted by a crow-step frieze (Plate 116). This courtyard is surrounded by a colonnade consisting of simple, square upright slabs of stone resembling stelae. The cube motif also occurs at the funerary monuments at Amrit, which usually consist of cubes, sometimes superimposed on each other and occasionally rock-cut, often surmounted by cylinders, pyramids or obelisks (Plates 128 and 129). Such monuments are a part of the ancient Semitic tradition of worshipping abstract forms that is so pronounced at Petra, with its emphasis on 'god-blocks'. Indeed, the ancient Semitic idea of the sacred cube reaches its culmination in the centre of Semitic worship today: the Ka'ba (which is simply Arabic for 'cube') at Mecca.

These elements are seen at their purest in the ancient south Arabian architecture of the early first millennium BC. Here, the entrances to temples are typically marked by rows of square monoliths, such as at the Moon Temples at Sirwah and Marib. The latter, which was capital of the ancient kingdom of Sheba, has the best extant examples. At the Temple of 'Ilmuqah known as *Arsh Bilqis*, the propylaeum consists of a line of six uncompromisingly square monoliths. Even their capitals, which are incorporated into the shafts, are entirely 'cubist', consisting of a series of smaller squares. A similar row of monoliths mark the entrance to the nearby temple known as *Awwam Bilqis* (Plate 134). The square and cubic form constantly recurs elsewhere at Marib. Altars usually take the form of a cube and are decorated in repeated rows of squares; columns are either square or polygonal, surmounted by capitals in the form of faceted squares. At the earlier Sheban capital at Sirwah nearby, even a frieze consisting of a row of ibex is reduced to abstract, cubist form (Plate 135).[343] The predominantly 'cuboid' appearance of ancient South Arabian architecture gives it a strangely elemental, almost modern – or, indeed, futuristic – appearance.

Plate 134 Propylaeum to the Temple of 'Ilmuqah (*Awwam Bilqis*) at Marib in Yemen

Plate 135 Ibex frieze at Sirwah in Yemen

It remained a constant theme of Yemeni architecture, with the landscape dominated by the very cuboid clusters of tower-houses. Indeed, the cubic form of mosques in southern Arabia down to the fourteenth century is noted as being derived from pre-Islamic models.[344]

Such abstract cuboid concepts with their emphasis on bold trabeate forms that characterised ancient south Arabian, north Arabian and Phoenician architecture appear through the Romanisation of Near Eastern architecture. The emphasis in eastern Roman architecture on trabeate forms was a survival of this, as was its predilection for long colonnades. The columns themselves became cylindrical rather than square and were surmounted by Corinthian capitals rather than south Arabian cuboid ones, but conceptually they form a part of the same tradition. The emphasis on the cube appears elsewhere in eastern Roman architecture, such as the essentially cuboid form of the tetrapylon, or the popularity of mounting columns on top of cuboid pedestals (e.g., Plates 75, 125). Altars, too, occasionally took cubic form, such as Khirbet Tannur or the main altar at Baalbek. The square trabeate style of the temple colonnades of both Amrit and Marib re-emerged in the late Roman architecture of north Syria. Here, much of the architecture is characterised by the long porticoes, appearing in both domestic and religious buildings, that are almost invariably square monoliths rather than the more familiar Classical colonnades (Plates 57 and 68). This marks a resurgence of older, native architectural values over the Classical – it is notable that much of the architecture of the Dead Cities is a vernacular, folk architecture rather than a formal one.

The 'baroque' style

Roman architectural decoration, highly formalised in the West and following a rigid set of formulas to the point of severeness, becomes in the East something more relaxed. The forms of Classical architecture were rigidly dominated by strict rules of order and proportion that were almost invariably adhered to. In the East, however, the rules were relaxed, set formulas happily disregarded and the natural Near Eastern love of flamboyance and elaboration had free reign. This oriental variation on Classical architecture has often been dismissed as debased, and a Vitruvius or a Sir Banister Fletcher might well have had a fit. But it lent the monuments a spontaneity and humour that is so often lacking in the purer but colder Classical monuments further west. In the East, it becomes warmer, more living, more experimental. This more exuberant form is often described as 'Roman baroque'.

The term 'baroque' was first applied to a particular style of Roman architecture in a seminal study by Margaret Lyttelton.[345] Using the parallel of the conventional definition of Baroque, as applied to the architecture of seventeenth- and eighteenth-century Europe, the 'baroque' style was applied to the more flamboyant, exuberant forms of Graeco-Roman architecture, particularly in the areas of decoration, in contrast with the more strict, 'Classic' forms. Whilst Roman baroque occurred throughout the empire – most famously at Hadrian's Villa at Tivoli – it is mainly a feature of the North African and eastern provinces, particularly Syria.[346] Nearly all of the examples were drawn from here in Lyttelton's study.

Features of this style are the highly elaborate, flowing and curved façades, often conveying a sense of movement. Entablatures are alternatively recessed and breaking forward, as are the pediments (Figures 75 and 80, Plates 8, 14, 49, 51, 96 and 132). Pediments can be triangular or semicircular, can be broken, break forward, or interrupted to frame a tholos

Figure 118 Interior façade of Tomb 36 at Palmyra (After Schmidt-Colinet)

or other feature (Plates 8, 14 and 49). Niches and miniature pediments are used as additional embellishments, usually having no function other than decorative (Plates 11, 17, 48, 96, 114, 115, 102 and 120). Often, such niches are framed by pilasters and a pediment, the so-called 'Syrian niche' (Plate 143). This feature is discussed in more detail below. Decoration is liberal to the point of profligacy – indeed, such façades can appear almost organic. This is almost literally true for the most famous baroque façades, those at Petra, which are cut from the living bedrock. The interior façade of the recently published Tomb 36 at Palmyra also copies the 'Pompeian style' baroque façades (Figure 118).[347]

Similar baroque façades are the *kalybe*, that probably Nabataean monument already related above to the Petra façades (Figures 79 and 80, Plate 51). Many nymphaea, closely related to the *kalybe*, and many gateways also belong to this style (Plate 96). The nymphaeum at Miletus in Asia Minor is perhaps the most elaborate and most famous example of such a baroque nymphaeum, but the Near East could boast ones almost as opulent, such as those at Jerash and Beth-Shean. Such baroque façades were also a feature of theatre *scenae frons*, which they resembled very closely, both in terms of embellishment and the sense of theatricality which characterised so much of eastern architecture (Plate 49). Baroque entrances usually formed the propylaea to elaborate temple complexes, such as those of the Artemis Temple at Jerash or the Hadad Temple at Damascus (Plate 115). In such cases the architecture expressed the sense of gorgeous, elaborate procession and ritual which were a feature of these. Occasionally, baroque entrances could also be civic arches, such as those at Palmyra or the North Gate at Jerash (Plate 15). The façades of other civic monuments could also be highly baroque, the most famous example being the Library of Celsus at Ephesus. Many interiors were similarly elaborate. Baths – throughout the empire – were positively encrusted with decoration, while the elaborate baroque temple interiors, such as Niha, Baalbek or Palmyra, were a feature of the East (Figure 100, Plates 118 and 119). A unique monument that is often cited as typifying the baroque style is the so-called Temple of Venus at Baalbek, which consisted of a circular tholos adorned with niches surrounded by a colonnade supporting a scalloped entablature and standing on a scalloped plinth. A second-century AD tomb at Shaqqa in the Hauran has a similar baroque plan, with its exterior walls ornamented with deep exedrae (Figure 119).[348]

Mixed orders and the insertion of additional elements into an entablature or column were other features of the baroque style in the East – the horror of the architectural historian and nightmare of the architectural restorer! The colonnade of the second-century Cardo at Apamaea, for example, was of the Corinthian order, but the entablature combined Doric, Ionic and Corinthian elements (Plate 136), and many of the columns had spiral fluted shafts (Plate 137). Spiral columns have a long pedigree in Syria, going back at least to the early second millennium BC, where they adorned the Old Assyrian temple at Tell Leilan.[349] Their popularity continued into the Islamic period, occurring, for example, on the entrance to the Umayyad palace of Qasr al-Hayr Sharqi.[350] The pilaster capitals of the temple at Slim in the Hauran were of a hybrid Ionic and Corinthian style (Plate 138), and at the Temple of Bel at Palmyra the peripteral colonnade was Corinthian while the exterior pilasters of the cella were Ionic (Plate 112). Eastern variations of capitals, particularly Corinthian, were common.[351] Additional elements were often also inserted. For example, colonnades, particularly street colonnades, usually had cubic pedestals under their bases (Plates 75 and 125). This tends to be a feature of the East, and might be related to older Semitic 'cuboid' styles discussed above. Furthermore, columns occasionally had projecting brackets two thirds up their shafts to hold statues (Plates 77, 100 and 137). This occurs most famously on the Palmyra colonnades, both in the Bel

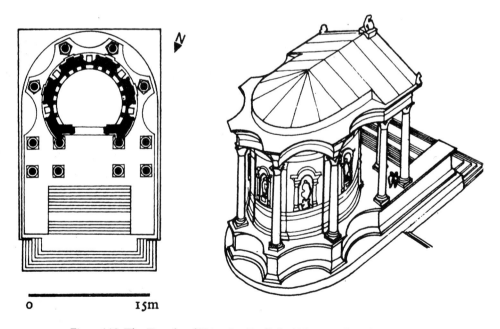

o   15m

Figure 119 The Temple of 'Diana' at Baalbek. (After Ward-Perkins, Butler)

Plate 136 Colonnade at Apamaea combining a Doric frieze with
Corinthian columns

Temple and along the streets. But they also occur at Apamaea and Qanawat in Syria as
well as at Olba, Pompeiopolis and Castabala in Cilicia. At the Apamaea agora, many of the
columns have curious, floriated bulbous bases inserted between the foot of the shaft and
the column base proper (Plate 139), a feature that is also found at the Hellenistic 'Palazzo
del Colonne' at Ptolemais in Libya. An additional element consisting of a projecting
bracket decorated with a frieze was also inserted between the capitals and the architrave
of the Jerash North Tetrapylon (Figure 75). Alternatively, elements of an entablature
might be left out altogether, such as the temenos wall of the Jerash Zeus Temple, which
consists only of a cornice and frieze without an architrave (Plate 140).

Many of the features of Roman baroque have been depicted in a famous series of first-
century BC architectural wall paintings at Pompeii. These styles, particularly the broken
and segmented pediments, curved and segmented entablatures, tholoi framed by broken
pediments, alternating projecting and recessed façades, have been traced to Ptolemaic
Alexandria of the second century BC. The more curvilinear and fragmented nature of
such architecture is regarded as a result of native Egyptian building techniques, such as the
bending of reeds and the shorter structural lengths of the date-palm trunk. This particular
baroque style is seen as deriving almost wholly from Ptolemaic Egyptian architecture,
rather than from Roman.[352] Another important but surprisingly neglected – albeit late –
source that depicts similar fantasy houses to those depicted on the Pompeii wall paintings
are the early eighth-century mosaics on the Umayyad Mosque in Damascus (Figure

Plate 137 Spirally fluted colonnade at Apamaea

120).[353] These mosaics depict a series of baroque Classical façades, where curved and broken elements – particularly the broken pediment – also figure prominently.

The liberal encrustation of entire wall surfaces with elaborate decoration derives from architecture further east, probably India. It is often said that much of oriental architecture consists of four convenient walls upon which to lavish decoration. Whilst form occupies just as important a place, it is nonetheless true that the emphasis on decoration is perhaps the main feature that characterises much of oriental architecture, displaying as it does a horror of blank wall surfaces. The elaborate surface decoration of Islamic architecture belongs firmly within this tradition, as does much of eastern Roman baroque. The tradition is demonstrated very graphically – and appropriately – in the Hellenistic and Hellenistic-derived Gandharan architecture of north-western India. The Gandharan style has already been discussed above in the section on Roman artistic influence in Chapter 4. One of its central features was the combination of basic Classical architectural features – pilasters and entablatures, mainly in the Corinthian order – with elaborate architectural decoration – particularly niches and sculptures – to cover entire wall surfaces. This is mainly seen in the vast numbers of Buddhist monastic complexes which are the predominant feature of Gandharan architecture (Figure 22, Plates 141 and 142).

The emphasis on decoration in Gandharan architecture is an Indian element grafted onto the Classical. This same emphasis characterises Mauryan architecture of the fourth–second centuries BC on, for example, shrines at Bharhut, Sanchi and Sarnath and the cave façade at Bhaja (Figure 121). It later became a universal feature of Indian architecture, for example at the cave façades of Ajanta and Karli in the first few centuries AD. Indeed, the sheer weight of architectural decoration on Indian monuments often obscures any form

Plate 138 Hybrid Ionic-Corinthian order on the Temple at Suwaylim

that they might have had.[354] The Gandharan and Indian origins of aspects of Roman baroque are explored in more detail below, when we focus on the 'Syrian niche'. Suffice for the moment to observe that the Hellenistic medium is the one element common to both Gandharan and eastern Roman architecture.

The other element common to both is Iranian architecture. Achaemenid influences upon Mauryan art have been long recognised, and just as the impact of Hellenism on India resulted in an Indo-Greek style, its impact further west created a 'Graeco-Iranian' style. This is seen throughout the Iranian world and beyond, from Kuh-i Khwaja in Seistan to Hatra, Dura Europos and Palmyra in Mesopotamia and Syria. The baroque façade of Tomb 36 at Palmyra, for example, can be related to the Parthian palace façade from Ashhur.[355] Whilst not always relating directly to Roman baroque, the importance of the Achaemenid Empire from the sixth to fourth centuries for internationalism and the transmission of artistic ideas cannot be emphasised too strongly. Indeed, behind the

Plate 139 Column shafts and bases at the Apamaea agora

Plate 140 Entablature without an architrave from the Zeus Temenos at Jerash

Figure 120 Baroque house façades adorning the Umayyad Mosque at Damascus (After Förtsch)

dissemination of Classical art throughout Asia, the 'remarkably durable arts of Persia' not only survived but formed the underpinning for the formation and movement of other forms.[356] Against this background, both the distinct nature of Roman baroque in the east, and its borrowings from as far away as India, is entirely plausible. If this might appear too tenuous, one must only contrast our eagerness – almost an unseemly haste in some instances! – to accept western influence on India ('Romano-Buddhist' art for example) with the traditional resistance to the idea that such movements might be two-way.

Plate 141 Votive stupas at Taxila in Pakistan. Note rows of niches, Classical entablatures and Corinthian derived pilasters

389

Plate 142 Detail of the Stupa of the Two-Headed Eagle at Taxila:
a Mauryan arch framed in Corinthian pilasters and entablature

The 'Syrian niche'

One of the most distinctive Syrian features of Roman baroque is a decorative feature known as the 'Syrian niche'. This is a niche set into a wall – often to house a statue – framed by a pair of engaged colonnettes supporting a miniature pediment (Plate 143). They were used to great – and elaborate – effect to decorate long façades, most notably in the temenos walls of Baalbek and Palmyra (Plates 17 and 114). One authority includes the Syrian niche as part of a general category of 'elaborated walls' in Roman architecture. Whilst citing eastern examples, such as Baalbek or Palmyra, as the most imposing examples surviving, it is not known where they originated or why.[357]

The tradition of framed niches, however, is one of the most ubiquitous and enduring features of much of the architecture of western Asia and India. They first occur in the

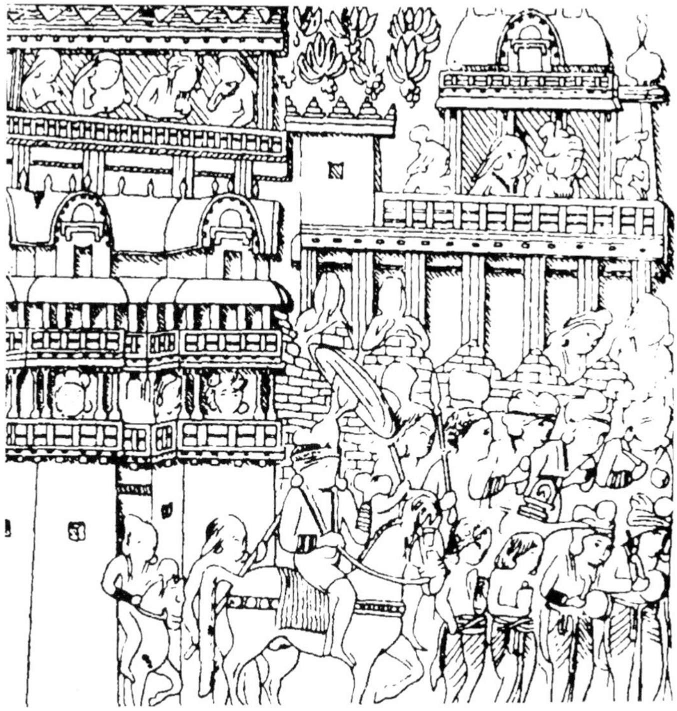

Figure 121 Mauryan decorative niches. A: Bharhut. B: Sanchi (After Reed/Michel)

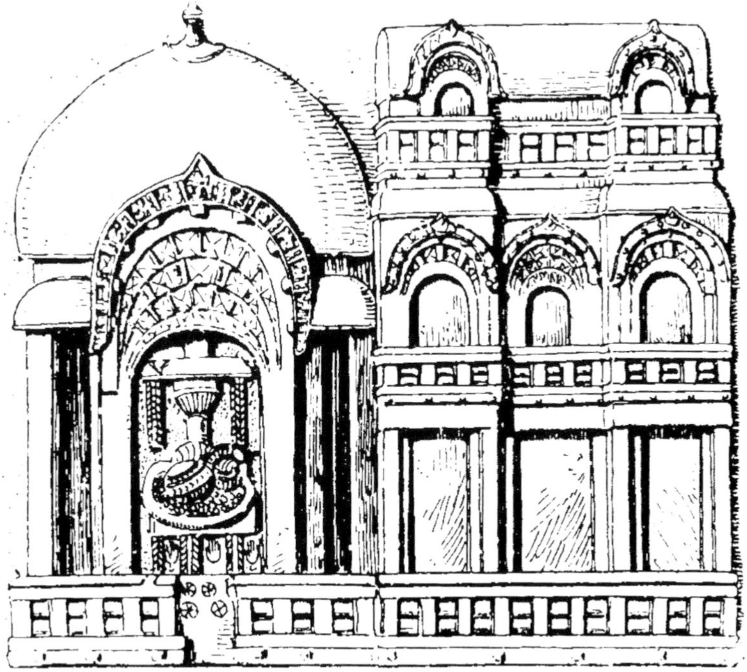

Buddhist architecture of Mauryan India, where they are used – like the Syrian niche – simply as a repeated, recurring decorative motif to adorn wall surfaces. They first occur, for example, at the second–first century BC façades at Bharhut, Sanchi and Bhaja, becoming characteristic of the cave architecture of Karli and Ajanta between the first and fifth centuries (Figure 121).[358]

The importance of the framed niche in Buddhist art is iconographical, deriving from the high regard given to the Buddha image. This is one of the commonest features of Buddhist art, where the Buddha image typically occurs within a frame. The earliest occurrence is the gold Bimaran Reliquary from Afghanistan, dating probably from the first century AD.[359] Thereafter, it becomes characteristic in Gandharan art, where Buddhist narrative reliefs or rows of seated Buddhas in niches are divided by Corinthian, or occasionally Persepolitan, columns. The best examples of the niche form in Gandharan architecture are from the category defined as 'inhabited caitya arches'.[360]

The form proved a remarkably popular and durable one in Indian architecture, surviving well into Islam. The decoration of the tomb façades in the extraordinary fourteenth–

Plate 143 'Syrian niche' on the Artemis Propylaeum at Jerash

eighteenth century necropolis of Thatta in Sind, for example, is liberally endowed with such framed arches, many of them flanked by engaged columns appearing remarkably like the Syrian niche. In Panjab, the Sohail Gate of the massive sixteenth-century Suri fortress at Rohtas is flanked by two 'Syrian niches' in much the same way that they were used to adorn temple propylaea in Roman Syria, and there are many more such occurrences elsewhere in Indian Islamic architecture (Plate 144).[361]

Further west, it proved equally enduring. The tradition of using repeated rows of niches purely for decorative effect to relieve wall surfaces became a feature of Parthian and Sasanian architecture. It occurs, for example, on the Parthian palaces at Nisa, Ashhur and Qal'a-i Yazdegird, as well as on Sasanian palaces at Firuzabad and Ctesiphon (Figure 122, Plate 145).[362] The remarkably baroque façade of the Parthian palace in Ashhur has been viewed as the inspiration for the Tomb 36 façade at Palmyra.[363] The idea was

Plate 144 Decorative niches used to flank the Sohail Gate in the sixteenth-century fort of Rohtas in Pakistan. Compare with Plate 116

Figure 122 The Parthian palace façade at Ashhur (After Andrae/Reuther)

enthusiastically adopted into Islamic architecture. We see exactly the same arrangement in large numbers of Islamic monuments before tile-work decoration in the fifteenth century smothered all other forms of surface embellishment. Examples include the tenth-century Tomb of Isma'il in Bukhara and the palaces at Samarra (Plate 146).[364]

Once again, one must look to the immensely international and enduring influence of the Achaemenid Empire to explain such links as wide apart in time and space as Mauryan India and the Roman East. Repeated rows of arches were used in Achaemenid architecture, most notably in the interiors of the palaces at Persepolis. In the Audience Hall of Xerxes, as well as the Private Apartments of both Darius and Xerxes, this is the main form of decoration.[365] The form in Iran has been traced back to the niches that adorned the early Iron Age columned halls of western Iran, for example at Hasanlu and Nush-i Jan.[366] Such niches are a far cry from the 'Syrian niches' of Roman baroque, and any resemblance might well be illusory. But like so much of the architecture related to Roman baroque, they nonetheless demonstrate the strength of the tradition throughout the East, in contrast to its paucity in the Classical architecture of the West.

Conclusion

The great flowering of architecture in the second and third centuries, when the cities of the Roman East were magnificently embellished, continues to impress visitors to this day. This was in accordance with the rest of the empire, all parts of which came in for similar embellishment. But this process had an additional element in the East. For there it not only marks an upsurge in wealth and stability, it also marks a native resurgence. Entire

Plate 145 Sasanian palace façade at Ctesiphon

Plate 146 Abbasid palace façade at Samarra

395

cities were monumentalised, great temples were enlarged, extended and rebuilt in dazzling proportions, but the embellishment was in the eastern way.

Observers have been dazzled by the Corinthian capitals which adorn these buildings, without looking beyond to the deeper architectural concepts which determine their basic form.[367] Ancient Near Eastern architectural forms had a tenacity which survived superficial Romanisation and still survive in the form of Islamic mosques to this day. Before the Macedonian and Roman conquests imparted an east–west political division on the Near East, the entire area was culturally far more unified than the brief, superficial appearance of Graeco-Roman art forms might imply.

It is possible to get a Mesopotamian or Iranian-style temple cella and dress it up in Graeco-Roman ornamentation. Never mind that the deity was Melqart, Dushara or Atargatis, it could always be called Zeus or Artemis. One might even throw a Corinthian colonnade around the outside of the sanctuary, as well as another around the extremely un-Classical-style temple courtyard to dazzle the worshippers who thronged there on holy days to sacrifice at the great altar that dominated it. Such colonnades would hardly disguise the very Semitic high places which the temple was equipped with, without which the gods would be affronted beyond belief. The magnificent arch through which one passed to enter the courtyard might be decorated with Classical statuary instead of the dragons and demons which embellished the Ishtar Gate, but it was still an earthly counterpart of the gateway to heaven. None of these frills made the temple Roman, it remained as it had always been, a Near Eastern temple familiar to the people who had been using it for thousands of years. Roman frills might be piled onto it, but the real architecture remained what it had always been: Near Eastern.

THE TRANSFORMATION OF AN EMPIRE

It is a common fallacy to contrast the outgoing curiosity of Europeans with the trad-itional incuriosity and inwardness of Asians, often cited in discussions of European expan-sion into the East, whether in antiquity or modern times. This fallacy still has a surprising tenacity.[1] Indeed, in one otherwise admirable survey of the interaction of East and West, it was written that 'when the ports of China and India were full of European and North American shipping, no junk or dhow had ever been seen in Seville, Bristol or Boston' and 'few non-Europeans other than the Turks even entered Europe . . . and we still do not really know why'.[2] The outgoing curiosity and expansion of Asian peoples into Europe began long before and continued long after the Greek and Roman expansion into the East: Phoenicians, Persians, Jews, Syrians, Arabs, Huns, Avars, Mongols and others, for example. These are largely beyond the present discussion. Suffice it to say that such fallacies do not stand up to scrutiny. At few other times in history was this more apparent than during the Roman Empire.

To begin with, the examination of Rome's direct and indirect expansion east of the frontiers reviewed in Chapter 4 must be contrasted with the converse: the expansion of Asia into Europe through the medium of the Roman world. The western movement of peoples and ideas forms an essential background to what was probably the greatest east–west intellectual movement in history: Christianity. The ensuing interchange culminated in an orientalisation of Europe.

The Arabs and the West

Near Eastern penetration and colonisation of Europe has a long history – certainly far longer than European colonisation of the East. It begins with the Phoenician outward expansion in the second millennium BC, and the conflict with Phoenicia's greatest colony – Carthage – over this expansion did more than anything else to thrust Rome onto the world stage. The eventual defeat of Carthage and collapse of its colonial empire did not bring about an end to this expansion. Quite the contrary, for the unification of the Mediterranean world under Rome brought Near Eastern communities in the wake of Rome's conquests in Europe. The Jewish Diaspora – which started before the destruction of Jerusalem by Titus in 66 – and the establishment of Jewish communities in every major city of the Mediterranean was a part of this broad pattern. In addition, Arab, Iranian and even Indian communities came west.

Substantial Arab minorities are recorded in most of the ports of southern Spain from the first few centuries AD: at Malaga, Cartagena, Seville and Cordoba. Pliny the Younger mentions the Syrian philosopher, Euphrates, at Rome in the early first century AD. Wealthy Near Eastern merchant colonies lived in Puteoli and Ostia in the second century AD. Indeed, with the cults of Tyrian Melqart, Egyptian Isis, Anatolian Cybele, Syrian Atargatis, Iranian Mithras, Nabataean Dushara, the various Syrian Baals of Jupiter Heliopolitanus, Jupiter Damascenus (Hadad) and Jupiter Dolichenus, and numerous other eastern cults known to flourish in Puteoli, it must have resembled an oriental city in the first few centuries AD. Apamaean, Palmyrene and Nabataean communities in Italy are also known, and there is a Palmyrene dedicatory inscription to Malakbel and a Nabataean dedicatory inscription to the Sun god in Rome. Safaitic inscriptions have also been found in Pompeii. Other Syrian merchant communities have been recorded in Spain and Gaul at Pannonia, Malaga, Lyons, Grenoble, Arles, Trier and elsewhere. In Lyons, for example, a bilingual inscription by Thayn bin Saʿd from Qanawat has been left by one of these Syrian merchant families. Such Syrian merchant communities became more influential after the adoption of Christianity, particularly in encouraging eastern forms of monasticism and the adoption of the crucifix as the Christian symbol. Salvian (who died in about 484) wrote of Syrian merchants in Marseilles, and there was known to have still been a Syrian merchant community in Narbonne as late as 589. After the fourth century Ravenna was noted for its Syrian influence, both in its mosaics and its religion, with a number of Syrian bishops recorded there. There was a Persian Patriarch, a former Zoroastrian, Mar Aba, who preached in Alexandria, Constantinople, and elsewhere in the Christian West. There was a Syrian bishop of Paris in the fifth century, and Aramaic was still being spoken in Orleans and Narbonne in the fifth and sixth centuries. Marseilles and Bordeaux still had a substantial Syrian population in the fifth century, mainly mercantile. In the first hundred years after the Muslim invasion, no less than six Popes were Syrian. One of these, Pope Sergius I (687–701), was particularly instrumental in introducing elements of Syrian liturgy and Christian belief into the Church of Rome. Theodore, the Archbishop of Canterbury from 669 to 690, was from Tarsus.[3]

After Emperor Severus Alexander's Persian war in 230–3, many 'Moorish', Arab and Iranian troops, mainly archers, were brought back and stationed in Germany. Syrian elements have been recorded in Roman army camps in Europe, particularly along the Danube frontier, where the Syrian cults of Aziz, Hadad and al-Uzza are known. On the British frontier, shrines to the Syrian Jupiter Dolichenus have been found at Caerleon, and shrines to Phoenician Astarte and Melqart have been found at Corbridge and Jupiter Heliopolitanus at Magnae, both near Hadrian's Wall. Near the end of the wall, at South Shields, a Palmyrene funerary memorial has been found associated with a Syrian community in Northumberland (Plate 147). The ancient name of the South Shields fort was Arbeia, a corruption of 'Arabs' (Plate 148), and the control of the river traffic at the mouth of the Tyne at that time was in the hands of an Arab community known as the 'Tigris boatmen'.[4]

The above survey, although brief, is enough to underline the interchange. The long and complex relationship between Rome and the Arabs, reviewed in Chapter 3, is also an integral part, as is the rise of Arab emperors of Rome, reviewed later in this chapter. Against this background, the Arab conquest of Spain in the early eighth century AD and the subsequent expansion into Sicily, Italy, southern France and even Switzerland[5] is not so much the first act in Islam's expansion as the last in a tradition of Near Eastern expansion into Europe. A tradition already thousands of years old by the time Tariq Ibn Ziyad crossed the Straits of Gibraltar (which preserves his name) with his seven hundred

Plate 147 Palmyrene funerary stele and inscription at South Shields

Muslim followers in 711. The fact that the Arab presence in Spain then endured for so long – nearly eight hundred years, longer even than the Romans themselves in Spain – is due to the power of traditions that stretch back deep into the past to the earliest Phoenician merchants.

India and the West

The amount of literature on the trade between the Roman Empire and India, together with the dramatic impact that the discovery of Roman and Roman-related finds in India had on western academic interest, has led to the assumption that such movement was

399

Plate 148 The Roman fort of 'Arabs' (Arbeia) at South Shields

one-way. But Indians and Indian influence came west too and the evidence can be found in both literary references and archaeological finds – indeed, there are more records of Indian delegations going west than the other way round.

Roman authors refer to delegations and their exotic gifts from India, Bactria, Scythia and elsewhere beyond Iran visiting the Roman Empire during the time of Augustus.[6] The most famous was the Indian king, Poros, who sent a mission to Augustus that included exotic gifts and was accompanied by a Brahman priest who later immolated himself at Athens.[7] Such visits continued throughout the imperial period: Hadrian and Antoninus Pius received 'Bactrian'[8] and Indian delegations, an Indian embassy to Elaga-balus passed through Edessa in about 218,[9] Indian and Bactrian ambassadors attended Aurelian's triumph over Palmyra, Constantine was supposedly venerated by Indians, and Julian received an embassy from Ceylon (Taprobane).[10] As late as the sixth century, sewn boats from India were still recorded as coming up the Red Sea.[11] Although usually described as 'ambassadors' in the Roman sources, they were more likely merchants rather than official diplomatic representations. One such trader was the Indian sailor who was shipwrecked on the Red Sea coast of Egypt in about 118 BC and later guided Ptolemaic expeditions to India.[12] The only possible exception was the envoy from King Poros mentioned by Strabo. This mission – particularly with its strong religious overtones – recalls the third-century BC diplomatic missions to the West sent by the Emperor Ashoka.[13] On the other hand there is no evidence that Rome sent official embassies to India or China, unlike, for example, the Parthians, who established official relations with China.[14]

Likewise, the 'gifts' were probably trade items rather than state exchanges of gifts. They were often described as precious goods and exotic animals. Whilst none of these have survived, there have been discoveries of oriental exotica, such as a first-century BC Indian ivory found in a house in Pompeii.[15] Indeed, the arrival of Indian sculpture even seems to have inspired a minor artistic fashion in 'Indianesque' portrait sculpture in Rome. This is seen in the series of first- and second-century AD Roman portrait busts that have Buddhist-style top-knots (Plate 149),[16] the *ushnisha*, which in Buddhist iconography symbolises the super-normal knowledge and consciousness of the Buddha. One of these portraits has been tentatively identified as Julius Bassianus of Emesa, the father of Julia Domna.[17] Another occurs in a second-century portrait of a young boy on a grave relief from Mambij in Syria, again suggesting influence from further east.[18] Such Indian

Plate 149 Indian-style bust of Julius Bassianus (?) in the Villa Borghese (© Archivio Fotografico Soprintendenza Beni Artistici e Storici di Roma)

influences on Roman art, however, in no way bear comparison with the Roman influences on Buddhist art discussed in Chapter 4.

The archaeological evidence adds substance to literary references. Indian pottery, including some with Tamil-Brahmin graffiti, has been found at the ancient sea trade entrepôt of Leukos Limen, modern Qusayr al-Qadim on the Egyptian coast of the Red Sea.[19] A possible Buddhist gravestone has been found at Alexandria, which assumes significance in the light of other Indian activity there discussed below.[20]

Far more archaeological evidence for Indian maritime penetration westwards occurs on the Persian Gulf. Quantities of Indian red-polished ware, for example, have been found – more, in fact, than the much-vaunted finds of Roman pottery in India. This distinctive ware spread around the Indian Ocean from the Gulf to Thailand. Architectural remains have been no less revealing: some artificial cave complexes on the Gulf have been tentatively identified as Buddhist, presumably religious communities that came in the wake of Indian trading colonies to the west. The converse, the Peutinger Table's much-vaunted Temple of Augustus at Musiris, still remains elusive, and even the 'Roman' remains at Arikamedu are open to doubt. Such Indian activity on the Gulf is supported by toponymic evidence of Indian-derived place names that can be found along the Gulf – again contrasting with the total lack of any Roman or otherwise western-derived place names in India.[21] This evidence emphasises the importance of this route over the Red Sea and Roman Egypt.[22]

One authority rightly emphasises the importance that the Indians played in this trade, as well as the Iranians and Arabs.[23] Throughout the history of commerce between India and the Roman world, the Arabs were the middlemen who both started off the trade and saw its end with the dawning of the Middle Ages. It was probably the Arabs, therefore, with the Iranians, Ethiopians and Indians themselves coming close behind, who dominated the trade far more than the Romans. Indeed, Roman sources often show confusion between Ethiopia and India.

Despite the body of evidence in India, both literary and archaeological, it still cannot be said for certain that there were colonies of Romans in India. There is, however, much better evidence for Indian colonies going west. The island of Socotra off the Indian Ocean coast of southern Arabia had a community of Indians in antiquity – the name of the island itself is derived from the Sanskrit *sukhatara-dvipa* meaning 'the most pleasant land'.[24] Armenia had a well-established colony of Indians from 130 BC to AD 300.[25] Indian and Chinese goods – presumably with merchants from those lands – came regularly up the Euphrates from the Persian Gulf to the annual trade fair at Batnae near Edessa from the second century AD right down to the sixth century.[26] Dion Chrysostom writes of an Indian merchant colony in Alexandria at the time of Vespasian, as well as Persians, Bactrians and Scythians,[27] and other documents describe colonies of Arabs and Indians controlling the trade in the Red Sea ports.[28]

The Cholas of southern India were the earliest and most widespread of the Indian maritime powers, with a mercantile empire stretching to Africa, Arabia and the Gulf made possible by superior sailing vessels of two and even three masts.[29] A highly developed and sophisticated system of native maritime trade was already in place in India by the first century AD. This had evolved over the previous 500 years, and had penetrated all over south and south-east Asia,[30] while a tradition of building large ocean-going vessels existed in Gujarat from the second century BC.[31]

In the field of literary influence, the flow was entirely one way, from India via Iran to the West, small though this may have been.[32] The first-century AD Fables of Phaedrus, for example, contain Jataka stories,[33] while the well-known early Christian work, *Barlaam and Joasaph* by St John Damascene, derives from the traditions of the early life of Gautama Buddha.[34] Iran was a major vehicle for transmitting Indian literary ideas to the West.[35] In Sasanian Iran a major literary genre was the *andarz-nama* or 'mirror for princes', which flourished in the time of Khusrau I. This continued into Islamic Iran, the most notable of which was the *Siyasat Nama* of Nizam ul-Mulk. The Iranians themselves might well have inherited the genre from similar Indian works, such as the third-century BC *Arthasastra* of Kautilya, written for Chandragupta Maurya. At the time that the genre was flourishing in Iran the first Byzantine 'mirror' appeared, written by Agapetus in the time of Justinian. The genre then continued into medieval and Renaissance Europe, the twelfth-century *King's Mirror* of Kink Haakon the Old of Norway or Machiavelli's *The Prince* being some well-known examples.[36]

Speculation has existed on the possibility of Stoicism being ultimately descended from the dispassionate approach to suffering and death so common in Indian philosophy, made from the initial contacts formed by the Greeks in India after Alexander.[37] The journeys of Apollonius of Tyana and the Apostle St Thomas are mentioned elsewhere as important events in these cross-cultural contacts.

Apart from the fertile ground of the Indo-Greek kingdoms (beyond the scope of this book) the main meeting ground of Indian and Graeco-Roman religious ideas would have been the international city of Alexandria. This was already one of the main centres for the eastern trade as we have seen (Chapter 4) and ideas arrived with the spices. Clement of Alexandria (*c.* AD 150–214), for example, makes reference to the Brahmans and the Buddhists.[38] Indeed, there is more concrete evidence for Indian communities in Alexandria than for Roman communities in southern India. It has even been suggested that the Indian element was a catalyst in the philosophical school of Alexandria that resulted in the formation of the mystical element in neo-Platonism, with many of the ideas of Plotinus of Alexandria in particular being cited as drawn directly from the Hindu *Upanishads*. One of Plotinus' main disciples, the neo-Platonist Porphyry (AD 233–305), wrote at length on the Brahmans, absorbing much of their ideas into his own teachings. Since Porphyry was probably a native of Batnae, the scene of a trade fair with Indian associations on the middle Euphrates (referred to above), the point of contact is obvious.[39] Much speculation has existed too on Indian origins for early Christian monasticism. This is generally attributed to initial beginnings in Egypt, but again the Indian contact with Egypt through Alexandria is an obvious point of contact.[40] Certainly it is possible to recognise – real or imagined – influence on early Christianity: St James, the brother of Christ, for example was a vegetarian and wore no wool or other animal products, only linen.[41] However one views the validity of such speculations about religious and philosophical contacts between India and the Roman world, there are no doubts about the Indian connections with ancient Greece through the Greek kingdoms of northern India.[42] With Rome owing so much to ancient Greece – particularly in the religious and philosophical sphere – there can be little doubt that many Indian ideas entered Rome through this indirect route.

The development of Buddhism in the Indian Subcontinent after 500 BC, with its emphasis on proselytisation and outwardness generally, stimulated an enormous expansion of the sea and land trade.[43] This, however, must be seen merely as a reaffirmation of an Indian tradition for outwardness and trade that was far older: of all the world's earliest civilisations, it was the Indus Valley that was the most widespread in the third and second millennia BC, with trade colonies established as far apart as north-eastern Afghanistan and Oman, and Indus-derived objects found throughout Central Asia and the Near East, as well as the Indian Subcontinent.[44] Buddhism, furthermore, was an outward religion, so that trade, Buddhism and the outward expansion of Indian civilisation generally would have been a part of the one movement – indeed, the rise of Buddhism in India directly stimulated the rise in trade throughout India and the neighbouring regions. The much-vaunted trade between India and the Roman World (discussed in Chapter 4) with all the ensuing contact and interchange, therefore, was more likely the result of stimuli from India, rather than the West.[45]

Julia Domna and the Arabs who ruled Rome

We have already seen above ('The Arabs and the West') how the Roman conquest of the Near East accelerated the movement of Arabs into the Mediterranean and Europe, a movement that began with the Phoenician colonisation of the first millennium BC and culminated in the Arab invasion of Europe in the eighth century AD. But it is not often realised that Arabs dominated the very heart of Rome as well, most notably with the emergence of Arab families who became Roman emperors in the third century.

The first of these families was – appropriately in the context of Semitic domination of the Mediterranean – of both Phoenician and Arab descent. The Phoenician side came from the aristocracy of Lepcis Magna in Africa. The Arab side came from the line of priest-kings who ruled the client kingdom of Emesa in Syria, reviewed in Chapter 3.

Septimius Severus and Julia Domna

There is a particularly revealing Roman portrait of 199 of a certain family group: a white-haired elder statesman, supremely confident at the peak of his powers; a dark, wavy-haired calculating woman; a youth whose features have been savagely erased; and a pampered, puffy-faced spoilt brat: Septimius Severus, Julia Domna, Geta and Caracalla (Plate 150. See also Plate 159).[46]

The happy family was probably Rome's most successful imperial dynasty[47] since the Julio-Claudians – and were as deeply flawed. But unlike the Julio-Claudians, the Severans hailed from distant corners of the empire, not from Rome itself or even Italy. Its founder was Septimius Severus (Plate 151). His birthplace was Lepcis Magna in North Africa in 145. Lepcis in origins was, like Carthage, a Phoenician colony. Even by Septimius' birth it still officially looked to Tyre as its traditional mother-city, rather than to Rome, despite its becoming formally a Roman colony in 112. Its population remained very close to its Phoenician roots – indeed Septimius himself was nicknamed 'Punic' on a number of occasions ('Punic Sulla', 'Punic Marius' etc.)[48] and spoke Latin with a Punic accent all his life, while his sister never spoke Latin properly at all (to the emperor's considerable embarrassment!).[49] Hence, his posting to Syria in about 180 as a young officer in the Roman army was probably seen by Septimius as a journey back to Phoenician roots.[50] Phoenicia obviously meant much to him: he revived (after he had become emperor) the ancient name of 'Phoenice' for the new province he created out of Syria, he travelled throughout the region, he consulted native Phoenician oracles.[51] It was at one of these oracles where he supposedly first heard of the Phoenician princess from Emesa (regarded

Plate 150 Portrait of Emperor Septimius Severus and his family: Julia Domna, Septimius Severus, Geta and Caracalla (© Antikensammlung, Staatliche Museen zu Berlin – Preussischer Kulturbesitz)

as being a part of Phoenicia) whose horoscope forecast she would marry a king. This was Julia Domna.

For it was not the Libyan father who dominated the dynasty but the Syrian mother – and her female relatives.[52] Julia Domna was the daughter of Bassianus, a descendant of the hereditary priest-kings of Emesa. Despite the obvious westernisation of this family – Roman names (although Bassianus derives from *basus*, an oriental title for priest),[53] Roman equestrian positions, etc. – there can be little doubt that it was Syrian first and foremost.[54] The family were to become the first ruling dynasty of Rome since the Flavians.[55]

It is not known whether Septimius actually met the young princess then – he was still married to his first wife Marciana, a native of Lepcis – but it seems more than likely. After all, Emesa's famous temple and its position as the seat of an important local family would have merited his attention, both as a young 'Phoenicophile' seeking his roots and as an important Roman officer. He obviously attracted enough personal attention during this period to be the butt of Antiochene jokes![56] Whether or not he met and remembered the young Julia Domna, he certainly remembered the horoscope – 'the fruitful offspring either of his superstition or his policy' as Gibbon dryly puts it[57] – concerning her destiny after he left. When Marciana (conveniently!) died during his subsequent posting at Lyons, he lost no time in sending for her. In this way Septimius Severus consolidated his Phoenician sentiments with his marriage in about 183 into one of Syria's oldest and

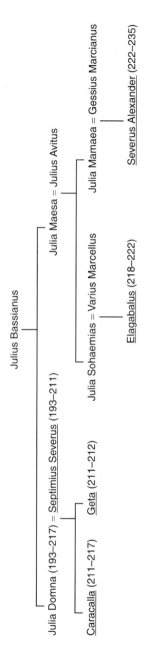

Family tree 3 The family of Julia Domna

Plate 151 Emperor Septimius Severus

most aristocratic families. Shortly afterwards, Septimius Severus, the Punic North African, conquered Rome: Hannibal could rest in peace.

But more important than the Punic emperor was the Syrian empress. Julia Domna became the real power behind both him and their son Caracalla. In taking control of the Roman Empire she aspired to make herself another Semiramis.[58] After Septimius Severus, more people from the East were incorporated into high positions in Rome through her influence – we read of Syrian tribunes, for example, in the Praetorian Guard.[59] It was probably she rather than Caracalla who was ultimately behind Caracalla's famous decree in 212 extending Roman citizenship to all free citizens of the empire, thus abolishing all legal distinctions between Romans and provincials.[60]

Julia Domna surrounded herself with a 'salon' of prominent literary and philosophical figures. One of her main protégés was the philosopher Philostratus, a disciple of the remarkable mystic Apollonius of Tyana. The religion of Apollonius interested Julia Domna immensely, and she commissioned Philostratus to write a life of him so that his teachings could be more widely disseminated. Apollonius was born in Tyana in Cappadocia sometime in the early first century AD. He espoused an extreme form of mysticism and asceticism, whose beliefs appear to combine elements of Pythagoreanism and even Brahmanism. Renouncing the drinking of alcohol, the eating of meat, the wearing of wool, and hot baths, he maintained a severe abstinence from all luxuries throughout his life. He believed in reincarnation and claimed to speak all languages, including those of birds and animals. These he venerated and advocated their complete

407

protection. Apollonius supposedly undertook a journey to the East, travelling through Iran to India, where he held conversations with the Magi and the Brahmans, as well as several secular rulers such as the Parthian King Vardanes in AD 43/4. On his return he attracted a wide following, and his cult was seen as a rival to that of Christ. Indeed, it is tempting to see Philostratus' *Life of Apollonius* as a deliberate Graeco-Roman answer to the Gospels. As late as the beginning of the fourth century, Apollonius was being held by pagans as a viable alternative to Christ with his philosophy contrasted with Christianity.[61] Whether or not this is so, Julia Domna's patronage of the cult certainly prepared the ground for Christianity.[62]

Caracalla and Geta

Septimius died whilst on campaign in Britain in 211. His eldest son was Antoninus, better known under his nickname, Caracalla. Caracalla would probably have succeeded his father as sole emperor, but his dissolute ways and obsessive ambition – even amounting, on one famous occasion in Britain, to an attempt on the life of Septimius himself – led his father to have grave doubts about the desirability of leaving the empire to one so unsuitable. In the end, he left it to both sons, Caracalla and his younger brother Geta, hoping that joint rule would temper the more unsavoury side of Caracalla's character. Septimius' decision could not have been worse, for it simply turned Caracalla's hatred of his brother into an obsession.

Of the two sons, Caracalla at first seemed to be the better choice: his youth was exemplary while Geta was a foppish dandy.[63] Events were soon to reveal Caracalla in his true colours. To end the sibling rivalry between Caracalla and Geta, a meeting was called presided over by their mother. The outcome was merely further divisiveness. Indeed, the empire was to be divided between the two, reinforcing a precedent begun by Marcus Aurelius and Lucius Verus – but this time, both players in the game originated from an eastern family and would look to the East. Caracalla was to get the West, Geta the East. Whilst the capital of the western empire was to remain at Rome, Caracalla anticipated Constantine in choosing Byzantium as his headquarters. Geta's headquarters was to be Chalcedon (opposite Byzantium), with either Antioch or Alexandria as his capital.[64] Whilst the events foreshadowed the momentous decisions of Diocletian and Constantine, the overriding impression is of two spoilt boys squabbling over their toys.

The spoilt Caracalla proved dissatisfied with merely a half an empire. He pursued his brother relentlessly, eventually having him killed in his mother's arms. Thus the half-Punic, half-Syrian[65] boy ended up with the lot. But the ghost of Geta and an eastern empire remained to haunt Caracalla. Having begun his reign with a fratricide Caracalla followed up Geta's murder with more butchery, eradicating everything and everybody remotely connected to Geta.[66] He then proceeded to exorcise the ghost of an eastern empire. He not only consciously aped Alexander the Great but even claimed he was a reincarnation,[67] then in 214, in pathetic emulation, set out for the East. He proceeded to Alexandria, Geta's choice as capital, and wiped out half the male population of the city in an appalling act of treachery and genocide.[68] Dio writes 'in spite of the immense affection which he professed to cherish for Alexander, [Caracalla] all but utterly destroyed the whole population of Alexander's city'.[69] But for Caracalla, Alexandria was not so much Alexander's as Geta's city.

Having finally satiated his grudge against Geta with the blood of the Alexandrians,

Plate 152 Emperor Caracalla (© Antikensammlung, Staatliche
Museen zu Berlin – Preussischer Kulturbesitz)

Caracalla set his eyes on Iran. He first grandly proposed uniting the two empires by a marriage to the daughter of King Artabanus of Parthia – a proposal consciously recalling Alexander's marriage to the Persian Princess Statira and the fusion of East and West. But Caracalla's proposal was further treachery. At first spurned, Caracalla's suit was finally accepted by Artabanus. The groom and his vast (and heavily armed!) entourage entered Mesopotamia in grand style and proceeded to Ctesiphon for the marriage. Artabanus had prepared a lavish royal wedding reception for him in the fields outside the city. Leaving their arms and their horses behind, the Parthians were caught totally unprepared for Caracalla's ruse. The Romans massacred the unarmed Parthian warriors in their thousands, with Artabanus himself (and the doubtless relieved bride) only just managing to escape. Caracalla left the blood-soaked wedding field and turned back westwards, claiming 'victory' over the entire East.[70] But the East and the Parthians had not yet finished with Caracalla. On his way back, Caracalla stopped off at Crassus' fateful battlefield at Carrhae where he was finally murdered.[71]

Julia Domna had followed her son to Antioch, as much to be near him as to wield power through him – as well, presumably, to return to her homeland. On receiving news of her son's death, she foresaw her own subsequent loss of power, so hastened a death already made inevitable from advanced breast cancer by fasting to death.[72] But Julia

Plate 153 Empress Julia Domna (© Roma, Musei Capitolini)

Domna left an equally forceful woman to succeed her as the power behind the throne, her sister Julia Maesa (Plate 154).

Caracalla's portraits are particularly revealing. An idealised bust in the Hermitage shows him as the 'beautiful youth' that the Roman mob so loved. The features of the pampered brat in the Berlin tondo are still easily recognisable in the adult, although the over-indulged plumpness disappears. Instead, the over-indulgence is replaced by a quick, uncontrolled temper suggested by the scowl depicted in the immensely powerful New York Metropolitan portrait, which otherwise displays youthful good looks. But the good looks are marred by the scowl, which also suggests underlying cruelty, and the 'designer stubble' simply suggests affectation. Subsequent portraits of Caracalla growing older mark inevitable regression. By the time that the Berlin Staatliche bust was made the designer stubble is replaced by a short beard, the youthful good looks have given way to coarser, heavier features, only the cruel – but by now deeply suspicious – scowl remains (Plate 152). Finally, the University of Pennsylvania granite portrait depicts a hideous image: a coarse, thoroughly brutalised tyrant where the ever-permanent scowl has become a baleful glare, unsoftened even by affectation or self-indulgence.[73]

His mother's portraits do not appear much better (Plate 153). Indeed, it is easy to see where Caracalla got his looks from: of the two boys, only the short-lived Geta appears to take after his father. Or perhaps it is just that the few surviving portraits of the youthful

Plate 154 Julia Maesa (© Roma, Musei Capitolini)

Geta are unmarred by the cruelty that characterises his brother, giving a superficial resemblance to the kinder features of Septimius.[74] Julia Domna is not bad-looking, but all portraits – medallions, coins, sculptures – seem to convey an image of subtlety and scheming, suggested perhaps by a mouth which appears locked in an expression of perpetual calculation, with eyes that are never direct.[75] Only in a bust in Munich do her features appear warmer and more relaxed – or perhaps it is just that her hair is let down here.[76] But whatever the expression, her portraits convey a far more powerful personality than either her son or her husband. No sloe-eyed, empty-headed eastern floozy here, interested only in harem intrigues! Small wonder she became the power behind the throne of two emperors. Such a pity that Caracalla, who in some ways had some admirable characteristics (he was good with the army, for example), never inherited her force of personality. But both he and Julia Domna were obsessive people, obsessed with the pursuit of power as much as with each other. One wonders whether a Roman relief of the Severan period depicting Mars and Venus contains more than a hint of Caracalla and Julia Domna.[77]

Elagabalus and Baal

Apart from a brief interlude by the Emperor Macrinus, Caracalla was succeeded by his second-cousin Elagabalus (see Family tree 3).[78] Elagabalus was the grandson of Julia Domna's equally redoubtable sister Julia Maesa (Plate 154), the son of her daughter Julia

Sohaemias. In Elagabalus we have one of the most curious – and most maligned – emperors ever to receive the Roman purple. His name was the same as his grandfather's, Bassianus, and after he became emperor he adopted the name of Marcus Aurelius Antoninus. Elagabalus was merely his title as hereditary high-priest at the Temple of Emesene Baal. But Elagabalus – or Heliogabalus, a variation[79] – is the name under which he has entered history. The youthful Bassianus-Elagabalus was the hereditary high-priest of this temple.

Elagabalus was also endowed with the fatal combination of youthful good looks, immense wealth and a scheming, ambitious grandmother. Following the death of Caracalla and the elevation of Macrinus, Syria was flooded with disaffected troops after the humiliation of the Second Battle of Carrhae (see Chapter 2). They were also smarting under the rule of Macrinus, having enjoyed greater privileges under Caracalla who had been as popular with the army as he was unpopular with historians and portraitists. Julia Maesa had two grandsons, Elagabalus and Alexander, sons of her daughters Sohaemias and Mamaea respectively, both born to the hereditary priesthood of the temple. Elagabalus was the elder of the two cousins by six years, hence high-priest. Rather ungallantly his grandmother spread the rumour that Elagabalus was the illegitimate offspring of a union between Caracalla and Sohaemias. The army loved it, bought it, and proclaimed the sixteen-year-old boy-priest emperor in Emesa in 218.[80]

The Emperor Elagabalus then proceeded to Rome, taking all the trappings of his cult with him. The sources describe him and his religious rites as 'frenzied orgies' and 'a frenzy of arrogance and madness',[81] with details of his private life even more lurid. Such descriptions have all the disapproving relish of a prude in a brothel, and can be dismissed as mere propaganda – similar Roman descriptions of cannibalism and other such unspeakable orgies in Christian rites have, after all, long been relegated to the dustbin.[82] With the more lurid details stripped away, there are some details that have a ring of truth and even bring out a more likeable side to Elagabalus' character. He had a rather endearing propensity for practical jokes, for example, such as his practice of seating his more pompous dinner guests on 'whoopee cushions' that let out a farting noise, or placing his drunk dinner guests after they had fallen asleep into a room with wild, but (unknown to the guests) perfectly tamed and harmless, beasts![83] Frenzied depravity or mere youthfulness (he was, after all, only sixteen)? Contemporary censure and outrage at Elagabalus' giving women – his mother, Julia Sohaemias, and his grandmother, Varia – a place in the Senate, or at promoting freedmen to high office,[84] should surely attract nothing but praise in our own days of feminist and socialist political correctness. Indeed, even the author of the most scurrilous of the stories in the *Augustan History* has to concede: 'However, both these matters and some others which pass belief were, I think, invented by people who wanted to depreciate Heliogabalus to win favour with Alexander.'[85] Contrasting with the almost universal condemnation of Elagabalus, John Malalas alone of the Romans wrote warmly of this emperor.[86]

But it is Elagabalus' religion rather than his 'depravities' that are of real interest.[87] Through the welter of Roman prejudice, the sources reveal some real details. The references, for example, to 'wild dancing' by themselves hardly indicate perversion, as forms of dance were an accepted religious rite in many eastern cults, surviving in some cases to this day.[88] Carrying a parasol, whilst raising eyebrows in Rome in antiquity, was nothing more than the almost universal oriental symbol of kingship from earliest times until the Islamic Middle Ages.[89] Elagabalus' ritual procession involving himself, his senators and his cult object – the black stone or *Elagabal* – was one of the most fundamental rites of eastern religions that is reflected so strongly in the architecture as we have seen, and was to be adopted into Christianity.[90]

Part of his 'religious depravity' involved placing the black stone cult object of Elah-Gabal in a chariot for religious procession. This may have formed a part of the ritual 'migration' of the god that the numismatic evidence from Emesa suggests.[91] His much-derided 'marriage of the deities'[92] of Emesene Baal, first with the statue of Trojan Pallas and then with Carthaginian Urania, was surely not madness but sound religious and political policy: fusion and syncretism between East and West deserves praise rather than the ridicule that has been heaped upon this action. After all, he also associated the Jews, Samaritans and Christians with the cult[93] so that worship of his god might accommodate every religion – and it is significant that the Temple of Elagabal that he built on the Palatine (Figure 6) was near an earlier temple to Adonis.[94] Elagabalus' choices of 'consort' too are significant. He did not choose the more regular Graeco-Roman deities, but chose, first, an eastern deity, Pallas, brought to Rome by Aeneas from Troy, and then Carthaginian Urania which, like Emesene Baal, was Phoenician. Was Elagabalus merely trying to fit into what were already commonly accepted eastern religious practices in Rome? Re-establishing an eastern connection that began at the foundation of Rome with Aeneas and the Trojan Pallas?

Above all, one can hardly censure Elagabalus for continuing his hereditary religious rites after becoming emperor. After all, he never plotted to become emperor, his grandmother did. Elagabalus was a priest first, and being brought up as high-priest would have been sincere and punctilious in his beliefs and practices; the purple was thrust upon him, he never chose it. As the high-priest of the cult, Elagabalus would feel bound to continue his rituals in Rome. He may, it is true, have executed 'many famous and wealthy men who were charged with ridiculing and censuring his way of life',[95] but what high-priest and absolute emperor would not retaliate for insults to his beliefs? Many a better emperor killed for less reason.

Alas, Elagabalus was before his time, and it would be several more generations before the Romans accepted an eastern religion wholeheartedly, and longer still before they accepted real religious syncretism. Instead, Elagabalus' religion simply alienated the conservative establishment and the ever-powerful Praetorian Guard. Elagabalus slowly but inevitably lost popularity to his younger cousin, Alexander, arousing increasing jealousy in him. In the end the fickle Praetorian Guard – never a good judge of emperors, as history proved on numerous occasions – butchered Elagabalus and his mother, dumping the bodies in a sewer. Severus Alexander was proclaimed emperor in his place.

We thus leave the rather sad figure of Emperor Elagabalus, a tragic enigma lost behind centuries of malignment.[96] He was an unsuccessful emperor, it is true. But he was a sincere priest, which is what he was born to be. Born and brought up to the cloistered ceremonies of an eastern religion rather than the cynical power games of Rome's byzantine politics, he was a Syrian and a priest first, and only a Roman and an emperor second. Above all he was young: his only fault was extreme youth. From sixteen when he first ascended the throne to nineteen when he was finally butchered after a reign of merely 'three years, nine months and four days'[97] is surely too young for so much to be thrust upon anybody. One of his few surviving portraits, in the Capitoline Museum in Rome, shows a rather pathetic figure: a cocky youth with a wispy, pubescent moustache, but with a sense of overwhelming youth, vulnerability and uncertainty, despite the cockiness (Plate

Plate 155 Emperor Elagabalus (© Roma, Musei Capitolini)

155).[98] One is left feeling sorrow for the boy rather than any condemnation for the Emperor.

But perhaps the ghost of Elagabalus was to triumph after all. For his Sun god did, in the end, receive its rightful place in the Roman pantheon. The cult may have been received with revulsion when Elagabalus tried to thrust it upon the unwilling Romans, but, when the Emperor Aurelian resurrected it as part of a great eastern victory, it had gained in respectability (not to mention attractiveness: the temple in Rome was loaded with immense riches by Aurelian). This was because the Emperor Aurelian attributed his victory against Zenobia outside Emesa in 272 to divine intervention from the Emesene Sun god. As a result, he paid his respects at the temple immediately after the battle and afterwards built a magnificent temple to the Sun god of Elagabal in Rome, decorating it with the trophies looted from Palmyra.[99] The Sun god cult then achieved wide popularity in the western Roman world, a prime adherent being Constantine before he favoured Christianity. Elagabalus' Sun cult, therefore, not only paved the way for Christianity, it was later actually grafted on to Christianity to make it more palatable, and to this day Christian churches still face the direction of the rising Sun.[100]

Severus Alexander and the end of a dynasty

Like Elagabalus, Alexander[101] was born to the Emesene priesthood, but being six years his junior was never high-priest. He was born at Arqa in present-day northern Lebanon where a few remains mark his birthplace (in modest contrast to Lepcis Magna or Shahba). Coming to Rome at the age of nine in the wake of Elagabalus, he was not subject to such Syrianising influences as Elagabalus was, being brought up more as a Roman (although on his return to Syria, it is notable that 'the inhabitants of the provinces looked up to him as a god').[102] He was one of the wisest and most moderate emperors of the chaotic third century, and his portraits (such as the bust in the Hermitage) combine youth with mildness. But like all members of his family, he was dominated by his women-folk. His mother, Julia Mamaea, younger daughter of Julia Maesa, was the last of that extraordinary line of redoubtable Syrian women who ruled Rome behind their sons and husbands. Mamaea was no exception, and was on hand at all times to advise and guide her son in the ways of the imperial world, accompanying him even into the field. Indeed, Gibbon extols Mamaea's virtues above Domna's, awarding her much of the credit for Alexander's exemplary reign. Her portraits show that she inherited all the strength of character of her aunt, but without the calculation – Julia Maesa's position after all was already established by a family of emperors before her. Her face is confident but more inward looking – and she appears the prettiest of her family.[103] She was also known to be favourably disposed towards Christianity, although not practising herself.

The other trait that Severus Alexander shared with other members of his family was a destiny with the East: it dominated his life – and destroyed him in the end. He returned to Syria in response to the new threat from Sasanian Iran.[104] Despite conducting his campaign 'with such discipline and amid such respect, that you would have said that senators, not soldiers, were passing that way',[105] his armies suffered disaster. He retired from the East discredited. His popularity with the army consequently plummeted, exacerbated by the army's resentment at being ruled by a 'mother's boy' and a woman (note that the resentment was entirely sexist, never racist: there was no hint of resentment at either Alexander or Mamaea being Syrian). Matters reached a head after his Iranian disasters when Alexander was commanding a campaign on the Rhine frontier. The soldiers dispatched both Mamaea and Severus Alexander while he clung to his mother's arms, proclaiming the brutish Thracian giant and former shepherd, Maximinus, as emperor. Rome's extraordinary line of Phoenicio-Syrian emperors finally came to an end.[106]

In this powerful family of Syrian women who dominated their husbands and sons, and through them the empire, one senses almost a matriarchy. Apart from the emperors themselves, husbands and fathers are very shadowy figures. It was the first (and last) time that women were given places in the Senate. Whenever the dynasty looked like failing it would be a female relative from Emesa who would be called upon to take over the helm at Rome, not a male. Caracalla, Elagabalus and Alexander may well have been dominated by their mothers. But they cannot stand condemned for mere macho reasons. After all, Elagabalus was merely sixteen when proclaimed emperor and Alexander only thirteen, both still boys when a mother's influence is only natural. Caracalla was undoubtedly a tyrant of the worst sort, but he was good with the army. This is what counted when it came to the real business of running Rome, which was protecting the borders. Even Elagabalus had sound albeit flawed intentions. And apart from the disasters in the East, Severus Alexander's fourteen-year rule was as mild and wise as his portraits depict him

Plate 156 Emperor Severus Alexander (© Roma, Musei Capitolini)

(Plate 156).[107] Herodian's epitaph is thus a fitting one: '[Alexander] ruled for fourteen years without blame or bloodshed so far as it affected his subjects. A stranger to savagery, murder and illegality, he was noted for his benevolence and good deeds.'[108] Even the *Augustan History* writes of Severus Alexander as the perfect prince in 'an awkward imitation of the *Cyropaedia*'.[109] Gibbon sees him as the greatest and wisest of emperors since the golden age of the Antonines, whose exemplary reign could serve as a model for modern princes.[110] Aurelius Victor goes even further when he states that Alexander saved Rome from collapse.[111] This most noble – and aptly named – 'Roman' thus formed a fitting end to Rome's extraordinary dynasty of Phoenicio-Syrian emperors.

Aftermath

There was a footnote to the Emesene dynasty of emperors. In 253 Gallus, Aemilian and Valerian were contending for power in Italy. With Rome's back turned on the East, Shapur was able to invade Syria and capture Antioch.[112] In the power vacuum left by the temporary collapse of Roman rule, another priest of Emesa, Samsigeramus, supposedly inflicted a defeat on Shapur outside Emesa. As a result of its great victory, Emesa proclaimed a new emperor. This new emperor was a young Emesene called Sulpicius Antoninus who assumed the purple under the name Uranius Antoninus. It is unclear from the sources whether Samsigeramus and Uranius were the same person, or two related people. Samsigeramus was priest of the temple of Aphrodite. In the often confusing way of eastern syncretism, the deity Urania was equated to both the Phoenician Astarte/Aphrodite and the Arabian Allat,[113] so they may have been the same. At first, Uranius simply regarded himself as a younger colleague to Valerian, but it inevitably became a direct challenge. With the immense wealth of the Emesene temple treasury behind him, Uranius for a while even issued his own coinage. The coinage came to an end in 255, either because the gold from the Emesene Sun temple was exhausted or because Valerian eventually put him down. The fate of Uranius is not known.[114]

The 'Emperor Uranius', last of the Emesene Sun-kings, was seen as a champion of the Roman cause against Iran. He had everything behind him: wealth, dynastic roots, and a great victory against Rome's greatest enemy. But Valerian, for all his failures, had the trump card: Rome itself. Uranius' brief two years of glory was probably the last claim by a representative of Julia Domna's family for the imperial purple.[115] Whilst there is no conclusive evidence that Uranius belonged to this family, it seems likely that he did. A near contemporary and local source, the so-called *Sibylline Oracles* that were probably written in Emesa, in fact describe him as the 'last of all' of the priests who 'came from the Sun'.[116] Indeed, given the hereditary nature of the Emesene high-priesthood, as well as his adoption of the dynastic name of Antoninus and pretensions to the purple, the implications are that he was related, however distantly.[117]

Philip the Arab

The story of the 'Emperor' Uranius is to anticipate events. Before then, another Arab emperor was established in Rome who had no connection to the Emesene dynasty.[118] This was Marcus Julius Philippus, known as Philip the Arab,[119] a native of the small town of Shahba in southern Syria. Philip's origins as the son of a bandit from Trachonitis, which Shahba formed a part of, has been rejected as later Roman anti-Arab prejudice.[120] One country's 'bandit' is in any case another's aristocrat, the two usually amounting to the same thing. In 243 Philip became the praetorian prefect of Gordian III, then on campaign in the East against Iran. After Gordian's death, Philip was proclaimed emperor by the troops in the East in 244. He then swiftly negotiated a peace treaty with Shapur – Sasanian rock reliefs depict him on bended knee before the mounted figure of Shapur (Plate 26)[121] – and returned to Rome. Philip's reign was brief – just five years – but it was a stable one in the unstable third century. Rome enjoyed an important respite. It came to an end only too soon when he and his son (prematurely proclaimed as Philip II) were eliminated in 249 in a revolt by Trajan Decius.[122]

Although a brief reign, Philip's was particularly important in the annals of Rome. This was for a number of reasons. First, the year 248 was the year of the Millennium. Rome celebrated a thousand years of its existence, a thousand years from its origins as a minor town to becoming the greatest empire of the world. Certainly a thousand-year Reich is reason enough for the event to be remarkable, but what made it even more remarkable was that the Roman emperor who presided over and presented the games, as the ultimate Roman and embodiment of Roman civilisation, was an Arab. A native of a country that the worthy rustics who founded the city would never have heard about, let alone dreamt that they would one day be ruled by someone from there – and ruled as one of their own, not as a foreign conqueror. In some ways this makes Philip's reign as remarkable as that of

Trajan's or Hadrian's, for nothing else demonstrated just how far in every way Rome had come by the middle of the third century.

The second reason is more important, although more controversial. For it was Philip, not Constantine, who was Rome's first Christian Emperor. Philip's Christianity has always been a subject of considerable controversy, not least because of the paucity of its support amongst the sources. The main source is Eusebius, whose account of him attending services and receiving confession leaves little doubt on the matter.[123] Another source claims that Philip converted so that the Millennium would be Christian and not pagan.[124] Pagan sources, on the other hand, are almost completely silent.[125] Modern scholarship has ranged from complete rejection to complete affirmation, with most taking the middle road conceding that Philip at least 'dabbled' in Christianity.[126] Why, therefore, is it Constantine's Christianity that has taken primogeniture over Philip's?

Later Christian propagandists have tried to minimise Philip's Christianity in order to emphasise Constantine's. But more important, Constantine actually proclaimed Christianity for political rather than religious reasons (and did not, in fact, formally become a Christian until his deathbed). Philip, on the other hand, did no such thing: paganism remained Rome's official 'religion', while a Roman citizen's private beliefs – even the emperor's – were of little concern to the public so long as they remained private. It is argued that Philip's acts, such as the secular games and the deification of his father, were inconsistent with Christian behaviour (although even Constantine was deified).[127] But such acts were entirely consistent with Philip's behaviour: a local boy made good – one who, furthermore, had to go far to secure his position in an unstable environment – was hardly going to publicise some obscure eastern belief in the heart of Rome so soon after Elagabalus' debacle. He would have kept quiet about it and been even more scrupulous to follow Roman public ceremonial to the letter. But the precedent was nonetheless made, and the importance of Philip's conversion as a precedent for Constantine cannot be overestimated.[128]

If Philip's reign was important for anticipating Constantine and Christianity, it was also important for anticipating the rise of the Arabs to domination. Whilst one can doubt the Arab identity of the Emesene emperors (and even there it must be remembered that coins of both the Severan emperors and Philip the Arab often depict Syrian deities, such as Hadad and Atargatis),[129] it is impossible to reject the Arab credentials of Philip. As his nickname implies, Philip was Arab. Portraits depict him with the features and tight curly hair that one sees in Syria even today (Plate 157).[130] Whether Philip in fact felt in any way 'Arab' in the modern sense is unlikely, nor did either Philip or the Severan emperors represent any 'Arab lobby' at Rome. Philip – and the Severan emperors – were Romans above all. But that is irrelevant. What is important is what Philip meant to the Arabs themselves: that one of their own number could aspire to the world's highest office and succeed. It forms as much a landmark in the Arabs' self-awareness as it did in the Roman awareness of them as more than merely tent-dwellers. Philip signified more than anything else that the Arabs were no mere barbaric nomads of little account on the fringes of the civilised world, but had become an increasing factor on the world stage. His reign is one of the more important in the chain of events that culminated in the eventual triumph of the Arabs in the seventh century when the Near East ceased to be Roman and became Arab.[131]

Plate 157 Emperor Philip the Arab (© Monumenti Musei e Gallerie Pontificie)

Lepcis Magna: Roman city in Africa and the orientalisation of Europe

Europe, Asia, Africa: the Roman Empire spanned all three continents and Roman civilisation incorporated native European and Classical Greek cultures as well as Phoenician, Near Eastern and African. At Septimius Severus' great city of Lepcis Magna in Libya[132] we see all elements combined in one of the most monumental and eclectic cities of the Roman Empire, a city that is at once Roman, African and oriental. But it is the oriental elements that, under Septimius' transformation of his native city, predominate: Lepcis Magna was a conscious oriental transplant in the West. More than anything else, the architecture of Lepcis Magna reflects the historical processes of the third century that ultimately transformed Europe. It is also where so much of what has been discussed in this book can be focused, both architectural and historical.

Most of Rome's cities in North Africa were originally of Phoenician foundation, albeit incorporating earlier Libyan elements. These were mainly established in the great age of Phoenician colonial expansion between the ninth and seventh centuries BC, the most famous of which was the foundation of Carthage in 814–813 BC.[133] Lepcis Magna,[134] along with its sister colonies in Tripolitania of Sabratha and Oea (Tripoli), may have been sub-colonies of Carthage rather than founded directly by Tyre, although as late as the mid-second century AD Lepcis Magna still regarded Tyre as its traditional mother city, despite having been Roman for some three centuries. The point is an important one that ran far deeper than mere folk memory: later building activity in Lepcis was to demonstrate that its citizens never forgot their Near Eastern heritage.

The native Libyan[135] element in Rome's North African cities is well attested from history and was as much a constant element then as it is now. Important native kingdoms such as the Numidians, Mauretanians and Garamantaeans at different times both challenged and supported Roman rule there. Even after the Numidians and Mauretanians had been incorporated directly into the empire, the position of the various Hamitic tribes remained a vital one throughout: major tribal revolts, such as the Austurian, occurred in the fourth century with devastating effect, while the lack of tribal support in the sixth century was one of the more important factors in the ultimate failure of the Roman reconquest of North Africa under Justinian. Much of the Donatist movement of late antiquity also contained nationalist elements: native Hamitic Donatism versus foreign Roman orthodoxy. Finally, the native Libyans would have made up the bulk of the population in the countryside as well as an indeterminate, but significant, portion of the cities, both in Phoenician and Roman times.

These native elements do not appear much in the material remains of the Roman cities. It must be remembered, however, that many of these 'Roman' cities – particularly further inland – have Libyan names, such as Dougga, Ammaedara (Haidra), Theveste (Tebessa) and others, reflecting Libyan foundation before either Phoenician or Roman and presumably a substantial Libyan presence since.[136] The only significant Libyan remains are to be found in the former Garamantaean kingdom in the desert areas of the interior of Libya, where both African (Egyptian) and Mediterranean elements exist in the monumental architecture.[137] Outside the desert areas, the Libyan element is most visibly present in the funerary architecture, such as the spectacular second-century BC Numidian mausoleum of Ateban at Dougga, which incorporates Ionian, Lycian, Hellenistic, Phoenician and possibly even Persian elements in an extraordinarily eclectic monument. A similar monument has recently been restored at Sabratha. The most extraordinary of all – indeed, perhaps some of the most extraordinary funerary monuments in the entire Mediterranean region – is the monumental necropolis of the fourth–sixth century AD Libyan settlement at Ghirza in Tripolitania. Here, almost every architectural style known – as well as a few completely new innovations! – is reflected in a range of some fourteen tombs in two cemeteries. Some reflect Palmyrene funerary architecture, and their general baroque exuberance also reflects (mocks?) eastern Classical prototypes.[138] The Libyan element in Roman North Africa, therefore, was both strong and long-lasting.

Like the Libyan, the Phoenician element is not easily visible on a superficial level, but becomes more so on closer inspection.[139] Most of the cities were Phoenician foundations (when not Libyan) and this is probably reflected in the town plans – the rather trite observation that grid plans reflect Roman influence and haphazard street plans Phoenician does not necessarily hold true, as we have seen.[140] More tangible are the many temples dedicated to deities such as Saturn, Hercules, Liber Pater or Juno Caelestis. Whilst often superficially conforming to standard patterns of Roman temple architecture, the deities worshipped were thinly disguised Phoenician ones: Baal Hammon, Melqart, Shadrapa and Astarte respectively. Some in fact bore little resemblance to Roman prototypes, despite their Classical veneer: the crescent layout seen, for example, at the Temple of Juno Caelestis at Dougga or the Temple of Baalat at Thuburbo Majus, was a popular one with no counterpart in Roman architecture.

The Phoenician element existed most tenaciously, however, in the population themselves. Official inscriptions were bilingual, in Punic and Latin, for several centuries after the Roman conquest, the names of most of the leading citizens recorded in inscriptions were Phoenician, and the bulk of the population spoke Punic (often to the exclusion of any other language, as in the case of Septimius Severus' own sister) until the end of Roman rule, as St Augustine was to bemoan in the fifth century. The very ease and thoroughness of the conquest by the Arabs, ethnic and linguistic first cousins of the Phoenicians, in the seventh century bears witness to the Phoenician make-up of the urban population. The overwhelming Phoenician character of Roman North Africa was one of the most important and constant aspects of Roman rule there, being a vital factor in the transmission of Christianity to the West as we shall see.

At Lepcis Magna archaeology reveals traces of a sixth–fifth century BC Phoenician settlement at the mouth of the harbour and underneath the theatre (Figure 123). It is not known how far the present town plan reflects a Phoenician layout, nor how far the Phoenician town spread, although the existence of a cemetery under the theatre suggests that this area was extramural. The Roman-period Old Forum, therefore, laid out in the late first century BC, might well have formed the heart of the Phoenician town; the earliest temple there, dating from the Augustan period, is to the Phoenician patron deity of Lepcis, Shadrapa, equated with Roman Liber Pater, so might well be on the site of an earlier Phoenician temple.

Expansion in the early Roman period was both rapid and dramatic. The monumental market was built in 8 BC, the Old Forum between 5 BC and AD 54, the theatre in AD 1, another market (the Chalcidium) in AD 11–12, the Arch of Augusta Salutaris between AD 27 and 30 and the Arch of Tiberius in AD 35–6. Where identified, nearly all were endowed by wealthy Phoenician citizens: both the market and the theatre by Annobal Rufus, the Chalcidium by Iddibal Caphada Aemilius, the Temple of Rome and Augustus in the Old Forum by Caius, son of Hanno, and the Capitolium, also in the Old Forum, by Balyathon and Bodmelqart.

Both the wealth and the administration were still firmly in the hands of the older Phoenician aristocracy. The wealth that enabled such rapid expansion derived from two sources: trade with the interior and olive plantations. Lepcis lay at the end of a trade route that led southwards to the Garamantaean kingdom and further, a fact which determined its initial foundation by the commercially minded Phoenicians. Gold, ebony, ostrich eggs and feathers, slaves, exotic wild animals and other African products flowed through Lepcis Magna's increasingly more sophisticated port facilities, a trade which expanded rapidly with the opening of the European markets after the Roman conquest. The city's hinterland furthermore had been extensively cultivated with olives by the Phoenicians, who had introduced both sophisticated agriculture and the olive to North Africa. In Julius Caesar's peace settlement of 46 BC following the defeat of Pompey, a massive fine of three million pounds of olive oil annually – the equivalent of the produce of over a million trees – was imposed on Lepcis for its support of Pompey. This provides some indication of the amount of land under olive cultivation and the wealth that it generated, for Lepcis was easily able to afford it, particularly after the Roman conquest created an almost insatiable demand for olive oil in Europe.[141] The Arch of Tiberius, as well as the paving of the city streets at the same time, for example, were paid from the income of just one set of

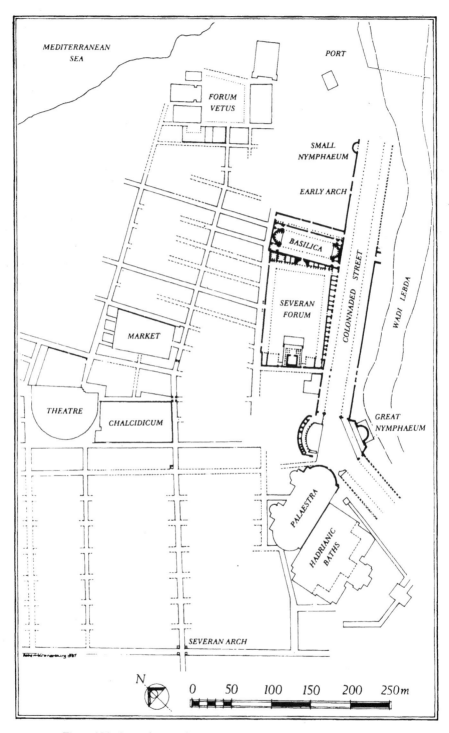

MEDITERRANEAN
SEA

PORT

FORUM
VETUS

SMALL
NYMPHAEUM

EARLY ARCH

BASILICA

COLONNADED STREET

SEVERAN
FORUM

WADI LEBDA

MARKET

THEATRE

CHALCIDICUM

GREAT
NYMPHAEUM

PALAESTRA

HADRIANIC
BATHS

SEVERAN ARCH

N

0   50   100   150   200   250m

Figure 123 Central area of Lepcis Magna (After Ward-Perkins)

lands. Annobal Rufus and his fellow philanthropists were presumably some of the many olive oil barons who profited from this boom. Thus, the city was doubly endowed with renewable sources of income which it was able to lavish on its buildings – it is significant that much of the emphasis was on market facilities in this first phase of monumentalisation.

The city's embellishment from this wealth culminated in the early second century AD with the elaborate Baths of Hadrian, dedicated in 126–7, modelled closely after the great imperial baths at Rome. To this and the existing monuments can be added several water installations, a second forum (unlocated, identified from inscriptions only), a massive amphitheatre and circus complex outside the city, and considerable engineering works enlarging and modifying the harbour to cope with the increasing shipping. By the middle of the second century, therefore, Lepcis Magna was a monumental city with all the standard urban trappings of a provincial Roman city sharing in the prosperity of the rest of Roman Africa, albeit a little more prosperous than most outside Carthage. The architecture was Roman above all, despite the Phoenician citizens who paid for it. The theatre, markets, baths, forums, circus and hippodrome hardly differed from the standard provincial architecture of the Roman West – even the Old Forum, with its possible Phoenician origins and temple to a Phoenician deity dominating it and Punic inscriptions to Phoenician benefactors, might just as easily belong to some country town in Italy, Gaul or Spain. To this, with the accession of one of Lepcis Magna's Phoenician elite to the Roman purple at the end of the second century, came one of the most dramatic and sudden transformations ever to affect a Roman city, when a monumental city of the Roman East was transplanted virtually wholesale over the existing western Roman fabric.

For Septimius Severus transformed his native town in two ways, the one long-recognised and easily apparent, the other more subtle but more radical. On becoming emperor, vast sums were lavished to transform it into one of the most monumental cities of the Roman world. But Septimius' transformation, and the city that Lepcis became, was almost wholly eastern in character. The transformation is seen in two areas: the Severan Arch and a whole new quarter that comprised a plaza, a nymphaeum, a colonnaded street, and a forum–basilica complex (Figure 123).

The Severan Arch is often dismissed as hurriedly erected and over-ornamented (Plate 158).[142] Both criticisms are valid, but its structural and aesthetic drawbacks detract from its significance. The arch is a 'triumphal' arch in the tradition of the great commemorative arches of Rome, such of those of Titus, Constantine or Septimius Severus himself. North Africa has many such arches (usually commemorating the Severan dynasty) but these are far simpler structures; in terms of elaboration and monumentality, that at Lepcis belongs with the imperial style of Rome rather than the more provincial ones elsewhere in North Africa (particularly now that it can be viewed in all its glory following the recent restoration). But what sets the Lepcis arch apart is that it is a four-way arch or tetrapylon, unlike most of the others, which are generally of the more standard single or triple arch types. Whilst tetrapylons exist in North Africa (the Arch of Marcus Aurelius in Tripoli, for example, or the Arch of Trajan at Lepcis itself), they were unusual; the form, as we have seen,[143] was a product of the Near East, where they occur frequently. The eastern princess, Julia Domna, is accordingly depicted with the remainder of the imperial family on two of the reliefs on the Lepcis arch (Plates 159 and 160). Julia Domna and the tetrapylon style are not the only oriental elements present. The siege of an oriental city (perhaps Hatra?) is also depicted, while the marble reliefs themselves – imported Proconnesian

Plate 158 The Severan Arch at Lepcis Magna

marble from the Sea of Marmara – were almost certainly carved by eastern artists, possibly from Aphrodisias in Asia Minor.[144] Indeed, the main relief on the attic storey, which depicts the triumphal procession of Septimius in a chariot with his two sons Caracalla and Geta, exhibits a tendency to frontality regardless of the direction they face (Plate 160). As well as anticipating Byzantine styles, this is characteristic of late antique Syrian and Mesopotamian art, more familiar in the art of Palmyra or Dura Europos, that probably originated in earlier Arabian art.[145] Overall, the 'baroque' flamboyance and elaboration of the monument also recalls eastern baroque prototypes: the over-elaboration of the Aphrodisias Tetrapylon, for example, or the broken pediments of the Petra façades (Plates 8 and 14). Whilst the great triumphal arches of imperial Rome express the triumphs of Rome, its emperors and Roman values, that at Lepcis is expressed almost wholly in an oriental vocabulary.

The Severan Arch is only an isolated monument, but in Septimius Severus' new monumental city of Lepcis we see a far more deliberate attempt to turn Lepcis Magna into an oriental city. The massive expansion of the harbour facilities reflects merely an economic need (although it appears that many of the new installations of the Severan-period harbour were meant more for show than for practical use), but one of the harbour-side temples was to a Syrian deity. This was the Temple of Jupiter Dolichenus on the south side of the harbour. Unfortunately too little of it survives – little more than the

Plate 159 Relief of the Severan family on the Arch at Lepcis Magna. The Emperor faces his two sons, Caracalla and Geta; Julia Domna looks on

Plate 160 Processional relief on the Arch at Lepcis Magna: the Emperor with Caracalla and Geta (whose features are erased) behind. Note tendency to frontality

steps and a much ruined podium – to determine whether it contained the standard Syrian trappings of high place, canopied adyton, exterior altar and temenos that we have reviewed in Chapter 7. But the rest of the new Severan quarter contains many more Syrian elements.

The quarter begins at the eastern end of the palaestra in front of the Hadrianic baths (Figure 124). Here, there is an awkward junction formed by the end of the palaestra with the street leading from the theatre to the north-west and the two new colonnaded streets that were built north-east to the harbour and south alongside the Hadrianic Baths. To mask – or mark – this, a circular plaza was planned (Figure 125). Such an irregular meeting of many disparate elements presents almost insuperable architectural problems, but the solution was both masterly and typical of the eastern Roman world. Although never finished (and now obscured by overbuilding) this circular plaza recalls that at Jerash, similarly built to mark an awkward junction, and others in the Roman Near East that we have reviewed elsewhere (Figures 37 and 64).[146]

The plaza was dominated on the south-eastern side by a monumental new nymphaeum, consisting of a massive exedra flanked by two arches aligned onto the sidewalks of the colonnaded streets to the south and north-east (Plate 161). Once again, this is more characteristic of the monumental nymphaea of the Roman East than of the fountains of the West. It closely follows that peculiar type of monument, strictly speaking not nymphaea, found only in Roman Syria, the *kalybe* or monumental façade for the display of statuary. Such *kalybes* appear to have no counterpart in western Roman architecture. Another, much ruined, Severan exedra of uncertain function, alongside the colonnaded street to the north-east, might also be a *kalybe*. Whether nymphaea in the conventional sense or *kalybes* along Syrian lines, the closest architectural parallels are once again in eastern Roman architecture rather than western (Figure 79, Plate 51).[147]

The most pronounced oriental feature of Severan Lepcis is, of course, the great

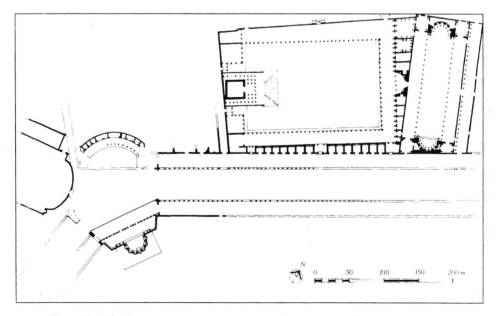

Figure 124 The Severan monumental quarter at Lepcis Magna (After Ward-Perkins)

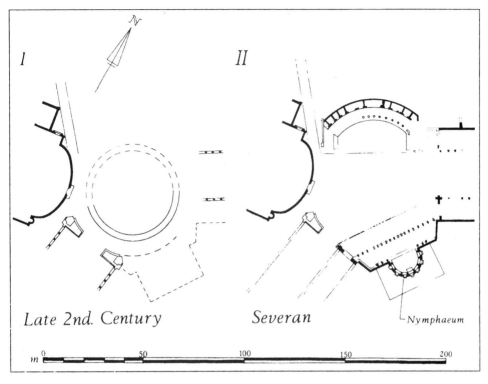

Figure 125 The circular plaza and nymphaeum at Lepcis Magna (After Ward-Perkins)

Plate 161 The Severan nymphaeum at Lepcis Magna. Compare with Plate 51

427

colonnaded street that led to the harbour, flanked by the new Severan forum (Figure 124). Some 400 metres in length and about 41 metres wide (with sidewalks), it forms a monumental approach from the newly enlarged Severan harbour. Colonnaded streets culminating in (or beginning with) a circular plaza are an entirely eastern urban feature as we have seen, with no occurrences in the Roman West (Figure 64). This is the sole occurrence of the arrangement outside the Near East[148] and more than any other monument at Lepcis represents a deliberate orientalism. Like colonnades in the East, those here are mounted on square pedestals, but unlike the trabeate colonnades of eastern cities (with the sole exception of Damascus), that at Lepcis is surmounted by arcades. This was, however, just as unusual a feature in the West as it was in the East at the time and anticipates Diocletian's arceate Palace at Spoleto by nearly a century and a half. Capitals, both here and in the forum alongside, were a combined lotus and acanthus style that is mostly found in Egypt as well as Syria and Anatolia.

The great forum with its basilica alongside was the crowning glory of the new Severan city (Figures 124 and 126, Plate 162). This complex has been compared with the great imperial forums of Rome itself, such as that of Trajan. At first, the Severan Forum might seem to be the one 'western' exception to an otherwise conscious architectural orientalism. After all, the forum is an entirely western architectural concept, with few counterparts in the East, and the basilica, forming an integral part of it alongside, is wholly western in inspiration and architectural development as we have seen in Chapter 7. The forum forms a vast rectangle, enclosed by unusually high walls of superb quality masonry, with entrances on both longitudinal walls. The interior is surrounded on three sides by splendid arcaded colonnades, decorated with Medusa heads in the spandrels. The centre of the fourth, south-western, side is dominated by a huge octastyle temple raised on a magnificent podium. Decoration is lavish to the point of vulgarity throughout, carried out on a 'money no object' basis. Immense slabs of deeply carved Proconnesian marble

Figure 126 Restored view of the Severan Forum and Temple at Lepcis Magna (After Ward-Perkins)

Plate 162 The Severan Forum at Lepcis Magna

adorn both forum and basilica, with the marble pilasters of the basilica almost certainly carved by the same eastern artists who worked on the Triumphal Arch. Colossal monolithic columns are of pink granite imported from upper Egypt. Everything about the complex was built to impress and overawe, in terms of scale, lavishness and sheer, opulent wealth.

But despite the western origins of the forum and comparisons with the great imperial forums of Rome, the architectural inspiration of the Severan Forum is once again from the East. Architecturally, western forums were far less unified, less enclosed, more cluttered, consisting of unenclosed plazas with temples, shops and other public buildings jostling each other for space – the Old Forum at Lepcis is a classic example. The Severan Forum is far more unified, and its high surrounding walls impart an exclusiveness to its compound, cutting it off from the surrounding city rather than forming an integral part of it as other forum plazas do. Most of all, instead of the standard 'forum package' of a Capitolium – a temple to the official cult of Jupiter, Juno and Minerva – with other temples to official city cults, that at Lepcis is dominated by just the one single temple, to which the vast courtyard in front of it appears entirely subservient (Figure 126). Architecturally, it appears to have been inspired most directly by the imposing temple compounds of Syria, similarly enclosed in sumptuously decorated colonnaded enclosures. On entering the great courtyard of the Severan Forum one is reminded overwhelmingly not so much of the Forum of Trajan in Rome but of Baalbek or Palmyra's Temple of Bel – or, for that matter, the Temple of Jupiter Hadad at Damascus or of Artemis at Jerash (Plate 4). The arrangement of a temple on a podium at one end of an immense open space recalls the Temple of Jupiter Heliopolitanus at Baalbek in particular, a temple we have already noted for its associations with the Severan dynasty (Figure 4).[149] Baalbek is also perhaps the only other building complex in the Roman world that matches the Severan Forum in sheer, overstated arrogant wealth. This is not to suggest that the Severan Forum at Lepcis is an eastern temple compound; its function as a forum is not in doubt. But the architectural and conceptual inspirations are striking, and it is significant that the temple that dominates Lepcis Magna's great new compound was dedicated neither to the official Roman triad nor to Rome and Augustus, but to the Severan family itself. The dedication was probably made by Caracalla in 216,[150] by which time the Severan family was dominated above all by Julia Domna and, through her, firmly connected to a line of oriental priest-kings, traditional guardians of one of the most opulent and exotic of oriental temples.

The hand of a single master architect, overseeing all of the Severan building activity from the Tetrapylon to the Harbour, has been recognised in these works, an architect whose eastern origins cannot be in doubt.[151] And behind the anonymous eastern architect the shadow of Septimius Severus looms large. But no other emperor before had embellished his home town on anywhere near the same scale: Septimius lavished more money on his birthplace than he did on Rome itself, and more than any other emperors lavished on their birthplace. For example, Falacrina in Italy or Italica in Spain, the former the birthplace of Vespasian, the latter of Trajan and Hadrian, remained small, unembellished provincial towns throughout antiquity. Other wealthy Phoenician citizens at Lepcis had endowed their city with monuments, but the works of Annobal Rufus, Bodmelqart and their fellow members of the local aristocracy were in a very different category from those of Septimius. Apart from sheer scale, former endowments at Lepcis had belonged unambiguously within the sphere of western Roman architecture, despite their Phoenician sponsors. Septimius' buildings are eastern imports.

Septimius Severus was fascinated by the lands of his Phoenician forebears to the east, but behind either Septimius Severus or his anonymous architect one can detect at Lepcis Magna the hand of his wife, Julia Domna, uppermost. The enormous influence that this redoubtable Syrian princess wielded throughout the Roman world through her husband and son has been described earlier in this chapter. The prodigious wealth of the Emesene temple which her family controlled is manifest in the 'money no object' rebuilding of Lepcis, endowments that no previous emperor had been able to afford for a provincial city. Through her and the Severan dynasty of oriental princesses and emperors which she (rather than her husband) founded, the East came to Rome. The fact that both her home town of Emesa in Syria and her 'adoptive' town of Lepcis Magna in Libya today are known under the same modern Arabic name of Homs may be no more than a coincidence. But it is a particularly appropriate one.

The Severan buildings at Lepcis Magna are more than a collection of architectural curiosities. At Lepcis we see the embodiment in stone of so much of what can only be called the Severan Revolution. The East had come to Rome to stay, and was to leave its permanent mark on all subsequent Roman history. Oriental cults were anticipating Christianity. The combination of Phoenician and Syrian religious ideas were to anticipate monotheism. The division of the empire into East and West by Caracalla and Geta were to anticipate Diocletian's reforms. The priest-emperor Elagabalus was to anticipate both the Popes of Rome and the Christian emperors of Constantinople in the centralising of all secular and religious power. The emphasis on dynasticism, clung to perhaps tenuously but always tenaciously (and usually by the Syrian women of the dynasty) anticipated the transformation of the Roman imperium into a hereditary monarchy. The architecture anticipated the great Imperial foundations of late antiquity. In the end of the client states and the extension of Roman citizenship to all free members of the empire we see the beginnings of the centralised, monolithic Byzantine state. Soon after the Severans, Rome was to see, in Philip, the first Christian emperor.

But most of all, with the rise of real provincials to supreme power, not only provincials from North Africa and Syria, but natives of those areas rather than descendants of Italian colonists, we see the beginning of the marginalisation of the city of Rome itself. Septimius paid more attention to transforming Lepcis than he did to Rome, a city he spent much of his life as emperor away from. Caracalla anticipated Constantine in choosing Byzantium as his capital – indeed, Septimius Severus was the first emperor to significantly embellish this otherwise little-known city. In massively enlarging and embellishing Lepcis Magna, Septimius may even have been anticipating Constantine in moving the capital of Rome itself. Under subsequent emperors the city of Rome was to become less and less a factor in Roman affairs. In the stones of Lepcis Magna the long march to Constantinople had begun.

From Paganism to Christianity

It is not often appreciated just how revolutionary a step the adoption of Christianity was for a European people. So closely is Christianity now associated with European civilisation that it is simply taken for granted. Indeed, Christianity is regarded as fundamental to the very *definition* of Europe and Western identity[152] – throughout history Christianity has been used as a stick with which to beat non-Europeans, as a way of underlining the difference between East and West, 'them' and 'us'. But to begin with, Christianity for the West was a radical, revolutionary idea, far more revolutionary than Communism or other nineteenth-century radical movements in Europe in our own era. For unlike Communism, which was rooted in European political and philosophical ideas already old by the time it was implemented, Christianity in antiquity was a completely alien idea with no counterparts and few points of contact in European religion or philosophy. In the transition from European paganism to Christianity, the question of how such an alien, non-European idea became so implanted on such infertile soil that it has become one of the fundamental definitions of European identity, is one of the most important questions in history, and perhaps the most important historical process in the development of European civilisation.

The transition from paganism to Christianity has recently come in for greater scrutiny.[153] In order to understand the process, three distinct transitions that Christianity had to make in establishing itself in the West must be recognised. There is the obvious spatial transition, from East to West, but less obvious is the conceptual transition, from the eastern to the western mind, as well as a class transition (with no intention of imparting a Marxist interpretation to history intended) from carpenter's assistant to world emperor.

Religion in pagan Rome

To begin with, it is important to understand the position of religion in Roman society. There was a strong, clear-cut division between public and private religion. We have already seen how this division is reflected in the beginnings of Christian architecture.[154]

Public religion consisted of the official cults of the Roman Empire: the cult of the Capitoline triad of Jupiter, Juno and Minerva, the cult of Rome and Augustus, the cult of the deified Emperor, and similar official cults designed to guarantee the civic welfare of the empire. These official cults, the nearest Rome had to an official 'religion' before Christianity, were a part of public life. Their temples occupied prominent positions in the public spaces of every town in the empire (outside the East). Observation of them was an essential duty of everybody holding public office, from the emperor to the common soldier, and participation in their rites was demanded as a demonstration of loyalty to the state. Women, holding neither public nor military office, were naturally exempt – a minor point, but one that was to have immense ramifications in the transition to Christianity, as we shall see.

Alongside the official cults were a vast range of private religions and cults. These reflected the religious beliefs of the vast majority of the empire, and could be – and often were – entirely personal. The personal religions were of no interest to the state, so long as they did not interfere with the observation of the official cults. There was an almost unlimited number of private cults, gods and religions. St Augustine enumerates an astonishing variety: gods of virtually every aspect of daily life, gods of the household, gods of various professions, patron gods of different localities, religions and cults of different peoples of the empire, even purely personal gods.[155] The pantheon was effectively unlimited. An individual was free to worship his own private religion in any way he pleased (so long as it did not transgress Roman laws against witchcraft, black magic or similar disapproved rites), and it was usually carried out in the private home or in relatively minor neighbourhood shrines and temples. It was into this sphere of Roman private religion that Christianity first entered and became a part of, along with cults of Mithras, Isis, Baal and the numerous other mystery and eastern cults that became increasingly popular.

From slave to master

It must be emphasised that Christianity was very much a religion of the lower classes, even the slaves, in the beginning. For such a religion to work its way up to the aristocracy and the highest in the land – the emperor – requires some explanation. Mere persuasive power of the religion itself is alone not enough, the distance between slave and master was too great, with few points of contact.

That Christianity appealed to the underclasses of Roman society is not itself surprising; its egalitarianism, its message to the humble, its promises of hope are well enough known not to need reiterating. More important, its conscientious objection to the performance of official Roman rites would have made it spread to the underclasses more easily, who were under no such obligation. From Rome's underclasses to its rulers is still a great transition, but there is one area where both extremes of the social spectrum came into regular and intimate contact: the household. By far the majority of slaves in the Roman world were household servants, rather than inmates of the galleys or the gladiatorial schools so beloved by cinema. The upper classes who naturally had the most contact with household slaves were the housebound women; the larger – and hence wealthier and more prominent – the household, the larger the number of slaves and the larger the contact between Christian servant and pagan mistress. It was through the servants – literally over the kitchen sink – that the women of Rome first learnt of Christianity. It comes as little surprise to learn that so many of the early Christians – and early Christian martyrs – were women, women moreover from the noblest households with the greatest numbers of servants. Sienkiewicz's novel *Quo Vadis*, whilst fictional, provides a very true picture in this respect. We even read of Christian women in the imperial household (such as Marcia, the mistress of Commodus) as early as Marcus Aurelius, while by the time of the Severans Christianity had touched the very top of the imperial female household (for example Julia Mamaea, mother of Emperor Severus Alexander). The relationship of high-born Roman lady to servant girl was a common theme in early Christianity, borne out, for example, in the story of the martyrdoms of St Perpetua and St Felicity at Carthage (where women generally represented a high proportion of the martyrs). Persecution of Christians was assured of high attendance in the arenas: not only was it women being butchered (and they were often displayed bare-breasted), but high-born women at that.[156] Any mob would love it.

From there the transition was but a short step. The husbands, of course, would not and could not have any truck with their wives' religion: being high-born they had public duties to perform which were incompatible to Christianity. But the children were another matter: the mothers were able to pass their religion on to their sons, the future holders of public office. The transition from slave to ruler was complete. Without adhering to any current 'politically correct' feminist view of history, the fact is nonetheless true that Christianity's first great triumph represents a triumph of feminism, one of women's greatest triumphs in history.

From Iran to Rome

The conceptual transition was an even greater one, for Christianity had virtually no common ground in western religious thought upon which to graft its ideas, despite efforts to see common ground in visions, ritual, philosophers or other aspects of western paganism. To understand this it is necessary to outline a number of different areas, both in which Christian religious ideas were rooted in the East, and through which contacts were made with the West. They can be summarised in terms of the religious ideas of Iran, Anatolia, the Semitic world (other than Judaeo-Christianity), and the pagan Sun cult. From there, the third and final transition, the physical one from East to West, becomes far more understandable.

Zoroastrianism was the world's first credal religion, reason enough for it to be fundamental to the development of any later monotheism. Its founder, Zoroaster, may have lived 1700–1500 BC, although he is generally regarded as having lived in about 1000–900 BC in Bactria.[157] Suffice to say it was substantially earlier than Christianity. But mere primogeniture does not alone make it essential to an understanding of Christianity; Zoroastrianism contained many more elements that found their way into Christianity. It was the first religion with a concept of a hopeful hereafter offering a day of judgement, salvation, resurrection and paradise, rather than some vague, amorphous netherworld such as existed in Greek or Judaic traditions. The dualism which dominates Zoroastrian belief – the conflict between the forces of light and darkness – is echoed in Christianity by its emphasis on good versus evil, as well as heaven and hell, god and Satan. This dualistic belief has been suggested as an explanation for the eastern orientation of the early churches: east, being the source of light, symbolised good, as opposed to the west, the source of darkness symbolising evil.[158]

More than that is the Zoroastrian notion of deity representing the abstract concept of purity and goodness, of the universal single god, of god the creator.[159] The idea that 'God is good' has become so much an accepted part of Christian faith that it is merely taken for granted, but it must be remembered that the idea was quite revolutionary in the western world in antiquity: the pagan gods – the gods of the Greeks and Romans – were good, bad, indifferent, in fact reflected the full range of human behaviour, the only difference from humankind being their immortality. They were rarely, if ever, *good*! Even the god of the Old Testament was to a large extent a severe, vengeful god; the Christian god owes more to Zoroastrianism than to Judaism.

The Zoroastrian conflict between good and evil was not indefinite, for it was believed that a redeemer – the *saoshyant* – would ultimately appear and overthrow the forces of darkness forever, ushering in a new era of rule by the forces of light that would last for eternity. This *saoshyant*, moreover, was to be born of a virgin from the prophet Zoroaster's lineage.[160] The implications for the development of Christianity are obvious, although the idea of a redeemer or saviour was common to a number of other ancient eastern religions, both pagan and monotheist.[161] The Christian reverence for a sacred book springs mainly from Judaism with its reverence for the Torah, but it might equally stem from the Zoroastrian reverence for the sacred *Avesta*. Of far greater implications for Christianity was the position of the hereditary priesthood, or Magi, in the Zoroastrian religion. The institution of the Magi is one of the most fundamental in Iranian tradition. Its exact origins are hazy: it probably antedates Zoroaster, going back to early Iranian origins in Central Asia. When Indo-Iranian tribes migrated to India in the second millennium BC the idea of an hereditary high-priesthood was taken with them and became the Brahmans, the Indo-Iranian overlay on Indian Hinduism. The institution of the Magi followed Iranian migrations to the Iranian plateau too, becoming a specific religious caste of the Medes. It was grafted onto Zoroastrianism and has remained an integral part of Iranian society to this day: many important Iranian dynasties, such as the Sasanians, the Barmakids, the Samanids and the Safavids, began as hereditary priestly families (Zoroastrian, Buddhist or Sufi), and today, Iran is the only country in the Islamic world which has a structured priestly hierarchy (the mullahs and ayatollahs). The institution of a priesthood had no counterpart in the West. The Judaic institution of the Pharisees only occurred, it must be stressed, *after* Judaism came into contact with – and under the influence of – Zoroastrianism during the Babylonian exile.[162] Pagan Rome had many priests, of course. But their function was strictly limited to the temples they were attached to; there was never any structured hierarchy, no concept of administering to a flock or of overseeing the religion, in both spiritual and administrative terms, such as became familiar under the Church. The Magi of Zoroastrian Iran was the only institution of a structured priesthood in the ancient world. The idea entered Christian mythology with the visit of the Three Magi to the infant Christ[163] – symbolically, the old monotheistic religion giving its blessing to the new one being born in Bethlehem.

The Iranian institution of the Magi was to have immense repercussions for the West politically as well as religiously. Under the Sasanian Shah Shapur I[164] in the third century AD, the religious reforms of the Zoroastrian high-priest Kartir established for the first time a monotheistic religion as a structured, state religion and the Zoroastrian 'church' as an extension and instrument of Iranian state policy. This was the culmination of a movement originally begun by Tansar, high-priest under Shapur's father, Ardeshir, who writes in his *Testament*: 'Know that royal authority and religion are two brothers in perfect agreement with each other.'[165] The position that Kartir created, of arch-priest with state responsibilities to oversee both official religious formalities and religious orthodoxy, foreshadowed the Papacy of Christianity.[166] Such a revolutionary step might have found precedent in Buddhism, such as Kanishka's patronage of Buddhism in the first century AD or even Ashoka's in the third century BC. The precedent thus set by the Iranians was soon followed by the Romans. Constantine, a short time later, established his own state monotheistic and monolithic church, a structure that was to be an instrument of state policy and a means for centralising his own rule – as well as a means, ironically, for combating Iran.[167] The ensuing structure became the keystone of all subsequent European history. Constantine's subsequent letter to Shapur extolling the virtues of Christianity seems to have been an echo of Abgar's letters to fellow rulers following his conversion over a century before, or even Ashoka's letters to the Hellenistic rulers of the West following his conversion to Buddhism in the third century BC.[168]

So far, only the influences of Iranian religious ideas have been outlined, with few physical points of contact with the West. Western contact with the Iranians was one of the most important and perennial factors of ancient history. This had two strands, in both Judaism and Hellenism. The first had the most immediate effect on Judaism, hence Christianity, for it must be stressed that much of the formation of canonical Judaism took place during and immediately after the Babylonian Exile when it came into intimate contact with Zoroastrianism. The contact transformed Judaism.[169]

Iranian contact with Hellenism is the other strand, beginning with the contacts formed with the Greek world in the days of the first Persian Empire of Cyrus the Great, and his successors with important Zoroastrian influences on Greek philosophy (which, it must be emphasised, originated in Asia Minor, not mainland Greece).[170] The contact, amounting to an obsession, was renewed by Alexander and became a constant theme of Roman imperial history, as much of this book has shown. It seems hardly necessary to look further for points of contact, so fundamental and so perennial has this peculiar Iranian relationship been. But several vehicles by which Iranian religious ideas came west are worth emphasising. The Romans themselves related their ancient cult of Vesta to the Zoroastrian fire cult, in particular to the great Fire Temple of Adhur Gushnasp at Shiz in Azerbaijan,[171] and Kartir himself claimed to have introduced Zoroastrianism to Antioch and other parts of the occupied Roman East during the Persian campaigns of the third century.[172]

In this context it is important to remember the existence of Iranian kingdoms – survivals of the Achaemenid Empire – *within* the Graeco-Roman world. These were the kingdoms in Anatolia founded by Iranian aristocratic families – often former satraps of the Persian Empire – following the death of Alexander: the kingdoms of Pontus founded in 302 BC by Mithradates, of Cappadocia founded in 255 BC by Ariarathes, and of Commagene founded in about 163 BC by Ptolemaeus.[173] There was also an Iranian element in the kingdom of Edessa, as we have seen, and a very strong Iranian element – both cultural and dynastic – in Armenia. Iranian elements have also been observed in the Nabataean kingdom.[174] In fact Iranian communities existed throughout Asia Minor, beyond the Iranian kingdoms, and Zoroastrianism survived throughout the Roman period in these communities.[175]

All of these 'neo-Persian' kingdoms survived into the Roman period.[176] The wars with Pontus – the three 'Mithradatic Wars' fought between Rome and Mithradates VI – in the first century BC were one of the more significant events in Rome's expansion into the

East, with a token Pontic kingdom under King Darius surviving as a client of Rome until 37 BC. Cappadocia and Commagene also became clients of Rome following Pompey's settlement of the East in 63 BC until both were annexed in the first century AD: Cappadocia in AD 17 after the death of its last king, Archelaus, and Commagene after the death of Antiochus IV in AD 72.

Commagene was the only one of these neo-Persian kingdoms whose royal family bore mainly Hellenistic names, despite their claims to Iranian aristocratic descent, whereas both the Pontic and Cappadocian royal families retained Iranian names throughout. Although all of the rulers became increasingly Hellenised after the first few generations – it is unlikely that any of them spoke Persian in the end – they retained considerable Iranian sentiment and character, particularly in the field of religion. Iranian priests – the Magi – who had come into Anatolia in the Achaemenid period remained as an import-ant religious group in these kingdoms throughout the Hellenistic and into the Roman period. The Magi were particularly prominent in the kingdom of Cappadocia. Strabo, Diodorus, Pausanias and Appian all describe the rites of the Magi and fire worship in Asia Minor.[177] The important first-century AD Cappadocian religious figure, Apollonius of Tyana, whose cult was put forward as an alternative to Christ as we have seen,[178] may well have been descended from the Cappadocian Magi (spiritually if not genetically).[179] We also learn of Magi practising in Syria, Mesopotamia, Arabia and Egypt, with instances even in the western Mediterranean, as late as the fourth century.[180] Zoroastrianism sur-vived in Anatolia as late as AD 562 – and was recognised by Rome as lying to some extent within Sasanian religious jurisdiction.[181] The Zoroastrian concept of the *saoshyant*, the saviour, arrived in the Hellenistic world through the Anatolian Iranian kingdoms in the second century BC in the tradition of the Oracle of Hystaspes. By the Christian era the Oracle of Hystaspes had become equated with Christ.[182] The Temple of Comana in Pontus became an important centre for the cult of Anaïtis, the Iranian Anahita or 'Persian Artemis', which became grafted on to the Anatolian Artemis cult. Anahita was one of the main cults of Iran throughout antiquity that incorporated elements of Zoroastrianism, so became in Pontus an important vehicle for the transmission of religious ideas. The cult was administered by hereditary Magi, presumably descendants of those who came from Iran in the Achaemenid period (the term for 'high-priest' for this cult is derived from the Iranian title *mawbed* for 'priest), who also became priests for other cults, even, on occasion, of a Temple of Rome.[183] Pausanias' description of the temples at Hypaipa and Hiero-caesarea in Lydia in the second century AD are virtually 'classic' Zoroastrian.[184] The Christian regard for holy water might have derived from the cult of Anahita, where holy water is central to its ritual. Holy water in Christianity, however, might equally have evolved from Nabataean religious practice[185] or even the cult of Atargatis, both of which had water central to their ritual. The rulers of Commagene, despite their Greek names, prac-tised an Iranian dynastic cult that incorporated Ahuramazda, Mithras and Verethragna, equated with Zeus, Apollo–Helios–Hermes, and Heracles respectively. This extraordin-ary syncretic cult is depicted sculpturally, epigraphically and spectacularly at Antiochus I's (69–31 BC) great dynastic complex on the top of Mt Nemrud in the middle of his kingdom, which was attended by Magi 'in the Persian fashion'. The spread of Mithraism elsewhere throughout Europe was known to have been helped by Commagenians.[186] The cult of Jupiter Dolichenus, which achieved considerable popularity throughout the Roman world spreading westwards as far as northern Britain, had its origins at Doliche in the Commagenian kingdom. Its iconography probably derives from the Hittite god

Teshup, but of more significance in the present context is that alone of Roman cults, that of Jupiter Dolichenus had a structured, hereditary clergy, surely deriving from the Iranian Magi. Dolichenus altars also bore a superficial resemblance to Zoroastrian fire altars.[187]

It comes as no surprise to learn that all of these former Iranian kingdoms became important centres of early Christianity, both for its development and its spread. The bishopric of Pontus, particularly under St Gregory in the third century, was one of the most important Christian centres in the East,[188] while the vast numbers of churches that still litter the landscapes of Cappadocia and Commagene today – the underground churches, for example, or the Binbir Kilise (the 'Thousand and One Churches') of the Black Mountain – attest to its strength and tenacity in those regions. In this context, it is worth recalling that Armenia, a similarly Iranised kingdom in Anatolia, was the first kingdom in the world to proclaim Christianity a state religion (with the possible exception of Edessa). The Magi of Anatolia simply became the priests of Christianity.

Of equal importance for the transmission of Iranian religious ideas to the West was Mithraism, the architectural remains of which have been found throughout the Roman world from the Euphrates to Hadrian's Wall, particularly along the northern frontiers.[189] Several emperors, from Nero to Galerius, toyed with Mithraism, and so popular did Mithraism become – particularly in the army – that for a while it even looked as though it might pre-empt Christianity in becoming the main religion of the empire. It never did nor could – it excluded women – and Roman Mithraism was substantially different from its Iranian origins.[190] Nonetheless, there were Iranian elements in Roman Mithraism and Iranian ideas broadly flowed into the Roman world through it.[191]

Another Iranian religion that entered the West in late antiquity was Manichaeism.[192] Manichaeism was a syncretic religion, proclaimed by the Iranian prophet Mani in the third century AD, that incorporated many elements of Zoroastrianism and acknowledged Zoroaster, Buddha and Jesus as the predecessors of Mani. It also incorporated elements of Gnosticism and neo-Platonism.[193] The Prophet Mani himself actively proselytised in the Roman Empire, accompanying Shapur's armies in the mid-third century into Syria.[194] He sent missions to Alexandria and elsewhere who converted, amongst others, Zenobia of Palmyra (according to Manichaean documents) and 'the religion of the Apostle [Mani] flourished in the Roman Empire'.[195] During the time of Diocletian a Manichaean schismatic called Boundos practised in Rome. He also taught in Persian, and his schism was called the Daristhenians, a Persian-derived word.[196] Manichaeism achieved wide popularity throughout the Roman world before it was condemned as a heresy by the Church. But it survived into the Middle Ages among the Cathars of France and the Bogomils of the Balkans, until they were finally exterminated. Although it was formed some centuries after Christianity – indeed, it incorporated Christianity – it is important to remember that much of Christian practice in its present form did not become doctrine until the fourth century and even later. Iranian religious ideas may well have entered Europe through Manichaeism, despite its later date, influencing much of medieval Christianity. One need only recall that St Augustine, more than anybody else the father of western Christianity, began life as a Manichee.

There was another Iranian religious element that had a profound, albeit indirect, effect on the growth of Christianity in the Greek mind. This came via Alexander. One of the most controversial acts (to his contemporaries) of Alexander's career was his insistence upon *proskynesis*, the Persian ritual obeisance, during and after his Central Asian campaign. Failure to observe it meant death to Greeks and Macedonians on several occasions (most notoriously to Alexander's 'friend' Cleitus in Samarkand, whom Alexander personally impaled). The increasing numbers of Iranians in Alexander's court and army saw nothing wrong with *proskynesis*, being standard practice before a Persian monarch. But to the Greeks and Macedonians it was abhorrent to the point of blasphemy. For *proskynesis* was reserved solely for a god, and Alexander's insistence on it implied divine status. In the end, Alexander had his way and it became standard, if reluctant, practice at his court in recognition of Alexander's spurious claim to be the son of god (of Zeus Ammon). The cult of the living god in a king was then renewed under the Seleucids, especially Antiochus Epiphanes, when it was imposed as an official cult to unify disparate peoples.[197] Alexander thus paved the way for the idea of Christ in the Greek mind, that a man could be at once human and divine, god and the son of god. The Greek reluctance to admit, through *proskynesis*, divine status in Alexander continued to plague the Greek mind for another thousand years with their obsession over the human and divine natures of Christ.

But whether or not Christianity has incorporated elements of Iranian religious ideas into its beliefs and practice is perhaps not the issue here. The real issue is that the spread of Iranian religions westwards *paved the way* for Christianity; it made it that much easier for similar or parallel ideas in Christianity – regardless of whether they are Iranian in origin or not – to take root when they did arrive.[198]

From Anatolia to Rome

Anatolia was another source for one of the most important aspects of the Christian religion (apart from the contact with Iranian religion reviewed above). The mother-goddess fertility cult was one of the main cults of ancient Anatolia, embedded deep in Anatolian prehistory, with evidence found in excavations of Neolithic sites going back to the seventh millennium BC. In Archaic Ionia in the seventh century BC, the Greek cult of Artemis was grafted onto it, producing in architecture one of the Seven Wonders of the World at Ephesus. But the cult of Ephesian Artemis had little, if any, resemblance to the goddess more familiar from Classical Greek mythology, and the Temple of Artemis at Ephesus was the embodiment in stone of the ancient Anatolian mother-goddess, the Classical style of its architecture notwithstanding, as well as elements of the Iranian Anahita cult.[199] In Ephesus, Christianity – in the person of St Paul – encountered some of its stiffest resistance with opposition from the 'Diana of the Ephesians'. Hence, it simply merged with the cult. For according to Christian tradition, several years after the death of Jesus the Virgin Mary was brought to Ephesus where she lived out her days in retirement – her purported house outside Ephesus is still a place of veneration today. The cult of the Virgin was simply grafted onto the cult of Ephesian Artemis.

Indirect support is found in the west of the Mediterranean many centuries before Mary. In Spain and southern Gaul, Phocaean Greek colonists from the coast of Asia Minor had taken the cult of Ephesian Artemis with them when they colonised the area in about 600 BC, founding, amongst other cities, the port of Marseilles. This was followed up by deliberate missionary expansion of the cult throughout the Roman world.[200] The cult of the Virgin Mary, strongest still today in these parts, found ready ground when it arrived almost a thousand years later. The graft was complete.

From the Semitic East to Rome

Even more than Anatolia or Iran, it was naturally enough the religions of the Semitic world which contributed most to Christianity. The Judaic roots of Christianity hardly need reiterating here.[201] Up until the time of Hadrian, the Jerusalem Christians – and their bishops – were Jews, and Jerusalem Christianity was still virtually a Judaic sect. It was only after Hadrian and his creation of Aelia Capitolina out of the ashes of Jerusalem – and the consequent expulsion of Jews – that the church of Jerusalem began to consist of gentiles.[202]

Of more interest here are the non-Judaic Semitic elements in Christianity. Perhaps the most important idea was that of the congregation – probably the most revolutionary concept that Christianity brought to the West after the concepts of monotheism or a structured priestly hierarchy. Again, the suggestion that the idea was a revolutionary one might raise eyebrows today, it has become so integral a part of accepted Christian practice. But the idea that all members of a community meet on set days to participate in communal worship was completely alien to western pagan practice. The public cults demanded participation only from the few officials in going about their public duties, while the private religions of the majority were practised individually in the home or the neighbourhood shrines. There was no concept of religious congregation. In the Semitic East, however, the idea was almost universal. We have already observed[203] how this concept was expressed architecturally in the East in the vast temple compounds built to accommodate mass worship, temples which had no counterpart in the West despite their superficial Classical embellishment. We have also traced how this concept determined the development of Christian architecture, with the adoption of the basilica form. Suffice to say here that the great temple compounds at Palmyra, Baalbek, Damascus, Jerash, Petra and elsewhere in the East reflect its universal practice in pagan Semitic usage, surviving in the great mosque courtyards of Islam.

Also central to most Semitic religion was the abstract concepts of deity. Again, this has already been reviewed in the architectural discussions in Chapter 7. It is only necessary to reiterate how so many ancient Semitic deities were represented in abstract – and often cubic – forms. Such were the ubiquitous 'god-blocks' of Nabataean religious architecture, or the black stone of the Temple of Elagabal of Emesa, or similar black stones of Phoenician temples to Melqart. Indeed, the *baetyls*, usually the stone blocks symbolising their gods, were a feature of ancient temples of the Near East, even after the influence of Greek and Roman art had personified the gods into shadows of western likenesses. When the prosaic Romans first entered these Semitic temples they were often baffled by the absence of images, the abstract concept of deity being at that time being alien to the western mind.

A cult practised initially at Edessa, which became fairly commonly practised all over northern Syria before Christianity, was that of the virgin mother and child. Women in fact traditionally held a high position at Edessa. As well as being incorporated into Christianity, the belief in the virgin and child also entered Islam. The iconography of the virgin and child probably had its origin in Egyptian depictions of Isis and the infant Horus, although it is notable that virtually the same iconography appears in an early AD Gandharan sculpture from northern Pakistan depicting the seated goddess Hairiti and child (Plate 30).[204]

Another belief common to many ancient Semitic religions was the concept of rebirth and resurrection. This was particularly prevalent in Phoenician religion, where it was a part of the cult of Melqart. Melqart was often Hellenised as Adonis, and was related to the ancient Sumerian Dummuzi, Biblical Tammuz, where rebirth and resurrection figured highly. In this context it is worth noting that Bethlehem was originally sacred to Tammuz.[205] When Phoenician colonists took the cult of Melqart to the West it was equated by the Romans with Hercules. Another popular Semitic cult throughout the East was that of the Sun god. This went under various guises – including Elagabal of Emesa and Heliopolitanus of Baalbek – but was adopted by the Greeks and Romans under the name Helios. Much more will be said of the Sun cult below, but for the moment it is worth observing that with the advent of Christianity the cult of the prophet Elias easily replaced the cult of the Sun god in the East simply because of the similarity in names.[206] Long before Christianity had supplanted paganism in the Semitic Near East, therefore, it is clear that most of the elements of Christian belief were already in place.

In addition to Iranian, Anatolian and Semitic religions, other Near Eastern religious ideas contributed to the acceptance of Christianity amongst the Romans. The part played by Egyptian religion is beyond the scope of this book,[207] but apart from the iconography of Isis and Horus mentioned above, attention must be drawn to the Egyptian monk St Anthony and the origins of monasticism in Egypt, Mesopotamia (the Tur Abdin) and Syria.[208] From further afield, elements of Buddhist and other Indian religious ideas probably entered the Near East to affect Christianity. The spread and influence of India in the West has been traced earlier in this chapter, with implications for the origins of Stoicism, neo-Platonism and Christian monasticism, so need not be repeated here. Suffice to say that the movement was a very real one. Of more concern for Christianity perhaps is the origin of relic worship, which figured so largely in medieval Christianity. The only other religion which places such a high – or higher – emphasis on relic worship is Buddhism. In this context it is significant that the first recorded case of the cult of relic worship in Christianity is the Apocryphal Acts of St Thomas, the apostle to India, concerning the miraculous cure of Misdaeus, an Indian king.[209]

From East to West

We must finally consider the physical journey that Christianity made to the West. Most evidence points to Christianity spreading in the East before it spread to the West[210] – indeed, at first Christianity looked set to become as much a definition of the East as Islam later became, and it may well have not taken root in the West. Shapur I's deportations of Syrian Christians following his campaigns in the 260s probably added much to the spread of Christianity throughout the Iranian world,[211] so that by 484 it was possible for a Christian Synod to be held in Ctesiphon, patronised by the shah himself. Here the Nestorian sect was proclaimed as the official, national Iranian brand of Christianity to underline Iran's differences with the Roman Empire and Roman orthodoxy.[212] It hardly survived in Iran (except in pockets) although it did spread further east, where it still survives. But in the early days at least, Christianity showed all indications of remaining in the region of its origins and spreading further east, not west. How, therefore, did this change?

To begin with, the position of Antioch was crucial in this interchange.[213] We have already reviewed the position of Antioch as an imperial Roman capital.[214] Equally important was its religious position. Antioch's cosmopolitan nature as a meeting and mingling of Hellenism with the ancient Semitic and Jewish communities has been long emphasised, and the cosmopolitan nature of Antioch takes precedence over either its Roman or Syrian character. An Iranian and Zoroastrian element has been discerned at Antioch even before its foundation, and the Iranian campaigns of the third century resulting in the capture of Antioch had a strong religious element, being accompanied by both the Zoroastrian state high-priest and the Prophet Mani.[215] It even saw delegations come through the city from far-off Bactria and India. Zoroastrian Magi rubbed shoulders in the street with Semitic priests, Jewish rabbis, Greek philosophers, and a host of eastern holy men, prophets and mystics of all descriptions. It became a religious melting pot where all religions were tolerated. It all made very receptive ground for the development of the first Christian church. Hence, it became the first teaching ground for both St Peter and St Paul.

Indeed, it was at Antioch that they were first named 'Christians' by the Roman authorities, to distinguish them from the Jews. For it was in Antioch that Christianity first became an organised religion — Antioch even claimed primacy over Rome because the first church of Antioch was founded by Peter himself before he went to Rome. However true the claim, Antioch remained central to the subsequent development and spread of Christianity. Theophilus, the Bishop of Antioch from 169 to 188, was the first to proclaim the Gospels as a divine revelation on the same footing as the Old Testament. In Antioch it was first made possible for Christianity to spread among the Gentiles. In Antioch Christianity first attracted converts of real wealth, which gave the new religion the first injection of money required to facilitate its spread. And Antioch's position at the centre of international communications not only facilitated the spread of Christianity, it also encouraged other religions to come in and meet — an encouragement boosted by the traditional Syrian love of religious experimentation.

Beyond Antioch, there were, of course, the proselytising journeys made by St Peter and St Paul, well enough known not to require reiterating. But by themselves they were hardly enough for their religion to spread amongst the Romans, and their effect was minimal — and greatly exaggerated by later Christian propagandists. For to begin with, the numbers of Christians in the Roman Empire before the second century was tiny.[216] It was amongst Jewish exile groups around the Mediterranean that Christianity found its first converts. The Jewish Diaspora certainly played its part, and Christianity was viewed by the Romans merely as a sect of Judaism, until St Paul underlined publicly — and judicially — its difference, thereby opening Christianity to the Gentiles. He also thus opened up Christianity to persecution: as a Jewish sect, the Romans, who followed an official policy of tolerating Judaism, tolerated it; separated from Judaism, they were under no such obligation.[217] The bloodbaths of the arenas followed. There is little evidence that the martyrdoms inspired conversions or even revulsion, nor were they as numerous as commonly believed, Christian propagandists notwithstanding. On the contrary, the sports of the arena were nothing more than spectacles, and for the spectators it mattered little whether the victim was a Christian or a common criminal. Conversions to Christianity following an afternoon in the arena had as little chance of succeeding as taking up the profession of robbery after watching a thief being dismembered. All evidence suggests that the persecutions were very effective indeed. By themselves, pagan persecutions would probably have succeeded in exterminating Christianity from the West as thoroughly as did the later Christian persecutions of Manichaeism in France and the Balkans, or of Islam in Spain.

A far more effective vehicle for carrying eastern religious ideas to the West was a people who came west a thousand years before the Jews did. These were the Phoenicians. The Phoenicians had penetrated many of the coastal regions of the western Mediterranean: Sicily, North Africa, Spain, Malta and Sardinia, to name just the main areas of influence. Even after Rome's defeat of the Carthaginians, Phoenician influence remained strong, particularly in North Africa where it was strongest, as we have seen above in the discussion on Lepcis Magna, remaining down until the Islamic conquest.

The Phoenicians brought their religions with them, and the Roman towns of North Africa are littered with the remains of temples to Shadrapa, Melqart, Astarte, Baal, Hathor and other deities, thinly disguised under tenuous Roman equivalents. Central to much of Phoenician religious belief was the very Semitic abstract concept of deity, as well as the concept of rebirth and resurrection, already reviewed above. Cadiz (Gadir), for example, the Phoenicians' main city on the Spanish mainland, had a famous temple dedicated to Phoenician Melqart. This temple preserved its Semitic characteristics until long after it had been absorbed into the Roman cult of Hercules: the absence of figural representation puzzled the Classical authors, and the central feature of the Melqart cult, both in Cadiz and elsewhere in Phoenician Spain, was the cycle of annual resurrection.[218] Christianity was certainly planted on fertile ground in Spain when it eventually arrived.

Another central fact of Phoenician religious practice was the *tophet*. This gruesome rite, associated with the cult of Baal-Cronos, consisted of the sacrifice of young children, infants and babies to the god by fire. It was by no means a universal Phoenician practice, but confined mainly to the Phoenicians of North Africa, most notably at Carthage. The sacrifices were usually of high-born children, preferably the first born. As many as 500 children were recorded as being immolated in a single ritual at Carthage. Because of the horrific nature of the *tophet*, it has come under considerable and sceptical scrutiny by archaeology in recent years, but the evidence confirms it as a fact of Phoenician society.[219] Modern scholarship has attempted to explain the *tophet* as a form of Phoenician upper-class birth control. Such an explanation is, of course, nonsense, an attempt to rationalise an ancient and distasteful practice in entirely modern-day terms. The *tophet* was simply a sacrifice, a very personal self-sacrifice of a possession greater than life itself to one's profoundest beliefs. In ancient terms it makes sense, as an expression of sheer, unquestioning faith that is inconceivable now; in modern terms it is a superstition that defies explanation. But the *tophet* was fact.

The Phoenician *tophet* in North Africa was to have a profound effect on early Christianity, even though the practice had long been suppressed by the Romans. For in North Africa, the concept of self-sacrifice, the Christian cult of martyrdom, was already firmly implanted long before Christianity arrived. Sacrifice, an abstract god, resurrection, all the elements were there. The Semitic Phoenicians of Carthage must have welcomed with relief this new Semitic religion as a revival of their ancient ways and most treasured beliefs, a renaissance after centuries of Romanisation.[220] It comes as very little surprise, therefore, to learn that the greatest spread of early Christianity outside the East was Carthage and the North African provinces. North Africa was probably the first area in the West to have a majority Christian population. So many of the first Christian martyrs were from North Africa – St Perpetua and St Felicity have already been mentioned, St Cyprian of Carthage was probably the most prominent Christian martyrdom after St Paul, and there were many others. Carthage rapidly became the most important bishopric in the empire after Rome itself. It was in North Africa that the first major schism in Christendom occurred, with the Donatist movement in the early fourth century. In the following century there emerged from North Africa the father of western Christendom, St Augustine of Hippo. Phoenician Africa was the most Christian of all provinces, and with good reason.

As well as being Phoenician and Christian, North Africa was *Roman*. Parallel to the Phoenician influence, the North African provinces were subject to more Romanisation than any other part of the empire outside Italy, with the possible exception of Gaul. The hundreds of Roman towns there, unlike the Roman cities of the East, were virtually identical to their counterparts in Italy. North Africa in Roman times was culturally an extension of Europe: before Islam imposed a north–south division on the Mediterranean, the cultural step from Africa to Europe did not exist. From this contact between Roman and Phoenician, the movement of Christianity to Europe was entirely smooth and logical.

There were several more steps, one of the most important also connected with the Phoenicians. This was the rise to the imperial purple of a Phoenician from North Africa, Septimius Severus. Through Septimius, other Phoenicians from North Africa were awarded important posts throughout the empire. The Phoenician religious impact by these means, however, was only minimal compared to the Phoenician impact through North Africa reviewed above. Where the Severan dynasty had most religious impact was through the Syrian family that the dynasty married into, Julia Domna and her relatives. This has already been discussed at length earlier in this chapter, but it is worth emphasising the religious aspects of the Syrian dynasty here. The 'Syrian dynasty' were, of course, Romans. Modern notions of nationalism did not exist then, least of all any 'Syrian' or Arab nationalism, and Rome was the universal identity. But the dynasty were nonetheless orientalisers above all, accelerating a process that had begun in Rome long before and was to culminate in Christianity. Being descended from priests themselves, the dynasty made religion – eastern religion – a major factor at Rome: Julia Domna encouraged eastern cults such as Apollonius of Tyana; Caracalla brought the Isis cult to Rome, where it enjoyed great support;[221] Elagabalus actually imposed the cult of Emesene Baal officially at Rome; Julia Maesa showed favourable disposition towards Christianity.[222] Eusebius in fact describes the family as consisting mainly of Christians.[223] Even amongst that most deeply conservative of all Roman subjects, the Jews, the Severan favour towards Judaism is reflected in a dedicatory inscription at Qisyon in Galilee in honour of Septimius Severus, Julia Domna, Caracalla and Geta – the only dedication by Jews in honour of a Roman emperor ever to be found in Palestine.[224] Furthermore, the orientalising of the Roman monarchy, which was accelerated under Diocletian and came to a head under Constantine, actually begun under the Severans, and is seen through the coins.[225] Although not Christians themselves, the Emesene dynasty did make the eventual acceptance of Christianity and Rome's drive to the East that much more feasible at Rome when it did come. It comes as no surprise to learn that during the Severan era, we find the world's first state proclaiming Christianity as its official religion. This was the kingdom of Edessa, with the conversion of Abgar the Great.[226] Shortly after the Severan period we even find in Rome the first Christian emperor. This was the Emperor Philip the Arab and the importance of Philip's conversion as a precedent for Constantine cannot be overestimated.[227]

Finally, it is left to discuss the position of the Sun cult in Rome in terms of this transition. The cult of the Sun in the Roman Empire bore many characteristics of incipient monotheism. It certainly implanted the idea of a single, all-powerful god into the minds of the Romans. It was a particularly popular one in the pre-Christian Near East among the Arabs. It existed in various forms: the cults of Palmyrene Malakbel, Jupiter Heliopolitanus at Baalbek and Elagabal at Emesa, for example, were different manifestations of the Sun cult.[228] This contributed to the rapid spread of Christianity amongst the Arabs during the first few centuries AD, for the cult of Christ was often identified with the Sun: Christ had risen at sunrise and the resurrection was equated with the rising, the second coming was expected from the east, early churches often faced the east.[229] Emperor Elagabalus brought the Emesene Sun cult to Rome in the early third century where he tried to make it the supreme cult of the Roman pantheon. It ended in ignominious failure as we have seen, but later in the third century the Emesene Sun cult was to prove triumphant when the Emperor Aurelian brought it to Rome following his victory over Palmyra. The great Sun Temple that Aurelian built in Rome, adorned with booty from the sack of Palmyra, had its dedication ceremony (*natalis*) on 25 December. The Sun cult was then particularly promoted by Aurelian, not merely as another addition to the pantheon but as a Roman national cult. Following Aurelian, the Sun cult found its most enthusiastic supporter in Constantine. Constantine's cultivation of the cult of the Sun – Sol Invictus – was incipient monotheism. In the third century Sol, Apollo and Mithras were sometimes interchangeable, but under Constantine, Sol emerged supreme. From Sol Invictus to Christianity the step was almost negligible. After his conversion, much of Christian practice was made more palatable by altering it to accommodate the Sun cult: churches faced east to the rising sun,[230] the day of worship was changed from the Sabbath to the day of the Sun, the birthday of the Sun on 25 December became one of the most important dates in the Christian calendar.[231] To this day, Christian worship has remained equated with the sun.

The oriental revolution

Constantine has been described as 'the most influential man in all history'.[232] But our perception of the momentousness of Constantine's revolution is almost entirely retrospective and not appreciated by his contemporaries. Whilst contemporary historians (such as Aurelius Victor) certainly appreciated Constantine's greatness, it was as a great general and emperor rather than as a philosopher or religious reformer; his Christianity passes almost unnoticed (except, of course, for Christian historians such as Eusebius, who had axes to grind) – Eutropius, for example, makes no mention of his Christianity and even states that on his death he was deified in the same way that all good pagan emperors were.[233] Emperors did what emperors do, mere mortals not to question why, and the matter of their mere religion was never regarded as particularly interesting or important, except when it might provide a juicy anecdote or two, such as Elagabalus' antics. If one were to go on contemporary accounts alone, the conversion to Christianity seems to pass virtually unnoticed.[234]

The Roman Empire was never entirely to let go of paganism. It has been pointed out[235] that Constantine's conversion was really a fluke, and not a result of any historical inevitability, nor could it be assumed that Christianity would necessarily become the official religion. Quite the contrary, Christianity was a small minority and lower-class religion and showed all signs of remaining so. Iran, for example, where Christianity enjoyed a far higher profile, did not become Christian. If Julian had not died during his eastern campaign but had continued with a long reign, he might well have succeeded in reinstating paganism. Even Constantine himself favoured pagan philosophers towards the end of his life.[236] In the 390s there was another pagan revival in Rome under Arbogast. In the later years of the Emperor Zeno's reign there were the efforts by Leontius in Syria to restore paganism. Leontius was crowned a rival emperor in Tarsus in 484, holding court in Antioch until his defeat in 488. Even in that most Christian period of Constantinople under Justinian, one of the emperor's most senior officers, the great codifier Tribonian, was quite openly a pagan.[237] In the early tenth century the Emperor Alexander flirted with paganism, admittedly rather pathetically so.[238] Indeed, paganism was never to entirely desert Rome right until the bitter end: immediately before the fall of Constantinople to the Turks in 1453, the man who has been described as the last of the 'Classical' philosophers of a tradition stretching back to Plato and Anaximander, the great Byzantine scholar Pleithon, promoted pagan ideas. He advocated the reorganisation of the empire along Platonic lines, God was referred to as Zeus, and his philosophy contained elements of Zoroastrianism in addition to paganism and neo-Platonism.[239]

The East might be the source of Christianity, but the move of Rome there had equal if not greater importance from deep within Rome's pagan past, Constantine's Christianity notwithstanding. The symbolism of the return to Troy and Rome's legendary roots was not lost on the Romans, whether pagan or Christian. Both the ecclesiastical historian Sozomen as well as the anonymous *Byzantine Life of Constantine*, for example, write of Constantine's foundation of Constantinople as a Third Troy almost as much as a Second Rome. They and the pagan historian, Zosimus, emphasise Constantine's first choice of Troy for the site.[240] In Constantine's dedicatory column in the heart of his great new forum in Constantinople, the statue of Pallas and other relics of Rome's pagan past were implanted alongside a fragment of the true cross. Christianity was all very well, but the New Rome had to be a New Troy as well as a New Jerusalem.

The history and development of early Christianity is heavily western-biased, for obvious reasons. But for the first few hundred years, all evidence points to eastern predominance: literary, archaeological, and political. Indeed, Christianity at first probably spread quicker and sooner through the Iranian world and even India than the Roman world, although it is far less well documented.[241] The Christianisation of western Europe was hundreds of years later. Whilst conceding the (rather embarrassing!) actual origin of Christianity in the East, Christianity very soon becomes 'western' and western in character; Christianity is 'us', not 'them' – the arrival of Islam was a godsend (no pun intended!) to Christianity, serving to emphasise an east/west, them/us division.[242] But both the origins and the first few centuries of the development of Christianity were almost wholly oriental. This cannot be emphasised too strongly when considering the definition of European civilisation in Christian terms. Constantine's revolution, therefore, was a true orientalisation of Rome.

The term 'revolutionary' has been used in a number of contexts to describe the transition from paganism to Christianity. The term has been chosen carefully, for it is used with the full political ramifications that the term suggests today. For it must be remembered that the new elements that Christianity brought into the Roman world, such as the idea of an organised, structural hierarchy exercising spiritual and temporal authority over large numbers of people, or the idea of members of a community gathering together to exercise their beliefs, posed very real *political* challenges to Roman authority. No other movement in the ancient world ever had these very real political strengths as integral parts of its framework. Never mind the religion itself, never mind the church fathers and the great martyrs, never mind the philosophic and moral message of Christianity. It was these very revolutionary, entirely oriental political strengths that posed the real challenges to Roman authority. One need hardly look further for the answer as to why Christianity won.

East and West

Character and prejudice

It is now appropriate to review the cultural character of the Near East under Roman rule, a subject that has come under increasing scrutiny in recent years.[243] A frequent assumption is made of the supposed domination of the Near East by western values, western institutions and western character. One authority, for example, states firmly that 'Every aspect of [Near Eastern] society and culture was influenced both by Greek civilisation and by the progressive extension of Roman rule.'[244] The assumed recognition of 'Greek' institutions – hence 'character' – in the Roman Near East is one of the most invidious manifestations of western misconceptions, and 'it has long been customary to search the middle east microscopically for any evidence of something Greek – almost to the exclusion of the existing cultures'.[245] For example, inscriptional evidence for a town assembly is naturally translated into the Greek language as *boule*,[246] and a mere reference to a *boule* at Philadelphia leads to the sweeping statement that 'we need not seriously doubt that Philadelphia possessed the normal constitutional structure of a Greek city'.[247] Similar misunderstandings are made of Palmyra's 'senate' being evidence of Romanisation.[248] But an assembly is a very ancient, entirely native, Near Eastern tradition. At its most simple level it consists of a meeting of tribal elders, such as still exists today in many traditional Arab societies, owing nothing to any perceived primogeniture of Greek civilisation. An Arab visitor to Rome, for example, would describe its senate as a *majlis*, in no way implying the existence of Arab institutions in Rome. By itself, the mention of a *boule* does not suggest the existence of a Greek institution, and as often as not is simply nothing more than the new Roman colonial administrators' translation of older native institutions into a 'language' that they understood.[249]

So much of the perceived evidence for the Graeco-Roman 'character' is interpreted from inscriptions. Problems arising from inscriptions have been emphasised in Chapter 1. Suffice to reiterate here that inscriptions – particularly those of a foreign occupier – hardly imply such thing as 'character': they are by their very nature propagandistic. It is as if an assessment were attempted of the Palestinian West Bank based solely on modern Israeli road signs which mention only Jewish settlements, not Palestinian. The comparison is a valid one, and one modern authority emphasises that inscriptions on ancient 'road signs' – milestones – as well as many other military inscriptions, were erected not so much to mark distances, as modern milestones are, but to display slogans for official propaganda.[250] The mere presence of a Greek inscription in the Wadi Sirhan prompts speculation regarding the Roman penetration, domination and western 'character' generally of inland Arabia.[251] But if similar speculation on an 'Arab' character or cultural influence were attached to, for example, the presence of Safaitic inscriptions at Pompeii, at best it would attract scorn, at worst it would be dismissed. At Damascus, the presence of a few Greek inscriptions prompts the assumption that ' . . . our evidence reveals *only* the Greek-speaking population of a Greek city' with the evidence for Semitic character entirely ignored.[252] Believing inscriptions is a little bit like believing what you see on television. Their value as historical evidence, therefore, needs to be treated with immense caution.

Much is loaded onto the evidence of Greek or Latin names in the Near East, which are minutely analysed for evidence of Greek speakers, Greek population and Greek character. For example, assumptions are made for the presence of Latin-speaking population – hence 'character' – from the Latin inscriptions and Latin names at Bosra.[253] But Latin inscriptions merely prove that some Latin-speakers instructed some masons to make inscriptions, and do not necessarily have any bearing on the character of a settlement or the make-up of its population. The predominance of Arab names in, say, Iran or Nigeria or Indonesia hardly negates the Iranian, Nigerian of Indonesian character of those places, whilst a similar analysis of modern British names (betraying origins as diverse as Hebrew, Latin and Nordic, often occurring in the one name) could never be taken as evidence for non-British character.

Negative evidence – the paucity of Semitic inscriptions – has been cited to support the notion that Greek was the predominant language in the Near East.[254] This is to commit one of the most cardinal of archaeological mistakes: the lack of an object merely implies the lack of evidence, not that the object never existed. From such misconceptions it becomes a short – but slippery! – step towards describing the Near East as 'unambiguously Greek' in its essential character.[255] But a 'Syrian' in the Greek or Latin sources would by definition be one who spoke Aramaic, even if he spoke Greek as well: there was no notion of nationality in the modern sense, so that only language would be meant by terms in the sources such as 'Syrian' or 'Arab'. Indeed, the rapid 're-emergence' of Aramaic in late antiquity demonstrates that Semitic languages never disappeared throughout the Graeco-Roman interregnum.[256] The question of how much Greek versus Semitic languages were spoken is apparent with the Islamic conquest, when Greek disappeared virtually overnight to be replaced by the native Semitic tongue (in this case Arabic). Unlike Europe, where Latin survives in the Romance languages, there is virtually no trace of Greek in the languages of the Middle East today. The Greek linguistic presence to which many historians give so much weight from the narrow evidence of the inscriptions, therefore, was always superficial.

Astonishingly, even native Near Eastern elements have been adopted as part of the cultural package of perceived 'western character'. Nowhere is this more pronounced than in the perceptions of Christianity, where Christianity is viewed as Greek, hence 'western' and 'us' as opposed to Near Eastern and 'them'.[257] For example, 'both the pagan and the Christian culture of this area . . . [can be seen] as derivatives of Greek culture'[258] with Christianity cited in terms of evidence for Hellenism. The same authority concludes that 'if we think of "culture" in the full sense . . . then we can find in the Roman Near East only two established cultures: Greek and Jewish'.[259] Any 'eastern' character of Judaic culture is doubted merely on the grounds that Judaea is too near the Mediterranean, so therefore must be 'western' in character. The Near Eastern character of the entire Phoenician and Levantine civilisations is thus casually wiped out.[260]

Anti-oriental prejudices have been noted in Chapter 1 and throughout this work. By ignoring the bulk of the evidence – which is the material remains – and concentrating too exclusively on the limited evidence of the inscriptions, a false picture has been painted that simply belittles the native culture of the Near East. Any use of the term 'Arab' or even 'Syrian' in a cultural context is often treated with extreme scholarly – even commendable – scepticism; with any similar use of the term 'Greek', however, scholarly caution is thrown to the winds and it is accepted rather too readily. A salutary contrast is provided by a recent site guide published in Syria,[261] where the remains of Rasafa are described as 'Arab' throughout. Such terminology would normally be dismissed out of hand as nationalistic, but is just as valid a term for Rasafa as our own 'Byzantine' or 'Roman' would be, if not more so. The persistent denial of any native Near Eastern culture or character in the Roman period would be perceived by an Arab or other native of the modern Middle East to be not just contentious, but arrogant and confrontational. In the end, the scholarship of such works is tempered by regret for the prejudice, and they become no different from the words of Rose Macaulay quoted at the beginning of Chapter 7.

Such conclusions may have been forgivable in a previous era, but entirely ignore the vast wealth of material remains that are overwhelming evidence for a vigorous, native Near Eastern culture, even apart from Christianity (which – and it seems to require emphasising! – is native to the Near East, not to Greece). By focusing on the material remains, it is hoped that this work offers a much-needed balance.

The view from the East

The fond picture of the 'barbaric' nations of the East happily basking under the Pax Romana and receiving the blessings of western civilisation may, to some extent, be true – and the monuments stand as mute reminders of this. But the 'natives', despite the questionable advantages of Roman rule, resented the Roman presence. Earlier folk memories of the domination of the East by the Persian Empire hearkened back to a golden age. Iranian rule was marked by a toleration, mildness and respect that had its founder, Cyrus, hailed as a prophet by the Jews and as the hero of an epic by the Greeks[262] – and had the Iranians welcomed back to the Roman East as liberators on a number of occasions. When reading our Roman sources for the East, therefore, one must constantly guard against bias: they give only the viewpoint of the rulers, not of the ruled. Talmudic sources, for example, describe Roman officials as 'bandits'.[263] The Judaean hatred of the Romans that culminated in suicidal revolts on a number of occasions need hardly be emphasised here. Even when 'basking' under Roman rule, the native populations of the Near East would flock to any banner raised in revolt, as they did to Mithradates in the first century BC or Mawiyya in the fifth century AD or various pretenders throughout. Perhaps nothing illustrates the hollowness of Roman rule in the Near East more than the rapidity and thoroughness of the Arab conquest in the seventh century. In the West, conquests of the Roman Empire ushered in a dark age; in the East it ushered in a renaissance.[264]

This marks a fundamental difference between Roman rule in the East and the West. In the West, the memory of Roman rule remained a golden age which was constantly invoked, right down until the modern era. Mussolini's conscious emulation of ancient Rome in the twentieth century had its counterpart in Rienzi's quixotic revival in the fourteenth. Since its collapse in the West, Europe's efforts to revive the Roman Empire have been tributes to this memory, from Charlemagne's coronation as Roman Emperor in 800 to the end of the empire's latest incarnation, the Holy Roman Empire, in 1806. At times, it even seemed that Rome's influence in Europe was strongest beyond its ancient frontiers. The barbarians who invaded from the north sought to become Roman, not to overturn Rome. Two countries in modern Europe who follow the Roman church, Ireland and Poland, were never within the imperial boundaries, while the one nation who laid most claim to being the 'Third Rome', Russia, lay well beyond, and it was the Prussian kings who styled themselves 'Caesar' (Kaiser). In a sense, Rome continued its conquests in the West long after it had collapsed, and the West has lain under its shadow ever since.

This was never matched in the East. The Romans, if not actually regarded with hostility, were regarded as transitory outsiders by the far older and stronger civilisations of the East. Even though the empire lasted far longer in the East, it was more ephemeral, for after its collapse the legacy virtually vanishes. Greek and Latin have left no mark on modern Middle Eastern languages – there is no counterpart in the East to the European Romance languages. When there was a renaissance of Semitic civilisation with the advent of Islam, the pre-Classical civilisations of Mesopotamia were evoked as well as those of Iran: the Macedonians and Romans were merely looked upon as interlopers. With the possible exception of a branch of the Seljuk Turks, who named their state the 'Sultanate of Rome', the Roman Empire was never evoked,[265] nor was it looked upon as any golden age. In the West, the Romans were the civilisers; in the East, it was the Romans who were on the receiving end of civilisation.

Some years ago it might have been possible to take, as it were, a bird's-eye view of Rome in the East. One would have seen all of the Near East basking under the Roman Empire, packed with Graeco-Roman cities, replicas of those in the Roman West. They were adorned with great and marvellous buildings whose styles emanated from Rome, the streets were thronged with sophisticated people – Near Eastern natives it is true but by now enjoying the benefits and civilisation of Rome, speaking Greek, copying Greek and Roman lifestyles and worshipping in temples to Zeus, Artemis and Heracles. One could even look past the imperial boundaries further east, to Iran and beyond. A view that might be marred by the occasional defeat at the hands of the Iranians, but compensated by rumours of lost Roman legions as far as China, of the art workshops of the Indian borderlands and Central Asia being trained by Roman master-craftsmen to turn out imitations of the imperial style. One would even see Romans strolling along the Silk Road, while in the south of India prosperous merchants from far-off Campania would be establishing strings of colonies, miniature Romes, on the shores of the Bay of Bengal and bringing the whole of India within the Roman financial system.

A view that must now be considerably modified. Scratch a Temple of Zeus and we find a Baal or a Hadad, scratch a 'Roman' city and we find something that is Near Eastern. The Corinthian colonnades vanish like a mirage to reveal forms and ideas rooted in the East, not West. The influences of Greek and Roman rule are there, of course. But the real picture now emerging is of cities, religious practices, lifestyles, architecture and a civilisation that remained overwhelmingly Near Eastern throughout the nine centuries of domination by Macedonians and Romans.

From its inception in 27 BC to its final collapse in May 1453, Rome was the longest-lived empire in history, with 164 emperors (including sole empresses) from Augustus to Constantine Dragases invested with the imperial purple. Its influence on all subsequent European civilisation is incalculable and the effects of the Roman Empire can still be felt today – indeed, some of its institutions still survive. In short, it was the world's most successful empire.

But such a statement can only be a personal opinion, a value judgement. In history there are few absolutes. Most of all, in order to understand Rome and appreciate it fully, it is necessary to see it in all of its breadth and richness, not just as a 'European' or 'Western' civilisation. Of the 1,480 years of the Roman Empire's existence, approximately half of that time was spent in the Near East, longer if one includes those parts of the East (mainly Anatolia) beyond the scope of this book. The influence of Rome on the East for those seven centuries was profound, and it would be a mistake of the first order to under-estimate that influence. Enough books have been written about that for the point not to require reiterating. But more profound was the influence of the East upon Rome. The process was invariably a two-way one, with ultimately the eastern element predominat-ing. A failure to understand this process and this influence is a failure to appreciate Rome itself. Ultimately, it is a failure to appreciate the legacy of Roman civilisation. This legacy is as much eastern as western, as much oriental as occidental, both to Europe and the world as a whole.

Triumph of the East

In the year AD 248, the city and people of Rome held one of the greatest triumphs in their history. They celebrated the millennium of the traditional foundation of Rome by Romulus and Remus. A thousand years from the birth of a small village to the centre of the greatest empire the world had seen. Rome and the Caesars could well be doubly triumphant, and games, feasts and gifts were disbursed by a munificent emperor on a lavish scale. But ironically, the Roman emperor who presided over this greatest and most Roman of all triumphs was not a Roman himself, nor was he from anywhere in Europe. He was from the East: the Emperor Philip the Arab. Philip the Arab formed the latest episode in a long story: the story of Rome's fascination with the East. The story is to a large extent the story of Rome itself, one of antiquity's greatest civilisations and mightiest empires that cannot be fully understood without understanding that fascination. It was a fascination of the new world for the old, of the exotic for the mundane, a love affair that even took literal form with the story of Antony and Cleopatra. Ultimately, it would be the East that took over Rome: one of the many ironies of our story is that the city of Rome itself was to end up as Rome's own imperial outpost, a Roman backwater.

The origins of this fascination lie in the very foundations of Rome, which go back in myth even beyond Romulus and Remus to a place far distant. This was Troy. In the ashes of Troy a native of Asia wrote one of the greatest tragic epics of all times. It was a Roman epic poet who turned this tragedy into a triumph. For out of the ashes, Rome was born: Homer's Trojan heroes were led by Aeneas from the burning walls of Troy to found a New Troy on the banks of the Tiber at Rome. But the ultimate outcome of Virgil's great epic lay many hundreds of years after the death of Virgil himself, an outcome which neither Homer nor Virgil could ever have conceived – but which both epic poets would have appreciated. For it was a latter-day Aeneas, the Emperor Constantine, who led the descendants of Virgil's Trojan heroes away from a crumbling, ramshackle Rome back to the East to found the New Rome at Byzantium, on the opposite shores of the Sea of Marmara to Troy. Troy had achieved its greatest triumph. More than anything else, the story of Rome is a story of the East more than of the West: a triumph of the East.

NOTES

Chapter 1

1 E.g. Roaf 1990: 214.
2 See, for example, Sherwin-White and Kuhrt (1993) for the Seleucids, and Narain (1957) for the Indo-Greeks.
3 Benjamin Isaac's (1992: 20–1) admirable study is one of the few to remark on anti-oriental prejudice in modern scholarship when dealing with the Roman East, and Irfan Shahid's series of studies (1984a, 1984b, 1989) is one of the few to be written from the Near Eastern viewpoint. It is perhaps both significant and salutary that the one authority is an Israeli and the other an Arab. See also Edward Said's essay on the subject (*Orientalism* 1978).
4 Gibbon 1 (1900: 116, 118), the latter in the context of Septimius' campaign against Niger.
5 Millar 1993.
6 Dodgeon and Lieu 1991: 5, referring to the Shapur inscription at Naqsh-i Rustam.
7 Dodgeon and Lieu 1991: 2.
8 Smallwood in Williamson and Smallwood 1981: 144.
9 Millar 1993: 218.
10 W. Hamilton and A. Wallace-Hadrill in the Penguin Classics edition of his work.
11 Aubet 1993: 23–5.
12 Millar 1993: 318.
13 Millar 1993: 329.
14 Millar 1993: 449, 462.
15 Millar 1993: 471.
16 Sherwin-White and Kuhrt 1993.
17 McDonald 1992 and 1993. For Pompeii see Gysens in Cimino 1994: 79.
18 Although one must be wary of attaching too much to this: it may only reflect a greater preservation of material remains in a desert environment, rather than any real distribution in antiquity.
19 MacDonald 1992: 303; MacDonald 1993.
20 Trimingham 1979: 92; Al Khraysheh 1992.
21 Millar 1993: 201, 493.
22 E.g. by Millar (1993) throughout his book – to the extent, even, of labouring the point.
23 See Sherwin-White and Kuhrt 1993. Whether Alexander was a Hellenophile or Hellenophobe cannot be gone into here, but whilst the first interpretation is the most popular, the latter is equally possible.
24 Wiesehöfer 1996: 183–91.
25 Even Ardeshir I's much vaunted Sasanian claim that Rome should restore its western Achaemenid satrapies had its Parthian precedent under Artabanus III – see Herodian 6. 2; Dio 80. 3; Tacitus *Annals* 6. 31. There is much controversy concerning how much later Iranian dynasties identified with the Achaemenids. See Frye 1967: 249–50; Frye 1984: 278; Whitby 1994: 234–5; Wiesehöfer 1996: 130–6, 165–71; Roaf in Curtis *et al.* 1998.
26 Frye 1963: 23.
27 Although Procopius refers to 'Byzantium' and 'Byzantines', but never 'Byzantine Empire'.
28 Herodian 3. 1. 4.

Chapter 2

1 And even the British who, in their incursions into the North-West Frontier and Afghanistan in the nineteenth century, chose to see signs of Alexander everywhere. See Lee, 1996: 74–8.

2 See, for example, Litvinsky 1996: chapters 2–4. Persian sources for this period have survived in Firdausi and al-Tabari. Whilst literary works such as the *Shahnameh* cannot be considered historical sources in the same way that the Graeco-Roman tradition of historiography can, they do provide a valuable insight into Iranian attitudes, in much the same way, for example, that a recent study has used Juvenal for its insight into attitudes, rather than historical fact. See Braund 1989.

3 I am indebted to Leonard Harrow for bringing my attention to these later Persian poetic sources, and for translating many of the passages. Much the same imagery survives, for example, in the *Siyasat-nama* of Nizam al-Mulk. See also Browne 1902.

4 al-Tabari 4. 705–6.

5 al-Tabari 4. 742–4; al-Biruni *Chronology*: 104–6.

6 According to al-Tabari 4. 648, for example, Rome paid tribute to Luhrasp, one of the mythical kings of Persia, and recognised him as 'King of Kings'.

7 Luttwak 1976. See also Isaac 1992: 28–33 and 265.

8 E.g., Moses Khorenats'i (2. 2) describes how Arses, the first Parthian ruler (third century BC), sought alliance and friendship with Rome. Whilst historically unlikely, this does at least reflect Iran's non-aggressive attitude towards Rome. See also Isaac 1992 and Rubin 1986.

9 A point Isaac (1992: 403) emphasises with reference to Aelius Gallus' campaign into Arabia.

10 Cf. Isaac 1992: 19–21. See also his remarks on p. 421.

11 Our main source for these events are Appian 11.

12 Although Antiochus' 'conquest' of India is doubtful. See Sherwin-White and Kuhrt 1993: 197–201.

13 Appian 11.'6. 30–6.

14 For accounts of these events see Green 1990: Part Five and to a lesser extent Lang 1978: chapter 6 and Hitti 1957: chapter 17. The main sources are Plutarch's *Lucullus* and *Pompey*, Books 11–12 of Appian, and Books 36–7 of Dio. See also Moses Khorenats'i 2.

15 Plutarch *Pompey*; Appian 12. 17. 116–17; Eutropius 6.14.

16 Though Crassus, ever jealous of Pompey, whenever his name was mentioned with the title 'the Great' would always cynically remark, 'How big is he?' See Plutarch's *Crassus*.

17 Appian 9. 8. 48.

18 Dio 36. 16. 1.

19 The 'naphtha' which the Armenians used to great effect against the Roman siege engines. See Dio 36. 1. 2.

20 Appian 12. 14. 94 and 12. 15. 97.

21 Dio 36. 46. 2.

22 Appian 9. 8. 49–50; 12. 16. 106.

23 Dio 37. 7; Plutarch *Pompey*; Moses Khorenats'i 2. 15.

24 The main sources for this are Josephus, Plutarch's *Crassus* and Dio.

25 E.g., see Ingholt 1954; Safar and Mustafa 1974; Colledge 1977.

26 Bivar (1983: 49–50) in fact sees Crassus' motives as a legitimate effort to support Roman sympathisers to the Parthian throne rather than simply unprovoked aggression.

27 See Bivar 1983: 50–2 for the Suren–Rustam connection. For the later Armenian connections, see Moses Khorenats'i II. 28, and Lang 1978: 155–6.

28 Probably King Abgar of Edessa. See Bivar 1983: 53, and Chapter 3 in this volume.

29 Such good tactics and better intelligence simply earned the Iranians and Ariamnes accusations by the defeated Romans of unsportsmanlike betrayal. Since the Syriac sources actually imply that Ariamnes was betraying the Iranians rather than the Romans, such accusations are probably nothing more than a Roman cover-up for failure. See Segal 1970: 12.

30 It is not certain whether he was killed by the Iranians or by the Romans themselves. See Dio 40. 27. 2.

31 Dio 51. 6–7.

32 Dio 49. 20. 4.

33 Dio 49. 19. Moses Khorenats'i (2. 20) actually attributes Pakores' death to Herod.

34 Mark Antony's invasion of Iran is discussed in Chapter 4.

35 Phraates IV's son by the Italian slave girl Musa, who for a while even ruled jointly with her son after the death – possibly by poison – of Phraates IV.

36 For accounts of these events see Herrmann 1977: chapters 2 and 3, Frye 1963: chapter 5, Frye 1984: 233–8, Hitti 1957: chapter 21, Bivar 1983: 48–58; Stoneman 1990: chapter 4; Millar 1993: 2.1; Kennedy 1996. The main sources are Plutarch's *Sulla* and *Crassus*; Books 47–9 of Dio.

37 Aurelius Victor 5.

38 Explored in more detail in 'Judaea, Herod the Great and the Jewish Revolt' in Chapter 3.

39 This is discussed further in Chapter 3, 'Arabia and the Nabataeans'.

40 Historians are often reluctant to accept this most simple and ancient of motives for imperial expansion, but search always for more complex reasons of 'grand strategy', even for the most blatant of aggressors from Sargon to Hitler. Benjamin Isaac (1992) is almost alone in recognising this aspect of Rome's aggressive intentions towards Iran.

41 See Bivar 1983: 586–91, Lightfoot 1990 for an account of this campaign. The campaign is also described in Dio 48. 17–30; Moses Khorenats'i 2. 55.

42 Even as late as the mid-fourth century, Trajan's exploits were still being compared to Alexander: see Dodgeon and Lieu 1991: 176. See also Aurelius Victor 13 (claiming Trajan conquered all nations between the Euphrates and Indus!); John Malalas 11. 4–7; Birley 1976, p. 51 (quoting Eutropius as the source); Maricq 1959; Frye 1984: 242.

43 See Smallwood 1966.

44 Indeed, whilst much is made of the Euphrates 'frontier', it was only a comparatively short stretch of the middle Euphrates that ever actually formed the boundary.

45 Lightfoot 1990: 126.

46 This is explored in more detail in Chapter 5.

47 Dio 71. 2. The ease with which the Romans claimed to have taken Ctesiphon virtually as a matter of course during so many of their Parthian campaigns, but without any long-term effect, makes one suspect the sources somewhat, or even whether it was actually taken.

48 Which even have Romans crossing the Indus at one point! See Aurelius Victor 13; Millar 1993: 111–18.

49 In fact the ease of Avidius Cassius' campaign is probably explained more by the smallpox epidemic among the Iranians rather than any real Roman prowess. The Romans in turn contracted it during their occupation of Ctesiphon and carried it to Europe. See Bivar 1983: 593–4.

50 Millar 1993: 117; *Augustan History* Avidius Cassius: 156. See also Eadie in Kennedy 1996b: 136–7.

51 Indeed, the fact of him being a native Syrian was no drawback, as Dio 72. 22. 2 refers to him as 'an excellent man and the sort one would desire to have as emperor'.

52 Our main sources for the following events are Herodian, Dio 75–6, and *Augustan History*.

53 Herodian 2. 8. 1–10; *Augustan History* Pescennius Niger: 226. See also Eadie in Kennedy 1996b: 137–8.

54 He was an Italian. See Dio 75. 6. 1.

55 See Chapter 8, 'Julia Domna and the Arabs who ruled Rome'.

56 Herodian 3. 4. 3–5. Though ironically, it was Niger who had been proclaimed a 'new Alexander'. See Dio 75. 6. 2.

57 Herodian 3. 4. 7–9.

58 *Augustan History* Septimius Severus: 215.

59 Which is situated on a broad steppe, and not according to Herodian 3. 9. 4 'located on top of a lofty mountain'. See also Dio 76. 10.

60 Herodian 3. 9. 9–12. See also *Augustan History* Sept. Sev.: 214–16.

61 According to Millar 1993: 122. He also subdivided Britain into two provinces for similar reasons. See Herodian 3. 8. 1.

62 For 'Ain Sinu see Oates 1968; for Castra Maurorum see Ball 1989a. See also Kennedy and Northedge in Northedge *et al.* 1988. The large numbers of 'Roman' sites in this region identified from the air by Aurel Stein, however, almost invariably turn out on investigation to be later. See Gregory and Kennedy 1985.

63 Indeed, the whole field of Rome in the East is almost top-heavy with studies of the frontier (the so-called *limes* system) from several international conferences to an impressive array of publications. See Kennedy and Riley 1990 for the main evidence. For Dura Europos, see Hopkins 1979.

64 See Chapter 8, 'Julia Domna and the Arabs who ruled Rome'.

65 Herodian 4. 14. 2–3; Zosimus 1. 6–10.

66 Herodian 4. 15. 5.

67 According to Moses of Khorenats'i (2. 17), Crassus' war – and his defeat! – was in fact fought against the Armenians, not the Iranians. A similar confusion between the Armenians and Iranians in this war occurs in John Malalas' (11. 3) account.

68 Those that survive indirectly in, for example, Firdausi or al-Tabari, reveal almost wholly a concern with the East.

69 The evidence of the material remains is analysed in more detail in subsequent chapters.

70 Appian 9. 8. 48. The title was probably borrowed by the Iranians from the ancient Urartians. See Frye 1964, 1967: 249–5 and 1984: 74. Frye (1984: 267) even suggests that the Roman cult of the deified emperor might be related to the dynastic cult of the Kushan kings of the eastern Iranian world. See Boyce and Grenet 1991: 30–3 and refs for the cult of god-kings amongst the Seleucids. For the Persian origins of royal purple, see Xenophon *Anabasis* 1. 2.

71 Appian 17. 14. 940.

72 Perhaps nothing demonstrates more the thoroughness of subsequent Roman rejection of its past republicanism than out of all the 164 Roman emperors, from Augustus to Constantine XI, there is not a single one named after its great republican leaders: not a single Emperor Marius or Sulla or Gracchus.

73 Herodian 5. 2. 4.

74 The sources for these wars are admirably covered by Dodgeon and Lieu 1991. See also Frye 1984.

75 The last Arsacid king of Armenia was King Artaxias IV, 423–28; see Lang 1978: 163. Armenia has long been a storehouse for forgotten dynasties: Moses Khorenats'i (2. 8) mentions that members of the Median royal family lived on as princes in Parthian Armenia, and medieval Armenian noble families traced their descent variously from the Assyrians, the Chinese and ancient Hebrews! See Lang 1978: 165. In the East a Parthian dynasty continued to rule in Seistan under the early Sasanian emperors; see A. K. Nikitin, 'Coins of the Last Indo-Parthian King of Sakastan (A Farewell to Ardamitra)', *South Asian Studies* 10 (1984), 67–70.

76 The last Achaemenid emperor was Darius III Codomanus, who perished in the invasion of Alexander of Macedon. But Darius was succeeded by the supposed (in the western sources) 'pretender', who assumed the royal name of Artaxerxes IV on his assumption of power. Ardeshir's name thus marks a direct continuity, more so even than if he were called Cyrus or Darius. However, the apparent continuity between the Sasanians and Achaemenids is probably just a western interpretation and not that of the Sasanians themselves. For opposing interpretations contrast Roaf with Herrmann in Curtis *et al.* 1998.

77 Syncellus. Dodgeon and Lieu 1991: 9–10. Frye (1984: 284–5), however, discusses the possible Parthian and eastern origins of the Sasanian dynasty.

78 See Chapter 8.

79 Herodian 6. 2; Dio 80. 3; Dodgeon and Lieu 1991: 16–17. Ardeshir I, however, was not the first Iranian king to issue such a challenge to Rome; the Parthian Artabanus III issued a similar challenge in AD 35. See Tacitus *Annals* 6. 31. Note, however, Frye's (1976: 1–2) salutary remarks: 'Although the Byzantine Greeks regarded their Sasanian enemies through the centuries' old glasses fashioned by Herodotus and other Classical authors, the Persians had forgotten much of their past by the third century AD. When Herodian, (6. 2) as well as other authors, assumes that Ardeshir, the first Sasanian king, intended to restore the empire of Cyrus and Darius, the historian of the Roman emperors is only drawing upon his own knowledge, and not on the presumed memory of the Persians for their own past. The Persians probably did retain a tradition about their former glory and grandeur, with a belief that once they had ruled most of the world, but the pretensions of the Sasanids to rule were more of an epic, almost eschatological, nature than a right based on the reading of history books. It is, I believe, a fundamental difference between the Byzantine and Sasanian Empires, so alike in other matters, that the

Byzantines had read their Thucydides and Herodotus, whereas the Persians had not, indeed could not, read their Behistun inscription.'

80 Such comparison with the fifth- and fourth-century BC wars between Greeks and Persians was not lost on the Romans: Aurelius Victor (24) actually calls Ardeshir 'Xerxes'.

81 Herodian 6. 6. 1–3; 5. 10. Alexander's disasters are recounted by Herodian, our most reliable source. But according to other, less reliable, sources (e.g., Aurelius Victor, Festus, Eutropius, the *Augustan History* – see Dodgeon and Lieu 1991: 26–32), Alexander's campaigns were entirely victorious against the Sasanians. See also Zosimus 1. 12–13.

82 All sources are summarised in Dodgeon and Lieu 1991: 34–67. An account from the Iranian viewpoint is given by Frye 1984: 296–302, the main source of which is Shapur himself.

83 Shapur, Frye 1984: 371. According to most Roman sources, however, Gordian was killed by his own officers, possibly as part of a plot by Philip. See Dodgeon and Lieu 1991: 36–44; Eadie in Kennedy 1996b: 144–5.

84 Ammianus Marcellinus 23. 5. 2–3; John Malalas 18. 87. See also in Downey 1961: 256–62 and 587–95; Dodgeon and Lieu 1991: 51–4.

85 See Chapter 4, 'Survivors of Edessa'.

86 Quoted in Downey 1961: 257. See also Lieu 1986: 477.

87 See Chapter 4, 'Survivors of Edessa'. See Dodgeon and Lieu 1991: 57–65 for a summary of the sources. See also Firdausi *Shahnama* Book 25. At Bishapur, one of the palaces excavated is believed to have been built for Valerian. See Matheson 1976: 239–40.

88 See Chapter 3, 'Palmyra and Queen Zenobia'.

89 Aurelius Victor 38; John Malalas 12. 34; Frye 1984: 305.

90 Although sources differ on the fate of Numerianus. John Malalas 12. 35; Dodgeon and Lieu 1991; 112–19.

91 Dodgeon and Lieu 1991: 122–34 and 136–8; Kennedy and Riley 1990; Blockley 1992.

92 Indeed, Shapur even 'ascended the throne' before he was born, according to some sources. Dodgeon and Lieu 1991: 143.

93 Dodgeon and Lieu 1991: 143–63; Libanius *Oration* 19 translated in Lieu and Montserrat 1996; *Chronicon Paschale* 350.

94 Ammianus Marcellinus 19. 2.

95 Our main sources for the following events are: Ammianus Marcellinus Books 22–5; Zosimus; John Malalas; Libanius *Orations* 17, 18 and 24: 'The lament over Julian', 'Funeral oration over Julian' and 'Upon avenging Julian'; *Chronicon Paschale* 363; and Book 1 of al-Tabari. For other sources, see Dodgeon and Lieu 1991: 231–74. Of the many modern works on Julian, see Bowersock 1978.

96 E.g., Zosimus (3. 3) compares Julian's victory over the Celts on the Rhine to Alexander's victory over Darius III; Libanius (*Oration* 15) compares him to Alexander and likens his war against the Persians to the Trojan Wars. See also the *Artemisii Passio* quoted in Dodgeon and Lieu 1991: 238 and again in Lieu and Montserrat 1996: 236; also Blockley 1992: 25.

97 Libanius *Oration* 15. 1.

98 According to the *Artemisii Passio* (quoted in Lieu and Montserrat 1996: 236). This is our only source for this incident.

99 Ammianus Marcellinus 23. 3. 1 and 23. 3. 7; Zosimus 3. 11–13. According to Ammianus, Julian's speech to the troops was at Callinicum.

100 John Chrysostom, quoted in Dodgeon and Lieu 1991: 252.

101 Libanius *Oration* 18. 261–2.

102 John Malalas 13. 22.

103 Though see note in Chapter 8, 'From Paganism to Christianity', for paganism and Roman emperors after Julian.

104 Julian's death was never satisfactorily cleared up, the only general agreement being that Iran had nothing to do with it. Libanius implies that it was a Roman, and elsewhere an Arab conspiracy is implied. Wallace-Hadrill (p. 464, his notes to the Penguin Classic edition of Ammianus) suggests that Julian, in being in the centre of the battle without armour, was deliberately courting death as an honourable way out of the disastrous situation into which he had led his army. See Libanius *Oration* 18. 274, 24. 6–8. For the 'Arab conspiracy' theory, see *Artemisii Passio* 69–70, Gregory Nazianzus 13, John Lydus and Philostorgius, all quoted in

Dodgeon and Lieu 1991: 239, 251, 254 and 266, and Chapter 3, 'The Tanukhids and Queen Mawiyya'.
105 Libanius *Oration* 18. 1 and 283.
106 Zosimus 3. 26–9.
107 According to Zosimus and Libanius it was the Romans, though according to John Malalas (13. 27) it was Shapur, imagining Julian to be still alive.
108 Zosimus 3. 32.
109 Zosimus 3. 33–5.
110 General accounts from differing standpoints are in Frye 1984: 324–34 and Norwich 1988: 181–266. See now also Greatrex 1998 (the latter not read before going to press).
111 Parker 1986a: 149.
112 Jones 1966: 8.
113 Chegini and Nikitin in Litvinsky 1996: 58.
114 Frye 1983: 149–54; Rubin 1986; Isaac 1992: 74–5 and 229–30.
115 E.g., Nizam al-Mulk's *Siyasat Nama* where he is held up throughout as the ideal king of the past for modern kings – in this case Sultan Alp Arslan – to emulate.
116 Procopius 1. 25. 1–4.
117 Whitehouse and Williamson 1973: 38–9. See also Chapter 4.
118 See the section on the Dead Cities in Chapter 6.
119 Procopius 2; John Malalas 18. 26–76.
120 Though much of Khusrau Parviz's military prowess is probably attributable more to his generals than himself. See Whitby 1994.
121 *Chronicon Paschale* 614–28; Sebeos; Palmer 1993. For a different viewpoint from the usual western sources, see al-Biruni *Chronology*: 105 (although he refers to the Roman emperor as Phocas, not Heraclius).
122 The words were actually uttered by the last Shah, Muhammad Reza Pahlavi, on the steps of the tomb of Cyrus the Great at Pasargadae on the occasion of his '2,500th Anniversary of the Iranian monarchy' in 1970. They are still often quoted – in irony – in Iran today.
123 Frye 1984: 335–7. See also Chapter 4.
124 Howard-Johnson 1994.

Chapter 3

1 Braund 1984.
2 Frye 1984: 275–81; Wiesehöfer 1996: 144–5.
3 Sullivan 1977b: 910.
4 In Chapter 8, 'From Paganism to Christianity'.
5 There is even an extraordinary suggestion that the Iranian province of Hyrcania to the south-east of the Caspian for a while in the first century AD became a client state of Rome in response to Hyrcanian requests to Rome for help. Hyrcania corresponds roughly to modern Gurgan in north-eastern Iran. The suggestion, despite receiving some support in Tacitus, certainly cannot be true, but is nonetheless interesting in view of the curious architectural connection reviewed in Chapter 7. See Tacitus *Annals* 14. 25 and Frye 1984: 240.
6 Gawlikowski in Alcock 1997: 41.
7 Although the Idumaeans of Judaea and Herod himself have been labelled 'Arab' by Shahid 1984a: 145–60.
8 Millar (1993), for example, treats any use of the term 'Arab' or even 'Syrian' in a cultural context with extreme – and quite commendable – scholarly scepticism. But the same authority accepts unquestionably any similar use of the term 'Greek', with all the cultural connotations that such a term implies. When it comes to the Greeks, the term is accepted rather too hastily, with the character of the whole area of the Arab Near East under review described as 'Greek'.
9 See Chapter 8, 'Julia Domna and the Arabs who ruled Rome'.
10 Isaac 1992: 235. Shahid (1984a: 1–14, 145–60) in fact sees Pompey's invasion of the Near East as a frustration of Arab self-assertion: but for Pompey, the Arabs would have emerged as the predominant civilisation of the Near East in the first century BC and not the seventh century AD (with a minor peak in Arab self-assertion in the third century with the Emesene dynasty, Philip

the Arab, and the rise of Palmyra). The same authority also sees the entire history of Rome in the Near East mainly in terms of a Roman-Arab confrontation, with the period from settlement of Pompey in 64 BC to the battle of Yarmuk in 636 as exactly 700 years. This is probably going too far. Interestingly, whilst hailing leaders such as Herod rather dubiously as an 'Arab' Shahid is almost entirely silent about the emperors Elagabalus and Alexander, who have far more claim to 'Arab' credentials than Herod does.

11 See Dussaud 1955; Hitti 1964: Part I; Trimingham 1979; Shahid 1984a, 1984b, 1989.
12 Shahid 1984a: 7–8 and 19–21.
13 Tidrick 1989. The prejudices go right back; see, for example, Ammianus 14. 4. 1 who writes 'The Saracens . . . we never found desirable either as friends or enemies.'
14 MacDonald 1993: 326. See also Gawlikowski in Alcock 1997: 39, 45.
15 Shahid (1984b: 1–28) I believe goes too far in seeing the entire history of the Arab *foederati* in terms of Roman-Arab relations, or an 'Arab problem'. See also Chapter 1, and Isaac 1992: 72ff and 119.
16 See the remarks in Chapter 1.
17 MacDonald 1993: 346 and 388.
18 See Seyrig 1959, Chad 1972 and Sullivan 1977a for accounts of this kingdom.
19 Millar 1993: 34.
20 Seyrig 1959.
21 We know only the Graeco-Latin forms of the Emesene names Iamblichus, Samsigeramus and Sohaemus, and their original Arabic forms of Yamlikel, Shamshigeram and Suhaym are not always certain. See: Chad 1972: 134–44; Shahid 1984a: 41–2; Baldus 1996: 374. Their derivations are explained further below.
22 Ammianus 14. 8. 9.
23 Also called Iamblichus II, depending upon which Iamblichus one takes as the first: the shaikh of the second century BC near Apamaea, or the son of Sampsigeramus of Arethusa in the first century BC used here. Chad 1972 rather confusingly uses both systems: Iamblichus, the son of Sampsigeramus, is I in his text but II in his dynastic table at the end.
24 Josephus *Antiquities* 14. 129. Ptolemaus may have been the son of Iamblichus – see Chad 1972: 41–3.
25 Dio 50. 13; 51. 2.
26 Jidejian 1975a: 19–22.
27 Seyrig 1952–3; Chad 1972: 54–8.
28 Millar 1993: 302.
29 See below, Judaea.
30 Frye 1984: 243.
31 Chad 1972.
32 Chad 1972: 92; Millar 1993: 84.
33 For the religious associations of 'Samsigeramus', see below.
34 In Chapter 8, 'Julia Domna and the Arabs who ruled Rome' and 'From Paganism to Christianity'.
35 Herodian 5. 3. 5.
36 See, for example, Frazer 1911–36: 4(1). 34–6.
37 Delbrueck 1948: 21.
38 Chad 1972: 134–8; Baldus 1996: 374.
39 Chad 1972: 141–3; Shahid 1984a: 41–2.
40 Chad 1972: 143–4.
41 See also Seyrig 1971: 340–5, and Stoneman 1992: 141–6 for accounts of the Sun cult of Elagabal.
42 Delbrueck 1948: 22–3, figure A; Seyrig 1971: figure 2; Baldus 1996: plate 1. The recurrent 'cubic' motif is discussed further in Chapter 7, 'The trabeate style'.
43 Herodian 5. 3. 4–6.
44 Chad 1972: 123; Burns 1997: 130.
45 Dussaud 1927: 284; Burns 1992: 234–5; Ball 1997: 67.
46 Herodian 5. 3. 4–6.
47 Though John Malalas (12. 27) implies it is in Emesa. His statement, however, is suspect since he

says it was built by Gallienus, when we know it was built earlier – and he does not in any case specify that it was the Sun Temple.

48 Delbrueck 1948: 24. An incident related in Damascius' *Life of Isidore* (quoted in Stoneman 1992: 142–3) also suggests that venerated 'god-stones' such as Sol Elagabalus travelled in some sort of cycle. See also Baldus 1996: 374.

49 Turcan 1996: 181–2.

50 That the deity was a mountain god is well known; see Baldus 1996: 374.

51 *Augustan History*. Dodgeon and Lieu 1991: 92–3. See also 'Palmyra' below, and Chapter 8, 'From Paganism to Christianity'.

52 Cf. Millar 1993: 218.

53 Dussaud 1942–3; Lankester Harding 1963; Jidejian 1975a; Ragette 1980; Ward-Perkins 1981: 314–21.

54 John Malalas 11. 22 and 13. 37; *Chronicon Paschale* 379.

55 Dussaud 1942–3; Seyrig 1971; Turcan 1996: 148–58.

56 *Chronicon Paschale* 379.

57 Teixidor 1977: 52–60.

58 Dussaud 1942–3; Seyrig 1971: 345–8.

59 See *Chronicon Paschale* 297 for the martyrdom of St Gelasinus in Heliopolis. Al-Biruni (*Chronology*: 187), a native of Khwarazm, records Baalbek's fame for the Sun cult in the eleventh century.

60 Dussaud 1942–3.

61 See section on high places in Chapter 7.

62 Although it is significant that the cult of Sabazius was sometimes assimilated to Bacchus. See Turcan 1996: 315–25.

63 E.g., Wheeler's essay 'Size and Baalbek' in *Alms for Oblivion* (London) 1966: 157–63 and Ward-Perkins 1981: 317.

64 These monoliths, known as the *trilithon*, were famous even in antiquity – see *Chronicon Paschale* 379.

65 Ammianus 14. 8. 5–13. See also Millar 1993: 211 and 214.

66 Millar 1993: 266–7.

67 For example, it is often confusing whether and when the Decapolis cities came under Roman or Nabataean administration in the first century, while in the third century they continued to describe themselves as belonging to Coele Syria, even *after* Septimius Severus created a new province of Coele Syria out of *northern* Syria, i.e., excluding the Decapolis. See Millar 1993: 423–4.

68 Jidejian 1975a: 32–3.

69 Turcan 1996: 155.

70 Jidejian 1975a: 32–3.

71 Millar 1993: 302.

72 Jidejian 1975a: 22.

73 Ibid.

74 Turcan 1996: 153 and 157.

75 Turcan 1996: 149–53.

76 Turcan 1996: 180–4.

77 Dio Cassius 37. 17. 4.

78 Strabo 16. 2. 40; Josephus *Antiquities* 14 and *Jewish War* 1. 154.

79 Rome only really 'acquired' Judaea in 63 BC; it did not annex it until much later, but only exerted indirect control over it.

80 Dio 36. 20–1.

81 In fact Pompey first went into Palestine in response to ravages of the Phoenician coast of Syria from Palestine. See Dio 37. 15. 2.

82 See, for example, Josephus *Jewish War* 2. 340–425.

83 Indeed, Jewish revolts against the all-pervasive 'Westernisation' within its own ranks – both the Hellenistic kind and later the Roman kind – bears many similarities with the Iranian Islamic Revolution of our own day.

84 For this section, Josephus is the main source. For modern works, see Smallwood 1976, Schurer

1973–87. For biographies of Herod see Perowne 1957, Grant 1971, Hadas-Lebel 1993, Kokkinos 1998.

85 Eusebius (1. 6) is at pains to emphasise Herod's foreignness, though to call Herod an 'Arab', as Shahid (1984a: 43–4 and elsewhere) does, is untenable.

86 Although this first snub by Egypt's great seductress did not discourage Herod from making another bid for Cleopatra's charms (not without a little encouragement, if Josephus is to be believed!): in 34 BC, with Antony safely away on his Parthian campaign, Herod stepped in, dancing attendance on her and showering her with lavish gifts while escorting her through his territory back from Syria. He hastily withdrew his attentions, however, when his friend safely returned from the Parthian campaign to resume his attentions. See Josephus *Jewish War* 1. 363; *Antiquities* 15. 96–9.

87 Smallwood 1976: 30.

88 For the buildings of Herod, see now Roller 1998. Whilst the Temple was certainly Herod's greatest achievement, it is possible that Herod's building activity elesewhere is greatly exaggerated, especially by Josephus, whose main source it must be remembered were the memoirs of Herod himself. Herod's boastings, therefore, may often have been little more than statements of intent that had little effect on the ground; outside the Temple, the fact remains that definitely established physical evidence of Herodian building activity is still comparatively rare.

89 Busink 1970–80. See also 'Temenos temples' in Chapter 7.

90 Josephus in *Jewish War* 5. 136–257 gives a very detailed description of the Herodian and other buildings at Jerusalem. See also Roller 1998.

91 An epithet that in fact may never have existed, being merely a mistranslation of Herod 'the Elder' to distinguish him from younger members of his family bearing the same name. The title does not appear on any coins or inscriptions. See E. Mary Smallwood's notes to Josephus, *The Jewish War*, trans. G. A. Williamson (London 1981), 417, n. 17.

92 A point emphasised by Braund 1984: Part II, chapter 2.

93 Josephus *Antiquities* 14. 110–12.

94 Herod's endowments have been taken as evidence of Jewish settlement – see Smallwood 1976: 82.

95 Although Sebaste in particular contained many Roman features, its temple followed essentially eastern models. See Chapters 5 and 7.

96 Though his grandson, King Agrippa I, had some Hasmonaean blood in him.

97 Though this event may simply be anti-Herodian propaganda. See Smallwood 1976: 103–4.

98 There was at least one other son – confusingly also called Herod. It was he who was probably the husband of Herodias and father of Salome according to Josephus, rather than Philip in the Biblical version.

99 See Chapter 5.

100 Formerly ruled by a separate Arab prince, associated with Emesa – see above.

101 The chief source is, of course, Josephus' *Jewish War*. See also Dio. For modern accounts, see Smallwood 1976 and Schurer 1973–87.

102 One questions, however, whether Jewish refusal to sacrifice to Rome and Augustus is not overstated. After all, temples to Rome and Augustus in the East are conspicuous by their absence – compared, for example, to North Africa, where every town had one – so that one is left wondering whether *anybody* in the East bothered with this ritual? See also Chapter 7.

103 Josephus' escape from his companions advocating mass suicide – he was the only survivor of the suicide 'pact' – is fairly explicitly put down to trickery on Josephus' part in the Slavonic version of the *Jewish War*. See Appendix F in the Penguin translation (1981) by G. A. Williamson and E. Mary Smallwood.

104 This prophecy is related by Suetonius, *Vespasian* 5, as well as by Josephus in *The Jewish War* 3, 407 and Dio 65. 1. 4.

105 With further adventures in the meantime. It was captured by the Visigoths during their sack of Rome in 410 and taken to Spain, where it passed into Vandal hands, eventually ending up in the Vandal capital of Carthage in North Africa after 439. Following Belisarius' reconquest of the Vandal kingdom in 534 it was taken to Constantinople, where Justinian ordered it to be finally restored to Jerusalem. It remained in Jerusalem, however, only for a short time, being captured along with other holy relics by the Persians under Khusrau II Parviz in 614 and taken

to Iran. That is the last we hear of it; it may lie at the bottom of the volcanic lake of Takht-i Sulaiman, site of the Iranian holy city of Shiz, where the captured relics were taken to. See Chapter 4, 'Mark Antony and Iran'.

106 Josephus (6. 423) actually puts the number of dead at 1,100,000 and the number of prisoners at 97,000, out of a total population of 3,000,000 (2. 279), which seem unrealistically high figures, a figure followed by John Malalas (10. 45). Tacitus, however, (*History* 5. 13) puts the total population of Jerusalem at the time of the siege at a more realistic 300,000 (probably based on a military census), five times less than Josephus' estimate. I have, therefore, divided Josephus' casualty figures by five.

107 Although the Emperor Julian had intentions of rebuilding it and may well have done so had he lived – an event that would have produced as much Jewish ambivalence as Herod's rebuilding. See Ammianus Marcellinus 23. 1. Also Shahid 1984b: 131–2.

108 See Rappaport 1989. Dio 68. 32 gives the improbable number of over half a million perishing in this revolt.

109 Mor 1989.

110 Dio 69. 12–14; Eusebius 2. 6.

111 Dated in Jewish tradition to the same date as the fall of Jerusalem in the first Jewish Revolt.

112 Isaac 1992: 353–4.

113 The last fact underlined by Isaac (1992: 105).

114 Josephus *Antiquities* 14. 69–72. There might even have been more Jews in the Persian Empire than in Judaea. It is certainly probable that eastern Jewry as a whole probably dates from Nebuchadnezzar's diaspora rather than Titus'. Judaism took root in many countries of the Iranian world very early on: the Afghans, for example, traditionally see themselves as descended from the tribes of Israel (see Juzjani, *Tabaqat-i Nasiri* and Caroe 1958: 3–7) present-day Islamic fundamentalism notwithstanding, and extensive Jewish remains dating from the tenth century have been found in central Afghanistan (Ball 1982, 1: 133–4 and 267–8). The former name of Maimana in Afghanistan, too, was *Yahudan* (Le Strange 1905: 424). In Iran itself, one of the greatest of all centres of Persian civilisation, Isfahan, was first called *Yahudieh*, being founded as a Jewish community settled there by the Sasanians (not by Nebuchadnezzar, as Le Strange, 1905: 203, states), and the name still survives as the oldest quarter in Isfahan today.

115 Although Josephus (*Jewish War* 1. 2 and 2. 377) states they never received any – or only negligible amounts – Dio (65. 4. 3) says that there were significant numbers of Jews from beyond the Euphrates fighting alongside the defenders of Jerusalem.

116 Josephus *Jewish War* 2. 397.

117 This was written just after the assassination of Yitzhak Rabin in 1995.

118 Josephus *Jewish War* 1. 7.

119 Smallwood in Williamson and Smallwood 1981: 17–18. Indeed, the passion of Josephus' argument for writing Near Eastern history by a Near Eastern native from a Near Eastern viewpoint, that comes across strongly in both the Preface to his *Jewish War* and his *Concerning the Antiquity of the Jews* has a very modern ring. Compare the similar (though less well-written) passion by a fellow-countryman: Edward W. Said's *Orientalism* (London 1978).

120 See earlier in this Chapter, 'Rome and the Arabs'.

121 Strictly speaking, there does not appear from the sources or inscriptions to have ever been a state called 'Nabataea', although Josephus refers to it (or Nabatene) as a general area. See Glueck 1965: 47, Hammond 1973. The state was called 'Arabia', dominated by an Arab tribe called the 'Nabataeans'. However, it is more convenient here to refer to the kingdom as Nabataea rather than Arabia which, apart from its more imprecise meaning covering a large area of the Near East, is used more specifically as the Roman Province of Arabia which replaced the Nabataean kingdom. Bowersock's excellent book (1983: chapters 1–5) provides the best and most up-to-date overview and summary of the available literary, epigraphical and archaeological evidence, flimsy though this often is. See also Parker 1986a.

122 See Chapter 5, 'The Decapolis'.

123 Though Bowersock (1983: 14) is very sceptical of the Hebrew and Assyrian references to the Nabataeans, stating that 'their history seems to be irrevocably dark before the year 312 BC.' See also Hammond 1973: 11–13.

124 The material culture – particularly the pottery – of the Edomites and Nabataeans shows a remarkable degree of continuity that would simply not be apparent from the literary sources alone, which imply cultural displacement. See, for example, Browning 1989: 31–5 .

125 Or before the Judaean campaign according to Dio 37. 15. 1–2 and Appian 12. 16. 106.

126 Dio does not seem to mention Trajan's annexation of Arabia. The sources are in fact confused, as they also refer to northern Mesopotamia – the Hatran state – as 'Arabia'. See Dio 68. 31 for Trajan's failed campaign against Hatra in 'Arabia'.

127 Or 60 BC according to Negev 1977: 542. The name 'Malichus' is problematic. It is really a title rather than a personal name, meaning 'king' (cf. Arabic *malik*), but was treated as a personal name by the Greeks and Romans. In a sense, therefore, all Nabataean kings were 'called' Malichus. Hence, it is uncertain when a reference in the sources to 'Malichus' is referring to a specific Nabataean king or just any king. This has led to many problems of chronology. Similar confusions between titles and personal names occur elsewhere in the Eastern client kingdoms, e.g., the Abgars of Edessa, the Samsigerami of Emesa, etc., when a title can become a personal name or vice versa. Cf. the Caesars of Rome! The term 'Malichus' was, however, used as a name as well as a title: the Tyrian philosopher Porphyry was called Malichus before he changed his name.

128 See Chapter 4.

129 Bowersock 1983: 54–7.

130 Moses Khorenats'i 2. 29.

131 2 Corinthians 11. 32–3. Rome may have awarded Damascus to Nabataea after a raid on Damascus by the Arabs of Chalcis – see Emesa, above.

132 Bowersock 1983: 73.

133 Millar 1993: 408.

134 Millar (1993: 414) emphasises the 'noiseless' nature of the disappearance of the Nabataean kingdom, with virtually nothing known of Trajan's campaign or of resistance, if any. See also the discussion by Freeman in Kennedy 1996b.

135 As the depiction of Bactrian camels on Trajan's Province of Arabia coins and Bowersock (1983: 84) suggest. It has even been argued that Hadrian effectively abandoned Trajan's conquest and Arabia remained beyond direct Roman administration until Septimius Severus. See Lander 1986.

136 Although Glueck (1965: 259–65) argues for a strong interrelationship between Nabataea and Parthia, manifested by artistic parallels.

137 Although there is indirect evidence that Roman forces were being transferred to the Near East at the time as if to expect trouble – see Bowersock 1983: 81–2.

138 Strabo 16. 2. 21.

139 Strabo 16. 4. 26. See also Negev 1977: 555.

140 Negev 1977: 523–6 quoting Diodorus Siculus.

141 Roller (1998) emphasises Herod's hydrological building works throughout the Near East as a Roman element, borrowed from his friend Agrippa's attention to such works in Rome, forgetting that Herod was half Nabataean. Such works in the Near East, therefore, must be viewed as a Nabataean element, not Roman.

142 See, for example, various essays presented in Daum 1988. See also Crone 1987: Part I.

143 For dates see McKenzie 1990.

144 See Chapter 7 for further discussion on the architecture of the Nabataeans.

145 McKenzie 1990: chapter 3.

146 As well as other Near Eastern pagan religions. This is explored further in Chapter 8, 'From Paganism to Christianity'.

147 The architectural aspects are analysed in more detail in Chapter 7, 'High places'.

148 Hammond 1973: 49, 98–9, 102–3.

149 Quoted in Browning 1989: 214.

150 Indeed, Browning (1989: 110–11) observes that the 'god-blocks' are usually located near water courses, implying some form of water-worship.

151 Strabo 16. 4. 26.

152 This is explored in Chapter 7, 'Circumambulatories'.

153 Wright 1969.

154 Hammond 1973: 49, 94.
155 Boyce and Grenet 1991: various refs.
156 Huff 1998.
157 Negev 1977: 657; Glueck 1965: 98–9, pls 106–8.
158 Hammond 1973: 54.
159 Parr 1968, McKenzie 1990: 144–7, 162–5.
160 McKenzie 1990: 140–3, 159–61.
161 In the section on funerary architecture in Chapter 7.
162 Other Nabataean links with Iranian religion and religious architecture are pointed out elsewhere in this work.
163 McKenzie 1990: 114.
164 Browning 1979; Starcky and Gawlikowski 1985; Stoneman 1992; Dodgeon and Lieu 1991: chapter 4.
165 The only source for his fourth tribe, to which Udaynath and Zenobia belonged, is al-Tabari 4 (1987: 138).
166 Teixidor 1977: 107–8; Drijvers 1982a: 36 .
167 For Mark Antony's campaign see Isaac 1992: 141.
168 There is no evidence that this was a 'Senate' in the Graeco-Roman sense, hence evidence for a Greek 'character' of Palmyra, as Millar (1993: 326) supposes. Cf. Frye 1984: 220. Gawlikowski in Alcock 1997: 44. See also Chapter 8, 'East and West': 'Character and Prejudice'.
169 The arguments for either the Camp or Baths of Diocletian being on the site of a royal palace are inconclusive.
170 Or a 'republic of merchants' – Gawlikowski in Alcock 1997: 44.
171 Gawlikowski 1994a, 1996a.
172 In Chapter 4, 'Rome in India'.
173 Not at Kharg Island as previously thought from Ghirshman's (undated) excavations there have suggested; see Haerinck 1974 and Whitehouse in Begley and De Puma 1991: 217. See also Frye 1984: 276, Collingwood and Wright 1965 and Turcan 1996: 173–6.
174 A point emphasised by Graf 1989: 114–15.
175 Stoneman 1992: 76–9.
176 Zosimus 1. 39.
177 Stoneman 1992: 5.
178 Duchess of Cleveland, *The Life and Letters of Lady Hester Stanhope*, London (1914), 159–60.
179 *Augustan History*. Dodgeon and Lieu 1991: 80–4; al-Tabari 4 (1987: 138–50).
180 See also 'The Tanukh and Queen Mawiyya', below.
181 Both Arab and Manichaean sources contain information about the two sisters not mentioned in the Classical sources. See al-Tabari 4 (1987: 138–50) and Klimkeit 1993: 202–3 and 208–9, with references. Zenobia was also called Na'ilah according to al-Tabari, and Queen Tadi or Nafsha according to Manichaean documents (although the latter name might be referring to her sister – there is confusion).
182 Lane Fox 1986: 570; Graf 1989: 147; Stoneman 1992: 152–3; Klimkeit 1993: 202–3 and 208–9; Lieu 1994: 26–30.
183 *Augustan History*. Dodgeon and Lieu 1991: 83.
184 *Augustan History*. Dodgeon and Lieu 1991: 83.
185 Stoneman 1992: 130.
186 Stoneman's (1992: chapter 6) excellent summary of intellectual life in third-century Syria as the background to Zenobia's 'Palmyrene court school' merely underlines its intellectual impoverishment within an otherwise extremely rich Syrian literary context.
187 Even the traditional association of the great fortress on the Euphrates at Halabiya with Zenobia cannot be demonstrated by the material remains. See Lauffray 1983.
188 Stoneman 1992: 155.
189 Dodgeon and Lieu 1991: 68–110, 275–99; Klimkeit 1993: 202–3 and 208–9.
190 Aurelius Victor 33.
191 The word is Zosimus' (1. 37).
192 Graf 1989: 153–4.
193 John Malalas 12. 28; Graf 1989: 143–4.

194 According to Manichaean documents from China, Zenobia received Manichaean missionaries in Alexandria. See Klimkeit 1993: 202–3.
195 Zosimus 1.44.
196 Eutropius (9.13–15) writes of him as of 'unrestrained temper . . . excessively inclined to cruelty'.
197 Zosimus 1.50–1.
198 The importance of this is further emphasised in Chapter 9, 'Julia Domna and the Arabs who ruled Rome' and 'From Paganism to Christianity'.
199 See Bowersock 1983: 132–5. See also 'The Tanukh and Queen Mawiyya' later in this chapter.
200 It must also be remembered that the area Zenobia fled to was also her traditional tribal grounds.
201 Zosimus 1.54–58; John Malalas 12.30. Dodgeon and Lieu 1991: 101, 108–9. Note, however, that the name 'Zenobius' and its variations in Rome did not necessarily denote descent from Zenobia.
202 John of Antioch. Dodgeon and Lieu 1991: 100.
203 Zosimus 1.52 lists Aurelian's army.
204 These are known from archaeological discoveries, as well as those listed in the *Augustan History* (Dodgeon and Lieu 1991:97–8) in the Sun Temple at Rome as loot from Palmyra.
205 Zosimus 1.60–1; *Augustan History*. Dodgeon and Lieu 1991: 101–3. See also Baranski 1994, who emphasises Aurelian's destructiveness.
206 See, for example, Graf's (1989: 143) references to Zenobia's 'Arab army' or Stoneman's (1992: 118) remarks.
207 E.g., Graf 1989.
208 See the discussion by Eadie in Kennedy 1996b: 148–50. See also Millar 1993: 334–5 and 337.
209 Downey 1961: 265–6.
210 Shahid 1984a: 39–41, 149–50.
211 Downey 1961: 268.
212 Warmington (1974: 321) notes that much of the Mediterranean and Egyptian trade 'was ruined' as a result of the sack of Palmyra.
213 Stoneman 1992: 17 and 54. See also Millar 1993: 325–6.
214 Millar 1993: 326.
215 Bowersock 1983: 132–5. See also 'The Tanukh and Queen Mawiyya', later in this chapter.
216 E.g., John Malalas 12.26.
217 Graf 1989.
218 Shahid 1984b: 15. See, however, Crone 1987.
219 Dodgeon and Lieu 1991: 84–5.
220 Stoneman 1992: 152–3; Klimkeit 1993: 202–3, 208–9.
221 See also Graf 1989: 155–6.
222 Teixidor 1977: 122–6.
223 Teixidor 1977: 134–40.
224 Saggs 1962: 299–358; Oates 1986: 152–4, 170–6.
225 Gawlikowski 1994a, 1994b.
226 Such processional ways are analysed in detail in Chapter 7, 'Sacred and processional ways'.
227 Strictly speaking, the name 'Edessa' refers just to the city rather than the kingdom. The name of the kingdom, of which Edessa was the capital, was Osrhoene. The ancient name of Edessa was Orhai, from which both Osrhoene and Urfa, the modern name of the city, derive. The name Edessa, however, is more conventionally used for both the city and the kingdom. By far the best study of the Kingdom of Edessa is Segal 1970. See also Drijvers 1980; Ross, (forthcoming).
228 Segal 1970: 23–4, 29–30.
229 Segal 1970: 23–4.
230 Saggs 1962: 145–53; Segal 1970: 5; Saggs 1984: 120–1.
231 Donner 1986.
232 Segal 1970: 27–30. See also Chapter 7, 'Funerary architecture'.
233 Segal 1970: 1–2.
234 E.g., see Algaze 1989: 571–608.
235 Saggs 1962: 145–53.

236 Segal 1970: 5–6.
237 Segal 1970: 7–8.
238 Though Millar (1993: 47) characteristically denies the native Semitic character of Edessan culture, recognising only the Greek – even going so far as to distort the meaning of Schlumberger's (1960) title in support of his refutation: Schlumberger was discussing Greek art in this context, not the culture!
239 Moses Khorenats'i 2. 26–7.
240 Indeed, Edessa is generally considered a part of Armenia by Moses Khorenats'i 2. 28, 34.
241 Segal 1970: 18–20, 31–3.
242 Tacitus *Annals* 12. 10.
243 Moses Khorenats'i 2. 34.
244 Iran dethroned Abgar after Carrhae and the throne remained vacant for a year. Segal 1970: 10–12; Bivar 1983: 53.
245 Moses Khorenats'i 2. 28.
246 Moses Khorenats'i 2. 29. See also 'The Nabataeans', above.
247 Dio 68. 30. 2.
248 Called 'king of the Persians' in the *Augustan History* Sept. Sev.: 217–18. See also the mosaic portrait of him discussed in Drijvers 1982b.
249 Quoted by Segal 1970: 24–5.
250 Probably on the site of the present Makan Ibrahim Mosque – see Segal 1970: 24–6. Fragments of it were reused in the mosque at Harran – see Mango 1982: 119–20. After it was rebuilt in the sixth century it became one of the most famous churches in the East – see Krautheimer and Curcic 1986: 219.
251 Segal 1970: 17. They are also interpreted as sacred pools to Atargatis – see later in this chapter.
252 There is no evidence that it was a temple, although the columns may have had some religious function; see below, also Chapter 7, 'Funerary architecture'. See Segal 1970: 26–7.
253 Segal 1970: 31. See also Chapter 4.
254 Michael the Syrian, Dodgeon and Lieu 1991: 35; Millar 1993: 151.
255 *Paikuli* H; Frye 1983: 130. He may have been related to the Lakhmid Arab dynasty of Hira, a client state of Iran. See 'The Tanukh and Queen Mawiyya', below.
256 Shahid 1984a: 46.
257 E.g., Tacitus *Annals* 12. 12.
258 See Drijvers 1980, 1982a; Teixidor 1977; Stoneman 1992: 138–41 for discussions of the religions of Edessa.
259 Peña 1996: 203.
260 Klimkeit 1993: 1–26.
261 Al-Biruni *Chronology*: 186, *India* I: 21.
262 For Ashoka's edicts, see Bloch 1950, Thapar 1961: 250–66. This and other Indian embassies are discussed further in Chapter 8, 'From India to Rome'.
263 Lucian; Segal 1970: 51; Turcan 1996: 133–43; Peña 1996: 205. The Mambij Atargatis cult also incorporated elements of Zoroastrianism. See Boyce and Grenet 1991: 356–7.
264 See Glueck 1965: 391–2 for a discussion of sacred pools associated with the Atargatis cult in Nabataea. Tanks of sacred fish are a well-known religious practice – both now and in antiquity – from elsewhere further east. E.g., see A. Schimmel, 'The martyr-mystic Hallaj in Sindhi folk-poetry', *Numen* 9 (1962), 161–200.
265 Their distinctive head-dress, as depicted on mosaics and sculpture, in fact survived in the region until the nineteenth century. See Segal 1970: 38–40.
266 Though not strong enough to prevent Abgar V aiding Nabataea in a war against Herod Antipas. But perhaps the Jewish lobby at Edessa – who traditionally hated the Herodians – were behind this war after all.
267 Eusebius 1. 13. See also Procopius 2. 12. 20–30; Moses Khorenats'i 2. 30–3. Copies of the correspondence were also preserved in a number of inscriptions throughout Anatolia and Macedonia. See also Segal 1970: 62–3, 71–2; Lane Fox 1976: 278–80.
268 Moses Khorenats'i 2. 30.
269 Bloch 1950; Thapar 1961: 250–66.
270 Eusebius 2. 1. 2–13.

271 The church, supposedly of fifth-century foundation, is mainly twelfth century and later. See Kleiss *et al.* 1974. Its association with St Thaddeus so far from Edessa has obvious implications for the historical geography of the kingdom and its relations with Adiabene.

272 Segal 1970: 64–5.

273 Bardaisan; Eusebius 4. 30; Segal 1970: 35–9. See also Drijvers 1980.

274 Bardaisan: 59; Shahid 1984a: 47.

275 Drijvers (1980: 14) considers the claim apocryphal.

276 Segal 1970: 60–1.

277 Segal 1970: 66, 105; Klimkeit 1993: 202–3, 208–9.

278 Lieu 1994: 38–45.

279 See also Ball 1989b.

280 Klimkeit 1993: 1–26.

281 Parker 1986a: 150.

282 Shahid 1984b: 21–2.

283 This still survives amongst the Pathans of Afghanistan and Pakistan as the traditional equestrian sport of *naiza-bazi* or tent-pegging, from where it was adopted into British military sports. The common denominator of both Pathan and Arab traditions was, of course, ancient Iran, from where the medieval European sport of jousting also derives.

284 Bowersock 1983: 157.

285 For the Tanukh see Hitti 1964: 81–2; Trimingham 1979; Bowersock 1983: 132–47; Shahid 1984b; al-Tabari 4 (1987: 128–50).

286 Frye 1984: 307. Also *Paikuli*.

287 Trimingham 1979: 93–4; Shahid 1984b.

288 Al-Biruni *Chronology*: 48–9, although in the end he concludes that Dhu'l-Qarnayn is to be identified with one of the Yemeni princes of the pre-Islamic Himyarite dynasty. See also the *Qur'an*.

289 Though Shahid (1984b: 38–42) dates this raid to after Imru'l-Qays' defection to the Romans.

290 Lieu 1994: 36–7.

291 Shahid 1984b: 56–9.

292 Quoted by Bowersock 1983: 138–9. Also quoted and extensively discussed by Shahid 1984b: 31–53. Much has been written about the Namara inscription with its reference to Imru'l-Qays as 'king of all the Arabs'. This does indeed remain an important document, both historically and linguistically, for pre-Islamic Arab history, and it is rightly considered to be one of our most important sources for the history of this period. But it is, after all, just a single monumental inscription that might be nothing more than an empty boast of little real foundation. Inscriptions are by their very nature propaganda. It is as dangerous to pin too much on them as it would be to write history from official newspaper headlines.

293 Shahid 1984b: 546–80.

294 Libanius *Oration* 24. 6–8; Shahid 1984b: 129–30.

295 Shahid 1984b: chapter 4.

296 The main source for Queen Mawiyya – or Mavia in the Byzantine sources – is Sozomen 6. 38. 7 and Pacatus. The main modern studies are Trimingham 1979: 96–100, Bowersock 1980 and Shahid 1984b: chapter 4 and pp. 532–44.

297 Such as the Arab chief Aspebatos. Aspebatos, who had converted to Christianity in 420, was made a bishop and was settled in Palestine, presumably with his tribe. See Isaac 1992: 235–49. According to Frye (1984: 316), however, the family was Iranian, from Gurgan (ancient Hyrcania). The name is actually a Persian title, *sepahbod*, meaning army commander.

298 If the Arab 'Chasidat' mentioned in the Anasartha inscription of 425 can be identified with Mawiyya's otherwise anonymous daughter. See Shahid 1984b: chapter 6.

299 Ammianus Marcellinus 31. 16. 5. See also Spiedel 1977: 727.

300 If this second Anasartha inscription recording the death of a virtuous Arab lady called Mawiyya in 425 can be identified with her. See Mouterde and Poidebard 1945: pl. xxxii; Shahid 1984b: chapter 6.

301 Parker 1986a: 149–50.

302 Al-Tabari 4 (1987: 139).

303 Musil 1928: 154–5.

304 Trimingham 1979: 95; Shahid 1989.

305 For the Ghassanids see Trimingham 1979: 178–88, Hitti 1957: 401–6, Hitti 1964: 78–81, Megdad 1982: 271–3, Parker 1986a: chapter 8; Shahid 1978, 1989. Unfortunately I had not had the opportunity to examine Shahid 1995 before going to press.

306 Hence, 'Yamani' is a common family name for many Arabs.

307 Procopius 1. 17. 47–8. The Greek term *phylarchos* is problematic, being variously used to translate 'king', 'shaikh' or even 'high-priest'. Since the Greeks generally used *basilios* for 'king', it seems likely that 'shaikh' is meant here, or at least 'over-shaikh'.

308 Procopius 1. 17. 29–48.

309 Procopius 1, 17. 36–40 and 2. 1.

310 Sauvaget 1939.

311 Hoag 1975: 22. See also Burns 1992: 197–8; Ball 1997: 104–6. This building is also discussed further in Chapter 7.

312 In a recent site guide published in Syria (*Al-Rassafa: Metropolis of the Syrian Desert* by Wafa Ayash, Damascus 1994), the remains of Rasafa are described as 'Arab' throughout. Such terminology would normally be dismissed out of hand as nationalistic by western scholarship, but in fact it is just as valid a term for Rasafa as our own 'Byzantine' or 'Roman' would be, if not more so.

313 Trimingham 1979: 258–9.

314 Hitti 1957: 406.

315 Bowersock 1983: 147.

Chapter 4

1 Wheeler's (1954) classic, but now outdated, work has long been the standard account of this presence.

2 Cimino 1994: 12–14, quoting various Latin authors. For Cyrus' vision see Frye 1963: 109–11.

3 Suetonius *Nero* 19.

4 According to Strabo 2. 13. 3, an account, now lost, was written of this campaign by Dellius, a friend of Antony's who accompanied him as one of the army commanders. Our main source for this campaign is Plutarch *Antony* as well as Strabo 2. 13 and Dio 49. 24–32. See also Minorsky 1945 and Bivar 1983: 58–65.

5 See Chapter 2.

6 Such as Judaea and Nabataea. See Chapter 3.

7 Moses Khorenats'i (2. 22) in fact attributes the entire defeat of Antony's force to the Armenians.

8 According to Moses Khorenats'i 2. 23, who, in writing a national Armenian history, had every reason to play down Armenian defeats and Roman successes. See also Lang 1978: 139.

9 Dio 49. 32. 2.

10 Tacitus *Annals* 12.13. Stein 1940: 324–46; Boyce and Grenet 1991: 84–6 and refs; Sherwin-White and Kuhrt 1993: 77 and refs.

11 For Takht-i Sulaiman see Schippmann 1971: 339–41; Herrmann 1977: 113–18 and Matheson 1976: 102–4 and references.

12 Minorsky 1945; Bivar 1983: 63–4; Boyce and Grenet 1991: 70–9.

13 Kleiss 1973; Herrmann 1977: 82.

14 Herodian 6. 6. 1–3. See also Chapter 2.

15 See Chapter 2. See also Minorsky 1945.

16 This expedition is related in Strabo 16. 4. 22–4, and (more briefly) Dio 53. 29 and Pliny 6. 32. 160–2. For modern accounts see Pirenne 1961: 93–124; Isserlin 1984; Sidebotham 1991: 20–30; Groom 1996.

17 Bowersock 1983: 96–9.

18 Strabo 1. 2. 32. For the Egyptian 'Land of Punt' in Hatshepsut's records and the story of the visit of the Queen of Sheba to King Solomon in 1 Kings 10, see Hourani 1995: 7–8.

19 Identified by Sir Lawrence Kirwan with Aynuna in Saudi Arabia. See Groom 1996: 5.

20 Dio 52. 29. 8 calls it 'Athlula', Strabo 16. 4. 24, 'Athrula', known in south Arabian inscriptions as Yathil. See Doe 1983: 127–8.

21 See Doe 1983: 120–4.
22 Bowersock 1983: Appendix I. Shahid (1984b: 72–4), however, argues for a third-century AD date for this inscription, arguing that it formed a part of Imru'l-Qays' Arabian campaign during the time of Constantine, but this seems dubious. See Chapter 3, 'Tanukh and Queen Mawiyya'.
23 Hammond 1973: 22–5.
24 The *Periplus* (26) refers to the capture of Eudaemon Arabia – Aden – by Romans, but this is generally thought unlikely (see Miller 1969: 14–16). Herodian in fact describes a further exped-ition into south Arabia by Severus during his Mesopotamian campaign in 192: 'Severus hurried on into Arabia Felix . . . [and] destroyed many towns and village there . . . and plundered the countryside' (Herodian 3. 4. 3). This is almost certainly untrue, and Herodian is presumably confusing the Arabs of Arabia Felix with the Arabs of Mesopotamia, who would have inhabited the upper Tigris and Euphrates at that time. This was, in fact, probably Xenophon's 'Arabia' – see Donner 1986. Shahid (1984b: 72–4) also postulates a third-century AD campaign into south Arabia during the time of Constantine, basing his argument partly on the Barraqish inscription, but this too seems doubtful.
25 Plutarch *Crassus*.
26 See Holt 1989: 55 n. 20 for a summary of sources. Lieu (1986) views this as part of a broader tradition of removing conquered peoples in the ancient Near East, e.g., Assyrian deportations, Babylonian exile of the Jews, etc.
27 The Afghans traditionally claim to be descended from the lost tribes of Israel. See Caroe 1958: 3–7.
28 Pliny *Natural History*: 6. 47.
29 Staviskij 1995: 201–2.
30 Herrmann *et al.* 1993: 43; see also Bader *et al.* 1995: 39–50.
31 When the Syriac *Chronicle of Se'ert* identifies them as descendants of Alexander. See Lieu 1986; see also, 'Survivors of Edessa', below.
32 Dubs 1957. See also Boulnois 1966: 64ff, Ferguson 1978: 599–601, Franck and Brownstone 1986: 114–5 and Ishjamts 1994: 163–4. For the historical background to this story, see also Ma and Sun 1994: 240–3 and Zadneprovskiy 1994: 463–8. The whole story, however, has been passionately rejected by Raschke 1978: 679–81 (who describes Dubs' interpretation of the facts as 'a work of fiction of moderate interest'), although Ishjamts 1994: 163–4 and Staviskij 1995: 200–2 accept it.
33 Staviskij 1995: 201.
34 Lieu 1986: 6.
35 Pigulevskaya 1963: various refs; Tafazzoli and Khromov in Litvinsky (1996) 92–3; Wiesehöfer 1996: 218–19.
36 Matheson 1976: 156–7.
37 But see the important discussion on city plans in Chapter 7.
38 See Chapter 7, however, for possible eastern origins of this type of monument. Ghirshman 1956: 148–9; Matheson 1976: 238–41 and references; Herrmann 1977: 101–5.
39 Supposedly built, according to al-Tabari (4. 690), after Queen Khumani, the mythical daughter of Artaxerxes, sent armies against Rome capturing large numbers of POWs. For the Band-i Qaysar and other 'Roman' bridges, see Reuther 1938–9: 570–1; Pope 1938–9: 1228–30; Matheson 1976: 140, 152, 156; Herrmann 1977: 97–8.
40 All fully published now in *Iranische Denkmäler*. Darabgird: Trümpelmann 1975; Bishapur 3: Herrmann and Howell 1981; Bishapur 1 and 2: Herrmann, MacKenzie and Howell 1983; Naqsh-i Rustam: Herrmann, MacKenzie and Howell 1989. See also Wiesehöfer 1996: 160–1.
41 Sarre in Pope 1938/9: 596; Herzfeld 1941: 314–7; Trümpelmann 1975.
42 MacDermot 1954; Herrmann 1977: 92–4; Herrmann and Howell 1981; Whitby 1994: 235–6.
43 Shapur *Res Gestae* in Frye 1984.
44 Sarre in Pope 1938/9: 597; Bivar 1972: 269–76; Whitby 1994: 236.
45 Herzfeld 1941: 318–19. The fifth and lowest panel was only discovered in 1975; see Sarfaraz 1973 and 1975.
46 Herrmann in Curtis *et al.* 1998: 42.
47 Frye 1963: 247–53; Lieu 1986; Dodgeon and Lieu 1991: 163.
48 According to the Syriac *Chronicle of Se'ert*, the main source for this story, but they were more

likely to have been descendants of the prisoners of Carrhae, still maintaining their 'Roman' identity.

49 See Le Strange 1905: 408 for the church north of Herat. For an excellent overview of Christianity in Central Asia, including the Christian remains at Merv, see Litvinsky and Vorobyeva-Desyatovskaya in Litvinsky 1996: 421–6. See also Wiesehöfer 1996: 200–5.

50 Theophylact Simocatta 5. 6. 9–10; Lieu 1986: 499.

51 See Chapter 8.

52 Lieu 1986: 487.

53 Ever since Warmington's classic account of this was published in 1928 (new edn 1974) there has been an increasing literature on this subject. The standard for many years was Part 3 of Wheeler 1954; important publications since have been Miller 1969, Raschke 1978, Sidebotham 1986: 20–47, Begley and De Puma 1991, Cimino 1994, Boussac and Salles 1995 and Reade 1996 (the last two I have not consulted), to name but a few of the many books on the subject. See also Schmittenhenner (1979) for a review of the literary evidence.

54 See Warmington 1974 for the extreme 'colonialist' view (albeit first published in 1928 when British India was at its height). Parisher (1991: 225–6) sees the idea that the foreigner played the dominant role in Indian commercial relations with the West as entirely colonial and post-colonial.

55 Cimino 1994: 10, with bibliography.

56 The best compendium of these sources is in McCrindle 1901. See also Sastri 1927. For the *Periplus* see below.

57 McCrindle 1901: 103–4; Warmington 1974: 43 and 394b; Sidebotham in Begley and De Puma 1991: 30–5.

58 Casson in Begley and De Puma 1991: 10. Even if one allows for much smaller Arab-style Indian-Ocean-going ships, rather than the massive Roman grain-carrying tubs of the Mediterranean on which Casson bases his calculation, the figure is still formidable.

59 Pliny 12. 41. 84; also 6. 26. 101; Wheeler 1954: 142; Miller 1969: 223–30; Sidebotham in Begley and De Puma 1991: 26–31; Cimino 1994: 17–8 and 141. Raschke (1978: 634–7) largely dismisses Pliny's evidence. See also Sidebotham 1986.

60 Translations of *Periplus* by Schoff (1912), Huntingford (1980) and Casson (1989). See also Warmington 1974: 43, Wheeler 1954: 141–52, Miller 1969: 16–20; Whitehouse 1990; Casson in Begley and De Puma 1991: 8.

61 For the Yavanas see Tarn 1951: 254–8; Narain 1957: App. I; Warmington 1974: 60–8, 112, 261–2; Deo in Begley and De Puma 1991: 39; Raman in Begley and De Puma 1991: 125ff; Cimino 1994: 64–70. The whole question of the Yavanas and foreigners generally in Indian literature is fully discussed in Parisher 1991: esp. chapter 7.

62 About the only variant *not* derived from Ionia is, surprisingly, the name 'Ionian Sea' on the west coast of Greece, which has no linguistic connection to 'Ionia'.

63 As Boardman's (1994: 24) cautionary note emphasises.

64 Deshpande in Cimino 1994: 175–6.

65 For a summary of the numismatic evidence see Raschke 1978: 665–73; Turner 1989 (the latter I have not consulted); Cimino 1994: 135–42; Gupta in Cimino 1994: 168–9. I am also indebted to a joint lecture on the numismatic and archaeological evidence given by David MacDowall and James Howell entitled 'Roman and sub-Roman finds in India' at the British Academy on 12 December 1994.

66 Ray (1994: 178) sees these as possibly reflecting the trade in wood for boat construction in India, rather than direct trade in other commodities with the Mediterranean.

67 A point emphasised by Deo (in Begley and De Puma 1991: 39) in his discussion of this evidence.

68 Will in Begley and De Puma 1991.

69 Orton in Begley and De Puma 1991. A similar argument has raged about the relationship between the earlier – fourth-century BC – 'northern black-polished ware' from India and Hellenistic 'black gloss ware' from the West. See Erdosy in Allchin 1995: 100–5 and Whitehouse in McNicoll and Ball 1996: 25–6 for the arguments.

70 For a summary of the archaeological evidence see Gysens, Colazingari and Deshpande in Cimino 1994: 148–57 and 182–3. I am also indebted to the joint lecture on the numismatic and

archaeological evidence given by David MacDowall and James Howell entitled 'Roman and sub-Roman finds in India' at the British Academy on 12 December 1994.

71 Stern in Begley and De Puma 1991.
72 De Puma in Begley and De Puma 1991: 82–112.
73 Deo in Begley and De Puma 1991; Raman in Begley and De Puma 1991; Gupta, Raman and Deshpande in Cimino 1994: 167–83.
74 Wheeler 1946, 1954: 173–9; Casal 1949; Allchin 1995: 147–9. New excavations by the University Museum, Pennsylvania, and Madras University were carried out between 1989 and 1992; see Begley 1996 (not consulted at the time of writing).
75 Wheeler 1954: 174–5.
76 Raman and Comfort in Begley and De Puma 1991. It must be pointed out, however, that the terra siggilata was found in the industrial area, not in the houses (of which none were excavated).
77 Wheeler 1954: 178–9.
78 Whitehouse 1990: 490.
79 Ray 1994: 49 and 69.
80 The archaeological evidence for trade between Mesopotamia and the Indus civilisation since the third millennium BC hardly needs reiterating here. See, for example, Hourani 1995: 6–11 and Roaf 1990: 98 for a summary of the evidence.
81 Begley in Begley and De Puma 1991: 7; Gupta in Cimino 1994: 171–3.
82 Wheeler 1954: 147–8.
83 Cosmas Indicopleustes 11; Whitehouse and Williamson 1973: 32–3; Ball 1986a: 110–12; Whitehouse 1996. For Christian remains on and near the Gulf, see for example Ghirshman 1960, Whitehouse 1974: 21–3, Ball 1986: 103, Okada 1992, King 1996.
84 Eusebius 5. 10, 3.1; Lane Fox 1986: 278. For Apollonius, see Chapter 8, 'Julia Domna and the Arabs who ruled Rome'.
85 Procopius 1. 20. 9–13. Cosmas Indicopleustes (11. 337) writes that Taprobane (Ceylon) was 'much frequented by ships from all parts of India and from Persia and Ethiopia, and it likewise sends out ships of its own'. No mention is made of Rome. See also Whitehouse and Williamson 1973 and refs; Rubin 1989; Carswell in Begley and De Puma 1991: 199; Coningham and Allchin in Allchin 1995: 172; Whitehouse 1996.
86 Warmington 1974: 145–260; Miller 1969: 25; Raschke 1978: 650.
87 For the Roman involvement in the Persian Gulf trade see: Ammianus Marcellinus 14. 3. 3; Hourani 1995: 13–7; Whitehouse and Williamson 1973; Williamson 1972; Warmington 1974: 86–7, 131, 138; Gawlikowski 1994a, 1996a; Ray 1994: 53–7; Whitehouse 1996; Potts 1997; Whitehouse, forthcoming. Sidebotham (1986: 15–17) in fact comments on the extreme paucity of Roman objects found in south Arabian archaeology.
88 See Whitehouse's (in Begley and De Puma 1991) important cautionary notes on this matter.
89 Warmington (1974: 184–219, 258–60) summarises the Indian and Far Eastern products that the Arabians and Ethiopians kept secret from the Romans. See also Sidebotham 1986: 15. Raschke (1978: 654–5), however, argues for an East African origin of cinnamon.
90 Warmington 1974: 250–1.
91 As Raschke (1978: 673) cautiously notes.
92 Casson 1989: 75.
93 Ray 1994: 74–5.
94 Buccellati and Kelly-Buccellati in Weiss (1985: 221–2).
95 Casson in Begley and De Puma 1991.
96 Ray 1994: 176–80.
97 Crone 1987: Part I; Hourani 1995: chapter 3; Ministry of Information, Oman (1979); Severin (1982).
98 Whitehouse and Williamson 1973.
99 Crone 1987; Hourani 1995: chapter 1.
100 Main studies are: Wheeler 1954; Ferguson 1978; Raschke 1978; Staviskij 1995; Graf 1996.
101 Frye 1984: 275–81
102 Translated by Schoff 1914. See his extensive commentary, as well as Fraser 1996: 88–93 and references.
103 Pliny 6. 52; Strabo 11. 7; see also Staviskij 1995: 191–2.

104 Staviskij 1995: 192.
105 Ptolemy 1. 11. 4–8, 1. 12.2–10, 6. 16. 1–8, 6. 21.1 See Cary and Warmington 196–7, Ferguson 1978: 594. At modern Tashkurghan, a major stopping place on the Karakorum Highway between Islamabad and Kashgar, there are some remains of an old fort and town, which is undated, although important seventh–fourth century BC graves have been excavated in the vicinity. See Ma and Wang in Harmatta (ed.) 1994: 210–11. However, Tashkurghan is a common Turkish name in Central Asia: another Tashkurghan, for example, is the first town in Bactria after crossing the Hindu Kush from the south in Afghanistan, although the citadel mound there has revealed nothing earlier than fifteenth century. See Ball 1982: 269. Stein (1912, 1: 345) tentatively identifies the 'Stone Tower' of Hsiuen Tsiang with the site of Charkhlik further east in Xinjiang, to the south of the Takla Makan Desert.
106 Le Strange 1905: 314–15; none of the surface pottery, on superficial examination, could be dated, however, earlier than the ninth century – personal observation.
107 Stein 1912: 2. 359–61; Von Le Coq 1928: 56–7, 93–5.
108 Yate 1888: 151–8; Dupree 1980: 116–18.
109 As we have observed above, 'Survivors of Edessa'.
110 Zhang Guang-da, and Litvinsky and Vorobyova-Destyatovskaya in Litvinsky 1996: 298 and 421–6.
111 This was Rabban Sauma. See Rossabi 1992.
112 Dubs 1957; Boulnois 1966: 71; Warmington 1974: 130–1, 262 and 394g; Ferguson 1978: 594–5; Graf 1996.
113 Chinese envoys in Bactria in the late second century BC discovered to their surprise Chinese goods that arrived via India. See Miller 1969: 255–6.
114 Ferguson 1978: 591–9; Raschke 1978: 615–19; Graf 1996.
115 Warmington 1974: 125–6, 394f, 204–6; Ray 1994: 111–13.
116 Ball 1982: Sites 17, 122, 404, 428, 1000, 1065, 1087; Staviskij 1995: 192–200.
117 See Ball 1982: Site 122 for references.
118 E.g., Taddei in Cimino 1994: 214–16.
119 Whitehouse 1989a.
120 Whitehouse 1989a, 1989b: 95.
121 Procopius 1. 20. 9. Even as late as the sixth century Cosmas Indicopleustes records silk as coming entirely by sea. See Miller 1969: 25.
122 See Ferguson 1978: 585, 590–1 and 595, and Raschke 1978: 625–30 for summaries of this evidence. For the Byzantine coin finds in the Tarim, see Zhang Guang-da in Litvinsky 1996: 292.
123 Gawlikowski 1994a, 1996a.
124 *Periplus*; see also Raschke 1978: 630.
125 See, for example, Sinor 1990.
126 See, for example, the map in Klimberg-Salter (1976) – or the vast number of guerrilla supply routes that sprang up through the mountains separating Afghanistan and Pakistan following the Soviet invasion.
127 An uncle of the better known baron of that name, the 'Red Baron'. See Richtofen 1877: 454.
128 Boulnois 1966.
129 Gibbon 1: 54–6.
130 E.g., at the formal opening of the Iran–Turkmenistan rail link at the border town of Sarakhs in Iran on 13 May 1996, attended by eight regional heads of state.
131 For example, the series of specialist academic publications coming under the 'UNESCO Silk Roads Project' is only one of many such usages now in vogue in academia. Staviskij (1995: 191), for example, refers to the existence of the 'Great Silk Road' as 'indisputable'.
132 Raschke (1978: 621–2) in fact writes 'There is no reason to assume that efforts to organise the entire Silk Route from Syria to China enjoyed any lasting success until the later political expansion of the Arabs and Mongols.'
133 Raschke 1978: 622–3.
134 See Ronan and Needham 1978: chapter 6.
135 See Zwalf 1996: 67–9 for a summary of the controversy. See now also Allchin et al. 1997 (which I have not consulted).

136 Tarn 1951 and Narain 1957 are the main studies. See also Bernard in Harmatta 1994.
137 Illustrated together, for example, in Higuchi 1984: 129.
138 Soper 1951; Errington and Cribb 1992: 118–35, 'Classicizing statuary'; Boardman 1994: 125–45, with the 'Trojan horse' relief on p. 136; Zwalf 1996: pls 92, 98, 157, 340, 355–77, 470–1.
139 Boardman 1994: 143.
140 E.g., virtually any of the stuccos illustrated in Barthoux 1930; Zwalf 1996: pls 595–629, especially 616–19 from Hadda, and the uninhibited realism of the delightful 'laughing youth' of pl. 626. For the 'Antinous Bodhisattva' see Barthoux 1930: pl. 37. For the Heracles relief see Boardman 1994: 141–4.
141 Rowland 1977: 167–70.
142 See Boardman 1994: 122–3; Zwalf 1996: 67–9 for summaries of the controversy.
143 Foucher 1905–51; Boardman in Errington and Cribb 1992: 36–7; Boardman 1994: 122–3.
144 Francfort 1979a; Boardman 1994: 116–17.
145 Rowland 1977: 121.
146 E.g., Wheeler 1949; Soper 1951; Wheeler 1954: chapter 13; Wheeler 1968: 149–71; Warmington 1974: 190–9; Rowland 1977: Part 3; Whitehouse 1989b; Santora in Cimino 1994: 225–7.
147 The dates of whom are a minefield, best avoided.
148 See Soper 1951. These 'embassies' are discussed more fully in Chapter 8, where they are interpreted differently.
149 Whitehouse 1989b: 94–5; Boardman 1994: 119.
150 Discussed in the previous section on the Silk Route, 'Rome in Central Asia and China'.
151 Whitehouse 1989b.
152 Pietrzykowski 1985–6.
153 Boardman 1994: 99–108.
154 Rowland 1977: 134.
155 Stein 1912, 1: 274 and 284; fig. 95.
156 Boardman 1994: 150–1.
157 Stein 1912; Rowland 1977: 186–7; Bussagli 1978: 21–4; see also C. Paula, *The Road to Miran* (London 1994).
158 Marshak and Negmatov in Litvinsky 1996: 273 and fig. 33. The she-wolf motif is in any case associated with the legendary origins of the Turks in Siberia.
159 Bussagli 1978: 25–9.
160 Boardman 1994: 148–51.
161 Apart from various press reports, the main accounts are to be found in *The Art Newspaper* 65, December 1996, and in the *SPACH (Society for the Preservation of Afghanistan's Cultural Heritage) Newsletter* 2, December 1996. See also Ball (1997a and b), review of Zwalf 1996, in *Journal of the Royal Asiatic Society*. The reports make horrific reading: the Begram glassware, for example, gone or smashed, as well as virtually all of the Gandharan sculpture. At Hadda, many of the clay and stucco sculptures were smashed by iconoclasts when they were in the process of being excavated in the 1930s, while the outstandingly well-preserved sculptures of the Tepe Shotor – including the Heracles relief and the Fish Porch – complex at Hadda was blown up in about 1980.
162 Allchin and Fabrègues in Errington and Cribb 1992: 46–8.
163 These 'embassies' and their ramifications are discussed in more detail in Chapter 8.

Chapter 5

1 Grainger 1995: 180. See also Woolf in Alcock 1997: 1–14.
2 Jones 1971: 247.
3 Millar 1993: 6–7.
4 Just as it cannot be assumed from the modern twinning of a British city with one in Europe that the city, and its inhabitants, consciously associated themselves with a European city.
5 Jones' (1971: 228–9) comments on the Greek and native names of the cities. Sherwin-White and Kuhrt (1993: 141–9) comment on the superficial Hellenisation of the Near East.

6 Only those which came under direct Roman rule are examined; those which formed more a part of the client states have been examined separately in Chapter 3.

7 Downey 1961, 1963; Green 1990: 160–4; Roller 1998: 214–16.

8 Grainger 1990: 37–8, 41–50, 55–6, 58–60.

9 Jones 1971: 242–3.

10 Downey 1961: 154–7, 168, 171–2, 197. The 'amphitheatre' may have been a hippodrome, as is now argued for Caesarea. See Porath 1995.

11 Downey 1961: 173–84.

12 Downey 1961: 206–29.

13 Downey 1961:239–41.

14 See, for example, Lieu 1986: 477.

15 See 'Shapur II, Constantius and the disaster of Amida' in Chapter 2.

16 Downey 1961: 318–27.

17 The 'Iranophile' element at Antioch is emphasised elsewhere in this book, e.g., Chapters 2, 3 and below. For the Iranian 'pre-foundation' see Boyce and Grenet 1991: 354–6.

18 E.g., see Braidwood 1937, Burney 1977 and Roaf 1990, with maps and references. See also further in this chapter.

19 Herodian 2. 7. 8–10; 3. 14. 6–9; 4. 2. 1; 6. 7. 4.

20 Chapter 7.

21 Isaac 1992: Appendix II.

22 Downey 1961: 262; 271.

23 John Malalas 12. 38.

24 Bowersock 1978: 95–6.

25 Norwich 1988, 2: 33.

26 Grainger 1990; Millar 1993: 236–63.

27 For example Millar (1993: 236–7) writes that 'there is hardly the slightest evidence to suggest that in any one of these cities there was conscious continuity with the populations which had lived there before the Macedonian conquest'.

28 E.g., Grainger 1990 and most recently by Millar 1993: 237.

29 Grainger (1995: 15–30) characterises the area as one of population and urban collapse during the Achaemenid period, but admits problems with the archaeology.

30 Abu Assaf in Weiss 1985: 347–50; Seton-Williams 1967: 16–33.

31 Moorey 1980; Peltenburg et al. 1995: 1–28.

32 Matthiae 1980: 51–7.

33 E.g., see Woolley 1953; Haines 1971.

34 Downey 1961, 1963; Grainger 1990.

35 Woolley 1953: chapter 10.

36 See the section on high places in Chapter 7.

37 Sauvaget 1934; Grainger 1990; Burns 1992: 143–5; Ball 1997: 119–20; Roller 1998: 228.

38 J. and E. Legarce, *Ras Ibn Hani. Archéologie et Histoire* (Damascus 1987). See also their reports in CRAI 1978–86.

39 Balty 1981 and 1988. See also Grainger 1990; Burns 1992: 45–50; Ball 1997: 102–3

40 Balty 1981: 18–31.

41 Strabo 16. 2. 10; Millar 1993: 250.

42 The Apamaea colonnaded streets are discussed further in Chapter 7.

43 Balty and van Rengen 1993.

44 In 'Emesa and the Sun kings' in Chapter 3, and in 'Julia Domna and the Arabs who ruled Rome' in Chapter 8.

45 Sauvaget 1941; Burns 1992: 28–43, 52–3; Ball 1997: chapter 8.

46 Frézouls 1977; Grainger 1990: 40–1; Burns 1992: 70–2.

47 Monceaux and Bosse 1925; Grainger 1990: 40–1; Burns 1992: 199.

48 Millar 1993: 437–88.

49 Pigulevskaya 1963: various refs; Mango 1982: 118; Gawlikowski 1996b. See now Kennedy 1998 (which I was unable to consult before going to press).

50 Pigulevskaya 1963: various refs; Burns 1992: 199–210 and refs.

51 Mango 1978: 24, 29; Lauffray 1983; Kennedy and Riley 1990: 117–18; Burns 1992: 122–4.

52 Spanner and Guyer 1926; Mango 1978: 24, 26, 52–5; Krautheimer and Curcic 1986: 151–6, 261–2; Kennedy and Riley 1990: 116–17; Burns 1992: 203–6; Ball 1997: 163–6.

53 See Hopkins 1979 for a general account and guide to the main sources. For recent excavations see Leriche and al-Mahmoud 1994 and Leriche *et al.* 1992. See now Leriche and Gelin 1997. See also Burns 1992: 114–19; Ball 1997: 171–4

54 Although Hopkins (1979: 200–3) sees oriental (Parthian) elements both in the origin and the architecture of the Mithraeum at Dura Europos.

55 Kraeling *et al.* 1956; Welles 1967.

56 Ward-Perkins 1981: 347–53.

57 Millar 1993: 469–70.

58 Pigulevskaya 1963: chapter 4; Mango 1982; Krautheimer and Curcic 1986: 301 and refs.

59 Preusser, C. (1911) *Nordmesopotamische Baudenkmäler.* Leipzig; Mango 1982.

60 See Chapter 2.

61 Mango 1978:24–7; J.Crow, 'Dara, a Late Roman Fortress in Mesopotamia', *Yayla* 4 (1980), 12–20.

62 Pigulevskaya 1963: 77; Burns 1992: 70 and refs.

63 Oates 1968.

64 Grainger 1990; Aubet 1992; Millar 1993: 264–95. See now also Sperber 1998 (which I was unable to consult before going to press).

65 Jones 1971: 230–1, 233–4.

66 Aubet 1993: 23–5.

67 Seyrig 1951; Rey-Coqais 1974; Burns 1992: 44–5, 50–1, 224–7 and refs; Ball 1997: 109–15.

68 See Chapter 7.

69 Boulanger 1966: 194.

70 The monumentalised birthplaces of Septimius Severus and Philip the Arab – see ' "Roman" Arabia: Bosrta and Shahba' (this chapter) and 'Lepcis Magna: Roman city in Africa and the orientalisation of Europe' (Chapter 8).

71 Jidejian 1996.

72 Jidejian 1968: chapters 9 and 10.

73 See 'From Paganism to Christianity' in Chapter 8.

74 Hitti 1957: 325–7; Jidejian 1975b; Lauffray 1977; Millar 1993: 279–81, 527–8; Butcher and Thorpe 1997; Roller 1998: 220–2.

75 Personal observation. See also the report in the *BANEA Newsletter* 10 (1997): 31–2.

76 Hitti 1957: 309.

77 Although current excavations have cast doubt upon Lauffray's (1977) reconstruction of ancient Beirut – see Butcher and Thorpe 1997.

78 See 'Julia Domna and the Arabs who ruled Rome' in Chapter 8.

79 Jidejian 1996; Roller 1998: 237–8.

80 Will 1952; Brundage 1958; Van Berchem 1967.

81 See also 'From Paganism to Christianity' in Chapter 8.

82 Lifshitz 1977a; Holum *et al.* 1988, with refs; Roller 1998: 133–44.

83 Holum *et al.* 1988: 105.

84 See Chapter 7.

85 And not in the 'Italian style', as Roller 1998: 88 and 92–3 writes. Its excavators wrote 'of Roman influence not a trace' – Crowfoot *et al.* 1942: 35. For these western versus eastern elements, see Chapter 7.

86 Millar 1993: 296.

87 For overviews, see Bietenhard 1977, Browning 1982: chapters 1 and 2, and Bowsher 1987. See also Millar 1993: 408–14; Graf 1995.

88 Jones 1971: 258–9; Bowsher 1987.

89 Cf. Bowsher 1987.

90 This is explored in more detail in Chapter 7.

91 Graf 1986.

92 Millar 1993: 412–13.

93 Bowersock 1983: 91–2.

94 Watzinger and Wulzinger 1921; Sauvaget 1949; Burns 1992: 72–98; Millar 1993: 310–19; Ball 1997: chapter 4.

95 Dussaud 1922; Freyberger 1989b; Millar 1993: 310–19.
96 See Chapter 7, particularly the section on 'Temenos temples'.
97 Despite this, Millar (1993: 312–14) writes that 'the dominant culture and historical perspective of the city [Damascus] were by now Greek' immediately after describing the temple which – even by his own description – exhibits fundamentally *non*-Greek characteristics. The overwhelming archaeological evidence for equating Jupiter Damascenus with Hadad is not even considered.
98 Butler 1903: 35–61; Butler 1907–20: 346–51; Sartre 1981; Ward-Perkins 1981: 339–41; Burns 1992: 191–4; Ball 1997: 79–82.
99 A restored version can be seen in the University Museum at Princeton, made from plaster casts of the masonry fragments found when excavating it.
100 Kraeling 1938, particularly chapter 2 by Fisher and chapter 3 by Kraeling; Browning 1982; Zayedine 1986 and 1989; Segal 1988: chapter 2; Seigne 1994.
101 McCown in Kraeling 1938: 159–67.
102 Segal 1988: chapter 1; Northedge 1992; Hadidi 1992.
103 Jones 1971: 240.
104 See 'The *kalybe*' in Chapter 7.
105 Such as that which Millar (1993: 412–13) sees 'unambiguous' evidence for.
106 Lenzen and Knauf 1987.
107 Lenzen 1994.
108 Lifshitz 1977b; Foerster and Tsafrir 1993.
109 Jones 1971: 241.
110 Frye 1984: 77–8.
111 Millar 1993: 423.
112 Smith and McNicoll 1992.
113 Wagner-Luse 1978, 1979, 1982; Weber and Khouri 1989; Kerner 1997; Hirschfeld 1997.
114 Mare 1992, 1997.
115 Segal 1997: 15–16, 153–4 and refs; Roller 1998: 169.
116 The quantity and quality of Bosra's standing remains has inspired a number of impressive studies, architectural, archaeological and epigraphic. See Butler 1903, Sartre 1985, Dentzer 1986a. See also Ward-Perkins 1981: 345–7; MacAdam 1986b; Segal 1988: chapter 3; Burns 1992: 61–8; Ball 1997: 72–8.
117 Dentzer 1986.
118 Peters 1983.
119 Segal's (1988: 63) comment on the lack of decorative detail at Bosra, when compared to other cities of Roman Arabia, is entirely explicable by the extremely hard nature of the building material.
120 Roman governor to Nabataean contractor: 'Colonnade the damn street in your barbarous Syrian fashion if you must, but for pity's sake, *don't* make it basalt!'
121 MacAdam 1986b: 176.
122 Millar 1993: 492.
123 Sartre 1985.
124 Butler 1903: 376–96; Segal 1988: chapter 4; Freyberger 1992; Burns 1992: 216–19; Ball 1997: 82–4.
125 Millar 1993: 531.

Chapter 6

1 Butler 1903: 12.
2 Seven hundred is the figure normally cited, but Peña (1996: 12) puts the figure at 'around 820'.
3 The Dead Cities have been extensively studied ever since they first came to notice in the nineteenth century in several series of multi-volume studies. See: De Voguë 1865–77; Butler 1903, 1907–20, 1929; Tchalenko 1953–8; Tate 1992; Peña 1996; Biscop 1997. For the religious aspects of the Dead Cities and their relationship to the state see Hammond 1987. For an excellent overview of both the Dead Cities themselves and the research, see the review article by Foss 1995: 213–23. For other general overviews see: Souaf 1957; Boulanger 1966: 395–418;

Ward-Perkins 1981: 326–6; Krautheimer and Curcic 1986: 137–56; relevant sections of Burns 1992; Ball 1997: chapter 9; Tate in Alcock 1997: 55–71.

4 Foss 1995: 222.
5 Peña 1996: 57–9.
6 Tchalenko 1053–8: pl. XXI.
7 These and other elements are discussed in more detail under 'Fabric and styles' in Chapter 7.
8 Despite Peña's (1996: 197) rather puzzling words that 'there are so few vestiges of the secondary and local roads . . . in the region'.
9 Tate 1992.
10 Donced-Vôute 1988; J. Balty 1977.
11 E.g., see Levi 1946.
12 Peña 1996: 201–3. These and the Nabataean high places are discussed further in Chapter 7.
13 Peña 1996: 39.
14 Peña 1996: 86–8; 116.
15 See 'Fabric and styles' in Chapter 7.
16 Peña 1996: 136–40.
17 Peña 1996: 63–4.
18 Peña 1996: 52–4.
19 See also 'High places' in Chapter 7.
20 Peña 1996: 63, 76, 96–100.
21 Foss 1995: 222.
22 Peña 1996: 39–40.
23 Peña 1996: 121–5.
24 Tate 1992; Peña 1996: 34–8. Though it is not certain whether these might be grape presses for wine.
25 Although the predominantly rustic nature of the finds and the lack of fine and luxury finds might create a false impression of rusticity. The Dead Cities were, after all, deserted slowly and peacefully (see below) rather than through destruction, so that everything of any value would have been taken from the sites in antiquity.
26 Peña (1996: 17–25), however, sees the initial settlements as a part of the colonisation and Romanisation policies of Trajan and Hadrian, and regards the settlements as essentially Roman in character, not native.
27 De Vogüë 1865–77.
28 Butler 1903, 1907–20.
29 Tchalenko 1953–8.
30 Sodini et al. 1980; Tate 1992; Biscop 1997.
31 Wilkinson, T. J. 1989, 1992.
32 Kenrick and Northedge in Matthers 1981: 439–71.
33 Courtois 1973.
34 Haines 1971.
35 Wilkinson in Marfoe et al. 1986: 38–46.
36 Gawlikowski in Alcock 1997: 37–54.
37 Schlumberger 1951.
38 Lassus 1936.
39 Burns 1992: 197–8; Ball 1997: 104–6.
40 E.g., see Akurgal 1990: 341–6 and refs; Taskiran 1993.
41 Mayerson 1960; Shereshevski 1991. For a good summary of recent work and overview, see Foss 1995: 223–34. See also Hirschfeld in Alcock 1997: 72–88. See now also Negev 1998.
42 Piccirillo 1985; Peterman 1994: 554–7.
43 Piccirillo 1985.
44 Watson 1996.
45 See Graf 1995 and refs.
46 Butler 1903; Barkay et al. 1974; MacAdam 1983; Dentzer 1986a; De Vries 1986 and 1990; Graf 1992; Burns 1992, various refs; De Vries in Peterman 1994: 552–3; Kennedy and Freeman 1995; Ball 1997: chapter 5
47 Jones 1971: 284–90; MacAdam 1983.

48 De Vries in Peterman 1994: 552–3. Also De Vries 1986 and 1990. See now De Vries 1998 (the latter I have been unable to consult before going to press).
49 See also 'Rome and the Arabs' in Chapter 3.
50 Kennedy and Freeman 1995.
51 Barkay *et al.* 1974.
52 This is discussed further in 'Circumambulatories' in Chapter 7.
53 Wilkinson and Tucker 1995: 58–77; see also Bartl 1996, Lyonnet 1996, and Simpson 1996, all in Bartl and Hauser 1996.
54 Millar 1993: 427.
55 Grainger 1995: 192–3.
56 See, for example, Ball *et al.* 1989: 41–4; Wilkinson and Tucker 1995: 77–88.
57 Foss 1995: 221.

Chapter 7

1 Macaulay 1977.
2 In Millar's (1993) constant denial of native character in the Roman Near East, for example.
3 E.g., MacDonald 1986.
4 Segal 1997: 2–5.
5 Millar 1993: 255 (writing of Mambij/Hierapolis and other cults – the italics are Millar's) and 354.
6 E.g., Millar (1993: 531) in referring to Philippopolis – Shahba – describes it as 'the most complete expression of the export to the edge of the steppe of the Graeco-Roman ideal of a city' while the hint of a grid system even in towns as far away as Xinjiang in China, such as Karakhoja, are described by western authorities as 'Roman'. See Von Le Coq 1928: 56.
7 E.g., Wheeler (1964: 46) writes with reference to Dougga and Thuburbo Majus, 'casual and un-Roman streets wind amongst conventional Roman buildings'.
8 See, for example, Owens 1991: 28–9.
9 Owens 1991: 30–4.
10 Owens 1991: 38–50.
11 Aubet 1993.
12 Fantar 1987: 113.
13 E.g., see Wheeler 1964: 46.
14 Jidejian 1968: 16.
15 Owens 1991: 51–6.
16 Owens 1991: 70.
17 As emphasised by Owens 1991: chapter 2.
18 Schwartz in Weiss 1985: fig. 7.
19 Strommenger 1985.
20 Kühne 1989–90: 308–23.
21 Hiorns 1956: 10–12.
22 Noted by Coningham in Allchin 1995: 51.
23 Allchin and Allchin 1982: 171–83. See also Wheeler 1968.
24 Erdosy in Allchin 1995: 111; Allchin 1995: 142–6.
25 Though there is controversy over its date. See Allchin 1995: 187–8 for a discussion.
26 See Rangarajan's plans of the Kautilyan city and fortified camp layouts, reproduced in Allchin 1995: figs 11–5–8. Kautilya is also discussed by Allchin 1995: 222–31. It is described in the Kautilya *Arthasastra* 2. 3–4 and 10–1.
27 See, for example, the sites of Altin Dilyar and Deh Nahr-i Jadid in Bactria for Achaemenid town plans. For older circular town plans, see Dashli 3 or Kutlug Tepe. Ball 1982: Sites 38, 257, 288, 666. See also Francfort 1979b.
28 See, for example, Emshi Tepe and Jiga Tepe in Bactria. Ball 1982: Sites 314, 475. It is often, too, forgotten, that the 'archetypal' Hellenistic implant in Central Asia, Ai Khanum on the Oxus, does *not* follow the Hippodamian town plan. See Ball 1982: Site 19.
29 This culminated, for example, in the foundation by al-Mansur of the round city of Baghdad. See Creswell 1958: 163–83 for a summary of its origins.

30 Parrot 1956: pl. I.
31 Burney 1957: 49–50, fig. 11; 1977: fig. 141; Summers 1993.
32 Barnet and Watson 1952: fig. 1; Burney 1977: 195.
33 Sarkhosh Curtis and Simpson 1997: 139–40.
34 Helms 1982: 11–13; Ball in McNicoll and Ball 1996: 392–4, fig. 2.
35 Grainger 1990: 61–2, 86–7.
36 Barghouti 1982.
37 Grainger (1990: 85–6) in fact comments on the uncertainty of Seleucid street layouts in Syria.
38 See the cautionary remarks by Barghouti 1982: 209–11.
39 Peters 1983.
40 Segal 1997: 5–8.
41 Browning 1979: 81–6.
42 Jidejian 1968: 114.
43 Peters 1983: 274. For the street see McKenzie 1990: 35–6 and refs.
44 Khouri 1986b: 123–9; McKenzie 1990: 172 and refs.
45 Dentzer 1985.
46 Donner 1986: 40.
47 Dalley and Goguel 1997.
48 All probably came under Nabataean administation for part of their history – and were at least within the broader Nabataean cultural sphere. See Chapter 3, 'Arabia and the Nabataeans'. For Damascus, see Bowersock 1983: 68.
49 McCown in Kraeling 1938: 159–67. Much of this and other observations at Jerash are based upon personal experience.
50 Herodian 5. 6; *Augustan History*, Heliogabalus.
51 Quoted in Millar 1993: 317–18.
52 For Alahan see Mango 1978: 40; for Gemili personal observation. I am greatly indebted to David Price-Williams for showing this latter fascinating monument to me.
53 Spanner and Guyer 1926; Mango 1978: 24, 26, 52–5; Krautheimer and Curcic 1986: 151–6, 261–2; Burns 1993: 203–6. The 'Church of St Sergius' is now identified as the Church of the Holy Cross.
54 See Oates 1986: 152–6.
55 Matheson 1976: 227–10 and refs.
56 Or modern restoration, such as at Apamaea and Jerash!
57 Balty 1981.
58 Jidejian 1996: 177–80.
59 For Beirut see Lauffray 1977. New excavations currently for progress might alter this picture. It must also be borne in mind that Beirut, exceptionally for eastern Roman cities, was very much a western transplant, so may never have had a colonnaded street, for reasons outlined below. At Pella, the first–fourth century city was all but obliterated by fifth–seventh century rebuilding; no trace, for example, has been found in excavation of its nymphaeum, despite its detailed depiction on coins. See Smith and McNicoll 1992: 119–44; Segal 1997: 152 n.3.
60 Donner 1992: 40, 47–8, 54–5, 63–5, 70, 75–6, 87–94.
61 See, for example, Downey 1961: 173, n. 45; Lassus 1972; McDonald 1986: 43–4; Segal 1997: 5–53, especially table pp. 48–9. For Apamaea see Balty 1981: 46–51 and Balty 1988. For others, see: Sauvaget 1934 and Saadé 1976 (Latakia); Frézouls 1977 (Cyrrhus); Taylor 1986: figure 90; Netzer and Weiss 1995 (Sepphoris); Holum *et al.* 1988: 175–6 (Caesarea); Denton in Peterman 1994: 554–5 (Madaba); Saliou 1996 (Palmyra).
62 For examples of colonnaded streets in Anatolia see Akurgal 1990: 105, 144, 326, 339 and references.
63 Wheeler 1964: 48–9; Ward-Perkins 1981: 363, 384–91 and 393–5; El-Saghir *et al.* 1985; Ward-Perkins 1993; Sear 1982: 197–8 and 205–6.
64 Donner 1992: 82–3.
65 See Chapter 8, 'Lepcis Magna: Roman city in Africa and the orientalisation of Europe'.
66 Sear 1982: 210–11. Here, however, they are piers rather than columns (pers. obs.).
67 Wheeler 1964: 144–6; Ward-Perkins 1981: 449–50; Sear 1982: 263–5.
68 With the possible exception of the Decumanus at Damascus. See Segal 1997: 12.

69 Downey 1961: 318. For the Diocletianic camps at Palmyra and Luxor, see Starcky and Gawlikowski 1985.
70 Ward-Perkins 1981: 449–50, Sear 1982: 269.
71 Balty 1994.
72 John Malalas 10. 8, 10. 23, 11. 24; Downey 1961: 173–9, 183–4, 196, 213–5, 477–9 and 500–1.
73 John Malalas 10. 8.
74 Lassus 1972; Balty 1994.
75 Kraeling 1938; Segal 1977: 5.
76 For Madaba see Denton in Peterman 1994: 554–5. For Anjar see Hoag 1975: 18–20.
77 Schlumberger 1978: 70–3, pls 24 and 97.
78 See Chapter 6.
79 MacDonald 1986: 43–4.
80 Ward-Perkins 1981: 150–5, 238–9; MacDonald 1986: 43–4; Roller 1998: 216.
81 MacDonald 1986: 43–4; Barghouti 1982: 217; Segal 1997: 5–9. For stoas see, for example, Ward-Perkins 1981: 256, Sear 1982: 239–42, Akurgal 1990: 72, 192, 212–19 and references.
82 Segal 1997: 5–8.
83 Postgate 1994: 76–9, 192–3.
84 Barghouti 1992: 217; Ball 1997: 39, 186–7.
85 As ʿad and Stepniowski 1989; Schlumberger 1978: 70–3, pls 24 and 97.
86 Matthiae 1977: fig. 12; Frankfort 1976: 282. Near Eastern origins for the trabeate style of colonnaded streets is discussed further below.
87 MacDonald 1986: 43.
88 John Malalas 10. 8 and 10. 23; see also Josephus *Antiquities* 17. 148, *Wars* 1. 425.
89 Ammianus Marcellinus 23. 2. 5.
90 E.g., Butler 1907–20: 233 (Bosra); Crowfoot *et al.* 1942 (Sebaste); Segal 1997: fig. 45 (Jerusalem); Browning 1979: 87–8 (Palmyra); Browning 1982: figs 11, 25, 73 (Jerash); Holum *et al.* 1988: fig. 128 (Caesarea); Browning 1989: fig. 17 (Petra). An exception is my own reconstruction of the Cardo at Jerash in Khouri 1986a: 26, where the question (and the sky!) is left open.
91 Wilkinson 1975: 118–20.
92 Segal 1997: 40.
93 The eastern side where it is flanked by the West Baths.
94 MacDonald 1986: 83–4.
95 MacDonald 1986: 80.
96 The four-way arch is discussed as a type in MacDonald 1986: 87–92.
97 MacDonald 1986: 155–6.
98 Ward-Perkins 1981: 236–7
99 Brogan and Smith 1984: figs 65 and 66.
100 Tchalenko 1953–8: pls XLIII, LXXXV. See also this chapter, 'Funerary architecture'.
101 MacDonald 1986: 88–9; Segal 1997: 140–9.
102 Haynes 1965: 73–4 and 92, Bartoccini 1931 (Lepcis Magna); Vermeule 1968: 336–49; Kinch 1890 (Thessalonike); Aurigemma 1969 (Tripoli); Ward-Perkins 1981: 454–9 (Thessalonike); Erim 1992: 22–3; Ward-Perkins 1995 (Severan Lepcis).
103 This is argued further in Chapter 8.
104 Donner 1992: 47–8, 63–5, 75–6, 87–94.
105 Mouterde and Poidebard 1945: 80–1, pl. LII.
106 Segal 1997: 140–9; Creswell 1969: 455–7; Butler 1903: 393 (Shahba); Sauvaget 1934: 88–91 (Latakia); Kraeling 1938: 103–16 (Jerash South Tetrapylon); Downey 1961: 173–9 (Antioch); Michalowski 1962: 10–54, 78–100 (Palmyra); Peters 1983; Sartre 1985: 120 (Bosra); Ball 1986b (Jerash North Tetrapylon); Holum *et al.* 1988: 176.
107 Hoag 1975: 18–20 (Anjar). In Damascus an Umayyad tetrapylon was recorded just south of the Friday Mosque as part of a ceremonial way leading from the Palace of Walid to the Mosque. In Beth-Shean, an Umayyad tetrapylon has recently been identified among the Roman ruins (see Hamis 1997). I am very grateful for Finbarr Flood for this information on both Beth-Shean and Damascus.
108 Akurgal 1990: 167–8.
109 Schippmann 1971: abb. 9, 38.

110 Reuther 1938–9: 428; Herzfeld 1941: 301–2, pl. xcvii
111 Schippmann 1971: 369–76; Kleiss 1973
112 Reuther 1938–9: 550–9; Pope 1965: 65–73; Mostafavi 1967: 43–7; Schippmann 1971: 212–15, Abb. 28; 13–21, Abb. 2; 282–91, Abb. 39; 430–7, Abb. 70. The 'Sasanian palace' at Sarvistan has recently been argued to be a fire-temple complex of the eighth–tenth century. See Bier 1986. The identification of many of the exposed *chahar taqs* as fire temples is largely myth. See Boucharlat 1985.
113 Pope 1965: 81–5, 100–1, 172–7, 185–9.
114 Pope 1965: figs 105, 136, 144.
115 Pope 1938–9: 1199, 1218–19, fig. 512.
116 Ward-Perkins 1981: 56–7, 101–4, 169–70; Sear 1982: 96–102.
117 See Mallowan and Rose 1935: 25–34 for the Mesopotamian Neolithic origin of the dome. For the continuation of this tradition today see Ball 1997: pl. 84.
118 See, for example, Beazley and Harveson 1982: 23–6 and 49–56. Although relatively recent, the mud dome of the ice-house at Bam, measuring 20 m. in diameter (personal observation), which is half the size of the dome of St Peter's in Rome, two-thirds the size of St Sophia's in Istanbul, or the same size as the Dome of the Rock in Jerusalem, is probably the greatest mute testimony to the strength of the dome tradition in Iranian architecture.
119 In addition to Segal 1997: ch. 3, part 1, see: Sauvaget 1941 (Aleppo); Spanner and Guyer 1926 (Rasafa); Jidejian 1975a (Baalbek); Watzinger and Wulzinger 1921; Sauvaget 1949 (Damascus); McKenzie 1990: 131–3 (Petra).
120 The only one of this category at Jerash. The supposed arch assumed from foundations and even reconstructed at the junction of the Cardo and the Oval Plaza (Browning 1982: 80, 133, fig. 25; Segal 1997: 133) could not have existed. They were merely piers that formed the junction of the Cardo colonnades with those of the Oval Plaza, and are too slight to have supported the type of arch that is reconstructed.
121 Segal 1997: 129–40. For others, see: Starcky and Gawlikowski 1985 (Palmyra); Hopkins 1979 (Dura Europos).
122 Although the famous reconstruction of the Ishtar Gate in the Vorderasiatische Museum in Berlin is probably due as much to preconceived notions of Roman triumphal arches as to the archaeological remains themselves, which when discovered were hardly above foundation level.
123 Oates 1986: 152–6 (Ishtar Gate); Herzfeld 1941: pl. li; Pope 1965: 33 (Persepolis); Roaf 1990: 192–3, 204–5, 211.
124 Michell 1989: 179–89.
125 Balty 1981: 56–8.
126 Downey 1961: 173–84.
127 As implied by the Arab name for the Damascus Gate, *Bab al-Amud*, or 'Gate of the Column', and confirmed by its depiction in the Madaba mosaic. See Wilkinson 1975.
128 Piccirillo 1993: 37, pls 337, 347.
129 Boulanger 1966: 174–5; Segal 1970: 26–7; Browning 1979: 169; Taylor 1986: fig. 14.
130 Davies 1997.
131 Bouchier 1916: 176; Hitti 1957: 354. For the Commagene monuments see: Akurgal 1990: 346–52 and references; Sanders 1996.
132 Segal 1970: 26–7, 51.
133 Peña 1996: 205.
134 Peña 1996: 105–6.
135 Piccirillo 1990: 44.
136 Peña 1996: 221.
137 Herrmann 1977: 103–5.
138 Wheeler 1968: 127–45; Allchin 1995: 251–8.
139 See Michell 1989: 270, 284.
140 Hoag 1975: 93–4; T. Leiston, 'Mashhad al Nasr', *Muqarnas: an annual on the visual culture of the Islamic world* 13 (1996).
141 Segal 1997: 152–68.
142 Donner 1992: 39–40, 47–8, 63, 75–6.

143 Downey 1963: 203; Jidejian 1968: 116; Browning 1979: 159–60; Balty 1981: 76; Taylor 1986: fig. 16.
144 Butler 1903.
145 Amer and Gawlikowski 1985.
146 Butler 1903.
147 Waheeb and Zuhair 1995.
148 See Chapter 5, 'Bosra', and Peters 1983.
149 The use of the term 'basilica' in its later, Christian, sense is discussed later in this chapter, in the section on Christian architecture.
150 Downey 1963: 75–6, 179–81.
151 Lauffray 1977. Current excavations have recently doubted Lauffray's interpretation of the remains – see Butcher and Thorpe 1997.
152 Crowfoot *et al.* 1942: 32–7; Segal 1997: 58.
153 Holum *et al.* 1988: 130.
154 Northedge 1992: 56; Hadidi 1992; Segal 1997: 60–1.
155 Segal 1997: 59–60.
156 Freyberger 1989a: Abb. 1.
157 Kraeling 1938: 153–8; Browning 1982: 131–3.
158 The suggestion is based on the existence of higher columns in the colonnades of both streets that might suggest entrances to some single, large complex in this area. Segal 1988: 34; Khouri 1986a: 86. Current excavations (summer 1998) might clarify this.
159 Amer and Gawlikowski 1985; Segal 1997: 55–7.
160 Owens 1991: 154.
161 Downey 1963: 56–7.
162 Sauvaget 1949; Balty 1981: 69–74; Hopkins 1979.
163 Martin-Bueno 1989, 1994.
164 See Segal 1997: 55–67 and references for forums and market places in Palestine, Arabia and southern Syria.
165 Peters 1983: 275.
166 Fisher in Kraeling 1938: 153–8. It is particularly unfortunate that the single column erected in the centre of the plaza detracts from the open unified sweep of this masterpiece. It was erected only a few years ago merely as a gimmick for the Jerash Festival.
167 Donner 1992: 64–5, 87–94.
168 Personal observation.
169 Donner 1992: 40, 47–8.
170 Downey 1961: 173–84.
171 Wheeler 1965: fig. 26.
172 MacDonald 1986: 53–4.
173 Ward-Perkins 1981: 410–13.
174 Doe 1983: 124–5, 160–5.
175 See Gawlikowski 1982. The *hawtah* and other possible links with south Arabian architecture are explored further below, in the sections on temenos temples and the trabeate style.
176 Boulanger 1966: 255.
177 Lindner *et al.* 1984; McKenzie 1990: 151–3, 159–61.
178 This is analysed in greater detail later, in the section on funerary architecture.
179 Donner 1992: 40, 54–5.
180 Peters 1983: 274.
181 Segal 1997: 67–81.
182 Tchalenko 1953–8: pls XIX–XX.
183 Butler 1903 (Bosra and Shahba); Kraeling 1938 (Jerash); Downey 1963: fig. 24 (Antioch); Browning 1979: 139–42 (Palmyra); Balty 1981: 53–5 (Apamaea); Hirschfeld and Solar 1981 (Hammat Gader); Foerster and Tsafrir 1993 (Beth Shean).
184 Ward-Perkins 1982: 325, 338, 345; Dodge 1990.
185 See, e.g., Segal 1994.
186 Sear 1997.
187 Boulanger 1966: 178.

188 Grainger (1990: 85) remarks on the lack of Greek theatres in Syria.

189 Although Caesar's theatre at Antioch might have been a rebuilding of an earlier Greek theatre – neither the sources nor the archaeological evidence give any clue. See Downey 1963: 76.

190 Jidejian 1968: 115. Note that its present location on the site is not the place it was originally found.

191 Kloner 1988; Gatier 1990: 204; Porath 1995.

192 Downey 1961: 156–7–although it may have been a hippodrome, like Caesarea.

193 Ammianus Marcellinus 14. 7. 1–2.

194 Porath 1995.

195 Peters 1983: 274–5. See Segal 1988: 83, for the possible identification of a hippodrome at Shahba. See also: Kehrberg and Ostracz 1997 (Jerash); Jidejian 1996: 188–96 (Tyre).

196 E.g., Gregory and Kennedy 1985, Freemen and Kennedy 1986; French and Lightfoot 1989; Kennedy and Riley 1990; Isaac 1992; Gregory in Kennedy (ed.) 1996; Kennedy 1996b.

197 Isaac 1992: 133.

198 Kennedy and Riley 1990: 125 (Bosra); Balty and Rengen 1993 (Apamaea); Gawlikowski 1996b (Zeugma). The identification of the square outline north of Bosra as the legionary headquarters has been refuted by Peters 1983: 275, but confirmed by MacAdam 1986b: 176.

199 Hopkins 1979; Gawlikowski 1984; De Vries 1986 and 1990: 9. The identification of this has recently been questioned: Millar 1993: 132–3.

200 Sack 1985.

201 Ward-Perkins 1981: 342–3, Sartre 1985: 123.

202 Butler 1903–5: 255–60; Peters 1983: 274.

203 See Roller 1998.

204 Will and Larché 1991.

205 Downey 1963: 235.

206 Kennedy and Riley 1990: chapter 7.

207 Kennedy and Riley 1990.

208 Isaac 1992: 408–9.

209 Gregory in Kennedy (ed.) 1996.

210 Hodgson 1989; Napoli 1997; Crow 1995.

211 Cameron 1993b: 118.

212 Wilhelm, G. (1989) *The Hurrians* (Warminster): 10–11.

213 Killick 1984; Gasche, Killick *et al.* 1987.

214 Josephus *Jewish War* 1, 103; Kokhavi 1989.

215 Ball 1982: 145.

216 Rakhmanov 1994.

217 Bader, Gaibov and Koshalenko 1995: 49–50; Chegini and Nikitin in Litvinsky (1996): 58.

218 Bader, Gaibov and Koshalenko 1995.

219 Strabo 11. 516; Tarn 1951: 117–18; Barthold 1977: 112–13.

220 Frye 1977 and 1984: 3.

221 Bivar and Fehevari 1966.

222 Kiani 1982, Charlesworth 1987.

223 Charlesworth 1987: 165 n. 2.

224 Dio 41. 61. 1; Herodian 6. 7. 8 and 7. 2. 1; Petersen 1966.

225 *Augustan History*: Hadrian 11. 2; Aurelius Victor 20; Eutropius 8. 19.

226 Turcan 1996: 209–10.

227 See Chapter 8, 'Arabs and the West'.

228 Millar 1993: 310–11, 505.

229 Roller (1998: 92–3) exaggerates the prevalence of Italian-style temples to Rome and Augustus in the East.

230 Boulanger 1966: 255, 315. For Husn Sulaiman, see below.

231 Taylor 1986.

232 Foerster and Tsafrir 1993: 8–12.

233 Unless it is Baalbek, as is postulated in 'The great Temple of Emesene Baal' in Chapter 3.

234 Busink 1970–80 (Jerusalem); Watzinger and Wulzinger 1921 (Damascus); Dussaud 1922

(Damascus); Jidejian 1968: 114–15 (Byblos); Kanellopoulos in Peterman 1994: 544–5 (Amman); Butler 1907–20: 228; Peters 1983: 273–4 (Bosra); Fischer *et al.* 1984 (Kedesh); Watson and Tidmarsh in Peterman 1994: 557–8 (Pella); Bowsher 1987: 63; Fischer in Kraeling 1938: 125–38 (Jerash).

235 Jidejian 1975a, Ragette 1980 and refs. See also 'The great Temple of Emesene Baal' in Chapter 3.

236 Zeus Kasios is known from the sacrifice made by the Emperor Julian referred to by John Malalas 13. 9. For the others, see: Tchalenko 1953–8: 106–11; Callot and Marcillet-Jaubert 1984; Taylor 1986: figs 135–9; Turcan 1996: 171–2.

237 Callot and Marcillet-Jaubert 1984.

238 Butler 1903: 346–51; Boulanger 1966: 545; Gogräfe 1993.

239 Seyrig 1951; Teixidor 1977: 50–2.

240 Millar (1993: 266 and 71–3) ignores the physical evidence of the material remains to see no evidence for any Semitic element in the cult of Baetococaea, and describes the structure as a purely 'Roman' building.

241 Kraeling *et al.* 1956: pl. LVII.

242 Fisher in Kraeling 1938: 125–38; Browning 1982: 85–92; Parapetti 1989.

243 Ward Perkins 1981: 417–18.

244 Some of the late Hellenistic and Roman period temples in Anatolia also belong within this tradition, such as the Temple of Athena at Pergamon, the Temple of Augustus at Antioch-in-Pisidia, and the Temple of Zeus at Aezani. See Lyttelton 1987.

245 Hatra: Colledge 1967: 129–34; Safar and Mustafa 1974; Herrmann 1977: 59–61; Kangavar: Reuther 1938–9: 413–14; Herrmann 1977: 107; Fard 1996. Khurha: Herrmann 1977: 38; Boyce and Grenet 1991: 90 and personal observation.

246 Personal observation.

247 Compare Fard 1996: 32 and 40.

248 Fard 1996: 9–15, 23–47.

249 A secondary element, for Hatra, is the deity itself: the Sun god cult in its various manifestations was a particularly popular one throughout the Roman East (the Temple of Emesene Baal, for example), ultimately spreading throughout the Roman world.

250 Reuther 1938–9: 428; Herzfeld 1941: 301–2, pl. XCVII.

251 Isakov 1982: fig. 9; Marshak and Negmatov in Litvinsky 1996: 237, fig. 2, I, II and X.

252 Schippmann 1971.

253 Wright 1985b: 244–5.

254 Moortgat 1969: 6, 20, 25, 57, 77, 160; Frankfort 1976: 43, 108; Roaf 1990: 60–3, 101, 192; Postgate 1994: 111–13.

255 In the section on public squares, above. See also Doe 1983: 124–5, 160–5.

256 The 'columns' are in the form of rectangular stele, and are discussed further in the section on the trabeate style. The courtyard is often described as an artificial lake, but this is more likely a result of recent hydrological changes rather than original design. See Dunand and Saliby 1985.

257 Postgate 1994: 123–4, 132.

258 This is discussed more in the section on 'Christian architecture' later, in this chapter. The concept of the congregation is elaborated again in Chapter 8, 'From Paganism to Christianity'.

259 Peña 1996: 143–5.

260 Teixidor 1977: 50–2; Sherwin-White and Kuhrt 1993: 61, 65.

261 E.g., see Gawlikowski 1982; Doe 1983: 160; Serjeant 1983; Lewcock 1986: 37–9.

262 Quoted in Millar 1993: 272–3.

263 Peña 1996: 141.

264 Ragette 1980: 34–5.

265 Palmyra see Starcky and Gawlikowski 1985; Baalbek see Jidejian 1975a; Petra see Joukowsky 1997; Qanawat see Freyberger 1993; Jerusalem depicted in the Dura Europos Synagogue, see Kraeling *et al.* 1956: pl. LVII; Suwayda recorded in the nineteenth century, see Butler 1903: 76; Nablus depicted in the Church of St Stephen mosaic at Kastron Mefaa, see Piccirillo 1993: pl. 351.

266 Ward-Perkins 1981: 314–16, 324, 332–3, 340, 356–7; Browning 1979: 99–125, 134–7, 163–8 (the Palmyra temples); Browning 1982 (the Jerash temples); Parapetti 1982, 1986 and 1989

(Jerash Artemis); Seigne 1986 (Jerash Zeus); Krencker and Zschietzschmann 1938 (Husn Sulaiman); Crowfoot *et al.* 1942 (Sebaste); Kanellopoulos in Peterman 1994 (Amman); Browning 1989, McKenzie 1990 (Petra temples); Negev 1977 (Nabataean temples); Ragette 1980 (Baalbek); Gogräfe 1993, 1996 (Isriya); Wright 1985 (Petra Dushara); Dentzer 1985 (Si'); Freyberger 1989c, 1991, 1992 and 1993 (Sanamayn, Slim, Shahba, Qanawat Helios); Tchalenko 1953–8: pls VIII, XLII (Burj Baqirha, Shaikh Barakat); Butler 1903: 76, 345 (Isriya, Suwayda, Atil, Qanawat, Mushannaf).

267 Lyttelton 1974.
268 Taylor 1986: figs 17–19, 167.
269 Ward-Perkins 1981: 322–3.
270 Moortgat 1969: 20–5, 77, 95, 161; Frankfort 1976: 42, 106, 205; Wright 1985b: 239–40.
271 Butler 1929: 13–15.
272 Moortgat 1969: 59, 95; Frankfort 1970: 276. Wright (1985b: 136 and 241) refers to it as the 'Old Mediterranean Temple Type'.
273 Krautheimer 1986: 137–56, 301–3.
274 Negev 1977: 606–20; Butler 1903; Glueck 1965 (Khirbet Tannur); al-Muheisen and Villeneuve 1994; Al-Muheisin, Villeneuve and Peterman in Peterman 1994: 540–2 (Khirbet adh-Dharih); Savignac and Horsfeld 1935; Kirkbride 1960 (Ramm).
275 Schlumberger 1951: 93–106.
276 Glueck 1965: 160 and refs. See Boyce and Grenet 1991: 172–9 and Shkoda 1998 for a discussion of Achaemenid and Graeco-Bactrian circumambulatory temples, where the origin might be in earlier Bactrian domestic architecture.
277 Schippmann 1971: 8–11, 57–70, 97–9, 129–34, 142–53, 212–15, 233–51, 251–8, 266–74, 309–57, Abb.1, 13, 18, 20, 28, 37, 38, 44; Reuther 1938–9: fig. 103 (Hatra); Herzfeld 1941: figs 398 (Imamzadeh Husain), 399 (Masjid-i Sulaiman) and pl. 97 (Kuh-i Khwaja); Herrmann 1977: 102 and Sarfaraz 1973 (Bishapur); Summers 1993: 93 (Altintepe). The circumambulatory of the Temple of the Sun at Hatra has been interpreted as a fire temple; see Duchesne-Guillemin 1983: 870. See also Stronach, D. (1967) 'Urartian and Achaemenian Tower Temples', *JNES* 26: 278–88 and Stronach 1985.
278 Though see Chapter 3, 'Nabataean religion' for a discussion of other possible Iranian religious influences on Nabataean religion.
279 Amy 1950. See also Negev 1973.
280 Negev 1973.
281 See in particular the reconstructions of the temple at Slim or the Dushara Temple at Petra; Wright 1985: fig. 2, Freyberger 1991: Abb. 3.4, 5.6.
282 For reconstructed elevations of these façades, see: Butler 1907–20: 366–402 (Si'); Klinkott 1989: Abb. 11 (Dmayr); Ragette 1980: 36–7 (Baalbek); Browning 1982: 160 (Jerash). For Rabbah and Sur, see Negev 1977: figs 14, 16.
283 The latter where Emperor Julian offered sacrifice during his eastern campaign. See John Malalas 13. 19.
284 MacDonald 1986: 69–70.
285 Peña 1996: 201–3.
286 Khouri 1986b: 123–9, McKenzie 1990: 172 and refs. It may have been Edomite in origin. See Lindner *et al.* 1997.
287 Horsfield and Conway 1930; Parr 1960; Hammond 1973: 52.
288 Glueck 1965.
289 Amy 1950: 82–3.
290 Negev 1973.
291 Boyce and Grenet 1991: various refs.
292 Roaf 1990: 104–6, 143.
293 See the distribution map in Roaf 1990: 105.
294 In 'Nabataean religion' in Chapter 3.
295 Butler 1907–20: figs 76, 90; Butler 1929: figs 85, 98, 155, 169; Tchalenko 1953–8: pls XVI, XXII, LXXVI, CXIII; Mango 1978: 80–1; Krautheimer 1986: 152–5.
296 Donner 1992: 45, 56, 69.
297 Piccirillo 1993: 34–5 and 324–5, pls 209 and 674.

298 Peña 1996: 146–8.
299 Creswell 1958: 44–81. An alternative inspiration for the minaret has been seen in the stylite pillar cults of northern Syria and elsewhere; see Peña 1996: 221, and above.
300 Butler 1929; Crowfoot 1941; Krautheimer 1986.
301 E.g., Butler 1929, Wilkinson 1984, Peña 1996.
302 Although Peña (1996: 72, 235–9) sees both the arceate form as an eastern (Persian) feature and Syria as the origin of much Christian architecture in Visigothic and Asturian Spain.
303 'From Paganism to Christianity' in Chapter 8.
304 Krautheimer 1986: 23.
305 Crowfoot 1941: 1–4; Welles 1967; Hopkins 1979; Krautheimer 1986: 27–8.
306 Peña 1996: 63.
307 Butler 1929: chapter 2.
308 E.g., Butler 1929: 191, Crowfoot 1941: 37–46, Mango 1978: 48–9, 52–5, 104, Krautheimer 1986: 129, 138–9, 144–9, 229–30.
309 Allchin 1995: 244–6; Krautheimer and Curcic 1986: 74.
310 The chaitya halls of Indian temples and the apses of Christian churches have been seen elsewhere as having a common origin, albeit in Greece or Ionia, and then travelling via Persia to India. See Thompson 1969.
311 Creswell 1924. See also Wilkinson 1981.
312 Butler 1903: 97, 159–66; Tchalenko 1953–8: pls XLIII, LXXXV; Burns 1992: 55–8; Seigne and Morin 1995.
313 Burns 1992: 137, 61, 198–9, 206, 222 and refs; Tchalenko 1953–8: pls XLIV, LXI, LXII.
314 Schmidt-Colinet in Alcock 1997: 166–70.
315 Butler 1903: 99–102; Tchalenko 1953–8: pl. CXLI.
316 Schmidt-Colinet in Alcock 1997: 161–3. See also Mango 1982: 117.
317 Pirenne 1963; Mango 1982: 117; Millar 1993: 465.
318 Collart 1973; Taylor 1986: pl. 95 (Qalʿat Faqra); McKenzie 1990: 114 (Petra); Gogräfe 1995 (Sirrin).
319 Dunand and Saliby 1985; Burns 1992: 44–5; Ball 1997: 114–15.
320 Brogan and Smith 1984.
321 Jidejian 1996: 167–74.
322 Wright 1985b: 324–9.
323 Schmidt-Colinet in Alcock 1997: 163–5.
324 Starcky and Gawlikowski 1985.
325 Colledge 1976.
326 Akurgal 1990: 255–66.
327 Akurgal 1990: 270–6.
328 Tchalenko 1953–8: pl. LXI.
329 The best source book now is McKenzie 1990.
330 Unless they functioned as ossuaries, as suggested in 'Nabataean religion' in Chapter 3.
331 Listed in the most recent, McKenzie 1990.
332 Translated by W. J. Jobling in McKenzie 1990: 35.
333 McKenzie 1990: 113, 144–8.
334 Lindner et al. 1984; McKenzie 1990: 150–1, 159–61.
335 Dodge 1990.
336 Although Peña (1996: 72) sees the curvilinear style of the church architecture of Syria as belonging to a Persian tradition.
337 Lyttelton 1974: 15.
338 What Zayedine (1991: 55–6 and figs 47–9) characterises as the 'Arabian' style.
339 Hammond 1973: 49–50, 95–96; McKenzie 1990: 159.
340 It occurs, for example, depicted on a Middle Assyrian altar depicting Tukulti-Ninurta I (1343–1207 BC) paying homage to a square cult object. See Harper et al. 1995: 112–13.
341 Gawlikowski in Alcock 1997: 47–9.
342 Aubet 1992: 212–15.
343 E.g., Doe 1983, Daum 1988, Breton 1992.
344 B. Finster, 'The architecture of the Rasulids', in Daum 1988: 258–60.

345 Lyttelton 1974.
346 Although MacDonald (1986: 220, 232) denies the emphasis on the East, seeing such buildings as the Temple of Venus at Baalbek or the Petra façades as not belonging to the baroque tradition.
347 Schmidt-Colinet in Alcock 1997: 165 and refs.
348 Butler 1903: 396–7.
349 Weiss 1985: figs 44 and 45.
350 Grabar *et al.* 1978.
351 Schlumberger 1933; Invernezzi 1995.
352 McKenzie 1990: chapters 5 and 8.
353 Förtsch 1993.
354 E.g., Rowland 1977: figs 15, 35, 38, 42, 46, 60; Michell 1989: 319–21; Allchin 1995: figs 12.14, 12.15, 12.18.
355 Schmidt-Colinet in Alcock 1997: 167–70. This connection is discussed further in the section on Syrian niches, below.
356 Boardman 1994: 108.
357 MacDonald 1986: 203–7.
358 E.g., Rowland 1977: figs 15, 35, 38, 42, 46, 60; Michell 1989: 319–21; Allchin 1995: figs 12.14, 12.15, 12.18.
359 Full bibliographies in Ball 1982: 58–9; Zwalf 1996.
360 E.g., Zwalf 1996: pls VI, 141, 143, 270–6.
361 Personal observation. See also, for example, Dani 1982.
362 E.g., Herrmann 1977: 34, 57, 67–72, 126–7.
363 Schmidt-Colinet in Alcock 1997: 167–70.
364 Pope 1965: 81–5.
365 Matheson 1976: 224–34 and refs.
366 See Roaf and Stronach 1973: 129–40.
367 The refreshing exception, as always, being Ward-Perkins (1981: chapter 12) in his outstanding general survey of eastern Roman architecture. See now also Freyberger 1998, which I have not been able to examine before going to press.

Chapter 8

1 See, for example, Warmington 1974: 1 (written in 1928) or, most recently, Roberts 1985.
2 Roberts 1985: 176 and 232.
3 Pliny *Letters* 1. 10; Dio 69. 8. 3; Bouchier 1916: 175–7; Hitti 1957: 346–8, 353–55; Glueck 1965: 377–80; Brown 1971: 158; Jones 1971; Bowersock 1983: 115–17; Starcky 1984; Houston 1990; Gysens in Cimino 1994: 79; Litvinsky and Destyatovskaya in Litvinsky 1996: 424; Peña 1996: 229, 232–4; Turcan 1996.
4 Herodian *Alexander*; *Augustan History* Alexander; Bouchier 1916: 177; Collingwood and Wright 1965; Drijvers 1980: 183–5; Harris 1965; Dodgeon and Lieu 1991: 30; Peña 1996: 230; Turcan 1996: chapter 3.
5 Reinaud, *Invasions des Sarrazins en France, et de France en Savoie, en Piemont et en Suisse*, trans. in Sherwani 1964. See also Hitti 1957: 346–8, 353–5.
6 E.g., Aurelius Victor 1; see also Cimino 1994: 12–16.
7 Strabo 15. 1. 4 and 15. 1. 73; Dio 54. 9. His tomb containing his ashes at Athens was inscribed with the following epitaph: 'Here lies Zarmanochegas, an Indian from Bargosa, who immortalised himself with the ancestral customs of the Indians.' See also Dio 54. 9. 8.
8 References to 'Bactria' by the Roman sources are an anachronism, the kingdom of Bactria having disappeared in the first century BC. They are probably references to the Kushan Empire of Central Asia and the Indian borderlands from the first century BC to the third AD. See Staviskij 1986.
9 Segal 1970: 31, quoting Bardaisan.
10 Quoted in Cimino 1994: 19–24. See also McCrindle 1901: 9–10, 77–8, 167, 213, 214; Wheeler 1954: 160–2; Warmington 1974: 36–8, 138–9.
11 Procopius 1. 19. 23–6.

12 Strabo 2. 3. 4; Pliny 2. 168. See also McCrindle 1901: 97; Begley in Begley and De Puma 1991: 6–7.
13 Bloch 1950; Thapar 1961: 250–66.
14 The Roman 'embassy' of 166 mentioned in Chinese sources is generally thought to be mercantile rather than diplomatic – the single coin of Marcus Aurelius found near Saigon notwithstanding. See Chapter 4.
15 Cimino 1994: 119–21.
16 Cimino 1994: 126–7.
17 Though probably on little more grounds than that of finding a suitable worthy Oriental – there was no Indianising element in the Emesene royal house.
18 Parlasca in Weiss 1985: 408, fig. 204.
19 Begley in Begley and De Puma (eds) 1991: 4; Sidebotham in Begley and De Puma 1991: 33–4; Ray 1994: 66.
20 Fraser 1972: 81 n. 391 discusses this gravestone and other evidence for Indians at Alexandria. Suggestions that some of the rock-cut monuments at Petra might be Hindu temples, however, are untenable: Goetz (1974) views one of the 'god-blocks' in the outer Siq at Petra as a Hindu temple, but it fits more into Nabataean architecture than Indian.
21 Though the evidence of Indian-derived place names on the Gulf might be illusory: cf. The 'East India' docks in London!
22 Williamson 1972; Whitehouse and Williamson 1973; Ball 1976, 1986, 1989b; Whitehouse in Begley and De Puma 1991; Ray 1994: 25–7, 172–5.
23 Whitehouse in Begley and De Puma (eds) 1991: 217–18.
24 *Periplus* 30; Hourani 1995: 22; Crone 1987: 35–6; Ball 1989b: 4.
25 Warmington 1974: 27–8.
26 Ammianus Marcellinus 14. 3. 3; Procopius 2. 25. 3; Hourani 1995: 41; Warmington 1974: 138.
27 McCrindle 1901: 215. Warmington 1974: 76.
28 Sidebotham in Begley and De Puma 1991: 31–2.
29 Warmington 1974: 64–6.
30 Ray 1994: 11–47, 87–120.
31 Ray 1994: 176.
32 Despite efforts to see an ancient Buddhist religious tract, *The Questions of Milinda*, as a Socratic dialogue – see Tarn 1951: 414–36. Tafazzoli and Khromov in Litvinsky (1996): 91.
33 Warmington 1974: 72.
34 See the Introduction by G. R. Woodward and H. Mattingly in the Loeb edition of St John Damascene. See also Gregorios 1985: 33.
35 Wiesehöfer 1996: 217–19.
36 Frye 1976: 7–8. On the *Arthasastra* see Allchin 1995: 187–94. On the *Siyasat Nama* see Frye 1975.
37 Gregorios 1985: 31.
38 McCrindle 1901: 183–4; Gregorios 1985: 31; see also Ray 1994: 66.
39 McCrindle 1901: 169–71.
40 Gregorios 1985: 33–4.
41 Eusebius 2. 23.
42 In addition to references already cited, see, for example, various essays in Doshi 1985. Tarn 1951 and Narain 1957 are the classic accounts of the Greeks in India.
43 See Ball 1989b.
44 See, for example, Chakrabarti 1990.
45 Ball 1976, 1986, 1989b. See also Ray 1994.
46 A wood tondo of 199 in the Staatliches Museum, Berlin – illustrated, for example, on the front cover of the Penguin Classic edition of the *Augustan History*. See also Kleiner 1992: 321–2.
47 The term 'dynasty' is used in the strict sense of family kinship here, not in the adoptive sense as the Antonines were.
48 *Augustan History* Pescennius Niger: 230.
49 *Augustan History* Septimius Severus: 215 and 220.
50 It is a great pity that Severus' autobiography, which Herodian II, ix, 4 refers to, is no longer extant.

51 The Temple of Bel at Palmyra – or Apamaea, according to Dio 79. 8. 6.

52 The names of the Emesene women were all Arabic in origin: Domna from *Dumayna*, Maesa from *Masa*, Sohaemia from *Suhayma*, 'black', Mammaea from *Mama*. See Shahid 1984a: 41–2.

53 Turcan 1996: 166, where it often occurs in the priesthood of Dolichenus. It is probably a mistake in any case to read too much into the presence or lack of Roman names in Syrian families, as Millar 1993 (especially chapter 13) does. The Arabic names almost universally used by modern Iranians, for example, does not detract from any Iranian character – far from it.

54 Herodian 5. 3. 2, for example, calls the family Phoenician, not Roman, and gives the derivation of Julia Maesa's name as Emesa.

55 See Turton 1974 for an account of this dynasty. See also Birley 1988; Shahid 1984a: 33–6; Grant 1996. Millar (1993: 302–3) has cautioned against the assumption of a connection between the family of the ancient kings of Emesa and the family of Julia Domna – and hence, the Severan dynasty of emperors. Equally, it must be remembered that there is no evidence that they were *not* connected. Indeed, the evidence of the historical sources implies overwhelmingly that there was a connection. The massive wealth that Julia Domna's family was able to command on a number of occasions (the coup that elevated Elagabalus, for example) could only have been the wealth of the Emesene royal house, famous for its fabulous wealth – see, for example, the discussion of this wealth in Baldus 1996. In addition, we have already seen how the Emesene royal family deliberately aligned itself with other important families through a policy of dynastic marriages: the royal houses of Judaea, Commagene and Armenia numbered amongst them. But whether or not the two families were related, the history of the Severans, one of Rome's most important imperial dynasties, cannot be fully understood without its background of the Emesene kings and their religion.

56 *Augustan History*, Septimius Severus: 210.

57 Gibbon 1. 112.

58 In the words of Dio 79. 23. 3.

59 Herodian 3. 11. 8.

60 Shahid 1984a: 34. Millar (1993: 141–59) sees the grant of *Colonia* status on Near Eastern cities by the various Syrian emperors from Caracalla to Philip as evidence for Romanisation, but surely it was the reverse: Syrian emperors granting favourable status to their own kind.

61 Lane Fox 1986: 606.

62 Philostratus *Life of Apollonius*. See also Bivar 1966: 43–4; Elsner in Alcock 1997: 178–80.

63 *Augustan History*, Caracalla: 250–1, Geta: 264–5.

64 Herodian 4. 3. 5–9.

65 Dio 78. 6. 1 writes 'Antoninus [Caracalla] belonged to three races; and he possessed none of their virtues at all, but combined in himself all their vices; the fickleness, cowardice, and recklessness of Gaul were his, the harshness and cruelty of Africa, and the craftiness of Syria'.

66 Herodian 3. 15. 4; 4. 6. 1–5; Dio 78. 1. 1–3; 78. 4–6, 12; *Augustan History*, Caracalla: 252–4.

67 Herodian 4. 8. 1–3; Dio. 78. 7; *Augustan History*, Caracalla: 251; see also Millar 1993: 142.

68 Herodian 4. 9; Dio 78. 22–3; *Augustan History*, Caracalla: 255.

69 Dio 78. 22. 1.

70 This incident is related by Herodian 4. 11, but does not appear in the account of the war given by Dio 79. 1–3.

71 Herodian 4. 13. 3–5; Dio 79. 5–6; *Augustan History*, Caracalla: 256; Zosimus 1. 6–10. To this day the ghost of the East still returns to haunt Caracalla, almost two millennia after his death. For the one thing more than anything else that is commonly associated with his name today is the immense baths he had built in Rome, 'in sheer bulk alone one of the most impressive buildings that have come down to us from antiquity' (Ward-Perkins 1981: 129). It has in modern times been converted into the world's largest outdoor opera house. As such, it is the regular venue for one of opera's greatest spectaculars: Verdi's grand eastern epic, *Aida*, set in ancient Egypt. Ironic indeed that the country whose capital he did so much to destroy is now associated more than ever with his name.

72 Dio 79. 23–24.

73 See Kleiner 1992: 322–4, and Richter 1948: front cover and fig. 107. See also the bust in the Farnese Collection in the National Museum of Naples. See also the description by John Malalas 11. 24.

74 E.g., the Munich bust – see Kleiner 1992: 326. See also the description by John Malalas 11. 23.

75 E.g., Kleiner 1992: 315–28.

76 See Goldscheider 1940: pl. 88.

77 Now in the Villa Albani, Rome. See Kleiner 1992: 349. Both Herodian (4. 9. 3) and Eutropius (8. 20) in fact hint of an Oedipan relationship.

78 *Augustan History*, Heliogabalus: 275–6; Zosimus 1. 11.

79 Elagabalus, for example, in Herodian, Heliogabalus in the *Augustan History* and Aurelius Victor.

80 Herodian 5. 4. See also Eadie in Kennedy 1996b.

81 Herodian 5. 8. 1; see also Aurelius Victor 23, *Augustan History* Heliogabalus, Zosimus 1. 11.

82 Indeed, it is surprising that otherwise respectable historians have been so selective in their acceptance or rejection of the more purple Roman descriptions of foreign religious rites.

83 *Augustan History*, Heliogabalus: 306–8.

84 Ibid. 298–9 and 304.

85 Ibid. 312.

86 Although he is, of course, much later. John Malalas, p. 158.

87 Turcan 1996: 176–83.

88 Such as the dervishes in Islam or the ceremonies in Ethiopian Christianity or the dancing in Judaism.

89 E.g., depictions of the ancient Persian kings at Persepolis (see Roaf 1983), or Sultan Mahmud of Ghazna in the twelfth century (see Nizam al-Mulk). See also Frazer 1911–36: 7 (1): 20 n. 1.

90 See Chapter 7, 'Sacred and processional ways'.

91 See Chapter 3, 'Emesa and the Sun Kings'.

92 Herodian 5. 6. 3–5.

93 *Augustan History*, Heliogabalus: 292; Downey 1961: 305.

94 Turcan 1996: 145.

95 Herodian 5. 6. 1.

96 Both the sources and the modern histories almost universally revile him, e.g., Gibbon 1: 143–8, or Birley 1976: 20: 'Elagabalus, the perverted Syrian youth.'

97 Gibbon 1. 143–8.

98 Kleiner 1992: 362–3.

99 Zosimus; *Augustan History*. Dodgeon and Lieu 1994: 92–3, 107. See also Will 1959, 1960.

100 The Sun cult is discussed further in 'From Paganism to Christianity', below.

101 It is curious that despite the long shadow Alexander the Great cast over the ancient world, Severus Alexander is the first Emperor – or ruler of any real note – to be named after him.

102 *Augustan History*, Alexander. Dodgeon and Lieu 1991: 21.

103 E.g., sculptures in the Capitoline Museum and the Louvre. See Goldscheider 1940: pls 90, 91, 94; Kleiner 1992: fig. 345.

104 See Chapter 2.

105 *Augustan History*, Alexander. Dodgeon and Lieu 1991: 21.

106 Herodian; *Augustan History*, Alexander; Zosimus 1. 11–12.

107 E.g., sculptures in the Louvre, Uffizi and the Capitoline. See Goldscheider 1940: pls 80 and 81; Kleiner 1992: 363–4.

108 Herodian 6. 8. 8.

109 Gibbon 1. 157 n. 95.

110 Gibbon 1. 149–66.

111 Aurelius Victor 24.

112 See Chapter 2.

113 Teixidor 1977: 68.

114 The main sources for Uranius are John Malalas 12. 26 and numismatic, summarised by Delbrueck 1948: 28–9, Dodgeon and Lieu 1991: 54–6 and Baldus 1996.

115 There was another Uranius who claimed the Bishopric of Emesa in *c.* 444, who might be a descendant. See Downey 1961: 467. Emesa was also the scene of another claim to the purple a short time later, by Quietus, which was put down by ʿUdaynath in about 263. See Dodgeon and Lieu 1991: 75–6.

116 Dodgson and Lieu 1991: 55.

117 Millar 1993. See also Bowersock 1983: 127–8; Isaac 1992: 227–8.
118 Though the name of Philip's wife, Ocatilia Severa, also an Arab, implies that some favours at least had been granted her family by the Severan dynasty. See Bowersock 1983: 123.
119 Aurelius Victor; Eutropius 9. 3; Shahid 1984a; Bowersock 1983: chapter 9.
120 Bowersock 1983: 123.
121 See 'Survivors of Edessa' in Chapter 4.
122 Zosimus 1. 19–22.
123 Eusebius 6. 34. A letter of Dionysius, the Bishop of Alexandria, also refers to emperors 'who were avowed Christians' before Valerian, which is presumably a reference to Philip. See Eusebius 7. 10.
124 Anonymous Velesianus, quoted in Lieu and Montserrat 1996: 45.
125 Aurelius Victor (28. 2) is the only pagan source for his Christianity. Although his Christianity is not mentioned, it is significant that Philip gets a bad press from Zosimus (1. 18), 'who had an axe to grind, and grind it he did. He was the last of the pagan historians' (Buchanan and Davis in the introduction to their translation of Zosimus, 1967).
126 E.g., Downey, 1961: 306–8, who rejects it, or Shahid 1984a: 36–7, 65–93, who supports it. Bowersock (1983: 125–7) takes the middle road. See also, Trimingham 1979: 58–60.
127 See Eutropius 10. 1–8.
128 Shahid 1984: 155–6.
129 Drijvers 1980: 89–90; Turcan 1996: 133–43.
130 Such as the bust of Philip in the Vatican Museum – see Kleiner 1992: 368–9.
131 Philip was not the last Roman emperor who was Arab. The Emperor Nicephorus I (802–11), or Niqfur in the Arabic sources, although heavily Romanised, was a descendant of the Ghassanid king Jabalah. The Isaurian or Syrian dynasty of emperors (717–802) whom Nicephorus displaced, whilst perhaps not Arab in the strict sense, were at least closely related to them – Emperor Leo III spoke Arabic as his first language, and their fanatic iconoclasm has been seen by some authorities to be derived from Islam. See Hitti 1963: 300 n. 2.
132 For accounts of Lepcis (or Leptis) Magna and its remains see: Wheeler 1964: 52–9 and refs; Haynes 1965; Ward Perkins 1981: 371–91; Birley 1988: 5–22; Raven 1993: various refs; Ward-Perkins 1993.
133 Aubet 1993.
134 The original Phoenician name was *Lpqy*, probably a native Libyan name. This was transcribed into Latin as *Lepcis*. Since this consonant cluster was difficult to pronounce by Latin speakers, it was usually vocalised as 'Leptis'. By the time of the later empire, this form had passed into official written usage as well, and has become the better known form today. The name survives today in the 'Wadi Libda' adjacent to the site.
135 The term 'Libyan' is used here to mean the native Hamitic or Berber North Africans in antiquity, rather than the modern North African country of that name.
136 Although native names do not necessarily represent a native presence: to take a modern example, the Australian aboriginal name of of Wollongong represents an entirely Anglo-Saxon city, not Aboriginal. Natives, if present at all, would be confined to slums.
137 See, for example, Daniels 1970.
138 See Di Vita 1968; Brogan and Smith 1984.
139 See, e.g., Ward-Perkins 1971.
140 See Chapter 7, 'Planned towns'.
141 Mattingly 1988: 21–42.
142 E.g., Ward Perkins 1981: 386.
143 See Chapter 7, 'Four-way arches'.
144 In addition to Ward-Perkins (1981), for the marble and artists at Severan Lepcis, see Walda and Walker 1984: 81–92.
145 Pietrzykowski 1985–6.
146 Chapter 7. See also MacDonald 1986: 53–4.
147 Jones and Ling in Ward-Perkins 1993.
148 Timgad has the only other properly colonnaded street in Roman North Africa.
149 See Chapter 4, 'Emesa'.
150 Ward-Perkins 1993: 53–4.

151 Ward Perkins 1981: 389–91.
152 Roberts 1985: 81–116.
153 Most notably, for example, in Lane Fox's recent (1986) admirable study. Lane Fox's account, however, only tells a part of the story, and I suspect a small part at that, nearly 800 pages notwithstanding. See also: MacMullen 1984; Markus 1990; Stark 1996; Lieu and Monserrat 1998. For a recent compilation of contrasting source material, see Lieu and Montserrat 1996. I am acutely aware that there is a simply vast theological literature – with a veritable sea of potential minefields! – on the subjects I cover in this section that it has not been possible to take on board. Nonetheless, the various points discussed here are still worth making in the context of this work. Note also the cautionary remarks of Boyce and Grenet 1991: 366, n. 16.
154 See Chapter 7, 'Early Christian architecture'.
155 St Augustine, *City of God* 4.
156 See, for example, the excellent account of the martyrdom of Perpetua and its background in Salisbury 1997.
157 For Zoroastrianism generally, see Boyce 1979. Some studies have put him as late as the sixth century BC and as early as about 2000 BC. Boyce, our main authority, (1979: 18) dates Zoroaster to 1700–1500 BC.
158 Boyce and Grenet 1991: 481; Peña 1996: 80.
159 'Second Isaiah, brought into contact in Babylon with Persian propagandists, developed in striking ways the belief in Yahweh as God alone and Creator of all, thus, it seems, both vying with Zoroaster's concept of Ahura Mazda as Creator of all that is good and at the same time rejecting his dualism' – Boyce and Grenet 1991: 361 and n. 2.
160 Boyce 1979: 42–3; Boyce and Grenet 1991: 451. See also Corbin 1976.
161 Although Boyce and Grenet (1991: chapter 11) stress the origin of the Judaeo-Christian belief in a day of judgement, a messiah and the physical resurrection in a hereafter in Zoroastrianism.
162 Boyce and Grenet 1991: chapter 11 with refs. On pp. 409–10 they discuss the possible derivation of the word Pharisee from 'Persians'.
163 Boyce and Grenet 1991: 448–56.
164 Or probably under Hormizd I in 272, rather than Shapur, according to Colpe 1983: 877–84.
165 Translated by Gutas 1998: 80–1.
166 Boyce 1979: chapters 6 and 7.
167 See Frye 1963: 247–9; Blockley 1992: 10–11; Wiesehöfer (1996: 199–200, 210–11) however, discards this view.
168 See section on Edessa in Chapter 3. For Constantine's letter, see Lane Fox 1986: 636–7.
169 Boyce 1979; Boyce and Grenet 1991: chapter 11.
170 For recent studies of these contacts – particularly religious – see, for example: Boyce and Grenet 1991: 361–71; Kingsley 1995; Stevenson 1997; Miller 1997 (which I have not yet read).
171 Procopius 2. 24. 1–3. For Adhur Gushnasp see Boyce and Grenet 1991: 70–9 and refs. For Vesta see Frazer 1911–36: 1 (2): chapter 14.
172 Dodgeon and Lieu 1991: 65.
173 Raditsa 1983.
174 Wright 1969. See also Chapter 3, 'Nabataean religion'.
175 Boyce and Grenet 1991: chapter 8. It is a mistake to assume, however, that an Iranian ethnic element necessarily remained in these populations simply because of the prevalence of Iranian religions, just as one cannot assume Palestinian or Arab elements in the populations of Roman Europe because of the popularity of Christianity.
176 Boyce and Grenet 1991: part 3 with refs; Turcan 1996: 200–1. See also Frazer 1911–36: 4 (1): 191–2.
177 Duchesne-Guillemin 1983: 872.
178 See 'Julia Domna and the Arabs who ruled Rome', above.
179 In fact the name 'Apollonius' was often consciously chosen by the Hellenised Iranians of Anatolia because of the equation of Greek Apollo with Iranian Mithras or (occasionally) Anahita. See Boyce and Grenet 1991: 250.
180 Colpe 1983: 826–31; Boyce and Grenet 1991: chapters 10 and 11; Kingsley 1995; Turcan 1996: Ch. 4.
181 Boyce and Grenet 1991: 239 and 256–7.

182 Colpe 1983: 831–4; Boyce and Grenet 1991: 376–87.
183 Raditsa 1983; Boyce and Grenet 1991: chapter 8.
184 Boyce and Grenet 1991: 235–8.
185 Although it is important to recall possible Iranian elements in Nabataean religion, discussed above.
186 Colpe 1983: 840–3; Boyce and Grenet 1991: 309–51; Turcan 1996: chapter 4. See also Sanders 1996.
187 Boyce and Grenet 1991: 352; Turcan 1996: 159–69.
188 Lane-Fox 1986: 532–8.
189 Turcan 1996: 209–15.
190 Although Hopkins (1979) sees more of an Iranian element in the Dura Mithraeum, and Mithraism was particularly popular among troops of eastern origin: Syrians, Palmyrenes and Commagenians. See Turcan 1996: chapter 4.
191 Colpe 1983: 853–6; Boyce and Grenet 1991: 468–90; Turcan 1996: chapter 4.
192 Widengran 1983, Klimkeit 1993, Lieu 1994.
193 Boyce and Grenet 1991: 460–5.
194 Dodgeon and Lieu 1991: 65.
195 Klimkeit 1993: 202–3, 208–9; Lieu 1994: chapter 2.
196 John Malalas 12. 42; Lieu 1994: 130–1.
197 Boyce and Grenet 1991: 30–3; Bosworth 1996: chapter 4. See also Frazer 1911–36: 1 (2): 50–1.
198 Cf. Elsner in Alcock 1997.
199 Boyce and Grenet 1991: chapter 8; Turcan 1996: chapter 1 and 254–8; Elsner in Alcock 1997: 180–91. See also Frazer 1911–36: 1 (1): 37–8.
200 Cook 1962: 59–60; Boardman 1980: 216–224; Turcan 1996: chapter 1; Elsner in Alcock 1997: 195.
201 Although note the Zoroastrian elements in Judaism stressed above.
202 Eusebius 4. 5; 5. 12.
203 Chapter 7, 'Temples'.
204 For virgin and child cults see Drijvers 1980: 120. For Hairiti and child see Zwalf 1996: pl. III. See also Hitti 1957: 256 and 333–5.
205 Frazer 1911–36: 4 (1): chapters 1–3, 5; Turcan 1996: 143–8.
206 Trimingham 1979: 79.
207 Turcan 1996: chapter 2.
208 Brown 1971: 96ff. Boyce and Grenet (1991: 477–8) also see the cult of Serapis as possibly beginning as an offshoot of Iranian Mithraism (*Sarapis* deriving from Persian *Shahrapat*, a manifestation of Mithras), although this is disputed, and in any case evolved along quite separate lines in the Roman world.
209 Lane Fox 1986: 446.
210 Lane Fox 1986: 278–80.
211 Lieu 1986.
212 Frye 1983: 148–9. Trimingham (1979: 160) sounds a cautionary note about 'Iranian' Christianity, which was a religion practised by non-Iranian minorities – mainly Aramaeans – in Iran, quite distinct from the Iranians themselves who for the main remained part of the official Zoroastrian 'church'.
213 Downey 1961: 272–316; Boyce and Grenet 1991: 254–6.
214 In 'Antioch the imperial city' in Chapter 5.
215 Cambyses founded a temple there during his Egyptian campaign on the site of the future city; see Boyce and Grenet 1991: 254–6. For the later religious missions see: Dodgeon and Lieu 1991: 65; Lieu 1994: 24–5.
216 Lane Fox 1986: 268–73.
217 Lane Fox 1986: 430–4.
218 Aubet 1993: 232–4; Turcan 1996: 169–70. See also Frazer 1911–36: 4 (1): chapter 5.
219 Aubet 1993: 207–17. See also Frazer 1911–36: 3: 168–79.
220 On the other hand, it must be pointed out that the Phoenician homeland in the Levant – particularly Tyre – remained a bulwark of paganism. See Jidejian 1996: 153.
221 *Augustan History* Caracalla: 258.

222 Shahid 1984a: 35–6.
223 Eusebius 6. 28.
224 Avi-Yonah 1961: 30.
225 Vermeule 1956–8.
226 See 'Edessa and the coming of Christendom' in Chapter 3.
227 See 'Philip the Arab' above.
228 The Palmyrene temple to Sol and Malakbel at Rome was equated with the sun. See Houston 1990. The latter two may have been one and the same cult, as postulated in Chapter 3, 'Emesa and the Sun Kings'. See also Seyrig 1971.
229 Teixidor 1977: 49.
230 Although this has been suggested to relate to Zoroastrian concepts, above.
231 Bird in Aurelius Victor: 150 n. 7; Lieu and Montserrat 1996: 75.
232 Norwich 1988: 32.
233 Eutropius 10.1–8.
234 The subject has recently come in for greater scrutiny. See, for example, Lane Fox 1986, Lieu and Montserrat 1996.
235 Jones 1966: 50 and 62.
236 Lieu and Montserrat 1996: 11.
237 Jones 1966: 50 and 62. Also Norwich 1988: 176–7.
238 Norwich 1988, 2: 12305.
239 See S. Runciman, *The Fall of Constantinople 1453* (1965), 14.
240 Sozomen 3.2; Zosimus 2. 30. 1; Lieu and Montserrat 1996: 127.
241 See Lane Fox 1986: 280–2 for a summary of the spread of Christianity through the East.
242 E.g., Millar (1993: 492) frequently cites Christianity in the Near East as evidence for 'Western' character as opposed to 'Eastern'.
243 Perhaps nowhere more so than by Millar 1993, where the assessment of 'character' of the Near East forms the main subject of his entire book. See also the discussion of Greek versus 'non-Greek' in Sherwin-White and Kuhrt 1993: 141–9; Laurence and Berry 1998.
244 Millar 1993: 235.
245 Sherwin White and Kuhrt 1993: 141.
246 E.g., Millar 1993: 417, referring specifically to Petra. There are many other such references elsewhere in his book. Cf. Frye 1984: 220, on the mistaken assumption of a Parthian 'Senate' by Greek and Latin authors. See also Grainger's (1995: 192–3) very salutary remarks on the Greek and Latin inscriptions in the East providing no convincing evidence for Roman style governing institutions, despite appearances.
247 Millar 1993: 411.
248 Stoneman 1992: 53–4.
249 Greek traveller to interpreter observing an Arab tribal assembly: 'What are they doing?'
Interpreter to Greek traveller: 'They're holding a *majlis*.'
Traveller: 'What's a *majlis*?'
Interpreter: 'Its a kind of assembly.'
Traveller: 'Ah, a *boule!*'
Traveller to a Greek author: 'The Arabs have a *boule*.'
Modern Classicist on reading Greek author: 'The Arabs had Greek institutions.'
250 Isaac 1992: 304–7.
251 E.g., Bowersock 1983: 96–9, Millar 1993: 138.
252 Millar 1993: 316 (my italics).
253 E.g., Sartre 1985; Grainger 1995: 180.
254 For example, Millar 1993: 456.
255 Indeed, in Fergus Millar's continual labouring of this very point, can one detect a certain triumphalism?
256 Gawlikowski in Alcock 1997: 46.
257 See also the conclusion to 'From Paganism to Christianity', above.
258 Millar 1993: 492.
259 Millar 1993: 517.
260 Millar 1993: 522.

261 Wafa Ayash *Al-Rassafa: Metropolis of the Syrian Desert* (Damascus 1994).
262 Isaiah 44–5; Xenophon *Cyropaedia*.
263 Isaac 1992: 82 and 283–4.
264 Umayyad and Abbasid civilisation hardly requires emphasising here. That early Islam was not only a civilisation but also a Semitic 'Renaissance' is hardly in doubt: the Syrians, for example, remained very much aware of their pre-Macedonian Semitic heritage, such as the Babylonian legacy, and viewed Islam in terms of a revival of this. See Gutas 1998.
265 Although Sultan Mehmet, in his conquest of Constantinople, felt very consciously that he was continuing the role of the Roman emperors.

BIBLIOGRAPHY

Ancient authors

In addition to the following sources, excellent compendiums have been made for certain subjects, such as McCrindle (1901) for the contact with India, or Dodgeon and Lieu (1991) for the wars with Sasanian Iran, or Le Strange (1905) for early Islamic sources, or Smallwood (1966) for the reigns of Nerva, Trajan and Hadrian, or Palmer (1993) for the seventh century.

Ammianus Marcellinus. *Roman History*. Loeb. Also *The Later Roman Empire (A.D. 354–378)*. Tr. W. Hamilton, notes by A. Wallace-Hadrill. Penguin, 1986.

Appian. *Roman History*. Loeb, 1912.

Augustan History. 3 vols. Loeb. Part of it also translated as *Lives of the Later Caesars* by A. Birley (Penguin Classic 1976).

Aurelius Victor. *De Caesaribus*. Tr. H. W. Bird. Liverpool, 1994.

al-Bal'ami. *Chronique de al-Tabari traduite sur la version Persane*. Tr. H. Zotenberg. Paris, 1958.

al-Biruni. *Chronology of Ancient Nations (Athar al-Bakiya)*. Tr. C. E. Sachau. London, 1879.

—— *India*. 2 vols. Tr. E. C. Sachau. London, 1910.

Bardaisan of Edessa. *The Book of the Laws of the Countries: Dialogue on Fate of Bardaisan of Edessa*. Ed. and tr. H. J. W. Drijvers. Semitic Texts with Translation, III. Assen, 1965.

Bible. The New English Bible, with Apocrypha. Oxford and Cambridge, 1970.

Chronicon Paschale 284–628 AD. Tr. M. and M. Whitby, 1989. Liverpool.

Cosmas Indicopleustes. *The Christian Topography*. Ed. E. O. Winstedt, Cambridge, 1909. Also *Topographie chrétienne*. Tr. W. Wolska-Conus. Paris, 1967–73. Also *The Christian Topography of Cosmas Indicopleustes, an Egyptian Monk*. Tr. J. W. McCrindle. Hakluyt Society 97, London, 1987.

Dio Cassius. *Dio's Roman History*. Tr. Earnest Cary. Loeb, 1914. Also *Lives of the Later Caesars*. Tr. A. Birley, Penguin, 1976.

Eusebius. *Ecclesiastical History*. Loeb, 1932. Also *The History of the Church*, tr. G. A. Williamson, ed. A. Louth, Penguin, 1989.

Firdausi. *Shahnama*. 6 vols. Tr. A. G. and E. Warner. London, 1912. See also translations and abridgements by J. and J. A. Atkinson, London, 1887, and Levy.

Herodian, *History of the Roman Empire from the death of Marcus Aurelius to the accession of Gordian III*. Tr. Edward C. Nichols. Berkeley and Los Angeles, 1961.

Isadore of Charax. *Parthian Stations*. Tr. W. H. Schoff. Philadelphia, 1914.

John Malalas. *Chronicle*. Tr. E. Jeffreys, M. Jeffreys and R. Scott. Melbourne, 1986.

Josephus. *Antiquities*. 9 vols. Tr. R. Marcus. Loeb, 1943.

—— *Jewish War*. Tr. G. A. Williamson, revised E. M. Smallwood. Penguin, London, 1981.

Juzjani, *Tabaqat-I Nasiri*. Tr. H. G. Raverty. Calcutta, 1881.

Kautilya. *Arthasastra*. Tr. R. P. Kangle, Bombay, 1960–5. Tr. also L. N. Rangarajan, Delhi, 1990.

Libanius. *Oration II. Antiochikos*. Tr. G. Downey (1959) *Proceedings of the American Philosophical Society* 103: 652–86.

—— *Selected Works*. 2 vols. Tr. A. F. Norman. Loeb, 1969–92.

Lucian. *The Goddesse of Surrye*. Tr. A. M. Harmon. Loeb, 1925.

Mas'udi. *Maruj adh-Dhahab*. Paris, 1861–77.

Moses of Khorenats'i. *History of the Armenians*. Tr. R. W. Thomson. Harvard, 1978.

Nizam al-Mulk. *Siyasat-nama or The Book of Government or Rules for Kings*. Tr. H. Darke. London 1978.

Pacatus. *Panegyric to the Emperor Theodosius*. Tr. C. E. V. Nixon. Liverpool Translated Texts, 1987.

Periplus of the Erythraean Sea. Tr. L. Casson, Princeton 1989. Also tr. G. W. B. Huntingford, London 1980, and W. H. Schoff, New York 1912.

Pliny. *Natural History*. Loeb, 1949.

Plutarch. *The Lives of the Noble Grecians and Romans*. Tr. J. Dryden, revised A. H. Clough (n.d.). New York. Also *Parallel Lives*. Loeb, 1926.

Procopius. *History of the Wars*. Tr. H. B. Dewing. Loeb, 1914.

Ptolemy. *Tetrabiblos*. Loeb, 1940.

Qur'an.

Sebeos. *History*. Tr. R. Bedrosian on *http://www.virtualscape.com/rbedrosian/seb1.htm*, 1985.

Shapur. *Res Gestae*. Tr. A. Maricq *Syria* 35, 1958: 295–360. Also in Frye 1984.

Sozomen. *Ecclesiastical History*. Tr. E. Welford. Nicene and Post-Nicene Christian Fathers, 2nd ser., 2. London.

Strabo. *Geography*. 8 vols. Ed. and tr. H. J. Jones. Loeb, 1983.

Suetonius. *The Twelve Caesars*. Tr. R. Graves. Penguin, 1957.

al-Tabari. *The History of al-Tabari*, 4: *The Ancient Kingdoms*. Tr. M. Perlman. Albany, 1987.

al-Tha'alabi. *Histoire des Rois de Perse*. Tr. H. Zotenberg. Paris, 1900.

Tacitus. *The Annals of Imperial Rome*. Tr. M. Grant. Penguin, 1956.

Xenophon. *Cyropaedia*. Tr. W. Miller. Loeb, 2 vols. 1914.

—— *The Persian Expedition*. Tr. R. Warner. Penguin 1965.

Zosimus. *Historia Nova. The Decline of Rome*. Tr. J. J. Buchanan and H. T. Davies. San Antonio, 1967.

Modern authors

Akurgal, E. (1990) *Ancient Civilizations and Ruins of Turkey* (7th edn). Istanbul.

Alcock, S. E. (ed., 1997) *The Early Roman Empire in the East*. Oxford.

Algaze, G. (1989) 'The Uruk Expansion', *Current Anthropology* 30: 571–608.

Al Khraysheh, F. (1992) 'Sites and tribes in Safaitic inscriptions' (in Arabic), in S. Tell (ed.) *Studies in the History and Archaeology of Jordan* IV. Amman and Lyon.

Allchin, B. and Allchin, R. (1982) *The Rise of Civilisation in India and Pakistan*. Cambridge.

Allchin, F. R. (1995) *The Archaeology of Early Historic South Asia. The Emergence of Cities and States*. Cambridge.

Allchin, R. *et al*. (eds, 1997) *Ghandaran Art in Context: East–West Exchanges at the Crossroads of Asia*. Delhi.

Amer, G. and Gawlikowski, M. (1985) 'Le sanctuaire impérial de Philippopolis', *Damaszener Mitteilungen* 2: 1–15.

Amy, R. (1950) 'Temple à Escaliers', *Syria* 27: 82–136.

As'ad, K. and Stepniowski, F. M. (1989) 'The Umayyad Suq in Palmyra', *Damaszener Mitteilungen* 4: 205–23.

Aubet, M. E. (1993) *The Phoenicans and the West. Politics, Colonies and Trade*. Cambridge.

Aurigemma, S. (1969) *L'Arco Quadrifonte di Marco Aurelio e di Lucio Vero in Tripoli*. Supplement to *Libya Antiqua* 3. Tripoli.

Avi-Yonah, M. (1961) *Oriental Art in Roman Palestine*. Rome.

Bader, A. N., Gaibov, V. and Košalenko, G. A. (1995) 'Walls of Margiana', in Invernizzi (1995): 39–50.

Baldus, H. R. (1996) 'Uranius Antoninus of Emesa. A Roman Emperor from Palmyra's neighbouring city and his coinage', *AAAS* 42: 371–7.

Ball, W. (1976) 'Two aspects of Iranian Buddhism', *Bulletin of the Asian Institute* 1, 4: 103–63.

—— (1982) *Archaeological Gazetteer of Afghanistan*. 2 vols. Paris.

—— (1986a) 'Some rock-cut monuments in southern Iran'. *Iran* 24: 95–115.

—— (1986b) 'The North Decumanus and North Tetrapylon at Jerash. Part B: the Architecture', in Zayadine: 385–409.

—— (1989a) 'Soundings at Seh Qubba, a Roman frontier station on the Tigris', in French and Lightfoot: 7–18.

—— (1989b) 'How far did Buddhism spread west? Buddhism in the Middle East in Ancient and Medieval Times', *al-Rafidan* X (Tokyo): 1–12.

—— (1997) *Syria. A Historical and Architectural Guide*. 2nd edn, London.

Balty, J. (ed. 1969–84) *Apamée de Syrie*. 3 vols, Brussels.

—— (1977) *Mosaïques de Syrie*. Brussels.

Balty, J. and Balty, J.-C. (1977) 'Apamée de Syrie, archéologie et histoire. I. Des origines à la Tétrachie', *ANRW* II, 8: 103–34.

Balty, J.-C. (1981) *Guide d'Apamée*. Brussels.

—— (1988) 'Apamea in Syria in the Second and Third Centuries A.D.', *Journal of Roman Studies* 78: 91–104.

—— (1990) 'Un portrait de Shahba-*Philippopolis* et l'iconographie de Phillipe de l'Arabe', in P. Matthiae, M. Van Loon and H. Weiss, *Resurrecting the Past: A Joint Tribute to Adnan Bounni*. Istanbul: 5–13.

—— (1994) 'Grande colonnade et quartier nord d'Apamée à la fin de l'époque hellénistique', *CRAI*: 77–101.

Balty, J.-C. and van Rengen, W. (1993) *Apamea in Syria: The Winter Quarters of the Legio II Parthica*. Brussels.

Baranski, M. (1994) 'The Roman army in Palmyra', in Dabrowa: 9–17.

Barghouti, A. N. (1982) 'Urbanization of Palestine and Jordan in Hellenistic and Roman Times', in Hadidi: 209–29.

Barkay, G. *et al.* (1974) 'Archaeological Survey in the Northern Bashan', *Israel Exploration Journal* 24: 173–84.

Barnet, R. D. and Watson, W. (1952) 'Russian Excavations in Armenia'. *Iraq* 14: 132–146.

Barthold, W. W. (1977) *Turkestan Down to the Mongol Invasion*. 4th edn. London.

Barthoux, J.-J. (1930) *Les Fouilles de Hadda. 3: Figures et figurines. Album photographique*. Paris and Brussels.

Bartl, K. and Hauser, S. (eds, 1996) *Continuity and Change in Northern Mesopotamia from the Hellenistic to the Early Islamic Period*. Berlin.

Bartoccini, R. (1931) 'L'Arco dei Severi di Leptis', *Africa Italiana* 4: 32–152.

Beazley, E. and Harverson, M. (1982) *Living with the Desert. Working Buildings of the Iranian Plateau*. Warminster.

Begley, V. (1996) *The Ancient Port of Arikamedu: New Excavations and Researches 1989–1992*. École Française d'Extrême-Orient. Paris.

Begley, V. and De Puma, R. D. (1991) *Rome and India. The Ancient Sea Trade*. Delhi.

Bier, L. (1986) *Sarvistan. A Study in Early Iranian Architecture*. Pennsylvania.

Bietenhard, H. (1977) 'Die syrische Dekapolis von Pompeius bis Traian', *ANRW* II, 8: 220–61.

Birley, A. R. (1976) *Lives of the Later Caesars*. London.

—— (1988) *Septimius Severus, The African Emperor*. London.

Biscop, J. L. (1997) *Deir Déhès: Monastère d'Antioncène*. Paris

Bivar, A. D. H. (1972) 'Cavalry equipment and tactics on the Euphrates frontier', *Dumbarton Oaks Papers* 26: 273–91.

—— (1983) 'The Political History of Iran under the Arsacids', in *Cambridge History of Iran* 3 (1): 21–99. Cambridge.

Bivar, A. D. H. and Fehevari, G. (1966) 'The walls of Tammisha', *Iran* 4.

Bloch, J. (1950) *Les Inscriptions d'Asoka, traduites et commentées*. Paris.

Blockley, R. C. (1992) *East Roman Foreign Policy: Formation and Conduct from Diocletian to Anastasius*. Leeds.

Boardman, J. (1980) *The Greeks Overseas*. London.

—— (1994) *The Diffusion of Classical Art in Antiquity*. London.

Bosworth, A. B. (1996) *Alexander and the East. The Tragedy of Triumph*. Oxford.

Boucharlat, R. (1985) 'Chahar Taq et temple de feu sasanide', in *De l'Indus aux Balkans. Receuil à la mémoire de Jean Deshayes*. (Paris): 461–78.

Bouchier, E. S. (1916) *Syria as a Roman Province*. Oxford.

Boulanger, R. (1966) *The Middle East. Lebanon – Syria – Jordan – Iraq – Iran*. Hachette World Guides, Paris.

Boulnois, L. (1966) *The Silk Road*. London.

Boussac, M.-F., and Salles, J.-F. (eds, 1995) *Athens, Aden, Arikamedu. Essays on the interrelations between India, Arabia and the Eastern Mediterranean*. New Delhi.

Bowersock, G. W. (1978) *Julian the Apostate*. London.

—— (1980) 'Mavia, Queen of the Saracens', *Studien zur antiken Sozialgeschichte. Festschrift Friedrich Vittinghof*. Kölner historische Abhandlungen 28: 477–95.

—— (1983) *Roman Arabia*. Cambridge, Mass.

Bowsher, J. M. C. (1986) 'The North Decumanus and North Tetrapylon at Jerash. 6. Inscriptions', in Zayadine: 384.

—— (1987) 'Architecture and Religion in the Decapolis: A Numismatic Survey', *Palestine Exploration Quarterly* 119: 62–9.

—— (1989) 'The Nabataean army' in French and Lightfoot: 19–30.

Boyce, M. (1979) *Zoroastrians, their Religious Beliefs and Practices*. London.

Boyce, M. and Grenet, F. (1991) *A History of Zoroastrianism. 3: Zoroastrianism under Macedonian and Roman Rule*. Leiden.

Braidwood, R. J. (1937) *Mounds in the Plain of Antioch. An Archaeological Survey*. Chicago.

Braund, D. C. (1984) *Rome and the Friendly King. The Character of Client Kingship*. London.

Braund, S. H. (1989) 'Juvenal and the East: satire as an historical source', in French and Lightfoot: 45–52.

Breton, J.-F. (1992) 'Le Sanctuaire de 'Athtar Dhu-Risaf à as-Sawda (République du Yemen)', *CRAI*: 429–53.

Brogan, O. and Smith, D. J. (1984) *Ghirza. A Libyan Settlement in the Roman Period*. Tripoli.

Brown, P. (1971) *The World of Late Antiquity*. London.

Browne, E. G. (1902) *A Literary History of Persia. 1: From the Earliest Times to Firdawsi*. London.

Browning, I. (1979) *Palmyra*. London.

—— (1982) *Jerash and the Decapolis*. London.

—— (1989) *Petra*. 3rd edn. London.

Browning, R. (1987) *Justininian & Theodora*. London.

Brümmer, E. (1985) 'Der Römishe Tempel von Dmeir', *Damsazener Mitteilungen* 2: 55–64.

Brundage, B. C. (1958) 'Herakles the Levantine: A Comprehensive View', *Journal of Near Eastern Studies* 16.

Brünnow, R. E. and Domaszewski, A. (1904–9) *Die Provincia Arabia*. 3 vols, Strasbourg.

Burney, C. A. B. (1957) 'Urartian Fortresses and Towns in the Van Region', *Anatolian Studies* 7: 37–54.

—— (1977) *From Village to Empire. An Introduction to Near Eastern Archaeology*. Oxford.

Burns, R. (1992) *Monuments of Syria. An Historical Guide*. London.

Bury, J. B. (1923) *History of the Later Roman Empire*. 2 vols, London.

Busink, T. A. (1970–80) *Der Tempel von Jerusalem von Salomo bis Herodes*. 2 vols, Leiden.

Bussagli, M. (1978) *Central Asian Painting from Afghanistan to Sinkiang*. London.

Butcher, R. and Thorpe, R. (1997) 'A note on excavations in central Beirut 1994–96', *JRA* 10: 291–306.

Butler, H. C. (1903) *Publications of the American Archaeological Expedition to Syria, 1899–1900*. Part II: *Architecture and Other Arts*. New York.

—— (1907–20) *Publications of the Princeton University Archaeological Expedition to Syria (1904–5, 9). Division II, Section A – Southern Syria. Division II, Section B – Northern Syria*. Leiden.

—— (1929) *Early Churches in Syria, 4th to 7th Centuries*. Princeton.

Callot, O. and Marcillet-Jaubert, J. (1984) 'Hauts-lieux de Syrie du Nord', in *Temples et sanctuaires* ed. G. Roux. Paris.

Cameron, A. (1993a) *The Later Roman Empire*. London.

—— (1993b) *The Mediterranean World in Late Antiquity AD 395–600*. London.

Campbell, D. B. (1986) 'What Happened at Hatra? The Problems of the Severan Siege Operations', in Freeman and Kennedy: 51–8.

Caroe, O. (1958) *The Pathans 550 B.C.–A.D. 1957*. Oxford.

Cary, M. and Warmington, E. H. *The Ancient Explorers*. Harmondsworth.

Casal, J.-M. (1949) *Fouilles de Virampatnam-Arikamedu*. Paris.

Casson, L. (1989) *The Periplus of the Erythraean Sea*. Princeton.

Chad, C. (1972) *Les Dynastes d'Émèse*. Beirut.

Chakrabarti, D. K. (1990) *The External Trade of the Indus Civilisation*. Delhi.

Charlesworth, M. (1987) 'Preliminary report on a newly-discovered extension of "Alexander's Wall" ', *Iran* 25: 160–5.

Cimino, R. M. (ed. 1994) *Ancient Rome and India. Commercial and Cultural Contacts between the Roman World and India*. Delhi.

Collart, P. (1973) 'La Tour de Qalaat Fakra', *Syria* 50: 137–64.

Colledge, M. A. R. (1967) *The Parthians*. London.

—— (1976) *The Art of Palmyra*. London.

—— (1977) *Parthian Art*. London.

Collingwood, R. B. and Wright, R. (1965) *Roman Inscriptions of Britain*. London.

Colpe, C. (1983) 'Development of religious thought', in *Cambridge History of Iran* 3 (2): 819–65.

Cook, J. M. (1962) *The Greeks in Ionia and the East*. London.

Corbin, H. (1976) *Spiritual Body and Celestial Faith. From Mazdean Iran to Shîʾite Iran*. Princeton.

Costa, P. M. (1977) 'Further comments on the bilingual inscription from Baraqish', *Proceedings of the Seminar for Arabian Studies* 7: 33–6.

Courtois, J.-C. (1973) 'Prospection dans la Vallée de l'Oronte', *Syria* 50: 53–94.

Creswell, K. A. C. (1924) *The Origin of the Plan of the Dome of the Rock*. British School of Archaeology in Jerusalem Supplementary Papers 2. London.

—— (1958) *A Short Account of Early Muslim Architecture*. Harmondsworth.

—— (1969) *Early Muslim Architecture*. 1 (2), Oxford.

Crone, P. (1987) *Mecca and the Rise of Islam*. Princeton.

Crow, J. G. (1995) 'The long walls of Thrace', in C. Mango and G. Dagron (eds), *Constantinople and its Hinterland*. Aldershot: 100–24.

Crowfoot, J. W. (1941) *Early Churches in Palestine*. London.

Crowfoot, J. W., Kenyon, K. M. and Sukenik, E. L. (1942) *The Buildings at Samaria*. London.

Cumont, F. (1906) *Oriental Religions in Roman Paganism*. New York.

Curtis, V. S. *et al.* (eds, 1998) *The Art and Archaeology in Ancient Persia. New Light on the Parthian and Sasanian Empires*. London.

Dabrowa, E. (ed., 1994) *The Roman and Byzantine Army in the East*. Krakow.

Dalley, S. and Goguel, A. (1997) 'The Sela' Sculpture: A Neo-Babylonian rock relief in southern Jordan', *ADAJ* 41: 169–76.

Dani, A. H. (1982) *Thatta: Islamic Architecture*. Islamabad.

Daniels, C. (1970) *The Garamantes of Southern Libya*. North Harrow.

Daum, W. (ed., 1988) *Yemen. 3000 Years of Art and Civilisation in Arabia Felix*. Innsbruck and Frankfurt.

Davies, P. E. J. (1997) 'The politics of pepetuation: Trajan's Column and the art of commemoration', *AJA* 101, 1: 41–65.

De Voguë, M. (1865–77) *Syrie centrale, architecture civile et réligieuse du Ier au VII siècle*. 2 vols, Paris.

De Vries, B. (1986) *Umm El-Jimal in the First Three Centuries A. D*. Oxford.

—— (1990) *Umm el-Jimal, 'Gem of the Black Desert'. A Brief Guide to the Antiquities*. Amman.

—— (1998) *Umm El-Jimal: A Frontier Town and its Landscape in Northern Jordan. 1: Fieldwork 1972–1981*. JRA Suppl Series 26.

Debevoise, N. (1938) *A Political History of Parthia*. Chicago.

Delbrueck, R. (1948) 'Uranius of Emesa', *Numismatic Chronicle* 8: 11–29.

Dentzer, J.-M. (1985) 'Six campagnes de fouilles à Si': Développement et culture indigène en Syrie méridionale', *Damaszener Mitteilungen* 2: 65–83.

—— (1986a) 'Les Sondages de l'arc nabatéen et l'urbanisme de Bosra', *CRAI*: 62–87.

—— (ed., 1986b) *Hauran I: Recherches archéologiques sur la Syrie du sud á l'époque hellénistique et romaine. IFAPO* 124. Paris.

Dentzer, J.-M., Blanc, P.-M. and Mukdad, A. (1993) 'Nouvelles recherches franco-syriennes dans le quartier est de Bostra Ash-sham', *CRAI*: 117–47.

Di Vita, A. (1968) 'Influences grecques et tradition orientale dans l'art punique de Tripolitaine', *MEFRA* 80: 70–83.

Dodge, H. (1990) 'Impact of Rome in the East', in M. Henig (ed.), *Architecture and Architectural Sculpture in the Roman Empire*. Oxford University Committee for Archaeology, Monograph 29, Oxford.

Dodgeon, M. H. and Lieu, S. N. C. (1991) *The Roman Eastern Frontier and the Persian Wars* (AD 226–363). *A Documentary History*. London.

Doe, B. (1983) *Monuments of South Arabia*. Naples and Cambridge.

Donced-Voûte (1988) *Les Pavements des églises byzantines de Syrie et du Liban. Décor, archéologie et liturgie*. 2 vols, Louvain.

Donner, F. (1986) 'Xenophon's Arabia', *Iraq* 48: 1–14.

Donner, H. (1992) *The Mosaic Map of Madaba*. Kampen, Netherlands.

Doshi, S. (ed. 1985) *India and Greece. Connections and Parallels*. Bombay.

Downey, G. (1939) 'Procopius on Antioch', *Byzantion* 14: 361–78.

—— (1961) *A History of Antioch in Syria*. Princeton.

—— (1963) *Ancient Antioch*. Princeton.

Drijvers, H. J. W. (1980) *Cults and Beliefs at Edessa*. Leiden.

—— (1982a) 'Pagan cults in Christian Syria', in N. G. Garsoïan *et al.* (eds) *East of Byzantium: Syria and Armenia in the Formative Period*. Washington.

—— (1982b) 'A tomb for the life of the King: a recently-discovered Edessene mosaic with a portrait of King Abgar the Great', *Le Muséon* 95, 1–2: 167–89.

Dubs, H. H. (1957) *A Roman City in Ancient China?* China Society Sinological Series no. 5, London.

Duchesne-Guillemin, J. (1983) 'Zoroastrian religion', in *Cambridge History of Iran* 3 (2): 866–908.

Dunand, M. and Saliby, N. (1985) *Le Temple d'Amrith dans la pérée d'Aradus*. Paris.

Dupree, L. (1980) *Afghanistan*. Princeton.

Dussaud, R. (1903) *Mission scientifique dans les régions désertique de la Syrie Moyenne*. Paris.

—— (1922) 'Le Temple de Jupiter Damascenien et ses transformations aux époques chrétienne et musulmane', *Syria* 3: 219–50.

—— (1927) *Topographie historique de la Syrie antique et médiévale*. Paris.

—— (1942–3) 'Temples et cultes de la triade héliopolitaine à Ba'albek', *Syria* 23: 33–77.

—— (1955) *La Pénétration des Arabes en Syrie avant l'Islam*. Paris.

Eadie, J. W. (1989) 'Strategies of economic development in the Roman East: the Red Sea trade revisited', in French and Lightfoot: 113–20.

Elderkin, G. W. (1934) *Antioch on the Orontes I–III.* Princeton.

El-Saghir, M., Golvin, J.-C. *et al.* (1986) *Le Camp romain de Lougsor.* Cairo.

Endress, G. and Kruk, R. (eds, 1997) *The Ancient Tradition in Christian and Islamic Hellenism.* Leiden.

Erim, K. T. (1992) *Aphrodisias. A Guide to the Site and its Museum.* Istanbul.

Errington, E. and Cribb, J. (eds, 1992) *The Crossroads of Asia. Transformation in Image and Symbol in the Art of Ancient Afghanistan and Pakistan.* Cambridge.

Fantar, M. H. (1987) 'Kerkouane: a Punic city at Cape Bon', in A. Khader and D. Soren (eds) *Carthage: A Mosaic of Ancient Tunisia.* New York.

Fard, S. K. (1374 *shamsi*; 1996) *The Anahita Temple Kangavar. Archaeological Excavations and Surveys: The Reconstruction and Architectural Restoration of the Nahid Temple and Taghe-Gera.* (In Persian). Tehran.

Ferguson, H. (1978) 'China and Rome', *ANRW* II: 581–603.

Fischer, M. (1995) 'The basilica of Ascalon: marble imperial art and architecture in Roman Palestine', in Humphreys (ed.): 121–50.

Fischer, M., Ovadiah, A. and Roll, I. (1984) 'The Roman temple at Kedesh, Upper Galilee: a preliminary study', *Tel Aviv* 11: 146–72.

Foerster, G. and Tsafrir, Y. (1993) 'The Beth-She'an Excavations Project 1988–91', *Excavations and Surveys in Israel* 11: 3–32.

Förtsch, R. (1993) 'Die Architekturdarstellungen der Umaiyadschenmoschee von Damaskus und die Rolle ihr antiken Vorbilder', *Damaszener Mitteilungen* 7: 177–212.

Foss, C. (1995) 'The Near Eastern countryside in late antiquity: a review article', in Humphreys: 214–34.

Foucher, A. (1905–51) *L'Art gréco-bouddhique de Gandhara.* 2 vols, Paris.

Francfort, H.-P. (1979a) *Les Palettes du Gandhara.* Mémoires de la Délégation Archéologique Française en Afghanistan 23. Paris.

—— (1979b) *Les Fortifications en Asie centrale de l'âge du bronze à l'époque Kouchane.* Paris.

Franck, I. M. and Brownstone, D. M. (1986) *The Silk Road: A History.* New York.

Frankfort, H. (1976) *The Art and Architecture of the Ancient Orient.* London.

Fraser, P. M. (1972) *Ptolemaic Alexandria.* 2 vols, Oxford.

—— (1996) *Cities of Alexander the Great.* Oxford.

Frazer, J. G. (1911–36) *The Golden Bough.* 13 vols, London.

Freeman, P. and Kennedy, D. (eds, 1986) *The Defence of the Roman and Byzantine East.* 2 vols, Oxford.

French, D. H. and Lightfoot, C. S. (eds, 1989) *The Eastern Frontier of the Roman Empire. Proceedings of a colloquium held at Ankara in September 1988.* 2 vols, Oxford.

Freyberger, K. S (1989a) 'Einige Beobachtungen zur städtebaulichen Entwicklung des römischen Bosra', *Damaszener Mitteilungen* 4: 45–60.

—— (1989b) 'Unterschungen zur Baugeschichte des Jupiter-Heiligtums', *Damaszener Mitteilungen* 4: 61–86.

—— (1989c) 'Das Tychaïon von as-Sanamaïn. Ein Vorbericht', *Damaszener Mitteilungen* 4: 87–108.

—— (1991) 'Der Tempel in Slim: Ein Bericht', *Damaszener Mitteilungen* 5: 9–38.

—— (1992) 'Die Bauten und Bildwerke von Philippopolis', *Damaszener Mitteilungen* 6: 293–311.

—— (1993) 'Der "Peripteraltempel" in Qanawat', *Damaszener Mitteilungen* 7: 64–79.

—— (1998) *Die frühkaiserzeitlichen Heiligtümer der Karawanstation im hellenisierten Osten.*

Frézouls, E. (1977) 'Cyrrhus et la Cyrrhestique jusqu'à la fin du Haut-Empire', *ANRW* II, 8: 164–97.

Frye, R. N. (1963) *The Heritage of Persia.* London.

—— (1964) 'The Charisma of Kingship in Ancient Iran', *Iranica Antiqua* 6: 111–15.

—— (1967) 'Parthian and Sasanid Persia', in F. Millar, *The Roman Empire and its Neighbours.* London.

—— (1975) *The Golden Age of Persia.* London.

—— (1976) 'Irano-Byzantine commercial and diplomatic rivalry', *Bulletin of the Asia Institute* 1, 4: 1–18.

—— (1977) 'The Sasanian system of walls for defence', in M. Rosen-Ayalon (ed.) *Studies in Memory of Gaston Wiet* (Jerusalem): 7–15.

—— (1983) 'The Political History of Iran under the Sasanians', in *Cambridge History of Iran* 3 (1): 116–80. Cambridge.

—— (1984) *The History of Ancient Iran*. Munich.

Gasche, H., Killick, R. G. *et al.* (1987) 'Habl as-Sahr 1983–85: Nebuchadnezzar II's cross-country wall north of Sippar', *Northern Akkad Project Reports* 1. Ghent.

Gatier, P.-L. (1990) 'Un amphithéâtre à Bosra?', *Syria* 67: 201–6.

Gawlikowski, M. (1982) 'The sacred space in ancient Arab religions', in A. Hadidi (ed.) *Studies in the History and Archaeology of Jordan* I: 301–4. Amman.

—— (1984) *Palmyre VIII. Les Principia de Dioclétien ('Camp des Enseignes')*. Warsaw.

—— (1994a) 'Palmyra as a trading centre', *Iraq* 56: 1–26.

—— (1994b) 'A Fortress in Mesopotamia: Hatra', in Dabrowa (ed.): 47–56.

—— (1996a) 'Palmyra and its caravan trade', *AAAS* 42: 139–45.

—— (1996b) 'Thapsacus and Zeugma. The crossing of the Euphrates in antiquity', *Iraq* 58: 123–33.

Ghirshman, R. (1956) *Bîchâpour: Les mosaiques sasanides*. Paris.

—— (undated) *L'Îsle de Kharg dans la Golfe persique*. Tehran.

Gibbon, W. (1900) *The Decline and Fall of the Roman Empire*. 7 vols, ed. J. B. Bury, London.

Glueck, N. (1965) *Deities and Dolphins*. London.

Goetz, N. (1974) 'An unfinished early Indian temple at Petra', *East and West* 24: 245–8.

Gogräfe, R. (1993) 'Die Datierung des Tempels von Isriye', *Damaszener Mitteilungen* 7: 45–62.

—— (1995) 'Die Grabtürme von Sirrin (Osroëne)', *Damaszener Mitteilungen* 8: 165–.

—— (1996) 'The Temple of Seriane-Esriye', *AAAS* 42: 179–86.

Goldscheider, L. (1940) *Roman Portraits*. London.

Grabar, O. *et al.* (1978) *City in the Desert: Qasr al-Hayr East*. Cambridge, Mass.

Graf, D. F. (1986) 'The Nabataeans and the Decapolis', in Freeman and Kennedy: 785–96.

—— (1989) 'Zenobia and the Arabs', in French and Lightfoot: 143–67.

—— (1992) 'The Syrian Hauran', *Journal of Roman Archaeology* 5.

—— (1995) 'The *Via Nova Trajana* in Arabia Petraea', in Humphreys: 241–68.

—— (1996) 'The Roman East from the Chinese Perspective', *AAAS* 42: 199–216.

—— (1997) *Rome and the Arabian Frontier from Nabateans to Saracens*.

Grainger, J. D. (1990) *The Cities of Seleukid Syria*. Oxford.

—— (1995) 'Village government in Roman Syria and Arabia', *Levant* 27: 179–95.

Grant, M. (1971) *Herod the Great*. New York.

—— (1996) *The Severans: The Changed Roman Empire*. London.

Greatrex, G. (1998) *Rome and Persia at War, 502–532*.

Green, P. (1990) *Alexander to Actium. The Hellenistic Age*. London.

Gregorios, P. (1985) 'The monastic tradition', in S. Doshi (ed.) *India and Greece. Connections and Parallels*. Bombay.

Gregory, S. and Kennedy, D. (1985) *Sir Aurel Stein's Limes Report*. 2 vols, Oxford.

Groom, N. (1981) *Frankincense and Myrrh: A Study of the Arabian Incense Trade*. London.

(1996) 'The Roman expedition into South Arabia', *Bulletin of the Society for South Arabian Studies* 1: 5–7.

Gutas, D. (1998) *Greek Thought, Arabic Culture*. London.

Hadas-Lebel, M. (1993) *Flavius Josephus*. New York.

Hadidi, A. (ed., 1982) *Studies in the History and Archaeology of Jordan* I. Amman.

—— (1992) 'Amman-Philadelphia: aspects of Roman urbanism', in S. Tell (ed.) *Studies in the History and Archaeology of Jordan* 4: 295–8. Amman and Lyon.

Haerinck, E. (1974) 'Quelques monuments funéraires de l'Îsle de Kharg dans la Golfe persique', *Iranica Antiqua* 11: 134–67.

Haines, R. C. (1971) *Excavations in the Plain of Antioch. 2: The Structural Remains of the Later Phases.* Chicago.

Hamis, E. S. (1997) 'Two inscriptions on wall mosaics from the Umayyad period at Beth Shean', *Cathedra* Oct.: 45–64.

Hammond, D. D. (1987) *Byzantine Northern Syria, A. D. 298–610: Integration and Disintegration.* Los Angeles.

Hammond, P. (1973) *The Nabateans – Their History, Culture & Archaeology.* Gothenberg.

Harmatta, J. (ed., 1994) *History of Civilizations of Central Asia. 2: The Development of Sedentary and Nomadic Civilizations: 700 B.C. – A.D. 250.* Paris.

Harold Mare, W. (1997) 'The 1996 season of excavation at Abila of the Decapolis', *ADAJ* 51: 303–10.

Harper, P. (1995) *Discoveries at Ashur on the Tigris. Assyrian Origins.* New York.

Harris, E. and J. R. (1965) *The Oriental Cults of Roman Britain.* Leiden.

Haynes, D. E. L. (1965) *The Antiquities of Tripolitania.* Tripoli.

Helms, S. W. (1982) 'Excavations at "The City and the Famous Fortress of Kandahar, the Foremost Place in all Asia"', *Afghan Studies* 3–4: 1.24.

Herrmann, G. (1977) *The Iranian Revival.* Oxford.

Herrmann, G., Masson, V. M., Kurbansakhatov, K., *et al.* (1993) 'The international Merv project, preliminary report on the first season (1992)' *Iran* 31: 39–62.

Herrmann, G. and Howell, R. (1981) *The Sasanian Rock Reliefs at Bishapur. Part 1: Bishapur III, Triumph Attributed to Shapur I.* Berlin.

Herrmann, G., MacKenzie, D. N. and Howell, R. (1983) *The Sasanian Rock Reliefs at Bishapur.* Part 3, Berlin.

————— (1989) *Naqsh-i Rustam 6. The Sasanian Rock Reliefs at Naqsh-i Rustam. The Triumph of Shapur I.* Berlin.

Herzfeld, E. E. (1941) *Iran in the Ancient East.* Oxford.

Higuchi, T. (1984) *Gandhara Art of Pakistan.* Tokyo.

Higuchi, T. and Izumi, T. (eds, 1994) *Tombs A and C Southeast Necropolis Palmyra Syria.* Nara.

Hiorns, F. R. (1956) *Town-Building in History.* London.

Hirschfeld, Y. (1997) *The Roman Baths of Hammat Gader.* Jerusalem.

Hirschfeld, Y. and Solar, G. (1981) 'The Roman Thermae at Hammat Gader', *Israel Exploration Journal* 31: 179–219.

Hitti, P. K. (1957) *History of Syria. Including Lebanon and Palestine.* London.

—— (1964) *History of the Arabs from the Earliest Times to the Present.* London.

Hoag, J. D. (1975) *Islamic Architecture.* Milan and London.

Hodgson, N. (1989) 'The East as part of the wider Roman imperial frontier policy', in French and Lightfoot: 177–89.

Holt, F. L. (1995) *Alexander the Great and Bactria.* Leiden.

Holum, K. G., Hohlfelder, R. L., Bull, R. J. and Raban, A. (1988) *King Herod's Dream. Caesarea on the Sea.* New York.

Hopkins, C. (1979) *The Discovery of Dura Europos.* New Haven and London.

Horsfield, G. and Conway, A. (1930) 'Historical and topographical notes on Edom', *Geographical Journal* 86, 5: 369–88.

Hourani, G. (1995) *Arab Seafaring in the Indian Ocean in Ancient and Early Medieval Times.* Princeton. Revised and expanded by J. Carswell, 1995.

Houston, G. W. (1990) 'The Altar from Rome with inscriptions to Sol and Malakbel', *Syria* 67: 189–93.

Howard-Johnson, J. (1994) 'The official history of Heraclius' Persia campaigns', in Dabrowa: 57–87.

Huff, D. (1998) ' "Fire altars" and *astodans*', in Curtis *et al.*: 74–83.

Humphreys, J. H. (ed., 1995) *The Roman and Byzantine Near East*. Journal of Roman Archaeology Supplementary Series 14, Ann Arbor.

Ingholt, H. (1954) *Parthian Sculptures from Hatra*. New Haven.

Invernizzi, A. (1995a) 'Corinthian terracotta assembled capitals in Hellenized Asia', in Invernizzi (1995b): 3–12.

—— (ed., 1995) *In the Land of the Gryphons. Papers on Central Asian archaeology in antiquity.* (Monografie di *Mesopotamia*). Firenze.

Isaac, B. (1992) *The Limits of Empire. The Roman Army in the East*. Oxford.

—— (1997) *The Near East under Roman Rule*. Leiden.

Isakov, A. I. (1982) *Drevniy Pendzhikent*. Dushanbe.

Ishjamts, N. (1994) 'Nomads in eastern Central Asia', in Harmatta: 151–70.

Isserlin, B. S. J. (1984) 'The expedition of Aelius Gallus and other aspects of Roman penetration into Arabia', in *Studies in the History of Arabia II. Pre-Islamic Arabia*. Riyadh.

Jidejian, N. (1968) *Byblos through the Ages*. Beirut.

—— (1975a) *Baalbek-Heliopolis, 'City of the Sun'*. Beirut.

—— (1975b) *Beirut Through the Ages*. Beirut.

—— (1996a) *Tyre Through the Ages*. Beirut.

—— (1996b) *Tripoli through the Ages*. Beirut.

Jones, A. H. M. (1964) *The Later Roman Empire*. 3 vols, Oxford.

—— (1966) *The Decline of the Ancient World*. London.

—— (1971) *Cities of the Eastern Roman Provinces*. Oxford.

Joukowsky, M. S. (1997) 'Brown University archaeological excavations at the "Great" Southern Temple at Petra', *ADAJ* 51: 189–95.

Kehrberg, I. and Ostracz, A. A. (1997) 'A history of occupational changes at the site of the Hippodrome of Gerasa', *Studies in the History and Archaeology of Jordan* 4: 167–75. Amman.

Kennedy, D. L. (1986) '"European" Soldiers and the Severan Siege of Hatra', in Freeman and Kennedy: 397–409.

—— (1996a) 'Parthia and Rome: eastern perspectives', in Kennedy 1996b: 67–90.

—— (ed., 1996b) *The Roman Army in the East*. JRA Suppl. Series 18.

—— (1998) *The Twin Towns of Seugma on the Euphrates: Rescue Work and Historical Studies*. JRA Suppl. Series 27.

Kennedy, D. L. and Freeman, P. (1995) 'Southern Hauran Survey 1992', *Levant* 27: 39–73.

Kennedy, D. and Riley, D. (1990). *Rome's Desert Frontier from the Air*. London.

Kerner, S. (1997) 'Umm Qays-Gadara: a preliminary report 1993–1995', *ADAJ*: 51: 283–99.

Khouri, R. G. (1986a) *Jerash. A Frontier City of the Roman East*. London.

—— (1986b) *Petra. A Guide to the Capital of the Nabataeans*. London.

Kiani, M. Y. (1982). *Parthian Sites in Hyrcania, the Gurgan Plain*. Archaeologische Mitteilungen aus Iran, Ergänzungsband 9. Berlin.

Killick, A. C. (1986) 'Udruh and the Southern Frontier', in Freeman and Kennedy: 431–46.

Killick, R. G. (1984) 'Northern Akkad Project: excavations at Habl as-Sahr', *Iraq* 46: 125–30.

Kinch, K.-F. (1890) *L'Arc de Triomphe de Salonique*. Paris.

King, G. R. D. (1996) 'Abu Dhabi', *Bulletin of the Society for Arabian Studies* 1: 15.

Kingsley, P. (1995) 'Meetings with the Magi: Iranian themes among the Greeks, from Xanthus of Lydia to Plato's Academy', *Journal of the Royal Asiatic Society* 5, 2: 173–210.

Kirkbride, D. (1960) 'Le Temple Nabatéen de Ramm, son évolution architectural', *Revue Biblique* 67: 64–92.

Kleiner, D. E. E. (1992) *Roman Sculpture*. New Haven and London.

Kleiss, W. (1973) 'Qal'eh Zohak in Azerbaidjan', *Archaeologische Mitteilungen aus Iran* 6: 163–188.

Kleiss, W., Seihoun, H., Ter-Gregorian, K. and Haghnazarian, A. (1974) *S. Thadei' Vank*. Milan.

Klimberg-Salter (1976) *The Silken Thread*. Los Angeles.

Klimkeit, H.-J. (1993) *Gnosis on the Silk Road. Gnostic Parables, Hymns & Prayers from Central Asia.* San Francisco.

Klinkott, M. (1989) 'Ergebnisse der Bauaufnahme am "Tempel" von Dmeir', *Damaszener Mitteilungen* 4: 109–61.

Kloner, A. (1988) 'The Roman amphitheatre at Beth Guvrin: preliminary report', *Israel Exploration Journal* 38: 15–24.

Knobloch, E. (1972) *Beyond the Oxus. Archaeology, Art and Architecture of Central Asia.* London.

Kokhavi, M. (1989) *Afek-Antipatris.* (In Hebrew). Tel Aviv.

Kokkinos, N. (1998) *The Herodian Dynasty.* Sheffield.

Kraeling, C. H. (1938) *Gerasa: City of the Decapolis.* New Haven.

Kraeling, C. H., Torrey, C. C., Welles, C. B. and Geiger, B. (eds, 1956) *The Excavations at Dura Europos.* Part 1: *The Synagogue,* New Haven.

Krautheimer, R. and Curcic, S. (1986) *Early Christian and Byzantine Architecture.* 4th edn, London.

Krencker, D. and Zschietzschmann, W. (1938) *Römische Tempel in Syrien.* Berlin.

Kühne, H. (1989–90) 'Tell She Hamad/Dur-katimmu 1985–87', *Archiv für Orientforschung* 36–7: 308–23.

Lander, J. (1986) 'Did Hadrian abandon Arabia?' in Freeman and Kennedy: 447–53.

Lane Fox, R. (1986) *Pagans and Christians.* London.

Lang, D. M. (1978) *Armenia. Cradle of Civilization.* London.

Lankester Harding, G. (1963) *Baalbek: A New Guide.* Beirut.

Lassus, J. (1936) *Inventaire archéologique de la région au nord-est de Hama* 1–2.

—— (1972) *Les Portiques d'Antioche. Antioch on the Orontes V.* Princeton.

—— (1977) 'La Ville d'Antioche à l'époque romaine d'après l'archéologie', *ANRW* II, 8: 54–102.

Lauffray, J. (1977) 'Beyrouth archéologie et histoire, époques gréco-romaines. I. Période hellénistique et haut-empire romain', *ANRW* II, 8:135–63.

—— (1983) *Halabiyya-Zenobia.* Paris.

Laurence, R. and Berry, J. (eds, 1998) *Cultural Identity in the Roman Empire.* London.

Lee, J. L. (1996) *The 'Ancient Supremacy'. Bukhara, Afghanistan and the Battle for Balkh, 1731–1901.* Leiden.

Lenzen, C. J. (1992) 'Irbid and Beit Ras. Interconnected Settlements C. A. D. 100–900', in Zaghloul *et al.*: 299–301.

Lenzen, C. J. and Knauf, E. A. (1987) 'Beit Ras/Capitolias. A Preliminary Evaluation of the Archaeological and Textual Evidence', *Syria* 64: 21–46.

Leriche, P. and al-Mahmoud, A. (1994) 'Doura-Europos. Bilan des récherches recentes', *CRAI*: 395–420.

Leriche, P. *et al.* (1992) 'Doura-Europos Etudes 1990', *Syria* 69: 1–152.

Leriche, P. and Gelin, M. (1997) *Doura-Europos, Études IV, 1991–1993.* Paris.

Le Strange, G. (1905) *Lands of the Eastern Caliphate.* London.

Levi, D. (1946) *Mosaic Pavements of Antioch.*

Lewcock, R. (1986) *Wadi Hadramawt and the walled city of Shibam.* Paris.

Lieu, S. N. C. (1986) 'Captives, refugees and exiles: a study of cross-frontier civilian movements and contacts between Rome and Persia from Valerian to Jovian', in Freeman and Kennedy: 475–505.

—— (1994) *Manichaeism in Mesopotamia & the Roman East.* Leiden.

Lieu, S. N. C. and Montserrat, D. (1996) *From Julian to Constantine. Pagan and Byzantine Views. A Source History.* London.

—— —— (1998) *Constantine.* London.

Lifshitz, B. (1977a) 'Césarée de Palestine, son histoire et ses institutions', *ANRW* II, 8: 490–518.

—— (1977b) 'Scythopolis. L'histoire, les institutions et les cultes de la ville à l'époque hellénistique et impériale', *ANRW* II, 8: 262–94.

Lightfoot, C. S. (1990) 'Trajan's Parthian War and the Fourth-century Perspective', *Journal of Roman Studies* 80: 113–26.

Lindner, M. *et al.* (1984) 'New Explorations of the Deir-Plateau (Petra) 1982/1983', *Annual of the Department of Antiquities of Jordan* 28: 163–81.

Lindner, M. *et al.* (1997) 'An Iron Age (Edomite) Occupation of Jabal al-Khubtha (Petra)', *ADAJ* 51: 177–86.

Litvinsky, B. A. (ed., 1996) *History of Civilizations of Central Asia. 3: The Crossroads of Civilizations: A.D. 250 to 270.* UNESCO, Paris.

Luttwak, E. N. (1976) *The Grand Strategy of the Roman Empire.* Baltimore.

Lyttelton, M. (1974) *Baroque Architecture in Classical Antiquity.* London.

—— (1987) 'The Design and Planning of Temples and Sanctuaries in Asia Minor in the Roman Imperial Period', in S. Macready and F. H. Thompson (eds) *Roman Architecture in the Greek World*: 38–59. Oxford.

Ma Yong and Sun Yutang (1994) 'The Western Regions under the Hsiung-nu and the Han', in Harmatta: 227–46.

MacAdam, H. I. (1983) 'Epigraphy and village life in southern Syria during the Roman and early Byzantine periods', *Berytus* 31: 103–16.

—— (1986a) *Studies in the History of the Roman Provinces of Arabia. The Northern Sector.* Oxford.

—— (1986b) 'Bostra Gloriosa', *Berytus* 34: 169–85.

Macaulay, Rose (1977) *The Pleasure of Ruins.* London.

McCrindle, J. W. (1901) *Ancient India as Described in Classical Literature.* London.

MacDermot, B. C. (1954) 'Roman Emperors in the Sassanian Reliefs', *Journal of Roman Studies* 44: 76–80.

Macdonald, M. C. A. (1992) 'The distribution of Safaitic inscriptions in northern Jordan', in Zaghloul *et al.*: 303–7.

—— (1993) 'Nomads and the Hawran in the late Hellenistic and Roman periods. A reassessment of the epigraphic evidence', *Syria* 70: 303–413.

MacDonald, W. L. (1986) *The Architecture of the Roman Empire.* 2 vols, New Haven.

McKenzie, J. (1990) *The Architecture of Petra.* Oxford.

MacMullen, R. (1984) *Christianizing the Roman Empire A. D. 100–400.* Yale.

McNicoll, A. W and Ball W. (eds, 1996) *Excavations at Kandahar 1974 and 1975.* Oxford.

Mallowan, M. E. L. and Rose, J. C. (1935) 'Excavations at Tell Arpachiyah 1933', *Iraq* 2, 1: 25–34.

Mango, C. (1978) *Byzantine Architecture.* Milan and London.

Mango, M. M. (1982) 'The continuity of the Classical tradition in the art and architecture of northern mesopotamia', in N. G. Garsoïan *et al.* (eds) *East of Byzantium: Syria and Armenia in the Formative Period.* Washington.

Mare, W. H. (1992) 'Internal Settlement Patterns in Abila', in Zaghloul *et al.*: 309–14.

Marfoe, L. *et al.* (1986) 'The Chicago–Euphrates Archaeological Project 1980–1984: An Interim Report', *Anatolica* 13: 37–148.

Maricq, A. (1959) 'La Province d'Assyrie créé par Trajan', *Syria* 9.

Markus, R. A. (1990) *The End of Ancient Christianity.* Cambridge.

Martin-Bueno, M. (1989) 'Notes préliminaires sur le *Macellum* de Gerasa', *Syria* 66: 177–99.

—— (1992) 'The Macellum in the Economy of Gerasa', in Zaghloul *et al.*: 315–19.

Matheson, S. (1976) *Persia: an Archaeological Guide.* London and Tehran.

Matthers, J. (ed., 1981) *The River Qoueiq, Northern Syria, and its Catchment.* Oxford.

Matthiae, P. (1980) *Ebla: An Empire Rediscovered.* London.

Mattingley, D. (1988) 'The olive boom: Oil surpluses, wealth and power in Roman Tripolitania', *Libyan Studies* 17: 21–42.

Mayerson, P. (1960) *The Ancient Agricultural Regime of Nessana and the Central Negeb.* London.

Megdad, S. al (1982) 'Le Role de la Ville de Bosra dans l'histoire de la Jordanie aux Epoques Nabatéenne et Romaine', in Hadidi: 267–73.

Michalowski, K. (1962) *Palmyra – Fouilles polonaises II, 1960.* Warsaw.

Michell, G. (1989) *The Penguin Guide to the Monuments of India. 1: Buddhist, Jain, Hindu.* London.

Millar, F. (1993) *The Roman Near East, 31 BC–AD 337*. Cambridge, Mass.

Miller, D. O. (1994) *The Lava Lands of Syria: Regional Urbanism in the Roman Empire*. Ann Arbor.

Miller, J. I. (1969) *The Spice Trade of the Roman Empire*. Oxford.

Miller, M. C. (1997) *Athens and Persia in the Fifth Century. A Study in Cultural Receptivity*. Cambridge.

Ministry of Information, Oman (1979) *Oman, A Seafaring Nation*. Muscat.

Minorsky, V. (1945) 'Roman and Byzantine campaigns in Atropatene', *Bulletin of the School of Oriental and African Studies* 11: 243–65.

Monceaux, P. and Bosse, L. (1925) 'Chalcis ad Belum: Notes sur l'histoire et les ruines de la ville', *Syria* 6: 339–50.

Moorey, P. R. S. (1980) *Cemeteries of the First Millennium B.C. at Deve Hüyük near Carchemish*. Oxford.

Moortgat, A. (1969) *The Art of Ancient Mesopotamia*. London.

Mor, M. (1989) 'The events of 351–352 in Palestine – the last revolt against Rome?' in French and Lightfoot: 335–53.

Mostafavi, S. M. T. (1967) *Persian Architecture at a Glance*. Tehran.

Mouterde, R. and Poidebard, A. (1945) *Les Limes de Chalcis*. 2 vols, Paris.

al-Muheisen, Z. and Villeneuve, F. (1994) 'Découvertes nouvelles à Khirbet edh-Dharih (Jordanie), 1991–1994: autour de sanctuaire nabatéen et romain', *CRAI*: 735–78.

Musil, A. (1927) *Arabia Deserta*. New York.

—— (1928) *Palmyrena*. New York.

Napoli, J. (1997) *Recherches sur les fortifications linéaires romaines*. Rome.

Narain, A. K. (1957) *The Indo-Greeks*. Oxford.

Negev, A. (1973) 'The Staircase-Tower in Nabataean Architecture', *Revue Biblique* 80: 364–83.

—— (1977) 'The Nabataeans and the Provincia Arabia', *ANRW* II, 8: 520–686.

—— (1998) *The Architecture of Oboda: Final Report*. Jerusalem.

Netzer, E. and Weiss, Z. (1995) 'New evidence for late-Roman and Byzantine Sepphoris', in Humphreys: 164–76.

Northedge, A. (1992) *Studies on Roman and Islamic 'Amman'*. 1: *History, Site and Architecture*. Oxford.

Northedge, A., Bamber, A. and Roaf, M. (1988) *Excavations at 'Ana. Qal'a Island*. Warminster.

Norwich, J. J. (1988) *Byzantium. The Early Centuries*. London.

Oates, D. (1968) *Studies in the Ancient History of Northern Iraq*. London.

Oates, J. (1986) *Babylon*. London.

Okada, Y. (1992) 'Ain Sha'ia and the early Gulf churches: an architectural analogy', *al-Rafidan* 13: 87–93.

Owens, E. J. (1991) *The City in the Greek and Roman World*. London.

Palmer, A. (1993) *The Seventh Century in the West-Syrian Chronicles*. Liverpool.

Parapetti, R. (1982) 'The architectural significance of the sanctuary of Artemis at Gerasa', in Hadidi: 255–60.

—— (1986) 'The Italian activity within the Jerash project 1982–1983', in Zayadine: 167–204.

—— (1989) 'Scavi e restauri italiani nel santuario di Artemide 1984–1987', in Zayedine: 1–40.

Parisher, A. (1991) *Mlecchas in Early India. A Study in Attitudes towards Outsiders up to AD 600*. Delhi.

Parker. S. T. (1986a) *Romans and Saracens: A History of the Arabian Frontier*. Winona Lake.

—— (1986b) 'Retrospective on the Arabian frontier after a decade of research', in Freeman and Kennedy: 633–60.

—— (ed., 1987) *The Roman Frontier in Central Jordan. Interim Report on the* Limes Arabicus *Project, 1980–1985*. Oxford.

Parr, P. J. (1960) 'Excavations at Petra, 1958–59', *PEQ* 92: 124–35.

—— (1968) 'The Investigation of Some "Inaccessible" Rock-Cut Chambers at Petra', *PEQ*: 5–15.

Parrot, A. (1956) *Mission archéologique de Mari*, 1. Paris.

Peltenburg, E. J. *et al.* (1995) 'Jerablus-Tahtani, Syria, 1992–4: Preliminary Report', *Levant* 27: 1–28.

Peña, I. (1996) *The Christian Art of Byzantine Syria*. London.

Peña, I., Castellano, P. and Fernández, R. (1987) *Inventaire du Jébel Baricha*. Milan.

Perowne, S. (1957) *The Life and Times of Herod the Great*. London.

Peterman, G. L. (1994) 'Archaeology in Jordan', *American Journal of Archaeology* 98: 521–59.

Peters, F. (1983) 'City planning in Greco-Roman Syria. Some new considerations', *Damaszener Mitteilungen* 1: 269–77.

Petersen, H. (1966) 'New Evidence for the Relations Between Romans and Parthians', *Berytus* 16: 61–9.

Piccirillo, M. (1985) 'Rural settlements in Byzantine Jordan', in A. Hadidi (ed.) *Studies in the History and Archaeology of Jordan* 2: 257–61. Amman.

—— (1990) *Madaba, Mount Nebo, Umm er-Rasas. A Brief Guide to the Antiquities*. Amman.

—— (1993) *The Mosaics of Jordan*. Amman.

Pietrzykowski, M. (1985–6) 'The origins of the frontal convention in the arts of the Near East', *Berytus* 33–4: 55–60 and 135–8.

Pigulevskaya, N. (1963) *Les Villes de l'état iranien aux époques parthe et sassanide*. Paris.

Pirenne, J. (1961) *Le Royaume sud-arabe de Qataban et sa datation*. London.

—— (1963) 'Aux origines de la graphie syriaque', *Syria* 40: 101–37.

Pope. A. U. (ed., 1938–9) *A Survey of Persian Art*. 8 vols, Oxford.

—— (1965) *Persian Architecture*. London.

Porath, Y. (1995) 'Herod's "amphitheatre" at Caesarea: a multipurpose entertainment building', in Humphreys: 15–27.

Postgate, J. N. (1994) *Early Mesopotamia. Society and Economy at the Dawn of History*. London.

Raditsa, L. (1983) 'Iranians in Asia Minor', in *Cambridge History of Iran* 3 (1): 100–15.

Ragette, F. (1980) *Baalbek*. London.

Rakhmanov, S. A. (1994) 'The wall between Bactria and Sogd: the study on the Iron Gates, Uzbekistan', in Masson *et al.*, *New Archaeological Discoveries in Asiatic Russia and Central Asia*. Archaeological Studies 16: 75–8. St Petersburg.

Rappaport, U. (1989) 'The Jews between Rome and Parthia', in French and Lightfoot: 373–81.

Raschke, M. G. (1978) 'New studies in Roman commerce with the East', *ANRW* II, 9, 2: 604–1378.

Raven, S. (1993) *Rome in Africa*. 3rd edn, London.

Ray, H. P. (1994) *The Winds of Change: Buddhism and the Early Maritime Links of South Asia*. New Delhi.

Reade, J. (ed., 1996) *The Indian Ocean in Antiquity*. London and New York.

Reuther, O. (1938–9) 'Parthian Architecture. (A) History' and 'Sasanian Architecture. (A) History', in Pope: 411–44 and 493–578.

Rey-Coqais, J.-P. (1974) *Arados et sa Pérée aux époques grecque, romaine et Byzantine*. Paris.

Richter, G. M. A. (1948) *Roman Portraits*. New York.

Richthofen, K. von (1877) *China*. Berlin.

Roaf, M. D. (1983) *Sculptures and Sculptors at Persepolis*. London.

—— (1990) *Cultural Atlas of Mesopotamia and the Ancient Near East*. New York and Oxford.

Roaf, M. and Stronach, D. (1973) 'Tepe Nush-I Jan 1970: Second interim report', *Iran* 11: 129–40.

Roberts, J. M. (1985) *Triumph of the West*. London.

Roller, D. W. (1998) *The Building Program of Herod the Great*. Berkeley.

Ronan, C. A. and Needham, J. (1978) *The Shorter Science and Civilisation in China*, 1. Cambridge.

Ross, S. K. (forthcoming) *Roman Edessa 114–242 C.E.* London.

Rossabi, M. (1992) *Voyager from Xanadu*. Tokyo, New York and London.

Rowland, B. (1977) *The Art and Architecture of India. Buddhist. Hindu. Jain*. London.

Rubin, Z. (1986) 'Diplomacy and war in the relations between Byzantium and the Sassanids in the fifth century AD', in Freeman and Kennedy: 677–95.

—— (1989) 'Byzantium and South Arabia – the policy of Anastasius', in French and Lightfoot: 383–420.

Saadé, G. (1976) 'Exploration archéologique de Lattaquié', *AAAS* 26: 9–36.

Sack, D. (1985) 'Damaskus die Stadt "iutra muros" ', *Damaszener Mitteilungen* 2.

Safar, F. and Mustafa, M. A. (1974) *Hatra. The City of the Sun God* (in Arabic). Baghdad.

Saggs, H. W. F. (1962) *The Greatness that was Babylon*. London.

—— (1984) *The Might that was Assyria*. London.

Saliou, C. (1996) 'Du portique à la rue à portiques les rues à colonnades de Palmyre dans le cadre de l'urbanisme romain imperial: originalité et conformisme', *AAAS* 42: 319–30.

Salisbury, J. E. (1997) *Perpetua's Passion. The Death and Memory of a Young Roman Woman*. London.

Sanders, D. H. (ed. 1996) *Nemrud Dagi: The Hierothesion of Antiochus I.*

Sarfaraz, A. A. (1973) 'Discovery of a Major Sasanian Bas-relief', *Historical Studies of Iran* 2: 5–16.

—— (1975) 'A new discovery at Bishapur', *Iran* 13: 171.

Sarkhosh Curtis, V. and Simpson, S. J. (1997) 'Archaeological News from Iran', *Iran* 35: 137–44.

Sartre, M. (1981) 'Le Territoire de Canatha', *Syria* 58.

—— (1985) *Bostra: Des origines à l'Islam*. IFAPO. Paris.

Sastri, S. M. (1927) *McCrindle's Ancient India as described by Ptolemy*. Calcutta.

Sauvaget, J. (1934) 'Le Plan de Laodicée-sur-Mer', *Bulletin d'études orientales* 4: 81–114.

—— (1939) 'Les Ghassanides et Sergiopolis', *Byzantion* 14: 115–30.

—— (1941) *Alep*. Paris.

—— (1949) 'Le Plan antique de Damas', *Syria* 26: 314–58.

Savignac, R. and Horsfeld, G. (1935) 'Le Temple de Ramm', *Revue Biblique* 44: 245–78.

Schippmann, K. (1971) *Die Iranischen Feuerheiligtümer*. Berlin.

Schlumberger, D. (1933) 'Les Formes anciennes du chapiteau corinthien en Syrie, en Palestine et en Arabie', *Syria* 14: 283–317.

—— (1951) *La Palmyrène de nord-ouest*. Paris.

—— (1960) 'Descendants non-Méditerranéens de l'art grec', *Syria* 37: 131–66, 254–318.

—— (1978) *Lashkari Bazar. Un résidence royale ghaznévide et ghoride*. Paris.

Schmittenhenner, W. (1979) 'Rome and India: Aspects of Universal History during the Principate', *Journal of Roman Studies* 69: 90–106.

Schoff, W. H. (1914) *The Parthian Stations by Isidore of Charax*. Philadelphia.

Schumacher, G. (1891) 'Meine Reise in Ostjordanlande', *Zeitschrift des deutschen Palästinavereins* 15: 63–4.

Schurer, E. (1973–87) *History of the Jewish People in the Age of Jesus Christ (175 BC–AD 135)*. 3 vols, rev. and ed. G. Vermes, F. Millar and M. Goodman, Edinburgh.

Sear, F. (1982) *Roman Architecture*. London.

Segal, A. (1988) *Town Planning and Architecture in Provincia Arabia. The cities along the Via Traiana Nova in the 1st–3rd centuries C. E.* Oxford.

—— (1994) *Theatres in Roman Palestine and Provincia Arabia*. Leiden.

—— (1997). *From Function to Monument. An Architectural History of the Cities of Roman Palestine, Syria and Arabia*. Oxford.

Segal, J. B. (1970) *Edessa 'The Blessed City'*. Oxford.

Seigne, J. (1986) 'Recherches sur le sanctuaire de Zeus à Jerash', in Zayadine: 29–106.

—— (1994) 'Jerash romaine et byzantine: développement urbain d'une ville provinciale orientale', in Tell: 331–41.

Seigne, J. and Morin, T. (1995) 'Preliminary report on a mausoleum ât the turn of the BC/AD century at Jarash', *ADAJ* 39: 175–91.

Serjeant, R. B. (1983) 'San'a' the "Protected", *Hijrah*', in R. B. Serjeant and R. Lewcock (eds) *San'a'. An Arabian Islamic City*. London.

Seton-Williams, M. V. (1967) 'The excavations at Tell Rifa'at,' *Iraq* 21: 16–33.

Severin, T. (1982) *The Sindbad Voyage*. London.

Seyrig, H. (1951) 'Arados et Baetocaece', *Syria* 28: 191–220.

—— (1952–3) 'Antiquités de la nécropole d'Emèse', *Syria* 29 and 30.

—— (1959) 'Caractères de l'histore d'Émèse', *Syrie* 36: 184–192.

—— (1971) 'Le Culte de Soleil en Syrie à l'époque romaine', *Syria* 48: 337–73.

Shahid, I. (1978) 'Ghassan', *Encyclopaedia of Islam*. Leiden.

—— (1984a) *Rome and the Arabs*. Washington.

—— (1984b) *Byzantium and the Arabs in the Fourth Century*. Washington.

—— (1989) *Byzantium and the Arabs in the Fifth Century*. Washington.

—— (1995) *Byzantium and the Arabs in the Sixth Century*. 2 vols. Washington.

Shereshevski, J. (1991) *Byzantine Urban Settlements in the Negev Desert*. Beersheva.

Sherwani, H. K. (1964) *Muslim Colonies in France, Northern Italy and Switzerland*. Lahore.

Sherwin-White, A. N. (1984) *Roman Foreign Policy in the East, 168 BC to AD 1*. London.

Sherwin-White, S. and Kuhrt, A. (1993) *From Samarkhand to Sardis. A New Approach to the Seleucid Empire*. London.

Shkoda, V. (1998) 'Iranian traditions in Soghdian temple architecture', in Curtis *et al.*: 122–32.

Sidebotham, S. E. (1986) *Roman Economic Policy in the Erythra Thalassa 30 BC–AD 217*. Leiden.

—— (1991) 'Ports of the Red Sea and the Arabia–India trade', in Begley and De Puma: 12–38.

Sinor, D. (ed., 1990) *The Cambridge History of Early Inner Asia*. Cambridge.

Smallwood, E. M. (1966) *Documents Illustrating the Principates of Nerva, Trajan and Hadrian*. Cambridge.

—— (1976) *The Jews Under Roman Rule. From Pompey to Diocletian*. Leiden.

Smith, R. H. and McNicoll, A. (1992) 'The Roman Period', in A. W. McNicoll *et al.* (eds) *Pella in Jordan*. 2: 119–44, Sydney.

Sodini, J.-P., Tate, G., Bavant, B. and S., Biscop, J.-L. and Orssaud, D. (1980) 'Déhès (Syrie du Nord), Campagnes I-III (1976–1978)', *Syria* 57: 1–304.

Soper, A. C. (1951) 'The Roman style in Gandhara', *AJA* 55: 301–19.

Souaf, S. (1957) *Six Tours in the Vicinity of Aleppo*. Aleppo.

Spanner, H. and Guyer, S. (1926) *Rusafa. Die Wallfahrtsstadt des Heiligen Sergios*. Berlin.

Sperber, D. (1998) *The City in Roman Palestine*. Oxford.

Spiedel, M. P. (1977) 'The Roman Army in Arabia', *ANRW* II, 8: 687–730.

Starcky, J. (1984) 'Note sur les sculptures palmyréniennes du Musée du Grenoble', *Syria* 61: 37–44.

Starcky, J. and Gawlikowski, M. (1985) *Palmyre*. Paris.

Stark, R. (1996) *The Rise of Christianity: A Sociologist Reconsiders History*. Princeton.

Staviskij, B. J. (1986) *La Bactriane sous les Kushans*. Paris.

—— (1995) 'Central Asian Mesopotamia and the Roman world. Evidence of contacts', in Invernizzi 1995b: 191–203.

Stein, M. A. (1912) *Ruins of Desert Cathay*. 2 vols, London.

—— (1940) *Old Routes in Western Iran*. London.

Stevenson, K. B. (1997) *Persica*. Edinburgh.

Stoneman, R. (1992) *Palmyra and its Empire. Zenobia's Revolt against Rome*. Ann Arbor.

Strommenger, E. (1985) 'Habuba Kabira South/Tell Qannas and Jebel Aruda', in Weiss: 83–5.

Stronach, D. (1985) 'On the evolution of the early Iranian fire temples', in *Papers in Honour of Mary Boyce*. Leiden.

Sullivan, R. D. (1977a) 'The dynasty of Emesa', *ANRW* II, 8: 198–219.

—— (1977b) 'Papyri reflecting the eastern dynastic network', *ANRW* II, 8: 908–39.

—— (1977c) 'The dynasty of Judaea in the first century', *ANRW* II, 8: 296–354.

Summers, G. D. (1993) 'Archaeological evidence for the Achaemenid period in eastern Turkey', *Anatolian Studies* 43: 85–108.

Tarn, W. W. (1951) *The Greeks in Bactria and India*. Cambridge.

Taskiran, C. (1993) *Silifke (Seleucia on Calycadnus) and Environs*. Ankara.

Tate, G. (1992) *Les Campagnes de la Syrie du Nord 1*. IFAPO 133, Paris.

Taylor, G. (1986) *The Roman Temples of Lebanon. Enlarged edition*. Beirut.

Tchalenko, G. (1953–8) *Villages antiques de la Syrie du nord*. 3 vols, Paris.

—— (1973) 'Travaux en cours dans la Syrie du nord. 1. Le sanctuaire de Seih Barakat', *Syria* 50: 115–27.

Teixidor, J. (1977) *The Pagan God. Popular Religion in the Greco-Roman Near East.* Princeton.

Thapar, R. (1961) *Ašoka and the Decline of the Mauryas.* Oxford.

Thompson, H. O. (1969) 'Apsidal construction in the Ancient Near East', *PEQ* 101: 69–86.

Tidrick, K. (1989) *Heart Beguiling Araby. The English Romance with Arabia.* London.

Trimingham, J. S. (1979) *Christianity Among the Arabs in Pre-islamic Times.* London and New York.

Trümpelmann, L. (1975) *Das sasanidische Felsrelief von Darab.* Berlin.

Tsfrir, Y., Di Segni, L. and Green, J. (1994) *Tabula Imperii Romani: Iudaea-Palaestina.* Jerusalem.

Turcan, R. (1996) *The Cults of the Roman Empire.* Oxford (trans. of *Les Cultes orientaux dans le monde Romain*, Paris 1989).

Turner, P. (1989) *Roman Coins from India.* London.

Turton, G. (1974) *The Syrian Princesses. The Women Who Ruled Rome, AD 193–235.* London.

Van Berchem, D. (1967) 'Sanctuaires d'Hércule-Melqart', *Syria* 44: 73–338.

Vermeule, C. C. (1956–8) 'Eastern Influences in Roman Numismatic Art A.D. 200–400', *Berytus* 12: 85–99.

—— (1968) *Roman Imperial Art in Greece and Asia Minor.* Cambridge, Mass.

Von Le Coq, A. (1928) *Buried Treasures of Chinese Turkestan.* London.

Wagner-Luse, W. (1978) 'Umm Qais', *ZDPV* 94.

—— (1979) 'Umm Qais', *Revue Biblique* 86.

—— (1982) 'Umm Qais', *ZDPV* 98.

Waheeb, M. and Zuhair, Z. (1995) 'Recent excavations at the Amman nymphaeum. Preliminary report', *ADAJ* 39: 229–40.

Walda, H. and Walker, S. (1984) 'The art and architecture of Lepcis Magna: Marble origins by isotopic analysis', *Libyan Studies* 15: 81–92.

Ward-Perkins, J. B. (1971) 'Pre-Roman elements in the architecture of Roman Tripolitania', in F. Gadalla (ed.) *Libya in History*: 101–16. Benghazi.

—— (1981) *Roman Imperial Architecture.* London.

—— (1993) *The Severan Buildings at Lepcis Magna.* London and Tripoli.

Warmington, E. H. (1974) *The Commerce Between the Roman Empire and India.* 2nd edn, London.

Watson, P. (1996) 'Pella hinterland survey 1994: preliminary report', *Levant* 28: 63–76.

Watzinger, C. and Wulzinger, K. (1921) *Damaskus: die antike Stadt.*

Weber, T. and Khouri, R. G. (1989) *Umm Qais. Gadara of the Decapolis. A Brief Guide to the Antiquities.* Amman.

Weiss, H. (ed. 1985) *Ebla to : Art and Archaeology in Ancient Syria.* Washington.

Welles, C. B. (1967) *The Excavations at Dura Europos. Part II: The Christian Building.* New Haven.

Wheeler, R. E. M. (1946) 'Arikamedu: a Roman trading-station on the east coast of India', *Ancient India* 2: 17–124.

—— (1949) 'Romano-Buddhist Art: an old problem restated', *Antiquity* 23: 4–19.

—— (1954) *Rome Beyond the Imperial Frontiers.* London.

—— (1964) *Roman Art and Architecture.* London.

—— (1968a) *Flames Over Persepolis.* London.

—— (1968b) *The Indus Civilization.* Cambridge.

Whitby, L. M. (1989) 'Procopius and Antioch', in French and Lightfoot: 537–53.

Whitby, M. (1994) 'The Persian King at War', in Dabrowa: 227–63.

Whitehouse, D. (1974) 'Excavations at Siraf. Sixth interim report', *Iran* 12: 1–30.

—— (1989a) 'Begram reconsidered', *Kölner Jahrbuch für Vor- und Frühgeschichte* 22: 151–7.

—— (1989b) 'Begram, the *Periplus* and Gandharan art', *JRA* 2: 93–100.

—— (1990) 'The *Periplus Maris Erythraei*', *Journal of Roman Archaeology* 3: 489–3.

—— (1996) 'Sasanian maritime activity', in Reade.

—— (forthcoming) *Ancient Glass from Ed-Dur (Umm al-Qaiwan, UAE) Excavated by the Belgian Archaeological Expedition.*

Whitehouse, D. and Williamson, A. (1973) 'Sasanian Maritime Trade', *Iran* 11.

Widengran, G. (1983) 'Manichaeism and its Iranian Background', in *Cambridge History of Iran* 3 (2): 965–90.

Wiesehöfer, J. (1996) *Ancient Persia.* London.

Wilkinson, J. (1975) 'The streets of Jerusalem', *Levant* 7: 118–36.

—— (1981) Architectural procedures in Byzantine Palestine', *Levant* 13: 156–72.

—— (1984) 'What Butler saw', *Levant* 16: 113–28.

—— (1989) 'Jerusalem under Rome and Byzantium', in K. J. Asali (ed.) *Jerusalem in History.* London.

Wilkinson, T. J. and Tucker, D. J. (1995) *Settlement Development in the North Jazjira, Iraq.* Warminster.

Wilkinson, T. J. (1989) 'Extensive sherd scatters and land-use intensity: some recent results', *Journal of Field Archaeology* 16, 1: 31–46.

—— (1992) 'Off-site archaeology: land-use diversity in bronze age Upper Mesopotamia', *National Geographic Research and Exploration* 8, 2: 196–207.

Will, E. (1952) 'Au sanctuaire d'Héraclès à Tyr', *Berytus* 10: 1–12.

—— (1959) 'Une figure du culte solaire d'Aurélien: Jupiter Consul vel Consulens', *Syria* 36: 193–201.

—— (1960) 'Encore le sanctuaire syrien du Janicule', *Syria* 37: 201–3.

Will, E. and Larché, F. (1991) *Iraq al-Amir: Le Chateau du Tobiade Hyrcan.* 2 vols, Paris.

Williamson, A. (1972) 'Persian Gulf commerce in the Sassanian period and the first two centuries of Islam', *Bastan Chenassi va Honar-e Iran* 9–10: 97–109.

Williamson, G. A. (1964) *The World of Josephus.* London.

Williamson, G. A. and Smallwood E. M. (1981) *Josephus The Jewish War.* London.

Woolley, L. (1953) *A Forgotten Kingdom.* London.

Wright, G. R. H. (1969) 'Strabo on funerary customs at Petra', *PEQ* 101: 113–16.

—— (1985a) 'The Qasr Bint Fir'aun at Petra', *Damaszener Mitteilungen* 2: 321–5.

—— (1985b) *Ancient Building in South Syria and Palestine.* 2 vols, Leiden.

Yate, C. E. (1888) *Northern Afghanistan, or Letters from the Afghan Boundary Commission.* Edinburgh and London.

Zadneprovskiy, Y. A. (1994) 'The nomads of northern Central Asia after the invasion of Alexander', in Harmatta: 457–72.

Zaghloul, M. *et al.* (eds 1992) *Studies in the History and Archaeology of Jordan IV.* Amman.

Zayadine, F. (ed. 1986) *Jerash Archaeological Project 1981–1983.* I. Amman.

—— (ed. 1989) *Jerash Archaeological Project 1984–1988.* II. Paris.

—— (1991) 'Sculpture in ancient Jordan', in Bienkowski (ed.) *The Art of Jordan* (Liverpool): 31–61.

Zwalf, W. (1996) *A Catalogue of the Gandhara Sculpture in the British Museum.* 2 vols, London.

INDEX

Numbers in italics denote illustrations.